Basic Marketing
European Edition

- William D. Perreault, Jr.,
- E. Jerome McCarthy,
- Stephen Parkinson and
- Kate Stewart

D1347254

MCGRAW-HILL PUBLISHING COMPANY

London • New York • Burr Ridge, IL • St Louis • San Francisco • Auckland
Bogotá • Caracas • Lisbon • Madrid • Mexico • Milan • Montreal • New Delhi
Panama • Paris • San Juan • São Paulo • Singapore • Sydney • Tokyo • Toronto

Published by

McGraw-Hill Publishing Company

Shoppenhangers Road, Maidenhead, Berkshire, SL6 2QL, England
Telephone +44 (0) 1628 502500
Facsimile +44 (0) 1628 770224
Website http://www.mcgraw-hill.co.uk/textbooks/perreault

British Library Cataloguing in Publication Data
A catalogue record for this book is available from the British Library

ISBN 0-256-20402-0

Publisher: Alfred Waller
Desk Editor: Alastair Lindsay
Assistant Editor: Caroline Howell
Produced by Steven Gardiner Limited
Cover by Hybert Design

Printed and bound in Italy by Vincenzo Bona, Turin

CONTENTS

Preface   viii
Acknowledgements   xi and xii

✓ CHAPTER 1
Marketing's Role in the Organization
Marketing—What's It All About?   4
How Marketing and Production Create Value
   for Customers   4
Marketing Is Important   5
How Should We Define Marketing?   6
The Focus of This Text—Management-
   Oriented Marketing   6
Marketing's Role Has Changed a Lot
   Over the Years   7
What Does the Marketing Concept Mean?   8
Adoption of the Marketing Concept Has Not
   Been Easy or Universal   10
The Marketing Concept Applies in Non-Profit
   Organizations   13
The Marketing Concept, Social Responsibility
   and Marketing Ethics   14
The Management Job in Marketing   15
Summary   18
Questions and Problems   19
Suggested Cases   19

CHAPTER 2
Understanding the Changing Marketing Environment
The Marketing Environment Should Be
   Analysed at Three Levels   22
The Macro-environment   22
Technological Environment   23
Political Environment   25
Legal Environment   28
Cultural and Social Environment   29
The Competitive Environment   30
Responding to the Environment   32
Summary   33
Questions and Problems   33
Suggested Cases   34

CHAPTER 3
Understanding the Consumer Environment
Effective Marketing Begins by Understanding
   the Consumer   38
Demographic Dimensions of Consumer
   Behaviour   40
People with Money Make Markets   41
Spending Varies with Other Demographic
   Dimensions   47

National Stereotypes Are Common and
   Misleading   50
Consumer Behaviour—Why Do They Buy
   What They Buy?   51
The Behavioural Sciences Help Understand the
   Buying Process   51
Psychological Influences Within an Individual   52
Social Influences Affect Consumer Behaviour   56
Individuals Are Affected by the Purchase
   Situation   58
Consumers Use Problem-Solving Processes   58
Several Processes Are Related and Relevant to
   Strategy Planning   61
Summary   62
Questions and Problems   62
Suggested Cases   63

CHAPTER 4
Business and Organizational Customers and Their Buying Behaviour
Business and Organizational Customers—A Big
   Opportunity   68
Organizational Customers Are Different   69
Organizational Buyers Are Problem Solvers   69
Basic Methods and Practices in Organizational
   Buying   74
Buyer–Seller Relationships in Business Markets   75
Manufacturers Are Important Customers   79
Producers of Services—Smaller and More
Spread Out   80
Retailers and Wholesalers
   Buy for Their Customers   80
The Government Market   81
Summary   83
Questions and Problems   83
Suggested Case   85

CHAPTER 5
Getting Information for Marketing Decisions
Marketing Managers Need Information   88
Marketing Information Systems Can Help   88
What is Marketing Research?   91
The Scientific Method and Marketing Research   93
Five-Step Approach to Marketing Research   93
Defining the Problem—Step 1   94
Analysing the Situation—Step 2   95
Getting the Problem-Specific Data—Step 3   97
Interpreting the Data—Step 4   102
Solving the Problem—Step 5   104
International Marketing Research   104

How Much Information Is Needed?   105
Summary   105
Questions and Problems   106
Suggested Case   107

CHAPTER 6
Market Segmentation, Targeting and Positioning

A Three-Stage Approach to Marketing Planning   110
Types of Opportunities to Pursue   111
International Opportunities Should
   Be Considered   113
Market Segmentation   113
What Dimensions Are Used to Segment
   Markets?   115
Targeting   119
A Seven-step Approach to Segmenting
   Product Markets   120
Seven-step Approach Applies in
   Business Markets   123
Segmenting International Markets   123
More Sophisticated Techniques   124
Positioning Helps Identify
   Product-market Opportunities   124
Summary   126
Questions and Problems   127
Suggested Cases   127

CHAPTER 7
Elements of Product Planning for Goods and Services

The Product Area Involves Many Strategy
   Decisions   132
What Is a Product?   132
Differences in Goods and Services   134
Whole Product Lines Must Be Developed   135
Product Classes Help Plan Marketing
   Strategies   136
Consumer Product Classes   136
Convenience Products—Purchased Quickly
   with Little Effort   138
Shopping Products—Are Compared   138
Speciality Products—No Substitutes Please!   139
Unsought Products—Need Promotion   140
One Product May be Seen as Several Consumer
   Products   140
Business Products Are Different   141
Business Product Classes—How They
   Are Defined   141
Capital Investment—Major Capital Items   141
Accessories—Important But Short-lived
   Capital Items   143
Raw Materials—Farm and Natural Items Are
   Expense Items   143

Component Parts and Materials—Important Expense
   Items   143
Supplies—Support Maintenance, Repair and
   Operations   144
Professional Services   145
Managing Products Over Their Life Cycles   145
Product Life Cycles Should Be Related to
   Specific Markets   148
Product Life Cycles Vary in Length   149
Planning for Different Stages of the Product
   Life Cycle   150
Summary   153
Questions and Problems   154
Suggested Cases   155

CHAPTER 8
New-Product Development and Branding

New-Product Planning   160
An Organized New-Product Development
   Process is Critical   161
New-Product Development: A Total
   Company Effort   168
Need for Product Managers   169
Branding Is a Strategic Issue   169
Branding—Why It Developed   170
Conditions Favourable to Branding   171
Achieving Brand Familiarity is a Challenge   172
Protecting Brand Names and Trademarks   175
What Kind of Brand to Use?   175
Who Does the Branding?   176
The Strategic Importance of Packaging   176
What Is Socially Responsible Packaging?   177
Guarantees Are a Part of Strategy Planning   178
Summary   179
Questions and Problems   180
Suggested Cases   180

CHAPTER 9
Place and Development of Channels of Distributions

Place Decisions Are an Important Part of
   Marketing Strategy   184
Place Decisions Are Guided by 'Ideal'
   Place Objectives   184
Channel System May be Direct or Indirect   188
Discrepancies and Separations Require
   Channel Specialists   190
Channels Must Be Managed   191
Vertical Marketing Systems Focus on
   Final Customers   192
The Best Channel System Should Achieve Ideal
   Market Exposure   193
Channel Systems can be Complex   195

Summary	196
Questions and Problems	197
Suggested Case	197

CHAPTER 10
Logistics and Distribution

Physical Distribution Gets It to Customers	200
Physical Distribution Customer Service	200
Physical Distribution Concept Focuses on the Whole Distribution System	201
The Transportation Function Adds Value to a Marketing Strategy	204
Which Transportation Alternative Is Best?	205
Economies of Scale in Transportation	206
The Storage Function and Marketing Strategy	207
Specialized Storage Facilities Can Be Very Helpful	208
The Distribution Centre—A Different Kind of Warehouse	209
Physical Distribution Challenges and Opportunities	210
Summary	213
Questions and Problems	214

CHAPTER 11
Retailers, Wholesalers and Their Strategy Planning

Wholesalers and Retailers Plan Their Own Strategies	218
The Nature of Retailing	218
Planning a Retailer's Strategy	218
Conventional Retailers—Try to Avoid Price Competition	220
Expand Assortment and Service—To Compete at a High Price	221
Evolution of Mass-Merchandising Retailers	221
Some Retailers Focus on Added Convenience	223
Retailing on the Internet	224
Retailing Types Are Explained by Consumer Needs Filled	224
Why Retailers Evolve and Change	225
Retailer Size and Profits	226
Location of Retail Facilities	227
Differences in Retailing in Different Countries	229
What Is the Future of Retailing	229
What is a Wholesaler?	230
Different Kinds of Wholesalers Have Different Costs and Benefits	230
Merchant Wholesalers Are the Most Numerous	231
Agents Are Strong on Selling	233
Comeback and Future of Wholesalers	236
Summary	237
Questions and Problems	238
Suggested Cases	239

CHAPTER 12
Promotion—Introduction to Integrated Marketing Communications

Communications Are a Corporate Issue	242
Several Promotion Methods Are Available	242
Plan, Integrate and Manage the Promotions Mix	244
Methods Depend on Promotion Objectives	246
Promotion Requires Effective Communication	247
Adoption Processes Can Guide Promotion Planning	249
How Typical Promotion Plans Are Mixed and Integrated	251
Integrated Direct-Response Promotion Is Very Targeted	254
The Customer May Initiate the Communication Process	254
Promotion Mixes Vary Over the Life Cycle	256
Setting the Promotion Budget	258
Summary	260
Questions and Problems	261
Suggested Case	261

CHAPTER 13
Advertising and Public Relations

Advertising and Marketing Strategy Decisions	266
The Importance of Advertising	266
Advertising Objectives Are a Strategy Decision	269
Objectives Determine the Kinds of Advertising Needed	270
Coordinating Advertising Efforts with Cooperative Relationships	271
Choosing the 'Best' Medium—How to Deliver the Message	273
Planning the 'Best' Message—What to Communicate	277
Advertising Agencies Often Do the Work	280
Measuring Advertising Effectiveness Is Not Easy	283
How to Avoid Unfair Advertising	284
Public Relations and Publicity	285
Summary	288
Questions and Problems	289
Suggested Case	290

CHAPTER 14
Personal Selling

The Importance and Role of Personal Selling	294
What Kinds of Personal Selling Are Needed?	297
Order Getters—Develop New Business Relationships	298
Order Takers—Maintain and Nurture Relationships	299

Contents

Supporting Salesforce—Informs and Promotes
in the Channel 301
The Right Structure Helps Assign
Responsibility 302
Information Technology Provides Help 304
Sound Selection and Training to Build
a Salesforce 304
Compensating and Motivating Salespeople 305
Personal Selling Techniques—Prospecting
and Presenting 307
Summary 311
Questions and Problems 312
Suggested Case 312

✓ CHAPTER 15
Sales Promotion and Direct Marketing

Sales Promotion—Stimulating Change 316
Challenges in Managing Sales Promotion 317
Sales Promotion in an International Context 319
Sales Promotion for Different Targets at
Different Times 319
Direct Marketing 322
Ethical Issues 326
Summary 326
Questions and Problems 327

CHAPTER 16
Pricing Objectives and Policies

Price Has Many Strategy Dimensions 332
Objectives Should Guide Strategy Planning
for Price 333
Profit-oriented Objectives 334
Sales-oriented Objectives 335
Status Quo Pricing Objectives 336
Most Firms Set Specific Pricing Policies—
To Reach Objectives 336
Price Flexibility Policies 337
Price-Level Policies—Over the Product
Life Cycle 338
Most Price Structures Are Built Around
List Prices 343
Discount Policies—Reductions From
List Prices 343
Allowance Policies—Off List Prices 345
Extra Value 346
List Price May Depend on Geographic
Pricing Policies 346
Legality of Pricing Policies 347
Grey Markets 347
Summary 348
Questions and Problems 349
Suggested Case 350

CHAPTER 17
Price Setting in the Business World

Price Setting is a Key Stategy Decision 354
Some Firms Just Use Mark-ups 354
Average-cost Pricing Is Common and Can
Be Dangerous 357
Marketing Manager Must Consider Various
Kinds of Costs 358
Some Firms Add a Target Return to Cost 361
Break-Even Analysis Can Evaluate Possible
Prices 361
Marginal Analysis Considers Both Costs
and Demand 363
Demand-Oriented Approaches for Setting
Prices 369
Pricing a Full Line 371
Bid Pricing and Negotiated Pricing Depend
Heavily on Costs 372
Summary 373
Questions and Problems 374
Suggested Cases 375

CHAPTER 18
Developing Innovative Marketing Plans

Marketing Planning Process Is More Than
Assembling the Four Ps 380
Blending the Four Ps Requires Understanding of
a Target Market 381
Forecasting Target Market Potential and Sales 386
Forecasting Company and Product Sales by
Extending Past Behaviour 387
Predicting Future Behaviour Calls for
More Judgement 389
Analysis of Costs and Sales Can
Guide Planning 389
The Marketing Plan Brings All the Details
Together 390
Companies Plan and Implement Whole
Marketing Programmes 393
Planning for Involvement in International
Marketing 394
Summary 397
Questions and Problems 398
Suggested Cases 398

CHAPTER 19
Implementing and Controlling Marketing Plans

Good Plans Set the Framework for
Implementation and Control 402
The Role of Information in Implementation
and Control 403

Effective Implementation Means that Plans
Work as Intended 404
Control Provides Feedback to Improve Plans
and Implementation 406
Sales Analysis 406
Performance Analysis Looks for Differences 407
A Series of Performance Analyses May Find
the Real Problem 408
Marketing Cost Analysis 410
Planning and Control Combined 412
The Marketing Audit 414
Summary 416
Questions and Problems 417
Suggested Case 417

CHAPTER 20
Managing Marketing's Link with other Functional Areas
Marketing in the Broader Context 422
Financial Resources to Implement Marketing
Plans 422
Production Must Be Coordinated with the
Marketing Plan 426
Accounting Data Can Help in Understanding
Costs and Profits 431
Building Quality into the Implementation
Effort 435
People Put Plans into Action 439
Summary 441
Questions and Problems 442
Suggested Cases 442

Appendix A
Economics Fundamentals
Products and Markets as Seen by Customers
and Potential Customers 446
Markets as Seen by Suppliers 450
Demand and Supply Interact to Determine
the Size of the Market and Price Level 451

Demand and Supply Help Us Understand the
Nature of Competition 452
Summary 456
Questions and Problems 456

Appendix B
Marketing Arithmetic
The Operating Statement 458
Detailed Analysis of Sections of the Operating
Statement 460
Computing the Stockturn Rate 461
Operating Ratios Analyse the Business 462
Mark-ups 463
Return on Investment (ROI) Reflects Asset Use 464
Questions and Problems 465

Cases
1. McDonald's 'Seniors' Restaurant 468
2. Pillsbury's Häagen-Dazs 468
3. Republic Polymer Company 470
4. Lilybank Lodge 470
5. Sophia's Ristorante 471
6. Runners World 472
7. Paper Suppliers Corporation 474
8. Mixed Media Technologies 475
9. Enviro Pure Water 476
10. WeddingWorld.com 477
11. Outdoor World 479
12. Furniture to Go 480
13. Wire Solutions 481
14. Plastic Master 482
15. Deluxe Foods, Ltd 483
16. Aluminium Basics Co. 485
17. Romanos Take-Away 486

Glossary 489
Illustration Credits 503
Author Index 507
Subject Index 511

Basic Marketing Satisfies Customers' Needs

Basic Marketing is intended as a first book in marketing. Building on the classic 4Ps organization the book offers students clear explanations and helpful frameworks and 'how to do it' perspectives that build students' understanding of marketing. It motivates and stimulates students with carefully integrated, current examples. There is a focus on marketing strategy planning throughout. This means that topics are developed in an integrated way—so that (1) students see the relationships between the elements of the marketing mix and (2) the target market opportunity.

The text is designed to make sure that students get a good feel for a market-directed system and how he or she can help it—and a business—run better. We believe that marketing is important and interesting and we want every student who reads *Basic Marketing* to share our enthusiasm.

This European edition of *Basic Marketing* and all the other teaching and learning materials that accompany it have been designed around the students' needs. In creating this edition we have taken one of the most successful American marketing textbooks and adapted it to the European marketplace. We highlight some of those changes in this preface, but first it is useful to put the European edition in a longer term perspective.

Building on Pioneering Strengths

Basic Marketing pioneered an innovative structure— using the 'four Ps' with a managerial approach—for the introductory marketing course. It quickly became one of the most widely used business textbooks ever published because it organized marketing ideas so that readers could both understand and apply them.

It has been 39 years since publication of the first edition of *Basic Marketing*. During that time there have been constant changes in marketing management. Some of the changes have been dramatic, and others have been subtle. Throughout all of these changes this textbook and the supporting materials that accompany it have been more widely used than any other teaching materials for introductory marketing. It is gratifying that the 'four Ps' has proved to be an organizing structure that has worked well for *millions* of students and teachers.

Continuous Innovation and Improvement

Of course, this position of leadership is not the result of a single strength, or one long-lasting innovation. Rather, the text's four Ps framework, managerial orientation and strategy planning focus have provided to be foundation pillars that are remarkably robust and powerful in supporting and encompassing new developments in the field. Our objective is to provide a flexible, high-quality text and choices from comprehensive and reliable support materials—so that lecturers and students can accomplish their learning objectives. Careful thought has been given to pedagogy. For example, the European edition gives the reader:

- Completely integrated coverage of the role of marketing in building relationships.
- A chapter on marketing's links with other functional areas.

Critically Revised, Updated and Rewritten

This text and all the supporting materials have been critically revised, updated and rewritten. Clear and interesting communication has been a priority. *Basic Marketing* is designed to make it easy, interesting and fast for students to grasp the key concepts of marketing. Careful explanations provide a crisp focus on the important 'basics' of marketing strategy planning.

Attention is given to changes taking place in today's dynamic markets. *Throughout* the text we have integrated discussion and examples of

- Relationship building in marketing.
- The importance of customer satisfaction and retention.
- International perspectives.
- Ethical issues.

Similarly, we have also integrated new material on such important and fast-evolving topics as:

- Integrated marketing communications, including direct-response promotion.
- The expanding role of information technologies in all areas of marketing.
- Return on quality and quality management (with special emphasis on service quality).
- The increasing channel power of large retail chains.
- Competitor analysis.
- Marketing control, including marketing analysis.

20 Chapters—with an Emphasis on Marketing Strategy Planning

The emphasis of *Basic Marketing* is on marketing strategy planning. Twenty chapters introduce the important concepts in marketing management and help the student see marketing through the eyes of the marketing manager. The organization of the chapters and topics is carefully planned. It is possible to rearrange and use the chapters in many different sequences—to fit different needs. All of the topics and chapters fit together into a clear, overall framework for marketing strategy planning.

The first chapter deals with the nature of marketing and the contribution of marketing to profit and non-profit organizations. Chapters 2, 3 and 4 focus on the environment in which marketing takes place, paying particular attention to the European consumer and business markets. Chapter 5 deals with marketing information and how it is collected and used for marketing decision making. Chapter 5 is a contemporary view of getting information—from marketing information systems and marketing research—for marketing management planning. Marketing managers develop marketing strategies to satisfy specific target markets and this is the focus of Chapter 6. The emphasis is on identifying target markets with market segmentation and positioning approaches.

The next group of chapters—Chapters 7 to 17—is concerned with developing a marketing mix out of the four Ps: Product, Place (involving channels of distribution, logistics and distribution customer service), Promotion and Price. These chapters are concerned with developing the 'right' Product and making it available at the 'right' Place with the 'right' Promotion and the 'right' Price—to satisfy target customers and still meet the objectives of the business. These chapters are presented in an integrated, analytical way, so students' thinking about planning marketing strategies develops logically.

Chapters 7 and 8 focus on Product planning for goods and services as well as on new-product development and the different strategy decisions that are required at different stages of the product life-cycle concepts.

Chapters 9 through 11 focus on Place. Chapter 9 introduces channels of distribution, with special emphasis of the need for channel members to cooperate and coordinate to better meet the needs of customers. Chapter 10 focuses on the fast-changing arena of logistics and the strides that firms are making to reduce the costs of storing and transporting products while improving the distribution service they provide customers. Chapter 11 provides a clear picture of retailers, wholesalers and their strategy planning. This composite chapter helps students see why the major changes taking place in retailing are reshaping the channel systems for many consumer products.

Chapters 12 to 15 deal with Promotion. These chapters build on the concept of integrated marketing communications, which is introduced in Chapter 12. Advertising, public relations and personal selling are dealt with in Chapters 13 and 14, respectively. Sales promotion and direct marketing are described in Chapter 15.

Chapters 16 and 17 deal with Price. Chapter 16 focuses on pricing objectives and policies, including consideration of pricing in the channel and the use of discounts, allowances and other variations from a list price. Chapter 17 covers cost-oriented and demand-oriented pricing approaches. Its careful coverage of marketing costs helps equip students with an appreciation of the cost-conscious business.

Chapter 18 reinforces the integrative nature of marketing management and builds up to a specific framework for creative marketing plans and programmes. Chapter 19 offers complete coverage of marketing implementation and control and shows the importance of control-related information and its availability.

Chapter 20 discusses the links between marketing and other functional areas. The marketing concept says that people in an organization should work together to satisfy customers at a profit. The chapter also details how total quality management approaches can improve implementation, including implementation of better customer service.

Careful Integration of Special Topics

Some textbooks treat 'special' topics—such as relationship marketing, international marketing, services marketing, marketing for non-profit organizations, marketing ethics, and business-to-business marketing—in separate chapters. We have deliberately avoided doing that because we are convinced that treating such topics separately leads to an unfortunate compartmentalization of ideas. We think they are *too important to be isolated in that way*. Instead, they are interwoven and illustrated throughout the text to emphasize that marketing thinking is crucial in all aspects of our society and economy.

Basic Marketing Motivates High Involvement Learning

In each *Basic Marketing* chapter, behavioural objectives are included on the first page of each chapter. Within chapters, major section headings and second-level headings immediately show how the material is organized and summarized in the text. Further, we have placed graphics key points materials near the concepts they illustrate to provide a visual reminder of the ideas, and show vividly how they apply in the business world. Each chapter also contains a brief Internet exercise related to that chapter's content. All of these aids help the student to understand important concepts. End-of-chapter questions and problems offer additional opportunities. They can be used to encourage students to investigate the marketing process and develop their own ways of thinking about it. These can be used for independent study or as a basis for written assignments or class discussion.

Varied Types of Cases

Understanding of the text material can be deepened by analysis and discussion of specific cases. *Basic Marketing* features several different types of cases. Each chapter starts with a case study developed specifically to highlight that chapter's teaching objectives. Other cases are provided within the chapter in a highlighted box. Each case illustrates how a particular company has developed its marketing strategy, with emphasis on topics covered in that chapter. All of these cases provide an excellent basis for critical evaluation and discussion.

In addition, there are several suggested cases at the end of each chapter. The focus of these is on problem solving. They encourage students to apply, and really get involved with, the concepts developed in the text. These case-based exercises stimulate a problem-solving approach to marketing strategy planning, and give students hands-on exerience that shows how logical analysis of alternative strategies can lead to improved decision making.

The Responsibilities of Authorship

In closing, we return to a point raised at the beginning of this preface. *Basic Marketing* has been a leading textbook in marketing since its first edition. It is committed to delivering the very best teaching and learning materials possible. Fulfilling this commitment requires a process of continuous improvement. Improvements, changes and development of new elements must be ongoing. Thoughtful criticisms and suggestions from students and teachers alike have helped to make *Basic Marketing* a success in America, Canada and Australasia. Building on that foundation, we expect this first European edition to be successful. We encourage your feedback.

Stephen Parkinson
Kate Stewart

ACKNOWLEDGEMENTS

Special thanks go to the reviewers for this edition who were:

Dr David Birks, School of Management, University of Bath, UK

Dr Joan Buckley, Department of Management and Marketing, University College Cork, Ireland

Professor Francis Buttle, School of Management, Cranfield University, UK

Dr Sara Carter, Senior Research Fellow, Department of Marketing, University of Strathclyde, UK

Dr Kenneth R. Deans, Department of Marketing, University of Strathclyde, UK

Sue Wild, Department of Hospitality and Tourism Management, Manchester Metropolitan University, UK

Professor Geoff Lancaster, Professor of Business Policy, University of Lincoln and Humberside, UK

Professor Dale Littler, Manchester School of Management, UMIST, UK

Professor Rob Menko, School of Economics, Erasmus University Rotterdam, The Netherlands

Professor Luiz Moutinho, Business School, University of Glasgow, UK

Dr Ko de Ruyter, Associate Professor of Marketing and Marketing Research, Maastricht University, The Netherlands

Professor Ingmar Tufvesson, Department of Business Administration, Lund University, Sweden

Dr Ricky Wilke, Marketing Institute, Copenhagen Business School, Denmark

Dr Veronica Wong, Business School, University of Warwick, UK

ACKNOWLEDGEMENTS

The development and production of the first European Edition of Basic Marketing is to the credit of many people and organisations. It is impossible to list all those who had an input but we do want to express our appreciation to those who have played the most significant roles.

Alistair Lindsay of McGraw-Hill has brought us along the author's learning curve, managing the project in an unflappable style. His commitment and sound judgement have provided reassurance when complications bedevilled the project.

Support has been forthcoming from our colleagues. In particular, Hazel Cameron has provided expertise with technolgy that was beyond us. That she has done so with enthusiasm and completely without fuss is much appreciated. As well as doing his doctorate and teaching, Mike Flynn found time to source materials from advertising agencies and businesses. He is a model multi-tasker and we are indebted to him. In the midst of our other responsibilities, the University of Ulster has given us time, space and resources to prepare the manuscript. We gratefully acknowledge this assistance.

Thanks are also due to the anonymous reviewers who said kind things about the text and who also made suggestions for its improvement: we have tried to incorporate your ideas.

We are indebted to the organisations that allowed us to reproduce their materials here. These materials help to illustrate the practical realities of marketing management. A textbook must encapsulate existing knowledge, while bringing new perspectives and organisation to enhance it. Many marketing scholars, students and practioners have shaped our thinking. We are grateful acknowledge these contributors.

It is appropriate to salute the work of the original authors, Bill Perreault and Jerome McCarthy. Their contribution to marketing as a discipline has been immense. In providing the foundation text, so many students have been helped to think about marketing with clarity and insight. Their enthusiasm for marketing and for this project is contagious. We are proud to be your co-authors for the edition.

Responsibility for any errors or omissions is ours, but the book would not have been possible without the assistance of many others. Our sincere appreciation goes to all those who helped in their own special way.

Stephen Parkinson
Kate Stewart

Basic Marketing
European Edition

CHAPTER 1
Marketing's Role in the Organization

When You Finish This Chapter, You Should

1 Know what marketing is and why you should learn about it.

2 Be able to recognize a market oriented organization.

3 Understand the contribution of marketing to profit and non-profit organizations.

4 Understand marketing's role in responding to environmental change.

5 Understand what a marketing manager does.

6 Recognize the main elements of the marketing mix.

7 Understand the important new terms (shown in colour).

When it's time to get up in the morning, does your Philips alarm clock wake you with a buzzer or by playing your favourite radio programme? Is the programme playing rock, classical or country music or perhaps an advertisement for a BMW car? Will you put your Levi's jeans on, your shirt from Benetton and your Nikes, or do you need to wear something more formal? Will breakfast be Kellogg's Corn Flakes, or some extra large eggs and Dutch bacon? Will it be decaffeinated Maxwell House Coffee grown in Colombia or instant orange juice? When you leave home, will it be in a Renault car, on a Honda bike or by public transport?

Your day has only just begun and already you have encountered many different examples of marketing. Marketing affects every aspect of our lives—often in ways we don't even consider.

Around the world people wake up each day to different experiences. A family in China may have little choice about what food it will eat or where its clothing will come from. A farmer in the mountains of Jakarta may awake in a barren hut with little more than the hope that he can raise what he'll need to survive. A housewife in Tokyo may have many choices, but not be familiar with products that have names like Maxwell House, Renault and Benetton.

This chapter explores these differences. You'll see what marketing is all about and why it's important to you. We will also look at what marketing managers do, and how the practice of marketing assists both profit and non-profit organizations.

MARKETING—WHAT'S IT ALL ABOUT?

Marketing is more than selling or advertising

When asked to define marketing, most people, including some business managers, say that marketing means 'selling' or 'advertising'. While it is true that these are parts of marketing there is much more to marketing than this.

What has marketing got to do with an Oasis concert?

To illustrate some of the other important things that are included in marketing, think about a concert by one of your favourite bands. Some fans are willing to travel long distances and pay large sums of money to see and hear their favourite performers. Others are content to buy the albums and watch the videos. Major bands usually have management teams who look after the commercial interests of the band. To do this effectively the management team will make decisions, such as:

1. Analyse the needs of fans and decide in which countries and cities to stage concerts.

2. Predict what types of fans are likely to come to concerts and make sure that the right merchandise such as T shirts, records and souvenir programmes will be available.

3. Estimate how many records are likely to be sold over the next few years and control new releases to optimize sales between new and old releases.

4. Promote new releases to radio shows and the music press.

5. Manage personal appearances of the band to promote new releases.

6. Negotiate contracts with record companies.

7. Organize tours to different countries, dealing with local agents to select the right venues and local promotion of the concerts.

8. Design and manage the stage set.

These activities are part of a process called *marketing* that helps make sure that the right goods and services are produced and find their way to consumers. Our first example shows that marketing includes much more than selling or advertising. This book deals with each of these elements in detail.

HOW MARKETING AND PRODUCTION CREATE VALUE FOR CUSTOMERS

Production is a very important economic activity. Whether for lack of skill and resources or just lack of time, most people don't make the most of the products they use. Picture yourself, for example, building a 21-speed bicycle, a compact disc player or a digital watch starting from scratch! We also turn to others to produce services like health care, air transportation and entertainment.

By thinking about the customer, Dolmio makes it easier for customers to use the product.

There are obvious advantages when people or organizations, specialize in producing products or services. Specialists are able to produce these products or services more efficiently and therefore more economically than any of us would do if we produced them for ourselves. Through exchange of money for such products or services everyone benefits. Market-based economies allow exchanges to take place to everyone's benefit.

Musicians, like mousetraps, don't sell themselves

Some people would suggest that production is more important than marketing. Their attitude is reflected in the old saying: 'Make a better mousetrap and the world will beat a path to your door'. In other words, they think that if you just have a good product, your business will be a success. The 'better mousetrap' idea probably wasn't true in the past, and it certainly isn't true today. In modern economies, the grass grows high on the path to the Better Mousetrap Factory if the new mousetrap is not properly marketed. We have already seen, for example, that there's a lot more to marketing Oasis than just making records. This is true for most goods and services.

Vespa is a symbol of creativity and entrepreneurial drive. It has been sold worldwide since 1946, and is always being renewed through new models which combine technology, design and reliabilty.

Marketing decisions focus on consumer needs. It doesn't make sense to provide goods and services consumers don't want when there are so many things they do want or need. Let's take our 'mousetrap' example a step further. Some customers don't want *any kind* of mousetrap. They may want someone else to produce a service and exterminate the mice for them, or they may live where mice are not a problem. Marketing is concerned with what customers want and it should guide what is produced and offered. This is an important idea that will be developed later. The role of marketing management in creating value for customers is considered late in the chapter. First, we discuss the value of studying marketing and then define marketing.

MARKETING IS IMPORTANT

Marketing is important to every consumer

One reason for studying marketing is that you as a consumer pay for the cost of marketing activities. In advanced economies, marketing costs about 50 per cent of customer expenditure[1]. Marketing also affects almost every aspect of your daily life. All the goods and services you buy, the stores where you shop and the radio and TV programmes paid for by advertising are there because of marketing. Even your *curriculum vitae* is part of a marketing campaign to sell yourself to an employer! Some courses are interesting when you take them, but never relevant again once they're over. Not so with marketing, you'll be a consumer dealing with marketing for the rest of your life.

Marketing will be important to your job

There are many exciting and rewarding career opportunities in marketing in areas such as sales, advertising, product management, marketing research and distribution. Even if your career is not in marketing, it is more than likely that you will work with marketing people. Knowing something about marketing will therefore be useful and may add to your professional effectiveness. Marketing is important to the success of every organization. Remember, a company that cannot successfully sell its products does not need accountants, financial managers, production managers, personnel managers, computer programmers or credit managers.

Marketing concepts and techniques also apply to non-profit organizations. Many of these have a marketing manager, and the same basic principles are used in marketing ideas, politicians, public transport, healthcare services, conservation, museums and even universities.[2]

Marketing affects economic growth

Another important reason for studying marketing is that marketing plays a big part in economic growth and development. Marketing stimulates research and new ideas resulting in new goods and services. Marketing gives customers a choice among products. If these products satisfy customers, fuller employment, higher incomes and a higher standard of living can result. An effective marketing system is important to the future of all national economies.

HOW SHOULD WE DEFINE MARKETING?

Our definition of marketing is as follows: Marketing seeks to accomplish an organization's objectives by anticipating customer or client needs and directing a flow of products and services to satisfy those needs, making the optimum use of available resources.

Applies to profit and non-profit organizations

First, this definition applies to both profit and non-profit organizations. Profit is the objective for most business firms. Other types of organizations may have other objectives, for example to seek more members or promote the acceptance of an idea, such as a road safety campaign. Customers may be individual consumers or business firms. Clients could include non-profit organizations, government departments or even foreign nations. While most customers and clients pay for the goods and services they receive, others may receive them free of charge or at a reduced cost through private or government support.

More than just persuading customers

Too many executives still think that marketing is just selling and advertising. They feel that the job of marketing is to 'get rid of' whatever the company happens to produce. In fact, the aim of marketing is to identify customers' needs and meet those needs so well that the product almost 'sells itself.' This is true whether the product is a physical good, a service, or even an idea. If the whole marketing job has been done well, the customers do not need much persuading. They should be ready to buy.

Begins with customer needs

Marketing should begin with potential *customer needs,* not with the production process. Marketing should try to anticipate needs. Then marketing, rather than production, should determine what goods and services are to be developed, including decisions about product design and packaging; prices or fees; credit and collection policies; use of distributors and agents; transporting and storing policies; advertising and sales policies; and, after the sale, installation, customer service, warranty and perhaps even disposal policies.

Marketing does not do it alone

This does not mean that marketing should try to take over production, accounting and financial activities. Rather, it means that marketing by interpreting customers' needs should provide direction for these activities and try to coordinate them. After all, the purpose of a business or non-profit organization is to satisfy customer or client needs. It is not to supply goods and services that are convenient to produce and *might* sell.

THE FOCUS OF THIS TEXT—MANAGEMENT-ORIENTED MARKETING

Because most of you are preparing for a career in management, this text will take a managerial perspective and will be concerned with practical approaches to managing marketing decisions. The ideas and decision areas that will be discussed throughout this text apply to a wide variety of marketing management situations. They are important not only for large and small business firms but also for all types of public sector and non-profit organizations. They are useful in both domestic and international markets, and can be applied regardless of whether the organization's focus is on marketing physical goods, services or an idea or cause. They are equally critical whether the relevant customers or clients are individual consumers, businesses or some other type of organization. In short, every organization needs to think about its markets and how effectively it meets its customers' or clients' needs.

To get a better understanding of marketing, the perspective of the marketing manager is adopted. The case of Manchester United Football Club (MUFC) is a useful illustration of marketing in practice.[3] Such has been the club's success on and off the pitch that it has attracted a purchase offer from BskyB for £625 million. In 1997 MUFC again announced record profits to its shareholders. Turnover increased by 65 per cent on the previous year and amounted to nearly £90 million. The year's profits nearly doubled to over £26 million as the club benefited from lucrative non-footballing activities. The contribution from gate receipts, formerly its staple income, was overtaken by off-the-field businesses such as merchandising, sponsorship and catering. An analysis of MUFC's turnover shows the sources of its revenue: gate receipts 34 per cent; merchandising 33 per cent; television 14 per cent; sponsorship and royalties 13 per cent; and conference and catering 6 per cent.

Television income increased as a result of a better deal with BskyB and participation in the European

Champions Cup. Conference and catering revenues were enhanced by better usage of the ground and the new North Stand. An Umbro kit contract also improved revenue from sponsorship and royalties. In common with other Premier League clubs, MUFC offers three main replica kits with each kit having a two-year cycle. The club uses wholesale, retail and mail-order activities to achieve high merchandise sales. An MUFC museum is a further extension of the brand. Pre-season tours of the Far East also ensure that the brand is promoted overseas.

Manchester United Football Club has achieved great success in terms of football, retail sales and ticket demand. The ingredients of such success are interdependent. Investment in players and facilities needs to be continuous if the team is to win championships. This, in turn, fuels support, sponsorship and other deals, off the pitch. In short, MUFC, like many famous international clubs, is a brand in its own right. For this reason, many football clubs have employed commercial managers to deal with these business activities.

The commercial managers need to ensure that the brand, like any other asset, is carefully managed. The right merchandise needs to be made available at the right time and priced to meet the needs of the fans. Manchester United has many overseas fans who would never be able to attend a game in Manchester. A critical issue is to ensure that overseas distribution of the product range, through intermediaries, is effective. It is also important to cater for the needs of these fans through the regular club magazine. Relations with the press, television and other media are an important part of the marketing management job.

Making marketing decisions is not easy. Each decision, as the MUFC case shows, affects other areas. Knowing what basic decision areas have to be considered helps to plan a more successful strategy. This chapter aims to give a framework of the marketing management decision areas that make up the rest of this book.

MARKETING'S ROLE HAS CHANGED A LOT OVER THE YEARS

It is clear that marketing decisions are very important to a firm's success. But marketing hasn't always been so complicated. In fact, it is only in recent years that an increasing number of producers, wholesalers, retailers and non-profit organizations have adopted modern marketing thinking. Instead of focusing only on producing or selling *products*, these organizations focus on *customers* and try to integrate an organization-wide effort to satisfy them.

Marketing activities can be seen in terms of five different stages of development (1) simple trade, (2) production orientation, (3) sales orientation, (4) marketing as a business activity and (5) marketing as an organization-wide activity. Different economic systems, and different organizations will have reached different levels in the extent of development of marketing.

Early stress on simple trade

When societies first moved away from a subsistence economy where each family raised and consumed everything it produced, traders played an important role. Early 'producers for the market' made products that were needed by themselves and their neighbours. As bartering became more difficult, societies moved into the simple trade era: a time when families traded or sold their 'surplus' output to local intermediaries. These specialists resold the goods to other consumers or distant distributors. This was the early role of marketing and it is still the focus of marketing in many of the less developed areas of the world. In most developed countries throughout Europe and the rest of the world things didn't change much until the Industrial Revolution brought larger factories over a hundred years ago.

From the production to the sales era

From the Industrial Revolution until the 1930s, most West European companies placed greatest emphasis on production. Demand for many products and services was considerably in excess of demand and the majority of organizations could afford to ignore the need to focus on customer needs rather than production capability. The production era is a time when a company focuses on production of a few specific products perhaps because few of these products are available in the market. 'If we can make it, it will sell' is management thinking characteristic of the production era. Because of product shortages, many nations including many of the newly independent countries of Eastern Europe continue to operate with production era approaches

By about 1930, production capacity in many markets in the industrialized western nations was exceeding demand. Coupled with a worldwide recession the problem wasn't now just to produce but became how to beat the competition and win customers. This led many firms to enter the sales era.

The sales era is a time when a company emphasizes the role of selling existing products to beat the competition. Mass production techniques developed rapidly and required concentrated effort on sales to move the output from production to the customer. During the Second World War resources were reallocated to military purposes in most countries and the balance between supply and demand changed. For the duration of hostilities demand for many consumer products was considerably in excess of supply, leading to rationing. However, following the end of the Second World War production capacity, which had been dedicated to military purposes, became available for the production of consumer goods. In the 1950s and early 1960s this led to a rapid increase in the production of goods and services. Companies readopted a sales-oriented approach stressing the role of selling to ensure that production capacity was fully utilized.

Marketing as a separate business activity

For most firms in advanced economies, the sales era continued well through the 1950s. By the early 1960s, sales were growing rapidly in most parts of the economy. However, markets were becoming more competitive and supply was again greater than demand. Companies need to determine how best to compete. Increasingly it was recognized that long-run competitiveness was more

likely when the company focused its activities on meeting customer needs, rather than trying to sell everything it could produce. Someone and something was needed to tie together the efforts of research, purchasing, production, distribution and sales, and to focus these activities on meeting the needs of the customer.

As this situation became more common, a focus on sales was replaced by a focus on meeting customer needs through applying the marketing concept. In some organizations this led to the establishment of a marketing department. Obviously not every organization can afford to set up a complete marketing department. Many organizations simply gave the responsibility for marketing to specific individuals to carry out.

Marketing as a corporate activity

Many organizations now recognize the importance of marketing and have at least one person with specific responsibility for marketing activities. However, there is still a considerable gap between this stage of development and the final stage where marketing is seen as a corporate-wide activity involving every member of the organization. In this organization everyone recognizes the importance of working together to meet customer needs. Such organizations have truly understood the meaning of the marketing concept.

WHAT DOES THE MARKETING CONCEPT MEAN?

A concept is an idea or way of thinking about a particular situation. Concepts are useful devices which enable us to organize our thinking and behaviour in a particular way. The marketing concept suggests how organizations should behave in terms of customers and competition. Broadly stated the marketing concept stresses the belief that an organization should aim *all* its efforts at anticipating and satisfying its *customers* at a profit. The marketing concept is a simple but very powerful idea as illustrated in Exhibit 1–1.

Adopting a marketing orientation is a strategic and far-reaching change for an organization. Too often marketing is thought of only in the narrow sense of an advertising campaign or a special promotion. For example, many people use the term 'marketing a product' when they really mean promoting a product. The marketing of a product or service is much more than promoting it.

The marketing orientation is not really a new idea—it has been around for a long time. But some managers act as if they are stuck at the beginning of the production

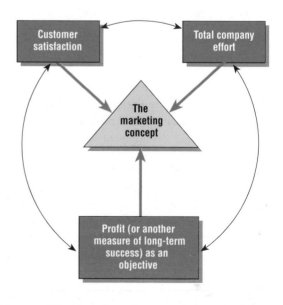

Exhibit 1–1 Organizations with a Marketing Orientation Carry Out the Marketing Concept

era when there were shortages of most products. They show little interest in customers' needs. These managers still have a production orientation making whatever products are easy to produce and *then* trying to sell them. They think of customers existing to buy the firm's output rather than of firms existing to serve customers and more broadly the needs of society. Think about the last time you experienced poor service when you were buying a specific product. Was the assistant really paying attention to meeting your needs or more concerned with making a sale?

Well-managed firms have replaced this production orientation with a marketing orientation. A marketing orientation means trying to implement the marketing concept. Instead of trying to get customers to buy what the firm has produced, a marketing-oriented firm tries to produce what customers need. For example, Amazon is an Internet bookseller. Once you have purchased books from Amazon, the company uses that information to make sure that you get information on the sort of books that you like when you next visit their website.

Three basic ideas are included in the definition of the marketing concept: (1) customer satisfaction, (2) a total company effort and (3) profit not just sales as an objective. In non-profit organizations profit is replaced by efficient use of resources. These ideas deserve more discussion.

 Internet Exercise

Amazon is one of the world's biggest booksellers. Visit their web site (**www.amazon.com**) and find the listing for this book. Is the book cheaper at Amazon? What information does a customer need to give Amazon and how can they use that information for marketing purposes?

Meet customer needs

The central focus of effective marketing is meeting customer or client needs. Organizations, which stress other goals, such as the individual concerns of managers or other staff, in determining the direction and activities will not succeed in the long run. The only valid purpose of an organization is to meet the needs of its customers.

Work together to do a better job

Ideally, all managers should work together because the output from one department may be the input to another. It is the combined efforts of the organization that have an impact on the final customer. But some managers tend to build 'fences' around their own departments as seen in Exhibit 1–2. There may be meetings to try to get them to work together but they come and go from the meetings worried only about protecting their own 'territory'.

We use the term *production orientation* as a shorthand way to refer to this kind of narrow thinking—and lack of a central focus in a business firm. But keep in mind that this problem may be seen in sales-oriented sales representatives, advertising-oriented agency people, finance-oriented finance people, directors of non-profit organizations, and so on. It is not just a criticism of people who manage production. They aren't necessarily any more guilty of narrow thinking than anyone else.

The 'fences' come down in an organization that has accepted the marketing concept. There are still departments, of course, because specialization makes sense. But the total system's effort is guided by what customers want instead of what each department would like to do.

A. A business as a box
   (most departments have high fences)

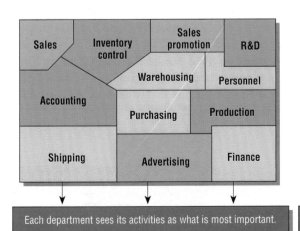

B. Total system view of a business
   (implementing marketing concept; still have
   departments but all guided by what customers want)

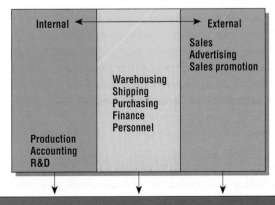

Exhibit 1–2

This worldwide advertising campaign features famous people who were once refugees. It is intended to bring home the message that many refugees contribute a great deal to their newly adopted countries.

In such a firm, it is more realistic to view the business as a box with both internal and external activities as shown in Exhibit 1–2B. Some internal departments such as production, accounting and research and development (R&D) are mainly concerned with affairs inside the firm. The external departments are concerned with outsiders sales, advertising and sales promotion. Finally, some departments, warehousing, shipping, purchasing, finance, and personnel work with both insiders and outsiders.

The important point is to have a guiding focus that *all* departments adopt. It helps the organization to work as a total 'system' rather than a lot of separate parts. The marketing concept specifies the high-level objective of customer satisfaction that is logical for each and every part of the system. It also specifies a profit or resource utilization objective, which is necessary for the system's survival. Organizations that stress the importance of marketing orientation do not have such internal barriers.

In commercial organizations survival and success require a profit

Commercial organizations must satisfy customers or the customers won't continue to 'vote' for the firm's survival and success with their money. But firms must also keep in mind that sales revenue from customers comes at a cost. It may cost more to satisfy some needs than any

customers are willing to pay. So profit, the difference between a firm's revenue and its total costs, is the 'bottom-line' measure of the firm's success and ability to survive. It is the balancing point that helps the firm determine what needs it will try to satisfy with its total (sometimes costly) effort.

Non-profit organizations must use resources efficiently

Non-profit organizations, such as charities or those operating in healthcare and education, must find a mechanism to use their resources efficiently. They are not primarily concerned with profit. Typically they have insufficient funds to meet all the needs of their clients, and must make compromises on who to support and which services to provide. Marketing skills can offer a way to determine where needs exists and help to determine how such needs can be satisfied to meet the objectives of the organization.

In a non-profit organization the marketing concept stresses the importance of anticipating and satisfying client needs within the resources that are available. Many non-profit organizations are only recently becoming aware of the need to identify different sets of customer or client needs. For example in healthcare many public healthcare organizations are only now beginning to recognize that patients are consumers with needs to be satisfied.[5]

ADOPTION OF THE MARKETING CONCEPT HAS NOT BEEN EASY OR UNIVERSAL

The marketing concept seems so logical that you would think it would have been quickly adopted. But this isn't the case. Many firms are still production oriented. In

fact, the majority are either production oriented or regularly slip back that way and must consciously refocus on customers' interests in their planning. It is very easy to lose sight of what the customer actually wants, particularly if the company has been in business for a long time, serving existing customers.

The marketing concept was first accepted by consumer products companies such as Unilever, Heinz and Mars. Competition was intense in their markets and trying to satisfy customers' needs more fully was a way to win in this competition. Widespread publicity about the success of the marketing concept helped spread the message to other firms.

Producers of industrial commodities—steel, coal, paper, glass and chemicals—have accepted the marketing concept slowly, if at all. Similarly, many companies manufacturing for other companies have been slower to accept the marketing concept in part because they are so close to final consumers that they 'feel' they really know their customers. When the product or service is highly technical and the customer is dependent on the technical skills of the manufacturer, the supplying company can be slow to adopt marketing.

Service industries are catching up

'Service' industries, including airlines, banks, stockbrokers, lawyers, doctors, accountants and insurance companies, were slow to adopt the marketing concept too. But this has changed dramatically in the last decade, partly due to changes in government regulations. In some situations such changes have forced many of these businesses to be more competitive. In other markets changes have allowed suppliers to adopt marketing approaches which have historically not been allowed.

Banks used to be open for limited hours that were convenient for bankers not customers. Many closed during lunch hour! But now financial services are less regulated, and banks compete with other financial service providers such as American Express. The banks stay open longer, often during the evenings and on Saturdays. They also offer more services for their customers such as automatic banking machines that take credit cards or a 'personal banker' to give financial advice. Most banks now heavily advertise their special services and interest rates so customers can compare bank offerings.[6] Banking has now become an international business. As more people travel abroad, and do so more frequently, there is an increasing demand for international banking services. Automatic teller machines are now linked across many European countries. For example a German traveller can now draw out pesetas in Barcelona from a local cash machine—a major advance on a few years ago when international currency transactions were much more complex.

There are often substantial barriers to adoption

While it might seem obvious that organizations should adopt a market-focused approach, many do not seem to have become marketing oriented. Their attention is still focused on the products or services which they provide, rather than the needs of their customers. These problems are particularly acute in markets where the concept of a customer-oriented culture is only recently being accepted. For example in the CIS (formerly the Soviet Union) organizations operated until relatively recently in a centrally planned economy where consumer requirements were secondary considerations behind the efficient use of scarce resources. When there are basic shortages of many necessities the concept of meeting customer requirements is less important than basic economic survival.

As the economy moves from a situation where production is centrally planned to one driven by market forces, considerable changes are required such as the need to replace state-controlled organizations with private sector organizations. The rate of adoption of a market-focused approach is also influenced by the experience and attitudes of consumers. Consumers with relatively little experience of a market-driven system are less sure of how to respond to changes in the way that products or services are provided. Their initial expectations of service may be limited and their tolerance of poor service high.

Organizations that have accepted the marketing concept actively search for information about customers and competition, and, this information is regularly collected and analysed. Such organizations do not believe that marketing is the responsibility of one department. Rather, they consider the whole organization to be involved in managing relationships with customers and develop an appropriate culture to ensure that everyone takes on this responsibility.[7]

It is easy to slip into a production orientation

The marketing concept may seem obvious, but it's very easy to slip into a production-oriented way of thinking. For example, a retailer might prefer only weekday hours and avoid nights, Saturdays and Sundays when many customers would prefer to shop. Or a company might rush to produce a clever new product developed by its scientists and engineers rather than first finding if it will fill an unsatisfied need. Many firms in high-technology businesses fall into this trap. They think that technology is the source of their success, rather than realizing that technology is only a means by which customer needs are met.

Take a look at Exhibit 1–3. It shows some differences in outlook between adopters of the marketing concept

Topic	Marketing Orientation	Production Orientation
Attitudes towards customers	Customer needs determine company plans.	They should be glad we exist, trying to cut costs and bringing out better products.
Product offering	Company makes what it can sell.	Company sells what it can make.
Role of marketing research	To determine customer needs and how well company is satisfying them.	To determine customer reaction, if used at all.
Interest in innovation	Focus on locating new opportunities.	Focus is on technology and cost cutting.
Importance of profit	A critical objective.	A residual, what's left after all costs are covered.
Role of customer credit	Seen as a customer service.	Seen as a necessary evil.
Role of packaging	Designed for customer convenience and as a selling tool.	Seen merely as protection for the product.
Inventory levels	Set with customer requirements and costs in mind.	Set to make production more convenient.
Transportation arrangements	Seen as a customer service.	Seen as an extension of production and storage activities, with emphasis on cost minimization.
Focus of advertising	Need-satisfying benefits of products and services	Product features and how products are made.
Role of salesforce	Help the customer to buy if the product fits customer's needs, while coordinating with rest of firm.	Sell the customer, don't worry about coordination with other promotion efforts or rest of firm.
Relationship with customer	Customer satisfaction before and after sale leads to a profitable long-run relationship.	Relationship is seen as short term—ends when a sale is made.

Exhibit 1–3 Some Differences in Outlook between Adopters of the Marketing Concept and the Typical Production-Oriented Managers

and typical production-oriented managers. As the exhibit suggests, the marketing concept if taken seriously is really very powerful. It forces the company to think through what it is doing and why. And it motivates the company to develop plans for accomplishing its objectives.

Where does competition fit?

Some critics say that the marketing concept doesn't go far enough in today's highly competitive markets. They think of marketing as 'warfare' for customers and argue that a marketing manager should focus on competitors,

not customers. That view, however, misses the point. The marketing concept idea isn't just to satisfy customers but to do it at a profit through an integrated, company-wide effort. Profit opportunities depend not only on outdoing some other firm but also on doing the right thing. In fact, often the best way to beat the competition is to be first to find and satisfy a need that others have not even considered. The competition between Pepsi and Coke illustrates this.

Coke and Pepsi were spending fortunes on promotion—fighting head-to-head for the same cola customers. They put so much emphasis on the competitor that they missed opportunities. They neglected the major retailers that distributed their products for them. This neglect encouraged retailers to develop their own brands of cola, frequently at lower prices with high levels of consumer acceptance, rapidly gaining market share at the expense of Coke and Pepsi. A marketing opportunity emerged for one soft drinks manufacturer to become a major supplier to retailers in the United States and Europe. Today retailer brands of cola challenge Coke and Pepsi for leadership position on many supermarket shelves.

THE MARKETING CONCEPT APPLIES IN NON-PROFIT ORGANIZATIONS

Newcomers to marketing thinking
The marketing concept is as important for non-profit organizations as it is for business firms. However, prior to 1970 few people paid attention to the role of marketing in facilitating the types of exchanges that are typical of non-profit situations. Now, marketing is widely recognized as applicable to all sorts of public and private non-profit organizations ranging from government departments, healthcare organizations, educational establishments and religious groups to charities, political parties and arts organizations. Some non-profit organizations operate just like a business. For example, there may be no practical difference between the gift shop at a museum and a for-profit shop located across the street. On the other hand, some non-profit organizations do differ from business firms in a variety of ways.

Support may not come from satisfied 'customers'
As with any business firm, a non-profit organization needs resources and support to survive and achieve its objectives. Yet support often does not come directly from those who receive the benefits the organization produces. For example, the World Wildlife Fund for Nature protects animals. If supporters are not satisfied with its efforts—don't think the benefits are worth what it costs to provide them—they will, and should, put their time and money elsewhere.

Just as most firms face competition for customers, most non-profit organizations face competition for the resources and support they need. A student organization will collapse if potential members join other organizations. A shelter for the homeless may fail if supporters decide to focus on some other cause, such as AIDS education. A community theatre group that decides to do a play that the actors and the director like never stopping to consider what the audience might want to see may find that the audience goes somewhere else.

What is the 'bottom line'?
As with a business, a non-profit organization must take in as much money as it spends or it won't survive. However, a non-profit organization does not measure 'profit' in the same way as a firm. The key measures of long-term success against which possible plans are measured are also different. Charities, universities, symphony orchestras and hospitals, for example, are all seeking to achieve different objectives and different measures of success are needed.

Profit guides business decisions because it reflects both the costs and benefits of different activities. In a non-profit organization, it is sometimes more difficult to be objective in evaluating the benefits of different activities relative to what they cost. However, if everyone in an organization agrees to *some* measure of long-run success, it helps serve as a guide to where the organization should focus its efforts. For example some hospitals use measures of patient satisfaction as an indicator of their effectiveness.

May not be organized for marketing
Some non-profit organizations face other challenges in organizing to adopt the marketing concept. Often there is no one who has overall responsibility for marketing. An accountant may keep the books, and someone may be in charge of 'operations'—but marketing may somehow seem less crucial, especially if no one understands what marketing is all about. Even when some leaders do the marketing thinking, they may have trouble getting unpaid volunteers with many different interests to all agree with the marketing strategy. Volunteers tend to do what they feel like doing!

The marketing concept provides focus
We have been discussing some of the differences between non-profit and business organizations. However, the marketing concept is helpful in *any* type of organization. Success is unlikely if everyone doesn't pull together to strive for common objectives that can be achieved with the available resources. Adopting the marketing concept helps to bring this kind of focus. After all, each organization is trying to satisfy some group of consumers in some way.

Throughout this book, we'll be discussing the marketing concept and related ideas as they apply in many different settings. Often we'll simply say 'in a firm' or 'in a business'—but remember that most of the ideas can be applied in *any* type of organization.

THE MARKETING CONCEPT, SOCIAL RESPONSIBILITY AND MARKETING ETHICS

Society's needs must be considered

The marketing concept is so logical that it's hard to argue with it. Yet when a firm focuses its efforts on satisfying some consumers to achieve its objectives there may be negative effects on society. This means that marketing managers should be concerned with social responsibility— a firm's obligation to improve its positive effects on society and reduce its negative effects. Being socially responsible sometimes requires difficult trade-offs. Consider, for example, the environmental problems created by CFCs, chemicals used in hundreds of critical products including fire extinguishers, refrigerators, cooling systems for offices, insulation and electronic circuit boards. We now know that CFCs deplete the earth's ozone layer. The result is a possible 'global warming' and exposure to cancer-causing ultraviolet radiation. Yet it is not possible to immedi- ately stop producing and using all CFCs. For many products critical to society, there is no feasible short-term substitute for CFCs. Du Pont and other producers of CFCs are working hard to balance these conflicting demands. Yet you can see that there are no easy answers for how these conflicts should be resolved.

Should all consumer needs be satisfied?

The issue of social responsibility in marketing also raises other important questions. For example, how far should organizations go in making a profit at the expense of environmental concerns such as pollution and waste? Should products and services be produced that damage consumers' health, yet can still be legitimately sold (for example, cigarettes or alcohol). There are no easy answers to these questions.

CO-OPERATIVE BANK MINI CASE

Some organizations have successfully adopted an ethical platform and have used this as a form of promotion in the marketplace—the Body Shop is an obvious example. In the United Kingdom, one bank in particular has taken an ethical stand. The Co-op Bank looked like many other British or European banks—straight, corporate and a little dull. In the early 1990s the bank did a survey to find out why customers had chosen the bank. A proportion of customers, it discovered, had chosen the bank because of its principles. Apart from being part of the co-operative movement, the bank had also taken a stance against South Africa in the 1980s.

Given the results of the survey the bank decided to take advantage of the opportunity. It developed and publicized an ethical policy. Among other things, this promised not to lend to those engaged in animal testing for cosmetics, hunting, the fur trade, tobacco manufacture or those who supply arms to repressive regimes. This has enabled the bank to attract more customers who care about ethical issues. Many of the bank's customers are middle-class people with left-of-centre views and who appreciate the bank's ethical policy.

Although such a policy is appealing to some people, others are less tolerant. The bank is constantly scrutinized by the media and others to check that it is adhering to the ethics it has publicized. Meanwhile other banks are much less under scrutiny. The Co-op Bank has also had advertising rejected because the content did not please a particular magazine. *Vogue* magazine turned down an advertisement that revealed a row of rabbits behind a beautiful woman, with the catchline 'We don't invest at face value'. The magazine claimed that the advertisement was 'tediously controversial'.[8]

What if it cuts into profits?

Being more socially conscious often seems to lead to positive customer response. For example, Gerber had great success when it improved the nutritional quality of its baby food. And many consumers have been eager to buy products that are friendly to the environment (even at a higher price).

Yet as the examples above show there are times when being socially responsible conflicts with a firm's profit objective. Concerns about such conflicts have prompted critics to raise the basic question: Is the marketing concept really desirable? Many socially conscious marketing companies are trying to resolve this problem. Their definition of customer satisfaction includes long-range effects as well as immediate customer satisfaction. They try to balance consumer, company *and* social interests. This book will be discussing many of the social issues faced by marketing management throughout the text.

The marketing concept guides marketing ethics

Organizations that have adopted the marketing concept are concerned about marketing ethics as well as broader issues of social responsibility. It is simply not possible for a firm to be truly consumer-oriented and at the same time intentionally unethical in decisions or actions that affect customers. Individual managers in an organization may have different values. As a result, problems may arise when some-

one does not share the same marketing ethics with others in the organization. One person operating alone can damage a firm's reputation and even survival. Because the marketing concept involves a company-wide focus, it is a foundation for marketing ethics common to everyone in a firm and helps to avoid such problems.

To be certain that standards for marketing ethics are as clear as possible, many organizations have developed their own written codes of ethics. Consistent with the marketing concept, these codes usually state at least at a general level the ethical standards that everyone in the firm should follow in dealing with customers and other people. Many professional societies have also adopted such codes.

THE MANAGEMENT JOB IN MARKETING

The marketing management process is the process of (1) *planning* marketing activities, (2) directing the *implementation* of the plans and (3) *controlling* these plans. These stages are shown in Exhibit 1–4. Planning, implementation and control are basic jobs of all managers but here we will emphasize what they mean to marketing managers.

Marketing planning begins with an assessment of the environment

The first stage in effective marketing planning is to understand the environment in which the organization

is operating. Changes in technology, demographic changes, such as increasing life expectancy, economic recession or boom or changing political environments, will all influence customer expectations and ultimately the products or services that they buy.

Marketing managers must seek attractive new opportunities as customers' needs change or as the organization's ability to meet customers' needs changes. Consider Parker Brothers, a company that seemed to have a 'Monopoly' in family games. While it continued selling board games, firms such as Atari and Nintendo

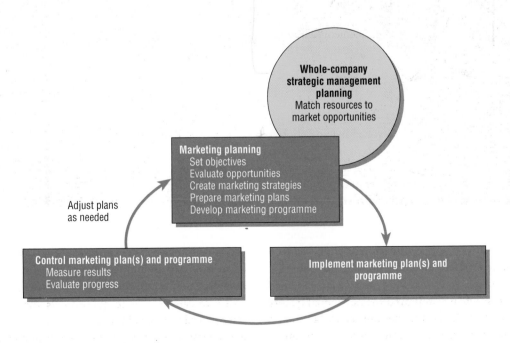

Exhibit 1–4 The Marketing Management Process

zoomed in with 'video game' competition. Of course, not every opportunity is good for every company. Really attractive opportunities are those that fit with what the whole company wants and is able to do.

Chapter 2 examines the major environmental factors that can influence the way in which customers behave.

Understanding customer needs is critical in marketing planning

The behaviour of individual customers is influenced by a wide range of factors, including individual attitudes and experience, family and friends, and different cultures. Effective marketing decisions can only be made once we understand what motivates the customer. It is only then that we can develop products or services that really meet their needs.

Chapter 3 examines what is currently known about consumer behaviour, and shows how this understanding is used in developing appropriate marketing programmes. Many companies sell products or services to other organizations. Chapter 4 looks at how organizations behave when they are buying products or services and shows how knowledge of the organizational customer can be applied in developing effective marketing programmes.

Marketing information must be collected systematically and regularly

Information on markets, competitors and customers is critical if the company is to develop good marketing plans. This means that the organization needs to set up and manage good systems to collect and use marketing information. Chapter 5 describes what should be included in a good marketing information system and also describes how to design and implement marketing research.

Marketing strategies reflect internal strengths and weaknesses and market opportunities and threats

Strategic marketing planning involves making choices about which markets to serve. Since it is unlikely that the organization will have the resources to make the same level of investment in every market, then choices must be made about where and how to direct resources. These choices depend on systematically collected information about the company's strengths and weaknesses and on the attractiveness of each market. Chapter 6 describes this strategic planning process in detail.

The marketing mix is designed to meet the needs of the target segment

Once the marketing strategy has determined which markets to focus on, and a decision has been made about how much marketing effort is justified for each market, appropriate marketing mixes must be developed for each market. The best marketing mix will combine product, price, promotion and place in a way which meets customer expectations better than the competition or matches competitive offers at lower cost.

There are many marketing mix decisions

There are many possible ways to satisfy the needs of target customers. A product can have many different features and quality levels. Service levels can be adjusted. The package can be of various sizes, colours or materials. The brand name and warranty can be changed. Various advertising media—newspapers, magazines, radio, television, posters—may be used. A company's own salesforce or other sales specialists can be used. Different prices can be charged. Price discounts may be given, and so on.

In Fiat's case these elements are the specification of different engine sizes, different designs and comfort levels. Prices vary reflecting the costs of producing the vehicle and the competitive environment where the cars are sold. Cars are advertised in different ways to present the car favourably to potential customers. Distribution decisions involve making sure that the cars are available when and where customers require them, and ensuring that the garages that sell those cars are providing appropriate standards of customer service. With so many possible variables, the question is: Is there a framework to organize all these decisions and simplify the selection of marketing mixes? The answer is: Yes.

The four 'Ps' make up a marketing mix

It is useful to reduce all the variables in the marketing mix to four basic ones:

Product Promotion Place Price

It helps to think of the four major parts of a marketing mix as the 'four Ps.' Exhibit 1–5 emphasizes their relationship and their common focus on the customer—'C'.

Each of the four Ps contributes to the whole

All four Ps are needed in a marketing mix. In fact, they should all be tied together. But is any one more important than the others? Generally speaking, the answer is no—all contribute to one whole. When a marketing mix is being developed, all (final) decisions about the four Ps should be made at the same time. That's why the four Ps are arranged around the customer (C) in a circle to show that they all are equally important.

Other 'P's may also matter

Some writers have suggested that there are more than four Ps in the marketing mix. For example in service

of new product or service development. Branding is a further critical issue.

Place decisions get the product or service to the customer

It would be of little use producing a product or service if it is not available to customers. Chapter 9 looks at the role of distribution systems in making products available to customers. Chapter 10 examines logistics and distribution decisions that determine levels of customer service and product availability. Most of us rely on retailers for many of the products which we buy. Some retailers rely in turn on wholesalers to supply products. Chapter 11 considers the role of retailers, and wholesalers, as members of the marketing channel.

industries the *People* dimension is also important as is *Physical* environment. However, in this book we will stick to the original four Ps approach. This has been widely used and is well accepted by both practitioners and academics alike.[9]

Let's sum up the discussion of marketing mix planning thus far. A *Product* is developed to satisfy the target customers. We find a way to reach our target customers—*Place*. We use *Promotion* to tell the target customers (and intermediaries) about the product that has been designed for them. We set a *Price* after estimating expected customer reaction to the total offering and the costs of getting it to them. The range of strategy decision areas organized by the four Ps is shown as Exhibit 1–6

Product decisions define the business

Chapters 7 and 8 look at product decisions in some detail because the product or service that the organization provides is central in determining its marketing programme. Product decisions include choices about the range and variety of products as well as the process

Organizations communicate to their customers using a variety of promotional tools.

Chapter 12 introduces the concept of integrated marketing communications. Chapter 13 then discusses the role of advertising and public relations. In chapter 14 attention is given to the role of personal selling and then in Chapter 15 the role of two other major communications tools: sales promotion and direct marketing is discussed.

Pricing decisions are critical elements of the marketing mix

There is a wide range of considerations which influence pricing decisions. These include the costs of supply and the willingness of customers to pay. Competitive pricing decisions are also critical. Chapter 16 considers pricing objectives and policies and Chapter 17 looks at how companies actually set prices in the real world.

Product	Place	Promotion	Price
Physical good	Objectives	Objectives	Objectives
Service Features	Channel type	Promotion blend	Flexibility
Quality level	Market exposure	Salespeople	Level over
Accessories	Kinds of	Kind	product life
Installation	middlemen	Number	cycle
Instructions	Kinds and	Selection	Geographic terms
Warranty	locations of	Training	Discounts
Product lines	stores	Motivation	Allowances
Packaging	How to handle	Advertising	
Branding	transporting	Targets	
	and storing	Kinds of ads	
	Service levels	Media type	
	Recruiting	Copy thrust	
	middlemen	Prepared by	
	Managing	whom	
	channels	Sales promotion	
		Publicity	

Exhibit 1–6 Strategy Decision Areas Organized by the Four Ps

Marketing plans fill out marketing strategy

A marketing plan is a written statement of a marketing strategy *and* the time-related details for carrying out the strategy. It should spell out the following in detail: (1) what marketing mix will be offered, to whom (that is, the target market) and for how long, (2) what company resources (shown as costs) will be needed at what rate (month by month perhaps) and (3) what results are expected (sales and profits perhaps monthly or quarterly). The contents of the marketing plan are described in detail in Chapter 18.

Control is analysing and correcting what you've done

The control job provides the feedback that leads managers to modify their marketing strategies. To maintain control, a marketing manager uses a number of tools such as computerized sales reporting systems. As we talk about each of the marketing decision areas, we will discuss some of the control problems. This will help you understand how control keeps the firm on course or shows the need to plan a new course.

All marketing jobs require planning and control

At first, it might appear that planning and control are of concern only to high-level management or in really large companies. This is not true. Every organization needs planning and without control it's impossible to know if the plans are working. Implementing and control decisions are discussed in Chapter 19.

Marketing people work with other members of the organization

While market-oriented strategy planning is helpful to marketers, it is also needed by accountants, production and personnel people and all other specialists. A market-oriented plan lets everybody in the firm know what ballpark they are playing in and what they are trying to accomplish. In other words, it gives direction to the whole business effort. An accountant can't set budgets if there is no plan, except perhaps by mechanically projecting last year's budget. Similarly, a financial manager can't project cash needs without some idea of expected sales to target customers and the costs of satisfying them. Chapter 20 looks at the linkages between marketing and other functional areas within the company.

Finally it is important to view some of the criticisms which are made of marketing as an activity in a consumer-oriented world. Each chapter discusses some of the ethical issues in marketing and leaves you to make up your own mind about the ethics of specific marketing decisions.

SUMMARY

Marketing's role within a marketing-oriented firm is to provide direction for a firm. The marketing concept stresses that the company's efforts should focus on satisfying target customers at a profit. Production-oriented firms tend to forget this. Often the various departments within a production-oriented firm let their natural conflicts of interest lead them to building fences. The job of marketing management is one of continuous planning, implementing and control. The marketing manager must constantly study the environment seeking attractive opportunities and planning new strategies. Possible target markets must be matched with marketing mixes the firm can offer. Then, attractive strategies—really, whole marketing plans—are chosen for implementation. Controls are needed to be sure that the plans are carried out successfully. If anything goes wrong along the way, this continual feedback should cause the process to be started over again with the marketing manager planning more attractive marketing strategies.

A marketing mix has four main variables: the four Ps—Product, Place, Promotion and Price. Most of this text is concerned with developing profitable marketing mixes for clearly defined target markets. So, after several chapters on analysing target markets, each of the four Ps will be discussed in greater detail.

QUESTIONS AND PROBLEMS

1. Define the marketing concept in your own words and then explain why profit is usually included in this definition.
2. Define the marketing concept in your own words and then suggest how acceptance of this concept might affect the organization and operation of your university.
3. Distinguish between 'production orientation' and 'marketing orientation', illustrating with examples.
4. Does the acceptance of the marketing concept almost require that a firm view itself as a 'total system?'
5. Distinguish clearly between a marketing strategy and a marketing mix. Use an example.
6. Why is the customer placed in the centre of the four Ps in the text diagram of a marketing strategy (Exhibit 1–5)? Explain, using a specific example from your own experience.
7. Explain in your own words what each of the four Ps involves.

SUGGESTED CASES

1. McDonald's 'Seniors' Restaurant
3. Republic Polymer Company

REFERENCES

1. E.H. Shaw, 'A review of empirical studies of aggregate marketing costs and productivity in the United States', *Journal of the Academy of Marketing Science*, Fall 1990, pp. 285–92.
2. C.H. Lovelock and C.B. Weinberg, *Marketing for Public and Nonprofit Managers*, Wiley, New York, 1984.
3. Manchester United Football Club Ltd, Annual Report, 1997; B. Potter and D. Millward, 'Man Utd says yes to Murdoch', *Electronic Telegraph*, 9 September 1998, Issue 1202; N. Bunyan, 'Manchester United's £47 shirts—with added zip', *Electronic Telegraph*, 17 April 1998, Issue 1057.
4. K. Kohli and B.J. Jaworski, 'Market orientation', *Journal of Marketing*, vol. 54, no. 2, 1990, p. 1 (18 pages); E. Gummesson, 'Marketing-orientation revisited', *European Journal of Marketing*, vol. 25, no. 2, 1991, p. 60 (16 pages); G.J. Hooley, 'The marketing concept: putting the theory into practice', *European Journal of Marketing*, vol. 24, no. 9, 1990, pp. 7–24.
5. V. Hayden 'How to increase market orientation', *Journal of Management in Medicine*, vol. 7, no. 1, 1993, pp. 29–46.
6. M.J. Baker, 'Bank marketing—myth or reality?' *International Journal of Bank Marketing*, vol. 11, no. 6, 1993, pp. 5–11.
7. F.E. Webster, 'Defining the new marketing concept', *Marketing Management*, vol. 2, no. 4, 1994, p. 23 (9 pages); F. Webster, 'Executing the new marketing concept', *Marketing Management*, vol. 3, no. 1, 1994, pp. 9–16.
8. M. Doyle, 'Co-op reaps green dividend', *The Daily Telegraph*, 18 April 1998, p. 31; <www.co-operativebank.co.uk/ethics.html>.
9. C. Grönroos, 'Marketing redefined', *Management Decision*, vol. 28, no. 8, 1990, p. 5 (5 pages); C. Vignali and B.J. Davies, 'The marketing mix redefined and mapped', *Management Decision*, vol. 32, no. 8, 1994. pp. 11–16.

CHAPTER 2
Understanding the Changing Market Environment

When You Finish This Chapter, You Should

1 Understand the importance of analysing the impact of the macro-environment, competitive environment and consumer environment on the company's marketing decisions.

2 Identify the main elements of the macro-environment.

3 Recognize the influence of economic and technical factors on marketing decisions.

4 Recognize the influence of legal and political influences on marketing decisions.

5 Recognize the influence of social and cultural factors on marketing decisions.

6 Understand the importance of competitive analysis in marketing planning.

7 Understand the important new terms (shown in colour).

The Winston family has been in business for over one hundred years in the North of England. Their business is haulage and transportation and in its founding years used horse-drawn carts to transport materials. From then the business has developed with the times. It invested in a fork lift that can handle large containers and now has a sizeable fleet of 80 lorries and trailers. Warehousing and warehouse leasing services are also part of the business. As a medium-sized freight firm it operates in a very dynamic environment over which it has little influence.

Government policy has determined that more freight ought to be carried by rail so as to lower the environmental impact of so much road traffic. For example, freight that could be carried on one train and six lorries, is currently carried on 40 lorries. However, the railways have in the past failed to invest in infrastructure and information technology. Taxes on lorries are likely to continue to rise: these are set according to the number of axles on the lorry. The maximum weight each lorry is allowed to carry may also change—this too is related to the number of axles on the trailer. For an outlay of about £2500, an extra axle can be added to the trailer, thus increasing its carrying capacity.

Winston Freight faces a dilemma. In order to grow it must invest in either a rail terminal or in modifying its existing fleet so as to take advantage of changes in taxes and weight regulations. To develop a rail facility will require extensive borrowing from banks and for it to be convinced that its money is safe. In addition, the business would need to be able to recruit staff who know the rail freight business and research suggests that there is a shortage of these. Planning permission from local authorities (councils) would also be required for the rail terminal. The company could, of course, develop a waiting policy. The problem is that competitors may seize the initiative.

There are considerable environmental pressures on freight companies, which will influence their marketing decisions for the foreseeable future. These include the pollution caused by exhaust gas, traffic congestion, safety on the roads, the green movement and government regulation. The whole of the transportation industry faces constant pressure from the macro-environment. There are many ways being considered by businesses to respond to such challenges.

THE MARKETING ENVIRONMENT SHOULD BE ANALYSED AT THREE LEVELS

The marketing management process begins with an understanding of the marketing environment. Organizations must understand the current challenges and potential threats that they face, if they are to develop successful plans. There are three parts to this environment. These are shown in Exhibit 2–1.

The broadest of these environments is the *macro-environment* within which every organization operates. This macro-environment includes economic, political, social and technical influences. Within this the organization competes with a range of others for individual markets. This is the organization's *competitive environment*. Finally the organization supplies products or services to specific customers. This is the *customer environment*. Changes in the organization's macro-environment can influence the competitive environment. Changes in the organization's competitive environment can influence consumer behaviour. It is important to monitor and predict changes at all three levels.[2]

In this chapter we will examine the nature of the organization's macro-environment and its competitive environment. Ultimately effective marketing decisions depend on having a thorough understanding of the consumer. In the next two chapters we will examine the

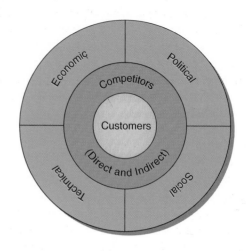

Exhibit 2–1 Dimensions of the Marketing Environment

organization's consumer environments. This chapter deals with broad environmental issues. In the next two chapters we turn to specific dimensions of European markets (particularly economic, demographic and social aspects of customers and markets).

THE MACRO-ENVIRONMENT

Economic dimensions

The economic and technological environment affects the way firms and the whole economy use resources. We will treat the economic and technological environments separately to emphasize that the technological environment provides a *base* for the economic environment. Technical skills and equipment affect the way an economy's resources are converted into output. The economic environment, on the other hand, is affected by the way all of the parts of a macro-economic system interact. This then affects such things as national income, economic growth and inflation. The economic environment may vary from one country to another, but economies around the world are linked.

Economic conditions change rapidly

The economic environment can, and does, change quite rapidly. The effects can be far-reaching and require changes in marketing strategy. Even a well-planned marketing strategy may fail if the country goes through a rapid business decline. As consumers' incomes drop,

they must shift their spending patterns. They may simply have to do without some products. A weak economy undermines consumer confidence, even among families whose income is not affected. When consumer confidence is low, many purchases, especially expensive ones, are delayed. Similarly, firms cut back on their own purchases. Many companies are not strong enough to survive such bad times.

Interest rates and inflation affect buying

Changes in the economy are often accompanied by changes in the interest rate—the charge for borrowing money. Interest rates directly affect the total price borrowers must pay for products. So the interest rate affects when, or if, they will buy. This is an especially important factor in some industrial markets. It also affects consumer purchases of homes, cars, furniture and other items usually bought on credit.

Interest rates usually increase during periods of inflation. Inflation is a fact of life in many economies. Some Latin American countries have had inflation at more than 400 per cent per year in recent years, in contrast, recent levels reached in many member states of the European Union are low. Still, inflation must be considered in strategy planning. When costs are rising rapidly, a marketing manager may have no choice but to increase prices. The decisions of individual marketing managers to raise prices adds to the macro-level inflation. In turn, that can lead to government policies that reduce income, employment *and* consumer spending.

The global economy is connected

In the past, marketing managers often focused their attention on the economy of their home country. It is no longer that simple. The economies of the world are connected and, at an increasing pace, changes in one economy affect others. Thus, turmoil in Asian economies in the late 1990s has had a bearing on the economies of the United States and Europe. One reason for this is that the amount of international trade is increasing and it is affected by changes in and between economies. Changes in the *exchange rate* show how much one country's money is worth in another country's money has an important effect on international trade. When the 'pound or krona is strong,' it's worth more in foreign countries. This sounds good—but it makes British or Swedish products more expensive overseas and foreign products cheaper in the United Kingdom and Sweden. Car manufacturers like Jaguar and Saab lose foreign customers to producers from other countries.

Within Europe, one of the major economic changes has been the introduction of a single European currency. Eleven countries joined the single currency on 1 January 1999: Austria, Belgium, Finland, France, Germany, Ireland, Italy, Luxembourg, Netherlands, Portugal and Spain. The United Kingdom, Sweden and Denmark decided not to join. Greece was not admitted, as it did not meet the economic criteria for joining. The euro is

a paper and electronic currency until 1 January 2002. National currencies of the 11 participating countries will be phased out after this date. Participating countries have a common interest rate, set by the European Central Bank located in Frankfurt.

The impact of the introduction of the euro will vary. Companies need to assess what their competitors are doing and what customers expect. One impact of the euro is that it is easier for customers to compare prices across countries. If the product is cheaper elsewhere then the customer may take their business away from the original supplier. Larger companies such as car manufacturers have asked their suppliers to switch to euros for invoices and price lists. Businesses may choose to price in euros, write invoices in euros, accept payment in euros or pay their own suppliers in euros. Converting to the euro as the base currency is the most demanding level of response to the single currency. Whatever response is chosen, it is clear that there are marketing implications as well as implications for accounting and information technology.[3]

A marketing manager is not immune from international economic forces just because his or her firm is not involved in foreign trade. New competition arises in the domestic market as foreign products gain a competitive edge due to their lower prices. Many companies find themselves helpless during such economic change. In fact, a country's whole economic system can change as the balance of imports and exports shifts, affecting jobs, consumer income and national productivity.

The marketing manager must watch the economic environment carefully. Changes in national and international economies can have an impact on competition and customers. The marketing manager needs to anticipate and respond to such changes. This may lead to changes in some aspect of the company's marketing mix such as a price increase or decrease.

TECHNOLOGICAL ENVIRONMENT

Benetton, the Italian clothing manufacturer, has grown from an initial investment of £1500 to a multinational organization with more than 6000 retail outlets in the past 20 years. The company is well known for its innovative styles and controversial advertising campaigns. However, its success is due in equal measure to the way in which it has introduced new ways of producing and distributing products in collaboration with its suppliers.

Traditionally the fibres in knitted garments are dyed before knitting. By reversing this and producing garments that can be dyed at any time after manufacture,

Benetton has increased its ability to respond quickly to fashion changes, and at the same time reduced the levels of stock, which need to be held. If the demand for a particular colour combination proves to be greater than the demand for other combinations, then stocks can simply be produced from the undyed garments. There is less waste and more rapid response to customers.[4]

The technological base affects opportunities

Underlying any economic environment is the technological base—the technical skills and equipment that affect the way an economy's resources are converted to output. Technological developments affect marketing in two ways: new products and new processes (ways of doing things). The Benetton case illustrates how changes in manufacturing have given the company a competitive advantage in terms of rapid product change to meet new market conditions.

Advances in information and communication technology make possible instant global communications. Computers allow more sophisticated planning and control of business. These process changes are accompanied by an exciting explosion of hitech products—from robots in factories to skin patches that dispense medicines, to home refrigerators that talk.

New technology has created important industries that didn't even exist a few years ago. Twenty years ago Microsoft did not exist. Now it is one of the most profitable companies in the world. The scale of the opportunities means that technology transfer from one part of the world to another is rapid. Many of the big advances in business have come from early recognition of new ways to do things. Marketers should help their firms to see such opportunities by trying to understand the 'why' of present markets, and what is keeping their firms from being more successful. Then, as new technological developments come along, the opportunity presented by those technologies can be assessed.

Internet technologies are reshaping marketing

The Internet is a system for linking computers around the world. The idea of linking computers in a network is not new. Although the Internet is described as a system, it might be more accurate to think of it as a collection of consistent hardware and software standards. Even so, the Internet expands the network concept to include any computer anywhere. The World Wide Web (WWW) facilitates the exchange of information. As a result, this new technology is radically changing many aspects of marketing.

As examples of this change, consider the marketing mix, starting with promotion. The invention of TV changed marketing because it suddenly made it possible for a sponsor to broadcast a vivid message to millions of people at the same time. Now the Internet makes it possible for that sponsor to select any of millions of messages and to simultaneously narrowcast any of them to millions of different individuals. It is just as easy for customers to request the information in the first place or to respond electronically once they have it. Thus, the Internet's capability radically changes our ideas about how firms communicate with customers and vice versa.

The Internet is creating totally different approaches to pricing. It allows consumers to be much better informed about prices for products and services. In addition, on-line auctions allow consumers to name their price for a product; the supplier then decides if they want to supply the product at that price. For example, with Priceline.com would-be passengers bid a price for travel between two destinations. If an airline is willing to issue a ticket at the bid price, the customer is obliged to buy. Airlines are able to sell seats that might otherwise go unsold and to assess whether it would pay to increase capacity. On-line auctions with their varying prices therefore facilitate the matching of supply and demand.

As for the place or distribution variable in the marketing mix, the Internet has been heralded as 'the end of geography'. Thus a business can offer its products worldwide from any local base, for example, Amazon.com is based in the United States but sells books and CDs to customers all over the world. Small local retailers can also offer their merchandise on the Internet, thereby reaching a much larger market. While many products will tend to be bought locally, customers may still use the Internet as a source of information on prices and product performance.

An outstanding Internet success story is that of the investment brokers Charles Schwab. The company decided in 1995 to develop a presence on the Internet and it is now by far the largest Internet brokerage in the world. Two features have contributed to the success of its web site. The company dropped its commission rate for on-line transactions, thus giving the web customer a cheaper service. However, the actual service itself was enhanced. On the web site (www.schwab.com) the customer can look up real-time quotations, news, historical financial data or use software tools. These allow the customer to set up their own asset allocation models, find the stocks and investment funds that fit the model and then put them through the company. Customers have free access to investment information for which many other brokers charge high fees. As the Charles Schwab example shows, the product may also change when it is sold through the Internet.[5]

Technology also poses challenges

The rapid pace of technological change opens up new opportunities, but it also poses challenges for marketers. For many firms, success depends on how quickly new ideas can be brought to market. It is easy for a firm to slip into a production orientation in the flush of excitement that follows a new discovery made through research and development (R&D). That makes it more important than ever for marketing thinking to guide the production process, starting at the beginning with decisions about where basic R&D effort will be focused.

Technology and ethical issues

Marketers must also help their firms decide what technical developments are ethically acceptable. For example, many firms have now installed a system to identify the telephone number of any incoming telephone call. When linked with a computer, this makes it possible for a firm to know which customer is calling, even before the customer says the first word. It also makes instantly available detailed information about what a customer has purchased in the past. This is a very powerful technology and some people feel that this sort of automatic number identification system is an invasion of privacy.

Similarly, with the growing concern about environmental pollution and the quality of life, some attractive technological developments may be rejected because of their long-run effects on the environment. Hygienically sealed drinks boxes, for example, are very convenient, but are difficult to recycle. In a case like this, what is good for the firm and some customers may not be good for the cultural and social environment, or be acceptable in the political and legal environment. Being close to the market should give marketers a better feel for current trends and help firms to avoid making serious mistakes.[6]

Environmental pollution is a problem which many consumers worry about. Texaco has stressed its attempts to minimize pollution.

POLITICAL ENVIRONMENT

Political pressures may change markets

National political environments can influence the way in which organizations operate in many ways. Different political parties have different agendas for the way in which a country should be managed, and as parties change, so the way in which a country's economy is managed will change. Governments make many different decisions which can affect the marketing environment. For example, decisions about interest rates, taxation of income and company profits can affect consumer and business expectations. Legislation about consumer and environmental protection can influence the way companies provide products or services.

Organizations attempt to lobby political interests

Because political decisions are important many organizations attempt to exert an influence by providing information to politicians and attempting to influence their point of view. This activity, known as *lobbying*, is engaged in by companies, trade associations, consumer groups and not-for-profit organizations. For example, trade associations representing companies that produce and sell alcohol lobby government about duties and taxes on alcohol. They would like these to be lowered, or, at the very least, not increased, in government budgets. Lobbying is increasingly important when companies operate in international markets where political decisions are influenced by international pressures.

Political factors are now an international concern

Every organization is now operating in international markets. Even if the firm does not sell its products or services overseas it is likely that overseas competitors will have entered the domestic market with their own products or services. Governments around the world have recognized the importance of trade between countries and have sought to encourage trading partnerships with other nations. The European Union (EU) is one of the most obvious examples of such collaboration.

While the aim of the EU is to encourage trade between member states there are still some barriers to establishing a truly international market. These barriers include problems of harmonizing national and international legislation. Local attitudes are often influenced by an interest in preserving industries that could not compete internationally, rather than by strict economic arguments. For example, years after beginning a campaign to create greater international competition in European energy markets, there is still a long way to go to achieve a real degree of competition among electricity and gas producers. In many European countries such producers are still state-owned monopolies that have resisted the pressures to allow new entrants.[7]

Nationalism can be limiting in international markets

Strong sentiments of nationalism, an emphasis on a country's interests before everything else, affects how macro-marketing systems work, as well as the work of many marketing managers. Nationalistic feelings can reduce sales, or even block all marketing activity, in some international markets. For many years, Japan has made it difficult for outside firms to do business there—in spite of the fact that Japanese producers of cars, colour TVs, VCRs and other products have established profitable markets in the United States, Europe and other parts of the world. The 'buy local' policy in many government contracts and business purchases reflects this same attitude in Europe. There is support for protecting European producers from foreign competition, especially producers of footwear, textiles, production machinery and cars.

Nationalistic feelings can determine whether a firm can enter markets because businesses often must get permission to operate. In some political environments, this is only a routine formality. In others, a lot of bureaucracy and personal influence are involved, and bribes are sometimes expected. This raises ethical issues for marketing managers. There are also legal issues since it

is illegal for European firms to offer such bribes. Clearly, that can make it difficult for a European firm to compete with a company from a country that does not have similar laws.

Regional groupings are becoming more important

Important dimensions of the political environment are likely to be similar among nations that have banded together to have common regional economic boundaries. An outstanding example of this sort of regional grouping is the economic unification of the countries in Europe. In the past, each of the countries of the European Union had its own trade rules and regulations. These differences made it difficult and expensive to move products from one country to the other, or to develop economies of scale. Now, the individual countries are reshaping into a unified economic superpower, what some have called the 'United States of Europe'. This unification has eliminated many barriers to inter-European trade. The increased efficiency is reducing costs and the prices that European consumers must pay, and creating millions of new jobs. The changes are by no means complete. The EU may expand to include at least 25 countries and 450 million people in the coming years.

Few people could have predicted the changes in the political environment that have brought about the massive changes in these markets. But the changes have dramatically altered opportunities available to marketing managers both in Europe and in other parts of the world. Europe is now the largest unified market in the world.

The unification of European markets

Of course, removal of some economic and political barriers will not eliminate the need to adjust strategies to reach submarkets of European consumers. Centuries of cultural differences will not instantly disappear nor may they ever do so. Yet the cooperative arrangement will give firms that operate in Europe easier access to larger markets, and the European countries will have a more powerful voice in protecting their own interests.

The political environment usually does not change as dramatically or as rapidly as it has in Europe. Some important political changes, both within and across nations, evolve more gradually. The development of consumerism is a good example.

Consumerism

Consumerism is a social movement that seeks to increase the rights and powers of consumers. In the last 30 years, consumerism has emerged as a major political force. The roots of the consumerist movement lie in the early 1960s, when increasing concern was expressed by many consumers about the potential problems that could be created by firms that were only interested in making profits rather than satisfying customer needs.

The basic rights of the consumer, to safety, to be informed, to choose and to be heard were originally stated by the American President Kennedy in a 'Consumer Bill of Rights'. Since then the voice of the consumer has become increasingly vocal on issues such as the impact of marketing on the environment—the so-called 'green' movement—and on ethical issues such as the sale of products or services that could damage the health and general well-being of consumers and the public at large.

It is clear that many organizations are influenced by consumerist issues in terms of the marketing decisions that they make. The recycling of packaging is one example, where attention is now being paid to using materials that can be used again (such as aluminium cans), and even the humble glass bottle is making a comeback, because it can be cleaned and reused several times. BMW emphasizes the extent to which the materials in its cars can now be recycled. Volvo builds its sales case around the safety of its cars.[8]

The organization, through its top management and marketing function must continue to pay attention to consumer concerns. The processes that are used to produce products, the products themselves, the way in which they are packaged and made available to the market may cause consumers and citizens concern. The old, production-oriented ways of doing things are no longer acceptable.[9]

GENETICALLY-MODIFIED FOOD

Macro-environmental forces are having a significant impact on the food industry. Developments in technology have enabled scientists to genetically engineer food. The technology has been described as akin to cross-breeding—adding a new gene to a plant or animal. Cross-breeding is limited in that it is possible with only the same species or close relatives. With genetic engineering, however, any genes can be mixed so theoretically there are no limits. For example, adding to strawberries an antifreeze protein from the flounder fish allows strawberries to be grown in cold climates. Some genetically modified cereals are already making their way into foodstuffs. Soya is used in 60 per cent of processed foods. The United States produces the majority of the world's soya and already about one-third of the crops is genetically modified (GM).

For businesses involved in the genetic engineering technology, the stakes are very high. Monsanto has spent around $1 billion on research and development while European companies such as Novartis, Zeneca and AgrEvo are also committed to GM foodstuffs. Mergers are alliances of companies within the overall agriculture and food sectors are taking place as companies try to position themselves to make profits for the future.

The big question is whether the European consumer will accept GM foods. If consumers are reluctant to buy these products then the investments are not going to be very profitable. Consumers have shown concern about the safety of GM crops and some 'eco-warriors' have vandalized them. Europeans think that they have better taste than Americans. Famed for their Mediterranean diet, high in fresh fruit, vegetables and olive oil, Europeans turn up their noses at scientifically created foods. What is the point of buying a tomato that has been engineered to taste better, but may prove harmful to health, when Mediterranean tomatoes taste wonderful anyway?

Europeans are anxious to know about the products they are eating and that GM foods are labelled as such. However, this is proving difficult, as most processed foods will have some genetically modified organisms present, even if the amount is very small. Member states rejected a European Commission recommendation to label foods with the wording 'may contain genetically modified organisms'. This was seen as too vague to give consumers confidence. On the other hand, proving whether a food contains GM organisms or not is simply impossible in many cases. As regulators, the EU is finding it difficult to reconcile all its interests—to protect consumers, support industry, respect national governments and maintain good trading relationships with the United States.

In the meantime, biotechnology and life sciences companies continue their investment in genetic engineering. Monsanto embarked on a $5 million advertising campaign to persuade European consumers of the merits of GM food. The campaign, run in France and the United Kingdom, suggests that GM will help to solve the world's food problems. Unusually for an advertising campaign, however, it also gives the contact details for organizations such as Greenpeace that hold opposing views.

Although many consumers are suspicious of biotechnology and its products, GM plants are expected to be easier and cheaper to produce. If that is the case, then the consumer may be won over by cheaper prices. In the United Kingdom, a GM, well-labelled tomato purée has been selling better than the conventional version for two years. The reason lies in it being 10–15 per cent cheaper than the alternative.[10]

LEGAL ENVIRONMENT

Changes in the political environment often lead to changes in the legal environment and in the way existing laws are enforced. Knowing all the relevant laws is sometimes difficult for a marketing manager, but it is important because the legal environment sets the basic rules for how a business can operate in society. It may severely limit some choices, but changes in laws and how they are interpreted also creates new opportunities. Allianz, a major German insurance company, has already taken steps to defend itself from fiercer competition at home as the EU deregulates the insurance market. Germany will be among those affected most by EU directives, which since July 1994, have allowed Europe's insurance companies to sell policies anywhere in the Union on the basis of regulations in their home states.

Local controls on the wording of policies and on rates have also been removed. In response, Allianz has reorganized the non-life side of its business into divisions serving three consumer groups—personal customers, small- and medium-sized commercial business and large industrial clients. The company is also preparing to adapt its products rapidly in response to changing demands.

 Internet Exercise

The World Trade Organisation is a very important force behind the global move to free trade, but trade disputes still emerge. Go to the WTO web site (www.wto.org) and find out how the WTO settles disputes. Do you think that this procedure favours the developed nations, the less-developed nations, or neither? Explain your thinking.

Trying to encourage competition

European economic and legislative thinking is based on the idea that competition among firms helps the economy. Therefore, attempts by business to limit competition are generally thought to be against the public interest and national governments spend a great deal of time trying to ensure that single companies do not dominate local markets. Paradoxically, the same governments frequently spend a great deal of time trying to ensure that domestic companies remain as suppliers in many markets and are not driven out by overseas competition. Frequently this is accomplished by preferential treatment to domestic suppliers in terms of investment incentives or different tax regimes (both now not allowed under EU competition rules).

There is sometimes an argument in favour of allowing companies to have high market shares when there are obvious advantages to the consumer. For example,

there may be economies of scale (see the discussion of this basic economic principle in Appendix A which follows Chapter 20), which make it more efficient for a few large suppliers to meet the needs of the market. Alternatively in some markets the costs of technological development may be such that companies with a small share of the market would never be able to recover their investment.

Each country has its own legal system with different laws and standards for product performance which can affect marketing decisions. Within the EU there are differences (sometimes large) between the standards operating in different countries. This has historically led to difficulties for manufacturers operating across national boundaries. For example, prior to harmonization of legislation, Philips, the Dutch manufacturer of televisions, had to produce eight different models of each television set to comply with the various national standards that existed throughout the community. Many of the advantages of the Union (the economies of large-scale production) were being lost. In the car industry alone, the costs of differing standards and regulations were estimated at being ecu286 million. The creation of a single market could lead to price reductions of up to 10 per cent due to economies of scale and greater competition between international suppliers with free access to each others' markets.[11]

Penalties for breaking the rules can be severe

In the majority of situations legislation has been designed in such a way as to encourage competition and discourage practices that may reduce competition. When companies are shown to have broken the rules then the penalties can be severe. The example of price fixing in the carton-board market shows what can happen when companies break the rules. The European Commission imposed record fines on 19 carton-board producers who had allegedly formed what it described as Europe's 'most pernicious' price-fixing cartel. Suppliers of carton-board in Western Europe face fines totalling ecu132.15 million (£104.27 million) with the cartel's 'ringleaders' bearing the brunt. Individual managers can also be held to be liable and subject to fines or imprisonment as a consequence of breaking the law. The cartel was uncovered in a series of unannounced inspections carried out simultaneously by the Commission after complaints by British and French carton-users' trade associations. The case is one of a number in which a cartel has been fined by the European Commission for distorting competition in the single market.

Consumer protection laws are not new

Some consumer protection is built into the legal systems of most countries. A seller has to tell the truth (if asked a direct question), meet contracts and stand behind the firm's product (to some reasonable extent). Beyond this, it is expected that vigorous competition in the market-place will protect consumers *so long as they are careful*.

Companies that are truly market oriented should not contemplate harming the customer in any way through the sale of dangerous products or services. They should also not be deceitful in the way in which they describe such products or services. Such companies should also be sensitive to environmental issues such as waste and pollution. However, this is an ideal situation and unfortunately many firms either deliberately or otherwise fail to meet these standards. Therefore most national governments have found it necessary to pass other laws. These cover a range of areas such as the use of customer databases, packaging and labels, credit practices, and environmental issues.

Consumerists and the law say: 'Let the seller beware'

The old rule about buyer–seller relations—*let the buyer beware*—has shifted to *let the seller beware*. The shift to pro consumer laws and court decisions suggests that there is more interest now in protecting consumers. This may upset production-oriented managers. But times have changed—and managers will just have to adapt to these new political and legal environments. After all, it is the consumers—through their government representatives—who determine the kind of economic system they want.

CULTURAL AND SOCIAL ENVIRONMENT

The cultural and social environment affects how and why people live and behave as they do—which affects customer buying behaviour and eventually the economic, political and legal environment. Many variables make up the cultural and social environment. Some examples are the languages people speak, the type of education they have, their religious beliefs, what type of food they eat, the style of clothing and housing they have, and how they view marriage and family. Because the cultural and social environment has such broad effects, most people do not stop to think about it, or how it may be changing, or how it may differ for other people.

A marketing manager cannot afford to take the cultural and social environment for granted. Although changes tend to come slowly, they can have far-reaching effects. Seeing the changes early may help in identifying big opportunities. Further, within any broad society the cultural and social environment may affect different subgroups of people in different ways. These differences require special attention when segmenting markets. In fact, dealing with these differences is often one of the greatest challenges when planning strategies for international markets.

Since we will discuss details of how the cultural and social environment relates to buying behaviour in Chapters 3 and 4, here we will just use an example to illustrate its impact on marketing strategy planning.

Changing women's roles

The shifting roles of women in society illustrate the importance of the cultural and social environment on marketing strategy planning. Forty years ago many people felt that a woman's role was in the home—first and foremost as a wife and mother. Women had less opportunity for higher education, and were completely shut out of many of the most interesting jobs. Obviously, there have been changes in that stereotyped thinking. With better job opportunities, more women are delaying marriage, and once married they are likely to stay in the workforce and have fewer children.

The entry of women into the job market boosted economic growth and changed society in many other ways. Many of the in-home jobs that were in the past done primarily by women, ranging from family shopping to preparing meals to doing volunteer work, still need to be done by someone. Some of these jobs have shifted to a husband or to children, which has in turn changed the target market for many products. Or, a working woman may look for help elsewhere. This has created opportunities for producers of prepared frozen meals, child-care centres, dry cleaners, financial services and the like.

Although there is still a big wage gap between men and women, the income generated by working women gives them new independence and purchasing power. For example, women now account for about half of the purchases of cars. Not long ago, many car dealers insulted a woman shopper by ignoring her or suggesting that she come back with her husband. Now the car companies have finally realized that women are important customers. It is interesting that Japanese car dealers, especially Mazda and Toyota, were the first to really pay attention to women customers. In Japan, fewer women have jobs or buy cars—the Japanese society is still very much male oriented. Perhaps it was the extreme contrast with the Japanese society that prompted these firms to pay more attention to women buyers.[12]

Changes come slowly

Most changes in basic cultural values and social attitudes come slowly. An individual firm cannot hope to encourage big changes in the short run. Instead, it is usually best to identify current attitudes and work within these constraints as it seeks new and better opportunities.

THE COMPETITIVE ENVIRONMENT

The competitive environment operates within the firm's macro-environment

Each of the areas of the macro-environment discussed in the last section can have a direct impact on the competitive environment that the company operates in. Economic recession in one country may force companies to compete overseas, increasing the level of competition in the overseas market. Technological breakthroughs may lead to new technologies that threaten existing suppliers in a market. Legislation may force national governments to reduce the level of protection given to domestic companies, thereby opening up markets to overseas competitors. Therefore the macro-environment and the competitive environment are directly related. Changes in the former will directly affect the latter.

The competitive environment is critical

Every organization competes with other organizations for customers or clients. Even non-profit organizations have competitors. For example charities compete with other charities for the support of the general public. Government organizations compete with other government organizations for a share of the national budget. Therefore it is important to keep a close eye on the competition and try to take competitive moves into account when developing marketing plans.

Choose opportunities that avoid head-on competition

The competitive environment affects the number and types of competitors the marketing manager must face—and how they may behave. Although a marketing manager usually cannot control these factors, it is often possible to choose strategies that will avoid head-on competition. Or, where competition is inevitable, to plan for it.

Economists describe four basic kinds of market (competitive) situations: pure competition, oligopoly, monopolistic competition and monopoly. Understanding the differences among these market situations is helpful in analysing the competitive environment, and our discussion assumes some familiarity with these concepts. (For a

review, see Exhibit A-11 and the related discussion in Appendix A which follows Chapter 20).

The economist's traditional view is that most product-markets head towards pure competition—or oligopoly—over the long-run. In these situations, a marketing manager competes for customers against competitors who are offering very similar products. Because customers see the different available products (marketing mixes) as close substitutes, competing firms are pressed to compete with lower and lower prices, especially in pure competition where there are likely to be a very large number of competitors. Profit margins shrink until they are just high enough to keep the most efficient firms in business.

Avoiding pure competition is sensible and certainly fits with our emphasis on target marketing. In fact the reasons for avoiding head-on competition help to explain why learning about effective target marketing is fundamentally different from learning about effective decision making in other areas of business. Accounting, production and financial managers for competing firms can learn about and use the same, standardized approaches and they will work well in each case. By contrast, marketing managers cannot just learn about and adopt the same 'good' marketing strategy that is being used by other firms. That just leads to head-on competition and a downward spiral in prices and profits. So target marketers try to offer customers a marketing mix that is better suited to their needs than competitors' offerings.

Competition-free environments are rare

Most marketing managers would like to have such a strong marketing mix that customers see it as uniquely able to meet their needs. This competition-free ideal guides the search for breakthrough opportunities. Yet monopoly situations in which one firm completely controls a broad product-market are rare in market-directed economies. Further, government regulation of monopolies is common. For example, in most parts of the world prices set by utility companies must be approved by a government agency. Although most marketing managers cannot expect to operate with complete control in an unregulated monopoly, they can move away from head-on competition.

Monopolistic competition is typical and a challenge

In monopolistic competition a number of different firms offer marketing mixes that at least some customers see as different. Each competitor is trying to get control (a monopoly) in its 'own' target market, but there is still competition because some customers see the various alternatives as substitutes. A subset of competing firms may even be in a head-on rivalry for the same customers with marketing mixes that are very similar. With monopolistic competition, each firm has it own down-sloping demand curve. But the shape of the demand curve and elasticity of demand depend on the extent to which competitors' products and marketing mixes are similar. Monopolistic competition is typical of the situation faced by the majority of marketing managers in developed economies.

In monopolistic competition, marketing managers sometimes try to differentiate very similar products by relying on other elements of the marketing mix. For example, in the detergent market considerable changes have taken place including moves from cardboard cartons to plastic containers, to refillable containers of different sizes and different levels of concentration of powders and liquids. Such approaches may not work, especially if there is little to prevent competitors from imitating the new ideas. Efforts to promote real, but subtle, differences may not be effective. If potential customers view the different offerings as essentially similar, the market will become more and more competitive and a firm must rely on lower costs to obtain a competitive advantage. On the other hand, real changes must offer significant benefit to customers or the competitive advantage will be lost.

Unilever, the leading Anglo-Dutch manufacturer of detergents, attempted to change the detergent market-place radically through its launch of 'power' detergents in 1994. Persil was a strong brand, which had a major market share. By incorporating manganese particles in the detergent the company was able to claim better cleaning properties. Unfortunately for Unilever, its major competitors very quickly claimed that use of this new detergent damaged clothes which were washed in the new detergent. This adverse publicity led to a considerable setback for the company.[13]

Analyse competitors to find a competitive advantage

The best way for a marketing manager to avoid head-on competition is to find new or better ways to satisfy customers' needs. The search for a breakthrough

opportunity, or at least some sort of competitive advantage, requires an understanding of customers and competitors. That is why marketing managers turn to competitor analysis—an organized approach for evaluating the strengths and weaknesses of current or potential competitors' marketing strategies. A complete development of the possible approaches for competitor analysis is beyond the scope of this book but we will briefly cover an approach that works well in many different market situations.

The approach is a logical extension of the marketing strategy planning framework. The basic idea is simple. The current (or planned) target market and marketing mix is compared with what competitors are currently doing, or are likely to do in response to your strategy. The initial step in competitor analysis is to identify potential competitors. It is useful to start broadly—and from the point of view of target customers. Companies may be offering quite different products to meet the same needs, but the companies are competitors if customers see them as offering close substitutes. For example, fax machines and email compete in the same generic market to meet consumers' communication needs. Identifying a broad set of potential competitors helps in understanding the different ways customers are currently meeting needs and sometimes points to new opportunities. Usually, however, marketing managers quickly narrow the focus of their analysis to the set of competitive rivals—firms who will be the closest competitors.

Rivals who are offering similar products are usually easy to identify. However, if a strategy involves a product concept that is really new and different, there may not be a current competitor with a similar product. In that case, the closest competitor may be a firm that is currently serving similar needs with a different product. Although such firms may not appear to be close competitors, they are likely to fight back perhaps with a directly competitive product, if another firm starts to take away customers.

Anticipate future competition

Even if no specific competitors can be identified, think about how long it might take for potential competitors to appear, and what they might do. It is easy to make the mistake of assuming that there will not be competition in the future or of discounting how aggressive competition may become. The problem is that a successful strategy will attract the interest of others who are eager to jump in for a share of the profit, even if profits only hold up for a short time. That is why it is important to find opportunities where you can sustain a competitive advantage over the longer run. Finding a sustainable competitive advantage requires special attention to competitor strengths and weaknesses. For example, it is very difficult to dislodge a competitor who is already a market leader simply by attacking with a strategy that has similar strengths. An established leader can usually defend its position by quickly copying the best parts of what a new competitor is trying to do. On the other hand, an established competitor may not be able to defend quickly if it is attacked where it is weak.

Business travellers have historically preferred air travel between Brussels, Paris and other continental countries to London. With the opening of the Channel tunnel travel time by rail between London and Continental capitals has fallen dramatically. If passengers are travelling from city centre to city centre, travel times from Brussels to London and Paris to London are now comparable with those needed to fly. Moreover, many passengers also prefer to travel by rail, finding it more relaxing and giving greater opportunity to work or plan meetings with colleagues.

The response of the airlines has been to increase the range of services offered to their most important customers—the business travellers—particularly in terms of refurbished and extended executive lounges and other passenger benefits. However, the fundamental differences between the two modes of transport may make it very difficult for the airlines to compete effectively in the future.

Seek information about competitors

A marketing manager should actively seek information about current or potential competitors. Although most firms try to keep the specifics of their plans secret, much public information may be available. For example, many firms routinely monitor competitors' local newspapers. In one such case, an article discussed a change in the competitor's sales organization. An alert marketing manager realized that the change was made to strengthen the competitor's ability to take business from one of her firm's key target markets. This early warning provided time to make adjustments. Other sources of competitor information include trade publications, alert sales staff, intermediaries and other industry experts. In business markets, customers may be quick to explain what competing suppliers are offering.

 ### Ethical issues may arise

The search for information about competitors sometimes raises ethical issues. For example, it's not unusual for people to change jobs and move to a competing firm in the same industry. These people may have a great deal of information about the competitor, but that raises questions about what information it would be ethical to use. Similarly, some firms have been criticized for going too far—like waiting at the rubbish tip to go through competitors' rubbish to find copies of confidential company reports.

Direct competition cannot always be avoided

Despite the desire to avoid highly competitive situations, especially pure competition, a firm may find that it cannot do this. The firm may already be in an industry before it becomes intensely competitive. Then, as some competitors fail, new firms enter the market, possibly because they do not have more attractive alternatives and can at least earn a living. In less developed economies, this is a common pattern with small retailers and wholesalers. New entrants may not even know how competitive the market is but they stay until they run out of money. Production-oriented firms are more likely to make such a mistake.

RESPONDING TO THE ENVIRONMENT

Many of the environmental forces discussed here will develop regardless of what is done by individual companies and their marketing managers. For example, interest rates will change, the workforce will contain more women, and the EU will pass legislation and regulations, and so on. The key point to appreciate is that businesses need to anticipate the changes and monitor them. They must also interpret the changes and decipher the business implications. On that basis, they can identify opportunities and threats and prepare for them. Marketing is the organizational function with greatest external focus on customers, competitors and other environmental forces. It is also the function that may provide the response to the environment's opportunities and threats. In many cases this response will involve a change to the marketing mix or the development of a new marketing strategy. As a response to changes in the marketing environment the company may decide to enter or withdraw from a market, new products may be developed and others deleted or adapted, the sales force may change in composition, new channels of distribution may be opened, a web site may be established, price levels may be changed and so on.

SUMMARY

Innovative strategy planning is needed for survival in our increasingly competitive markets. In this chapter, we discussed the variables that shape the environment of marketing strategy planning—and how they may affect opportunities. First we looked at the environments that are external to the firm. They are important because changes in these environments present new opportunities, as well as problems, that a marketing manager must deal with in marketing strategy planning.

The economic environment, including changes of recession or inflation, affects the choice of strategies. And the marketer must try to anticipate, understand and deal with these changes, as well as changes in the technological base underlying the economic environment.

The marketing manager must also be aware of legal restrictions—and be sensitive to changing political climates. The acceptance of consumerism has already forced many changes. Legal and political forces operate at national and international levels. The social and cultural environment relate to the context in which we live, our beliefs and values and our lifestyles. These issues will be addressed more fully in the following chapters. A manager must also study the competitive environment. How well established are competitors? Are there competitive barriers, and what effect will they have? How will competitors respond to a plan?

The marketing manager must monitor the environment and anticipate and identify the forces at work. Interpreting the changes in terms of their opportunity and threat is a key marketing task. Developing effective responses to the environment may mean changing elements of the marketing mix or developing a new marketing strategy. Clearly, marketing management is a challenging job that requires much integration of information from many disciplines.

QUESTIONS AND PROBLEMS

1. Discuss how economic issues such as interest rates and income levels impact on consumers and businesses. Choose an industry or sector and give examples.
2. Discuss how a company's financial strength may have a bearing on the kinds of products it produces. Will it have an impact on the other elements of the marketing mix as well? If so, how? Use an example in your answer.
3. Select an industry and describe the impact that changing technology has had on it over the past few years. What is its likely impact in the next five years?
4. How does the political environment affect businesses? Give examples of groups that may try to lobby government on particular business issues.
5. Does the elimination of trade barriers between countries in Europe eliminate the need to consider submarkets of European consumers. Why or why not?
6. Why is it necessary to have so many laws regulating business?
7. What and whom is the government trying to protect in its efforts to preserve and regulate competition?
8. Give and example of a significant cultural change that has occurred over the past decade. What are the marketing implications of this change?
9. In your own words, explain how a marketing manager might use competitor analysis to avoid situations that involve head-on competition.
10. The owner of a small grocery store—the only one in a small rural town—has just learned that a large chain plans to open a store nearby. How difficult will it be for the owner to plan for this new competitive threat? Explain your answer.

SUGGESTED CASES

5. Sophia's Ristorante
15. Deluxe Foods Ltd

REFERENCES

1. D. Sumner Smith, 'Wrestling with politicians', *The Sunday Times*, 16 August 1998, Business section, p. 10.
2. H.T. Suchard and J.C. Suchard, *Business Strategy and the Environment (UK)*, vol. 3, no. 3, 1994, pp. 16–32; D. T. Brownlie, 'The marketing audit', *Marketing Intelligence and Planning*, vol. 11, no. 1, 1993, pp. 4–13.
3. A. Garrett, 'Ready, steady, euro', *Management Today*, January 1999, pp. 50–53; I. Traynor and A. Brown, 'Day of the euro dawns', *The Observer*, 3 January 1999, Focus section, p. 13.
4. P. Dapiran, 'Benetton—global logistics in action', *International Journal of Physical Distribution & Logistics Management*, vol. 22, no. 6, 1992, pp. 7–11.
5. G. Hamel and J. Sampler, 'The e-corporation', *Fortune*, 7 December 1998, pp. 52–63; Erick Schonfeld, 'Schwab puts it all online', *Fortune*, 7 December 1998, pp. 64–68.
6. 'The Digital Factory', *Fortune*, 14 November 1994, pp. 92–110; 'Waking Up to the New Economy', *Fortune*, 17 June 1994, pp. 36–46; For more on privacy, see: 'Who's Reading Your Screen?' *Time*, 18 January 1993, p. 46; 'Nowhere To Hide', *Time*, 11 November 1991, pp. 34–40.
7. D. Marsh, L. Barber, R. Corzine, A. Hill, M. Wolf, H. P. Frohlich, I. Davidson, A. Jackson, R. Lapper, D. Dodwell, G. Mead, D. Gardner, N. Tait, C. Milton, P. Rawsthorne, M. Cassell, E. Balls, D. Goodhart, D. Green, J.S. Schwarz, W. Dawkins, R. Peston, A. Baxter, 'The European single market', *Financial Times*, 19 January 1993, Section III, pp. 1–7.
8. For more on 'green marketing' see special issue of *Journal of Marketing Management*, vol. 14, no. 6, July 1998.
9. R. Swagler, 'Evolution and applications of the term consumerism: Theme and variations', *Journal of Consumer Affairs*, Winter 1994, pp. 347–60.
10. C. Blackledge, 'Bitten but not smitten', *The European*, 17–23 August 1998, pp. 8–11; Robin McKie, 'Europe to lose gene harvest', *The Observer*, 27 December 1998, p. 22.
11. P. Cecchini, *The European Challenge of 1992: Benefits of the Single Market*, Gower/Commission of the EC, Aldershot, 1988.
12. For more on firms targeting women, see 'Nike has women in mind', *Advertising Age*, 4 January 1993, p. 36; 'BMW tailors for women', *Brandweek*, 11 April 1994, p. 4; 'In the Fast Lane', *Brandweek*, 5 July 1993, pp. 21–24.
13. R.O.D. Summers and N. Buckley, 'Soap wars: Washing of dirty linen leaves deep stains—When Unilever and Procter & Gamble clash everyone pays a price', *Financial Times*, 21 December 1994, p. 9.

CHAPTER 3
Understanding the Consumer Environment

When You Finish This Chapter, You Should

1 Know about population and income trends in European markets and how they affect marketers.

2 Know how consumer spending is related to family life cycle and other demographic dimensions.

3 Understand the economic man model of buyer behaviour.

4 Understand how psychological variables affect an individual's buying behaviour.

5 Understand how social influences affect an individual's and household's buying behaviours.

6 See why the purchase situation has an effect on consumer behaviour.

7 Know how consumers use problem-solving processes.

8 Understand the important new terms (shown in colour).

The word unisex somehow seems trapped in the 1970s, when entrepreneurs tried to persuade the children of the 1960s sexual revolution to sport the same haircuts, wear the same jeans and use the same toilets. Unisex, or the concept behind it, was central when Calvin Klein, the US fashion designer behind such bestselling fragrances as Obsession, Eternity and Escape, launched the scent cK one.

Whereas Eternity, Escape and other perfumes are aimed either at women or men, cK one is what Calvin Klein calls a 'shared fragrance' for the young consumers who, he believes, are happy to buy a scent created for both sexes. Calvin Klein Cosmetics, a subsidiary of Unilever, the Anglo-Dutch consumer products group, is known for big fragrances with big smells. Research suggested that there was a new generation of young consumers who wanted something new and fresh with a lighter smell that did not fit into the conventional categories.

Calvin Klein is not the only cosmetics company to have detected a demand from consumers for innovation in the fragrance market. After an uncertain period in which the industry has adopted a conservative approach to product development, a number of other groups—notably L'Oréal of France and Japan's Shiseido—have become more experimental. The prestige perfume market remained relatively resilient during the recession and has grown rapidly as economic conditions have improved.

Industry estimates suggest that retail sales have risen, yet profitability has been depressed by the expansion of big companies, such as France's Elf Sanofi and Estée Lauder of the United States, as well as L'Oréal, Shiseido and Unilever which has heralded a new era of escalating advertising budgets. The cost of launching a new fragrance worldwide rose in the mid-1990s to US$40 million (£26.6 million) thereby raising the risk of costly failures.

These pressures encouraged the industry to play safe in the presentation of new products. The most successful new scents of the 1990s—Tresor from L'Oréal and Champagne, Yves Saint-Laurent's first launch since its acquisition by Elf Sanofi—targeted the classic fragrance market by reflecting traditional images of luxury in their advertising.

The first sign that there was also a demand for something different was the runaway success of the fragrance Jean-Paul Gaultier, the ageing *enfant terrible* of French fashion. His scent has a fairly classic smell, but broke all the industry rules with its punky advertising campaign and a bottle (designed by Gaultier himself) in the form of a woman's torso encased in an aluminium can. The perfume was designed to capture the spirit of his fashion—witty, creative, slightly controversial. The strategy has worked with the brand a success, indicating to the industry avant garde. The advertising images used by the perfume houses had traditionally relied on pictures of classy women jumping out of private jets or fancy cars. Gaultier broke the mould.

L'Oréal responded with Eden, designed to appeal to the ecologically concerned consumers of the 1990s. Its advertising featured evocative rainforest scenes and the packaging uses a green bottle with no discernible brand name. The bottle is made from an opaline substance that changes colour to ensure that each one is unique.

But the most iconoclastic brand is undoubtedly cK one. Having decided to break new ground by launching a 'shared fragrance', Calvin Klein Cosmetics also adopted an innovative approach to marketing. It chose a tactically low price of £23 for a 100 ml bottle of cK one eau de toilette, against £32 for Obsession. It also introduced youth-oriented products, such as massage oil, and sold through unconventional outlets, such as music shops.

EFFECTIVE MARKETING BEGINS BY UNDERSTANDING THE CONSUMER

There are many different users of perfume

Think about the markets for perfume. How many different types of consumers can you identify? How do their needs differ and how do perfume producers cater for different needs? The market for perfume is very varied. There are different occasions when perfume is worn, for example a daytime fragrance is different from an evening or special occasion perfume, and the perfumes worn by young women are promoted differently from those worn by more mature customers. There are upmarket expensive perfumes, beyond the reach of those with limited income, and there are perfumes for the mass market. There has been a very rapid increase in the male cosmetics market in the last few years. Now men are as likely as women to use fragrances, typically in the form of aftershave, and frequently bought for the user as a gift.

In this market perfume manufacturers constantly search for new opportunities. These opportunities are defined in terms of target customers. For example, one target market could be the 'young independent female seeking a fragrance for use during the working day'. A second could be the 'mature married female seeking a fragrance for special occasions'. Once the target customer has been defined then the perfume can be developed to fit the profile of the target customer. The young independent female market seeking a fragrance for everyday use is likely to want a 'light' product that does not have too strong a fragrance. She may like to change and experiment with new perfumes on a regular basis, so new products are important in keeping this customer. Innovation in the way that the perfume is presented (i.e. its packaging and its image) may be important in attracting her attention. She may want a perfume that conveys a sense of fun.

In contrast the mature married female seeking a fragrance for special occasions is more likely to choose a 'heavier' fragrance. This may well be her favourite perfume for this purpose, and she may be less likely to experiment with new perfumes for such occasions. The image of the brand is equally important, and must convey the sense of occasion when it is right to use such a perfume. In her mind, some fragrances would suit a romantic evening, while others would be better for a formal event, such as a wedding or birthday celebration.

Target marketers focus on the customer

Target marketers believe that the *customer* should be the focus of all business and marketing activity. These marketers hope to develop unique marketing strategies by finding unsatisfied customers and offering them more attractive marketing mixes. They want to work in less competitive markets with more inelastic demand curves. Finding these attractive opportunities takes real knowledge of potential customers and what they want. This means finding those market dimensions that make a difference—in terms of population, income, needs, attitudes and buying behaviour.

Three important questions should be answered about any potential market:

1. Are there different types of customers in the market?
2. How big is the market?
3. Where is it?

Are there different types of customers in the market?

The first question is basic. Every customer has different needs, even if they are buying similar products. Usually it is possible to identify segments, or groups of customers with similar requirements. Each of these segments can then be satisfied with different marketing programmes. In this chapter and the next we will look at how our knowledge of consumer behaviour can be used to pick the right dimensions in the first place. Keep in mind that we aren't trying to make generalizations about average customers or how the mass market behaves, but rather how *some* people in *some* markets behave. You should expect to find differences.

How big is the market?

Once we have identified a market opportunity it is important to be able to determine the size of the market segment. This will be related to how many potential customers there are in the target segment and whether they are able to buy our product. Their ability and willingness to pay depends on such factors as their income and alternative ways in which they might spend this income.

Where is it?

We also need to identify where this market is geographically. As trade barriers have reduced within the European Union, so many companies have looked at the potential of overseas markets which they had never previously considered. Such markets may frequently be distant from their current markets, and one of the first questions is how to reach such markets. Should the company attempt to sell directly into the market? Should it find a local distributor to work with? How should it establish distribution points or warehouses to satisfy customers? Are there differences in languages or local cultures that mean that adaptation of the company's current marketing programme is necessary?

Market segmentation is the start of marketing planning

Once the company can establish the answers to these questions then it is in a position to begin the process of marketing planning. In Chapter 6 we will discuss the process of market segmentation and market selection in detail. You will see how organizations use information about the attractiveness of the market and their competitive strengths and weaknesses to make decisions about which market opportunities to pursue. Understanding the customer is the starting point for this activity.

In this chapter we focus on the final consumer. The chapter considers both demographic and behavioural dimensions. Demographic dimensions provide marketing managers with critical information about the size, location and characteristics of target markets. Behavioural dimensions help marketing managers to understand why customers behave in the way that they do. Such dimensions include the values and attitudes of consumers, the influence of family and friends on purchase behaviour and the broader influences of culture.

Much segmenting may be required

Marketers can learn a great deal about possible opportunities in different countries by studying available demographic data and trends. The examples we have considered here give you a feel, but keep in mind that much more useful data is available. For example, extensive data on every country in the world is available from Euromonitor easily accessible on a windows based CD-ROM. The types of data that are available are illustrated in Exhibit 3–1.

Demographic trends and forecasts
Economic indicators
Consumer expenditure patterns
Retailing and retail distribution
Advertising patterns and media access
Consumer market sizes
Consumer prices and costs
Households and house expenditure
Cultural indicators (e.g. literacy rates)
Pan European profiles of individual markets

Exhibit 3–1 Data available from Euromonitor, London[1]

After finding some countries or regions of possible interest (and eliminating unattractive ones), much more segmenting may be required. To illustrate how useful demographic dimensions can be in this effort, we will consider specific characteristics of the European market in some detail. Keep in mind, however, that similar ideas apply to other markets around the world.

DEMOGRAPHIC DIMENSIONS OF CONSUMER BEHAVIOUR

Marketers need a global perspective

Today most companies operate in global markets. Competition is increasingly international, and can come from any part of the world. Take a look at the country of origin of the products on your local supermarket shelf and you will see how international we have become. In other supermarkets in other countries you would see products from your country on display.

Marketing managers need a global perspective when they begin to look for market opportunities. It is increasingly important to have this point of view as political barriers to international trade reduce, and the costs of accessing and serving international markets fall. Nevertheless, it would be impossible to provide more than an overview of some of the major dimensions of every international market in a book such as this. Rather, we have chosen to give you an overview of some trends in global markets, and then move relatively quickly to a focus on European markets. Even with this limiting focus you will see that we cannot deal with every market in detail.

GUINNESS IN ASIA-PACIFIC

Although many companies have only recently discovered the potential of the Asia-Pacific markets, Guinness has had a presence there since the early part of this century. Those who went to the 'colonies' took it with them and distribution expanded from there. Guinness—a dark beer or stout—began its colonial life in Indonesia, but by 1930 was being drunk in Malaysia. The dark, bitter, viscous qualities appealed to health-conscious Chinese in Singapore, Malaysia and Hong Kong. It was sold through medical halls as a tonic and consumed in vast quantities as a disease deterrent. Although consumption per capita was actually quite low, profits were high because of the vast population and the beer's premium pricing. Over time and with the increasing affluence of the region, however, other beer companies have moved in and today there are many competing beers in Asia.

While westerners often talk about Asia-Pacific as if it were one homogeneous market it actually constitutes half of the world's population and is an array of markets. Research by Guinness in the growing Chinese markets shows that there are big differences in tastes and purchasing habits and expectations between younger and elder brothers in the same family. The research also suggests that consumers are getting closer in their needs. Beer is a universal product that plays a different role in each stage of a person's life.

The Guinness strategy aims for a consistent message that the product is distinctive and its core proposition is that of 'goodness'. Some of the execution of the communications varies across markets—for example labelling on the products may vary. Promotions do have to be tailored to match the different markets within the region. In Australia there is a well-established pub culture with session-drinking common so Guinness offered a branded leather jacket in exchange for drinking a certain amount. In Singapore, gambling and games of chance are very popular so the promotion involved giving away two BMWs (cars are very expensive there) in a game of chance.

The Chinese market represents a major opportunity for Guinness. By the year 2000 China may well be the largest beer market in the world. It has 600 breweries and the economy is growing at such a rate that the average consumer income doubles every six years. Clearly any beer company would like a part of such a vast market but for Guinness the market is a particular challenge. For a start most of the beer drunk in China is lager and most drinking takes place on-trade, usually in restaurants. As a heavy dark beer, Guinness is not the most appropriate product. For this reason, a new product—Guinness Special Light—was developed.

One of the best environments in which to drink Guinness is in an Irish pub. So Guinness has been helping entrepreneurs to establish Irish pubs in China and elsewhere. The investor owns the pub, but is supported and advised by Guinness. A Dublin-based company designs and builds the Irish pub and then flat-packs them to their destination where they are reassembled. Irish staff, Irish music and Irish food all help to re-create the atmosphere of the Irish pub. In such an atmosphere, Guinness is the drink of choice. Guinness have found that these pubs attract ex-pats and that they tend to bring along locals to introduce them to things Irish, including Guinness beer. So far Guinness reckons that its penetration in Asia will always be lower than in Europe but the sheer size of the market means that the pubs in Asia already generate twice the volumes of Guinness products than their western counterparts.[2]

Get the facts straight

It is widely thought that the income of consumers in Japan has grown rapidly in the last decade, that there is a vast and largely untapped market in China, and that many people in Ethiopia live in desperate poverty. It is also clear that demographic dimensions vary within countries: there are lots of retired people in southern Spain, many Dutch speak English, and the population in many rural communities is declining rapidly. Generalities like these may be partly true—but 'partly true' isn't good enough when it comes to making marketing strategy decisions. Fortunately, much useful information is available on the demographic dimensions of consumer markets around the world. Most of it is free because it has been collected by government agencies. When valid data is available, managers have no excuse for basing their decisions on guesses. Look at the data in this chapter and the next one in terms of selecting relevant market dimensions and estimating the potential in different market segments. Also, check your own assumptions against this data.

PEOPLE WITH MONEY MAKE MARKETS

Markets consist of people with money to spend. So it makes sense to start with a broad view of how population, income and other key demographic dimensions vary for different countries around the world. This will help you to see why so many firms are pursuing opportunities in international markets. We also give some examples to emphasize that depending on half-truths will not work in increasingly competitive international markets.

Marketers search for growing markets

Although a country's current population is important, it provides only a snapshot of the market. The population trend is also important. Generally, population growth is expected in most countries. But how rapidly? And will output increase faster than population? These are important questions for marketers. The answers affect how rapidly a country moves to higher stages of development and becomes a new market for different kinds of products.

Population, income and other demographic dimensions help to answer these questions. Exhibit 3–2 shows where long-term world population growth will come from. Notice the expected growth of countries in the Middle and Far East. India (with a population of about 920 million) and China (with a population of almost 1.2 billion) are getting even larger. You can see why so many firms from all over the world want to reach consumers in these countries now that trade barriers are relaxing. Although many of the countries in South America and Africa have much smaller populations, they too are growing at a rapid rate.

Population is becoming more concentrated

The population in some countries is spread over a very large area. Population density is important to marketers. If the population is very spread out, as it is in some countries in the former eastern Europe, it is difficult and expensive for marketers to deliver products or services at the time that consumers want them. This is especially a problem in countries that do not have efficient highway and rail systems. Similarly, a widely spread population may make promotion more difficult, especially when there are language differences or when communication systems are poor.

For example, there are approximately 10 million people in the Czech Republic. The population has grown at 2 per cent per annum over the last 10 years. There are 10 major cities with more than 100 000 inhabitants, but only 25 per cent of the population live in those cities. Prague, the capital, has 1.2 million inhabitants or approximately 10 per cent of the Czech population. Transport systems are emerging from state-owned organizations to private companies, but much of the transport and distribution infrastructure is still relatively underdeveloped, making it expensive and time consuming to reach consumers with many products or services.

The extent to which the people of a country are packed in and around urban areas varies considerably. In the United States, Venezuela, Australia, Israel and Singapore, for example, the percentage of people who live in urban areas is very high (see Exhibit 3–3). By contrast, in China and Afghanistan less than 20 per cent of the people live in major urban areas. People everywhere are moving off the farm and into industrial and urban areas. Shifts in population, combined with already dense populations, have led to extreme crowding in some parts of the world. And the crowding is likely to get worse.

The trend towards urbanization around the world is a key factor that has prompted increased interest in international markets. For many firms, the concentration of people in major cities has simplified place and promotion strategy decisions. This is especially the case for major cities in the wealthiest nations. Affluent, big city consumers often have similar lifestyles and needs. Thus, many of the products that are successful in Hamburg, Geneva or Paris are also likely to be of interest in Rome or Athens. However, it is important to keep in mind that

EXHIBIT 6=1   Population Added between 1994 and 2020

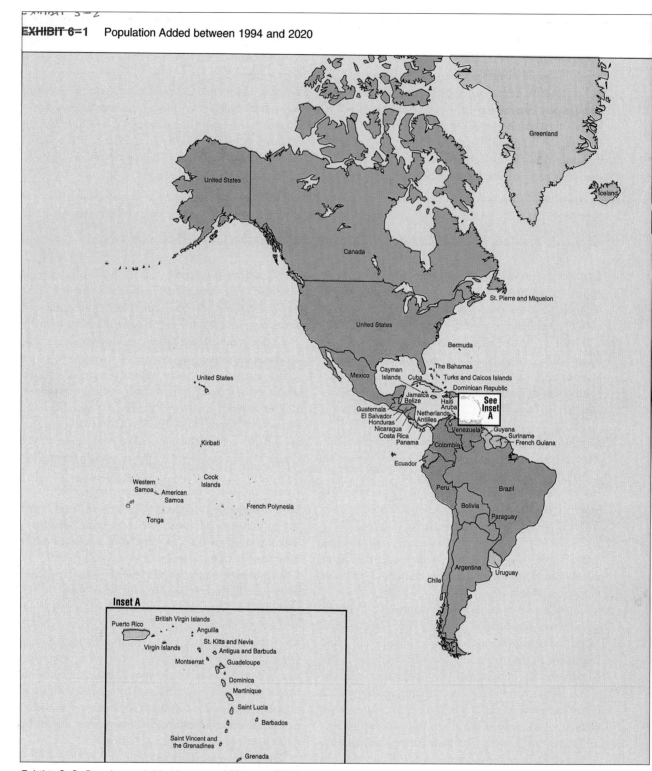

Exhibit 3–2 Population Added between 1994 and 2020

many of the world's consumers, whether they are crowded in cities or widely spread in rural areas, live in deplorable conditions. For them, there is little hope for an escape from the crush of poverty. They certainly have needs but they do not have the income to do anything about the needs.

There's no market when there's no income
Profitable markets require income—as well as people. The amount of money people can spend affects the products they are likely to buy. When considering international markets, income is often one of the most important demographic dimensions. The best available measure of total

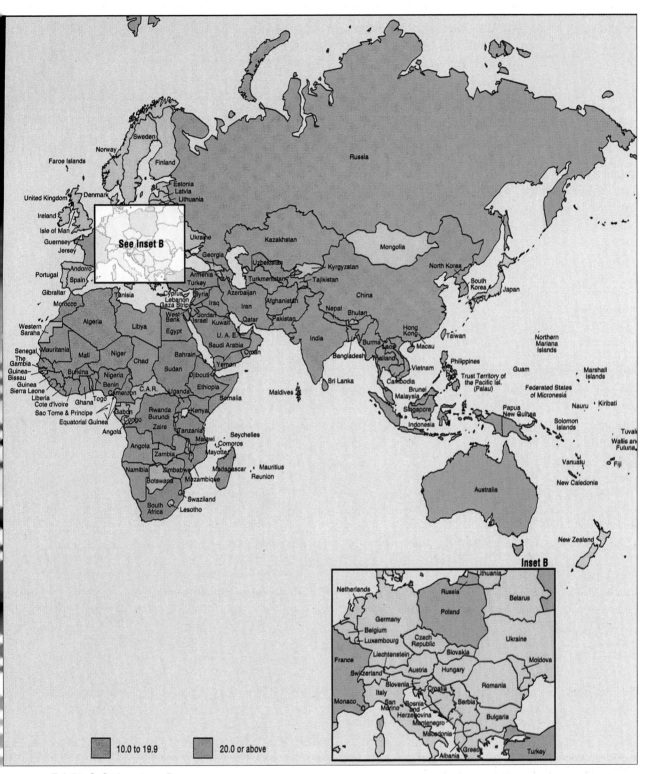

Exhibit 3–2 *(continued)*

income in most countries is **gross domestic product (GDP)**—the total market value of goods and services produced in an economy in a year. Unfortunately, GDP measures are not ideal for comparing very different cultures and economies. For instance, do-it-yourself activities, household services and the growing of produce or meat by family members for their own use are not usually figured as part of GDP. Since the activities of self-sufficient family units are not included, GDP can give a false picture of economic well-being in less developed countries.

However, gross domestic product *is* a useful measure and sometimes it is the only available measure of market

Country	2000 Population (000s)	1990–2000 Percentage Annual Population Growth	1997 Years for Population to Double	1997 Population Density (people per sq. mile)	1997 Percentage of Population in Urban Areas	1995 GNP (millions of $US)	1995 GNP per Capita	1995 Percentage Annual GNP Growth	1995 Literacy Percentage
Afghanistan	26 668	5.9	25	95	18	3 154	192	0.0	31.5
Algeria	31 788	2.3	29	32	50	44 609	1 600	3.0	61.6
Argentina	37 218	1.3	56	34	87	278 431	8 030	−5.0	96.2
Australia	18 950	1.1	100	6	85	337 909	18 720	3.0	100.0
Bangladesh	132 081	1.8	35	2 424	16	28 599	240	4.0	38.1
Brazil	169 545	1.2	48	50	76	579 787	3 640	3.0	83.3
Cameroon	15 966	2.9	25	81	44	8 615	650	3.0	63.4
Canada	29 989	1.2	127	8	77	537 695	19 380	2.0	96.6
Chile	14 996	1.3	46	50	86	59 151	4 160	10.0	95.2
China	1 253 438	1.0	67	339	29	744 890	620	10.0	81.5
Colombia	39 172	1.7	33	93	70	70 263	1 910	3.0	91.3
Croatia	5 044	−0.0	–	230	74	15 508	3 250	−1.0	95.7
Cuba	11 131	0.5	102	257	54	23 000	2 068	1.4	97.6
Ecuador	12 360	2.0	30	109	59	15 997	1 390	1.0	90.1
Egypt	68 437	2.0	34	169	44	45 507	790	2.0	51.4
Ethiopia	63 514	2.8	25	136	15	5 722	100	6.0	35.5
Finland	5 115	0.3	257	43	65	105 174	20 580	4.0	100.0
France	59 079	0.4	204	278	74	1 451 051	24 990	2.0	100.0
Germany	85 684	−0.1	–	622	85	2 252 343	27 510	1.7	100.0
Ghana	19 272	2.4	24	204	36	6 719	390	4.0	64.5
Greece	10 735	0.6	1733	210	72	85 885	8 210	2.0	96.7
Haiti	6 901	1.3	39	621	32	1 777	250	4.0	45.0
Iceland	280	0.9	79	7	92	6 686	24 950	2.0	100.0
India	1 012 909	1.7	36	843	26	319 660	340	6.0	52.0
Indonesia	219 267	1.6	40	297	31	190 105	980	7.0	83.8
Iran	71 879	2.3	26	107	58	158 000	2 449	3.0	72.3
Iraq	24 731	2.9	25	133	70	44 872	2 298	5.0	70.8
Israel	5 852	2.6	47	705	90	87 875	15 920	7.0	95.6
Italy	57 807	−0.0	–	507	67	1 088 085	19 020	3.0	98.1
Jamaica	2 669	0.8	41	626	50	3 803	1 510	0.0	85.0
Japan	126 582	0.2	289	825	78	4 963 587	39 640	1.0	100.0
Kenya	30 490	2.4	27	131	27	7 583	280	7.0	78.1
Kuwait	2 420	1.3	32	302	96	28 941	17 390	3.0	78.6
Libya	6 294	3.7	19	8	85	20 323	4 671	−6.0	76.2
Madagascar	15 295	2.8	21	63	22	3 178	230	2.0	45.7
Malaysia	21 610	2.1	31	161	51	78 321	3 890	9.0	83.5
Mexico	102 912	1.9	32	131	71	304 596	3 320	−9.0	89.6

Exhibit 3–3 Demographic Dimensions for Representative Countries

potential. Exhibit 3–4 gives a GDP estimate for 18 European countries. You can see that Germany, France, the United Kingdom and Italy have the biggest share of European GDP. This is why so much trade takes place between these countries, and why many firms see them as the more important markets.[3]

Income growth expands markets

On the other hand, the fastest *growth* in GDP is not necessarily in those countries with the largest GDPs. For example, while the GDP of Switzerland remained relatively constant between $100 and $105 billion from 1988 to 1993, during the same period GDP in Spain

Country	2000 Population (000s)	1990–2000 Percentage Annual Population Growth	1997 Years for Population to Double	1997 Population Density (people per sq. mile)	1997 Percentage of Population in Urban Areas	1995 GNP (millions of $US)	1995 GNP per Capita	1995 Percentage Annual GNP Growth	1995 Literacy Percentage
Morocco	32 229	2.1	35	176	51	29 545	1 110	–7.0	43.7
Mozambique	19 614	3.3	26	60	28	1 353	80	3.0	40.1
Nepal	24 364	2.4	31	429	10	4 391	200	4.0	27.5
Netherlands	15 893	0.6	223	1 195	61	371 039	24 000	2.0	100.0
Nicaragua	4 729	2.8	23	94	63	1 659	380	21.0	65.7
Nigeria	117 328	3.0	23	305	16	28 411	260	4.0	57.1
North Korea	25 491	1.7	39	523	61	21 000	894	3.0	99.0
Norway	4 461	0.5	204	37	74	136 077	31 250	4.0	100.0
Pakistan	141 145	2.1	25	440	28	59 991	460	5.0	37.8
Panama	2 821	1.7	37	92	55	7 235	2 750	4.0	90.8
Peru	26 198	1.8	32	50	70	55 019	2 310	8.0	88.7
Philippines	80 961	2.2	30	661	47	71 865	1 050	6.0	94.6
Poland	39 010	0.2	573	329	62	107 829	2 790	8.0	100.0
Romania	20 996	–0.2	–	241	55	33 488	1 480	7.0	97.9
Russia	147 938	–0.5	–	22	73	331 948	2 240	–4.0	99.5
Saudi Arabia	22 246	3.4	23	24	80	133 540	7 040	–1.0	62.8
Singapore	3 620	1.8	64	14 369	100	79 831	26 730	10.0	91.1
Somalia	10 880	2.7	22	41	24	1 047	156	0.6	24.0
South Africa	44 018	1.7	46	90	57	130 918	3 160	3.0	81.8
South Korea	47 351	1.0	75	1 212	74	425 000	9 437	9.0	98.0
Spain	39 545	0.2	1 386	204	64	532 347	13 580	3.0	97.1
Sri Lanka	19 377	1.2	47	751	22	12 616	700	5.0	90.2
Sudan	35 530	2.9	33	36	27	7 759	285	–1.3	50.6
Sweden	9 052	0.6	4 077	56	83	209 720	23 750	3.0	100.0
Switzerland	7 374	0.8	231	472	68	286 014	40 630	1.0	100.0
Syria	17 759	3.4	25	227	51	15 780	1 120	6.0	70.8
Taiwan	22 214	0.9	73	1 739	75	264 000	12 390	7.9	93.0
Tanzania	31 045	2.2	23	86	21	3 703	120	4.0	67.8
Thailand	61 164	1.1	63	301	19	159 630	2 740	8.0	93.8
Turkey	66 618	1.7	43	213	63	169 452	2 780	8.0	82.3
Uganda	21 891	2.5	24	267	11	4 668	240	11.0	61.8
Ukraine	50 380	–0.6	–	217	68	84 084	1 630	–13.0	98.8
United Kingdom	58 894	0.3	433	628	90	1 094 734	18 700	2.0	100.0
United States	274 943	1.0	116	76	75	7 100 007	26 980	2.0	99.5
Venezuela	23 596	2.0	33	66	85	65 382	3 020	3.0	91.1
Vietnam	78 350	1.7	43	598	20	17 634	240	8.0	93.7
Zimbabwe	11 777	1.5	26	77	31	5 933	540	–1.0	85.1

Exhibit 3–3 (continued)

went from $190 to $210 billion. GDP tells us about the income of a whole nation, but in a country with a large population that income must be spread over more people. GDP per person is a useful figure because it gives some idea of the income level of people in a country. For example, Exhibit 3–4 shows that GDP per capita in Norway, Switzerland, Denmark, Sweden and other northern European countries is relatively high.

Disposable income

Families do not get to spend all of their income. **Disposable income** is what is left after taxes. Out of this

	1977	1980	1985	1987	1988	1989	1990	1991
EU								
Austria	796	995	1 348	1 481	1 566	1 673	1 801	1 928
Belgium	2 842	3 519	4 856	5 208	5 564	6 032	6 422	6 743
Denmark	279	374	615	700	732	767	799	828
Finland	130	193	335	392	434	487	515	481
France	1 918	2 808	4 700	5 337	5 735	6 160	6 510	6 764
Germany							2 684	2 684
Germany, East[a]	164	187	232	254	261	240	190	
Germany, West	1 198	1 471	1 821	1 991	2 096	2 224	2 425	
Greece	964	1 711	4 618	6 259	7 572	8 805	10 551	12 889
Ireland	6	9	18	20	23	25	27	28
Italy[b]	214	388	811	984	1 092	1 194	1 312	1 427
Luxembourg	103	133	205	237	250	283	300	319
Netherlands	275	345	428	441	457	485	516	542
Portugal	626	1 256	3 524	5 177	6 003	8 141	9 585	10 957
Spain	9 178	15 209	28 201	36 144	40 159	45 044	50 145	54 901
Sweden	370	531	867	1 024	1 115	1 233	1 360	1 447
United Kingdom	146	232	357	424	471	516	551	575

Exhibit 3–4 Trends in Total Gross Domestic Product 1977–96 (National Currencies).

disposable income, together with gifts, pensions, cash savings or other assets, the family makes its expenditures. Some families do not spend all of their disposable income and save part of it. Therefore, when trying to estimate potential sales in target markets, we should distinguish among income, disposable income and what consumers actually spend.

It is dangerous to assume that where GDP per capita is high then consumers may have more purchasing power. For example, high rates of personal tax in Denmark and Sweden reduce the amount of disposable consumer income. Lower rates of personal tax in other European countries increase the amount of disposable income. Nevertheless, GDP per capita is a useful first measure of market potential.

Discretionary income is elusive

Most families spend a good portion of their income on such 'necessities' as food, rent or house payments, car and home furnishings payments, and insurance. A family's purchase of 'luxuries' comes from discretionary income—what is left of disposable income after paying for necessities. Discretionary income is an elusive concept because the definition of necessities varies from family to family and over time. It depends on what they think is necessary for their lifestyle. A colour TV might be purchased out of discretionary income by a lower-income family but is considered a necessity by a higher-income family. But if many people in a lower-income neighbourhood buy colour TVs, then

they might become a 'necessity' for the others and severely reduce the discretionary income available for other purchases. Many families with young or growing children do not have enough discretionary income to afford the lifestyles seen on TV and in other mass media. On the other hand, some young adults and older people without family responsibilities have a lot of discretionary income. They may be especially attractive markets for stereos, cameras, new cars, foreign travel and various kinds of recreation such as tennis, skiing, boating, concerts and restaurants.

Expenditure data tells how target markets spend

Obviously, wealthy families spend more money than poor ones—and on different things. But how it is spent—and how spending varies for different target markets—is important to marketers. There are considerable variations across different European countries in the way in which household income is spent. Exhibit 3–5 shows the varying distribution of different household appliances across a sample of countries. Of course the distribution of household appliances in different countries may reflect more than just differences in income levels in each country. There are also major cultural and social reasons why certain products may be more likely to be used in one European country than another. It is up to the marketing manager to look behind the basic statistics to determine where these influences lie and work out what their effects might be.[4]

	1992	1993	1994	1995	1996	% growth 1977–96	Total $ billion 1996	c
EU								
Austria	2 046	2 118	1 955	2 352	2 463	209.4	232.8	28 719
Belgium	7 102	7 285	7 621	7 936	8 370	194.5	270.3	26 611
Denmark	851	873	929	958	1 010	262.5	174.2	33 270
Finland	477	480	509	546	595	357.6	129.5	25 264
France	7 011	7 083	7 380	7 663	7 866	310.1	1 537.6	26 359
Germany	2 813	2 854	2 978	3 041	3 540		2 352.5	28 716
Germany, East[a]								
Germany, West								
Greece	14 832	16 760	23 196	25 553	29 576	2 968.0	122.9	11 713
Ireland	30	32	35	39	43	660.6	69.7	19 601
Italy[b]	1 507	1 559	1 641	1 692	1 944	808.2	1 259.6	22 012
Luxembourg	339	355	361	367	400	288.3	12.9	31 354
Netherlands	563	574	600	618	662	140.7	392.5	25 204
Portugal	12 307	12 980	13 755	15 073	16 395	2 519.0	106.3	10 838
Spain	59 002	60 904	64 673	69 722	73 661	702.6	581.6	14 659
Sweden	1 442	1 442	1 517	1 635	1 644	344.4	245.2	27 804
United Kingdom	597	631	668	700	737	405.0	1 151.4	19 803

Exhibit 3–4 (continued)

SPENDING VARIES WITH OTHER DEMOGRAPHIC DIMENSIONS

Spending varies over the family life cycle

Income has a direct bearing on spending patterns, but many other demographic dimensions are also useful in understanding consumer buying. Marital status, age and the age of any children in the family have an especially important effect on how people spend their income. Put together, these dimensions tell us about the life-cycle stage of a family. Exhibit 3–6 shows a summary of stages in the family life cycle. In our discussion, we will focus on the traditional flow from one stage to the next, as shown in the middle of diagram. However, as shown at the top and bottom of the exhibit, divorce does interrupt the flow for many people; after a divorce, they may recycle through earlier stages.

Young people and families accept new ideas

Singles and young couples seem to be more willing to try new products and brands, and they are careful, price-conscious shoppers. Younger people often earn less than older consumers, but they spend a greater proportion of their income on discretionary items because they do not have the major expenses of home ownership, education and growing families. Many people are delaying marriage, waiting longer to get married. Younger families, especially those with no children, are still accumulating durable goods, such as cars and home furnishings.

They spend less on food. It is only as children arrive and grow that family spending shifts to soft goods and services, such as education, medical and personal care. This usually happens when the family head reaches the 35–44 age group. To meet expenses, people in this age group often make more purchases on credit, and they save less of their income.

Divorce is an increasing reality that disrupts the traditional family life-cycle pattern. Divorced parents do not spend like other single people. The mother usually has custody of the children, and the father may pay child support. The mother and children typically have much less income than two-parent families. Such families spend a larger percentage of their income on housing, childcare and other necessities, with little left for discretionary purchases. If a single parent remarries, the family life cycle may start over again.

Reallocation for teenagers

Once children become teenagers, further shifts in spending occur. Teenagers eat more, want to wear expensive clothes, and develop leisure and education needs that are hard on the family budget. The parents may be forced to reallocate their expenditures to cover these expenses, spending less on durable goods, such as appliances, cars, household goods and housing.

Percentage of Households with:	Austria	Belgium	Finland	France	HOUSEHOLD Germany
Compact Disc	32	20	35	64	21
Freezer	66	57	83	81	48
Dishwasher	36	22	42	44	44
Telephone	88	81	90	95	98
Microwave	34	10	71	56	55
Washing machine	83	85	82	90	94
					WESTERN EUROPEAN
Homes with TV sets (%)	99	98	96	98	99
As a percentage of TV homes:					
Homes with VCR	68	54	69	68	62
Homes with full cable service	37	90	30	9	81
Homes with teletext	58	24	44	–	63
Daily reach, all TV (%)	67	85	85	83	87
Average daily viewing (min)	143	159	148	193	195

Note: ¹Data refer to German language television only.

Exhibit 3–5 Distribution of Household Appliances in Different European Countries

Kookai is a French clothing company geared towards the needs of the teenage adolescent market.

Teenagers also begin to earn money in their own right, much of which is discretionary income, particularly if they are still living at home.

Selling to the empty nesters

An important category is the **empty nesters**—people whose children are grown and who are now able to spend their money in other ways. Usually these people are in the 50–64 age group. But this is an elusive group because some people marry later and are still raising a family at this age. Empty nesters are an attractive market for many items. They may have paid for their homes, and the big expenses of raising a family are behind them. They are more interested in travel, small sports cars and other things they couldn't afford before. Much depends on their income, of course. But this is a high-income period for many workers, especially white-collar workers.

| EQUIPEMENT | | | | | | | | |
Ireland	Italy	Netherlands	Portugal	Spain	Sweden	Switzerland	UK	USA
45	8	66	2	29	66	45	20	–
97	63	60	52	24	78	69	39	–
23	32	16	27	14	50	46	19	–
83	90	98	79	86	96	98	92	99
63	22	43	24	35	68	27	66	–
90	89	93	91	95	74	96	91	–
TELEVISION DATA								
99	99	98	99	99	98	94	98	98
68	67	68	54	60	70	62	87	75
37	–	96	–	3	39	79	9	61
39	60	75	–	32	73	56	56	–
87	80	69	83	91	72	71[1]	76	–
200	218	157	159	214	139	129[1]	194	242

Exhibit 3–5 *(continued)*

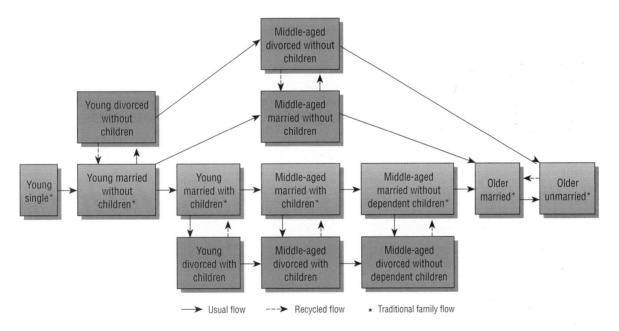

Usual flow — — → Recycled flow * Traditional family flow

Exhibit 3–6 Stages in Modern Family Life Cycles

Senior citizens are a growing market

Finally, the **senior citizens**—people over 65—should not be neglected. The number of people over 65 is increasing rapidly because of modern medicine, improved sanitary conditions, and better nutrition. This group is a growing percentage of the population. Our senior citizens are more prosperous than ever before. Their income is lower than in their peak earning years, but most do have money to spend. They don't just get by on social security. Older people also have very different needs. Many firms are already catering for senior citizens and as the population ages, more businesses will be attracted to serving this growth market. Keep in mind, however, that older people are not all the same. With a group this large, generalities can be dangerous. Different senior citizen target markets have different needs and require different marketing strategies.

NATIONAL STEREOTYPES ARE COMMON AND MISLEADING

We all have our own prejudices

When you think of different nationalities what pictures come to mind? Do you have a particular set of expectations of different countries that influences your expectations? Many people do have such prejudices which influence their perceptions of different nationalities. For example, many tourists to the United Kingdom rarely venture beyond London, Edinburgh and Stratford-on-Avon if they come for a first visit. For them, the United Kingdom is London with its histori- cal attractions, shopping and nightlife, Edinburgh castle and Shakespeare's birthplace. Unless such tourists venture any further these perceptions colour their subse- quent expectations of the United Kingdom.

In the same way it is very dangerous to think of other markets in terms of such national stereotypes. There is no such thing as a typical Spaniard or a typical Italian, and it would be a mistake to base marketing decisions entirely around such perceptions, even if they frequently prove correct. (See boxed example.)

HOW THE FRENCH AND BRITISH SEE THE CHANNEL TUNNEL

Advertising of the Channel tunnel varied in Britain and France. British newspaper advertisements for the Channel tunnel showed cartoon-like figures snoozing their way through the tunnel or driving down tree-lined French roads. The French press advertising campaign, by contrast, featured Napoleon, Churchill and Queen Victoria giving their blessing to the venture.

These different approaches reflect national attitudes to the European engineering project. For the sceptical British, who had become used to a stream of stories about problems in the £10 billion project, the approach had to be gentle, humorous and coaxing. For the French, who regarded the tunnel with Gallic pride as a natural extension of their record-breaking, high-speed rail network, the tunnel had to be presented with all due ceremony.

This two-pronged advertising strategy—which initially caused some controversy on the Eurotunnel board—was part of a wider marketing strategy which had to address important pricing, distribution and public relations issues. Some people wanted the UK campaign to be triumphal about the achievement represented by the tunnel. But research by Eurotunnel and its adver- tising agency, DDB Needham, showed that with the problems completing the venture such an approach left people cold.

'We realized our ads could not be pompous. They had to be light-hearted while at the same time explaining why people should use the tunnel. The board did not like that idea at first. They said that they had worked so hard on the project. But in the end the market research swung the argument.'[5]

Ethnic markets are becoming more important

Nationality is only one of many ways of analysing markets. Markets can also be analysed in terms of differ- ent ethnic groupings. Such groupings can be people of different religions or race. Ethnic markets are frequently found across more than one country, and can be of signifi- cance to the marketer in formulating his or her market- ing plan. The Muslim community is one of the largest and most important ethnic groups with many people in different European countries sharing a set of common beliefs about family life. Products promoted to this ethnic group must reflect the set of values held by these people. For example, such values tend to stress a subservient role for women. However, within this very large ethnic group there can still be considerable differences. Some Muslims, predominantly the young, have rejected the values that put females into a secondary role behind men and sought to take on more 'western' lifestyles. Others, including many young Muslims, have adopted more extreme stances going back to the fundamental practice of their religion. Any organization that seeks to provide services or sell to this group needs to take account of such differ- ences within this broad ethnic grouping.

CONSUMER BEHAVIOUR—WHY DO THEY BUY WHAT THE...

In the last section, we discussed basic data on population, income and consumer spending patterns. This information can help marketers predict basic *trends* in consumer spending patterns. Unfortunately, when many firms sell similar products, demographic analysis isn't much help in predicting which specific products and brands consumers will purchase—and why. Many other variables can influence consumers and their buying behaviour. To better understand why consumers buy as they do, many marketers have turned to the behavioural sciences for help. In the second part of this chapter, we will explore some of the thinking from economics, psychology, sociology and the other behavioural disciplines.

Specific consumer behaviours va... different products and from one target ... In today's global markets, the variations a... ... makes it impractical to try to 'catalogue ... ine detailed possibilities for all different market situations. For example, how and why a given consumer buys a specific brand of shampoo may be very different from how that same consumer buys motor oil; and different customers in different parts of the world may have very different reactions to either product. But there are *general* behavioural principles—frameworks—that marketing managers can apply to learn more about their specific target markets. Our approach focuses on developing your skill in working with these frameworks.

THE BEHAVIOURAL SCIENCES HELP UNDERSTAND THE BUYING PROCESS

Economic needs affect most buying decisions

Most economists assume that consumers are **economic men and women**—people who know all the facts and logically compare choices in terms of cost and value received to get the greatest satisfaction from spending their time and money. A logical extension of the economic-man theory led us to look at consumer spending patterns. This approach is valuable because consumers must at least have income to be in a market. Further, most consumers do not have enough income to buy everything they want. So, most consumers want their money to stretch as far as it can. This view assumes that most consumer behaviour is guided by economic needs. **Economic needs** are concerned with making the best use of a consumer's time and money, as the consumer judges it. Some consumers look for the lowest price. Others will pay extra for convenience. And others may weigh price and quality for the best value. Some economic needs are:

1. Economy of purchase or use.
2. Convenience.
3. Efficiency in operation or use.
4. Dependability in use.
5. Improvement of earnings.

Uncle Ben's has extended customer benefits by providing a variety of different recipe suggestions.

Clearly, marketing managers must be alert to new ways to appeal to economic needs. Most consumers appreciate firms that offer them improved value for the money they spend. But improved value does not just mean offering lower and lower prices. Many consumers face a 'poverty of time' and appreciate carefully planned place decisions that can make it easier and faster for customers to make a purchase. Products can be designed to work better, require less service, or last longer. Promotion can inform consumers about their choices, or explain product

...ts in terms of measurable factors like operating costs or the length of the guarantee.

The 'economic value' that a purchase offers a customer is an important factor in many purchase decisions. However, most marketing managers think that buyer behaviour is not as simple as the economic model suggests. A product that one person sees as a good value may be of no interest to someone else. So, buying behaviour needs to take a broader view.

How we will view consumer behaviour

Many behavioural dimensions influence consumers. Let's try to combine these dimensions into a model of how consumers make decisions. Exhibit 3–7 shows that psychological variables, social influences, and the purchase situation all affect a person's buying behaviour. We'll discuss these topics in the next few pages. Then we'll expand the model to include the consumer problem-solving process.

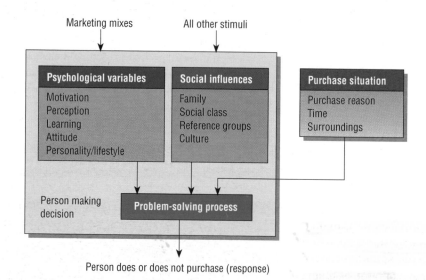

Exhibit 3–7 A Model of Buyer Behaviour

PSYCHOLOGICAL INFLUENCES WITHIN AN INDIVIDUAL

Here we will discuss some variables of special interest to marketers—including motivation, perception, learning, attitudes and lifestyle. Much of what we know about these *psychological (intrapersonal) variables* is drawn from ideas originally developed in the field of psychology.

Needs motivate consumers

Everybody is motivated by needs and wants. **Needs** are the basic forces that motivate a person to do something. Some needs are concerned with a person's physical well-being. Other needs are concerned with the individual's self-view and relationship with others. Needs are more basic than wants. **Wants** are 'needs' that are learned during a person's life. For example, everyone needs water or some kind of liquid, but some people also have learned to want 'Perrier with a twist of lemon'. When a need is not satisfied, it may lead to a drive. The need for liquid, for example, leads to a thirst drive. A **drive** is a strong stimulus that encourages action to reduce a need. Drives are internal—they are the reasons behind certain behaviour patterns. In marketing, a product purchase is the result of a drive to satisfy some need.

Some critics imply that marketers can somehow manipulate consumers to buy products against their will. But marketing managers can't create internal drives in consumers. Most marketing managers realize that trying to get consumers to act against their will is a waste of time. Instead, a good marketing manager studies what consumer drives, needs and wants already exist and how they can be satisfied better.

Consumers seek benefits to meet needs

We all are a bundle of needs and wants. Exhibit 3–8 lists some important needs that might motivate a person to some action. This list, of course, is not complete. But thinking about such needs can help you see what *benefits* consumers might seek from a marketing mix. When a marketing manager defines a product market, the needs may be quite specific. For example, the food need might be as specific as wanting a thick-crust pepperoni pizza—delivered to your door hot and ready to eat.

Several needs at the same time

Some psychologists argue that a person may have several reasons for buying—at the same time. Maslow is well known for his five-level hierarchy of needs. We will discuss a similar four-level hierarchy that is easier to apply to consumer behaviour. The four levels are illustrated in Exhibit 3–9, along with an advertising slogan that illustrates how a company has tried to appeal to each need. The lowest-level needs are physiological. Then come safety, social, and personal needs. To help memorize these needs, think of PSSP needs.

The **physiological needs** are concerned with biological needs—food, drink, rest and sex. The **safety needs** are concerned with protection and physical well-being (perhaps involving health food, medicine and exercise). The **social needs** are concerned with love, friendship, status and esteem, things that involve a person's interaction with others. The **personal needs**, on the other hand, are concerned with an individual's

Types of Need	Specific Examples			
Physiological needs	Hunger Sex Rest	Thirst Body elimination	Activity Self-preservation	Sleep Warmth/coolness
Psychological needs	Aggression Family preservation Nurturing Playing-relaxing Self-identification	Curiosity Imitation Order Power Tenderness	Being responsible Independence Personal fulfilment Pride	Dominance Love Playing-competition Self-expression
Desire for . . .	Acceptance Affiliation Comfort Esteem Knowledge Respect Status	Achievement Appreciation Fun Fame Prestige Retaliation Sympathy	Acquisition Beauty Distance—'space' Happiness Pleasure Self-satisfaction Variety	Affection Companionship Distinctiveness Identification Recognition Sociability
Freedom from . . .	Fear Pain Harm	Depression Imitation Ridicule	Discomfort Loss Sadness	Anxiety Illness Pressure

Exhibit 3–8 Possible Needs Motivating a Person to Some Action

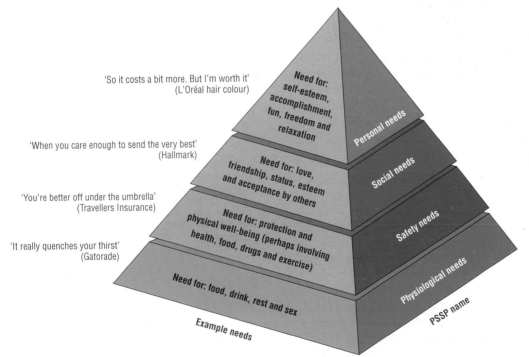

'So it costs a bit more. But I'm worth it'
(L'Oréal hair colour)

'When you care enough to send the very best'
(Hallmark)

'You're better off under the umbrella'
(Travellers Insurance)

'It really quenches your thirst'
(Gatorade)

Need for: self-esteem, accomplishment, fun, freedom and relaxation — Personal needs

Need for: love, friendship, status, esteem and acceptance by others — Social needs

Need for: protection and physical well-being (perhaps involving health, food, drugs and exercise) — Safety needs

Need for: food, drink, rest and sex — Physiological needs

Example needs · PSSP name

Exhibit 3–9 The PSSP Hierarchy of Needs

need for personal satisfaction, unrelated to what others think or do. Examples include self-esteem, accomplishment, fun, freedom and relaxation.

Motivation theory suggests that we never reach a state of complete satisfaction. As soon as lower-level needs are reasonably satisfied, those at higher levels become more dominant. This explains why marketing efforts targeted at affluent consumers in countries with advanced economies often focus on higher-level needs. It also explains why these approaches may not be of much use in many parts of the world where consumers' most basic needs have not been met. It is important to see, however, that a particular product may satisfy more than one need at the same time. In fact, most consumers try to fill a *set* of needs rather than just one need or another in sequence.

It seems obvious that marketers should try to satisfy different needs. Yet, seeing specific consumer needs may require careful analysis. Consider, for example, the lowly vegetable peeler. Marketing managers for OXO International realized that many people, especially young children and senior citizens, have trouble gripping the handle on the typical peeler. OXO redesigned the peeler with a bigger handle that addressed this physical need. They also coated the handle with dishwasher-safe rubber. This makes cleaning more convenient, but it also makes it safer to use the sharp peeler when the grip is wet. The attractively designed grip also appeals to consumers who get personal satisfaction from cooking and who want to impress their guests. Even though OXO priced the peeler much higher than most kitchen utensils, it has sold very well because it appeals to people with a variety of needs.[6]

Perception determines what is seen and felt

Consumers select varying ways to meet their needs. Some of this is because of differences in **perception**—how we gather and interpret information from the world around us. We are constantly bombarded by stimuli—advertising, products, shops—yet we may not hear or see anything. This is because we apply the following selective processes:

1. **Selective exposure**—our eyes and minds seek out and notice only information that interests us.
2. **Selective perception**—we screen out or modify ideas, messages and information that conflict with previously learned attitudes and beliefs.
3. **Selective retention**—we remember only what we want to remember.

These selective processes help explain why some people are not affected by some advertising—even offensive advertising. They just don't see or remember it! Even if they do, they may dismiss it immediately. Some consumers are sceptical about any advertising message.

Our needs affect these selective processes. And current needs receive more attention. For example, banks advertise details of loans continuously. However, we are unlikely to pay much attention to such advertising until we need a loan. Marketers are interested in these selective processes because they affect how target consumers get and retain information. This is also why marketers are interested in how consumers *learn*.

Learning determines what response is likely

Learning is a change in a person's thought processes caused by prior experience. Learning is often based on direct experience: a girl tastes her first Häagen-Dazs ice-cream cone, and learning occurs! Learning may also be based on indirect experience or associations. If you watch a Häagen-Dazs advertisement that shows other people enjoying a new flavour, you might conclude that you would like it too. Consumer learning may result from things that marketers do, or it may result from stimuli that have nothing to do with marketing. Either way, almost all consumer behaviour is learned.[7]

Experts describe a number of steps in the learning process. We have already discussed the idea of a drive as a strong stimulus that encourages action. Depending on the **cues**—products, signs, advertisements and other stimuli in the environment—an individual chooses some specific response. A **response** is an effort to satisfy a drive. The specific response chosen depends on the cues and the person's past experience.

Reinforcement of the learning process occurs when the response is followed by satisfaction—that is, reducing the drive. Reinforcement strengthens the relationship between the cue and the response. And it may lead to a similar response the next time the drive occurs. Repeated reinforcement leads to the development of a habit—making the individual's decision process routine. The relationships of the important variables in the learning process are shown in Exhibit 3–10.

The learning process can be illustrated by a thirsty person. The thirst *drive* could be satisfied in a variety of ways. But if the person happened to walk past a vending machine and saw a Coca-Cola sign—a *cue*—then he might satisfy the drive with a *response*—buying a Coca-Cola. If

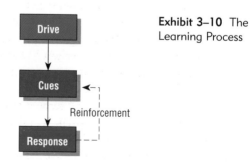

Exhibit 3–10 The Learning Process

the experience is satisfactory, positive *reinforcement* will occur, and our friend may be quicker to satisfy this drive in the same way in the future. This emphasizes the importance of developing good products that live up to the promises of the firm's advertising. People can learn to like or dislike Coca-Cola as reinforcement and learning works both ways. Unless marketers satisfy their customers, they are constantly trying to attract new ones to replace the dissatisfied ones who do not come back. Good experiences can lead to positive attitudes about a firm's product. Bad experiences can lead to negative attitudes that even good promotion won't be able to change. In fact, the subject of attitudes, an extremely important one to marketers, is discussed more fully in a later section.

Positive cues help a marketing mix

Sometimes marketers try to identify cues or images that have positive associations from some other situation and relate them to their marketing mix. Many people associate the smell of lemons with a fresh, natural cleanliness. Lemon scent is often added to household cleaning products—Persil dishwashing detergent and Pledge furniture polish, for example—because it has these associations. Similarly, many firms use ads that suggest that people who use their products have more appeal to the opposite sex.

Many needs are culturally learned

Many needs are culturally (or socially) learned. The need for food, for instance, may lead to many specific food wants. Many Japanese enjoy raw fish, and their children learn to like it. Few Europeans, however, have learned to like raw fish.

Attitudes relate to buying

An **attitude** is a person's point of view towards something. The 'something' may be a product, an advertisement, a salesperson, a firm or an idea. Attitudes are an important topic for marketers, because attitudes affect the selective processes, learning and eventually the buying decisions people make. Because attitudes are usually thought of as involving liking or disliking, they have some action implications. Beliefs are not so action-oriented. A **belief** is a person's opinion about something. Beliefs may help shape a consumer's attitudes but don't necessarily involve any liking or disliking. It is possible to have a belief, say, that Listerine (a mouthwash) has a medicinal taste, without really caring what it tastes like. On the other hand, beliefs about a product may have a positive or negative effect in shaping consumers' attitudes. For example, a person with a headache is unlikely to switch to a new pain-relief medicine unless she believes it will be more effective than what she has used in the past.

In an attempt to relate attitude more closely to purchase behaviour, some marketers have stretched the attitude concept to include consumer 'preferences' or 'intention to buy'. The intention to buy is of most interest to managers who must forecast how much of their brand customers will buy. Forecasts would be easier if attitudes were good predictors of intentions to buy. Unfortunately, the relationships usually are not that simple. A person may have positive attitudes towards a Jacuzzi but no intention of buying one.

Try to understand attitudes and beliefs

Research on consumer attitudes and beliefs can sometimes help a marketing manager get a better picture of markets. For example, consumers who have very positive attitudes towards a new product idea might indicate a good opportunity—especially if they have negative attitudes about competitors' offerings. Or they may have beliefs that would discourage them from buying a product.

Most marketers work with existing attitudes

Marketers generally try to understand the attitudes of their potential customers and work with them. We'll discuss this idea again when we review the way consumers evaluate product alternatives. For now, we want to emphasize that it is more economical to work with consumer attitudes than to try to change them. Attitudes tend to be enduring. Changing present attitudes, especially negative ones, is sometimes necessary but it is probably the most difficult job that marketers face.[8]

 Ethical issues may arise

Part of the marketing job is to inform and persuade consumers about a firm's offering. An ethical issue sometimes arises, however, if consumers have *inaccurate* beliefs. For example, many consumers are confused about what foods are really healthy. Marketers for a number of food companies have been criticized for packaging and promotion that take advantage of inaccurate consumer perceptions about the meaning of the words 'low-fat.' A firm's 'low-fat' yoghurt may have less fat or fewer calories than its other yoghurt, but that does not mean that the yoghurt is *low* in fat or calories. Similarly, promotion of a 'children's cold formula' may play on parents' fears that adult medicines are too strong, even though the basic ingredients in the children's formula are the same and only the dosage is different. Marketers must also be careful about promotion that might encourage false beliefs, even if the advertising is not explicitly misleading. For example, Nike doesn't claim that a kid who buys its football boots will be able to play World Cup standard football.

Dimension	Examples		
Activities	Work Hobbies Social events	Vacation Entertainment Club membership	Community Shopping Sports
Interests	Family Home Job	Community Recreation Fashion	Food Media Achievements
Opinions	Themselves Social issues Politics	Business Economics Education	Products Future Culture
Demographics	Income Age Family life cycle	Geographic area City size Dwelling	Occupation Family size Education

Exhibit 3–11 Lifestyle Dimensions (and some related demographic dimensions)

Personality affects how people see things

Much research has been done on how personality affects people's behaviour, but the results have generally been disappointing to marketers. A trait like neatness can be associated with users of certain types of products—like cleaning materials. However, marketing managers have not found a way to use personality in marketing strategy planning. As a result, the focus has moved from personality measures borrowed from psychologists to lifestyle analysis.

Psychographics focus on activities, interests and opinions

Psychographics or **lifestyle analysis** is the analysis of a person's day-to-day pattern of living as expressed in that person's activities, interests, and opinions, sometimes referred to as 'AIOs'. A number of variables for each of the AIO dimensions are shown in Exhibit 3–11, along with some demographics that are used to add detail to the lifestyle profile of a target market.

Lifestyle analysis assumes that marketers can plan more effective strategies if they know more about their target markets. Understanding the lifestyle of target customers has been especially helpful in providing ideas for advertising themes. Marketing managers for consumer products firms who are interested in learning more about the lifestyle of a target market sometimes turn to outside specialists for help. For example, SRI International, a research firm, offers a service called VALS 2 (an abbreviation for 'values, attitudes and lifestyles'). SRI describes a firm's target market in terms of a set of 'typical' VALS lifestyle groups (segments). An advantage of this approach is that SRI has developed very detailed information about the various VALS groups. For example, the VALS approach has been used to profile consumers in the United Kingdom, Germany, Japan and Canada as well as the United States. However, the disadvantage of VALS 2, and other similar approaches, is that it may not be very specific to the marketing manager's target market.[9]

SOCIAL INFLUENCES AFFECT CONSUMER BEHAVIOUR

We have been discussing some of the ways that needs, attitudes and other psychological variables influence the buying process. Now, we'll see that these variables, and the buying process, are usually affected by relations with other people. We will look at how the individual interacts with family, social class and other groups who may have influence.

Who is the real decision-maker in family purchases?

Relationships with other family members influence many aspects of consumer behaviour. We saw specific examples of this earlier in this chapter when we considered the effects of the family life cycle on family spending patterns. Family members may also share many attitudes and values, consider each other's opinions and divide up various buying tasks. Historically, most marketers targeted the wife as the family purchasing agent. Now, with more women in the workforce and with night and weekend shopping becoming more popular, men and older children are doing more shopping and decision making. In other countries, family roles vary. For example, in Norway women do most of the family shopping. Although one member of the family may go to the store and make a specific purchase, it is important in planning marketing strategy to know who else may be involved. Other family members may have influenced the decision or really decided what to buy. Still others may use the product. Surveys show that kids often have a big say in a family's choice of products such as clothes, cars, electronics, and health and beauty aids.

Family considerations may overwhelm personal ones

A husband and wife may jointly agree on many important purchases, but sometimes they may have strong personal preferences. However, such individual preferences may be changed if the other partner has different priorities. One might want to take a family holiday to Disneyland when the other wants a new video recorder and Sony large screen TV. The actual outcome in such a situation is unpredictable. The preferences of one spouse might change because of affection for the other, or because of the other's power and influence. Buying responsibility and influence vary greatly depending on the product and the family. A marketer trying to plan a strategy will find it helpful to research the specific target market. Remember, many buying decisions are made jointly, and thinking only about who actually buys the product can misdirect the marketing strategy.[10]

Social class affects attitudes, values and buying

Up to now we have been concerned with individuals and their family relationships. Now consider how society looks at an individual and perhaps the family in terms of social class. Almost every society has some social class structure. In most countries social class is closely related to a person's occupation, but it may also be influenced by education, where a person lives, income, possessions, social skills, and other factors, including the family into which a person is born. In most countries there is *some* general relationship between income level and social class. But the income level of people within the same social class can vary greatly, and people with the same income level may be in different social classes. So income by itself is usually not a good measure of social class. And people in different social classes may spend, save and borrow money in very different ways. For example, spending for clothing, housing, home furnishings, leisure activities, as well as choices of where and how to shop, often vary with social class. The class system is not rigid in most countries. Children start out in the same social class as their parents—but they can move to a different social class depending on their educational levels or the jobs they hold. By contrast, in India the social structure is much more rigid and it is difficult for an individual to move up in the class system.

Marketers want to know what buyers in various social classes are like. Several different approaches can be used. Simple approaches for measuring social class groupings are based on a person's *occupation, education* and *type and location of housing*. By using marketing research surveys or available census data, marketers can get a feel for the social class of a target market.

What do these classes mean?

One of the great values of the social class system of classifying markets is that such classifications often seem to be useful predictors of buying behaviour. Since social class is often determined by occupation, it is probably truer to say that someone's occupation, which is linked usually to education, is a good predictor of buying behaviour. Social class is not directly linked to income. People in the 'lower' social class groups may frequently have higher levels of income than those in higher social groups. A skilled engineer or car mechanic will frequently earn more than an office manager or teacher. However, there will be differences in the way that each of these groups spends this income. For example, the engineer or car mechanic may be more likely to spend money on family holidays or new furniture. The school teacher may be more likely to spend money on school fees for private education of her children.

Reference groups are relevant, too

A **reference group** is the people to whom an individual looks when forming attitudes about a particular topic. People normally have several reference groups for different topics. Some they meet face to face. Others they may just wish to imitate. In either case, they may take values from these reference groups and make buying decisions based on what the group might accept. We are always making comparisons between others and ourselves. So reference groups are more important when others will be able to 'see' which product or which brand is being used. Influence is stronger for products that relate to status in the group. For one group, owning an expensive car may be a sign of 'having arrived'. A group of environmentalists might view it as a sign of bad judgement. In either case, a consumer's decision to buy or not buy an expensive car might depend on the opinions of others in that consumer's reference group.

Reaching the opinion leaders

An **opinion leader** is a person who influences others. Opinion leaders are not necessarily wealthier or better educated. Opinion leaders on one subject are not necessarily opinion leaders on another subject. Capable homemakers with large families may be consulted for advice on family budgeting. Young women may be opinion leaders for new clothing styles and cosmetics. Each social class tends to have its own opinion leaders. Some marketing mixes are aimed especially at these people since their opinions affect others and research shows that they are involved in many product-related discussions with 'followers'. Favourable word-of-mouth publicity from opinion leaders can really help a marketing mix. The opposite is also true. If opinion leaders are not satisfied, they are likely to talk about it.

Culture surrounds the other influences

Culture is the whole set of beliefs, attitudes and ways of doing things of a reasonably homogeneous set of people. We can think of French culture, English culture or Dutch culture. It is still relatively early to think about a European culture, although there are signs that such a culture is beginning to develop. People within these cultural groupings tend to be more similar in outlook and behaviour. Sometimes it is useful to think of subcultures within such groupings. For example, within the Dutch culture, there are various religious and ethnic subcultures; there also tend to be different cultural forces in different regions of the country.

Culture varies in international markets

Planning strategies that take into consideration cultural differences in international markets can be even harder than for domestic markets. Each foreign market may need to be treated as a separate market, with its own submarkets. Ignoring cultural differences, or assuming that they are not important, almost guarantees failure in international markets. From a target marketing point of view, a marketing manager will probably want to aim at people within one culture or subculture. If a firm is developing strategies for two cultures, it often needs two different marketing plans.

INDIVIDUALS ARE AFFECTED BY THE PURCHASE SITUATION

Purchase reason can vary

The reasons why a person is buying a product can influence purchasing behaviour. For example, a student buying a pen to take notes might pick up an inexpensive BIC. But the same student might choose a Mont Blanc pen if it was to be a gift for a friend.

Time affects what happens

Time is also a purchase situation influence. When a purchase is made—and the time available for shopping—also influence behaviour. A leisurely dinner induces different behaviour than does a quick snack at McDonald's in the middle of a shopping trip.

Surroundings affect buying, too

Surroundings can affect buying behaviour. The excitement of an auction may stimulate impulse buying. Surroundings may discourage buying, too. For example, some people don't like to stand in a checkout queue and have others look at what they are buying, even if the other shoppers are complete strangers. Needs, benefits sought, attitudes, motivation and even how a consumer selects certain products all vary depending on the purchase situation. So different purchase situations may require different marketing mixes, even when the same target market is involved.

CONSUMERS USE PROBLEM-SOLVING PROCESSES

The variables we have been discussing affect *what* products a consumer finally decides to purchase. It is also important for marketing managers to understand *how* buyers use a problem-solving process to select particular products. Most consumers seem to use the following five-step problem-solving process:

1. Becoming aware of—or interested in—the problem.
2. Recalling and gathering information about possible solutions.
3. Evaluating alternative solutions—perhaps trying some out.
4. Deciding on the appropriate solution.
5. Evaluating the decision.[11]

Exhibit 3–12 presents an expanded version of buyer behaviour model in Exhibit 3–1. Note that this exhibit integrates the problem-solving process with the whole set of variables which we have been reviewing.

When consumers evaluate information about purchase alternatives, they may compare not only a product type in relation to other types of products, but also differences in brands within a product type *and* the shops where the products may be available. This can be a very complicated evaluation procedure, and, depending on their choice criteria, consumers may make seemingly 'irrational' decisions. If convenient service is crucial, for example, a buyer might pay list

Exhibit 3–12 An Expanded Model of the Consumer Problem-Solving Process

Marketing mixes   All other stimuli

Psychological variables
Motivation
Perception
Learning
Attitude
Personality/lifestyle

Social influences
Family
Social class
Reference groups
Culture

Purchase situation
Purchase reason
Time
Surroundings

Person making decision

Need-want awareness

Routinized response

Search for information

Feedback of information as attitudes

Set criteria and evaluate alternative solutions

Decide on solution

Postpone decision

Purchase product

Postpurchase evaluation

Response

---

price for an 'unexciting' car from a very convenient dealer. Marketers need a way to analyse these decisions.

 Internet Exercise

To make it easier for consumers to visualise how certain fashions will look together, the GAP's web site **(www.gap.com)** has a 'get dressed interactive' feature. Go to the GAP web site and check out this feature. Does it make it easier to evaluate a potential purchase?

Grid of evaluative criteria helps

Based on studies of how consumers seek out and evaluate information about products, researchers suggest that marketing managers use an evaluative grid showing features common to different products (or marketing mixes). For example, Exhibit 3–13 shows some of the features common to three different cars a consumer might consider.

The grid encourages marketing managers to view each product as a 'bundle' of features or 'attributes'. The

pluses and minuses in Exhibit 3–13 indicate one consumer's attitude towards each feature of each car. If members of the target market do not rate a feature of the brand with 'pluses', it may indicate a problem. The manager might want to change the product to improve that feature, or perhaps use more promotion to emphasize an already acceptable feature. The consumer in Exhibit 3–13 has a minus under petrol consumption for the Nissan. If the Nissan really gets better petrol consumption than the other cars, promotion might focus on mileage to improve consumer attitudes towards this feature and towards the whole product.

Some consumers will reject a product if *one* feature is below standard, regardless of how favourably they might regard the product's other features. The consumer represented in Exhibit 3–13 might avoid the Saab, which he saw as less than satisfactory on ease of service, even if it were superior in all other aspects. In other instances, a consumer's overall attitude towards the product might be such that a few good features

Brands	Common features			
	Petrol mileage	Ease of service	Comfortable interior	Styling
Nissan	−	+	+	−
Saab	+	−	+	+
Toyota	+	+	+	−

Note: Pluses and minuses indicate a consumer's evaluation of a feature for a brand.

Exhibit 3–13 Grid of Evaluative Criteria for Three Car Brands

could make up for some shortcomings. The comfortable interior of the Toyota (Exhibit 3–13) might make up for less exciting styling, especially if the consumer viewed comfort as really important.

Of course, consumers do not use a grid like this. However, constructing such a grid helps managers think about what evaluative criteria are really important to their target consumers, what consumers' attitudes are towards their product (or marketing mix) on each criterion, and how consumers combine the criteria to reach a final decision. Having a better understanding of the process should help a manager develop a better marketing mix.[12]

Three levels of problem solving are useful

The basic problem-solving process shows the steps consumers may go through while trying to find a way to satisfy needs, but it does not show how long this process will take or how much thought a consumer will give to each step. Individuals who have had a lot of experience solving certain problems can move quickly through some of the steps or almost directly to a decision. It is helpful, therefore, to recognize three levels of problem solving: extensive problem solving, limited problem solving and routinized response behaviour (see Exhibit 3–14). These problem-solving approaches are used for any kind of product.

Extensive problem solving is involved when a need is completely new or important to a consumer and when much effort is put into deciding how to satisfy the need.

For example, a music lover who wants higher quality sound might decide to buy a CD player, but not have any idea what to buy. After talking with friends to find out about good places to buy a player, they might visit several of the stores to find out about different brands and their features. After thinking about there needs some more, they might buy a portable Sony unit so they could use it in their flat and in her car.

Limited problem solving is involved when a consumer is willing to put *some* effort into deciding the best way to satisfy a need. Limited problem solving is typical when a consumer has some previous experience in solving a problem, but is not certain which choice is best at the current time. If our music lover wanted some new discs for there player, they would already know what type of music they enjoy. They might go to a familiar shop and check out what discs they had in stock for their favourite types of music.

Routinized response behaviour involves regularly selecting a particular way of satisfying a need when it occurs. Routinized response behaviour is typical when a consumer has considerable experience in how to meet a need and there is therefore no need for additional information. For example, our music lover might routinely buy the latest recording by her favourite band as soon as it is available. Most marketing managers would like their target consumers to buy their products in this routinized way. Routinized response behaviour is also typical for **low involvement purchases**—purchases that do not have high personal importance or relevance for the customer. Let's face it, buying a box of salt is probably not one of the burning issues in your life.[13]

Problem solving is a learning process

The reason problem solving becomes simpler with time is that people learn from experience, both positive and negative things. As consumers approach the problem-solving process, they bring attitudes formed by previous experiences and social training. Each new problem-solving process may then contribute to or modify this attitude set.

New concepts require an adoption process

When consumers face a really new concept, their previous experience may not be relevant to problem solving. These situations involve the **adoption process**—the steps individuals go through on the way to accepting or

Low involvement Frequently purchased Inexpensive Little risk Little information needed	**Routinized response behaviour**	**Limited problem solving**	**Extensive problem solving**	High involvement Infrequently purchased Expensive High risk Much information desired

Exhibit 3–14 Problem-Solving Continuum

rejecting a new idea. It is similar to the problem-solving process, but in the adoption process the role of learning is clearer—and so is promotion's potential contribution to a marketing mix.

In the adoption process, an individual moves through some fairly definite steps:

1. Awareness—the potential customer comes to know about the product but lacks details. The consumer may not even know how it works or what it will do.
2. Interest—*if* the consumer becomes interested, he or she will gather general information and facts about the product.
3. Evaluation—a consumer begins to give the product a mental trial, applying it to his or her personal situation.
4. Trial—the consumer may buy the product to experiment with it in use. A product that is either too expensive to try or isn't available for trial may never be adopted.
5. Decision—the consumer decides on either adoption or rejection. A satisfactory evaluation and trial may lead to adoption of the product and regular use. According to psychological learning theory, reinforcement leads to adoption.
6. Confirmation—the adopter continues to rethink the decision and searches for support for the decision that is, further reinforcement.[14]

Marketing managers for 3M, the company that makes Scotch tape, worked with the adoption process when they introduced Post-It note pads. Test market advertising increased awareness: they explained how Post-It notes could be applied to a surface and then easily removed. But test market sales were slow because most consumers were not interested. They didn't see the benefit. To encourage trial, 3M distributed free samples. Using the samples confirmed the benefit—and when the samples were used up consumers started buying Post-Its. As Post-It distribution expanded to other market areas, 3M used samples to speed consumers through the trial stage and the rest of the adoption process.[15]

Dissonance may set in after the decision

A buyer may have second thoughts after making a purchase decision. The buyer may have chosen from among several attractive alternatives—weighing the pros and cons and finally making a decision. Later doubts, however, may lead to **dissonance**—tension caused by uncertainty about the rightness of a decision. Dissonance may lead a buyer to search for additional information to confirm the wisdom of the decision and so reduce tension. Without this confirmation, the adopter might buy something else next time—or not comment positively about the product to others.

SEVERAL PROCESSES ARE RELATED AND RELEVANT TO STRATEGY PLANNING

Exhibit 3–15 shows the interrelation of the problem-solving process, the adoption process, and learning. It is important to see this interrelation and to understand that promotion can modify or accelerate it. Also note that the potential buyers' problem-solving behaviour should affect how firms design their physical distribution systems. If customers are not willing to travel far to shop, a firm may need more outlets to get their business. Similarly, customers' attitudes help determine what price to charge. Clearly, knowing how a target market handles these processes will aid marketing strategy planning.

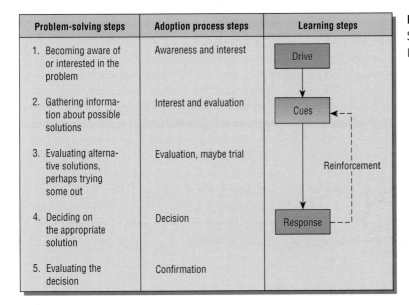

Problem-solving steps	Adoption process steps	Learning steps
1. Becoming aware of or interested in the problem	Awareness and interest	Drive
2. Gathering information about possible solutions	Interest and evaluation	Cues
3. Evaluating alternative solutions, perhaps trying some out	Evaluation, maybe trial	Reinforcement
4. Deciding on the appropriate solution	Decision	Response
5. Evaluating the decision	Confirmation	

Exhibit 3–15 Relation of Problem-Solving Process, Adoption Process and Learning (given a problem)

SUMMARY

In this chapter, we analysed the individual consumer in terms of broader demographic and behavioural variables. Broad demographic factors provide the market with the first ways of identifying market segments where there may be specific opportunities for the company. Demographic variables can indicate where the consumer is, how much the consumer is likely to buy and how to reach the consumer in terms of distribution and promotion activities.

We also considered the role of the buyer as a problem solver who is influenced by psychological variables, social influences and the purchase situation. All these variables are related, and our model of buyer behaviour helps integrate them into one process. Marketing strategy planning requires a good grasp of this material. Assuming that everyone behaves the way you do, or even like your family or friends do, can lead to expensive marketing errors.

Consumer buying behaviour results from the consumer's efforts to satisfy needs and wants. We discussed some reasons why consumers buy, and saw that consumer behaviour can't be fully explained by only a list of needs. We also saw that most societies are divided into social classes, a fact that helps explain some consumer behaviour. And we discussed the impact of reference groups and opinion leaders.

A buyer behaviour model was presented to help you to interpret and integrate the present findings, as well as any new data you might get from marketing research. As of now, the behavioural sciences can only offer insights and theories, which the marketing manager must blend with intuition and judgement in developing marketing strategies.

Marketing research may have to be used to answer specific questions. But if a firm has neither the money nor the time for research, then marketing managers have to rely on available descriptions of present behaviour and 'guesstimates' about future behaviour. Popular magazines and leading newspapers often reflect the public's shifting attitudes. And many studies of the changing consumer are published regularly in the business and trade press. This material will help your marketing strategy planning.

QUESTIONS AND PROBLEMS

1. Discuss the value of gross national product and gross national product per capita as measures of market potential in international consumer markets. Refer to specific data in your answer.
2. Name three specific examples of firms that have developed a marketing mix to appeal to the baby boom group of consumers.
3. Some demographic characteristics are likely to be more important than others in determining market potential. For each of the following characteristics, identify two products for which this characteristic is *most* important: (*a*) size of geographic area, (*b*) population, (*c*) income, (*d*) stage of life cycle.
4. Name three specific examples (specific products or brands—not just product categories) and explain how demand will differ by geographic location *and* urban–rural location.
5. Explain how the continuing mobility of consumers should affect marketing strategy planning in the future. Be sure to consider the impact on the four Ps.
6. Explain how the redistribution of income has affected marketing planning thus far—and its likely impact in the future.
7. Explain why mobile consumers can be an attractive market.
8. Why are marketing managers paying more attention to ethnic dimensions of consumer markets?
9. In your own words, explain economic needs and how they relate to the economic man model of consumer behaviour. Give an example of a purchase you recently made which is consistent with the economic man model. Give another example of a purchase that is not explained by the economic man model. Explain your thinking.
10. Explain what is meant by a hierarchy of needs and provide examples of one or more products that enable you to satisfy each of the four levels of need.

11. Cut out (or copy) two recent advertisements: one full-page colour advertisement from a magazine and one large display from a newspaper. Indicate which needs are being appealed to in each case.
12. Explain how an understanding of consumers' learning processes might affect marketing strategy planning. Give an example.
13. Briefly describe your own *beliefs* about the potential value of a driver-side airbag in a car, your *attitude* towards airbags, and your *intention* about buying a car with an airbag.
14. Explain psychographics and lifestyle analysis. Explain how it might be useful for planning marketing strategies to reach students as compared to the 'average' consumer.
15. Illustrate how the reference group concept may apply in practice by explaining how you are influenced personally by some reference group for some product. What are the implications of such behaviour for marketing managers?
16. Give two examples of recent purchases where your purchase decision was influenced by the specific purchase situation. Briefly explain how your decision was affected.
17. Give an example of a recent purchase in which you used extended problem solving. What sources of information did you use in making the decision?

SUGGESTED CASES

1. McDonald's 'Seniors' Restaurant
3. Republic Polymer Company
11. Outdoor World

REFERENCES

1. *World Marketing Data and Statistics 1995* (on CD-ROM), 1st edn, Euromonitor Ltd, London, 1995; *European Marketing Data and Statistics*, Euromonitor, London, 1995, contains specific data on European Markets 30th edition; *The Book of European Forecasts*, Euromonitor, London, 1995, contains market forecasts covering a wide range of sectors including socioeconomic trends, trade and industry development, marketing and media activities; *Consumer Europe*, 11th edn, Euromonitor, London, 1995.
2. J. Simms (1998), 'A stout defence', *Marketing Business*, March, pp. 16–20.
3. US Bureau of the Census, Reports WP/94 and WP/94-DD, *World Population Profile: 1994*, U.S. Government Printing Office, Washington, DC, 1994; US Bureau of the Census, *Statistical Abstract of the United States 1994*, U.S. Government Printing Office, Washington, DC, 1994, pp. 850–52; PC *Globe Maps 'N' Facts Software*, Broderbund, Novato, CA, 1993.
4. S. Vandermerwe, 'A framework for constructing Euronetworks' *European Management Journal*, March 1993, pp. 55–61; Y. Marbeau, 'Harmonization of demographics in Europe 1992: the state of the art', *Marketing and Research Today* (Netherlands), March 1992; pp. 33–50; G. Guido, 'Implementing a pan-European marketing strategy', *Long Range Planning*, October 1991, pp. 23–35.
5. C. Batchelor, 'How the French and British see the channel tunnel', *The Financial Times*, 10 February 1994, p. 14.
6. 'What works for one works for all', *Business Week*, 20 April 1992, pp. 112–13.
7. A. Hawkins and S.J. Hoch, 'Low-involvement learning: memory without evaluation', *Journal of Consumer Research*, September 1992, pp. 212–25; G. McWilliam, 'Consumers' involvement in brands and product categories', in M.J. Baker, (ed.) *Perspectives on Marketing Management*, Wiley, Chichester, 1992.

8. F. Dall'Olmo Riley, A. Ehrenberg and N. Barnard, 'Changes in attitudes and behaviour', in P. Anderrson (ed.), *Marketing Research and Practice*, 27th EMAC Proceedings, 1998, Track 6, pp. 13–32.

9. J. Waldrop, 'Markets with attitude', *American Demographics*, July 1994, pp. 22–33; 'New VALS 2 takes psychological route', *Advertising Age*, 13 February, 1989, p. 24; L.R. Kahle, S.E. Beatty and P. Homer, 'Alternative Measurement Approaches to Consumer Values: The List of Values (LOV) and Values and Life Styles (VALS)', *Journal of Consumer Research*, December 1986, pp. 405–10.

10. For more on children's influence in purchase decisions, see Sharon E. Beatty and Salil Talpade, 'Adolescent influence in family decision making: A replication with extension', *Journal of Consumer Research*, September 1994, pp. 332–41; For more on men's influence, see J.B. Ford, M.S. LaTour and T.L. Henthorne, 'Perception of Marital Roles in Purchase Decision Processes: A Cross-Cultural Study', *Journal of the Academy of Marketing Science*, Spring 1995, pp. 120–31; U. Yavas, E. Babakus and N. Delener, 'Family Purchasing Roles in Saudi Arabia: Perspectives from Saudi Wives', *Journal of Business Research*, September 1994, pp. 75–86; Rosemary Polegato and J.L. Zaichkowsky, 'Family Food Shopping: Strategies Used by Husbands and Wives', *Journal of Consumer Affairs*, Winter 1994, pp. 278–99.

11. Adapted and updated from J.H. Myers and W.H. Reynolds, *Consumer Behavior and Marketing Management*, Houghton Mifflin, Boston, 1967, p. 49. See also J.L. Zaichkowsky, 'Consumer behavior: yesterday, today, and tomorrow', *Business Horizons*, May/June 1991, pp. 51–8.

12. W.D. Hoyer, 'An examination of consumer decision making for a common repeat purchase product', *Journal of Consumer Research*, December 1984, pp. 822–29.

13. J. Brock Smith and J.M. Bristor, 'Uncertainty orientation: explaining differences in purchase involvement and external search', *Psychology & Marketing*, November/December 1994, pp. 587–608; P.G. Patterson, 'Expectations and product performance as determinants of satisfaction for a high-involvement purchase', *Psychology & Marketing*, September/October 1993, p. 449.

14. Adapted from E.M. Rogers with F. Shoemaker, *Communication of Innovation: A Cross Cultural Approach*, Free Press, New York, 1968.

15. '3M's aggressive new consumer drive', *Business Week*, 16 July 1984, pp. 114–22.

CHAPTER 4

Business and Organizational Customers and Their Buying Behaviour

When You Finish This Chapter, You Should

1 Know who the business and organizational customers are.

2 Understand the problem-solving behaviour of organizational buyers.

3 See why multiple influence is common in business and organizational purchase decisions.

4 Know the basic methods used in organizational buying.

5 Understand the different types of buyer–seller relationships and their benefits and limitations.

6 Know about the number and distribution of manufacturers and why they are an important customer group.

7 Know how buying by service firms, retailers, wholesalers and governments is similar to—and different from—buying by manufacturers.

8 Understand the important new terms (shown in colour).

THE QUEUE MANAGEMENT GROUP

Many service companies face problems with managing levels of demand. Supermarkets, restaurants, theme parks, banks and post offices all have to deal with varying levels of demand and respond to them accordingly. These demand fluctuations often mean that queues develop at some times while at others there is no queue yet staff are in place waiting to attend to customers. All of this leads to inefficiencies, with customers becoming disgruntled in queues and management wasting staff resources when customer demand is low.

One company that set out to solve these problems for service businesses is, appropriately enough, called Queue Management (QM). The Post Office is one of their biggest customers. The scale of the Post Office gives some indication as to the likely queuing problems—28 million customers per week; 170 core transactions offered; £500 million cash handled daily; 19 200 branches throughout the UK; branch size ranges from small village post offices that open for a few hours each week to central London branches with 24 counter staff at one time.

QM and the Post Office work in partnership to solve the post office queuing problem. This relationship developed after a chance meeting between executives from QM and the Post Office at a conference. QM spent more than 900 manhours on site and its project team worked closely with managers and staff at many branches. Only when it comes to proposing a solution, after extensive research, does QM enter into a financial arrangement with its clients. By the time clients become financially committed the view QM as partners and know that the products supplied are absolutely right for their specific needs.

Seven months after the initial contact with the Post Office, a prototype system was piloted. An adaptable barrier system marshals customers into a single queue with a head height screen at the front. When the next counter position is free the customer at the head of the queue hears a spoken instruction as to which member of staff is available. There is also an on-screen image of an arrow and number relating to the vacant counter position. A light simultaneously flashes at that position. This system gets over the problem of the perceived unfairness experienced by customers who see other queues moving more quickly under the traditional ways of queuing. After consultation with branch staff, QM also developed an information system to let management know footfall patterns, estimated customer waiting times, number of staff on duty and speed of service. Further new 'products' are being developed by QM, in response to the particular issues and problems that confront the Post Office.

QM's approach tends to mean that each client is treated differently. Project managers invest in researching the client's situation and developing a customized solution. Sometimes this innovation amounts to a new product which can subsequently be standardizded and sold to others. For the most part, however, QM's business is derived from working closely with clients, analysing and solving client problems.[1]

BUSINESS AND ORGANIZATIONAL CUSTOMERS—A BIG OPPORTUNITY

Most of us think about individual final consumers when we hear the term *customer*. But many marketing managers aim at customers who are not final consumers. In fact, more purchases are made by businesses and other organizations than by final consumers. In the markets served by the companies in the opening illustration, speed of service, quality of design and flexibility are important reasons why companies can win orders in this market, particularly at the expense of lower priced competitors from the Far East. The customers who are buying from these companies are buying to meet organizational needs, rather than personal needs and so the motivation is different from that of the final consumer. However, a successful marketing plan will still depend on developing a solid understanding of who these customers are, and how they buy. That is the focus of this chapter.

What types of customers are involved?

Business and organizational customers are any buyers who buy for resale or to produce other goods and services. Exhibit 4–1 shows the different types of customers in these markets. They include industrial manufacturers, producers of services, intermediaries and various non-profit organizations, including government agencies. These varied customers do many different jobs. Yet many of the segmenting dimensions that a marketing manager needs to describe their buying behaviour tend to be common across the different types of organization. There is a reason for this. Industrial firms originally developed many of the basic approaches for organizational buying. Other types of organization then adopted the best ideas, so there are many characteristics of buying behaviour that are common to them. That is why the different kinds of organizational buyers are often loosely referred to as 'industrial buyers' or 'intermediate buyers'. As we discuss organizational buying, we will interchange examples of buying by many different types of organization. Later in the chapter, however, we will highlight some of the specific characteristics of the different customer groups.

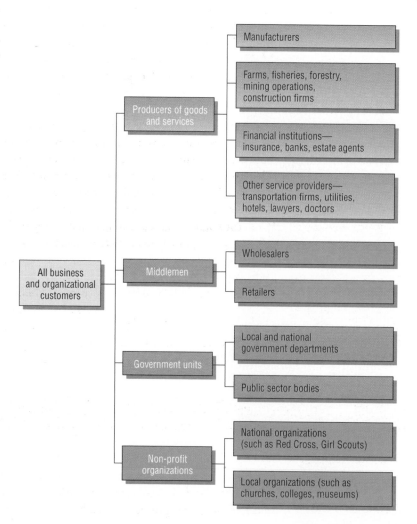

Exhibit 4–1 Examples of Different Types of Business and Organizational Customers

ORGANIZATIONAL CUSTOMERS ARE DIFFERENT

Organizations buy for a basic purpose

Like final consumers, organizations make purchases to satisfy needs. But it is often easier to understand an organization's needs because most organizations make purchases for the same basic reason. They buy goods and services that will help them meet the demand for the goods and services that they in turn supply to their markets. In other words, their basic need is to satisfy their own customers and clients. Technically this sort of demand is called 'derived demand', because the demand for such products and services is derived from the demand for the final products or services of the customer. A manufacturer buys because it wants to earn a profit by making and selling goods. A wholesaler or retailer buys products it can profitably resell to its customers. A local authority or council wants to meet its legal and social obligations to citizens. Similarly, a leisure club wants to help its members enjoy their leisure time.

Even small differences are important

Different types of customer may buy for the same basic purpose, but there are many variations in how they buy and why they pick specific suppliers. Understanding how the buying behaviour of a particular organization varies from others can be very important. These customers often make large purchases, and competition for their business is often intense. Even 'trivial' differences in buying behaviour may be important because success often hinges on fine tuning the marketing mix to precisely meet the target customers' needs.

Sellers often approach each organizational customer directly, usually through a sales representative. This gives the seller more chance to adjust the marketing mix for each individual customer. A seller may even develop a unique strategy for each individual customer. This is carrying target marketing to its extreme. But often that is what is necessary to be competitive when a customer's potential purchase volume is very large. In such situations, the individual salesperson takes much responsibility for strategy planning. The salesperson often coordinates the whole relationship between the supplier and the customer.

That may involve working with many people—including top management—in both firms.

Serving customers in international markets

Many marketers have discovered that there are good opportunities to serve business customers in different countries around the world. Specific business customs do vary from one country to another and the differences can be important. For example, a salesperson working in Japan must know how to handle a customer's business card with respect. Japanese think of a business card as a symbolic extension of the person who presents it. Thus, they consider it rude to write notes on the back of a card or put it in a wallet while the person who presented it is still in the room. While such cultural differences can be very important, the basic approaches marketers use to deal with business customers in different parts of the world are much less varied than those required to reach individual consumers. This is probably why the shift to a global economy has been so rapid for many firms. Their business customers in different countries buy in similar ways and are reached with similar marketing mixes. Moreover, business customers are often willing to reach out further than final consumers to work with a supplier who has developed a superior marketing mix.

Customers may expect quality certification

Business customers considering a new supplier or one from overseas may be concerned about product quality. This is becoming less of an obstacle because of ISO 9000. ISO 9000 is a way for a supplier to document its quality procedures according to internationally recognized standards. ISO 9000 assures a customer that a supplier has effective quality procedures in place, without the customer having to conduct its own costly and time-consuming audit. Some businesses will not buy from another business unless it has ISO 9000. To get ISO 9000 certification a company basically must prove to outside auditors that it documents in detail how the company operates and who is responsible for quality at every step.

ORGANIZATIONAL BUYERS ARE PROBLEM SOLVERS

Some people think of organizational buying as entirely different from consumer buying but there are many similarities. In fact, the problem-solving framework introduced in Chapter 3 can be applied here.

Three kinds of buying processes are useful

In Chapter 3, we discussed problem solving by consumers and how it might vary from extended problem solving to routine buying. In organizational markets, we can adapt these concepts slightly and work with three similar buying processes: a new-task buying process, a modified rebuy process, or a straight rebuy.[2] See Exhibit 4–2.

New-task buying occurs when an organization has a new need and the buyer wants a great deal of information. New-task buying can involve setting product specifications, evaluating sources of supply and establishing an order routine that can be followed in the future if results are satisfactory.

A straight rebuy is a routine repurchase that may have been made many times before. Buyers probably don't bother looking for new information or new sources of supply. Most of a company's small or recurring purchases are of this type—but they take only a small part of an organized buyer's time.

The modified rebuy is the in-between process where some review of the buying situation is done—though not as much as in new-task buying. Sometimes a competitor will get lazy enjoying a straight rebuy situation. An alert marketer can turn these situations into opportunities by providing more information or a better marketing mix.

Customers in a new-task buying situation are likely to seek information from a variety of sources. See Exhibit 4–3. How much information a customer will collect also depends on the importance of the purchase and the level of uncertainty about what choice might be best. The time

Characteristics	Type of process		
	New-task buying	Modified rebuy	Straight rebuy
Time required	Much	Medium	Little
Multiple influence	Much	Some	Little
Review of suppliers	Much	Some	None
Information needed	Much	Some	Little

Exhibit 4–2 Organizational Buying Processes

and expense of searching for and analysing a lot of information may not be justified for a minor purchase. But a major purchase often involves real detective work. After all, the consequences of a mistake can be very important.

Most buyers try to routinize buying

To save effort and expense, most firms try to routinize the purchase process whenever they can. When some person or unit wants to buy something, a requisition—a request to buy something—is filled out. After approval by some supervisor, the requisition is forwarded to the buyer for placement with the 'best' seller. Approved requisitions are converted to purchase orders as quickly as possible. Straight rebuys are usually made the day the

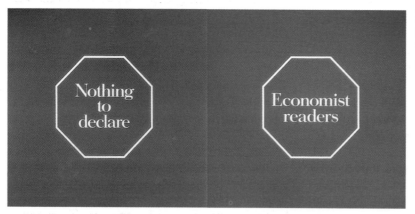

Business customers need good information for decision making. *The Economist* stresses this benefit to readers.

	Marketing sources	**Non-marketing sources**
Personal sources	• Salespeople • Others from supplier firms • Trade shows	• Buying centre members • Outside business associates • Consultants and outside experts
Impersonal sources	• Advertising in trade publications • Sales literature • Sales catalogues • Web page	• Rating services • Trade associations • News publications • Product directories • Internet news pointcasts

Exhibit 4–3 Major Sources of Information Used by Organizational Buyers

requisition is received, while new-task and modified rebuys take longer. If time is important, the buyer may place the order by telephone, fax or computer.

Computer buying is becoming common

Many buyers now delegate a large portion of their routine order placing to computers. They program the decision rules that tell the computer how to order and leave the details of following through to the machine. When economic conditions change, buyers modify the computer instructions. When nothing unusual happens, however, the computer system continues to routinely rebuy from regular suppliers as needs develop.

Being selected as a major supplier, and electronically linked to that customer, can lead to substantial sales and revenue. Such a buyer will be more impressed by an attractive marketing mix for a whole *line* of products than just a lower price for a particular order. It may be too expensive and too much trouble to change the whole buying system just because somebody is offering a low price on a particular day.[3]

It pays to know the buyer

In routine order situations, it is very important to be one of the regular sources of supply. For straight rebuys, the buyer (or computer) may place an order without even considering other potential sources. Sellers' sales representatives regularly call on these buyers—but *not* to sell a particular item. Rather, they want to maintain relations, become a source, and/or point out new developments that might cause the buyer to reevaluate his present straight rebuy procedure and give more business to the sales representative's company.

Shopping on the Internet provides opportunities

The logic of treating routine purchases as a rebuy is to reduce the time, hassle and risk of shopping around. On the other hand, use of the Internet and on-line order systems makes it easier for suppliers to attract customers who would otherwise just settle for the convenience of a preferred source. When a buyer can do a quick Internet search and check availability and prices of products, especially standardized items that are available from a number of vendors, differences in price become very visible. A vendor that does not offer superior value, perhaps through differentiated service or more convenience, may find it loses customers.

Inventory policy may determine purchases

Business customers generally try to maintain an adequate inventory, certainly enough to prevent stockouts or keep production lines moving. A retailer or wholesaler can lose sales quickly if products that are in demand are not on the shelf. On the other hand, keeping too much inventory is expensive. Firms are now paying more attention to inventory costs, and looking to their suppliers for help in controlling them. This often means that a supplier must be able to provide just-in-time delivery—reliably getting products there *just* before the customer needs them.

Just-in-time relationships between buyers and sellers require a lot of coordination. For example, a car producer may ask a supplier of car carpets to load the delivery lorry so that the colour and style is in the planned order of cars on the assembly line. This reduces the buyer's costs because the carpets will only need to be handled once. However, it may increase the supplier's costs. Most buyers realize they cannot just push costs back onto their suppliers without giving them something in return. Often what they give is a longer-term contract that shares both the costs and benefits of the working partnership. Just-in-time delivery arrangements are discussed in more detail in Chapter 10.

Reciprocity may influence buying

Reciprocity means trading sales for sales— 'If you buy from me, I'll buy from you.' If a company's customers also can supply products that the firm buys, then the sales departments of both buyer and seller may try to 'trade' sales for sales. Purchasing agents generally resist reciprocity but often face pressure from their sales departments. When prices and quality are otherwise competitive, an outside supplier seldom can break a reciprocity relationship. The supplier can only hope to become an alternative source of supply and wait for the competitor to let its quality slip or prices rise.

Purchasing managers are buying specialists

Many organizations, especially large ones, need buying specialists (purchasing managers). Purchasing managers are buying specialists for their employers. Most purchasing managers are well educated. In large organizations, they usually specialize by product area. Salespeople are frequently obliged to see the purchasing manager first— before they contact any other employee. These buyers hold important positions and take a dim view of sales representatives who try to go around them. Rather than being 'sold', these buyers want salespeople to provide accurate information that will help them buy wisely. They like information on new goods and services, and tips on potential price changes, supply shortages and other changes in market conditions.

Purchasing may be centralized

If a large organization has facilities at many locations, much of the purchasing work may be done at a central location. For example, Tengelman, the second largest retailer in Europe, handles most of its buying from its headquarters in Germany. When buying is centralized, a sales representative may be able to sell to facilities all over a country—or even across several countries—without leaving a base city. This makes selling easier for competitors, too, so the market may be extremely competitive. The importance of such big buyers has led some companies to set up 'national account' or 'key account' salesforces specially trained to cater for these needs. In Chapter 14 of this book you will see the work of such key account managers in more detail.

Economic and behavioural factors can both be important

Organizational buyers typically focus on economic factors when they make purchase decisions. Buyers try to consider the total cost of selecting a supplier and a particular product, not just the initial price of the product. In the business car-hire market competition is becoming increasingly fierce. There are few differentiating features between the major car-hire companies. They all have access to the same cars to include in their hire fleet. The standards of customer service are well defined and any new approach to meeting customer needs can easily be copied by competitors. Prices are therefore very competitive and similar from one company to the next.

However, behavioural factors are also relevant. Faced with no significant differences between different car-hire companies the business traveller is likely to be influenced by his or her perception of other factors. For example, how easy is it to hire the car? Do the check in procedures take long, and how convenient is it to return the vehicle at the end of the hire? Are all the charges carefully explained and are there any unexpected 'extras' in the bill? Although he or she will not

personally be paying for the hire cost, it will still be necessary to justify the expenses! Finally, does the car-hire company have the sort of car which the user would enjoy driving, particularly if the hire is for an extended period? This is an area where personal and organizational needs clearly overlap.

Purchases must be reliable

The matter of dependability deserves further emphasis. A hire car must be reliable and not let the user down. There would be nothing worse than missing an important business appointment because the hire car broke down. The consequences of product failure in other areas can be even more serious. If a production line has to be shut down because a supply of parts has not arrived from a supplier this can have a major impact on the operations of the company. Dependable product quality is important too. The cost of a small item may have little to do with its importance. For example, a short piece of wire with faulty insulation might cause a large piece of equipment to break down, and the costs of finding and correcting the problem could be completely out of proportion to the cost of the wire.

Vendor analysis can help to make better purchasing decisions

Considering all the economic factors relevant to a purchase decision is sometimes complex. A supplier or product that is best in one way may not be best in others. To try to deal with these situations, many buyers use vendor analysis—formal rating of suppliers on all relevant areas of performance. This may involve a team of managers visiting prospective suppliers to determine whether they are capable of meeting the customers' requirements. Companies that do not satisfy their customers that they are competent suppliers will not be

Business customers still respond to emotional appeals. The Audi A4 was Business Car of the Year in 1997.

considered for future orders. Evaluating suppliers and how they are working out results in better buying decisions.[4]

Behavioural needs are relevant too

Vendor analysis tries to focus on economic factors, but purchasing in organizations may also involve many of the same behavioural dimensions we discussed in Chapter 3. Modern buyers are human and they want friendly relationships with suppliers. Some buyers seem eager to imitate progressive competitors, or even to be the first to try new products. Such innovators might deserve special attention when new products are being introduced. Buyers are also human with respect to protecting their own interests and position in the company. That causes many buyers to want to avoid taking risks that might reflect badly on their decisions. They have to buy a wide variety of products from many sources and make decisions involving many factors beyond their control. If a new source delivers late or product quality is poor, you can guess who will be blamed. Marketers who can help the buyer avoid taking risks have a definite appeal. In fact, this may make the difference between a successful and unsuccessful marketing mix. A seller's marketing mix should satisfy *both* the needs of the buyer's company as well as the buyer's individual needs. Therefore, sellers need to find an overlapping area where both can be satisfied. See Exhibit 4–4 for a summary of this idea.

 Internet Exercise

The travel purchasing decision is different for the business travellers and the holidaymaker. Visit the Eurostar web site (**www.eurostar.com**) and click on the pages for Business Travel and Holidays Direct. How does the content of the two pages differ? What does this tell you about the business traveller's purchase criteria?

 Ethical conflicts may arise

Although organizational buyers are influenced by their own needs, most are real professionals who are careful to avoid a conflict between their own self-interests and company outcomes. Marketers must be careful here. A salesperson who offers one of his company pens to a buyer may view the gift as part of the promotion effort but the customer's firm may have a policy against a buyer accepting *any* gift. Most organizational buyers do their work with high ethical standards and expect marketers to work in the same way. Marketers need to take concerns about conflict of interest very seriously. Part of the promotion job in marketing is to identify and persuade different individuals who may influence an organization's purchase decision. Yet, the whole marketing effort may be put in a bad light if it even *appears* that a marketer has encouraged a buyer to put personal gain ahead of company interest.

Multiple buying influences in a buying centre

Much of the work of the typical purchasing manager consists of straight rebuys. When a purchase requisition comes in, the purchasing agent places an order without consulting anyone else. But, in some cases—especially new-task buying—multiple buying influence is important. Multiple buying influence means that several people—perhaps even top management—share in making a purchase decision. Possible buying influences are shown in Exhibit 4–5. They include:

1. *Users*—perhaps production line workers or their supervisors.
2. *Influencers*—perhaps engineering or R&D people who help write specifications or supply information for evaluating alternatives.

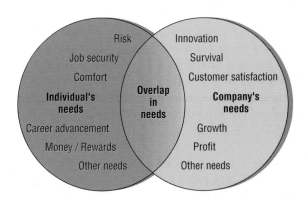

Exhibit 4–4 Overlapping Needs of Individual Influencers and the Customer Organization

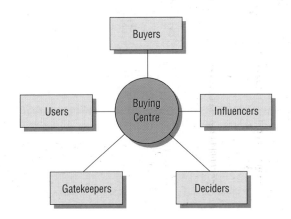

Exhibit 4–5 Multiple Influence and Roles in the Buying Centre

3. *Buyers*—the purchasing agents who have the responsibility for working with suppliers and arranging the terms of the sale.
4. *Deciders*—the people in the organization who have the power to select or approve the supplier—usually the purchasing agent for small items, but perhaps top management for larger purchases.
5. *Gatekeepers*—people who control the flow of information within the organization—perhaps purchasing agents who shield users or other deciders. Gatekeepers can also include receptionists, secretaries, research assistants and others who influence the flow of information about potential purchases.

An example shows how the different buying influences work.

Suppose Electrolux, the Swedish domestic appliance manufacturer, wants to buy a machine to stamp out various metal parts it needs. Different suppliers are eager for the business. Several people (influencers) help to evaluate the choices. A finance manager worries about the high cost and suggests leasing the machine. The quality control people want a machine that will do a more accurate job although it is more expensive. The production manager is interested in speed of operation and the quality of the final product. The production line workers and their supervisors want the machine that is easiest to use so workers can continue to rotate jobs. The company president asks the purchasing department to assemble all the information but retains the power to select and approve the supplier (the decider). The purchasing manager's administrative assistant (a gatekeeper) has been deciding what information to pass on to senior management as well as scheduling visits for salespeople. After all these buying influences are considered, one of the purchasing managers for the firm will be responsible for making recommendations and arranging the terms of the sale (the buyer).

It is helpful to think of a buying centre as all the people who participate in or influence a purchase. Different people may make up a buying centre from one decision to the next. This makes the marketing job difficult. The salesperson must study each case carefully. Just learning who to talk with may be hard, but thinking about the various roles in the buying centre can help. The salesperson may have to talk to every member of the buying centre, stressing different topics for each. This not only complicates the promotion job but also lengthens it. Approval of a routine order may take anywhere from a day to several months. On very important purchases, such as a new computer system, a new plant or major equipment, the selling period may stretch out to a year or more.[5]

BASIC METHODS AND PRACTICES IN ORGANIZATIONAL BUYING

Should you inspect, sample, describe or negotiate?
Organizational buyers (really, buyers of all types, including final consumers) use four basic approaches to evaluating and buying products: (1) inspection, (2) sampling, (3) description and (4) negotiated contracts. Understanding the differences in these buying methods is important in strategy planning, so let's look at each approach.

Inspection looks at everything
Inspection buying means looking at every item. It is used for products that are not standardized and require examination. Here each product is different—as in the case of livestock or used equipment. Such products are often sold in open markets, or at auction if there are several potential buyers. Buyers inspect the goods and either bargain with the seller or bid against competing buyers.

Sampling looks at some
Sampling buying means looking at only part of a potential purchase. As products become more stan-dardized, perhaps because of careful grading or quality control, buying by sample becomes possible. For example, a power company might buy miles of heavy electric cable. A sample section might be heated to the melting point to be certain the cable is safe. Prices may be based on a sample. Although demand and supply forces may set the general price level, the actual price may vary depending on the quality of a specific sample. For example, this kind of buying is used in grain markets where the actual price is based on a sample that has been withdrawn from a shipment of grain and analysed. People in less developed economies do a lot of buying by inspection or sampling, regardless of the product. The reason is scepticism about quality, or lack of faith in the seller.

Specifications describe the need
Description (specification) buying means buying from a written (or verbal) description of the product. Most manufactured items and many agricultural commodities are bought this way—often without inspection. When quality can almost be guaranteed, buying by

description—grade, brand or specification—may be satisfactory, especially when there is mutual trust between buyers and sellers. This method, of course, reduces the cost of buying and is used by buyers whenever practical. Services are usually purchased by description. Since a service is usually not performed until after it is purchased, buyers have nothing to inspect ahead of time.

Once the purchase needs are specified, it's the buyer's job to get the best deal possible. If there are several suppliers interested in the business, the buyer will often request competitive bids. Competitive bids are the terms of sale offered by different suppliers in response to the buyer's purchase specifications. If different suppliers' quality, dependability and delivery schedules all meet the specifications, the buyer will select the low-price bid. But a creative marketer needs to look carefully at the purchaser's specifications to see if there are other elements of his or her marketing mix that could provide a competitive advantage.

Negotiated contracts handle relationships

Negotiated contract buying means agreeing to a contract that allows for changes in the purchase arrangements. Sometimes, the buyer knows roughly what the company needs but cannot fix all the details in advance. The specifications or total requirements may change over time. This situation is common, for example, R&D work and in the building of special-purpose machinery or buildings. In such cases, the general project is described, and a basic price may be agreed, perhaps even based on competitive bids, but with provision for changes and price adjustments up or down. Or a supplier may be willing to accept a contract that provides some type of incentive, such as full coverage of costs plus a fixed fee or full costs plus a profit percentage tied to costs. The whole contract may even be subject to renegotiation as the work proceeds. While the marketing job varies depending on which buying process and methods a firm uses to make a particular purchase, the type of relationship a supplier has with the customer firm is sometimes an even more important consideration.

BUYER–SELLER RELATIONSHIPS IN BUSINESS MARKETS

Build relationships—for mutual benefits

In business markets, there are often significant benefits of a close working relationship between a supplier and a customer firm. Such relationships are becoming more common. Many firms are reducing the number of suppliers with which they work—expecting more in return from the select suppliers that remain. The best relationships involve real partnerships—where there's mutual trust and respect. For both the customer and supplier the basic benefit of a close relationship is improved profits through cooperation that reduces total costs. Closely tied firms can often share tasks at lower total cost than would be possible working at arm's length. Costs are sometimes reduced simply by reducing uncertainty and risk. A supplier is often willing and able to reduce its selling price significantly if a customer commits to large orders or orders over a longer period of time. With a larger sales volume the supplier may capture savings through economies of scale and reduced selling costs. The customer not only benefits from getting needed parts or services at lower cost but is also assured a dependable source of supply. Firms that work closely with fewer suppliers can focus their effort on working with suppliers to resolve joint problems. For example, it may cost both the supplier and the customer more to resolve the problems of a defective product after it is delivered than it would have cost to prevent the problem in the first place. But without the customer's help it may be impossible for the supplier to identify a solution to the problem. As the

head of purchasing at Motorola puts it: 'Every time we make an error it takes people at both ends to correct it.'

Relationships may reduce flexibility

Although close relationships can produce benefits, they are not always effective. Making a long-term commitment to a partner—any partner—may result is a loss of flexibility. In many markets, the forces of competition drive down costs and spur innovative marketing mixes; then the customer may be better off simply letting suppliers compete for the business. It may not be worth the customer's investment of time and energy to build a relationship with a supplier for purchases that are not particularly important or made that frequently. It may at first appear that a seller would *always* prefer to have a closer relationship with a customer, but that is not so. In situations where a customer doesn't want a relationship, trying to build one is likely to cost more than it is worth. Further, just because a customer is interested in a relationship doesn't mean that it always makes sense for the supplier. Many small suppliers have made the mistake of relying too heavily on relationships with too few customers. One failed relationship may bankrupt the business.

Relationships have many dimensions

There are many different aspects of buyer–seller relationships. Firms may have a close buyer–seller relationship in some ways and not be related at all in others.

Exhibit 4–6 Key Dimensions of Relationships in Business Markets

Thus, it is useful to know about five key dimensions that help characterize most buyers–seller relationships: cooperation, information sharing, operational linkages, legal bonds and relationship-specific adaptations. Purchasing managers for the buying firm and salespeople for the supplier usually coordinate the different dimensions of a relationship. However, as shown in Exhibit 4–6, close relationships often involve direct contacts between a number of people from other areas in both firms. We'll discuss each of these dimensions separately, but keep in mind that a given relationship might be high on some dimensions and low on others.

Cooperation treats problems as joint responsibilities

In cooperative relationships, the buyer and seller work together to jointly achieve both mutual and individual objectives. This doesn't mean that the buyer (or seller) will always do what the other wants, but rather that people in the two firms treat any problems that may arise as a joint responsibility. Low cooperation occurs when each firm focuses on working independently to achieve its own goals. Some buyers still see little need for co-operation. If one supplier cannot satisfy their objectives, there are others who can.

Through cooperation, National Semiconductor (NS) and Siltec—one of its major suppliers of silicon wafers—found clever ways to cut costs in spite of big increases in the cost of basic silicon. For example, workers at the NS plant used to throw away the expensive plastic cassettes that Siltec uses to transport the silicon wafers. Now Siltec and NS cooperate to recycle the cassettes. As NS's workers unpack the silicon they toss the empty cassettes into a shipping box—and when the box is full UPS delivers it back to Siltec. This helps the environment and also saves more that £200 000 a year, most of which Siltec passes along to NS as lower prices.[6]

Shared information is useful, but may be risky

Some relationships involve open sharing of information, even important proprietary information, that is useful to both the buyer and seller. This might include the exchange of cost data, discussion of demand forecasts and joint work on new product designs. Information might be shared personally or electronically through information systems. Information sharing can lead to better decisions, reduced uncertainty about the future and better planning. However, sometimes firms don't want to share information, especially if there is a risk that a partner might misuse it. For example, some suppliers claim that General Motors' former purchasing chief showed blueprints of their latest technology to competing suppliers. Information sharing usually requires trust in the partner. Violations of trust in a relationship are an ethical matter and should be taken seriously. However, as a practical matter, it makes sense for a firm—regardless of whether it is a supplier or customer—to know its partner well before revealing all.

Operational linkages share functions between firms

Operational linkages are direct ties between the internal operations of the buyer and seller firms. These linkages usually involve formal arrangements and ongoing coordination of activities between the firms. Shared activities are especially important when neither firm, working on its own, can perform a function as well as the two firms can working together.

For example, operational linkages are often required to reduce total inventory costs. Business customers want to maintain an adequate inventory. On the other hand, keeping too much inventory is expensive. Providing a customer with inventory when it is needed may require that a supplier be able to provide just-in-time delivery. Just-in-time systems are covered in more detail in Chapter 10. For now, note that just-in-time relationships between buyers and sellers usually require operational linkages (as well as information sharing). For example, a car manufacturer may want a supplier of car seats to deliver seats in the colour and style order of the cars on the assembly line. This reduces the buyer's costs because the seats only need to be handled once when they arrive. However, it means that the supplier's production of seats and systems for loading them on the lorry must be closely linked to the customer's production line.

Operational linkages may also involve the routinized activities of individuals. This might include design engineers, salespeople and service representatives who closely integrate themselves into a buying organization. They may participate in developing solutions to continuing problems, conduct regular maintenance checks on equipment or monitor inventory and coordinate orders. These people almost become part of the customer's operations. Linkages may be customized to a particular relationship, or they may be standardized and operate the same way across many exchange partners. For example, in the channel of distribution for grocery products many different producers are standardizing their distribution procedures and coordinating with retail chains to make it faster and cheaper to replenish grocery store shelves. When a customer's production line or other internal operations are dependent on those of a supplier, it may be difficult or expensive to switch to another supplier. Many buyers would rather avoid a relationship that increases their 'switching costs', but there is an incentive when the benefits of a relationship with a specific supplier more than offset the loss of flexibility.

Contracts spell out obligations

Many of the purchases in business markets are straightforward. The seller's basic responsibility in a transaction is to transfer title to goods or perform services, and the buyer's basic responsibility is to pay the agreed price. However, in some buyer–seller relationships the responsibilities of the parties are spelled out in a detailed legal agreement. An agreement may apply only for a short period, but long-term contracts are also common.

For example, a customer might ask a supplier to guarantee a 6 per cent price reduction for a particular part for each of the next three years and pledge to virtually eliminate defects. In return, the customer might offer to double its orders and help the supplier boost productivity. This might sound attractive to the supplier, but also require new people or facilities. The supplier may not be willing to make these long-term commitments unless the buyer is willing to sign a contract for promised purchases. The contract might spell out what would happen if deliveries were late or if quality was below specification. The contract might even cover what would happen if the supplier's factory burned down.

When a contract provides a formal plan for the future of a relationship, some types of risk are reduced. But a firm may not want to be legally 'locked in' when it is unclear how the future might affect the relationship. Alternatively, some companies figure that even a detailed contract isn't a good substitute for regular, good-faith reviews to make sure that the terms of a deal keep pace with changing business conditions so neither party gets hurt by something that is unforeseen. Harley-Davidson decided to use this approach. When Harley moved towards closer relationships with a smaller number of suppliers, its lawyers drafted a detailed, 40-page contract, but purchasing executives rejected it. It was replaced with a short statement of principles that should guide relationships between Harley and its suppliers. This 'operate on a handshake' approach is typical of relationships with Japanese firms such as Honda, and many other firms are now adopting it. It is great when it works, and a disaster when it does not.

Specific adaptations invest in the relationship

Relationship-specific adaptations involve changes in a firm's product or procedures that are unique to the needs or capabilities of a relationship partner. Industrial suppliers often custom design a new product for just one customer; this may require investments in R&D or new manufacturing technologies. Buying firms may also adapt to a particular supplier; a computer maker may design around Intel's memory chip, and independent photo processors say 'We use Kodak paper for the good look' in their advertising. However, buyers are often hesitant about making big investments that increase dependence on a specific supplier. Typically, they do it only when there isn't a good alternative—perhaps because only one or a few suppliers are available to meet a need—or if the benefits of the investment are clear before it is made. On the other hand, sometimes a buyer will invest in a relationship because the seller has already demonstrated a willingness to do so.

The relationships between Boeing, the giant aircraft manufacturer, and one of its suppliers, involves relationship-specific adaptation. Boeing is a big customer for machine tools—the equipment it uses to make aircraft parts. Like many other manufacturers, Boeing usually designed parts for its planes first and then the supplier whose machines met Boeing's specifications at the lowest price got the order. With that approach, neither firm did much adapting to the other. However, it didn't always produce a good result. Boeing had better success when it invited a small set of qualified suppliers to study its operations and recommend how a new landing-gear part could be designed so that the machines to produce them would be more efficient. One supplier, Ingersol, worked with Boeing to design the landing gear so that the total cost of both the parts and the machine to produce them would be lower. The design also helped Boeing speed up its production process. Ingersol put in all this work not knowing if it would win Boeing's business. The investment paid off with an $8 million contract.[7]

A seller may have more incentive to propose new ideas that save the customer money when the firms have a mutual investment in a long-term relationship. The customer firm usually rewards the seller with more orders or a larger share of its business, and this encourages future suggestions and loyalty by the supplier. In contrast, buyers who use a competitive bid system exclusively—either by choice or necessity, as in some government and institutional purchasing—may not be offered much beyond basic goods and services. They are interested primarily in price.

ALLIED SIGNAL BETS ON RELATIONSHIP WITH SOLE SUPPLIER

AlliedSignal is a large company that produces car parts and aerospace electronics. It is good at what it does, partly because it appreciates the benefits of close relationships with suppliers who know what they are doing. Consider its relationship with Betz Laboratories, a smaller firm that makes industrial water-treatment chemicals. Originally, Betz was just one of several suppliers that sold Allied chemicals to keep the water in its plants from blocking pipes and rusting machinery. However, Betz did not stop at selling commodity powders. It works to reduce all of the costs related to water use in Allied's plants.

High-level teams of Betz experts and engineers from Allied study water as it flows through a plant. They evaluate whether it is as safe as possible for the equipment and the environment, or whether water is being wasted. In less than a year, a team in one plant found £16 million in potential cost reductions. The ideas included using filtered river water instead of buying city water, and recycling water instead of paying high charges to dump it. By adding a few valves to recycle the water in a cooling tower, Betz was able to save 300 gallons of water a minute, which results in savings of over £66 000 a year. Because of cost-saving ideas like this, Allied's overall use of water treatment chemicals will decrease. Betz is now Allied's sole supplier, and its sales will double.[8]

Buyers and suppliers form partnerships

To be sure of dependable quality, a buyer may develop loyalty to certain suppliers. This is especially important when buying non-standardized products. When a supplier and buyer develop a working partnership over the years, the supplier practically becomes a part of the buyer's organization. Sometimes the buyer will design a product and simply ask the supplier to build and deliver it at a fair price. When a seller proposes a new idea that saves the buyer's company money, the buyer usually rewards the seller with a long-term contract, and this encourages future suggestions. In contrast, buyers who use a bid system exclusively, either by choice or necessity, as in some government and institutional purchasing, may not be offered much beyond basic goods and services. They are interested primarily in price. The price which industrial customers pay for a product or service is only part of the total cost. For example, with a production line there will be a series of ongoing costs such as maintenance and power usage. A more expensive system may have the disadvantage of a higher initial price but it may have higher levels of output and operate more reliably than competitive products. Loss of output through less efficient operation, and unexpected breakdowns are part of the hidden costs of ownership, which make up the total cost of operation. Effective marketing managers base their case to customers on this total cost argument rather than on the initial purchase price.

To make this sort of case to prospective customers means that the company needs to get very close to its customers and work with them on the specification of the production line. APV plc is a major international engineering group, with operations around the world. Its subsidiary companies manufacture a wide range of food processing equipment, typically in consultation with the major food manufacturers. You would be familiar with many of the snack-food products that come from production lines designed and built by APV for its international customers. The company bases its competitive success on its ability to design production systems which meet customer needs more effectively than competitors. Companies within the group possess the 'know how' necessary to build production systems capable of high-volume production, which are reliable and operate at low costs. When a customer wants a production line for a new product, for example a new confectionery bar, it will come to APV with its broad requirements in terms of volumes, product specification and when the launch of the product is planned. Engineers in APV will then design a production system capable of meeting the customer's needs. The design will involve close consultation with the customer, and modifications may be made to the original specification in line with accumulating experience of different design aspects. For example, the company may want a high rate of output, but it might not be possible to produce a reliable cooking process to ensure product consistency unless the production flow is slowed down. These types of compromise mean that APV and its prospective customers must work together very closely to develop new production systems. This type of industrial marketing process can take a long time but be very satisfying to become involved in when the final production line is up and running.

Powerful customers may control the relationship

A supplier may want to form a cooperative partnership, but that may not be possible when a large, powerful customer dictates how the relationship will work. In grocery markets there has been an increasing tendency towards fewer customers with increasing shares of the retail market. Each of these major customers has become very important to manufacturers of consumer products. If one of them decides not to stock a product (delist the product), then this can have very serious consequences for the manufacturer. These large customers have also introduced many new 'own label' brands in the last few years, and now manufacturer brands are under considerable pressure in many different product areas (for example detergents and cosmetics). For some manufacturers, the situation is now one of producing own-label brands for major retail customers, or going out of business. Even Heinz, one of the world's most famous manufacturer brands, has resorted to producing for the 'own-label' market.

Buyers may use several sources to spread their risk

Even if a firm has developed the best marketing mix possible, it may not get all of a business customer's business. Buyers often look for several dependable sources of supply to protect themselves from unpredictable events, such as strikes, fires or floods in one of their suppliers' plants. Still, a good marketing mix is likely to win a larger share of the total business—which can prove to be very important. Moving from a 20 per cent to a 30 per cent share may not seem like much from a buyer's point of view, but for the seller it is a 50 per cent increase in sales![9]

Variations in buying by customer type

We've been discussing dimensions and frameworks that marketing managers often use to analyse buying behaviour in many different types of customer organizations. However, it is also useful to have more detail about specific types of customers.

MANUFACTURERS ARE IMPORTANT CUSTOMERS

There are relatively few large manufacturers

One of the most striking facts about manufacturers is how few there are compared to final consumers. Typically a very few companies dominate the output of most sectors of manufacturing industry. Industrial marketers typically have anywhere between one and several thousand current customers, compared to the millions of potential final consumers. As a consequence it is often desirable to segment industrial markets on the basis of size because the larger companies do most of the purchasing.

Customers cluster in geographic areas

In addition to concentration by company size, industrial markets are concentrated in certain geographic areas. Internationally, industrial customers are concentrated in countries that are at the more advanced stages of economic development. Within a country, there is often further concentration in specific areas. For example, in Germany the steel industry is concentrated in the Ruhr Valley. In the United Kingdom, it is heavily concentrated in the north of England. Similarly, there is a high concentration of chemicals manufacturers concentrated around Rotterdam and The Hague in The Netherlands.

Much data is available on industrial markets by SIC codes

The products an industrial customer needs to buy depend on the business it is in. Because of this, sales of a product are often concentrated among customers in similar businesses. For example, clothing manufacturers are the main customers for buttons. Marketing managers who can relate their own sales to their customers' type of business can focus their efforts.

Detailed information is often available to help a marketing manager learn more about customers in different lines of business. Most national governments regularly collect and publish data by Standard Industrial Classification (SIC) codes—groups of firms in similar lines of business. The number of establishments, sales volumes and number of employees—broken down by geographic areas—are given for each SIC code. However, in many countries data on business customers is incomplete or inaccurate.

The SIC code breakdowns start with broad industry categories such as food and related products, tobacco products, textile products, clothing and so on. Within each two-digit industry breakdown, much more detailed data may be available for three-digit and fourdigit industries (that is, subindustries of the two- or three-digit industries). Four-digit detail is not available for all industries in every geographic area because a government does not provide data when only one or two factories are located in an area. Many firms find

their *current* customers' SIC codes and then look at SIC-coded lists for similar companies that may need the same goods and services. Other companies look at which SIC categories are growing or declining to discover new opportunities. If companies aiming at business target markets know exactly who they are aiming at, readily available data organized by SIC codes can be valuable. Most trade associations and private organizations that gather data on business markets also use SIC codes. SIC codes are not perfect. Some companies have sales in several categories but are listed in only one—the code with the largest sales. In addition, some newer businesses don't fit any of the categories very well. So, although a lot of good information is available, the codes must be used carefully.

PRODUCERS OF SERVICES—SMALLER AND MORE SPREAD OUT

Marketing managers need to keep in mind that the service side of the economy is large and has been growing fast. Service operations are also growing in some other countries. There may be good opportunities in providing these companies with the products they need to support their operations and there are also challenges.

Some service firms are big companies with international operations. Examples include credit card companies such as Master Card, Thomas Cook and Avis Car rental. These firms have purchasing departments that are like those in large manufacturing organizations. But, as could be expected, given the large number of service firms, most of them are small. They are also more spread out around the country than manufacturing concerns. Factories often locate where transportation facilities are good, where raw materials are available, and where it is less costly to produce goods in quantity. Service operations, in contrast, usually have to be close to their customers.

Buying may not be as formal

Purchases by small service firms are often handled by whoever is in charge. This may be a doctor, lawyer,

owner of a local insurance agency or manager of a hotel. Suppliers who usually deal with purchasing specialists in large organizations may have trouble adjusting to this market. Personal selling is still an important part of promotion, but reaching these customers in the first place often requires more advertising. In addition, small service firms may need much more help in buying than a large corporation.

One Japanese company, Canon, capitalized on such needs. Canon knew that Xerox, the familiar name in office copiers, was very successful selling to larger accounts. But Xerox's salesforce was not as good at serving the needs of smaller service firms like legal firms. Canon seized this opportunity. It developed promotion materials to help first-time buyers understand differences in copiers. It emphasized that its machines were easy to use and maintain. And Canon also used retail channels to make the copiers available in smaller areas where there wasn't enough business to justify using a sales rep. As a result, Canon has been very successful in this market.[10]

RETAILERS AND WHOLESALERS BUY FOR THEIR CUSTOMERS

Most retail and wholesale buyers see themselves as purchasing agents for their target customers, mindful of the old saying that 'Goods well bought are half sold'. Typically, retailers do *not* see themselves as sales agents for particular manufacturers. They buy what they think

they can sell. And wholesalers buy what they think their retailers can sell. They do not try to make value judgements about the desirability or worth of what they are selling. Rather, they focus on the needs and attitudes of *their* target customers.

Aldi and Netto are two major grocery retailers with outlets throughout Europe. Both of these grocery chains are focused on the low price, convenience end of the market. Their shops are unashamedly 'cheap and cheerful' and they have no pretences to copy other more 'upmarket' stores. Suppliers seeking to do business with either of these chains need to focus on maintaining low prices and reliable delivery. Price promotions are likely to include discounts for buying in bulk over a specified period of time. Orders will tend to be high in volume, but low in variety to a limited number of distribution points. Consumer promotions will be expected to feature money-off coupons. Each of these elements of the marketing programme is discussed in detail in later chapters.

Reorders are straight rebuys

Retailers and wholesalers usually carry a large number of products. A drug wholesaler, for example, may carry up to 125 000 products. Because they deal with so many products, most intermediaries buy their products on a routine, automatic reorder basis, straight rebuys, once they make the initial decision to stock specific items. Purchases are usually made at head office level, and the sales representative will usually deal with a well-informed buyer who is aware of the rates of sale of specific products, the competing alternatives for scarce shelf space and the overall profitability of individual lines. Sellers to these markets must understand the size of the buyer's job and have something useful to say and do when they call. For example, they might try to save the intermediary time by taking inventory, setting up displays or arranging shelves while trying to get a chance to talk about specific products and maintain the relationship.

Buyers watch computer output closely

Most larger firms now use sophisticated computerized inventory control systems. Scanners at retail checkout counters keep track of what goes out of the door—and computers use this data to update the records. Even small retailers and wholesalers are using automated control systems that can print daily unit control reports showing sales of every product on their shelves. This is important to marketing managers selling to such firms, because buyers with this kind of information know, in detail, the profitability of the different competing prod-

ucts. If a manufacturer's product is not moving, the retailer is not likely to be impressed by a salesperson's request for more in-store attention or added shelf space.

Buying and selling are closely related

In wholesale and retail firms, there is usually a very close relationship between buying and selling. Buyers are often in close contact with their firm's salespeople and with customers. The household buyer for a department store, for example, may even supervise the salespeople who sell household products. Salespeople are quick to tell the buyer if a customer wants a product that is not available—especially if the salespeople work on commission. A buyer may even buy some items to satisfy the preferences of salespeople. Therefore, the salespeople should not be neglected in the promotion effort.

Committee buying is impersonal

Some buyers—especially those who work for big retail chains—are annoyed by the number of wholesalers' and manufacturers' representatives who call on them. Space in their shops is limited and they simply are not interested in carrying every product that some salesperson wants them to sell. Consider the problem facing grocery chains. In an average week, 150 to 250 new items are offered to the buying offices of a large chain such as Aldi. If the chain accepted all of them, it would add 10 000 new items during a single year! Obviously, these firms need a way to deal with this overload. Because of situations like this, in some firms the major decisions to add or drop lines or change buying policies may be handled by a *buying committee*. The seller still calls on and gives a 'pitch' to a buyer, but the buyer does not have final responsibility. Instead, the buyer prepares forms summarizing proposals for new products. The forms are passed onto the committee for evaluation. The seller may not get to present his story to the buying committee in person. This rational, almost cold-blooded approach reduces the impact of a persuasive salesperson. Wholesalers' and manufacturers' marketing managers must develop good marketing mixes when buying becomes this sophisticated and competitive. And such situations are more common now that so many retailers use computers to improve sales analysis and inventory control.

THE GOVERNMENT MARKET

Size and diversity

Some marketers ignore the government market because they think that government bureaucracy is more trouble

than it's worth. They probably do not realize the sheer size of the government market In many countries, Government is the largest customer group. In addition to national governments, within the EU the European Commission is a major purchaser of products and services. Regular invitations to bid for government contracts are issued from the Commission in Brussels. These contracts are open to organizations from any of the member states of the EU.

Competitive bids may be required

Government buyers are expected to spend money wisely, in the public interest, so their purchases are usually subject to much public review. To avoid charges of favouritism, most government customers buy by specification using a mandatory bidding procedure. Often the government buyer is required to accept the lowest bid that meets the specifications. You can see how important it is for the buyer to write precise and complete specifications. Otherwise, sellers may submit a bid that fits the specifications but does not really match what is needed. By law, a government unit might have to accept the lowest bid, even for an unwanted product.

Writing specifications is difficult and buyers usually appreciate the help of well-informed salespeople. Salespeople *want* to have input on the specifications so their product can be considered or even have an advantage. One company may get the business, even with a bid that is not the lowest, because the lower bids do not meet minimum specifications.

 ## 'Rigged' specifications are an ethical concern

At the extreme, a government customer who wants a specific brand or supplier may try to write the description so that no other supplier will be able to meet all the specs. The buyer may have good reasons for such preferences—a more reliable product, prompt delivery or better service after the sale. This kind of loyalty sounds great, but marketers must be sensitive to the ethical issues involved. Laws that require government customers to get bids are intended to increase competition among suppliers, not reduce it. Specifications that are written primarily to defeat the purpose of these laws may be viewed as illegal 'bid rigging'.

The approved supplier list

Specification and bidding difficulties aren't problems in all government orders. Some items that are bought frequently, or for which there are widely accepted standards, are purchased routinely. The government unit simply places an order at a previously approved price. To share in this business, a supplier must be on the list of 'approved suppliers'. The list is updated occasionally, sometimes by a bid procedure. School supplies, construction materials and fuel are examples of products that are

typically bought this way. Buyers and sellers agree on a price that will stay the same for a specified period.

Negotiated contracts are common too

Contracts may be negotiated for items that are not branded or easily described, for products that require research and development, or in cases where there is no effective competition. Depending on the government unit involved, the contract may be subject to audit and renegotiation, especially if the contractor makes a larger profit than expected. In some situations the government may not want to go to open public tender for specific products or services. For example, in some sensitive areas of defence purchasing the government will prefer to negotiate with one or more domestic suppliers in order to maintain control over the supply and delivery of new systems. This is one situation where there is considerable political pressure on governments to buy from domestic rather than international suppliers.

Learning what government wants

Most national governments regularly produce invitations to manufacturing organizations to tender for the supply of specified products and services. Companies which are interested in supplying this market must make sure that they are included in the list of companies to which details are circulated. In many situations companies are invited to submit an application to become a qualified supplier. Details of the company are required in advance of specific purchase orders being placed. These details include financial information as well as information about expertise and previous related experience. If the company meets the criteria that have been set, then it is placed on a list of qualified suppliers. When requirements arise it will then receive a request to bid for a specific order. A similar process operates for some supplies to the European Commission

Dealing with foreign governments

Government agencies around the world spend a great deal of money and they are important target customers for some firms. But selling to government units in foreign countries can be a real challenge. In many cases a firm must get permission from the government in its own country to sell to a foreign government. Moreover, most government contracts favour domestic suppliers, if they are available. Even if such favouritism is not explicit, public sentiment may make it very difficult for a foreign competitor to get a contract. Or the government bureaucracy may simply nit-pick a foreign supplier with so much red tape that there's no way to win.

Is it unethical to 'buy help'?

In some countries government officials expect small payments just to speed up processing of routine paperwork, inspections or decisions from the local bureaucracy. Outright bribes, where government officials or their friends request money to sway a purchase decision, are common in some markets. In the past, marketers from some countries have just looked at such bribes as a cost of doing business. However, the climate is now changing and such approaches are less frequently accepted.

SUMMARY

In this chapter we considered the number, size, location and buying habits of various types of organizational customers—to try to identify logical dimensions for segmenting markets. We saw that the nature of the buyer and the buying situation are relevant. We also saw that the problem-solving models of buyer behaviour introduced in Chapter 3 apply here—with modifications.

The chapter focuses on aspects of buying behaviour that often apply to different types of organizational customers. However, some key differences in the manufacturer, intermediary and government markets are discussed.

A clear understanding of organizational buying habits, needs, and attitudes can aid marketing strategy planning. And since there are fewer organizational customers than final consumers, it may even be possible for some marketing managers (and their salespeople) to develop a unique strategy for each potential customer.

This chapter offers some general principles that are useful in strategy planning, but the nature of the products being offered may require adjustments in the plans. Different product classes are discussed in Chapter 7. Variations by product may provide additional segmenting dimensions to help a marketing manager fine-tune a marketing strategy.

QUESTIONS AND PROBLEMS

1. Compare and contrast the problem-solving approaches used by final consumers and by industrial buyers.

2. Describe the situations that would lead to the use of the three different buying processes for a particular product—lightweight bumpers for a pickup truck.

3. Compare and contrast the buying processes of final consumers and industrial buyers.

4. Briefly discuss why a marketing manager should think about who is likely to be involved in the buying centre for a particular purchase. Is the buying centre idea useful in consumer buying? Explain your answer.

5. If a non-profit hospital were planning to buy expensive MRI scanning equipment (to detect tumours), who might be involved in the buying centre. Explain your answer and describe the types of influence that different people might have.

6. Why would an industrial buyer want to get competitive bids? What are some of the situations when competitive bidding can't be used?

7. How likely would each of the following be to use competitive bids: (a) a small town that needed a road resurfaced, (b) a scouting organization that needed a printer to print its scouting handbook, (c) a hardware retailer that wants to add a new lawnmower line, (d) a grocery store that wants to install a new checkout scanner, (e) a professional association that wants to buy a computer to keep track of member subscriptions. Explain your answers.

8. Discuss the advantages and disadvantages of 'just-in-time' supply relationships from an organizational buyer's point of view. Are the advantages and disadvantages merely reversed from the seller's point of view?

9. IBM has a long-term negotiated contract with Microsoft, a supplier that provides the software operating system for IBM computers. Discuss several of the issues that IBM might want the contract to cover.

10. Discuss how much latitude a purchasing manager for a manufacturer has in selecting the specific brand and the specific source of supply for a product once it has been requisitioned by some production department. Consider this question with specific reference to pencils, paint for the offices, plastic materials for the production line, a large printing press and a new factory. How should the buyer's attitudes affect the seller's marketing mix?

11. Would a toy manufacturer need a different marketing strategy for a big retail chain, such as Toys "R" Us, than for a single toy store run by its owner. Discuss your answer.

12. How do you think a furniture manufacturer's buying habits and practices would be affected by the specific type of product to be purchased? Consider fabric for upholstered furniture, a lathe for the production line, cardboard for shipping cartons and lubricants for production machinery.

13. Explain how SIC codes might be helpful in evaluating and understanding business markets. Give an example.

14. Considering the nature of retail buying, outline the basic ingredients of promotion to retail buyers. Does it make any difference what kinds of products are involved? Are any other factors relevant?

15. The government market is obviously an extremely large one, yet it is often slighted or even ignored by many firms. 'Red tape' is certainly one reason, but there are others. Discuss the situation and be sure to include the possibility of segmenting in your analysis.

SUGGESTED CASE

3. Republic Polymer Company

REFERENCES

1. D.S. Smith, 'The enterprise network', *The Sunday Times*, 29 March 1998, Business section, p. 9.
2. M.D. Bunn, 'Taxonomy of Buying Decision Approaches', *Journal of Marketing*, January 1993, pp. 38–56; R. Tullous and J.M. Munson, 'Organizational purchasing analysis for sales management', *Journal of Personal Selling & Sales Management*, Spring 1992, pp. 15–26.
3. R.E. Plank *et al.*, 'The impact of computer usage by purchasing', *Industrial Marketing Management*, August 1992, pp. 243–48; J.W. Henke, Jr., A.R. Krachenberg and T. F. Lyons, 'Competing against an in-house supplier', *Industrial Marketing Management*, vol. 18, no. 3, 1989, pp. 147–54.
4. M. Bixby Cooper, C. Dröge and P.J. Daugherty, 'How buyers and operations personnel evaluate service', *Industrial Marketing Management*, vol. 20, no. 1, 1991, pp. 81–90; R. Germain and C. Dröge, 'Wholesale operations and vendor evaluation', *Journal of Business Research*, September 1990, pp. 119–30.
5. R.D. McWilliams, E. Naumann and S. Scott, 'Determining Buying Center Size', *Industrial Marketing Management*, February 1992, pp. 43–50; H.E. Brown and R.W. Brucker, 'Charting the industrial buying stream,' *Industrial Marketing Management*, February 1990, pp. 55–62.
6. 'Purchasing's new muscle', *Fortune*, 20 February 1995, pp. 75–83.
7. F. Dwyer, P. Schurr and S. Oh, 'Developing buyer–seller relationships', *Journal of Marketing*, April 1987, pp. 11–27; Sang-Lin Han, D.T. Wilson, and S.P. Dant, 'Buyer–supplier relationships today', *Industrial Marketing Management*, November 1993, pp. 331–38; A.J. Magrath and K.G. Hardy, 'Building customer partnerships', *Business Horizons*, January–February 1994, pp. 24–28; P. Dion, D. Easterling and S.J. Miller, 'What is really necessary in successful buyer/seller relationships?', *Industrial Marketing Management*, January 1995, pp. 1–10; M.U. Kalwani and N. Narayandas, 'Long-term manufacturer-supplier relationships: Do they pay off for supplier firms?', *Journal of Marketing*, January 1995, pp. 1–16.
8. 'The New Golden Rule of Business', *Fortune*, 21 February 1994, pp. 60–64.
9. C.O. Swift, 'Preferences for single sourcing and supplier selection', *Journal of Business Research*, February 1995, pp. 105–12.
10. Canon *1993 Annual Report*, 'Can anyone duplicate Canon's personal copiers' success?', *Marketing and Media Decisions*, Special Issue, Spring 1985, pp. 97–101.

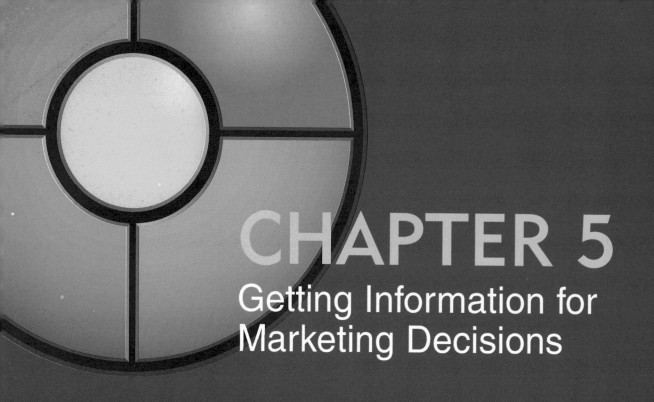

CHAPTER 5
Getting Information for Marketing Decisions

When You Finish This Chapter, You Should

1 Know about marketing information systems.

2 Understand a scientific approach to marketing research.

3 Know how to define and solve marketing problems.

4 Know about getting secondary and primary data.

5 Understand the role of observing, questioning and using experimental methods in marketing research.

6 Understand the important new terms (shown in colour).

Why does a Skoda have a heated rear windscreen? So you can keep your hands warm while you're pushing it. The Skoda has all the charm of the typical Eastern European product in the British mind—a dubious car of comical design, renowned only for its joke status. The complete repositioning of the brand has been one of the most daunting marketing challenges of recent years. The impetus for Skoda to attempt the seemingly impossible comes as a result of Volkswagen taking control of the Czech company and, in the United Kingdom, the establishment of Skoda Automobile UK, a wholly-owned subsidiary, to import the cars. The old Estelle model—the traditional Skoda of the joke—has been superseded, and Volkswagen has been improving the production processes, product strategy and the brand image.

Under Volkswagen management Skoda has been trying to improve their share of the UK car market. This has been a major marketing task. It is not about distribution strategy or retailing capacity—it is about changing the perception of a company that had come to epitomize much that was negative about Eastern Europe. In the United Kingdom, the brand is a victim partly of its own success: the jokes exist because Skoda has a considerable presence in the market. Elsewhere in Western Europe, the jokes would be meaningless and have therefore not taken root.

A tight marketing budget meant that objectives had to be clearly defined and focused. With no marketing department, the company's first stop was a market research consultancy, which carried out qualitative studies among three groups: current Skoda owners, 'suscepti-bles' who might be persuaded to buy a Skoda and 'rejecters' who would be unlikely to purchase. Skoda owners were found to be just normal people who were characterized by being honest, straightforward and disliking hype. They had a very clear-sighted view of the kind of purchases they wanted to make, wanting to pay no more than they needed. Skoda owners loved their Skodas and had even come to love the jokes. The only problem was that there weren't enough owners, which is why the next group, the 'susceptibles', became so important. Susceptibles were found to be atti-tudinally similar to Skoda owners. They had been put off by the jokes and by their lack of real awareness of the brand. If conditions were right, and they felt other people weren't going to laugh at them, they'd jump at the chance of owning a Skoda.

Working alongside the marketing research company, was an advertising agency, whose job it became to develop a strategy for awakening the interest of the susceptibles. They discovered it was not enough merely to point out the merits of the Skoda to potential purchasers. There was such a huge dissonance between what people had in their heads about what Skoda is and means, and what the company was presenting to them. So the marketing strategy emphasized exposure, making sure that people actually saw, touched and tried the cars. Journalists, comedians, disc jockeys and other careless Skoda joke artists, as well as potential customers, were persuaded, and sometimes paid, to take a test drive. Since then brand advertising has tried to address the perception issue with slogans such as: 'We've changed our cars; can you

'... your mind?' The target audiences ... een potential customers and the general public. VW's involvement with Skoda is also emphasized as the VW brand has strong quality and reliability associations.

More recently, Skoda has launched the Octavia, which has received excellent reviews from motoring journalists and sales success across Europe. The collection of market intelligence continues. Importers, dealers and customers meet with the company on a monthly basis. These meetings aim to share the large amount of knowledge these people have of the market and to set targets and plans accordingly.[1]

MARKETING MANAGERS NEED INFORMATION

Skoda cars have long been the subject of unfortunate jokes. The company wanted to change this position but recognized that this could not be achieved without a significant level of understanding about how customers and potential customers perceived the car. Market research into the view of current and potential Skoda owners provided some of the answers. The example shows how successful planning of marketing strategies requires information—information about existing Skoda owners as well as potential target markets and their likely responses to marketing mixes as well as about competition and other marketing environment variables. Information is also needed for implementation and control. Without good marketing information, managers have to use intuition or guesses and in today's fast-changing and competitive markets, this invites failure.

On the other hand, managers seldom have all the information they need to make the best decision. Both customers and competitors can be unpredictable. Getting more information may cost too much or take too long. For example, data on international markets is often incomplete, outdated or difficult to obtain. So managers often must decide if they need more information and, if so, how to get it. This chapter discusses how marketing managers can get the information they need to plan successful strategies. You will also see why managers actually need a strategy to deal with the collection and use of marketing data.[2]

MARKETING INFORMATION SYSTEMS CAN HELP

Marketing managers for some companies make decisions based almost totally on their own judgement with very little hard data. When it is time to make a decision, they may wish they had more information but by then it is too late, so they do without.

MIS makes available data accessible

There is a difference between information that is *available* and information that is readily *accessible*. Some information, such as the details of competitors' plans, is just not available. In other cases, information is available, but not without time-consuming collection. Such information is not really accessible. For example, a company may have records of customer purchases, what was sold by sales representatives last month or what is in the warehouse. But if this information is not available to the manager at the right time, it is not useful.

The first important step to improve things is to recognize that a systematic approach is required to collect and use marketing information. Professional marketing managers recognize that information can be a strategic resource, and deliberately design systems to collect relevant information and make it available within the firm, as and when it is required.

The formal name for such a system is a marketing information system or MIS. A marketing information system (MIS) is an organized way of continually gathering and analysing data to provide marketing managers with information they need to make decisions. In some companies, an MIS is set up by marketing specialists. In other companies, it is set up by a group that provides *all* departments in the firm with information. However, bear in mind that in many companies such systems are not as formal or as comprehensive as the title MIS suggests. Many companies do not have such formal systems, or are only now beginning to recognize the value of marketing information in marketing decision making. You will see in this chapter that it is possible to have a useful system without formally calling it an MIS. The technical details of setting up and running an MIS are beyond the scope of this course. But, you should understand what an MIS is so you know some of the possibilities. Exhibit 5–1 shows the elements of a complete MIS.

Faster and easier access to information

Basic MIS concepts are not very different today from the way they were 20 years ago. However, recent developments are having a radical impact on what information is available to marketing managers and how quickly. It is much easier today to set up and use an MIS. A short time ago connecting remote computers or exchanging data over networks was very difficult. Now it is standard and almost automatic. A manager with little computer experience can quickly learn to use an MIS. As a result, managers everywhere have access to much more information. Equally importantly, the type of information available is changing dramatically. For a long time managers have relied on computers mainly for

'number crunching'. The multimedia revolution in computing has lifted that limitation. Whether the marketing information takes the form of a marketing plan, report, memorandum, spreadsheet, database, presentation, photograph or table of statistics, it is all now computer generated. Thus, it can be easily stored and accessed by computer.

An Intranet helps in sharing information

The Internet is helping to make more information available and changing marketing itself. In addition, many firms, even quite small ones, have their own intranet—a system for linking computers within a company. An intranet works like the Internet. However, to maintain security, access to web sites on an intranet is usually limited to employees. Even so, information is available on demand and it is a simple matter to 'publish' new information as soon as it becomes available. So, information can be constantly updated. Prior to this decade such a capability was just a dream.

Useful marketing information comes from a wide range of sources

As Exhibit 5–1 illustrates, useful marketing information can come from a wide range of different sources. Sometimes a marketing manager might complain that there is too much information rather than too little. In addition to a wider range of government sources, commercial agencies regularly publish surveys of markets and competitors' activities are frequently reviewed in trade journals. The company's salesforce is regularly in contact with customers and potential customers and in one of the best positions to provide continuous feedback on developments in the marketplace. The finance

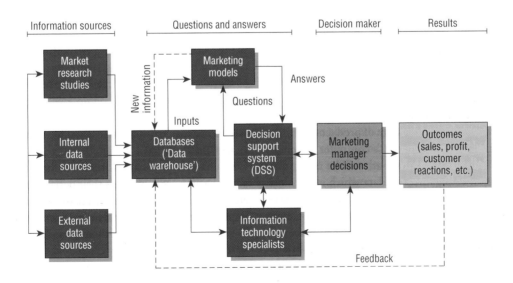

Exhibit 5–1 Elements of Complete Marketing Information Systems

USING RESEARCH PROFITABLY IN A SMALL BUSINESS

Sometimes it is possible to use research effectively even if resources are limited. PrintKraft, which was a small family-owned printing company, was losing money. Sales had been declining steadily over the last eighteen months and although there was no immediate danger of financial collapse, the family owners were concerned about the future. The firm had modern premises on a new industrial estate three kilometres from the centre of town.

The firm specialized in providing high-quality solutions to the printing needs of its customers. Concerned about the future the company's owner and managing director asked a marketing consultant to help to solve the problem. She felt that the problem was simply lack of awareness of the business in the company's target markets, but the consultant insisted on collecting some information first.

The consultant began by looking at the company's *invoices*. By analysing invoices for work completed over the past two years it was possible to build up a picture of the different types of customer which the company dealt with. Using *costing information* it was also possible to make a good first guess about the relative profitability of different types of customer. The analysis confirmed the owners, *instinct* that a decreasing number of customers were becoming increasingly important to the company. It also revealed that there had been little or no business from new customers in the past two years.

The next step was to *talk to existing customers*. Using the telephone the consultant contacted the 10 most important customers and asked them some initial questions about their printing requirements and how they met them. This initial *telephone survey* was very revealing. While each of these customers still sent major printing jobs to outside suppliers such as our company, they were increasingly using in-house printing capabilities to handle low-volume, lower-quality printing needs. Several of these customers had made significant investments in their own desktop publishing systems for this type of work.

The consultant then looked at some of the other smaller accounts. Much of this work was straightforward copying of black and white material, often in small and varying quantities. Looking in the *Yellow Pages* she found several small copying shops operating in the centre of town. A visit to one of these copying shops proved very revealing. Her first *observation* was that the shop was very busy, surprisingly so since she had chosen Saturday morning to visit. As she listened to other customers she was surprised to see that most were small businesses with a wide range of copying requirements.

She was also surprised to see the range of services provided. Although the technical quality of the work might not be so high, most of the customers seemed satisfied with the standard and it certainly was cost competitive, as a later comparison of *published price lists* showed. Many of these customers would have been seen as the target customers for our small printing firm. She made a mental note of the range of businesses that were getting work done in this way.

These customers also seemed to be combining work with family life. Printing jobs were brought in, requirements discussed with the staff and then the customers left the shop to do their own personal shopping, returning to collect the work in an hour or so.

Back in her office the consultant then looked at potential customers. The profile of existing customers showed the types of businesses which were currently buying printing services from the company. It was a relatively simple task to buy a complete list of companies from an *agency* matching the profile of the company's existing customer base. It wasn't really all that surprising to discover that the company was selling to only 15 per cent of all of the potential customers in the list. Of course, not all these potential customers might be in the market for the types of service provided by the company, but some further *telephone research* would provide a better indication of where the opportunities might be.

 ## Ethical issues in marketing research

The basic reason for doing marketing research is to get information that people can trust in making decisions. But, research often involves many hidden details. A person who wants to misuse marketing research to pursue a personal agenda can often do so. Perhaps the most common ethical issues concern decisions to withhold certain information about the research. For example, a manager might selectively share only those results from a research project that support his or her viewpoint. Others who are involved in a decision might never even know that they are getting only part of the truth. Or, during a set of interviews a researcher may discover that consumers are interpreting a poorly worded question in many different ways. If the researcher doesn't admit to the problem, an unknowing manager may rely on meaningless results.

Another problem involves more blatant abuses. It is unethical for a firm to contact consumers under the pretence of doing research when the real purpose is to sell something. For example, some political organizations have been criticized for surveying consumers to find out their attitudes about a candidate and various issues. Then, armed with that information, someone else calls back to solicit donations. Legitimate marketing researchers are very concerned about such abuses. If the problem were to become widespread, consumers might not be willing to participate in any research.

The relationship between the researcher and the manager sometimes creates an ethical conflict, especially when an outside firm does the research. Managers must be careful not to suggest that the only acceptable results from a research project are ones that confirm his or her existing viewpoint. Researchers are supposed to be objective, but that objectivity may be swayed if getting future jobs from the manager hangs on finding the 'right' results.

Effective research usually requires cooperation

Effective marketing research requires much more than just technical tools. It requires cooperation between researchers and marketing managers. Good marketing researchers must keep both marketing research *and* marketing management in mind to be sure their research focuses on real problems. Marketing managers must be involved in marketing research. Many marketing research details can be handled by company or outside experts. Marketing managers must be able to explain their problems and information needs. They should be able to communicate with specialists in the specialists' language. Marketing managers may only be users of research but they should be informed consumers, able to explain exactly what they want from the research. They should also know about some of the basic decisions made during the research process so they know the limitations of the findings.

For this reason, the discussion of marketing research will not emphasize mechanics but rather how to plan and evaluate the work of marketing researchers.[4]

THE SCIENTIFIC METHOD AND MARKETING RESEARCH

The scientific method—combined with the strategy planning framework introduced in Chapter 1 and discussed in detail in the next chapter—can help marketing managers to make better decisions. The scientific method is a decision-making approach that focuses on being objective and orderly in *testing* ideas before accepting them. With the scientific method, managers don't just *assume* that their intuition is correct. Instead, they use their intuition and observations to develop hypotheses—educated guesses about the relationships between things or about what will happen in the future. Then, they test their hypotheses before making final decisions.

A manager who relies only on intuition might introduce a new product without testing consumer response.

But a manager who uses the scientific method might say, 'I think (hypothesize) that consumers currently using the most popular brand will prefer our new product. Let's run some consumer tests. If at least 60 per cent of the consumers prefer our product, we can introduce it in a regional test market. If it doesn't pass the consumer test there, we can make some changes and try again.' The scientific method forces an orderly research process. Some managers don't carefully specify what information they need. They blindly move ahead, hoping that research will provide 'the answer'. Other managers may have a clearly defined problem or question but lose their way after that. These 'hit-or-miss' approaches waste both time and money.

FIVE-STEP APPROACH TO MARKETING RESEARCH

The marketing research process is a five-step application of the scientific method that includes:
1. Defining the problem.
2. Analysing the situation.
3. Getting problem-specific data.
4. Interpreting the data.
5. Solving the problem.

Exhibit 5–2 shows the five steps in the process. Note that the process may lead to a solution before all of the steps are completed. Or, as the feedback arrows show, researchers may return to an earlier step if needed. For example, the interpreting step may point to a new question or reveal the need for additional information before a final decision can be made.

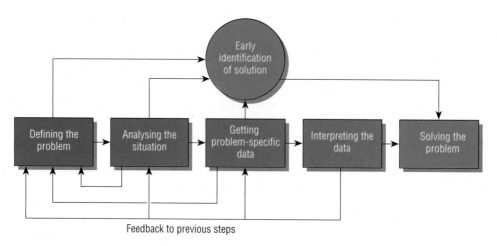

Exhibit 5.2 Five-step Scientific Approach to Marketing Research Process

DEFINING THE PROBLEM—STEP 1

Defining the problem is the most important, and often the most difficult, step in the marketing research process. It is worth taking some time over this stage to make sure that the objectives of the research are clearly defined. The best research on the wrong problem is wasted effort.

Finding the right problem level almost solves the problem

The strategy planning framework introduced in Chapter 1 can be useful here. It can help the researcher identify the real problem area and what information is needed. Do we really know enough about our target markets to work out all of the four Ps? Do we know enough to decide what celebrity to use in an advertising campaign or how to handle a price war in Belgium or Italy? If not, we may want to do research rather than rely on intuition.

The importance of understanding the problem—and then trying to solve it—can be seen in the introduction of One Shot, a laundry product developed to clean, soften and reduce static cling all in one step. Marketing managers were sure that One Shot was going to appeal to heavy users—especially working women with large families. As one manager summarized the situation, 'our research showed that while over 50 per cent of women were going back to work, 70 per cent were still responsible for the family wash … and 80 per cent use three different laundry products. These women are looking for convenience'. When marketing managers found that other firms were testing similar products, they rushed One Shot into distribution. To encourage first-time purchases,

they offered introductory price discounts, coupons and rebates. They also supported the sales promotion with heavy advertising on TV programmes that research showed the heavy users watched.

However, research never addressed the problem of how the heavy user target market would react. After the introductory price-off deals were dropped, sales dropped off too. While the product was convenient, heavy users weren't willing to pay the price for each washload. For the heavy users, price was a qualifying dimension. And these consumers did not like the pre-measured packets because they had no control over how much detergent they could put in. The competing firms recognized these problems at the research stage and decided not to introduce their products.

After the fact, it was clear that One Shot was most popular with college students, singles, and people living in small flats. They did not use much so the convenience benefit offset the high price. But the company never targeted those segments. It just assumed that it would be profitable to target the big market of heavy users.[5]

The moral of this story is that the strategy planning framework can be useful for guiding the problem definition step as well as the whole marketing research process. First, a marketing manager should understand the target market and what needs the firm could satisfy. Then, the manager can focus on lower-level problems, namely, how sensitive the target market is to a change in one or more of the marketing mix ingredients. Without such a framework, marketing researchers can waste time and money working on the wrong problem.

Confusing problems with symptoms

The problem definition step sounds simple and that is a danger. It is easy to confuse symptoms with the problem. Suppose a firm's MIS shows that the company's sales are decreasing in certain territories while expenses are remaining the same, resulting in a decline in profits. Will it help to define the problem by asking: How can we stop the sales decline? Probably not. This would be like fitting a hearing-impaired patient with a hearing aid without first trying to find out *why* the patient is having trouble hearing. When symptoms are mistaken for the problem, research objectives become confused. Relevant questions may be ignored while unimportant questions are analysed in expensive detail.

Setting research objectives may require more understanding

Sometimes the research objectives are very clear. A manager wants to know if the targeted households have tried a new product and what percentage of them bought it a second time. The manager might also want to know 'why' some did not buy or whether they had even heard of the product. Companies rarely have enough time and money to study everything so the research objectives need to be very focused. One good way is to develop a 'research question' list that includes all the possible problem areas. Then the items on the list can be considered more completely in the situation analysis step before final research objectives are set.

ANALYSING THE SITUATION—STEP 2

What information do we already have?

When the real problem has begun to surface, a situation analysis is useful. A situation analysis is an informal study of what information is already available in the problem area. It can help define the problem and specify what additional information, if any, is needed.

Pick the brains around you

The situation analysis usually involves informal talks with informed people. Informed people can be others in the firm, a few good intermediaries who have close contact with customers or others knowledgeable about the industry. In industrial markets, where relationships with customers are close, researchers may even call the customers themselves. Informed customers may have already worked on the same problem or know about a source of helpful information. Their inputs can help to sharpen the problem definition too.

Situation analysis helps educate a researcher

The situation analysis is especially important if the researcher is a research specialist who does not know much about the management decisions to be made or if the marketing manager is dealing with unfamiliar areas. They must both be sure they understand the problem area, including the nature of the target market, the marketing mix, competition and other external factors. Otherwise, the researcher may rush ahead and make costly mistakes or simply discover what is already known by management. The following case illustrates this danger.

A marketing manager at the home office of a large retail chain hired a research firm to do in-store interviews to learn what customers liked most—and least—about some of its shops in other cities. Interviewers diligently filled their questionnaires. When the results came in, it was apparent that neither the marketing manager nor the researcher had done their homework. No one had even talked with the local store managers! Several of the shops were in the middle of some messy physical development so all the customers' responses concerned the noise and dust from the construction. The research was a waste of money. The point is: even big companies make marketing research mistakes when they do not adequately undertake the situation analysis.

Secondary data may provide the answers—or some background

The situation analysis should also find relevant secondary data information that has been collected or published already. Later, in step 3, we will cover primary data—information specifically collected to solve a current problem. Too often researchers rush to gather primary data when much relevant secondary information is already available—at little or no cost! See Exhibit 5–3.

Secondary data is plentiful

Ideally, much secondary data is already available from the firm's MIS. Data that has not been organized in an MIS may be available from the company's files and reports. Secondary data also is available from libraries, trade associations and government agencies.

Many computerized database and index services are available through libraries and private firms. Much of this data is now distributed on CD-ROM or available on-line from remote systems. A vast range of data is also now available on the Internet, and on-line commercial services are growing at a rate which makes any current

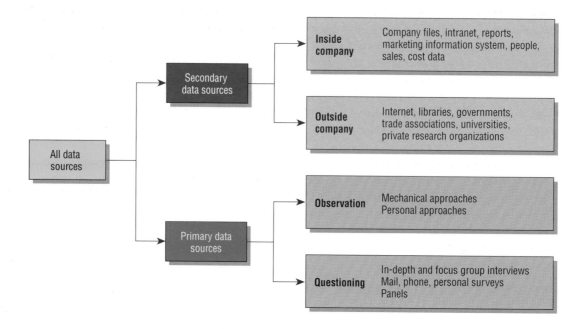

Exhibit 5.3 Sources of Secondary and Primary Data

list of sources out of date almost before it is published. Lockheed's DIALOGUE system, for example, allows a distant researcher to access a computer and get summaries of articles written on a specific subject. Similarly, ABI Inform is an on-line service that indexes a wide range of business periodicals. Anbar is another abstracting service that covers a wide range of business and academic publications. Business periodicals such as *The Financial Times* also allow on-line access to articles that can be retrieved by a key-word search. A computerized search can save time and help the researcher to be thorough. There are many tools for searching on the Internet. Most popular Internet browsers, like Netscape Navigator and Microsoft Internet Explorer, have a menu selection or button to activate an Internet search. In addition, there are hundreds of more specialized search engines. In general, a user specifies words or phrases to find and the search engine produces a list of hyperlinks to web sites where the search string is found.

Government data is inexpensive

Governments publish data on many subjects. Government data is often useful in estimating the size of markets. Almost all government data is available in inexpensive publications. Much of it is also available in computer form ready for further analysis. Sometimes it is more practical to use summary publications for leads to more detailed documents. For the UK market, one of the most useful summaries is the *Annual Abstract of Statistics*. It is like an almanac. It is issued each year and

gives summary tables from a wide range of published sources. Detailed footnotes are a guide to more specific information on a topic. Similarly, Eurostat, the statistical office for the European Union countries, and the Organisation for Economic Cooperation (in Paris) offer many publications packed with data on Europe.

Secondary data is very limited on some international markets. However, most countries have government agencies of use to the researcher. This can be supplemented by data from private agencies. For example, in Hungary the Hungarian Statistical Office can provide information on general demographic data such as the distribution of population by age and sex, the number of births, marriages and divorces. United Nations Statistics can help fill in background data on economic indicators such as trends in GDP, consumer prices and exports and imports. Young and Rubicam, a leading international advertising agency, has published data on the proportion of households with television, and the proportion of the population reading daily newspapers, while the Hungarian Advertising Association can provide data on the amount of advertising expenditure for specific product catagories.

Private sources are useful

Many private research organizations, as well as advertising agencies, newspapers and magazines regularly compile and publish data. Some information is available inexpensively as a customer service to clients of advertising agencies or buyers of advertising space or time. Often a company's suppliers can provide useful information. Specialist reports are published by agencies for specific market sectors or covering individual topics. For example Euromonitor, a major publisher of reports on European markets regularly publishes reports on topics as diverse as soft drinks in Europe, the international market for fast food, cosmetics and toiletries in Eastern Europe, Europe's major food companies, household cleaning products in Eastern Europe and European consumer lifestyles. Details of the last study will give you some idea of the level of analysis that may already have been made in a specialist report. The European consumer lifestyles study contains an analysis on a country-by-country basis of basic consumer demographics, social trends, employment patterns, the ownership of consumer goods, spending patterns, retail trade structures, leisure activities and the personal finance market. Having consulted secondary sources, it may not be necessary to conduct primary market research. At the very least secondary data provides background information useful for the design of primary research.

Situation analysis is useful

The virtue of a good situation analysis is that it can be very informative but takes little time. It is inexpensive compared with more formal research efforts such as a large-scale survey. It can help to focus further research or even eliminate the need for it entirely. The situation analyst is really trying to determine the exact nature of the situation and the problem. Hasty researchers may try to skip this step in their rush to get out questionnaires. Often these researchers find the real problem only when the questionnaires are returned and they must start over again. One marketing expert put it this way: 'Some people never have time to do research right the first time, but they seem to have time to do it over again.'

Determine what else is needed

At the end of the situation analysis, it can be seen which research questions from the list developed during the problem-definition step remain unanswered. Then the exact information needed to answer those questions can be determined. This often requires discussion between technical experts and the marketing manager. Often a written research proposal, a plan that specifies what information will be obtained and how, is used to be sure that no misunderstandings occur later. The research plan may include information about costs, what data will be collected, how it will be collected, who will analyse it and how, and how long the process will take. Then the marketing manager must decide if it makes sense to go ahead, that is if the time and costs involved seem worth while. It is foolish to pay £100 000 for information to solve a £50 000 problem! When the decision is not clearcut, marketing managers should know more about the next steps in the marketing research process.

GETTING PROBLEM–SPECIFIC DATA—STEP 3

Gathering primary data

The next step is to plan a formal research project to gather primary data. There are different methods for collecting primary data. Which approach to use depends on the nature of the problem and how much time and money are available. In most primary data collection, the researcher tries to learn what customers think about some topic—or how they behave under some conditions. There are two basic methods for obtaining information about customers: *questioning* and *observing*. Questioning can range from qualitative to quantitative research. Many kinds of observing are possible.

Qualitative questioning

Qualitative research seeks in-depth, open-ended responses, not 'yes' or 'no' answers. The researcher tries to get people to share their thoughts on a topic without giving them many directions or guidelines about what to say. A researcher might ask different consumers:

'What do you think about when you decide where to shop for food?' One person may talk about convenient location, another about service and others about the quality of the fresh produce. The real advantage of this approach is *depth*. Each person can be asked follow-up questions so the researcher really understands what *that* respondent is thinking. The depth of the qualitative approach gets at the details though a lot of judgement is involved in summarizing it all.

Some types of qualitative research do not use specific questions. For example, a cartoon may show a situation, such as a woman and a man buying coffee in a supermarket. The respondent may be asked to explain what the woman is saying to the man or the consumer might simply be shown a product or an advertisement and asked to comment. When Cadbury's were developing new boxed selections of chocolates, focus groups were shown mock-ups of the package and asked what they thought about it.

Focus groups stimulate discussion

The most widely used form of qualitative questioning in marketing research is the focus group interview, which involves interviewing 6 to 10 people in an informal group setting. The focus group also uses open-ended questions, but here the interviewer wants to get group interaction—to stimulate thinking and get immediate reactions. A skilled focus group leader can learn a lot from this approach. A typical session may last an hour so participants can cover a lot of ground. Sessions are often videotaped so different managers can form their own impressions of what happened. However, conclusions reached from watching a focus group session vary depending on who watches it! A typical problem—and serious limitation—with qualitative research is that it is hard to measure the results objectively. The results seem to depend so much on the viewpoint of the researcher. In addition, people who are willing to participate in a focus group—especially those who talk the most—may not be representative of the broader target market.

Focus groups can be conducted quickly and at relatively low cost. This is part of their appeal but there is a view that focus groups are being overused. It's easy to fall into the trap of treating an idea that comes out of a focus group as a 'fact' that applies to a broad target market. To avoid this trap, some researchers use qualitative research to prepare for quantitative research. Qualitative research can provide good ideas or hypotheses. But other approaches, perhaps based on more representative samples and objective measures, are needed to *test* the hypotheses.

Structured questioning gives more objective results

When researchers use identical questions and response alternatives, they can summarize the information quantitatively. Samples can be larger and more representative, and various statistics can be used to draw conclusions. For these reasons, most survey research is quantitative research—which seeks structured responses that can be summarized in numbers, like percentages, averages or other statistics. For example, a marketing researcher might calculate what percentage of respondents have tried a new product and then compute an average score for how satisfied they were with the experience.

Fixed responses speed answering and analysis

Survey questionnaires usually provide fixed responses to questions to simplify analysis of the replies. This multiple-choice approach also makes it easier and faster for respondents to reply. Simple fill-in-a-number questions are also widely used in quantitative research.

A questionnaire might ask an industrial buyer:[6] 'From approximately how many suppliers do you currently purchase electronic parts?' Fixed responses are also more convenient for computer analysis, which is how most surveys are analysed.

Internet Exercise

Perseus Development Corporation sells software that allows a use to create on-line questionnaires that can be distributed by e-mail or used on the Internet. To see samples of on-line questions, go to the Perseus web site (**www.perseus.com**) and then click on survey samples. Do you think it's more convenient for a consumer to complete a survey on-line or with pencil and paper?

Quantitative measures of attitudes too

One common approach to measuring consumers' attitudes and opinions is to have respondents indicate how much they agree or disagree with a questionnaire statement. A researcher interested in what target consumers think about frozen pizzas, for example, might include statements like those at the top of Exhibit 5–4. Another approach is to have respondents *rate* a product, feature or shop. Figure 5–4 shows commonly used rating 'scales.' Sometimes rating scales are labelled with adjectives like *excellent*, *good*, *fair* and *poor*.

Surveys by mail, telephone or in person

Decisions about what specific questions to ask, and how to ask them, are usually related to how respondents will be contacted—by mail, on the telephone or in person.

Mail surveys are the most convenient

The mail questionnaire is useful when extensive questioning is necessary. With a mail questionnaire, respondents can complete the questions at their convenience. They may be more willing to fill in personal or family characteristics because a mail questionnaire can be returned anonymously. The questions must be simple and easy to follow, because no interviewer is there to help. A big problem with mail questionnaires is that many people do not complete or return them. The response rate—the percentage of people contacted who complete the questionnaire—is often only around 10 per cent in consumer surveys. Another problem is that respondents may not be representative. People who are most interested in the questionnaire topic may respond but answers from this group may be very different from the answers of the typical less interested group. Mail surveys are economical if a large number of people respond but they may be quite expensive if the response rate is low. Further, it can take a month or longer to get the data and this is too slow for some decisions.

A. Please check your level of agreement with each of the following statements.

	Strongly Agree	Agree	Uncertain	Disagree	Strongly Disagree
1. I add extra toppings when I prepare a frozen pizza.	——	——	——	——	——
2. A frozen pizza dinner is more expensive than eating at a fast-food restaurant.	——	——	——	——	——

B. Please rate how important each of the following is to you in selecting a brand of frozen pizza.

	Not at all Important					Very Important
1. Price per serving						
2. Toppings available	——	——	——	——	——	——
3. Amount of cheese						
4. Cooking time	——	——	——	——	——	——

C. Please check the rating that best describes your feelings about the last frozen pizza you prepared.

	Poor	Fair	Good	Excellent
1. Price per serving	——	——	——	——
2. Toppings available	——	——	——	——
3. Amount of cheese	——	——	——	——
4. Cooking time	——	——	——	——

Exhibit 5–4 Sample Questioning Methods to Measure Attitudes and Opinions

Moreover, it is difficult to get respondents to elaborate on particular points. In markets where illiteracy is a problem, it may not be possible to get any response. In spite of these limitations, the convenience and economy of mail surveys makes them popular for collecting primary data.

Telephone surveys—fast and effective
Telephone interviews are growing in popularity. They are effective for getting quick answers to simple questions. Telephone interviews allow the interviewer to probe and really learn what the respondent is thinking. On the other hand, some consumers find calls intrusive and may refuse to answer any questions. Moreover, the telephone is usually not a very good contact method if the interviewer is trying to get confidential personal information—such as details of family income. Respondents are not certain who is calling or how such personal information might be used. Research firms—with up to 50 interviewers calling at the same time on long distance lines—can complete 1000 or more interviews in one evening. In addition, with computer-aided telephone interviewing, answers are immediately recorded on a computer, resulting in fast data analysis. The popularity of telephone surveys is partly due to their speed and high response rates.

Personal interview surveys—can be in-depth
A personal interview survey is usually much more expensive per interview than a mail or telephone survey. However, the interviewer can get and keep the respondent's attention. The interviewer can also help to explain

Market research was used to test the effectiveness of the commercials for Nivea Cosmetics

complicated directions and perhaps get better responses. For these reasons, personal interviews are commonly used for research on business customers. To reduce the cost of locating consumer respondents, interviews are sometimes done at a shop or in the street. Researchers have to be careful that having an interviewer involved does not affect the respondent's answers. Sometimes people will not give an answer they consider embarrassing or they may try to impress or please the interviewer. Further, in some cultures people do not want to give any information or believe that it might be used for other purposes than market research. This is also a problem in many low-income, inner-city areas.

Observing—what you see is what you get

Observing—as a method of collecting data—focuses on a well-defined problem. Here we are not talking about the casual observations that may stimulate ideas in the early steps of a research project. With the observation method, researchers try to see or record what the subject does naturally. They do not want the observing to *influence* the subject's behaviour. A museum director wanted to know which of the many exhibits was most popular. A survey didn't help. Visitors seemed to want to please the interviewer and usually said that all of the exhibits were interesting. Putting observers near exhibits, to record how long visitors spent at each one, didn't help either. The curious visitors stood around to see what was being recorded and that messed up the measures. Finally, the museum floors were waxed to a glossy shine. Several weeks later, the floors around the exhibits were inspected. It was easy to tell which exhibits were most popular, based on how much wax had worn off the floor!

In some situations, consumers are recorded on videotape. Later, researchers can study the tape by running the film at very slow speed or actually analysing each frame. This technique is used to study the routes consumers follow through a grocery outlet or how they select products in a department store.

Observing is common in advertising research

Observation methods are common in advertising research. For example, A.C. Nielsen has developed a device that adapts the observation method to television audience research. This machine is attached to the TV set in the homes of selected families. It records when the set is on and what station is tuned in. The results are widely used to rate the popularity of TV shows. Some claim that once families get used to the device, it no longer influences their behaviour. Note, however, that it records only what channel is on, not whether anyone is watching it.

Checkout scanners record purchases

Computerized scanners at retail checkout counters, a major breakthrough in observing, help researchers collect very specific and useful information. Often this type of data feeds directly into a firm's MIS. A.C. Nielsen uses consumer panels—a group of consumers who provide information on a continuing basis. Whenever a panel member shops for groceries, he or she gives an ID number to the checkout operator, who keys in the number. Then the scanner records every purchase—including brands, sizes, prices and any coupons used. For a fee, clients can evaluate actual customer purchase patterns—and answer questions about the effectiveness of their discount coupons. Did the coupons draw new customers, or did current customers simply use them to stock up? If consumers switched from another brand, did they go back to their old brand the next time? The answers to such questions are important in planning marketing strategies—and scanners can help marketing managers get the answers.

WHIRLPOOL HEATS UP SALES WITH MARKETING RESEARCH

Marketing managers at Whirlpool want to build a profitable, long-lasting relationship with the customers that they serve—and to bring new consumers into the fold. Each year the firm mails an appliance satisfaction survey to 180 000 households. Respondents rate all their appliances on dozens of dimensions. When a competing product scores higher, Whirlpool engineers take it apart to see why and build the best ideas into their new models. However, they don't just wait for competitors to figure things out first.

A new oven illustrates their approach. A survey showed that consumers wanted an oven with easy-to-clean controls. That did not seem consistent with previous sales patterns; the firm's MIS showed that models with knobs consistently outsold models with easier-to-clean push buttons. Rather than disregard the survey, Whirlpool designed a range with touch pad controls by listening to consumers at every step along the way. Consumers who played with computer simulations of the touch pad explained what they liked and did not like. Videotapes of consumers who tried prototype models in mall intercept interviews provided ideas to further refine the design. The result is a touch pad control that is easy to clean and so easy to use that consumers don't even need to read the manual.

Consumer research has been an even more important factor in Whirlpool's growth overseas. For example, until recently only about one-third of European households had a microwave oven. Whirlpool researchers learned that more people would buy if a microwave could crisp food as it heated it. Whirlpool designed a microwave with a broiler coil and other innovations. The result is an oven that is popular in Britain for frying bacon and eggs and in Italy for crisping pizza crusts.[6]

The use of scanners to 'observe' what customers actually do is changing consumer research methods. Companies can turn to a *single source* of complete information about customers' attitudes, shopping behaviour and media habits. The information available is so detailed that the possibilities are limited more by imagination and money than by technology.[7]

Experimental method controls conditions

A marketing manager can get a different kind of information with either questioning or observing, using the experimental method. With the experimental method, researchers compare the responses of two or more groups that are similar except on the characteristic being tested. Researchers want to learn if the specific characteristic, which varies among groups, *causes* differences in some response among the groups. For example, a researcher might be interested in comparing responses of consumers who had seen an advertisement for a new product with consumers who had not seen the advertisement. The 'response' might be an observed behaviour such as the purchase of a product, or the answer to a specific question such as: 'How interested are you in this new product?'

Marketing managers for Mars, the company that makes Snickers bars, used the experimental method to help solve a problem. Other confectionery and snack foods were taking customers. But why? Surveys showed that many consumers thought the bar was too small. But they also didn't want to pay more for a larger bar. Mars' managers wanted to know if making their bar bigger would increase sales enough to offset the higher cost. To decide, they conducted a marketing experiment.

The company carefully varied the size of bars sold in *different* markets. Otherwise, the marketing mix stayed the same. Then researchers tracked sales in each market area to see the effect of the different sizes. They saw a difference immediately. It was clear that the added sales would more than offset the cost of a bigger bar. So marketing managers at Mars made a decision that took them in the opposite direction from other companies.

Test markets of new products are another use of marketing experiments. The typical approach is for a company to try variations on its planned marketing mix in a few geographic market areas. The results of the tests help to identify problems or refine the marketing mix before deciding to go to broader distribution. However, alert competitors may disrupt such tests, perhaps by increasing promotion or offering retailers extra discounts.

The experimental method is not used as often as surveys and focus groups because it is hard to set up controlled situations where only one marketing variable is different. But it is also the case that many managers do not understand the valuable information to be derived from this method. Further, they may not like the idea of a researcher 'experimenting' with their business.

Syndicated research shares data collection costs

Some private research firms specialize in supplying data that are regularly collected and used by managers in many different client firms. Often the marketing manager subscribes to the research service and gets regular updates. Marketing managers from many different firms may have to make the same kinds of decisions and need the same type of data. The most economical approach in a situation like this is for one specialist firm to collect the data and distribute it to the different users, who share the cost. This is how A. C. Nielsen operates. There are many other firms that collect and distribute specialized types of data. For example, The Economist Intelligence Unit is a research firm that sells access to its surveys on home appliances and electronics, retail banking and insurance, and other product categories.

INTERPRETING THE DATA—STEP 4

What does it really mean?

When data has been collected it has to be analysed to decide what it all means. In quantitative research, this step usually involves statistics. Statistical packages, easy-to-use computer programs that analyse data, have made this step easier. As noted earlier, some firms provide *decision support systems* so managers can use a statistical package to interpret data themselves. More often, however, technical specialists are involved at the interpretation step.

Statistical data can be analysed in a variety of ways

The most common form of analysis of statistical data is simply to count the relative frequency with which individual responses are given. For example, a survey could tabulate how many respondents agreed or disagreed with a particular opinion. The researcher can then analyse the relative proportions of respondents in favour or against a particular point of view. Most surveys of peoples' voting intentions follow this format attempting to predict how many will for vote for each candidate at the next election.

Cross-tabulation is one of the most frequently used approaches for analysing and interpreting marketing research data. It shows the relationship of answers to two different questions. Exhibit 5–5 is an example. In this case, a telephone company was interested in learning more about customers who had adopted its touch-tone dialling service. The analysis shows that customers who had moved in the last year were much more likely than non-movers to have adopted the touch-tone service. So the researchers concluded that people who had just moved were a prime target market for the service.

Cross-tabulation is popular because the results are usually easy to interpret. There are many other approaches for statistical analysis and which is best depends on the situation. The details of statistical analysis are beyond the scope of this book. A good manager should know enough to understand what a research project can and cannot do.

Is the sample really representative?

It is usually impossible for marketing managers to collect all the information they want about everyone in a population—the total group they are interested in. Marketing researchers typically study only a sample, a part of the relevant population. How well a sample *represents* the total population affects the results. Results from a sample that is not representative may not give a true picture. The manager of a retail shop might want a phone survey to learn what consumers think about the store's hours. If interviewers make all of the calls during the day, the sample will not be representative. Consumers who work outside the home during the day won't have an equal chance of being included. Those interviewed might say the limited store hours are 'satisfactory.' Yet it would be a mistake to assume that *all* consumers are satisfied.

	Have You Moved in the Last Year?			
	Answers:	No	Yes	Total
Do You Have Touch-Tone	Yes	10.2%	23.4%	15.5%
Dialling at Your Home?	No	89.8	76.6	84.5
	Total	100.0%	100.0%	100.0%

Interpretation: 15.5% of people in the survey said that they had Touch-Tone Dialling in their homes. However, the percentage was much higher (23.5%) among people who had moved in the last year and lower (10.2%) among people who had not moved.

Exhibit 5–5 Cross-Tabulation Breakdown of Responses to a Phone Company Consumer Survey

Random samples tend to be representative

Getting a representative sample is very important. One method of doing so is random sampling, where each member of the population has the same chance of being included in the sample. Great care must be used to ensure that sampling is really random, not just haphazard. If a random sample is chosen from a population, it will tend to have the same characteristics and be representative of the population. 'Tend to' is important because it is only a tendency: the sample is not exactly the same as the population.

Much marketing research is based on non-random sampling because of the high cost and difficulty of obtaining a truly random sample. Typically the researcher will attempt to define a quota of people who should be represented in the sample. Provided any one respondent meets the quota criteria then that respondent can be included. For example, there are approximately 50 per cent men and 50 per cent women in the population as a whole. Any sample that is to represent the population should have at least the same proportions of men and women in the sample. Sometimes non-random samples give very good results, especially in industrial markets where the number of customers may be relatively small and fairly similar. Results from non-random samples must be interpreted, and used, with care.

Research results are not exact

An estimate from a sample, even a representative one, usually varies somewhat from the true value for a total population. Managers sometimes forget this. They assume that survey results are exact. Instead, when interpreting sample estimates, managers should think of them as *suggesting* the approximate value. If random selection is used to develop the sample, then methods are available for stating the likely accuracy of the sample value. This is done in terms of confidence intervals—the range on either side of an estimate that is likely to contain the true value for the whole population. Some managers are surprised to learn how wide that range can be.

Consider a wholesaler who has 1000 retail customers and wants to learn how many of these retailers carry a product from a competing supplier. If the wholesaler randomly samples 100 retailers and 20 say yes, then the sample estimate is 20 per cent. But with that information the wholesaler could be only 95 per cent confident that the percentage of all retailers is between 12 and 28 per cent.

The larger the sample size, the greater the accuracy of estimates from a random sample. With a larger sample, a few unusual responses are less likely to make a big difference. The nature of the sample, and how it is selected, makes a big difference in how the results of a study can be interpreted. Managers must consider this factor when planning data collection and ensure that the final results can be interpreted with enough confidence to be useful in marketing strategy planning.

Validity problems can destroy research

Even if the sampling is carefully planned, it is also important to evaluate the quality of the research data itself. Managers and researchers should be sure that research data really measures what it is supposed to measure. Many of the variables that are of interest to marketing managers are difficult to measure accurately. Questionnaires may assign numbers to consumer responses, but that still does not mean that the result is precise. An interviewer might ask: 'How much did you spend on soft drinks last week?' A respondent may be perfectly willing to cooperate—and be part of the representative sample—but just not be able to remember.

Validity concerns the extent to which data measures what it is intended to measure. Validity problems are important in marketing research because most people want to help and will try to answer, even when they know little about the subject. Further, a poorly worded question can mean different things to different people and invalidate the results. Managers must be sure that they only pay for research results that are representative and valid.

Poor interpretation can destroy research

Besides sampling and validity problems, a marketing manager must consider whether the analysis of the data supports the *conclusions* drawn in the interpretation step. Sometimes technical specialists pick the right statistical procedure—their calculations are exact—but they misinterpret the data because they don't understand the management problem. In one survey, car buyers were asked to rank five cars in order from 'most preferred' to 'least preferred'. One car was ranked first by slightly more respondents than any other car so the researcher reported it as the 'most liked car'. That interpretation, however, ignored the fact that 70 per cent of the respondents ranked the car *last*! Interpretation problems like this can be subtle but crucial. Some people draw misleading conclusions deliberately to get the results they want. A marketing manager must decide whether *all* of the results support the interpretation and if they are relevant to the problem.

Marketing manager and researcher should work together

Marketing research involves some technical details. The marketing researcher and the marketing manager must work together to ensure that the problem facing the firm is solved. If the whole research process has been a joint effort, then the interpretation step can move quickly to decision making and solving the problem.

SOLVING THE PROBLEM—STEP 5

The last step is solving the problem

In the problem-solution step, managers use the research results to make marketing decisions. Some researchers and managers are fascinated by the interesting bits of information that come from the research process. They are excited if the research reveals something that they did not know before. Ultimately, if research does not have action implications, it has little value and suggests poor planning by the researcher and the manager. When the research process is finished, the marketing manager should be able to apply the findings in marketing strategy planning—the choice of a target market or the mix of the four Ps. If the research does not provide information to help guide these decisions, the company has wasted research time and money.

We emphasize this step because it is the reason for and logical conclusion to the whole research process. This final step must be anticipated at each of the earlier steps.

INTERNATIONAL MARKETING RESEARCH

Research contributes to international success

Marketing research on overseas markets is often a major contributor towards international marketing success. Conversely, export failures are often due to a lack of home-office management expertise concerning customer interests, needs and other segmenting dimensions as well as environmental factors such as competitors' prices and products. Effective marketing research can help to overcome these problems.

Avoid mistakes with local researchers

Whether a firm is small and entering overseas markets for the first time or already large and well-established internationally, there are often advantages to working with local market research firms. These research suppliers know the local situation and are less likely to make mistakes based on misunderstanding the customs, language or circumstances of the customers they study.

As has been emphasized, however, it is still important for a marketing manager to work closely with the researchers to be certain that the research solves the manager's problem. Just because a researcher is expert on doing research in their local setting does not mean that he or she is expert on the specific marketing problems the manager needs to solve. Finding a research supplier with relevant experience helps to reduce the likelihood of problems. Many large research firms have a network of local offices around the world to help with such efforts. Similarly, multinational or local advertising agencies and intermediaries can often provide leads on identifying the best research suppliers.

Some coordination and standardization makes sense

When a firm is doing similar research projects in different markets around the world, it makes sense for the marketing manager to coordinate the efforts. If the manager does not establish some basic guidelines at the outset, the different research projects may all vary so much that the results can't be compared from one market area to another. When key questions and issues are studied in similar ways, comparisons across markets are possible. Such comparisons give a home-office manager a much better chance of understanding how the markets are similar and how they differ. This can be a key to knowing if it is appropriate for marketing strategies to be standardized across markets, or alternatively what customized approaches are necessary.

Multinational companies with operations in various countries often attempt to centralize some market research functions. One reason is to reduce costs or achieve research economies of scale. The centralized approach also improves the firm's ability to transfer experience and know-how from one market area or project to another.

The African, Asian and Australian unit of Eastman Kodak's International Photographic Division recognized the value of coordinating its marketing research activities. It appointed one or more market research specialists in each subsidiary company throughout the region. The specialists report to local marketing managers, but also receive research direction from expert research managers in the head office in the United States. Head office control ensures a high standard of research quality worldwide. For example, the head office coordinates the marketing research training that is handled on a regional basis. Centralized coordination also assures that research findings in any particular country can be meaningfully compared with other countries.

There is even greater opportunity and need to standardize and coordinate elements of a marketing information system in an international marketing operation. A custom market research survey designed to obtain primary data may only be used once and may need to focus on specifics of the local situation. Yet, by their very nature, computer databases and information systems are most useful when they are designed to include the same variables organized consistently over time. Without this, it is impossible for the manager to go into much depth in comparing and contrasting data from different markets.

HOW MUCH INFORMATION IS NEEDED?

Information is costly, but reduces risk

Good marketing information is beneficial, but dependable information can be expensive. A company may spend millions developing an information system. A large-scale survey can cost from £20 000 to £100 000, or even more. The continuing research available from companies such as A.C. Nielsen can cost a company well over £100 000 a year. And a market test for 6–12 months may cost hundreds of thousands of pounds per test market! Companies that are willing and able to pay the cost often find that marketing information pays for itself. They are more likely to select the right target market and marketing mix or to see a potential problem before it becomes a costly crisis.

What is the value of information?

The high cost of good information must be balanced against its probable value to management. Managers never get all the information they would like to have. Very detailed surveys or experiments may be too good or too expensive or too late if all the company needs is an immediate rough sampling of retailer attitudes towards a new pricing plan. Money is wasted if research shows that a manager's guesses are wrong and the manager then ignores the facts.

Marketing managers must take risks because of incomplete information. That is part of the management job. However, they must weigh the cost of getting more data against its likely value. If the risk is not too great, the cost of getting more information may be greater than the potential loss from a poor decision. A decision to expand into a new territory with the present marketing mix, for example, might be made with more confidence after a £25 000 survey. Just sending a sales representative into the territory for a few weeks to try to sell to the potential customers would be a lot cheaper. If successful, the business has the answer as well as some sales. Faced with many risky decisions, the marketing manager should only seek help from research for problems where the risk can be reduced at a reasonable cost.[8]

SUMMARY

Marketing managers face difficult decisions in selecting target markets and managing marketing mixes. In addition, managers rarely have all the information they would like to have—but they don't have to rely only on intuition. Good information can usually be obtained to improve the quality of their decisions.

Computers have helped marketing managers to become fully-fledged members of the information age. Both large and small firms are setting up marketing information systems (MIS), to be certain that routinely needed data is available and accessible quickly.

Marketing managers deal with rapidly changing environments. Available data is not always adequate to answer the detailed questions that arise. In those circumstances, a marketing research project may be required to gather new information.

Marketing research should be guided by the scientific method. The scientific approach to solving marketing problems involves five steps: defining the problem, analysing the situation, obtaining data, interpreting data and solving the problem. This objective and organized approach helps to keep research on target, reducing the risk of doing costly research that is not necessary or does not solve the problem.

The strategy planning framework can be helpful in finding the real problem. By finding and focusing on the real problem, the researcher and marketing manager may be able to move quickly to a useful solution, without the cost and risks of gathering primary data in a formal research project. With imagination, they may even be able to find the answers in the MIS or in other readily available secondary data.

QUESTIONS AND PROBLEMS

1. Discuss the concept of a marketing information system and why it is important for marketing managers to be involved in planning the system.

2. In your own words, explain why a decision support system (DSS) can add to the value of a marketing information system. Give an example of how a decision support system might help.

3. Discuss how output from an MIS might differ from the output of a typical marketing research department.

4. Discuss some of the likely problems facing the marketer in a small firm that has just purchased an inexpensive personal computer and modem to help to develop a marketing information system.

5. What would you have said if you had been writing the report for PrintKraft (see boxed example, p. 8)?

6. Explain the key characteristics of the scientific method and show why these are important to managers concerned with research.

7. How is the situation analysis different from the data collection step. Can both these steps be done at the same time to obtain answers sooner? Is this wise?

8. Distinguish between primary data and secondary data and illustrate your answer.

9. Go to the library and find (in some government publication) three marketing-oriented 'facts' concerning international markets that you did not know existed or were available. Record on one page and show sources.

10. Explain why a company might want to do focus group interviews rather than doing individual interviews with the same people.

11. Distinguish between qualitative and quantitative approaches to research—and give some of the key advantages and limitations of each approach.

12. Define what is meant by response rate and discuss why a marketing manager might be concerned about the response rate achieved in a particular survey. Give an example.

13. Prepare a table that summarizes some of the key advantages and limitations of mail, telephone and personal interview approaches for administering questionnaires.

14. Explain how you might use different types of research (focus groups, observation, survey and experiment) to forecast market reaction to a new kind of disposable baby nappy, which is to receive no promotion other than what the retailer will give it. Further, assume that the new nappy's name will not be associated with other known products. The product will be offered at competitive prices.

15. Marketing research involves expense—sometimes considerable expense. Why does the text recommend the use of marketing research even though a highly experienced marketing executive is available?

16. Discuss the concept that some information may be too expensive to obtain in relation to its value. Illustrate.

SUGGESTED CASE

5. Sophia's Ristorante

REFERENCES

1. D. Summers, 'Skoda', *The Financial Times*, 12 May 1994, p. 23; J. Simms, 'Time to get serious', *Marketing Business*, November 1998, pp. 24–28.

2. N.B. Zabriskie, A.B. Huellmantel, 'Marketing research as a strategic tool', *Long Range Planning*, vol. 27, no. 1, 1994, pp. 10–18.

3. J.T. Mentzer and N. Gandhi, 'Expert systems in marketing: Guidelines for development', *Journal of the Academy of Marketing Science*, Winter 1992, pp. 73–80; W.D. Perreault, Jr., 'The shifting paradigm in marketing research', *Journal of the Academy of Marketing Science*, Fall 1992, pp. 367–76.

4. 'The "Bloodbath" in market research', *Business Week*, 11 February 1991, pp. 72–4; 'Why products fail', *Adweeks Marketing Week*, 5 November 1990, pp. 20–25; B. Townsend, 'Market research that matters', *American Demographics*, August 1992, p. 58.

5. 'Call it Worldpool', *Business Week*, 28 November 1994, pp. 98–99; 'The gold mine of data in customer service', *Business Week*, 21 March 1994, pp. 113–14; 'How to listen to consumers,' *Fortune*, 11 January 1993, pp. 77–9; *1993 Annual Report*, Whirlpool.

6. For more detail on observational approaches, see S.J. Grove and R.P. Fisk, 'Observational data collection methods for services marketing: An overview', *Journal of the Academy of Marketing Science*, Summer 1992.

7. A.R. Andreasen, 'Cost-conscious marketing research', *Harvard Business Review*, July–August, 1983, pp. 74–81.

8. J. Bessen, 'Riding the information wave', *Harvard Business Review*, September–October 1993, pp. 150–61.

CHAPTER 6
Market Segmentation, Targeting and Positioning

When You Finish This Chapter, You Should

1 Understand the importance of segmentation, targeting and positioning

2 Know about the different kinds of marketing opportunities.

3 Understand why opportunities in international markets should be considered.

4 Have a knowledge of market segmentation.

5 Know three approaches to market-oriented strategy planning.

6 Know how to segment product markets into submarkets.

7 Know dimensions that may be useful for segmenting markets.

8 Know a seven-step approach to market segmentation.

9 Have a knowledge of positioning.

10 Understand the important new terms (shown in colour).

When personal computers first came on the scene, early business users needed a fast way to get quality hard copy of the text, spreadsheets and graphs produced by the software. Hewlett-Packard (HP) quickly recognized this need and came out with the LaserJet brand printer. HP's unique LaserJet was so flexible that it virtually created the desktop publishing boom. By the time competitors came along, HP offered even better printers, including high-capacity models for firms with computer networks. When HP's marketers saw fast growth in home computing, they targeted new easy-to-use models at families. To reach this new segment at a lower price, HP sent its sales-people to convince discount retailers to carry the printers. Many agreed to do just that because the printers were good value and HP's publicity, sales promotions and adver-tising attracted customers who were ready to buy. When Microsoft's Windows software showed consumers the possibilities of colour computing, HP was ready again. Its R&D on inkjet technology pioneered a new way for customers to do low-cost colour printing. As a result, HP's inkjets are the colour leaders and LaserJets still capture the bulk of all laser printer sales.

These past successes are not the only reason for HP executives to be confident. Rather, it is because HP is now making hefty profits with a strategy that targets innovators who want to use computers for digital colour photography. HP is meeting their needs with its line of PhotoSmart scanners, printers and digital cameras. HP marketers believe that colour digital imaging and printing will ultimately change how people think about photography and about HP.

Can HP compete with a photo giant like Kodak? Clearly, Kodak is positioned in consumers' minds as the leader in photogra-phy. Advertising constantly reminds us that a 'Kodak moment' is about great pictures. One-hour photo labs are in many towns and cities. They develop Kodak film and print it on Kodak paper. Many will even put pictures in digital form on a computer disk. HP has other disadvantages in the photographic battle. The quality of photos printed on the HP PhotoSmart printer is not quite as good. The colours do not last as well. The cost is twice as high and printing pictures is slow. On the other hand, HP is not trying to meet all photography needs. Rather it is focusing on specific target markets with needs that Kodak does not meet.

For example, many people want a quick and easy way to print photographs that they can download from the Internet. Similarly, Internet e-mail makes it cost less to send digital photographs to friends or business contacts all over the world. An estate agent can, for exam-ple, instantly send a picture of a house to a client in a distant city. Many photo buffs want to alter photographs on the computer, perhaps to include them in reports, brochures and adver-tising materials. Even children like to make their own greetings cards, calendars and brochures. Local photo labs do not address these needs, and Kodak does not (yet) produce a colour printer. In contrast, HP has many different PhotoSmart printers for different needs. Large format printers make poster-size photos and graphics needed for business presentations and advertising. Printers for kids come with video tutorials on a computer CD. HP is even moving into printers that work within a computer. One model of the PhotoSmart printer hooks directly to a digital camera. Another connects to Microsoft's Web TV set-top control box. HP is working on a printer that plugs into a telephone line. Publishers who want to use electronic delivery will be able to 'call' a subscriber's printer, thereby wiping out the delays and cost of printing and mailing.

Some of these markets are not large but they are growing fast and creating opportunities that HP is turning into profitable strategies. For example, each customer who buys an HP PhotoSmart printer uses ink cartridges and special paper. Selling these replacement supplies gives HP a profitable on-going relationship with the customer. In fact, inkjet supplies now produce approximately 25 per cent of HP's total profits. HP's market research suggests that sales of supplies will double if current users print just one extra colour page per week.

HP marketers know that they need the right marketing mix to achieve HP's growth objectives. They hope to extend distribution of inkjet cartridges through using super-markets and mass merchandisers rather than just relying on computer and office-supply stores that currently carry them. At the same time, HP is looking for ways to reduce the price for a cartridge to about the cost of a roll of film. Of course, product development also continues. This includes new inks with better colours, more precise print heads and Internet technologies that will make it easier to distribute pictures over the Internet. HP is working on a digital camera combined with a cellular phone that will allow the user to take a picture, instantly upload it to the Internet and send it somewhere else to be printed.

Marketers at HP may have missed opportunities related to photography if they had just defined markets in terms of computer products the company was already producing. Instead they are focused on the changing needs of different segments of customers and innovative ways that HP can leverage its strengths to serve these customers. In the future, as HP attacks other photographic markets, it will face new challenges and tougher competition. It needs to continue to spot opportunities and convert them into creative marketing strategies.[1]

A THREE-STAGE APPROACH TO MARKETING PLANNING

Three stages are involved in implementing marketing planning

Effective marketing planning makes the difference between success and failure. To build success, the company has to identify the range of markets that it should operate in, decide where to compete and, more importantly, where not to compete because of too strong competition. It has also to decide how to position itself against competition in such a way as to create a preference in customers' minds for its products.

Companies have gone through the three stages in implementing marketing planning, namely market segmentation, market targeting and positioning. Some people call this process STP marketing, using the first letters of each stage, thus Segmentation, Targeting and Positioning. Much of a marketing manager's time is spent on implementing these three activities as part of the marketing planning process. This chapter explores each of stages in detail.

Market segmentation is the process of selecting target markets and developing suitable marketing mixes. Such clusters or segments are the focal point for marketing programmes. Market targeting is the process of deciding in which markets to compete. Usually a firm's resources will not allow it to pursue every opportunity, even if they are all attractive. Finally, positioning is the process of designing a marketing programme, a marketing mix, which will give the company or brand a unique image in the market and in the mind of the customer.

Some firms do not use a market-based approach

Some production-oriented managers ignore the tough part of defining markets. To make the narrowing-down process easier, they just describe their markets in terms of *products* they sell. For example, producers and retailers of greetings cards might define their market as the greeting card market. This production-oriented approach ignores customers and it is customers who make a market. This narrow definition also leads to missed opportunities. Hallmark is a company that is not missing these opportunities. Instead, it aims at the personalexpression market. It offers all kinds of products that can be sent as memory makers, to express one person's feelings towards another. Hallmark has expanded far beyond holiday and birthday cards—the major greeting card days—to jewellery, gift wrap, plaques, candles and puzzles as well as to all-occasion and humorous cards. The company has succeeded by identifying a range of different occasions and developing products to meet each occasion.

Electrolux relaunched its product range across Europe as an 'upper mass-market' brand, because (so the company believes) the 45–55 age group are willing to react to a consistent appeal. The same products and advertising were used to position the brand in a common

Market segmentation allows companies to target specific groups of customers with products that fill their self-image. Ben Sherman focuses on independent young customers.

segment across all European countries. Electrolux continued to exploit strong national preferences by selling two 'local' brands in each major market in addition to the pan-European brand.[2]

When marketing managers really understand their target markets, they may see breakthrough opportunities. Adidas, the German sports shoe manufacturer, was under considerable pressure when Nike and Reebok entered its markets in the 1980s. Its response was to better define market segments and to introduce products more carefully positioned to meet the needs of target customers throughout Europe.[3]

TYPES OF OPPORTUNITIES TO PURSUE

Most people have unsatisfied needs and marketers can find opportunities all around them. Some opportunities seem obvious only after someone else identifies them. It helps to have a framework for thinking about the kinds of opportunities you may find. Exhibit 6–1 shows the four broad possibilities: market penetration, market development, product development, and diversification. Each of these will be covered separately, but some firms may pursue more than one type of opportunity at the same time.

Market penetration

Market penetration is trying to increase sales of a firm's present products in its present markets, probably

	Existing products	**New products**
Existing markets	Market penetration	Product development
New markets	Market development	Diversification

Exhibit 6–1 Four Basic Types of Opportunities

through a more aggressive marketing mix. The firm may try to increase the customers' rate of use or attract competitors' customers or current non-users. For example, Visa has increased advertising to encourage customers to use its credit card when they travel and to switch from using American Express. New promotion appeals alone may not be effective. A firm may need to add more shops in present areas for greater convenience. Short-term price cuts or coupon offers may help. BT has progressively cut the costs of many local telephone calls in the United Kingdom as part of a strategy to encourage greater usage of the telephone.

Obviously, effective analysis and planning is aided by a real understanding of why some people are buying now and what will motivate them to shift brands, buy more, or begin or resume buying.

Market development

Market development is trying to increase sales by selling existing products in new markets. This may only involve advertising in different media to reach new target customers. Or it may mean adding channels of distribution or new stores in new areas, including overseas markets. For example, McDonald's is reaching new customers by opening outlets in airports, office buildings, zoos, casinos, hospitals and military bases. There is now a branch of McDonald's in one of London's largest hospitals. It is also rapidly expanding into international markets with outlets in places like Russia, Brazil, Hong Kong, Mexico and Australia. Market development may also involve a search for new uses for a product, as when Kellogg encourages consumers to eat their product as a snack in the evening as well as the traditional breakfast food.

Product development

Product development is offering new or improved products for existing markets. Here, the firm should know the market's needs; it may see ways of adding or modifying product features, creating several quality

levels, or adding more types or sizes to satisfy them better. Computer software firms such as Microsoft boost sales by introducing new versions of popular programs. Microsoft has also developed other types of new products for its customers. It now sells computer books (some in the new CD-Rom format) and even computer hardware.

Diversification

Diversification is moving into totally different lines of business, which may include entirely unfamiliar products, markets or even levels in the production-marketing system. Richard Branson's Virgin empire has expanded from its origins in record production, to now include record stores, airlines, rail transport, insurance, clothing, drinks and pension schemes! The most challenging opportunities involve diversification. Here, both new products *and* new markets are involved. The further the opportunity is from what the firm is already doing, the more attractive it may look to the optimists and the harder it will be to evaluate. Opportunities that are far from a firm's current experiences involve higher risks and costs.

Which opportunities come first?

Usually, attractive opportunities are fairly close to markets the firm already knows. This may allow the firm to capitalize on changes in its present markets or more basic changes in the external environment. Most firms think first of greater market penetration. They want to increase profits where they already have experience and strengths. Marketers who have a good understanding of their present markets may also see opportunities in product development especially because they already have a way of reaching their present customers. But if the firm currently has as large a share as it can get in its present markets, it is especially sensible to think of market development. This involves finding new markets for their present products, including expanding regionally, nationally or internationally.

INTERNATIONAL OPPORTUNITIES SHOULD BE CONSIDERED

Advances in communications and transportation are making it easier and cheaper to reach international customers, even for small firms. Market opportunities are often no more limited by national boundaries than they are by the regional boundaries within a country. Around the world there are potential customers with needs and money to spend. Ignoring these customers does not make any more sense than ignoring potential customers in the same town. The real question is whether the firm can effectively use its resources to meet these customers' needs at a profit.

Develop a competitive advantage at home and abroad

If customers in other countries are interested in the products a firm offers, or could offer, serving them may make it possible to achieve better economies of scale. Lower costs and prices may give a firm a competitive advantage both in its home markets *and* abroad. This sort of competitive pressure may actually *force* a marketing manager to expand into international markets. Marketing managers who are only interested in local customers may be rudely surprised to find that an aggressive, low-cost foreign producer is willing to pursue those customers. Many companies that thought they could avoid the struggles of international competition have learned this lesson the hard way.

The marketing manager who carefully looks for international market development opportunities often finds them. Different countries are at different stages of economic and technological development, and their consumers have different needs at different times. For example, Western European manufacturers have found many new markets in Eastern European countries that were formerly not accessible.

A company that is facing tough competition, thin profit margins and slow sales growth at home may get a fresh start in another country where demand for a product is just beginning to grow. A marketing manager may be able to transfer marketing know-how, or some other competitive advantage, the firm has already developed. Tengelman, a large German retailer, has established a strong base of activities in Hungary, using its knowledge of retailing developed in its home market.

Unfavourable trends in the marketing environment at home, or favourable trends in other countries, may make international marketing particularly attractive. For example, population growth in many of the markets in the Western European countries has slowed and income is also levelling off. In most other places in the world, populations are increasing rapidly and incomes are rising. For many firms, growth, and perhaps even survival, will come only by taking aim at more distant customers.

MARKET SEGMENTATION

Market grid is a visual aid to market segmentation

It helps to picture a market as a rectangle with boxes that represent the smaller, more homogeneous product markets. Exhibit 6–2, for example, represents the broad product market of bicycle riders. The boxes show different submarkets. One submarket might focus on people who want basic transportation, another on people who want exercise, and so on.

Segmenting is an aggregating process

Marketing-oriented managers think of segmenting as an aggregating process, clustering together people with similar needs into a market segment. A market segment is a (relatively) similar group of customers who will respond to a marketing mix in the same way. For example, in Exhibit 6–2 the 'environmentalists' are bike riders who are motivated to use the bicycle, partly at least because of a desire to protect their environment. These

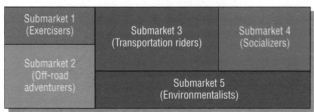

Broad product market (or generic market) name goes here
(The bicycle-riders product market)

Exhibit 6–2 A Market Grid Diagram with Submarkets

riders would be attracted by advertising that stressed the role of the bicycle in reducing exhaust emissions, and would be influenced by other green issues such as maintaining the countryside. The promotional campaigns developed for this group would feature these aspects of bike ownership strongly. In contrast the off-road adventurers would respond more to advertising that stressed the adventure element in bike usage, featuring cross-country activity. This group would be less concerned about environmental issues and more concerned with the durability of the bicycle and its ability to handle rough ground.

Incidentally one of the problems is that it would be difficult for the same bicycle manufacturer to appeal to both segments, if 'environmentalists' were also concerned about the impact of off-road adventurers on the countryside. This type of conflict between the apparent needs of different segments means that companies often have to choose to serve some segments and exclude others.

Clusters of customers

Here, the emphasis is on looking for similarities rather than basic differences in needs. Customers may have unique requirements. In an ideal world the company might like to meet each customer's requirements in a unique way. However, this would be too costly, and many people would not be able to afford the prices which manufacturers would have to charge to recover their costs. In some cases companies are now encouraging customers to select their unique product specification. Computer companies such as Dell and Gateway allow the customer to specify the exact features of the computer and then the company assembles and delivers it. The norm in consumer markets is that companies

seek to identify distinct segments of the market that they can serve effectively with the same marketing mix.

A few products are tailored to meet individual customer requirements

In some markets companies do not segment in this way. For example, in many business markets a manufacturer will often develop a unique product or service to meet an individual customer's needs, for example a new computer system, while in a consumer market, a customer who is willing to pay more might go to a tailor to get a suit made that is fitted exactly to his or her individual measurements. In many markets today increasing emphasis is on developing a company's skills so that individual needs can be met increasingly on an individual basis, while still keeping costs down. We discuss some of these approaches, termed mass customization later on in this book.

Customer needs provide the starting point for market segmentation

Consider a product market in which a customer's needs differ on two important segmenting dimensions: need for status and need for dependability. This is shown in Exhibit 6–3A, where each dot shows a person's position on the two dimensions. While each person's position is unique, many of them are similar in terms of how much status and dependability they want. So the segmentation approach would aggregate these people into three (an arbitrary number) relatively homogeneous submarkets—A, B and C. Group A might be called 'status oriented' and Group C 'dependability oriented'. Members of Group B want both and might be called the 'demanders'.

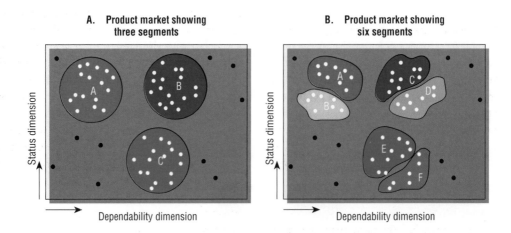

Exhibit 6–3 Every Individual Has His or Her Own Unique Position in a Market—Those with Similar Positions Can be Aggregated into Potential Target Markets

What are the limits of aggregation?

When segmenting markets, the desire is to aggregate individual customers into some workable number of relatively homogeneous target markets and then treat each target market differently. Look again at Exhibit 6–3A. Remember that three arbitrary segments were derived. As Exhibit 6–3B shows, there may really be six segments. Does this broad product market consist of three segments or six segments? Another difficulty with segmenting is that some potential customers just do not fit neatly into market segments. For example, not everyone in Exhibit 6–3B was put into one of the groups. Forcing them into one of the groups would have made these segments more heterogeneous and, as a consequence, harder to please. Further, forming additional segments for them probably would not be profitable. They are too few and not very similar in terms of the two dimensions. These people are simply too unique to be catered for and may have to be ignored, unless they are willing to pay a high price for special treatment. The number of segments that should be formed depends more on judgement than on some scientific rule. But the following guidelines can help.

Criteria for segmenting a broad product market

Ideally, effective market segments meet the following criteria:

1. *Homogeneous (similar) within*—the customers in a market segment should be as similar as possible with respect to their likely responses to marketing mix variables *and* their segmenting dimensions.
2. *Heterogeneous (different) between*—the customers in different segments should be as different as possible with respect to their likely responses to marketing mix variables *and* their segmenting dimensions.
3. *Substantial*—the segment should be big enough to be profitable.
4. *Operational*—the segmenting dimensions should be useful for identifying customers and deciding on marketing mix variables.

It is especially important that segments be *operational*. This leads marketers to include demographic dimensions such as age, income, location and family size. Information on these dimensions is usually readily available, and it is can be very useful in determining the size of markets and planning marketing mixes. In fact, it is difficult to make some place and promotion decisions without such information.

Avoid segmenting dimensions that have no practical operational use. A personality trait such as moodiness, for example, might be found among the traits of heavy buyers of a product, but how could this fact be used? Salespeople cannot give a personality test to each buyer. Similarly, advertising media buyers or copywriters could not make much use of this information. So although moodiness might be related in some way to previous purchases, it would not be a useful dimension for segmenting.

WHAT DIMENSIONS ARE USED TO SEGMENT MARKETS?

Segmenting dimensions guide marketing mix planning

Market segmentation forces a marketing manager to decide which product-market dimensions might be useful for planning marketing strategies. The dimensions should help guide marketing mix planning. Exhibit 6–4 shows the basic kinds of dimensions and their probable effect on the four Ps. Ideally, we would like to describe any potential product market in terms of all three types of customer-related dimensions, plus a product type description, because these dimensions will help us to develop better marketing mixes.

Many segmenting dimensions may be considered

Customers can be described by many specific dimensions. Exhibit 6–5 gives examples of some of the dimensions that are useful for segmenting consumer markets. As Exhibit 6–5 shows, some of these are behavioural dimensions and others are geographic and demographic dimensions. Exhibit 6–6 shows some additional dimensions for segmenting markets when the customers are businesses, government agencies or other types of organizations. Regardless of whether customers are final consumers or organizations, segmenting a broad product market may require using several different dimensions at the same time. Which ones are most important will depend on the specific product market.

With so many possible segmenting dimensions, and knowing that several dimensions may be needed to show what is really important in specific product markets, certain dimensions have to selected.

What are the qualifying and determining dimensions?

To select the important segmenting dimensions, it is useful to think about two different types of dimensions. Qualifying dimensions are the dimensions that are relevant to including a customer type in a product market.

Potential Target Market Dimensions	Effects on Strategy Decision Areas
1. Behavioural needs, attitudes and how present and potential goods and services fit into customers' consumption patterns.	Affects *Product* (features, packaging, product line assortment, branding) and *Promotion* (what potential customers need and want to know about the firm's offering, and what appeals should be used).
2. Urgency to get need satisfied and desire and willingness to seek information, compare and shop.	Affects *Place* (how directly products are distributed from producer to customer, how extensively they are made available, and the level of service needed) and *Price* (how much potential customers are willing to pay).
3. Geographic location and other demographic characteristics of potential customers.	Affects size of *Target Markets* (economic potential), *Place* (where products should be made available), and *Promotion* (where and to whom to target advertising and personal selling).

Exhibit 6–4 Possible Relation of Potential Target Market Dimensions to Marketing Strategy Decision Areas

Behavioural

Needs	Economic, functional, physiological, psychological, social, and more detailed needs.
Benefits sought	Situation specific, but to satisfy specific or general needs.
Thoughts	Favourable or unfavourable attitudes, interests, opinions, beliefs.
Rate of use	Heavy, medium, light, non-users.
Purchase relationship	Positive and ongoing; intermittent, no relationship, bad relationship.
Brand familiarity	Insistence, preference, recognition, non-recognition, rejection.
Kind of shopping	Convenience, comparison shopping, speciality, none (unsought product).
Type of problem-solving	Routinized response, limited, extensive.
Information required	Low, medium, high.

Geographic

Region of world, country	North America (United States, Canada), Europe (France, Italy, Germany), and so on.
Region in country	In the UK: Scotland, Wales, Northern Ireland, North-East England, North-West England, The Midlands, South-East England, South-West England.
Size of city	No city; population under 5000; 5000–19 999; 20 000–49 999; 50 000–99 999; 100 000–249 999; 250 000–499 999; 500 000–999 999; 1 000 000–3 999 999; 4 000 000 or over.

Demographic

Income	Under £5000; £5000–£9999; £10 000–£14 999; £15 000–£19 999; £20 000–29 999; £30 000–£39 999; £40 000–£59 999; £60 000 and over.
Sex	Male, female.
Age	Infant, under 6; 6–11, 12–17; 18–24; 25–34; 35–49; 50–64; 65 or over.
Family size	1, 2, 3–4, 5 or more.
Family life cycle	Young, single, young, married, no children; young, married, youngest child under 6; young, married, youngest child over 6; older, married, with children; older, married, no children under 18; older, single; other variations for single parents, divorced, etc.
Occupation	Professional and technical; managers, officials, and proprietors; clerical sales; craftspeople, foremen; operatives; farmers; retired; students; housewives; unemployed.
Education	Secondary school; third level; higher degree.
Race	White, Black, Hispanic origin, American Indian, Asian, Multiracial, and so on.
Social class	A, B, C^1, C^2, D, E.

Exhibit 6–5 Possible Segmenting Dimensions and Typical Breakdowns for Consumer Markets

Kind of relationship	Weak loyalty → strong loyalty to vendor
	Single source → multiple vendors
	'Arm's length' dealings → close partnership
	No reciprocity → complete reciprocity
Type of customer	Manufacturer, service producer, government agency, military, non-profit, wholesaler or retailer (when end user) and so on.
Demographics	Geographic location (region of world, country, region within country, urban → rural)
	Size (number of employees, sales volume)
	Primary business or industry (North American Industry Classification System)
	Number of facilities
How customer will use product	Installations, components, accessories, raw materials, supplies, professional services
	Decentralized → centralized
Type of buying situation	Buyer → multiple buying influence
	Straight rebuy → modified rebuy → new-task buying
Purchasing methods	Vendor analysis, inspection buying, sampling buying, specification buying, competitive bids, negotiated contracts, long-term contracts

Exhibit 6–6 Possible Segmenting Dimensions for Business/Organizational Markets

Determining dimensions are the dimensions that actually affect the customer's purchase of a specific product or brand in a product market. A prospective car buyer, for example, has to have enough money, or credit, to buy a car and insure it. The buyer must also have a driver's licence. This still does not guarantee a purchase. There must be a real need such as a job that requires a car or children that have to be taken to school. This need may motivate the purchase of *some* car. But these qualifying dimensions are not determining with respect to what specific brand or model car the person might buy. That would depend on more specific interests such as the kind of safety, performance or appearance the customer wants. Determining dimensions related to these needs will affect what specific car the customer purchases.

Determining dimensions may be very specific

How specific the determining dimensions are depends on whether the focus is on a general product type or a specific brand. See Exhibit 6–7. The more specific the focus, the more particular the determining dimensions may be. In a particular case, the determining dimensions may seem minor but they are important because they *are* the determining dimensions. In the car status-seekers market, for example, paint colours or the brand name may determine which cars people buy.

Internet Exercise

Courtyard by Marriott targets business travellers. Visit the Marriott web site **(www.marriott.com)** and identify the qualifying and determining dimensions for a business person choosing Courtyard over Marriott's other hotel options.

Qualifying dimensions are important

The qualifying dimensions help to identify the core features that must be offered to everyone in a product market. Qualifying and determining dimensions work together in marketing strategy planning. Note that each different submarket within a broad product market may be motivated by a different set of dimensions. In the snack-food market, for example, health food enthusiasts are interested in nutrition, dieters may care only about calories, and economical family shoppers, with more than average numbers of children, may want volume to fill them up. The related submarkets might be called: health-conscious snack-food market, dieters' snack-food market and children's snack-food market. They would be in different boxes in a market grid diagram for snack-food customers.

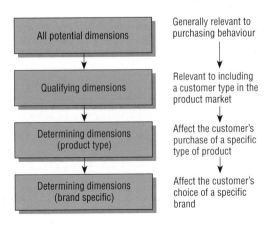

Exhibit 6–7 Finding the Relevant Segmenting Dimensions

Fiat has a range of cars for different market segments. The Fiat Seicento is produced for singles and families with small children.

Ethical issues in selecting segmenting dimensions

Marketing managers sometimes face ethical decisions when selecting segmenting dimensions. Problems may arise if a firm targets customers who are, in some way, at a disadvantage in dealing with the firm, or who are unlikely to see the negative effects of their own choices. For example, cigarette manufacturers have been criticized for targeting young teenage smokers with new brands. Sometimes a marketing manager must decide whether a firm should serve customers it really doesn't want to serve. For example, some hospitals only want to serve patients who do not smoke. They reason that the non-smokers have a better chance of survival from life-threatening surgery. Others discourage parents from bringing sick children to accident and emergency in the middle of the night. Different people may have very different opinions about what segmenting dimensions are ethical in a given situation. A marketing manager needs to take into consideration not only his or her own views, but also the views of other groups in society. Even when there is no clear answer about what is 'right', negative publicity may be very damaging.

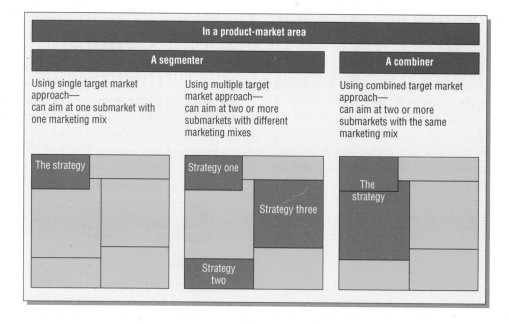

Exhibit 6–8 Target Marketers Have Specific Aims

TARGETING

Target marketers aim at specific targets

Given the idea that broad product markets may have submarkets, target marketers usually have a choice among many possible target markets. There are three basic ways of developing market-oriented strategies in a broad product market.

1. The single target market approach—segmenting the market and picking one of the homogeneous segments as the firm's target market.
2. The multiple target market approach—segmenting the market and choosing two or more segments, each of which will be treated as a separate target market needing a different marketing mix.
3. The combined target market approach—combining two or more submarkets into one larger target market as a basis for one strategy.

Note that all three approaches involve target marketing. They all aim at specific, clearly defined target markets. See Exhibit 6–8. For convenience, we will call people who follow the first two approaches the 'segmenters' and the people who use the third approach 'combiners'.

Combiners try to satisfy 'pretty well'

Combiners try to increase the size of their target markets by combining two or more segments. Combiners look at various submarkets for similarities rather than differences. Then they try to extend or modify their basic offering to appeal to these 'combined' customers with just one marketing mix. For example, combiners may try a new package, more service, a new brand or new flavours. But even if they make product or other marketing mix changes, they are not trying to uniquely satisfy smaller submarkets. Instead, combiners try to improve the general appeal of their marketing mix to appeal to a bigger 'combined' target market.

A combined target market approach may help achieve some economies of scale. It may also require less investment than developing different marketing mixes for different segments. That is especially attractive if a firm has limited resources. These potential benefits may make combining very appealing and may make it seem less risky.

Too much combining is risky

It is tempting to aim at larger combined markets instead of using different marketing mixes for smaller segmented markets. Care needs to be taken to avoid aggregating too far. As the target market enlarges, it becomes less homogeneous and individual differences within each submarket may begin to outweigh the similarities. This makes it harder to develop marketing mixes that can do an effective job of reaching and satisfying potential customers within each of the submarkets. A market has that been aggregated too far is vulnerable to the continual risk of innovative businesses chipping away at the various segments of the combined target market by offering more attractive marketing mixes to more homogeneous submarkets.

Segmenters try to satisfy 'very well'

Segmenters aim at one or more homogeneous segments and try to develop a different marketing mix for each segment. Segmenters usually do more adjusting of their marketing mixes for each target market, perhaps making basic changes in the product itself because they want to satisfy each segment very well. Instead of assuming that the whole market consists of a fairly similar set of customers (like the mass marketer does) or merging various submarkets together (like the combiner), a segmenter sees submarkets with their own demand curves, as shown in Exhibit 6–9. Segmenters believe that aiming at one, or some, of these smaller markets will provide greater satisfaction to the target customers and greater profit potential for the firm.

Segmenting may produce more sales

Note that segmenters are not settling for a smaller sales potential. Instead, segmenters hope to increase sales by getting a much larger share of the business in the market(s) they target. With segmentation, the target market may be so well satisfied that there is no real competition.

AFG Industries, a company that manufactures glass, had a small market share when it was trying to sell glass in the construction market. Then AFG's marketing managers focused on the special needs of firms that used tempered and coloured glass in their own production. AFG used a multiple target market approach and planned marketing mixes for 'niche' segments that didn't get attention from the bigger producers. Because of careful segmenting, AFG now sells 70 per cent of the glass for microwave oven doors and 75 per cent of the glass for shower enclosures and patio table tops. AFG also earns the best profit margins in its industry.

To segment or combine?

Which approach should be used? This depends on the firm's resources, the nature of competition, and—most important—the similarity of customer needs, attitudes and buying behaviour. In general, it is usually safer to

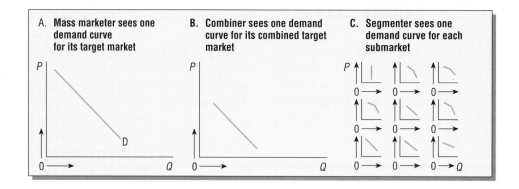

Exhibit 6–9 There May be Different Demand Curves in Different Market Segments

segment, that is, to try to satisfy some customers *very* well instead of many just *fairly* well. That is why many firms use the single or multiple target market approach instead of the combined target market approach. Procter & Gamble, for example, offers many products that seem to compete directly with each other. However, P&G offers tailormade marketing mixes to each submarket that is large enough, and sufficiently profitable, to deserve a separate marketing mix. This approach can be extremely effective but may not be possible for a smaller firm with more limited resources.

A smaller firm may have to use the single target market approach, aiming all its efforts at the one submarket niche where it sees the best opportunity.

Target marketers develop and implement complete strategies and are not limited to the segmenting tasks. In practice, this means that cost considerations probably encourage more aggregating, to obtain economies of scale, while demand considerations suggest less aggregating, to satisfy needs more exactly. Profit is the balancing point. It determines how unique a marketing mix the firm can afford to offer to a particular group.

A SEVEN-STEP APPROACH TO SEGMENTING PRODUCT MARKETS

A logical, seven-step approach to market segmentation will now be described. Chapter 5 discussed how marketing research could help fine tune some of the decisions made with this approach. Even without additional research this approach is effective and has led to successful strategies. It is especially useful for finding the determining dimensions for product types. When the need is to focus on dimensions for specific brands, especially when there are several competing brands, more sophisticated techniques may be needed. Each step of this approach will be reviewed separately, its importance explained and an ongoing example used to show how each step works. The example concerns people who need accommodation, in particular, the market for hotel guests.

1. Name the broad product market
First, the firm must decide in which broad product market it wishes to operate. This may be stated in the firm's objectives. Or if the firm is already successful in some product market, its current position might be a good starting point. It is better to build on the firm's

strengths while avoiding its weaknesses and the strengths of competitors. Available resources, both human and financial, will limit the possibilities, especially if the firm is just getting established.

Example. A firm has been building small hotels on the periphery of a large city and renting rooms to travellers. A narrow view, considering only the firm's current products and markets, might lead the firm to think only of more small motels. A wider view might see such hotels as only a small part of the total hotel market or even the total overnight accommodation needs market in the firm's geographic area. Taking a yet wider view, the firm could consider expanding to other geographic areas, or moving into other kinds of products such as apartments or restaurants. There has to be some balance between naming the product market too narrowly (same old product, same old market) and naming it too broadly (the whole world and all its needs). Here, the firm decided on the whole market of hotel users in one city because this is where the firm had some experience.

2. List potential customers' needs

The next step involved relates to the needs of all of the potential customers in the broad product market. These should be identified, perhaps by a 'brainstorming' exercise. Possible needs can be derived by thinking about *why* some people buy the present offerings in this broad product market.

Example. In the broad hotel guest market, it is fairly easy to list some possible needs: a private room and furnishings, safety and security, convenience (to something), parking, food and drink, entertainment, space for recreation, attractive interiors and good maintenance and service to assure trouble-free and comfortable stays.

3. Form homogeneous submarkets— i.e. 'narrow' product markets

Assuming that some people will have different needs from others, each submarket's needs can be used as a basis for forming different submarkets. This can be started by forming one submarket around some typical type of customer and then aggregate similar people into this segment as long as the same marketing mix could satisfy them. The important need dimensions and customer-related characteristics (including demographic characteristics) of each submarket should be ascertained. This will facilitate decisions on whether each new customer-type should be included in the first segment. This will also help later when naming the submarkets. For example, if the people in one market are young families looking for a good place to stay while on holiday, naming the submarket as 'family holiday-makers' indicates what the submarket wants and why.

People who are not homogeneous, that is who do not fit in the first segment, should be used to form a new submarket.

Example. A young family on holiday probably wants a hotel to provide a clean room that is large enough for adults and children, convenient parking, a location that is near tourist attractions, a pool for recreation with a lifeguard for safety, entertainment in the room (a TV and video movies) and perhaps a refrigerator or vending machine for snacks. A travelling executive, on the other hand, has quite different interests—a room with a desk, but *also* a good restaurant, fast transportation to and from an airport, more services (room service, dry cleaning, a way to send and receive faxes, and fast check-in)— all away from distracting noise from children.

4. Identify the determining dimensions

The need dimensions for each possible segment should be reviewed and the determining dimensions identified. Although the qualifying dimensions are important, perhaps reflecting core needs that should be satisfied, they are not the *determining* dimensions. Careful thinking about the needs and attitudes of the people in each possible segment will help to identify which are the determining dimensions. They may not seem very different from market to market, but if they are determining to those people then they *are* determining!

Example. With hotel customers, basic comfort needs (heating and cooling, a good bed, a clean bathroom), a telephone for communicating and safety and security are probably not determining. Everyone has these qualifying needs. Looking beyond these common needs helps to ascertain the determining dimensions, such as different needs with respect to recreation, restaurant facilities services and so on. See Exhibit 6–10.

5. Label the possible product markets

A market grid is a good way to help visualize the broad product market and its narrow product markets. The market grid may be drawn as a rectangle with boxes inside representing smaller, more homogeneous segments, as in Exhibit 6–10. The whole rectangle represents the broad product market, as labelled. Each of the boxes can be thought of as narrow product markets. Since the markets within a broad product market usually require very different dimensions, the same two dimensions should not be used to name the markets or to label the sides of the market grid boxes. Rather, just think of the grid as showing the relative sizes of product market segments. Then each segment can be labelled with its name.

Example. The following overnight guest submarkets can be identified: family holiday-makers, up-market executives, budget-oriented travellers, resort seekers, event-centred visitors, and long-stay guests. See Exhibit 6–10. Note that each segment has a different set of determining dimensions (benefits sought) that follows directly from customer type and needs.

6. Evaluate why product-market segments behave as they do

After naming the markets (step 5), the behaviour of each should be considered to understand how and why these markets behave the way they do. Different segments may have similar—but slightly different—needs. This may explain why some competitive offerings are more successful than others. It also can lead to splitting and renaming some segments.

Need dimensions (benefits sought)	Customer-related characteristics	Nickname of product market
1	Comfort, security, privacy, *family fun, recreation (playground, pool), entertainment (games room, films), child care and snacks.*	Couples and single parents with children who want a fun family experience; young, active and energetic.	**Family holiday-makers**
2	Comfort, security, privacy, *distinctive furnishings, attentive staff, prestige, status, easy access to airport and business meetings, express check-in and check-out, quality dining.*	Senior business executives with a big expense account who want to be 'pampered' with 'very important person' service and accommodations.	**Upmarket executives**
3	Comfort, security, privacy, *economy (no 'extras' to increase cost), convenience (to low-cost restaurants, motorways), free parking.*	Young people, retired couples, and salespeople who travel by car, pay their own expenses, and want a simple place to stay for one night—before moving on.	**Budget-oriented travellers**
4	Comfort, security, privacy, *home-like amenities (kitchenette, separate living room), laundry and exercise facilities, pleasant grounds, entertainment.*	Business people, out-of-town visitors, and others who stay in the same motel for a week or more; want many of the comforts they have at home.	**Long-stay guests**
5	Comfort, security, privacy, *socializing (lounges and public spaces), conference facilities (including catering for group meals), message and transportation services.*	Individuals who are attending events scheduled at the motel (a business meeting or conference, family reunion, etc.), often for several days.	**Event-centered visitors**
6	Comfort, security, privacy, *relaxation (golf), pleasure (fine dining, whirlpool bath), attractive views (elaborate landscaping), fun, variety (information/arrangements for theatre).*	Sophisticated couples with leisure time to relax and have 'adult' fun; they want to show their individuality and have discretionary income to spend.	**Resort seekers**

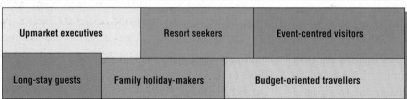

Exhibit 6–10 Segmenting the Broad Market for Hotel Guests in an Urban Area

Example. The resort seekers might have been treated as family holiday-makers in step 5 because the 'family' characteristic did not seem important. But with more thought, we see that while some of the resort seekers are interested in the same sort of fun and recreation as the family holiday-makers, the focus of the resort seekers is on adult fun, not activities with children. For them, getting away from the family holiday-makers' children may be part of the escape they want. Further, although the resort seekers are a higher income group similar to the up-market executives, they have different needs from the executives and probably should be treated as a separate market. The point here is that these market differences might only be discovered in step 6. It is at this step that the 'resort seekers' market would be named and a related row created to describe the new segment.

7. Estimate the size of each product-market segment

Remember, the objective is to find *profitable* opportunities. So now data on the product markets should be tied to demographic data, or other customer related characteristics, to make it easier to estimate the size of these markets. It is too early to estimate likely sales yet. Sales will depend on the competition as well as the particulars of the marketing mix. The more that is known about the possible target markets, the easier will be the subsequent tasks of forecasting and marketing mix planning. Fortunately, much data on the size of markets is available, especially demographic data. Introducing demographics adds a note of economic reality. Some possible product markets may have almost no market potential. Without some hard facts, the risks of aiming at such markets are great.

To refine the market grid, the inside boxes should be redrawn to give a better indication of the size of the various segments. This will help to highlight the larger and perhaps more attractive opportunities. Remember the relative sizes of the markets might vary depending on what geographic areas are considered. The market sizes might vary from city to city or from one country to another.

Market dimensions suggest the appropriate mix

Once all seven steps have been followed it should be possible to see the outlines of the kinds of marketing mixes that would appeal to the various markets. For example, based on the determining dimensions (benefits sought) in Exhibit 6–10, a hotel designed to appeal to the up-market executives might offer rooms with quality furniture, including a desk and chair for reading, a high-quality restaurant, extensive room service, special secretarial services (copying, dictation and fax) on an extra-cost basis, limousine pickup at the airport, someone to help with travel problems and pre-cleared check-in and check-out. The hotel might also provide a quiet bar and exercise room

and extras such as thick bath towels and a valet service for free shoe cleaning. It might also offer a business library and a free newspaper delivered every morning. Of course, the price for this special treatment would be high. It is also useful to think about what the executives would not want: facilities shared by families with young children!

While the discussion above focuses on the up-market executives, profitable marketing mixes might be developed for the other segments as well. For example, Hilton International has been successful with facilities designed for event-centred visitors. During the week many of their customers are there for business conferences, but on the weekend the focus is often on family events, such as meals and receptions related to a wedding or family reunion. In the United Kingdom, a relatively recent phenomenon is that of budget hotels. These are designed for budget-oriented travellers and provide basic, value-for-money accommodation. Typical of these budget hotels are Travel Inn, Holiday Inn Express, Formule 1, Ibis Lodges and Campanille.[4]

SEVEN-STEP APPROACH APPLIES IN BUSINESS MARKETS

A similar seven-step approach can be used for markets where the customers, or final users, are business organizations rather than individual consumers. The major change is in the first step of selecting the broad product market. The needs in business markets, especially in industrial settings, are often different. Business organizations usually make purchases to meet basic functional needs. Their demands are derived from final consumer demands, so the business or non-profit organization market is concerned with purchases that help produce finished goods or services. The functions these customers are concerned about include, but are not limited to, forming, bending, grading, digging, cutting, heating, cooling, conducting, transmitting, containing, filling, cleaning, analysing, sorting, training and insuring. They may buy physical goods and do the work themselves, or they may pay for someone else to provide the service as well.

Defining the relevant broad product market using both geographic dimensions and basic functional needs usually ensures that the focus is broad enough, that is, not exclu-

sively on the product now being supplied to present customers. But it also keeps the focus from vaguely expanding to 'all the business needs in the world'. As with consumer markets, it is better to focus on needs satisfied by products, *not* product characteristics themselves. New ways of satisfying the need may be found and completely surprise and upset current producers, if the product market is defined too narrowly. For example, desktop computers and printers now compete in what some producers thought was the typewriter market. Telephone calls, fax machines and electronic mail are replacing letters, further reducing the need for typing. Perhaps this broad product market is concerned with thought processing and transmitting. Certainly, the typewriter-view is too narrow. Market-oriented strategy planners try to avoid surprises that result from such tunnel vision.

After the first step in the seven-step approach, the other steps are similar to segmenting consumer markets. The main difference is that segmenting dimensions like those shown in Exhibit 6–6 and discussed in Chapter 4 are used.[5]

SEGMENTING INTERNATIONAL MARKETS

Success in international marketing requires even more attention to segmenting. There are over 140 nations with their own unique cultures! There can be significant differences in language, customs (including busi-

ness ethics), beliefs, religions, race and income distribution patterns from one country to another. The discussion of these in Chapter 3 should have indicated that the additional differences could complicate the segmenting process. What makes it even worse is that there is often less dependable data as firms move into international markets. While the number of variables increases, the quantity and quality of data decrease. This is one reason why some firms insist that local operations and decisions be handled by locals. They, at least, have a 'feel' for their markets.

Segmenting international markets may require more dimensions. But a practical method adds just one step before the seven-step approach discussed above. See Exhibit 6–11. First, segment by country or region— looking at demographic, cultural and other characteristics, including stage of economic development. This may help find reasonably similar submarkets. Then, depending on whether the firm is aiming at final consumers or business markets, the seven-step approach can be applied.

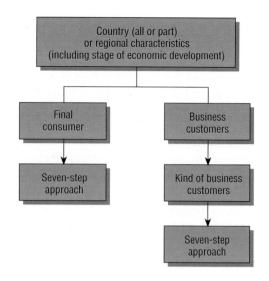

Exhibit 6–11 Segmenting in International Markets

MORE SOPHISTICATED TECHNIQUES

The seven-step approach is inexpensive, logical and practical. Computer-aided methods can contribute to the process. A detailed review of the possibilities is beyond the scope of this book. A brief discussion of some approaches will give an overview of how computer-aided methods work.

Clustering usually requires a computer

Clustering techniques try to find similar patterns within sets of data. Clustering groups customers who are similar on their segmenting dimensions into homogeneous segments. Clustering approaches use computers to do what previously was done with much intuition and judgement. The data to be clustered might include such dimensions as demographic characteristics, the importance of different needs, attitudes towards the product and past buying behaviour. The computer searches all the data for homogeneous groups of people. When it finds them, marketers study the dimensions of the people in the groups to see why the computer clustered them together. The results sometimes suggest new, or at least better, marketing strategies.

A cluster analysis of the toothpaste market, for example, might show that some people buy toothpaste because it tastes good (the sensory segment), while others are concerned with the effect of clean teeth and fresh breath on their social image (the sociables). Others are worried about decay or tartar (the worriers) and some are just interested in the best value for their money (the value seekers). Each of these market segments calls for a different marketing mix, although some of the four Ps may be similar.

Finally, a marketing manager has to decide which one (or more) of these segments will be the firm's target market(s). Clustering techniques are only an *aid* to the manager. Judgement is still needed to develop an original list of possible dimensions and then to name the resulting clusters.

Trade-off analysis helps develop the marketing mix

Another computer-based approach that is often used in segmenting markets is trade-off analysis (sometimes called 'conjoint analysis'—a technique that helps to determine how important certain elements of the firm's marketing mix are to customers. The name for this approach comes from the idea that it shows how much money, in terms of a higher price, a customer would 'trade-off' for a particular product feature.

POSITIONING HELPS TO IDENTIFY PRODUCT-MARKET OPPORTUNITIES

Positioning is another important approach that shows how customers locate proposed and/or present brands in a market. Like cluster analysis and trade-off analysis, it requires some formal marketing research but may be helpful when competitive offerings are quite similar. The results are usually plotted on graphs to help show where the products are positioned in relation to competing products. Usually, the products' positions are related to two or three product features that are important to the target customers. Assuming the picture is reasonably accurate, managers then decide whether they want to leave their product (and marketing mix) alone or reposition it. This may mean *physical changes* in the product or simply *image changes based on promotion*. For example, most beer drinkers can't pick out their favourite brand in a blind test—so physical changes might not be necessary (and might not even work) to reposition a brand of beer.

The graphs for positioning decisions are obtained by asking product users to make judgements about different brands, including their ideal brand, and then using computer programs to summarize the ratings and plot the results. The details of positioning techniques, sometimes called 'perceptual mapping', are beyond the scope of this text. Exhibit 6–12 shows the possibilities.

Exhibit 6–12 shows the 'product space' for different brands of soap using two dimensions—the extent to which consumers think the soaps moisturize and deodorize their skin. For example, consumers see Dial as quite low on moisturizing but high on deodorizing. Lifebuoy and Dial are close together, implying that consumers think of them as similar on these characteristics. Dove is viewed as different and is further away on the graph. Remember that positioning maps are based on *customers' perceptions*: the actual characteristics of the products (as determined by a chemical test) might be different. The circles on Exhibit 6–12 show different sets (submarkets) of consumers clustered near their ideal

soap preferences. Groups of respondents with a similar ideal product are circled to show apparent customer concentrations. In this graph, the size of the circles suggests the size of the segments for the different ideals.

Ideal clusters 1 and 2 are the largest and are close to two popular brands—Dial and Lever 2000. It appears that customers in cluster 1 want more moisturizing than they see in Dial and Lifebuoy. However, exactly what these brands should do about this is not clear. Perhaps both of these brands should leave their physical products alone, but emphasize moisturizing more in their promotion to make a stronger appeal to those who want moisturizers. A marketing manager talking about this approach might simply refer to it as 'positioning the brand as a good moisturizer'.

Lava doesn't seem to satisfy any of the ideal clusters very well. Therefore, some attempt probably should be made to reposition it, either through physical or image changes. Alternatively, if Lava has really strong cleaning power, promotion might be used to encourage consumers to think more about this feature so that it will be viewed more favourably by some customers.

Note that ideal cluster 7 is not near any of the present brands. This may suggest an opportunity for introducing a new product—a strong moisturizer with some deodorizers. If some firm chooses to follow this approach, we would think of it as a segmenting effort.

Combining versus segmenting

Positioning analysis may lead a firm to combining, rather than segmenting, if managers think they can

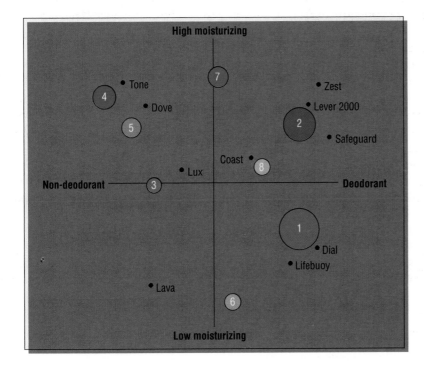

Exhibit 6–12 'Product Space' Representing Consumers' Perceptions for Different Brands of Bar Soap

make several general appeals to different parts of a combined market. For example, by varying its promotion, Coast might try to appeal to clusters 8, 1 and 2 with one product. These clusters are all quite similar (close together) in what they want in an ideal brand. On the other hand, there may be clearly defined submarkets and some parts of the market may be 'owned' by one product or brand. In this case, segmenting efforts may be practical, moving the firm's own product into another segment of the general market area where competition is weaker.

Positioning as part of broader analysis

The major value of positioning is to give managers an understanding of how customers see their market. It is a visual aid to understanding a product market. Positioning usually focuses on specific product features and, as such, is product oriented. There is the risk that important *customer-related* dimensions, including needs and attitudes, may be overlooked. However, as part of a broader analysis of target markets, positioning can be very useful. The first time such an analysis is done, managers may be shocked to see how much customers' perceptions of a market differ from their own, and for this reason alone, positioning is useful.

Premature emphasis on product features is a risk if the process starts with a product-oriented definition of a market, as in the soap example. This leads to positioning soaps against soaps. This can lead to a firm overlooking more basic shifts in markets. For example, bars might be losing popularity to liquid soaps. Or other products, such as bath oils or facial cleansers, may be part of the relevant competition. Such shifts would not be seen by looking only at alternative bar soap brands: the focus is just too narrow.

As is emphasized throughout the text, an understanding of potential needs and attitudes is required when planning marketing strategies. If customers are treating quite different products as substitutes, then a firm has to position itself against those products. It must avoid focusing on physical product characteristics that are not the determining dimensions of the target market.

SUMMARY

Creative strategy planning is needed for survival in our increasingly competitive markets. This chapter considered four basic types of opportunity—marketing penetration, market development, new product development and diversification—with special emphasis on why opportunities in international markets should be considered. We also discussed how to find attractive target market opportunities. The shortcomings of a too narrow product-oriented view of markets were emphasized.

Market segmentation, the process of naming and then segmenting broad product markets to find potentially attractive target markets, was discussed. Some people try to segment markets by starting with the mass market and then dividing it into smaller submarkets based on a few dimensions. This can lead to poor results. Instead, market segmentation should first focus on a broad product market, and then group similar customers into homogeneous submarkets. The more similar the potential customers are, the larger the submarkets can be. Four criteria for evaluating possible product-market segments were presented.

Once a broad product market has been segmented, marketing managers can use one of three approaches to market-oriented strategy planning: (1) the single target market approach, (2) the multiple target market approach and (3) the combined target market approach. In general, segmentation is advocated rather than an aggregation approach.

We discussed a practical—'rough-and-ready'—seven-step approach to market segmentation that works for both consumer and industrial markets and which, with minor additions, works well for international markets. It is also possible to use computer-aided segmenting approaches such as clustering techniques, trade-off analysis and positioning.

Marketing managers should understand the markets in which their business operates. By creatively segmenting markets, opportunities arise, even breakthrough opportunities, enabling firms to succeed against aggressive competitors offering similar products. Segmenting is basic to target marketing. It is through the practice of segmentation that more meaningful market segments are identified.

QUESTIONS AND PROBLEMS

1. Explain the major differences among the four basic types of opportunities discussed in the text and cite examples for two of these types of opportunities.

2. Explain why a firm may want to pursue a market penetration opportunity before pursuing one involving product development or diversification.

3. In your own words, explain several reasons why marketing managers should consider international markets when evaluating possible opportunities.

4. Give an example of a foreign-made product (other than car) that you personally have purchased. Give some reasons why you purchased that product. Do you think that there was a good opportunity for a domestic firm to get your business? Explain why or why not.

5. Explain what market segmentation is.

6. List the types of potential segmenting dimensions and explain which you would try to apply first, second and third in a particular situation. If the nature of the situation would affect your answer, explain how.

7. Explain why segmentation efforts based on attempts to divide the mass market using a few demographic dimensions may be very disappointing.

8. Illustrate the concept that segmenting is an aggregating process by referring to the admissions policies of your own university.

9. Evaluate the six submarkets identified in the market for hotels (Exhibit 6–10) with respect to the four criteria for selecting good market segments.

10. Review the types of segmenting dimensions listed in Exhibits 6–5 and 6–6, and select the ones you think should be combined to fully explain the market segment you personally would be in if you were planning to buy a new watch today. List several dimensions and try to develop a shorthand name, such as 'fashion-oriented', to describe your own personal market segment. Then try to estimate what proportion of the total watch market would be accounted for by your market segment. Next, explain if there are any offerings that come close to meeting the needs of your market. If not, what sort of a marketing mix is needed? Would it be economically attractive for anyone to try to satisfy your market segment? Why or why not?

11. Identify the determining dimension or dimensions that explain why you bought the specific brand you did in your most recent purchase of (a) soft drink, (b) shampoo, (c) shirt or blouse and (d) a larger, more expensive item, such as a bicycle, camera, boat and so on. Try to express the determining dimension(s) in terms of your own personal characteristics rather than the product's characteristics. Estimate what share of the market would probably be motivated by the same determining dimension(s).

12. Apply the seven-step approach to segmenting consumer markets to the market for off-campus apartments in your city. Then evaluate how well the needs in these market segments are being met in your geographic area. Is there an obvious breakthrough opportunity waiting for someone?

13. Explain how the first step in the seven-step approach to segmenting markets would have to be changed to apply it in industrial markets. Illustrate your answer.

14. Explain how positioning can help a marketing manager identify target market opportunities.

SUGGESTED CASES

4. Lilybank Lodge
15. Deluxe Foods Ltd

REFERENCES

1. W. Perreault and E.J. McCarthy, *Basic Marketing: A Global Managerial Approach*, 13th edn, McGraw-Hill, Boston, MA, 1999, Ch. 3.
2. A. Baxter, 'A clean sweep through Europe for Electrolux', *The Financial Times*, 3 October 1991, p. 12.
3. A. Brown, 'Adidas kicks back', *International Management*, July/August 1994, pp. 27–30.
4. J. Doward, 'Fast lane for rooms with a view of the motorway', *The Observer*, 8 November 1998, p. 8.
5. K. Helsen, K. Jedidi and W.S. DeSarbo, 'A new approach to country segmentation utilising multinational diffusion patterns', *Journal of Marketing*, October 1993, pp. 60–71; R. Abratt, 'Market segmentation practices of industrial marketers', *Industrial Marketing Management*, May 1993, pp. 79–84; S. Dibb and L. Simkin, 'Implementation problems in industrial market segmentation', *Industrial Marketing Management*, February 1994, pp. 55–64; R.L. Griffith and L.G. Pol, 'Segmenting industrial markets', *Industrial Marketing Management*, February 1994, pp. 39–46.

CHAPTER 7
Elements of Product Planning for Goods and Services

When You Finish This Chapter, You Should

1 Understand what 'Product' really means.

2 Know the key differences between pure goods and pure services.

3 Know the differences among the various consumer and business product classes.

4 Understand how the product classes can help a marketing manager plan marketing strategies.

5 Understand how product life cycles affect strategy planning.

6 Understand the important new terms (shown in colour).

Snickers—A Very International Brand

Just about every kiosk, petrol station, corner shop and retailer sells chocolate. Usually it's by the check-out counter—where consumers with a sweet tooth can buy on an impulse. And there's no shortage of choices, either. Companies like Nestlé, Cadbury, Mars and Suchard each have a line of different bars to appeal to different tastes and preferences. Mars, for example, offers varieties with familiar brand names such as Snickers, Milky Way, M&Ms and Twix.

It is difficult for new products to take loyal customers away from these venerable old brands—perhaps because it is even harder for new entrants to get retailers to allocate more shelf space. But that has not kept some firms from trying—or even succeeding. Marketing managers for Nestlés have been especially successful in developing new products. The Lion bar, for example, is one of Nestlé's strongest and most popular brands in Europe. Of course, the market for chocolate bars is not so competitive everywhere. Marketing managers for Mars, for example, got a fresh start—with less competition and greater prospects for future growth—when they decided to go into the Russian market after the breakup of the Soviet Union.

Without subsidies from the government, Russian confectionery factories didn't have hard currency to buy the imported cocoa and sugar they needed to produce high-quality chocolate. By 1992, there was virtually no locally produced chocolate in Russia. Some Turkish chocolate was available, but consumers rejected it because poor packaging allowed it to get stale before it even got to the store.

Years earlier, when Mars introduced Snickers bars in England, marketing managers changed the brand name to Marathon. They were concerned that Snickers sounded too much like knickers, a British term for women's underwear. Later, however, they changed back to Snickers so that they could promote the same brand name throughout all of Europe. Even though Russia uses a different alphabet than Western Europe, Mars stuck with the one-name policy. That meant that TV advertising had to teach consumers to recognize and pronounce the name. However, TV advertising in Russia cost about £8 000 a minute—only a fraction of the cost in the United States. And the Russian ads worked unusually well. Within a year 82 per cent of Russians recognized the Snickers name.

Now, among those who can afford luxuries such as chocolate, Snickers is a preferred chocolate bar and is one of the more affordable western status symbols. Mars has yet to make a big profit. However, as the market leader, Mars is building strong distribution channels and consumer loyalty. As incomes in Russia grow, sales and profits will as well. Establishing the Snickers name is an important step in the process.[1]

THE PRODUCT AREA INVOLVES MANY STRATEGY DECISIONS

The Snickers case highlights some important topics to be discussed in this chapter and the next. This chapter covers the issues of classifying products and the product life cycle. In Chapter 8, the focus is on new product development, branding and packaging.

In summary, these chapters address the product decisions made in the strategy planning of producers and channel members. Keep in mind that there are many decisions related to the Product area as shown in Exhibit 7–1.

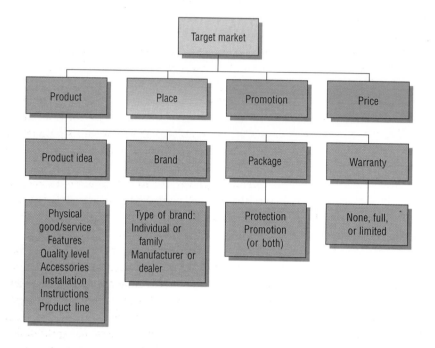

Exhibit 7–1 Strategy Planning for Product

WHAT IS A PRODUCT?

Customers buy satisfaction

First, it is useful to define what is meant by 'product'. When Renault sells a new Megane, is it just selling a certain number of nuts and bolts, some sheet metal, an engine and four wheels? When your local hardware store sells a tin of exterior paint is it just selling a tin of chemicals? When Air France sells a ticket for a flight to the Caribbean is it just selling wear and tear on an aircraft and some piloting services? The answer to all these questions is *no*. Instead, what these companies are really selling is the satisfaction, use or benefit the customer wants. All customers care about is that their cars look good and keep running. They want to protect their homes with paint, not analyse it. And when they take a trip on Air France, they really don't care how hard it is on the plane or the crew. They just want a safe, comfortable trip. In the same way, when producers and intermediaries buy a product, they are interested in the profit they can make from its purchase, through use or resale, not how the product was made.

Product means the need-satisfying offering of a firm. The idea of 'Product' as potential customer satisfaction or benefits is very important. Many business managers—trained in the production side of business—get wrapped up in the technical details. They think of Product in terms of physical components, like transistors and screws. These are important to *them*, but components have little effect on the way most customers view the product. Most customers think about products in terms of the total satisfaction they provide. Providing satisfaction may require a 'total' product offering that is really a complex combination, perhaps including the right kind of service, a physical good with the right features, useful instructions, a convenient package, a trustworthy warranty, and perhaps even a familiar name that cuts shopping risk by identifying a product that has satisfied the consumer in the past.

Product quality and customer needs

Because consumers buy satisfaction, not just parts, marketing managers must be constantly concerned with product quality. This may seem obvious, but the obvious is sometimes easy to overlook. In the 1980s, many European firms learned this lesson the hard way when Japanese, Taiwanese and Korean competitors stole market share by offering customers higher quality products.

But what does 'high quality' mean? Companies focus on better quality control in production, so that products work as they should and consumers really get what they think they are buying. But quality means more than that. From a marketing perspective, quality means a product's ability to satisfy a customer's needs or requirements. This definition focuses on the customer and how the customer thinks a product will fit some purpose. For example, the best credit card may not be the one with the highest credit limit but the one that is accepted where a consumer wants to use it. Similarly, the best quality clothing for casual wear at university or college may be a pair of jeans, not a pair of expensive designer trousers.

Among different types of jeans, the one with the strongest stitching and the most comfortable or durable fabric might be thought of as having the highest grade or *relative quality* for its product type. Marketing managers often focus on relative quality when comparing their products to competitors' offerings. However, a product with more features, or even better features, is not a high-quality product if the features are not what the target market wants or needs.

Quality and satisfaction depend on the total product offering. If biscuits get stale on the shelf because of poor packaging, the consumer will be dissatisfied. A broken button on a shirt will disappoint the customer, even if the laundry did a good job cleaning and ironing the shirt. A very fast and powerful computer is a poor-quality product if it makes occasional errors when doing arithmetic. A full-featured stereo VCR is a poor-quality product if it is hard for a consumer to programme a recording session, or if the seller does not answer the phone to respond to the customer's question.

Goods and/or services are the product

A product may be a physical *good* or a *service* or a *blend* of both. This view needs to be thoroughly understood. It is too easy to slip into a limited, physical-product point of view. We want to think of a product in terms of the needs it satisfies. If a firm's objective is to satisfy customer needs, service can be part of its product, or service alone may *be* the product and must be provided as part of a total marketing mix.

Exhibit 7–2 shows this expanded view of Product. It shows that a product can range from a 100 per cent emphasis on physical goods for commodities such as common nails to a 100 per cent emphasis on service such as advice from a lawyer. Regardless of the emphasis involved, the marketing manager must consider most of the same elements in planning products and marketing mixes. Given this, we usually won't make a distinction between goods and services but will call all of them *Products*. Sometimes, however, understanding the differences in goods and services can help to fine-tune marketing strategy planning. Some of these differences are considered next.

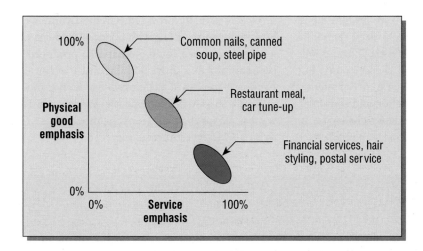

Exhibit 7–2 Examples of Possible Blends of Physical Goods and Services in a Product

DIFFERENCES IN GOODS AND SERVICES

Pure services differ from pure goods in a number of ways: services are intangible, the production and consumption of services are inseparable, and services cannot be transported or stored.

How tangible is the Product?

Because a good is a physical thing, it can be seen and touched. You can try on a Tommy Hilfegger shirt, thumb through the latest *Hello* magazine, smell Colombian coffee as it brews. A good is a *tangible* item. When it is bought the customer owns it. Before the actual purchase, it is usually relatively easy to evaluate the product.

On the other hand, a service is a deed performed by one party for another. When a customer is provided with a service, the customer cannot actually keep it. Rather, a service is experienced, used or consumed. After seeing a Touchstone Studios film, all that the customer has is a memory. The customer can ride on a ski lift in the Alps, but does not own the equipment. Services are not physical—they are *intangible*. A service cannot be held. Before purchase, it can be difficult for the customer to know exactly what they will get upon purchase.

Most products are a combination of tangible and intangible elements. BP petrol and the credit card to buy it are tangible—the credit the card grants is not. A Domino's pizza is tangible, but the fast home delivery is not. Indeed, in many cases it is the service factor that adds extra value and differentiates one goods company from another.

Is the product produced before it is sold?

Goods are usually produced in a factory and then sold. A Sony TV may be stored in a warehouse or store waiting for a buyer. By contrast, services are often sold first, then produced. Further, they are produced and consumed in the same time frame. A deed cannot be performed and then put on the shelf. Thus, goods producers may be far away from the customer, but service providers often work in the customer's presence.

The *inseparability* of the production and consumption of services gives rise to a quality challenge. In essence, the involvement of the customer and the service

employee is less reliable than the machinery in a traditional goods factory. That means that it is difficult to guarantee the level of service that the customer will receive. A worker in a Sony TV factory can be in a bad mood—and customers will never know. A faulty TV can be caught by a quality control inspector. By contrast, a rude bank clerk can drive customers away. The growing use of computers and machines in service businesses is partly an attempt to avoid this problem. An automatic teller machine is never rude but it cannot do everything.

Services can't be stored or transported

Services are perishable—they cannot be stored. This makes it harder to balance supply and demand. An example explains the problem. Belgacom, the Belgian national telephone company, is a major supplier of long-distance telephone services. Even when demand is high, during peak business hours or on Mother's Day, customers expect the service to be available. They don't want to hear 'Sorry, all lines are busy'. So Belgacom must have enough equipment and employees to deal with peak demand times. However, when customers are not making many calls, Belgacom facilities are idle. Belgacom might be able to save money with less capacity (equipment and people), but then it will sometimes have to face dissatisfied customers.

It is often difficult to have economies of scale when the product emphasis is on service. If a firm is serving a large group of customers, it may be able to justify adding more or better equipment, facilities, or people to do a better job. Services can't be produced in large, economical quantities and then transported to customers. In addition, *services often have to be produced in the presence of the customer*. So service suppliers often need duplicate equipment and staff at places where the service is actually provided. Crédit Lyonnaise sells investment advice along with financial products worldwide. That advice could, perhaps, be produced more economically in a single building in Paris. But Crédit Lyonnaise uses small facilities all over France and other countries so as to be conveniently available. Customers want a personal touch from the stockbroker telling them how to invest their money.[2]

In contrast to goods, services are said to be relatively intangible, inseparable and perishable. These characteristics are evident in the service of hair dressing. In addition, the hair dressing case allows us to see the marketing implications of the characteristics of services.

Imagine that you have just moved to a particular town or city. After a short period there, you decide that you need a hair cut and are considering having it restyled. How do you decide which salon to go to to book an appointment? Local friends and contacts may be asked for a recommendation. We might actually get an impression of the different hair salons by the hair styles of the people who recommend them.

Another alternative is to walk around town and have a look at the salons themselves. The location of the salon may give more clues as to what type of service to expect. The back street hairdresser with run down premises and no customers inside would suggest that it is not a popular venue. A few hand written notices promote discounts for senior citizens. If you want the latest in hair fashion, it may be wise to question the likelihood of getting a quality service there. Nevertheless, an immediate appointment is available.

On the other hand, in the centre of town there may be a very trendy salon. The premises are modern, and decorated with awards and qualifications won by the staff. Expensive brands of hair products are attractively merchandised. The salon has a number of stylists and assistants, all of whom are busy. The customers who you see are well dressed and about your age group. A price list (if one is visible at all) tells you that a restyle by one of the salon's partners is expensive. However, if you choose a junior stylist it would be less expensive. An immediate appointment is not available.

You may be able to relate to this scenario as a consumer. Now examine it in light of what has been said about goods and services. The characteristic of intangibility has a bearing on purchase behaviour. In the absence of a physical good to evaluate the consumer typically resorts to clues. The location, appearance and decor of the premises are signals of what to expect. Likewise, the clientele and price give an indication of whether this is likely to be the right service for the customer. Ironically, in this case it may actually be a good signal that an immediate appointment is not available! In the long run, if customers cannot be accommodated with appointments, the salon either has to recruit more stylists or risk turning away business. In addition, the premises and other tangible features have to be designed and maintained in a way that promotes the right image to customers and potential customers. This example illustrates the notion of the inseparability of production and consumption. The only way that a customer can have a hair cut is by being there when the stylist is actually doing it! Whether the customer chooses to come back again or to recommend the salon to others is down to many factors—the new hair style as well as the process of actually getting it.

To design and deliver quality service is a management challenge. Like all management, it helps if information is available on the nature of customers and their behaviour in relation to the particular type of product. Again, services can pose difficulties. Intangibility and inseparability make it difficult for researchers to identify the factors that are important to consumers and how they actually evaluate the quality of services.

Think about the whole Product

Providing the right product when and where and how the customer wants it is a challenge. This is true whether the product is primarily a service, primarily a good, or, as is usually the case, a blend of both. Marketing managers must think about the *whole* Product they provide, and then make sure that all of the elements fit together and work with the rest of the marketing strategy. Sometimes a single product is not enough to meet the needs of target customers and assortments of different products may be required.

WHOLE PRODUCT LINES MUST BE DEVELOPED

A product assortment is the set of all product lines and individual products that a firm sells. A product line is a set of individual products that are closely related. The seller may see them as related because they are produced and/or operate in a similar way, sold to the same target market, sold through the same types of outlet or priced at about the same level. Nestlé, for example, has many product lines in its product assortment, including coffee, tea, desserts and snacks. But Avis has one product line—different types of cars to rent. An individual product is a particular product within a product line. It usually is differentiated by brand, level of service offered, price, or some other characteristic. For example, each size of a brand of soap is an individual product.

Each individual product and target market may require a separate strategy. For example, Nestlé's strategy for selling tea in England is different from its strategy for selling confectionery in Hungary. The focus here is mainly on developing one marketing strategy at a time. Remember that a marketing manager may have to plan *several* strategies to develop an effective marketing programme for a whole company.

TO SEE THE ULTIMATE
MODERN ART,
JUST ASK THE TIME.

Swatch has developed a range of different watches to meet the
needs of different market segments.

PRODUCT CLASSES HELP PLAN MARKETING STRATEGIES

Every product does not have to be treated as unique when planning strategies. Some product classes require similar marketing mixes. These product classes are a useful starting point for developing marketing mixes for new products and evaluating present mixes. Exhibit 7–3 summarizes the product classes.

Product classes start with type of customer
All products fit into one of two broad groups based on the type of customer that will use them. Consumer products are products meant for the final consumer. Business products are products meant for use in produc-ing other products. The same product, for example Mazola Corn Oil, *might* be in both groups. Consumers buy it to use in their own kitchens but food processing companies and restaurants buy it in large quantities as an ingredient in the products they sell. Selling the same product to both final consumers and business customers requires (at least) two different strategies.

There are product classes within each group. Consumer product classes are based on *how consumers think about and shop for products*. Business product classes are based on *how buyers think about products and how they'll be used*. Consumer product classes are discussed first.

CONSUMER PRODUCT CLASSES

Consumer product classes divide into four groups: (1) convenience, (2) shopping, (3) speciality and (4) unsought. Each class is based on the way people buy products. See Exhibit 7–4 for a summary of how these product classes relate to marketing mixes.

Exhibit 7–3 Product Classes

Consumer Product Class	Marketing Mix Considerations	Consumer Behaviour
Convenience products		
Staples	Maximum exposure with widespread, low-cost distribution; mass selling by producer; usually low price; branding is important.	Routinized (habitual), low effort, frequent purchases; low involvement.
Impulse	Widespread distribution with display at point of purchase.	Unplanned purchases bought quickly.
Emergency	Need widespread distribution near probable point of need; price sensitivity low.	Purchase made with time pressure when a need is great.
Shopping products		
Homogeneous	Need enough exposure to facilitate price comparison; price sensitivity high.	Customers see little difference among alternatives, seek lowest price.
Heterogeneous	Need distribution near similar products; promotion (including personal selling) to highlight product advantages; less price sensitivity.	Extensive problem solving; consumer may need help in making a decision.
Speciality products	Price sensitivity is likely to be low; limited distribution may be acceptable, but should be treated as a convenience or shopping product (in whichever category product would typically be included) to reach persons not yet sold on its speciality product status.	Willing to expend effort to get specific product, even if not necessary; strong preferences make it an important purchase.
Unsought products		
New unsought	Must be available in places where similar (or related) products are sought; needs attention-getting promotion.	Need for product not strongly felt; unaware of benefits or not yet gone through adoption process.
Regularly unsought	Requires very aggressive promotion, usually personal selling.	Aware of product but not interested; attitude toward product may even be negative.

Exhibit 7–4 Consumer Product Classes and Marketing Mix Planning

CONVENIENCE PRODUCTS—PURCHASED QUICKLY WITH LITTLE EFFORT

Convenience products are products a consumer needs but is not willing to spend much time or effort shopping for. These products are bought often, require little service or selling, don't cost much, and may even be bought by habit.

The three types of convenience products—staples, impulse products and emergency products—are again based on *how customers think about products*, not the features of the products themselves.

 Internet exercise

Visit the Campbell's Soup web site (**www.camp-bellssoup.com**). Does the web site make it easy for you to get information? Does it want to make you spend more time and get more information? Explain your answer.

Staples—purchased regularly by habit

Staples are products that are bought often, routinely, and without much thought—like breakfast cereal, canned soup and most other packaged foods used almost every day in almost every household. Staples are usually sold in convenient places like local shops, petrol stations and supermarkets. Branding is important with staples. It helps customers cut shopping effort and encourages repeat buying of satisfying brands.

Impulse products—bought immediately on sight

Impulse products are products that are bought quickly—as *unplanned* purchases—because of a strongly felt need. True impulse products are items that the customer hadn't planned to buy, decides to buy on sight, may have bought the same way many times before, and wants right now. An ice-cream seller at a beach sells impulse products. If sunbathers do not buy an ice cream when he rings his bell, the need goes away, and the purchase won't be made later.

This buying behaviour is important because it affects Place—and the whole marketing mix—for impulse products. If the buyer does not see an impulse product at the right time, the sale may be lost. That is why retailers put impulse products where they will be seen and bought—near the checkout or in other heavy traffic areas. Grocery retailers sell chewing gum, chocolate bars and magazines this way.

Emergency products—purchased only when urgently needed

Emergency products are products that are purchased immediately when the need is great. The customer doesn't have time to shop around when its raining heavily or the car runs out of petrol. The price of the umbrella or recovery service won't be important. Meeting customers' emergency needs may require a different marketing mix—especially regarding Place. Some small local shops carry 'emergency' products to meet these needs, staying open from 7 a.m. until 11 p.m. and stocking fill-in items such milk or bread. A car breakdown service is available 24 hours a day. Customers don't mind the higher prices charged for these purchases because they need them urgently.

Increasing numbers of garages now stock a wide range of grocery products, newspapers and other staple products. Shell has recognized the potential of having this type of shop at many of its service stations. The Shell Shop has become today's equivalent of the old local 'corner' or convenience shop.

SHOPPING PRODUCTS—ARE COMPARED

Shopping products are products that a customer feels are worth the time and effort to compare with competing products. Shopping products can be divided into two types, depending on what customers are comparing: (1) homogeneous and (2) heterogeneous shopping products.

Homogeneous shopping products— the product must be low in price

Homogeneous shopping products are shopping products the customer sees as basically the same—and wants at the lowest price. Some consumers feel that certain sizes and types of fridges, television sets and washing machines are very similar and so they shop for the best price. Firms may try to emphasize and promote their product differences to avoid head-to-head price competition. For example, Shell may stress the performance enhancement from additives in its diesel fuel. If consumers do not think the differences are real or important, they will consider just price. Even some inexpensive products like butter or coffee may be considered homogeneous shopping products. *Some* people carefully read advertisements for the lowest food prices—and then go from shop to shop for bargains. They don't do this for staples.

Heterogeneous shopping products—the product must be right

Heterogeneous shopping products are shopping products the customer sees as different—and wants to inspect for quality and suitability. Furniture, clothing, cars and some cameras are good examples. Quality and style matter as much as price. It is harder to compare prices of non-standardized items. Once the customer has found the right product, price may not matter, as long as it is reasonable. This is also true when service is a major part of the product, as in a visit to a dentist or car repair service. You may have asked a friend to recom-mend a dentist who gives pain-free treatments without even asking what the dentist charges.

Branding may be less important for heterogeneous shopping products. The more consumers compare price and quality, the less they rely on brand names or labels. Retailers frequently carry competing brands so consumers won't go to a competitor to compare items. Often the buyer of heterogeneous shopping products not only wants—but expects—some kind of help in buying. If the product is expensive, the buyer may want *personalized* services, such as alteration of clothing or the installation of a dishwasher or washing machine.

SPECIALITY PRODUCTS—NO SUBSTITUTES PLEASE!

Speciality products are consumer products that the customer really wants—and makes a special effort to find. Shopping for a speciality product doesn't mean comparing—the buyer wants that special product and is willing to search for it. It is the customer's *willingness to search*—not the extent of searching that makes it a speciality product. Speciality products do not have to be expensive, once-in-a-lifetime purchases. Think of your last hair cut and how long you waited for the hairdresser you wanted. *Any* branded product that consumers insist on by name is a speciality product.

People have been observed at the chemists asking for a drug by its brand name and, when offered a chemi-cally identical substitute, actually leaving in anger. Marketing managers want customers to see their prod-ucts as speciality products and ask for them over and over again. Building that kind of relationship between the customer and the firm's offering isn't easy. It means satisfying the customer every time. However, that is easier and a lot less costly than trying to win back dissatisfied customers or attract new customers who may not be seeking the product at all.

Some products or services require extended search behaviour. *Pagine gialle* (Yellow Pages) helps customers with this search.

UNSOUGHT PRODUCTS—NEED PROMOTION

Unsought products are products that potential customers don't yet want or know they can buy. So they don't search for them at all. In fact, consumers probably won't buy these products if they see them unless Promotion can show their value. There are two types of unsought products. New unsought products are products offering really new ideas that potential customers don't know about yet. Informative promotion can help convince customers to accept or even seek out the product, ending their unsought status. Direct insurance, allowing the consumer to buy insurance over the telephone, rather than through a broker, weekend holiday breaks in destinations such as Prague and Florence, and mobile telephones are all now popular items. However, initially they were new unsought products because they were innovations and consumers did not know what benefits they offered.

Regularly unsought products are products such as life insurance and encyclopaedias that stay unsought but not unbought forever. There may be a need, but potential customers are not motivated to satisfy it. There is little hope that life insurance will move out of the unsought class. For this kind of product, personal selling is *very* important. Many non-profit organizations try to 'sell' their unsought products. For example, the Red Cross supplies blood to disaster victims. In order to have blood supplies available, the Red Cross needs to obtain blood from the public. Yet few of us feel the need to donate blood. For us, giving blood is an unsought product. So the Red Cross regularly holds blood drives to remind prospective donors of how important it is to give blood.

ONE PRODUCT MAY BE SEEN AS SEVERAL CONSUMER PRODUCTS

Product classes have been considered one at a time. Remember that customers vary. The same product might be seen in different ways by different target markets, at the same time. Because each of these markets sees the product differently, it may be appropriate to develop different marketing mixes.

A tale of four hotels

Hotels are a good example of a service that can be seen as four different kinds of consumer products. Some tired motorists are satisfied with the first hotel they come to—a convenience product. Others shop for basic facilities at the lowest price—a homogeneous shopping product. Some shop for the kind of place they want at a fair price—a heterogeneous shopping product. Others study tourist guides, talk with travelling friends, and telephone in advance to reserve a place in a recommended hotel—a speciality product.

Perhaps one hotel could satisfy *all* potential customers. But it would be hard to produce a marketing mix attractive to everyone—easy access for convenience, good facilities at the right price for shopping product buyers and qualities special enough to attract speciality product travellers. That is why very different kinds of hotels may at first seem to be competing with each other. In fact, they may be aiming at different markets.

Product class is likely to vary by country

The consumer product classes are based on how consumers see products—and how they shop for them. It is important to keep in mind that consumers in different countries are likely to vary significantly on these dimensions. For example, a product viewed as a staple by most consumers in France, or some similar affluent country might be seen as a heterogeneous shopping product by consumers in another country. Many of today's familiar consumer brands are seen as very desirable by consumers in former Eastern European countries. They are perceived to confer status on the consumer. However, the price is much higher when compared to local substitutes, and as a proportion of the consumer's budget, and the available choices might be very different. Similarly, a convenient place to shop often means very different things in different countries. Garages in many Eastern European countries have not developed the full range of services represented in outlets such as the Shell shop.

The product class idea works in different countries, but marketers must look at the products from the viewpoint of the target customers, not from the marketer's. Of course, marketing strategy planners need to know more about potential customers than how they buy specific products. Nevertheless, these classes are a good place to start strategy planning.

BUSINESS PRODUCTS ARE DIFFERENT

Business product classes are also useful for developing marketing mixes. Patterns of buying are frequently related to these product classes. Before looking at business product differences, however, we'll note some important similarities that affect marketing strategy planning.

One demand derived from another

The big difference in the business products market is derived demand—the demand for business products is derived from the demand for final consumer products. For example, car manufacturers buy about one-fifth of all steel products. Even a steel company with a good marketing mix will lose its sales to car manufacturers if demand for cars drops.[3]

Price increases might not reduce quantity purchased

The fact that demand for most business products is derived means that total *industry* demand for such products is fairly inelastic. To satisfy their customers' needs, business firms buy what they need to produce their own products, almost regardless of price. For example even if the cost of basic silicon doubles, Intel still needs it to make computer chips. The increased cost of the silicon won't have much effect on the overall price of the final computer or on the number of computers consumers demand.

Suppliers may face almost pure competition

Although the total industry demand for business products may be inelastic, the demand facing *individual sellers* may be extremely elastic if competitive products are similar and there are many sellers. To buy as economically as possible, sharp business buyers quickly tell suppliers that competitors are offering lower prices.

BUSINESS PRODUCT CLASSES—HOW THEY ARE DEFINED

Business product classes are based on how buyers see products and how the products will be used. Firms treat capital items and expense items differently. Products that become part of a firm's own product are seen differently from those that aid production. The relative size of a particular purchase can make a difference. A personal computer might be a major purchase for a small business, but relatively unimportant for a major multinational company such as Hoechst.

The classes of business products are: (1) capital investment, (2) accessories, (3) raw materials, (4) components, (5) supplies, and (6) professional services. Exhibit 7–5 relates these product classes to marketing mix planning.

CAPITAL INVESTMENT—MAJOR CAPITAL ITEMS

Capital investment, such as buildings, land rights and major equipment, is an important decision for the company. One-of-a-kind capital investments, such as office buildings and custom-made equipment, generally require special negotiations for each sale. Negotiations for capital investment involve top management and can stretch over months or even years.

Small number of customers at any one time

Capital investments are long-lasting products and, as such, are infrequent purchases. The number of potential buyers at *any particular time* is usually small. Custom-made machines may have only a half-a-dozen potential customers, compared to a thousand or more for standard machines. In the offshore oil industry a handful of major oil companies are the major customers for offshore production platforms. It usually takes several years to design and build such platforms and install them. Typically several hundred people will become involved in decisions about each aspect of the construction and installation of such systems, ranging from the consultants who design the offshore platform, to the engineers who are responsible for running the platform once it is installed and the finance personnel who are concerned with the costs of operating the platform, and the oil revenues which result.

Business Product Classes	Marketing Mix Considerations	Buying Behaviour
Capitol investment	Usually requires skilful personal selling by producer, including technical contacts, and/or understanding of applications; leasing and specialized support services may be required.	Multiple buying influence (including top management) and new-task buying are common; infrequent purchase, long decision period, and boom-or-bust demand are typical.
Accessory equipment	Need fairly widespread distribution and numerous contacts by experienced and sometimes technically trained personnel; price competition is often intense, but quality is important.	Purchasing and operating personnel typically make decisions; shorter decision period than for installations.
Raw materials	Grading is important, and transportation and storing can be crucial because of seasonal production and/or perishable products; markets tend to be very competitive.	Long-term contract may be required to ensure supply.
Component parts and materials	Product quality and delivery reliability are usually extremely important; negotiation and technical selling typical on less standardized items; replacement after market may require different strategies.	Multiple buying influence is common; competitive bids used to encourage competitive pricing.
Maintenance, repair and operating (MRO) supplies	Typically require widespread distribution or fast delivery (repair items); arrangements with appropriate intermediaries may be crucial.	Often handled as straight rebuys, except important operating supplies may be treated much more seriously and involve multiple buying influence.
Professional services	Services customized to buyer's need; personal selling very important; inelastic demand often supports high prices.	Customer may compare outside service with what internal people could provide; needs may be very specialized.

Exhibit 7–5 Business Product Classes and Marketing Mix Planning

Capital investment, a boom-or-bust business

Capital investment is a boom-or-bust business. When sales are high, businesses want to expand their own capacity rapidly. Sales to such companies will increase rapidly. If the potential return on a new investment is very attractive, firms may accept any reasonable price. But during a down-swing, buyers have little or no need for new capital investment, and sales fall off sharply. Since it often takes several months or even years to manufacture and install capital equipment it is frequently difficult to maintain an even flow of production activity.

May have to be leased or rented

Because capital investment is relatively expensive, some customers prefer to lease or rent. Leasing makes it easier for a firm to keep up with advancing technologies. Many firms lease computers so they can expand to bigger systems or incorporate new capabilities as they grow.

Specialized services are needed as part of the product

To increase the efficiency of capital investment and the expected return on the buyer's investment, suppliers sometimes include special services at no extra cost. Installing the machine in the buyer's plant, training employees in its use, and supplying repair services are good examples of services that can become part of the final product. Gateway computers, one of the leading international suppliers of personal computers, provides a free help desk service that deals with any queries from buyers once they have purchased the equipment.

There are likely to be multiple influences on choice

Because a major capital purchase can have an impact on many different aspects of the company, several people may be involved or influential in its purchase. For example, the production director may be concerned with the quality of output from a new production line. The marketing director may be more concerned with the ability of the line to handle a wide range of different products to meet varying market requirements, and the finance director may be most concerned with how much the machine costs and how the company will pay for it.

ACCESSORIES—IMPORTANT BUT SHORT-LIVED CAPITAL ITEMS

Accessories are short-lived capital items—tools and equipment used in production or office activities, such as copy machines, fax machines, portable drills, electric lift trucks and filing cabinets. Because these products cost less and last a shorter time than capital investment, multiple buying influences are less important. Users and purchasing agents, rather than top managers, may make the purchase decision.

More target markets requiring different marketing mixes

Accessories are more standardized than capital investment. And more customers usually need them. For example, IBM sells its robotics systems, which can cost over £1 million, as custom capital investment to large manufacturers. But IBM's Thinkpad computers are accessory equipment for just about every type of modern business all round the world. And these different types of customers are spread out geographically. The larger number of different kinds of customers and increased competition mean that accessories need different marketing mixes from capital investment.

Special services may be attractive

Ordinarily, engineering services or special advice is less important for simpler accessory equipment. Yet some companies manage to add attractive services to their accessories such as office furniture suppliers who offer decorating services and advice on office layout or computer sellers who help customers set up their software.

RAW MATERIALS—FARM AND NATURAL PRODUCTS ARE EXPENSE ITEMS

They become part of a physical good

Raw materials are unprocessed expense items, such as timber, iron ore, wheat and cotton, that are moved to the next production process with little handling. Unlike capital investment and accessories, *raw materials become part of a physical good and are expense items.* We can break raw materials into two types: (1) farm products and (2) natural products. Farm products include oranges, wheat, sugar cane, cattle, poultry, eggs and milk. Natural products include fish and game, timber and sugar beet, and copper, zinc, iron ore, oil and coal.

Raw materials involve grading, storing and transporting

The need for grading is one of the important differences between raw materials and other business products. Nature produces what it will and someone must sort and grade raw materials to satisfy various market segments. Top-graded fruits and vegetables may find their way into the consumer products market. Lower grades, which are treated as business products, are frequently used in juices, sauces and soups.

Raw materials are usually produced in specific geographic areas—in France wine is produced in world-famous regions such as Burgundy and Champagne, coal is produced in the major coal fields of Namur and the Ruhr valley, and olives are largely grown in southern Mediterranean countries such as Italy and Greece. Many raw materials—such as oranges and potatoes—are produced seasonally. Yet the demand for raw materials is geographically spread out and fairly constant all year. As a result, storing and transportation are important.

Large buyers may want long-term contracts

Most buyers of raw materials want ample supplies in the right grades for specific uses—fresh vegetables for Birds Eye's production lines or logs for Inveresk paper mills. To ensure steady quantities, raw materials customers often sign long-term contracts, sometimes at guaranteed prices, for a supplier's output. Natural products are usually produced by fewer and larger companies who can adjust supply to maintain stable prices. For example, the amount of iron ore mined in any one year can be adjusted up or down, at least within limits. Most natural products aren't perishable so they can be easily stored to wait for better market conditions.

COMPONENT PARTS AND MATERIALS—IMPORTANT EXPENSE ITEMS

The whole is no better than...

Components are processed expense items that become part of a finished product. They need more processing than raw materials and require different marketing mixes from raw materials—even though they both become part of a finished product.

Component *parts* include items that are (1) finished and ready for assembly or (2) nearly finished, requiring only minor processing (such as grinding or polishing) before being assembled into the final product. CD-Rom drives included in personal computers, airbags in cars, and motors for domestic appliances such as washing machines are examples. Component *materials* are items such as wire, paper, textiles or cement. They have already been processed but must be processed further before becoming part of the final product.

Components must meet specifications

Some components are custom-made. Much teamwork between the engineering staffs of both buyer and seller may be necessary to arrive at the right specifications. Top management may be involved in negotiating the price, especially if the price of the item is high or it is extremely important to the final product, and the purchasing company intends to produce high volumes of the final product. A major car manufacturer such as Volvo, works at any one time with literally thousands of individual suppliers. Each of these suppliers has their own suppliers. Together these companies form a network of organizations that needs to be managed carefully to produce cars efficiently and meet the needs of car buyers.

Other components are produced in quantity to accepted standards or specifications. Production people in the buying firm may specify quality but the purchasing manager who does the buying often wants several dependable sources of supply. Because components become part of the firm's own product, quality is extremely important. The buyer's own name and whole marketing mix are at stake so a buyer tries to buy from sources that help assure a good product. In such a situation, a buyer may even find it attractive to develop a close partnership with a single supplier who is really dedicated to the same objectives as the buyer.

Profitable replacement markets may develop

Since component parts go into finished products, a replacement market often develops. This *replacement market* can be both large and very profitable. Car tyres and batteries are two examples of components originally sold in the *original equipment market* (OEM) that become consumer products in the after market. The target markets are different—and different marketing mixes are usually necessary.

When Michelin sells its tyres to Fiat or Mercedes, negotiations take place at senior management level. Large quantities of tyres will be sold. Price negotiations are extensive, and the purchaser, Fiat or Mercedes, is very well informed about the suitability of the tyre for different vehicles as well as the likely costs of manufacture and the available margins. When tyres are supplied to such customers they are sent in large quantities to one central location, where they are fitted to the vehicle. When Michelin supplies the same tyres to the replacement market the marketing programme is different. Tyres must be widely distributed in much smaller quantities to a wide range of garages and specialist tyre centres close to the final customer. The right tyre must be available or the customer is quite likely to switch to another brand. Consumers are less well informed about the performance characteristics of tyres and will be more likely to buy on price, availability and branding.

SUPPLIES—SUPPORT MAINTENANCE, REPAIR AND OPERATIONS

Supplies can be divided into three types: (1) maintenance, (2) repair and (3) operating supplies—giving them their common name: MRO supplies.

Maintenance supplies include products such as paint, light bulbs and lubricants. Repair supplies are parts such as filters, bearings and gears needed to fix worn or broken equipment. Operating supplies include lubricating oils and greases, grinding compounds, typing paper, paper clips, coal or electricity, and insurance.

Important operating supplies

If operating supplies are needed regularly, and in large amounts, they receive special treatment from buyers. Many companies buy coal and fuel oil by the truck or tanker load. Usually there are several sources for such homogeneous products and large volumes may be purchased in highly competitive international markets. Or contracts may be negotiated, perhaps by top-level managers, to assure lower prices and a continuing supply.

Maintenance and small operating supplies

These products are like convenience products. They are so numerous that a purchasing agent cannot possibly be an expert in buying all of them. Each requisition for maintenance and small operating supplies may be for relatively few items. Although a purchase order may amount to only £1 or £2, handling it may cost £25 to £30. Branding may become important for such products because it makes product identification and buying easier for such 'nuisance' purchases. Breadth of assortment and the seller's dependability are also important when buying supplies. In many markets specialist intermediaries usually handle this type of small-volume, frequently purchased item.

PROFESSIONAL SERVICES

Professional services are specialized services that support a firm's operations. They are usually expense items. Engineering or management consulting services can improve the plant layout—or the company's efficiency. Computer services can process data. Design services can supply designs for a physical plant, products and promotion materials. Advertising agencies can help promote the firm's products and food services can improve morale. Here the *service* part of the product is emphasized. Goods may be supplied, as coffee and sandwiches are with food service, but the customer is primarily interested in the service.

Managers compare the cost of buying professional services outside the firm to the cost of having company people do them. For special skills needed only occasionally, an outsider can be the best source. Further, during the last decade, many firms have tried to cut costs by 'downsizing' the number of people that they employ. In many cases, work that was previously done by an employee is now provided as a service by an independent supplier. Catering and office cleaning services provided by specialist organizations such as Rentokil are now frequently contracted out. Clearly, the number of service specialists is growing in our complex economy.

MANAGING PRODUCTS OVER THEIR LIFE CYCLES

A life and death cycle is being repeated over and over again in product markets worldwide. Cellular phones are replacing short-wave radios, and also making it possible for people to communicate from places where it was previously impossible. Cassette tapes replaced vinyl records, and now CDs and digital audiotape are challenged by new formats. Switchboard operators in many firms were replaced with answering machines,

and now answering machines are losing ground as telephone companies offer new voice mail services. These innovations show that products, markets and competition change over time. This makes marketing management an exciting challenge. Developing new products and managing existing products to meet changing conditions is important to the success of every firm.

3COM CASE

When 3Com introduced its PalmPilot III Connected organizer in 1998, it was an evolution, not a revolution. This personal digital assistant (PDA) was not a radically new concept. Rather, it improved on the firm's earlier models. After all, in just two years 3Com had already sold a million units through distribution in 35 countries. The product development team did not want to add a lot of new gadgets that would make the tiny hand-held unit more complicated. The target market of busy managers also wanted the product to be simple. The PalmPilot's advantage is that it is easy to use and does a few important things very well. It stores thousands of names and addresses, tracks expenses, schedules meetings and priorities, and has a calculator. The company has positioned it as a 'connected organizer' because it can send data to another PalmPilot and easily links to the user's computer or can connect to e-mail.

If you were the marketing manager for a traditional pen and paper organizer business, you might see all this as revolution, not evolution. If one of your customers sees a PalmPilot and likes it, their traditional organizer becomes obsolete. High-powered PDAs are also taking business away from data watches, programmable calculators, laptops and digital pagers—all of which still seem relatively new. Some of these products may not even seem to be competitors but when a firm finds a better way to meet customer needs, it disrupts the old way of doing things.

The success of the PalmPilot and the growth of the PDA market are attracting a lot of direct competitors as well. Casio, IBM, Sharp, Psion, HP and others have all entered the market. The overall market is expected to triple by 2001. Even so, not every brand will succeed. Some of the first PDAs to go on the market failed. Apple rushed its Newton PDA through the development process to be first on the market. Problems persisted and the Newton did not meet customers' expectations. Of course, even a successful pioneer can sometimes lose out to a creative imitator, as happened with computer modems. Hayes was the early market leader, but 3Com's high speed US Robotics units and new cable modems overtook them. PalmPilot's connectivity plays to that strength.

With competition becoming more intense, the product manager has offered upgrade discounts to loyal owners of past models so as to maintain relationships with them. Owners can also register at the web site to receive updates about new software and services. Given the dynamism of the market, the future is impossible to predict. For companies such as 3Com, research and product development is a constant activity.[4]

Products go through life cycles. Consequently, product planning and marketing mix planning are important. Competitors are always developing and copying new ideas and products, making existing products out of date more quickly than ever. In Chapter 6 we emphasized the importance of the process of segmentation, targeting and positioning to develop effective marketing strategies. Businesses need to monitor their markets continuously to spot opportunities and identify potential threats from new competition or new technologies. Through this process it is able to identify specific segments where there may be opportunities to develop their business. They then targets their efforts on attractive segments and develop a marketing programme that they hope will be better than that offered by the competition. This programme includes all four elements of the marketing mix, namely Product, Price, Promotion and Place.

Successful marketing integrates the whole mix

A successful programme requires all the elements of the marketing mix combined in a way that meets the needs of the potential customer better than the competition. The marketing mix must offer a superior combination of product quality and availability. The brand must be presented in such a way that the target customers form a favourable view of the brand, and prices must be consistent with the overall marketing programme. This programme can vary over the life cycle of the product. The second half of this chapter explores how this poses challenges for marketing planning.

Product life cycle has four major stages

The product life cycle is divided into four major stages: (1) market introduction, (2) market growth, (3) market maturity and (4) sales decline. Products experience each of these stages at different times. At any one time a firm may also have a range of different products at different stages in their life cycles.

One company has recently announced the concept of 'time share' for expensive sports cars such as Ferrari and Lotus. Members of the scheme will be able to buy a number of months of usage allowing them to part-own cars that would have been far beyond their means. Such a concept is at the market introduction stage. It may prove popular and the market may grow rapidly. Alternatively the concept may not find a market.

Computers with multimedia capabilities, and the ability to access the Internet are at the growth stage in their development. The market for such products is growing rapidly and many different versions are emerging as the market develops. In contrast, in Denmark 97 per cent of households have television sets. The market is a mature one where most sales come from replacement purchases, rather than first purchase. Sales are relatively stable. Finally, few people today would buy a standard typewriter rather than a word processor or computer. Sales are declining and the long-term prospect for this product is limited.

For a number of reasons a firm's marketing mix usually must change during the product life cycle. Customers' attitudes and needs may change. The product may be aimed at entirely different target markets at different stages. And the nature of competition moves towards pure competition based around price or oligopoly based around distinctive product features. Further, total sales of the product, by all competitors in the industry, vary in each of its four stages. They move from very low in the market introduction stage to high at market maturity and then back to low in the sales decline stage. More importantly, the profit picture also changes. These general relationships can be seen in Exhibit 7–6. Note that sales and profits do not move together over time. *Industry profits decline while industry sales are still rising.*

Market introduction

In the market introduction stage, sales are low as a new idea is first introduced to a market. Customers are not looking for the product. They do not even know about it. Informative promotion is needed to tell potential customers about the advantages and uses of the new product concept. The concept of 'time share' for expensive cars would be a novel one for most people and would need to be explained carefully.

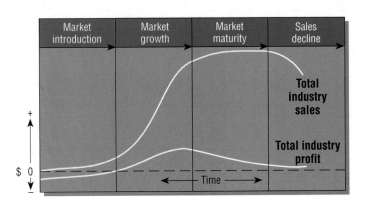

Exhibit 7–6 Life Cycle of a Typical Plant Product

Even though a firm promotes its new product, it takes time for customers to learn that the product is available. Most companies experience losses during the introduction stage because they spend a large amount of money on Promotion, Product and Place development. Of course, they invest the money in the hope of future profits.

Market growth

In the market growth stage, industry sales grow quickly, but industry profits rise and then start falling. The first into the market begins to make significant profits as more and more customers buy. However, competitors see the opportunity and enter the market. Some just copy the most successful product or try to improve it to compete better. Others try to refine their offerings to do a better job of appealing to some target markets. The new entries result in much product variety. Each of the alternative products is competing to establish itself as the industry standard. In the personal computer market there are many competing brands, which now offer multimedia capability, each trying to attract the customer with alternative specifications, functions and prices. This can create considerable confusion for the buyer who is not sure which machine to buy.

This is the time of largest profits *for the industry*. However, by the end of this phase industry profits begin to decline as competition increases. See Exhibit 7–6. Some firms make strategy planning mistakes at this stage by not understanding the product life cycle. They see the substantial sales and profit opportunities of the early market growth stage but ignore the fact that competition will soon follow. This can lead to companies finding themselves unable to cope with aggressive levels of competition. Marketing managers who pay attention to what the competition is doing are less likely to encounter this problem.

Market maturity

The market maturity stage occurs when industry sales level off and competition gets tougher. Industry profits

go down throughout the market maturity stage because promotion costs rise and some competitors cut prices to attract business. Less efficient firms cannot compete with this pressure and they drop out of the market. Even in oligopoly situations, there is a long-run downward pressure on prices. New firms may still enter the market at this stage, increasing competition even more. Note that late entries skip the early life-cycle stages, including the profitable market growth stage. They must try to take a share of the saturated market from established firms, which is difficult and expensive. The market leaders have a lot at stake, so they will usually fight hard to defend their market share and sales revenue. Satisfied customers who are happy with their current products typically won't be interested in switching to a new brand.

Virgin Airlines faces this dilemma as it attempts to develop its sales of passenger flights in competitive international markets, dominated by large national competitors such as Lufthansa, Iberia or Olympic Airlines. Its alternatives are to go 'head to head' against the competition, which is difficult for a company of its size to sustain or it can choose to specialize in specific markets (for example, North America and Japan) and target its efforts on creating a sustainable difference in service levels on such routes. Its marketing strategies to date have followed the second alternative.

Persuasive promotion becomes more important during the market maturity stage. Products may differ only slightly if at all. Most competitors have discovered the most effective appeals or have quickly copied the leaders. Although each firm may still have its own demand curve, the curves become increasingly elastic (responsive to price changes) as the various products become almost the same in the minds of potential consumers. Virgin's strategy has been to link its flights with the broader appeal of Virgin to the younger 'fun' segment of the market that would identify with other products such as the Virgin record stores.

In most developed European countries, the markets for cars, boats, television sets and many household appliances are in market maturity. This stage may continue for many years, until a basically new product idea comes along. Individual brands or models may come and go at in this stage.

Within individual product areas there can still be considerable change. For example, although the overall car market is mature in many European countries, two new product categories have emerged in the last five years, which have created essentially mini-markets, both of which have shown considerable growth, within an overall market that has remained relatively static. These are four-wheel-drive, off-road vehicles and large people carriers. The four-wheel-drive vehicle targets customers who want an off-road capability, rather than being restricted to conventional roads. These include the Range Rover and the Shogun. Such vehicles are often sold to people who never use the off-road capability. The people-carrier market targets customers who want to move larger families around in relative comfort. These vehicles include Renault's Espace, Ford's Galaxy and Volkswagen's Sharan. The four-wheel-drive and people-carrier products have also experienced the same patterns of introduction, growth and maturity. New segments have already emerged within the four-wheel-drive segment, for smaller versions of the original four-wheel-drive vehicle. For example, Landrover launched a smaller version of its Discovery, targeted unambiguously at the 'fun' segment of the market. This vehicle competes with Toyota's very successful Rav4.

Sales decline

During the sales decline stage, new products replace the old. Price competition from dying products becomes more vigorous, but firms with strong brands may make profits until the end. As the new products go through their introduction stage, the old ones may keep some sales by appealing to the most loyal customers or those who are slow to try new ideas. These conservative buyers might switch later thus smoothing the sales decline.

PRODUCT LIFE CYCLES SHOULD BE RELATED TO SPECIFIC MARKETS

Remember that product life cycles describe industry sales and profits for a *product idea* within a particular product-market. The sales and profits of an individual product or brand may not, and often do not, follow the life-cycle pattern. They may vary up and down throughout the life cycle, sometimes moving in the opposite direction of industry sales and profits. Further, a product idea may be in a different life-cycle stage in different markets.

Individual brands may not follow the pattern

A given firm may introduce or withdraw a specific product during any stage of the product life cycle. A 'me-too' brand introduced during the market growth stage, for example, may never get any sales at all and suffer a quick death. Or it may reach its peak and start to decline even before the market maturity stage begins. Market leaders may enjoy high profits during the market maturity stage, even though industry profits are declining. Weaker products, on the other hand, may not earn a profit during any stage of the product life cycle. Sometimes the innovator brand loses so much in the introduction stage that it has to drop out just as others are reaping big profits in the growth stage.

Strategy planners who naively expect sales of an individual product to follow the general product life-cycle pattern are likely to be rudely surprised. In fact, it might be more sensible to think in terms of product-market life cycles rather than product life cycles, but we will use the term *product life cycle* because it is commonly accepted and widely used.

Each market should be carefully defined

How broadly the product market is defined determines the actual product life cycle. For example, almost 63 per cent of all UK households own microwave ovens. Although microwave ovens are approaching the market maturity stage in this market, in many other countries they are still early in the growth stage. Even in European countries such as Switzerland, Denmark, Italy and Spain, fewer than 35 per cent of all households own microwave ovens. As this example suggests, a firm with a mature product can sometimes turn back the clock by focusing on new growth opportunities in international markets.

How broadly the needs of customers are defined in a product market also affects the product life cycles and the composition of the competition. If a market is defined broadly, there may be many competitors and the market may appear to be in market maturity. On the other hand, if the focus is on a narrow submarket, and a particular way of satisfying specific needs, then there may be much shorter product life cycles as improved product ideas come along to replace the old. Four-wheel-drive vehicles are an example of such a market within the broader overall car market.

PRODUCT LIFE CYCLES VARY IN LENGTH

How long a whole product life cycle takes, and the length of each stage, varies a lot across products. The cycle may vary from a few months, in the case of toys like the Mighty Morphin Rangers line, to possibly 100 years for petrol-powered cars. The product life-cycle concept does not tell a manager precisely *how long* the cycle will last. But a manager can often make a good guess based on the life cycle for similar products. Sometimes marketing research can also help. However, it is more important to expect and plan for the different stages than to know the precise length of each cycle.

Some products move rapidly

A new product idea will move through the early stages of the life cycle more quickly when it has certain characteristics. For example, the greater the *comparative advantage* of a new product over those already on the market, the more rapidly its sales will grow. Sales growth is also faster when the product is *easy to use* and if its advantages are *easy to communicate*. If the product *can be tried* on a limited basis, without a lot of risk to the customer, it can usually be introduced more quickly. Finally, if the product is *compatible* with the values and experiences of target customers, they are likely to buy it more quickly.

The fast adoption of the Netscape Navigator browser for the Internet's World Wide Web is a good example. Netscape offered real benefits. The Internet had been around for a while, but very few people used it because it was hard to access. Compared to existing ways for computers to communicate on the Internet, Navigator was easy to use and it worked well with pictures as data. It also offered a simple way to customize to the user's preferences. Free on-line downloads of software made it easy for consumers to try the product. Navigator worked like other Windows software that users already knew, so it was easy to install and learn. Further, it was compatible with their computers and how they worked. Most of the initial growth, however, was in the United States. In countries where computers were less common and where there were fewer computer networks, Navigator did not initially have the same ease of use.[5]

Product life cycles are getting shorter

Although the life of different products varies, in general product life cycles are getting shorter. This is partly due to rapidly changing technology. One new invention may make possible many new products that replace old ones. Tiny electronic microchips led to hundreds of new products, from calculators and digital watches in the early days to microchip-controlled heart valves and fax machines now. Fax machines can transmit a letter or illustration anywhere in the world over standard phone lines, in just minutes. They have changed how companies communicate and they have also taken business and profits away from overnight delivery services from companies such as DHL.

Some markets move quickly to market maturity, if there are fast copiers. In the highly competitive grocery products industry, cycles are down to 12 to 18 months for really new ideas. Simple variations of a new idea may have even shorter life cycles. Competitors sometimes copy flavour or packaging changes in a matter of weeks or months. Patents for a new product may not be much protection in slowing down competitors. Competitors can often find ways to copy the product idea without violating a specific patent. Worse, some firms find out that an unethical competitor simply disregards the patent protection. Patent violations by foreign competitors are very common. A product's life may be over before a case can get through patent-court bottlenecks. By then, the copycat competitor may even be out of business. These problems are even more severe in international cases because different governments, rules and court systems are involved.

Although life cycles are moving faster in the developed economies, keep in mind that many advances bypass most consumers in less developed ones. The latter struggle at the subsistence level, without an effective macro-marketing system to stimulate innovation. However, some of the innovations and economies of scale made possible in developed economies do trickle down to benefit these consumers. Inexpensive antibiotics and drought-resistant plants, for example, are making a life-or-death difference.

The early bird usually makes the profits

The increasing speed of the product life cycle means that firms must be developing new products all the time. Further, they must try to have marketing mixes that will make the most of the market growth stage, when profits are highest. During the growth stage, competitors are likely to introduce product improvements. Fast changes in marketing strategy may be required here because profits do not necessarily go to the innovator. Sometimes fast copiers of the basic idea will share in the market growth stage.

Sony, a pioneer in developing videocassette recorders, was one of the first firms to put VCRs on the market. Other firms quickly followed and the competition drove down prices and increased demand. As sales of VCRs continued to grow, Sony doggedly stuck to its Beta format VCRs in spite of the fact that most consumers were buying VHS-format machines offered by competitors. Not until a decade later did Sony finally surrender and offer a VHS-format machine. However, by then the booming growth in VCR sales had ebbed, and competitors controlled 90 per cent of the market. Although Sony was slow to see its mistake, its lost opportunities were minor compared to many European producers who sat on the sidelines and watched as foreign producers captured the whole VCR market. Copiers can be even faster than the innovator in adapting to the market's needs. Marketers must be flexible, *but also* they must fully understand the needs and attitudes of their target markets.[6]

The short happy life of fashions and fads

The sales of some products are influenced by fashion—the currently accepted or popular style. Fashion-related products tend to have short life cycles. What is currently popular can shift rapidly. A certain colour or style of clothing—flared jeans, miniskirts or four-inch-wide ties—may be in fashion one season and outdated the next. Marketing managers who work with fashions often have to make rapid product changes.

It is not really clear why a particular fashion becomes popular. Most present fashions are adaptations or revivals of previously popular styles. Designers are always looking for styles that will satisfy fashion innovators who crave distinctiveness. And lower cost copies of the popular items may catch on with other groups and survive for a while. Yet the speed of change increases the cost of producing and marketing products. Companies sustain losses due to trial and error in finding acceptable styles, then producing them on a limited basis because of uncertainty about the length of the cycle. These increased costs are not always charged directly to the consumer because some firms lose their investment and go out of business. But in total, fashion changes cost consumers money. Fashion changes are a luxury that most people in less developed countries simply cannot afford.

A fad is an idea that is fashionable only to certain groups who are enthusiastic about it. But these groups are so fickle that a fad is even more short-lived than a regular fashion. Many toys are fads but do well during a short-lived cycle. Some teenagers' music tastes are fads. Exhibit 7–7 summarizes the shape of typical life cycles for fashions, fads and styles. Note that the pattern for a style may go up and down as it comes back into fashion over time.

PLANNING FOR DIFFERENT STAGES OF THE PRODUCT LIFE CYCLE

Length of cycle affects strategy planning

Where a product is in its life cycle, and how quickly it is moving to the next stage, should affect marketing strategy planning. Marketing managers must make realistic plans for the later stages. Exhibit 7–8 shows the relationship of the product life cycle to the marketing mix variables. The next few chapters of this book discuss many of the terms in this figure in some detail.

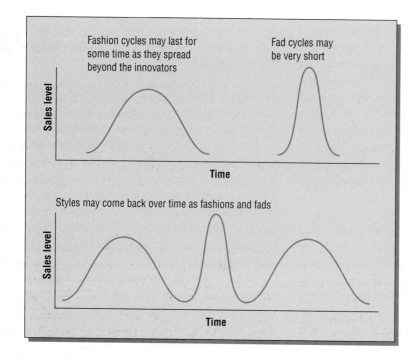

Exhibit 7–7 Patterns of Fashion, Fad, and Style Cycles for Fashion Products

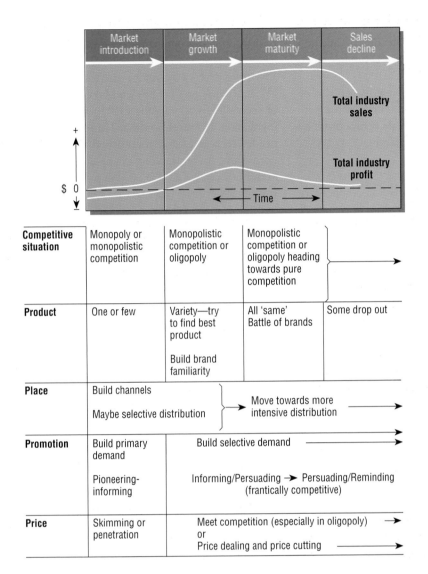

Exhibit 7–8 Typical Changes in Marketing Variables over the Product Life Cycle

	Market introduction	Market growth	Market maturity	Sales decline
Competitive situation	Monopoly or monopolistic competition	Monopolistic competition or oligopoly	Monopolistic competition or oligopoly heading towards pure competition	→
Product	One or few	Variety—try to find best product Build brand familiarity	All 'same' Battle of brands	Some drop out
Place	Build channels Maybe selective distribution	Move towards more intensive distribution →		→
Promotion	Build primary demand Pioneering-informing	Build selective demand → Informing/Persuading → Persuading/Reminding (frantically competitive)		
Price	Skimming or penetration	Meet competition (especially in oligopoly) → or Price dealing and price cutting →		

Introducing new products

Exhibit 7–8 shows that it is a substantial task to introduce a really new product and this should be reflected in the strategy planning. Money must be spent designing and developing the new product. Even if the product is unique, this does not mean that everyone will immediately come running to the producer's door. The firm will have to build channels of distribution, perhaps offering special incentives to win cooperation. Promotion is needed to build demand *for the whole idea*, not just to sell a specific brand. Because all this is expensive, it may lead the marketing manager to try to 'skim' the market—charging a relatively high price to help pay for the introductory costs.

The correct strategy, however, depends on how quickly the product life cycle is likely to move, that is, how quickly the new idea will be accepted by customers, and how quickly competitors will follow with their own versions of the product. When the early stages of the cycle will be fast, a low initial (penetration) price may make sense to help develop loyal customers early and keep competitors out.

Of course, not all new product ideas catch on. Customers may conclude that the marketing mix does not satisfy their needs, or other new products may meet the same need better. The success that eludes a firm with its initial strategy can sometimes be achieved by modifying the strategy. Videodisc players illustrate this point. They were a flop during their initial introduction in the home-entertainment market. Consumers did not see any advantage over cheaper videotape players. Some new opportunities have developed. For example, a new generation of video games uses laser videodiscs to store sounds and images. These games are really just a special application of multimedia computer systems that link videodisc players with a personal computer. The business market for these systems is also growing. Many firms are buying these systems as a selling aid.

Salespeople use them to make presentations, and they are also used for in-store selling. Customers can shop for products by viewing pictures on a computer video screen.[7]

The ability to change strategies rapidly can also be critical. Some firms are very flexible. They can compete effectively with larger, less adaptable competitors by adjusting their strategies more frequently.

Managing maturing products

It is important for a firm to have some competitive advantage as it moves into market maturity. Even a small advantage can make a big difference and some firms do very well by carefully managing their maturing products. They are able to capitalize on a slightly better product, or perhaps lower production and/or marketing costs. Or they are simply more successful at promotion, allowing them to differentiate their more or less homogeneous product from competitors. For example, car manufacturers such as Renault, Volkswagen, Rover and Saab, all attempt to differentiate their products through sustained advertising designed to build up a distinctive position in the minds of target customers in essentially the same market.

Product life cycles keep moving. That does not mean that a firm should just sit by as its sales decline. There are other choices. A firm can improve its product or develop an innovative new product for the same market. Or it can develop a strategy for its product (perhaps with modifications) targeted at a new market. For example, it might find a market in a country where the life cycle is not so advanced, or it might try to serve a new need. The old VW Beetle experienced successful sales in several overseas markets long after it was withdrawn from production in Germany. Or a firm can

withdraw the product before it completes the cycle and refocus on better opportunities. See Exhibit 7–9.

Improve the product or develop a new one

When a firm's product has won loyal customers, it can be successful for a long time, even in a mature or declining market. However, continued improvements may be needed to keep customers satisfied, especially if their needs shift. An outstanding example is Unilever's Persil brand (also called OMO and Skip in some markets). Introduced over 50 years ago, this washing powder has undergone many different formulations since its launch. Technically the product has changed, as new formulations became available, offering new benefits to customers. Equally importantly the presentation of the product through advertising has been carefully managed to reflect changing attitudes and lifestyles.

In early advertisements Persil was portrayed as essential to mother as she looked after the washing for her family. As roles changed and an increasing number of women took on independent roles outside the family, this stereotype became less appropriate and the portrayal of the brand shifted. Other members of the household were featured using the product. It became a friend of the whole family. This type of product improvement can help to extend the product life cycle.

On the other hand, a firm that develops an innovative new product may move to a new product life cycle. For example, by 1985 new liquid detergents were moving into the growth stage, and sales of powdered detergents were declining. To share in the growth-stage profits for liquid detergents and to offset the loss of customers from powdered Persil, Unilever introduced Persil Liquid. Although Unilever used the familiar Persil brand name, Persil Liquid appears to be a different

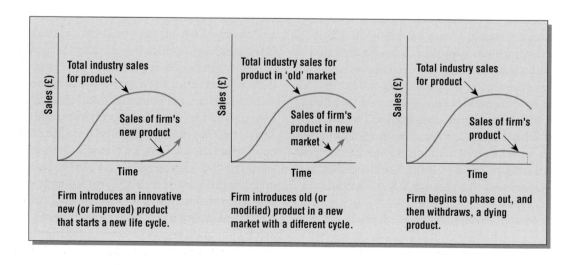

Exhibit 7–9 Examples of Three Marketing Strategy Choices for a Firm in a Mature Product Market

product concept that competes in a different product market. Even though powdered detergents in general appear to be in the decline stage, powdered Persil continues to sell because it still does the job for some consumers. Persil Tablets, introduced in 1998, are the next generation of products in the detergent market.[8]

It makes sense to think in terms of a wave of products. This means that the business can have products at different stages of the life cycle. Those that are making profits today can help to fund yesterday's breadwinners and the development and introduction of tomorrow's breadwinners. Although sound marketing strategy decisions can influence the shape and length of the product life cycle, products can still go into decline. By having new products coming onto the market and by adapting existing products, it is possible for businesses to avoid having to rely on a product that is in the decline stage.

Develop new strategies for different markets

It is clear that the same product may be in different life cycle stages in different markets. That means that a firm may have to pursue very different strategies for a product, at the same time, in different markets. In a mature market, a firm may be fighting to keep or increase its market share. But if the firm finds a new use for the product, it may need to try to stimulate overall demand. Du Pont's Teflon fluorocarbon resin is a good example. It was developed more than 50 years ago and has enjoyed sales growth as a non-stick coating for cookware, as insulation for aircraft wiring and as a lining for chemically resistant equipment. Marketing managers for Teflon have not waited for declining profits in those mature markets. They have constantly developed strategies for new markets where Teflon can meet needs. For example, Teflon sells well as a special coating for the wires used in high-speed communications between computers.[9]

Phasing out dying products

Not all strategies have to be exciting growth strategies. If prospects are poor in a product market, a phase-out strategy may be needed. The need for phasing out becomes more obvious as the sales decline stage arrives. Even in market maturity, it may be clear that a particular product is not going to be profitable enough to reach the company's objectives using the current strategy. Then, the wisest move may be to develop a strategy that helps the firm phase out of the product market, perhaps over several years.

Marketing plans are implemented as ongoing strategies. Salespeople make calls, inventory moves in the channel, advertising is scheduled for several months into the future, and so on. So the firm usually experiences losses if managers end a plan too abruptly. Because of this, it is sometimes better to phase out the product gradually. Managers order materials more selectively so production can end with a minimum of unused inventory, and they shift salespeople to other jobs. They may cancel advertising and other promotion efforts more quickly because there is no point in promoting for the long run. These various actions obviously affect morale within the company and they may also cause intermediaries to pull back. The company may therefore have to offer price inducements in the channels. Employees should be told that a phase-out strategy is being implemented and of the implications for their jobs, as the plan is completed.

Obviously, there are some difficult implementation issues here. But phase-out is also a *strategy* and it must be market oriented in order to cut losses. In fact, it is possible to milk a dying product for some time if competitors move out more quickly. This situation occurs when there is still ongoing, though declining, demand with some customers willing to pay attractive prices to get their favourite brand.

SUMMARY

In this chapter, we looked at Product very broadly. A product may be a physical good or it may be a service. Pure services differ from goods by being intangible, inseparable and perishable. In many cases, however, a product is some combination of goods and services such as a meal at a restaurant. From a marketing perspective, it is important that a Product is seen as *what satisfies the needs of its target market.*

In an effort to order out thinking on all of the different types of product that exist, we first classified products according to who buys them. This gave rise to

two broad classes of product—consumer products and business products. Consumer product classes are based on consumers' buying behaviour. Four consumer product classes were identified—convenience, shopping, speciality and unsought products. Business product classes are based on how buyers see the products and how they are used. Business product classes are installations, accessory equipment, raw materials, components, supplies and professional services. Typical marketing mixes for each of these classes can be found. The marketing mixes, for example, of convenience goods are very similar to each other but they, of course, differ from the typical marketing mixes of accessory equipment.

Remember that customers vary. Different target markets might see the same product in different ways, at the same time. Because each of these markets sees the product differently, it may be appropriate to develop different marketing mixes. The fact that different people may see the same product in different product classes helps explain why seeming competitors may succeed with very different marketing mixes.

The product life-cycle concept is especially important to marketing strategy planning. The product life cycle suggests that products move through introductory, growth, maturity and decline stages. Sales levels and profit levels characterize each of these stages. The marketing implications of the product life cycle are that the firm needs to actively manage the product by developing different marketing mixes, and even strategies, over the life of the product. By managing the Product element (development, extension, improvement and adaptation) and the other marketing mix elements, it is possible to influence the shape and length of the product life cycle.

QUESTIONS AND PROBLEMS

1. What do you understand by the term 'product'?
2. Discuss several ways in which physical goods are different from pure services. Give an example of a good and then an example of a service that illustrates each of the differences.
3. What products are being offered by a shop that specializes in bicycles? By a travel agent? By a supermarket? By a new car dealer?
4. What kinds of consumer products are the following: (*a*) watches, (*b*) cars, (*c*) toothpastes? Explain your reasoning.
5. Consumer services tend to be intangible and goods tend to be tangible. Use an example to explain how the lack of a physical good in a pure service might affect efforts to promote the service.
6. How would the marketing mix for a staple convenience product differ from the one for a homogeneous shopping product? How would the mix for a speciality product differ from the mix for a heterogeneous shopping product? Use examples.
7. Give an example of a product that is a *new* unsought product for most people. Briefly explain why it is an unsought product.
8. In what types of stores would you expect to find: (*a*) convenience products, (*b*) shopping products, (*c*) speciality products and (*d*) unsought products?
9. Cite two examples of business products that require a substantial amount of service in order to be useful.
10. Explain why a new firm of solicitors might want to lease, rather than buy, furniture.
11. Would you expect to find any wholesalers selling the various types of business products? Are retail stores required (or something like retail stores)?
12. What kinds of business products are the following: (*a*) lubricating oil, (*b*) electric motors, (*c*) a firm that provides landscaping and grass mowing for a building complex? Explain your reasoning.
13. How do raw materials differ from other business products? Do the differences have any impact on their marketing mixes? If so, what specifically.
14. For the kinds of business products described in this chapter, complete the following table (use one or a few well-chosen words).

1. Kind of distribution facility(ies) needed and functions they will provide.
2. Calibre of salespeople required.
3. Kind of advertising required.

Products	1	2	3
Capital investment			
Buildings and land rights			
Major equipment			
Standard			
Custom-made			
Accessories			
Raw materials			
Farm products			
Natural products			
Components			
Supplies			
Maintenance and small			
operating supplies			
Operating supplies			
Professional services			

15. Explain how industry sales and industry profits behave over the product life cycle.
16. Cite two examples of products that you feel are currently in each of the product life-cycle stages. Consider services as well as physical goods.
17. Explain how you might reach different conclusions about the correct product life-cycle stage(s) in the worldwide car market.
18. Explain why individual brands may not follow the product life-cycle pattern. Give an example of a new brand that is not entering the life cycle at the market introduction stage.
19. Discuss the life cycle of a product in terms of its probable impact on a manufacturer's marketing mix. Illustrate using personal computers.
20. What characteristics of a new product will help it to move through the early stages of the product life cycle more quickly? Briefly discuss each characteristic—illustrating with a product of your choice. Indicate how each characteristic might be viewed in some other country.

SUGGESTED CASES

1. Mcdonald's 'Seniors' Restaurant
2. Paper Supplies Corporation

REFERENCES

1. 'The eclipse of Mars', *Fortune*, 28 November 1994, pp. 82–92; 'In Moscow, the attack of the killer brands', *Business Week*, 10 January 1994, p. 40; 'Russia Snickers after Mars invades', The *Wall Street Journal*, 13 July 1993, p. B1ff.
2. S. Brown, R. Fisk and M.J. Bitner, 'The development and emergence of services marketing thought', *The International Journal of Service Industry Management*, vol. 5, no. 1, 1994, pp. 21–48; L.L. Berry, A. Parasuraman and V.A. Zeithaml, 'The service-quality puzzle', *Business Horizons*, September/October 1988, pp. 35–43.
3. W.S. Bishop, J.L. Graham and M.H. Jones, 'Volatility of Derived Demand in Industrial Markets and Its Management Implications', *Journal of Marketing*, Fall 1984, pp. 95–103.
4. Available from World Wide Web: <http://palmpilot.3com.com.>; 'The PalmPilot sequel is a hit', Fortune, 13 April 1998, pp. 154–56; 'The PalmPilot flies higher', *Business Week*, 23 March 1998, p. 20; 'A best seller gets better', *Newsweek*, 16 March 1998, p. 79; 'Palm-to-palm combat,' Time, 16 March 1998, pp. 42–44; '3Com again changes name of hot-selling PalmPilot', *Advertising Age*, 9 March 1998, p. 4; 'Apple drops Newton, an idea ahead of its time', *The Wall Street Journal*, 2 March 1998, p. B1ff.; 'What's in a name? Ask 3Com', *Business Week*, 26 January 1998, p. 6; 'Little computers, big new marketing battle', *The Wall Street Journal*, 17 November 1997, p. B1ff.; 'A rocket in its pocket,' Business Week, 9 September 1996, pp. 111–14; 'How Palm computing became an architect', *Harvard Business Review*, September–October 1997, p. 89.
5. 'Netscape's plan: survive, thrive—New focus is on digital economy', *USA Today*, 21 April 1998, p. 1Bff.; 'Netscape to share browser program code', *The Wall Street Journal*, 23 January 1998, p. B6; 'Special report: The Internet', *The Wall Street Journal*, 8 December 1997, pp. R1–32; 'Netspeed at Netscape', *Business Week*, 10 February 1997, pp. 78–86; 'A sea change for Netscape: Internet upstart shows muscle on the Web', *USA Today*, 6 February 1996, p. 1Bff.
6. 'Sony isn't mourning the "death" of Betamax', *Business Week*, 25 January 1988, p. 37; S.P. Schaars, 'When Entering Growth Markets,

Are Pioneers Better than Poachers?' *Business Horizons*, March/April 1986, pp. 27–36; M. Lambkin, 'Pioneering New Markets: A Comparison of Market Share Winners and Losers', *International Journal of Research in Marketing*, March 1992, pp. 5–22.

7. 'Multimedia goes Mainstream', *Business Marketing*, June 1991, pp. 20–22; 'A new spin on videodiscs', *Newsweek*, 5 June 1989, pp. 68–69.

8. A. Garrett, 'Soap tablets lever Persil to success', *The Observer*, Business section, 6 September 1998, p. 5; G. Alexander, 'P&G gambles on shake-up to beat crisis', *The Sunday Times*, 13 September 1998, Business section, p. 10; 'Ultra-clean—Retail cheers still more P&G concentrates', *Advertising Age*, 22 August 1994, p.1ff.

9. For more on rejuvenating mature products, see 'A boring brand can be beautiful', *Fortune*, 18 November 18 1991, pp. 169–77; R.F. Maruca and A.L. Halliday, 'When new products and customer loyalty collide', *Harvard Business Review*, November–December 1993, pp. 22–36; G.L. Gordon, R.J. Calantone, and C.A. di Benedetto, 'Mature markets and revitalization strategies: An American fable', *Business Horizons*, May/June 1991, pp. 39–50; 'Teflon is 50 years old, but Du Pont is still finding new uses for invention', *The Wall Street Journal*, 7 April 1988, p. 34.

CHAPTER 8
New-Product Development and Branding

When You Finish This Chapter, You Should

1 Know what is involved in designing new products and what constitutes a 'new product'.

2 Understand the new-product development process.

3 Understand the need for product or brand managers.

4 Understand the meaning of branding.

5 Know what conditions are more conducive to branding success.

6 Understand the strategic importance of packaging.

7 Know why warranties are an important part of the product or service.

8 Understand the important new terms (shown in colour).

For many years Volvo had a reputation of manufacturing safe, if somewhat boring, cars. While the company has led European car manufacturers in terms of its reputation for safety, the model ranges were uncompromisingly designed. Conscious of the need to develop new markets Volvo deliberately attempted to move away from its original position to project itself in a different way to its target markets.

The introduction of the high performance 850 series was a radical change in product policy for Volvo. Cars in this range were portrayed as high-performance cars with the same potential speeds and acceleration as several well-known sports cars. These cars were shown in ads in dangerous situations, where their performance and safety were major reasons used to explain their purchase.

More recently Volvo has developed a range of mid-sized cars, the S40 and V40 designed to compete in the market segment dominated by companies such as BMW and Mercedes. These model ranges move away from the traditional 'box-like' designs of former ranges. They are more 'rounded' in profile and the interiors have been designed to meet the expectations of drivers who would have been comparing the car against competitors such as BMW.

To meet the needs of different customers the new models have a variety of different optional extras, designed to allow the buyer to 'create' the car of his or her choice. While the basic models come equipped with antilock brakes, electric front windows, power steering, six-point stereo, driver's airbag, central locking and immobilizer, and side impact airbags, optional extras include sunroof, rear arm rest, remote locking, handling and suspension upgrades, air conditioning, electric rear windows, and automatic transmissions. In total there are over 14000 potential options for the prospective buyer to choose from.

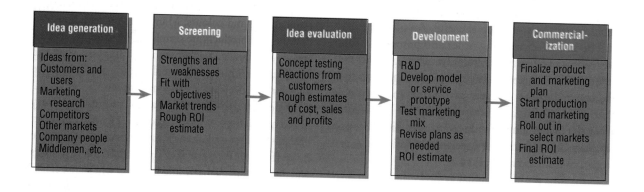

Exhibit 8–1 New-Product Development Process

itself or be rejected. Such a process may seem harsh, but experience shows that most new ideas have some flaw that can lead to problems and even substantial losses. Marketers try to discover those flaws early, and either find a remedy or reject the idea completely. Applying this process requires much analysis of the idea, both within and outside the firm—*before* the company spends money to develop and market a product. This is a major departure from the usual production-oriented approach in which a company develops a product first and then asks sales to 'get rid of it'.

Of course, the actual new-product success rate varies among industries and companies. Many companies *are* improving the way they develop new products. It is important to understand that if a firm does not use an organized process like this, it may bring bad or weak ideas to market, at a substantial loss.

Step 1—Idea generation

New ideas can come from a company's own sales or production staff, distributors, competitors, consumer surveys or other sources such as trade associations, advertising agencies or government agencies. By analysing new and different views of the company's markets and studying present consumer behaviour, a marketing manager can spot opportunities that have not yet occurred to competitors, or even to potential customers.

This aspect of product planning reflects basic market or customer orientation. Every company, big or small can benefit from listening to the customer, looking at the competition and reacting appropriately. For example, a small restaurant can analyse systematically the pattern of selections made from its menus to discover what is selling well and what is less popular. Visits to other competitive restaurants in the neighbourhood

would also provide information on competitive menus and prices. Suppliers, for example, of frozen desserts may have new ranges that would increase the potential variety of choice to restaurant users. A new chef with experience elsewhere will also bring new ideas.

No one firm can always be first with the best new ideas. In their search for ideas, companies should pay attention to what current or potential competitors are doing. For example, new-product specialists at Olivetti buy other firms' products as soon as they are available. Then they take them apart to see what the other firms are doing in the way of new ideas or improvements. British Airways talks to travel agents and constantly monitors the market to learn about new services offered by competitors. Many other companies use similar approaches.[4]

Research shows that many new ideas in business markets come from customers. Such customers frequently identify a need. Then they approach a supplier with the idea, perhaps even with a particular design or specification. The supplier then develops the product in collaboration with the customer. For example, a software house may be approached by a company with a request for a software solution to a particular business problem. The user may have already have defined what it wants from the software package and the supplier's job is to meet the specification. Such a customer can become the lead-user of the product, but the supplier may be able to sell the solution to other customers.

Ideas can also be come the company's own research and development work. Many companies sustain high levels of expenditure on R&D with the objective of developing new products for the future. When such products can be patented, for example in the case of many drugs, this can provide considerable competitive advantage.

BBA FRICTION-MINTEX DON LIMITED

'There is a large emphasis on customer needs now. In R&D we have spent a lot of time over the last few years to ensure that we fully understand customer requirements. Their needs are changing rapidly and the best way to understand that is to talk to customers'.

BBA Friction manufactures and supplies friction materials for braking and power transmission applications. Mintex Don produces brake linings that are supplied to many of the world's leading car, truck and bus manufacturers.

Realizing the fundamental differences in the markets it serves, Mintex Don reorganized into three separate business units—Light Vehicle Products, Heavy Vehicle Products and After Market. Although the basic product technology is similar for each business unit, the requirements for manufacturing planning, marketing and distribution are so different that a market-focused reorganization was necessary. Customer focus has significantly improved, as reported by customer satisfaction assessments, and so has company performance.

To describe Mintex Don as a supplier of brake linings belies the complexity and expertise that goes into developing and producing this most critical of components. Mintex Don is more precisely a supplier of 'friction technology'. A sophisticated combination of chemistry and engineering disciplines are required to meet the rapidly advancing customer requirements for brake performance. World class research and development, allied closely with exceptional manufacturing capability, is therefore essential.

Mintex Don Research and Development Division provides a research and development service to customers and Mintex Don's international manufacturing business. The R&D division has its own mission, which has been defined by consideration of both internal and external customer requirements. The role of R&D is seen as central to the success of the business and senior managers throughout the company are regularly informed about, if not regularly involved with, new-product development activities.

Following the reorganization into business units, R&D also restructured to focus on cars and heavy vehicles. Previously these two markets had been dealt with by the same R&D teams. The central research team interfaces between the two customer-focused units. In each unit there are three sections, namely engineering, product development chemists and testing. The engineers work extremely closely with customers, and to enhance this linkage new-product development teams are structured by customer. For example, one team many be developing with the Japanese transplants, one with Ford Motor Company, another with Rover Group, another with the French market, etc.

The role of the central research team is to provide support for the teams at each stage of product development. This research group includes a diverse range of specialists ranging from analytical chemists who design-out brake noise and other problems at an early stage, to process technologists who assess the best way to manufacture products for the next 5 to 10 years.

Equal emphasis is placed on manufacturing process development as it is on the development of the product itself. Mintex Don has invested heavily in an extensive preproduction laboratory, with all equipment mirroring that used in the factory except on a smaller scale. This ensures that anything R&D develop can be manufactured efficiently in full-scale production.

Scale-up is a vital issue for Mintex Don, and one that has in the past culminated in projects failing at the final hurdle. Lessons were learnt from failure. Changes were made which resulted in earlier involvement of manufacturing in the development cycle to ensure that product and process innovation occurred simultaneously.

The new-product development process has now been well documented with systematic procedures in place to monitor and control the whole process from concept to production. The R&D teams are also well trained in formal evaluative techniques for project appraisal (e.g. Tagucci, finite element analysis, etc.) and are assessed in terms of how well they have performed in the process, and not just how well the final product performs. This has generated an atmosphere where new-product development teams have the tools to manage the development process most effectively, and fear of failure does not limit creativity and innovative thinking.

However, Mintex Don realizes that it does not have all the answers and can learn from external sources. The importance of codevelopment has been recognized and new-product development frequently takes place with customers, suppliers and research institutions. Cooperation with key customers is seen as particularly vital, and frequently this will involve both the brake and vehicle manufacturers in a tripartite development initiative. The overriding consideration has to be for the whole car and not the friction material in isolation.

Mintex Don's R&D activities are recognized as being central to the success of the organization, but they are not viewed in isolation. Their role is defined in terms of how it can contribute to the success of the business as a whole, and to the success of its customers. Close links with internal and external customers are maintained through excellent communication systems and cross-disciplinary team working. This customer-focused R&D approach coupled with state-of-the-art manufacturing facilities and a market-driven organizational structure, has resulted in Mintex Don becoming a major force in a highly competitive market supplying increasingly demanding customers.[5]

Mintex Don illustrates the importance of using both customers and R&D to develop new ideas in a competitive market. They also illustrate how a systematic approach can show dividends.

Step 2—Screening

Screening involves evaluating the new ideas with the product-market screening criteria described in Chapter 6. Recall that these criteria include the combined output of a resource (strengths and weaknesses) analysis, a long-run trends analysis, and a thorough understanding of the company's objectives. Further, a good new idea should eventually lead to a product (and marketing mix) that will give the firm a competitive advantage, hopefully a lasting one. Opportunities with better growth potential are likely to be more attractive. Screening should consider how the strategy for a new product would hold up over the whole product life cycle. In other words, screening should consider how attractive the new product will be both in the short term and long term.

Screen based on consumer welfare

Screening should also consider how a new product will affect consumers over time. Ideally, the product should increase consumer welfare, not just satisfy a whim. Exhibit 8–2 shows different kinds of new-product opportunities. Obviously, a socially responsible firm tries to find desirable opportunities rather than deficient ones. This may not be as easy as it sounds, however. Some consumers want pleasing products instead of desirable ones. They emphasize immediate satisfaction and give little thought to their own long-term welfare. Some competitors willingly offer what consumers want in the short run. Generating socially responsible new-product ideas is a challenge for new-product planners, but consumer groups are helping firms to become more aware.

For example, in the food industry many suppliers face a dilemma. Should they continue to manufacture and supply food products that are attractive to the consumer such as full fat ice cream. Alternatively should they focus more on products which are healthy, but lack mass market appeal and higher sales volumes. The optimum solution would be to develop food products that are not only healthy but also highly profitable. In the ice-cream market frozen yoghurt is one such product.

Safety must be considered

Real acceptance of the marketing concept certainly leads to safe products. But consumers still buy some risky products for the thrills and excitement they provide—for example, bicycles, skis, hang gliders and bungee jumps. Even so, companies can usually add safety features and some potential customers want them. Each of the major European countries has its own codes of safety, which govern product performance. Frequently these have been harmonized, particularly for products such as domestic appliances that are sold across Europe. Since 1998, all products sold for the handicapped in the EU must have a 'Conformité Europeenne' mark to show that they conform to minimum standards, though manufacturers still face huge differences between countries.

Product safety complicates strategy planning because not all customers, even those who want better safety features, are willing to pay more for safer products. Some

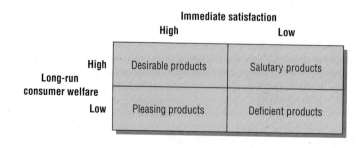

Exhibit 8–2 Types of New-Product Opportunities

features cost a lot to add and increase prices considerably. These safety concerns must be considered at the screening step because a firm can later be held liable for unsafe products. Pharmaceutical products must go through several years of clinical trials and testing before they are released for general use. This process may seem to be a potential waste of time and resources, but is essential if safety concerns about new drugs are to be addressed.

Products can turn to liabilities

Product liability means the legal obligation of sellers to pay damages to individuals who are injured by defective or unsafe products. Product liability is a serious matter. Liability settlements may exceed not only a company's insurance coverage but its total assets!

Courts in many European countries enforce a very strict product liability standard. Producers may be held responsible for injuries related to their products no matter how the items are used or how well they're designed. Product liability is a serious ethical and legal matter. Many countries are attempting to change their laws so that they will be fair to both firms and consumers. Until product liability questions are resolved, marketing managers must be even more sensitive when screening new-product ideas.

ROI is a crucial screening criterion

Getting by the initial screening criteria doesn't guarantee success for the new idea. But it does show that at least the new idea fits generally *for this firm*. If many ideas pass the screening criteria, a firm must set priorities to determine which ones go onto the next step in the process. This can be done by comparing the return on investment (ROI) for each idea—assuming the firm is ROI-oriented. The most attractive alternatives are pursued first.

Return on investment is related to sales and costs. It is important at an early stage to produce an initial estimate of the likely level of sales of a new idea. Forecasting is a difficult task, but nevertheless it is essential to get some overall indication of the level of return associated with investing in a particular product. Marketing can help by producing estimates of the overall market size and projecting what the income might be with different levels of market share. Experience in forecasting demand for related products can be helpful, but when the product is a completely new concept forecasting can be very difficult to get right. For example, how confident would you be today in predicting how many people would be using the Internet for banking in 10 years' time?

Firms also need an estimate of the costs of producing new products. These costs are established by consultation between production, design and product development. The BBA Friction-Mintex Don case showed that new-product development had to address the manufacturing process development throughout the project. It is important at an early stage to design the product in such a way that it can be manufactured easily. It is no good having an elegant product design which costs too much to manufacture or is difficult to produce at the right level of quality.

Finding new product ideas ought not to be left to chance. Companies need a formal procedure for seeking new ideas. The checkpoints discussed below should be reviewed regularly to assure a continual flow of new and sound ideas. A continual flow of ideas for new products allows a business to spot an opportunity early, while there is still time to take advantage of it. Although later steps eliminate many ideas, a company must have some that succeed.

Step 3—Idea evaluation

When an idea moves past the screening step, it is evaluated more carefully. Note that an actual product has not yet been developed and this can handicap the firm in getting feedback from customers. For help in idea evaluation, firms use concept testing—getting reactions from customers about how well a new product idea fits their needs. Concept testing uses market research ranging from informal focus groups to formal surveys of potential customers.

Companies can often get better estimates of likely costs, revenue and profitability at this stage. Market research can help to identify the size of potential markets. Informal focus groups are useful, especially if they show that potential users are not excited about the new idea. If results are discouraging, it may be best to kill the idea at this stage. Remember, in this hypothesis-testing process, we're looking for any evidence that an idea is *not* a good opportunity for this firm—and should be rejected.

Product planners must think about wholesaler and retailer customers as well as final consumers. Distributors may have special concerns about handling a proposed product. At a basic level packaging must be designed so that it fits onto the supermarket shelf. Round containers take up more shelf space than square ones, but are more appealing to customers. Many supermarkets operate standard fixture sizes which packs must fit onto. Packaging must protect the product as it travels through the distribution channel to the shelf. We return to the topic of packaging towards the end of this chapter.

Idea evaluation is often more precise in business markets. Potential customers are more informed and their needs focus on the economic reasons for buying rather than emotional factors. Further, given the derived nature of demand in business markets, most needs are already being satisfied in some way. New products frequently substitute for existing ones. This means that product planners can compare the cost advantages and limitations of a new product with those currently being used. By interviewing well-informed people, they can determine the range of product requirements and decide whether there is an opportunity.

For example, the printing technology used to produce this book is well understood. The capabilities of the machines that are currently used are well defined, and the printer knows the various costs of each stage of production. These costs include paper usage, printing inks and labour costs. Suppliers can estimate the impact of a new ink, paper or printing process on printing costs and calculate the potential demand. Discussions with printers would quickly reveal whether the printer also saw potential benefits.

Whatever research methods are used, the idea evaluation step should gather enough information to help decide whether there is an opportunity, whether it fits with the firm's resources, *and* whether there is a basis for developing a competitive advantage. With such information, the firm can estimate likely ROI in the various market segments and decide whether to continue the new-product development process.[6]

Step 4—Development

Product ideas that survive the screening and idea evaluation steps must now be analysed further. Usually, this involves some engineering to design and develop the physical part of the product. In the case of a new service offering, the firm will work out the details of what training, equipment, staff and so on will be needed to deliver on the idea. Input from the earlier efforts helps guide this technical work.

Computer-aided design (CAD) systems greatly facilitate design work. Designers can develop lifelike 3-D colour drawings of packages and products. Then the computer allows the manager to look at the product from different angles and views, just as with a real product. Changes can be made almost instantly. Once the designs are finalized they feed directly into computer-controlled manufacturing systems. Companies like Lucas and Daimler-Benz have found that these systems cut their new-product development time in half, giving them a lead on competitors. Even so, it is still good to test models and early versions of the product in the market. This process may have several cycles. A manufacturer may build a model of a physical product or produce limited quantities; a service firm may try to train a small group of service providers. Product tests with customers may lead to revisions—*before* the firm commits to full-scale efforts to produce the good or service. Software companies use this form of research, which they term

'beta-testing' to identify potential bugs and problems with new software before it is released to the whole marketplace.

With actual goods or services, potential customers can react to how well the product meets their needs. Using small focus groups, panels and larger surveys, marketers can get reactions to specific features and to the whole product idea. Sometimes that reaction kills the idea. For example, CocaCola Foods believed it had a great idea with Minute Maid SqueezeFresh, frozen orange juice concentrate in a squeeze bottle. CocaCola thought consumers would prefer to mix one glass at a time rather than find space for another two-litre jug in the refrigerator. When actually tested, however, SqueezeFresh flopped. Consumers loved the idea but hated the product. It was messy to use, and no one knew how much concentrate to squeeze in the glass.

In other cases, testing can lead to revision of product specifications for different markets. Sometimes a complex series of revisions may be required. Months or even years of research may be necessary to focus on precisely what different market segments will find acceptable. For example, Gillette's Mach 3 razor took seven years and nearly £500 million pounds to develop—see the Gillette case in the box that follows.

Firms often use full-scale market testing to get reactions in real market conditions or to test product variations and variations in the marketing mix. For example, a firm may test alternative brands, prices, or advertising copy in different test locations. Note that the firm is testing the whole marketing mix, not just the product. For example, a hotel chain might test a new service offering at one location to see how it appeals to customers.

Test marketing can involve the risk of giving information to competitors. However, *not* testing is also dangerous. Market tests can be very expensive. Nevertheless, an extensive amount of product and promotional testing takes place in a wide range of European markets before products are finally commercialized. This can range from testing advertisements to long-term product evaluation for many pharmaceutical products. This can uncover problems that otherwise might go undetected and destroy the whole strategy.

If a company follows the new-product development process carefully, the market test will provide a lot more information to the firm than to its competitors. Of course, the company must test specific variables rather than just vaguely testing whether a new idea will sell. After the market test, the firm can estimate likely ROI for various strategies to determine whether the idea moves on to commercialization.

In some sectors market tests are not practical. In fashion markets, for example, speed is extremely important, and products are usually just tried in market. Indeed, designers are usually very concerned to maintain tight security around their latest ideas until the seasons' fashions are formally launched at fashion shows. Durable products, which have high fixed production costs and long production lead times, may have to go directly to market. In these cases, it is especially important that the early steps be done carefully to reduce the chances for failure.

products annually. In 1997, 49 per cent of the company's sales came from products introduced in the last five years. The pace and scale of new-product development can be seen in the new products introduced in 1998: Duracell Ultra line of high technology alkaline batteries, the Braun Oral-B 3D plaque remover and the Mach 3 shaving system. The Mach 3 is the first triple-blade razor and the company argues that it is the most technologically advanced shaving system in history.

The shaving market is large. In 1997 Gillette had 66 per cent of the male shaving market and 70 per cent of the female shaving market. Gillette sold $2.9 billion worth of razors and blades. Gillette aim to be technologically dominant in its served markets. So, rather than compete on price or image, Gillette has made huge investments in new-product development. The Mach 3 was developed in Reading, England, at Gillette's R&D laboratory. Scientists set out to find a more efficient way of shaving and a successor product to its existing brand the Sensor Excel. In some respects the Mach 3 is an incremental development on the Sensor Excel. However, in the materials employed and the use of three blades the Mach 3 is a very new product.

Scientists came up with the technology to allow three-blade shaving. Using Silicon Graphics workstations to configure simulated shaving movements, Gillette was able to see how well a prototype blade would work without having to make the prototype. Using a project code name of Manx, the development work continued. Industrial designers were detailed to create a 'masculine, high-tech and aerodynamic' version of the product. Several hundred potential brand names were whittled down to four—Triad, Synchro 3, Vector 3 and Mach 3 before the last name was selected.

Market research with potential customers in the first out-plant shaving test assured the company that the product was a hit with the market. Shavers said it shaved smoothly, like a paint brush and left the skin feeling smoother. Achieving a closer and more comfortable shave was the ultimate aim of the R&D team. Having developed the product from 1992, the approach of commercialization in 1998 meant that production of the product in volume was the next stage. Gillette spent hundreds of millions of pounds installing state-of-the-art machines to mass produce the Mach 3. Workers had to sign confidentiality agreements and production of the Mach 3 was kept separate from the rest of the factory. The product was launched with a substantial advertising campaign and has achieved considerable market success. As production continues, the production machines are slowly being debugged and their speed is being ratcheted up. Already, the R&D team is at work on a successor product.[7]

Step 5—Commercialization

A product idea that survives this far can finally be placed on the market. First, the new-product people decide exactly which product form or line to sell. Then they complete the marketing mix—really a whole strategic plan. Top management has to approve an ROI estimate for the plan before it is implemented. Finally, the product idea emerges from the new-product development process—but success requires the cooperation of the whole company.

Putting a product on the market is expensive. Manufacturing or service facilities have to be set up. Goods have to be produced to fill the channels of distribution, or people must be hired and trained to provide services. Further, introductory promotion is costly, especially if the company is entering a very competitive market. Because of the size of the job, some firms introduce their products city by city or region by region, in a gradual 'roll out', until they have complete market coverage. Roll outs also permit more market testing although that is not their purpose. Rather, the purpose is to do a good job implementing the marketing plan. Marketing managers also need to pay close attention to control to ensure that the implementation effort is working and that the strategy is on target.

Rivalry in the vacuum cleaner market is fierce. The established companies have been shaken by the huge success of a newcomer to the market. The Dyson vacuum cleaner was launched on the market in the late 1980s. Within two years of its launch, the Dyson cleaner became the best selling cleaner in the British market, overtaking the established brands of Electrolux, Hoover, Panasonic, Miele and the rest. Dyson now dominates the market to an extent that is rare in a mature sector. It has more than half the market by value and a third by volume. How has a new product achieved such success?

The idea of developing new technology for vacuum cleaning belongs to the owner of the company—an entrepreneur called James Dyson. He pursued the idea and spent five years perfecting the new vacuum cleaner. After 5 127 prototypes he had a working model. However, existing manufacturers who were approached to buy the invention were disinterested. Using his own house to secure finance, Dyson therefore decided to make the cleaner under his own name and to take on the companies who had rejected his invention.

At £200, the cleaners are priced well above those of competitors but customers are prepared to pay the extra for the advertised better design of the cleaners and their better performance. The factory now makes 9 000 cleaners per day and has 600 workers assembling the distinctive yellow and grey bits of plastic. All staff, regardless of their job, spend the first day assembling a cleaner so that they know how the product works.

The firm has concentrated on the one product and managing the phenomenal growth of the business. Overseas distributors and subsidiaries handle sales in Australia, France, Germany, Turkey, Sweden, Holland and Israel. In America the product trades under the names of Fantom, Lightning and Fury and is manufactured under licence. The company hopes soon to be selling in Japan, the home of electrical appliance manufacture and marketing.

Dyson is working on new products and has 200 designers in his R&D department. The team are looking at what other products the company can successfully make. Dyson will not introduce any new product unless he is sure that it can beat anything the competition is providing. The company is keen to avoid small appliances that can be easily copied. Having a fortune of £400 million does cushion the risks in any future new-product development. However, such is the Dyson legend, that when any new products are launched the Dyson reputation will be at stake.[8]

NEW-PRODUCT DEVELOPMENT: A TOTAL COMPANY EFFORT

Top-level support is vital

Companies that are particularly successful at developing new goods and services seem to have one trait in common: enthusiastic top-management support for new-product development. New products tend to upset old routines that managers of established products often try in subtle but effective ways to maintain. So someone with top-level support, and authority to get things done, needs to be responsible for new-product development.

A new-product development department or team (committee) from different departments may help ensure that new ideas are carefully evaluated and profitable ones quickly brought to market—as the Mintex Don case illustrates. It is important to choose the right people for the job. Overly conservative managers may kill too many, or even all, new ideas. Or committees may create bureaucratic delays leading to late introduction and giving competitors a head start. A delay of even a few months can make the difference between a product's success or failure. Sometimes one committed manager can make the difference, see the Dyson case study.

Market needs guide R&D effort

Many new-product ideas come from scientific discoveries and new technologies. That is why firms often assign specialists to study the technological environment in search of new ways to meet customers' needs. Many firms have their own R&D group that works on developing new products and new-product ideas. Even service firms have technical specialists who help in development work. For example, a bank thinking about offering customers a new set of investment alternatives must be certain that it can deliver on its promises. We've touched on this earlier, but the relationship between marketing and R&D warrants special emphasis.

The R&D effort is usually handled by scientists, engineers and other specialists who have technical training and skills. Their work can make an important contribution to a firm's competitive advantage—especially if it competes in high-tech markets. However, technical creativity by itself is not enough. The R&D effort must be guided by the type of new-product development process discussed here.

From the idea generation stage to the commercialization stage, the R&D specialists, the operations people and the marketing people must work together to evaluate the feasibility of new ideas. It is not sensible for a marketing manager to develop elaborate marketing plans for goods or services that the firm simply cannot produce, or produce profitably. It also does not make sense for R&D people to develop a technology or product that does not have potential for the firm and its markets. Clearly, a balancing act is involved here. The critical point is the basic one emphasized throughout the whole book: marketing-oriented firms seek to satisfy customer needs at a profit with an integrated, whole-company effort.

A complicated, integrated effort is needed

Developing new products should be a total company effort. The whole process, involving people in management, research, production, promotion, packaging and branding, must move in steps from early exploration of ideas to development of the product and marketing mix.

Even with a careful development process, many new products do fail, usually because a company skips some steps in the process. Because speed can be important, it is always tempting to skip needed steps when some part of the process seems to indicate that the company has a really good idea. The process moves in steps, gathering different kinds of information along the way. By skipping steps, a firm may miss an important aspect that could make a whole strategy less profitable, or actually cause it to fail.

Eventually, the new product is no longer new and it becomes just another product. In some firms, at this point the new-product people turn the product over to production people and start to develop other new ideas. In other firms, the person who is the new-product champion continues with the new product, perhaps taking on the broader responsibility for turning it into a successful business.

NEED FOR PRODUCT MANAGERS

Product variety leads to product managers

When a firm has only one or a few related products, everyone in the company is interested in them. But when many new products are being developed, someone should be put in charge of new-product planning to be sure it is not neglected. Similarly, when a firm has products in several different product categories, management may decide to put someone in charge of each category, or each brand, to be sure that attention to these products is not lost in the rush of everyday business. Product managers or brand managers manage specific products, often taking over the jobs formerly handled by an advertising manager. That gives a clue to what is often their major responsibility—Promotion—since the products have already been developed by the new-product people. However, some brand managers start at the new-product development stage and carry on from there. In the next section you will see how brand management has become a major area of responsibility in many companies.

Product or brand managers are especially common in large companies that produce many kinds of products. Several product managers may serve under a marketing manager. Sometimes these product managers are responsible for the profitable operation of a particular product's whole marketing effort. Then they have to coordinate their efforts with others, including the sales manager, advertising agencies, production and research people, and even channel members. This is likely to lead to difficulties if product managers have neither control over the marketing strategy for other related brands nor authority over other functional areas whose efforts they are expected to direct and coordinate!

To avoid these problems, in some companies the product manager serves mainly as a product champion, concerned with planning and getting the promotion effort implemented. A higher-level marketing manager with more authority coordinates the efforts and integrates the marketing strategies for different products into an overall plan. The activities of product managers vary a lot depending on their experience and aggressiveness, and the company's organizational philosophy. Today companies are emphasizing marketing *experience* because this important job takes more than academic training and enthusiasm. Clearly someone must be responsible for developing and implementing product-related plans, especially when a company has many products.[9]

BRANDING IS A STRATEGIC ISSUE

There are so many brands that we take them for granted. In the grocery products area alone, there are more than 70 000 brands. Brands are of great importance to their owners. They help to identify the company's marketing mix and help customers to recognize the firm's products and advertising.

What is branding?

Branding means the use of a name, term, symbol or design—or a combination of these—to identify a product. It includes the use of brand names, trademarks and practically all other means of product identification. Branding may even extend to relating brands to colours. For example, Milka chocolate produced by Suchard has a distinctive purple wrapper. Pepsi now presents its cans in blue as distinct from Coke's red cans. Body Shop's 1500 stores throughout the world have a distinctive green livery.

The process of branding is a complex one. All of us have distinctive images of a company and its products or services. These images are the result of our experience of these products and services as customers or more generally when we see advertisements or when others tell us about their experiences. We also have images of competing products or services, which are constantly compared with specific brands.

Think about an expensive wrist-watch such as Tag Heuer or Rolex. What images do these two watches have in your mind? Both are expensive, but do they serve the same needs. If you look at the advertising you will see that Tag watches are clearly associated with sporting performance. Rolex are associated with exclusive lifestyles. They have different images or meanings to the customer. Which one would you like best as a gift if you were fortunate enough to have the choice? Today there are also many cheap copies of Rolex or other watches on the market. Why should anyone want to buy the 'real thing', when it is possible to buy a copy which is indistinguishable from the original, unless it is closely inspected? The reality is that the consumer still gets considerable personal satisfaction, which makes the 'real' watch worth buying, even at a high price. He or she still knows that it is the 'real thing'.

Others will share many of the thoughts that went through your mind as you read the last paragraph. Some will be unique to you as a consumer. Skilful marketing attempts to build lasting favourable impressions of products in the minds of carefully defined target markets. These impressions are created when the company develops and implements an effective marketing programme. Pricing decisions, distribution decisions and promotional decisions must all be coordinated in an effective and distinctive way. The next few chapters discuss in detail how this is done.

Brand names and trademarks

Brand name has a narrower meaning. A brand name is a word, letter or a group of words or letters. Examples include Kickers, Levis, Lego and BMW.

Trademark is a legal term. A trademark includes only those words, symbols or marks that are legally registered for use by a single company.

The word 'Mars' can be used to explain these differences. The Mars bar is branded under the brand name (whether it is spoken or printed in any manner). When 'Mars' is printed in a certain kind of script, however, it becomes a trademark. A trademark need not be attached to the product. It need not even be a word, it can be a symbol. These differences may seem technical but they are very important to business firms that spend a lot of money to protect and promote their brands.

BRANDING—WHY IT DEVELOPED

Brands provide identification

Some of the earliest brands can be traced back to Roman times. Visitors to Pompeii and Ostia Anticca can still see evidence of symbols in the mosaics denoting craftsmen and other traders. During the Middle Ages when craft guilds (forerunners of labour unions) and merchant guilds formed to control the quantity and quality of production, each producer had to mark his goods so output could be cut back when necessary. This also meant that poor quality, which might reflect unfavourably on other guild products and discourage future trade, could be traced back to the guilty producer. Early trademarks also protected the buyer, who could then know the source of the product.

More recently, brands have been used for identification. As companies grew in size and extended their operations nationally and internationally it became more important to establish a common identity that would be widely recognized and preferred by consumers. Companies that were able to build high market share and brand preference gradually took over from less efficient competitors. Lever Bros, the international manufacturer of soap products established many leading brands during this period. Many of these brands, such as Persil, still dominate their segments. Exhibit 8–3 shows the enduring power of many household brand names.

Many successful brands were established a considerable time ago, and have played a powerful role in the marketplace ever since. Today, familiar brands exist for most product categories, ranging from Campbells (soups and sauces) to Adidas (sports

UK brands	Product	1933 position	Current position
Hovis	Bread	1	1
Stork	Margarine	1	1
Kellogg's	Cornflakes	1	1
Gilette	Razors	1	1
Schweppes	Mixers	1	1
Colgate	Toothpaste	1	1
Kodak	Film	1	1
Hoover	Vacuum cleaners	1	1

Exhibit 8-3 Dominance of Leading Brands

equipment). Brands can differ in terms of familiarity. Some are recognized internationally. Benetton, the Italian fashion brand, is widely recognized in many countries. Its controversial advertising campaigns have reinforced its excellence in production and distribution to create an international presence. Others have only national or regional presence.

Brands make consumers' shopping easier

Well-recognized brands make shopping easier. Think of trying to buy groceries, for example, if you had to evaluate the advantages and disadvantages of each of 20 000 items every time you went to a supermarket. Many customers are willing to buy new things but, having gambled and won, they like to buy a familiar brand the next time. Even on infrequent purchases, consumers often rely on well known brands as an indication of quality. If consumers try a brand and do not like it, they know what to avoid in future purchases.

 Internet Exercise

Go to the Procter and Gamble web site **(www.pg.com)** and click on P&G Products. Find out the brand names of the different shampoos and the target markets to which they appeal?

Branding helps branders too

Brand promotion has advantages for branders as well as customers. A good brand name speeds up shopping for the customer and thus reduces the marketer's selling time and effort. In addition, when customers repeatedly purchase by brand, the brander is protected against competition from other firms. Sometimes a firm's brand name is the only element in its marketing mix that a competitor cannot copy.

Good brand names can improve the company's image, speeding acceptance of new products marketed under the same name. For example, many consumers quickly tried frozen Mars bars when they were introduced because they already knew they liked the original Mars bar. From a financial perspective, the money that Mars spent over the years to promote the original brand paid off again when consumers tried the new product. There is a limit to how far the brand name can be stretched to cover new brands. However, many new products introduced in recent years have followed the approach of extending a successful brand name. Volkswagen, the German car manufacturer, also sells a wide range of financial services. Virgin, perhaps better known for its record stores and airline, also sells financial services and vodka. Both of these companies have extended the brand name to cover services that do not immediately seem to be consistent with the business where they started.[10]

CONDITIONS FAVOURABLE TO BRANDING

Most firms, especially firms that sell consumer products, work hard to establish respected brands. On the other hand, some product categories have fewer well-known brands. For example, can you recall a brand name for timber, nails or electric extension cables? As these examples suggest, it is not always easy to establish a respected brand.

The following conditions are favourable to successful branding:

1. The product is easy to identify by brand or trademark.
2. The product quality is the best value for the price and the quality is easy to maintain.
3. Dependable and widespread availability is possible. When customers start using a brand, they want to be able to continue using it.
4. The demand for the general product class is large.

5. The demand is strong enough so that the market price can be high enough to make the branding effort profitable.

6. There are economies of scale. If the branding is really successful, costs should drop and profits should increase.

7. Favourable shelf locations or display space in stores will help. This is something retailers can control when they brand their own products. Producers must use personal selling to get favourable positions.

ACHIEVING BRAND FAMILIARITY IS A CHALLENGE

Brand acceptance must be earned with a good product and regular promotion. Brand familiarity means how well customers recognize and accept a company's brand. The degree of brand familiarity affects the planning for the rest of the marketing mix, especially where the product should be offered and what promotion is needed.

Five levels of brand familiarity

Five levels of brand familiarity are useful for strategy planning: (1) rejection, (2) non-recognition, (3) recognition, (4) preference and (5) insistence.

Some brands have been tried and found wanting. Brand rejection means that potential customers won't buy a brand unless its image is changed. Rejection may suggest a change in the product or perhaps only a shift to target customers who have a better image of the brand. Overcoming a negative image is difficult and can be very expensive. Brand rejection is a big concern for service-oriented businesses because it's hard to control the quality of service. A business traveller who gets a dirty room in a Great Western Hotel in Budapest, might not return to any Great Western anywhere. Yet it is difficult for Great Western to ensure that every chambermaid does a good job every time.

Some products are seen as basically the same. Brand non-recognition means final consumers do not recognize a brand at all, even though distributors may use the brand name for identification and inventory control. Examples include school supplies, pencils and inexpensive crockery.

BAILEYS

Since its launch in 1974, Baileys Irish Cream Liqueur has become the number one liqueur in the world and the 13th biggest selling spirit. It rivals Guinness as the world's most famous Irish brand. Baileys accounts for over 1 per cent of Irish exports in value terms and makes up 50 per cent of spirits exported from Ireland. It is distributed in over 130 markets world-wide and the company reckons that the brand is known and drunk by 500 million consumers.

The success of Baileys is due to huge investment and marketing support. In 1998, the company spent 65 million pounds on promoting the brand throughout the world, having spent an average of 50 million pounds a year since its inception. The challenge now is to recruit new drinkers to the brand and to encourage existing Baileys drinkers to drink it more often.

To date, its most successful markets are Ireland, Britain, Spain, the US and Germany. In North America Baileys sells about 12 million bottles per year. The company knows that 10 per cent of consumers drink 80 per cent of the total volume of Baileys sold there. On average they drink around 30 glasses of Baileys a year, still regarded as a very low level of consumption. Despite the impression that Baileys may be the older person's drink research shows that more than 60 per cent of its consumers are under 35 years of age, with a 50/50 split between male and female drinkers. Even for those customers who drink only a couple of glasses of Baileys a year, the Baileys brand has a very strong image.

As for new customers, Baileys is trying to penetrate Asia, Latin America, Russia and China. In many cases, high-quality western brands are favoured in Russia and China so Baileys has a head start. Japan is a difficult market that Baileys has yet to really get established despite spending quite a lot of money and time there. Of course, the Irish market is the most successful for the brand and more Baileys is drunk per capita in Ireland than anywhere else.

With such an established brand the temptation is to exploit it. However, the company stresses that they want to protect the brand and not milk it. Nonetheless, it is unique in the drinks industry because it has also become an integral part of the ice cream, chocolate and confectionery sectors. The company is also testing the market with a whiskey under the Baileys umbrella brand. Great care is taken with anything done under the Baileys trademark. Depending on the various benchmarks for evaluating the test, the company will decide when and if to roll out Baileys whiskey on a national and international basis.

Baileys is an exemplar brand. It has established itself in the national market and some international markets. Market research continually informs management about the customers and potential customers. The extension of the brand to other sectors has helped to enhance the brand's image and to build the success of Baileys. Grand Metropolitan who own the brand have recently merged with Guinness to form one of the world's drinks giants. They rightly regard Baileys as a truly global brand and an icon.[11]

Brand recognition means that customers remember the brand. This can be a big advantage if there are many 'nothing' brands on the market. Even if consumers cannot recall the brand without help, they may be reminded when they see it in a store among other less familiar brands.

An example from the mobile telephone market in the United Kingdom shows how creativity can be used to establish and promote a brand. 'Orange' took on established competitors in the mobile phone market. The market had been dull with none of the players having a distinctive identity. Qualitative research helped to develop a theme for advertising of the 'wireless future'. The Orange brand promoted positive themes with advertising designed to communicate specific advantages of the brand. In projecting a strong, confident and positive brand identity the company was very successful. Spontaneous awareness of Orange outstripped that for Vodaphone and Cellnet, the two established competitors. Research found that people not only were aware of Orange but that they associated the brand with benefits and value for money, and this led to actual purchases.[12]

Most branders would like to win **brand preference**— which means that target customers usually choose the brand over other brands, perhaps because of habit or favourable past experience.

Brand insistence means customers insist on a firm's branded product and are willing to search for it. This is an objective of many target marketers. Here the firm may enjoy a very inelastic demand curve.

The right brand name can help

A good brand name can help build brand familiarity. It can help tell something important about the company or its product. Exhibit 8–4 lists some characteristics of a good brand name. Some successful brand names seem to break all these rules, but many of them got started when there was less competition.

Companies that compete in international markets face a special problem in selecting brand names. A name that conveys a positive image in one language may be meaningless in another. Or, worse, it may have unintended meanings. GM's Nova car is a classic example. GM stuck with the Nova name when it introduced the car in South America; it seemed like a sensible decision because *Nova* is the Spanish word for star. However, Nova also sounds the same as the Spanish words for 'no go'. Consumers weren't interested in a no-go car and sales didn't pick up until GM changed the name.[13]

A respected name builds brand equity

Because it is difficult and expensive to build brand recognition, some firms prefer to buy established brands rather than try to build their own. The value of a brand to its current owner or to a firm that wants to buy it is sometimes called **brand equity**—the value

---

- Short and simple
- Easy to spell and read
- Easy to recognize and remember
- Easy to pronounce
- Can be pronounced in only one way
- Can be pronounced in all languages (for international markets)

- Suggestive of product benefits
- Adaptable to packaging/labelling needs
- No undesirable imagery
- Always timely (does not get out of date)
- Adaptable to any advertising medium
- Legally available for use (not in use by another firm)

Exhibit 8–4 Characteristics of a Good Brand Name

FÜR UNVERGESSLICHE MOMENTE. *Tiffany Solitärdiamantring Etoile in Platin oder 18 Karat Gold.*

TIFFANY & CO.

SINCE 1837

MÜNCHEN RESIDENZSTRASSE 11 089/29 00 43-0 FRANKFURT GOETHESTRASSE 29 069/92 00 77-0

NEW YORK TORONTO LONDON MUNICH FRANKFURT ZURICH MILAN FLORENCE TOKYO SEOUL TAIPEI HONG KONG SINGAPORE SYDNEY

of a brand's overall strength in the market. For example, brand equity is likely to be higher if many satisfied customers insist on buying the brand and if retailers are eager to stock it. That almost guarantees ongoing profits from the brand and increases the brand's value.

Keeping customers satisfied and loyal is what builds brand equity. Concern about brand equity is another reason that there is increasing attention to building closer relationships with customers. However, traditional financial statements don't show the future profit potential of having a large base of satisfied customers. Perhaps they should. Having that information would prompt a lot of narrow-thinking finance managers to view marketing efforts as an investment, not just as an expense that drains profits.

In the last few years, particularly in the United Kingdom, there has been increased interest in quantifying the value of the brand in the company's balance sheet. This was prompted by a number of highly publicized takeovers including Nestlé's acquisition of Rowntree, the leading United Kingdom chocolate manufacturer, and Ford's purchase of Jaguar, manufacturer of specialist upmarket motor cars. Rowntree had concentrated on building up a portfolio of confectionery products which were well known throughout Europe. These included the Lion Bar, Kit Kat and other leading chocolate products. Rowntree also had good presence in specialist retail outlets, which made the company attractive to Nestlé. Nestlé bought the company, following a protracted struggle with Jacobs Suchard, a rival chocolate manufacturer, acquiring as a result a wide portfolio of attractive brands without needing to invest in them to build up the market.

When Ford bought Jaguar it acquired the prestige of the Jaguar name, which allowed it to enter into markets which would never have considered buying a Ford, however well it had been built. Ford's manufacturing and distribution strengths now support the Jaguar brand name in markets where international competition from companies such as Lexus (owned by Toyota) is intense.

PROTECTING BRAND NAMES AND TRADEMARKS

European law protects the rights of trademark and brand name owners. By registering the trademark, a company can gain some protection against other companies seeking to use the same trademark to brand their own products. Typically trademarks need to be registered in each country to which the protection is to apply. In the United Kingdom trademarks are registered with the patents office. A scan of registrations indicates that registrations are sought for several reasons, including protection for licensing purposes (e.g. Body Shop), and desire to extend into other non-related sectors (e.g. Virgin).

Counterfeiting is accepted in some cultures

Even when products are properly registered, counterfeiters may make unauthorized copies. Many well-known brands—ranging from Levi's jeans to Rolex watches to Zantac ulcer medicine to Mickey Mouse T-shirts—face this problem. Counterfeiting is especially common in developing countries. For example, counterfeit copies of software programs like WordPerfect are available in hundreds of outlets in Taiwan—often selling for a dollar or two each. In China, most videotapes and CDs are 'bootleg' copies. Multinational efforts are underway to stop such counterfeiting, but they may meet with limited success. Counterfeiting is big business in some countries, and their government agencies do not want to deal with the problem. There are also differences in cultural values. In some countries, for example, counterfeiting is not seen as unethical.[14]

WHAT KIND OF BRAND TO USE?

Keep it in the family

Branders of more than one product must decide whether they are going to use a family brand—the same brand name for several products—or individual brands for each product. Examples of family brands are Whiskas cat food products (international), and Galbani cheese and salami products (Italy) and Zanussi appliances (international).

The use of the same brand for many products makes sense if all are similar in type and quality. The main benefit is that the goodwill attached to one or two products may help the others. Money spent to promote the brand name benefits more than one product, which cuts promotion costs for each product. Using a family brand makes it easier, faster and less expensive to introduce new products. This can be an important competitive advantage and it explains why many firms are expanding the number of products sold under family brand names.

A special kind of family brand is a licensed brand—a well-known brand that sellers pay a fee to use. For example, The Body Shop is a widely recognized retail outlet operating in many countries. Licence to use the Body Shop name is franchised (licensed) to independent operators. Each operator must adopt the same retailing format, use the same product ranges and promote products in the same way. Instructions to staff in terms of standards of dress, approach to customers and so on ensure that the brand is presented in a consistent way in every market. Some products may be adapted to suit local customers' preferences in an effort to increase international sales—whereas Body Shop trades strongly in Scandinavian countries it fares less well in America and France. Despite these local adjustments, the Body Shop brand identity is common throughout the world.

Individual brands for outside and inside competition

A company uses individual brands—separate brand names for each product—when it is important for the products to each have a separate identity, as when products vary in quality or type. Often these brands are also associated under one overall corporate name. Nestlé provides one of the best illustrations of a wide range of products which carry not only the individual brand names, but also the overall Nestlé brand as a symbol of overall quality. Next time you are in a supermarket try to count the number of Nestlé brands in different product categories such as beverages, confectionery and cake mixes.

If the products are really different, individual brands can avoid confusion. Some firms use individual brands with similar products to make segmentation and positioning efforts easier. Unilever, for example, markets Aim, CloseUp and Pepsodent toothpastes, but each involves different positioning efforts. Despite such reasoning, many firms that once used this approach have reorganized. Faced with slower market growth, they found they had plenty of competitive pressure from other firms. In addition the retailer's own brand is now a very important competitor in many product areas. The internal competition just made it more difficult to co-ordinate different marketing strategies. A few years ago the managers for the individual brands were fighting it out, often going after the same target market with similar marketing mixes. Now one manager has responsibility for developing a coordinated marketing plan for all products in the bar soap category. The result is a better-integrated effort.

Generic 'brands'

Products that some consumers see as commodities may be difficult or expensive to brand. Some manufacturers and distributors have responded to this problem with generic products—products that have no brand at all other than identification of their contents and the manufacturer or distributor. Generic products are usually offered in plain packages at lower prices. They are quite common in less developed nations.

WHO DOES THE BRANDING?

Manufacturer brands still dominate

Historically most brands were developed by manufacturers. Manufacturers sought to develop and sustain market share by establishing favourable positions in the minds of their target customers. Frequently such brands were supported by considerable amounts of advertising and promotion. The aim of such promotion was, and still is, to create a position where customers are prepared to pay more for certain products and services because of higher levels of perceived value. By consuming (and being seen to consume) certain brands consumers perceive a benefit that would not associate with other brands. Similarly many brands became a symbol of reliable product performance which is an equally important customer benefit.

Manufacturers such as Nokia (consumer electronics) rely on the brand name to attract consumers to their products. Distributors are prepared to stock such brands, because they are aware that customers will deliberately search for the brand and prefer it over competing alternatives. Part of the sales task has already been accomplished. On the other hand, the very power of individual brands gives manufacturers some control over distributors. Distributors must have the brands which consumers demand, and therefore the manufacturer is in a position to dictate margins and terms and conditions of sale.

Retailer brands are now becoming more important

In many consumer goods markets these pressures have led retailers and other distributors to develop their own brands (particularly in grocery products). Initially many retailer brands were poor substitutes for manufacturer brands, often offered at the cheap end of the market as low cost alternatives. However, this position has changed dramatically in recent years and now retailer brands increasingly dominate many product categories. There are several advantages to the retailer. Margins can be controlled directly. The presence of retailer brands puts more pressure on manufacturer brands and hence gives greater bargaining power to the retailer, and it is much more efficient to build and create a retail brand which covers several thousand products than advertise each product separately. Chapter 11 examines the retailer–manufacturer relationship in more detail.

Having discussed products and branding, we now turn to the issue of packaging. This too can add value or detract from a brand and its sales.

THE STRATEGIC IMPORTANCE OF PACKAGING

Packaging has two key functions—to promote the product and to protect the product. In one sense, therefore, packaging is a key element in the way in which the product is presented to the consumer. In another it is essential for product protection as it travels through the major channels of distribution. Ineffective packaging can undermine an otherwise good brand by spoiling its image or spoiling the contents.

Photocopying paper is essentially a commodity. Paper supplied from one manufacturer is essentially the same as paper supplied by a second manufacturer. However, each manufacturer attempts to differentiate itself in different ways from the others. If photocopying machines are to work effectively, the paper that is used should be of uniform quality and not damp. Packaging can help to ensure that the product supplied meets these criteria. It can also provide a promotional message about the product for example with details on how to reorder.

Packaging can be important to both sellers and customers. Packaging can make a product more convenient to use or store. It can prevent spoiling or damage. Good packaging makes products easier to identify and promotes the brand at the point of purchase and even in use.

Packaging can make the difference

A new package can make *the* important difference in a new marketing strategy—by meeting customers' needs better. A better box, wrapper, can or bottle may help create a 'new' product—or a new market. For example, Crest toothpaste is available in a neat squeeze-pump dispenser that makes less mess and leaves less waste.

Sometimes a new package improves a product by making it easier or safer to use. Kodak increased sales of its light-sensitive X-ray film by packing each sheet in a separate foil pack—making the film easier to handle. Many drug and food products now have special seals to prevent product tampering. Many medicines, for example, come in a tamper-resistant package that children cannot open. Gerber baby food is packaged in bottles that show the consumer if they have been opened prior to the consumer buying the product.

Packaging sends a message— even for services

Packaging can tie the product to the rest of the marketing strategy. Packaging for Eveready batteries features the pink bunny seen in attention-getting TV advertising and reminds consumers that the batteries are durable. Expensive perfume may come in a crystal bottle, adding to the prestige image.

In a way, the appearance of service providers or the area where a service is provided is a form of packaging. Disney sends the message that its parks are a good place for family holidays by keeping them spotless. Lawyers put their awards and qualifications on the wall so that clients know they provide a high-quality product. In addition, some firms try to 'package' their services so that there is a tangible reminder of the product. For example, the American Express Gold Card sends a signal that is understood worldwide.

Packaging may lower distribution and promotion costs

Better protective packaging is very important to manufacturers and wholesalers. They sometimes have to pay the cost of goods damaged in shipment, and goods damaged in shipment also may delay production or cause lost sales. Retailers also need good packaging. Protective packaging can reduce storing costs by cutting breakage, spoilage and theft. Packages that are easier to handle can cut costs by speeding price marking, improving handling and display and saving space.

A good package sometimes gives a firm more promotion effect than it could possibly afford with advertising. Customers see the package in shops when they are actually buying. For example, a recent study found that 81 per cent of consumers' purchase decisions on groceries are made at the shop. The package may be seen by many more potential customers than the company's advertising. An attractive package may speed turnover enough to reduce total costs as a percentage of sales.

Or it may raise total costs

In other cases, costs (and prices) may rise because of packaging. However, customers may be more satisfied because the packaging improves the product by offering much greater convenience or reducing waste. Packaging costs as a percentage of a manufacturer's selling price vary widely, ranging from 1 to 70 per cent. When sugar producers sell sugar in 45 kg bags, the cost of packaging is only 1 per cent of the selling price. In 1 kg and 2 kg cartons, it's 25 to 30 per cent. And for individual serving packages, it's 50 per cent. Consumers do not want to carry a 45 kg bag home. They are quite willing to pay more for convenient sizes. Restaurants use one-serving envelopes of sugar to eliminate the cost of filling and washing sugar bowls and because customers prefer the sanitary little packages.

WHAT IS SOCIALLY RESPONSIBLE PACKAGING?

Some consumers say that some package designs are misleading, perhaps on purpose. Who hasn't been surprised by a chocolate bar half the size of the package? Others feel that the great variety of packages makes it hard to compare values. One of the most pressing issues is the environmental impact of packaging. Consumers and businesses are increasingly concerned that packaging should not be wasteful and that it should be re-cycleable and biodegradeable.

 Ethical decisions remain

Although various laws provide guidance on many packaging issues, many areas still require marketing managers to make ethical choices. For example, some firms have been criticized for designing packages that conceal a 'downsized' product, giving consumers less for their money. Similarly, some retailers have been criticized for designing packages and labels for their private-label products that look just like, and are easily confused with, manufacturer brands. Furthermore, some producers quickly put their lawyers and engineers to work so they can copy a competitor's popular packag-ing innovation without violating the patent. Are efforts such as these unethical, or are they simply an attempt to make packaging a more effective part of a marketing mix? Different people will answer differently.

Some marketing managers have been criticized for promoting environmentally friendly packaging on some products, while simultaneously increasing the use of problematic packages on others. Empty packages now litter our streets, and some plastic packages will lie in a landfill site for decades. Some consumers like the convenience that accompanies these problems. Think about this next time you see a pile of cartons outside a fast-food outlet! Is it unethical for a marketing manager to give consumers with different preferences a choice, and to develop different marketing mixes to reach different target markets? Some critics argue that it is. Others praise firms that are taking steps to give consumers a choice.

Many critics feel that labelling information is too often incomplete or misleading. Do consumers really understand the nutritional information required by law? Further, some consumers want information that is difficult, perhaps even impossible, to provide. For example, how can a label accurately describe a product's taste or texture? But the ethical issues usually focus on how far a marketing manager should go in putting potentially negative information on a package. For example, should Häagen-Dazs label its ice cream 'this product will clog your arteries?' That sounds extreme, but what type of information *is* appropriate?[15]

Unit-pricing is a possible help

Some retailers, especially large supermarket chains, make it easier for consumers to compare packages with differ-ent weights or volumes. They use unit-pricing—which involves placing the price per gram (or some other stan-dard measure) on or near the product. This makes price comparison easier.

Universal product codes allow more information

To speed handling of fast-selling products, government and industry representatives have developed a univer-sal product code (UPC) that identifies each product with marks readable by electronic scanners. A computer then matches each code to the product and its price. Supermarkets and other high-volume retailers have been eager to use these codes. They reduce the need to mark the price on every item. They also reduce errors by cashiers, make it easy to control inventory and track sales of specific products. Exhibit 8–5 shows a univer-sal product code mark.

The codes help consumers too because they speed the checkout process. Also, most systems now include a printed receipt showing the name, size and price of each product bought. These codes will become even more widely used in the future because they do lower operating costs.

Exhibit 8–5 Illustration of a Universal Product Code

GUARANTEES ARE A PART OF STRATEGY PLANNING

Guarantee puts promises in writing

A guarantee explains what the seller promises about its product. Deciding on guarantee policies is part of strat-egy planning. A marketing manager should decide whether to offer a specific guarantee, and if so what the guarantee will cover and how it will be communicated to target customers. This is an area where the legal envi-ronment—as well as customer needs and competitive offerings—must be considered.

Some firms used to say their products were fully warranted or absolutely guaranteed. However, they did not state the time period or spell out the meaning of the guarantee. Now a company has to make clear whether it is offering a full or limited guarantee—and the law defines what full means. Most firms offer a limited guar-antee—if they offer one at all.

Guarantee may improve the marketing mix

Some firms use guarantees to improve the appeal of their marketing mix. They design more quality into their goods or services and offer refunds or replacement—not just repair—if there is a problem. Xerox uses this approach with its photocopying machines. Its three-year guarantee says that a customer who is not satisfied with a copier—for *any* reason—can trade it for another model. This type of guarantee sends a strong signal. A buyer doesn't have to worry about whether or not the copier will work as expected, service calls will be prompt or even that the Xerox salesperson or dealer has recommended the appropriate model.

Service guarantees

Customer service guarantees are becoming more common as a way to attract—and keep—customers. Pizza Hut guarantees a luncheon pizza in five minutes or it's free. There is more risk in offering a service guarantee than a guarantee on a physical product. An apathetic employee or a service breakdown can create a big expense. However, without the guarantee, dissatisfied customers may just go away mad without ever complaining. Providing a service guarantee also removes some of the uncertainty associated with buying services.

If customers claim on a guarantee, the company can clearly identify the problem. Then the problem can be addressed so it does not happen again to other customers. Service guarantees also seem to be effective in creating repeat customers. Customers who complain can become a very loyal and profitable group if their complaints are satisfactorily handled.

Guarantee support can be costly

Customers might like a strong guarantee, but it can be expensive, even economically impossible for small firms. Backing-up guarantees can also be a problem. Some customers abuse products and then demand a lot of service on warranties. The cost of guarantee support ultimately must be covered by the price that consumers pay. This has led some firms to offer guarantee choices. The basic price for a product may include a guarantee that covers a short time period or that covers parts but not labour. Consumers who want more or better protection pay extra for an extended guarantee or a service contract.

SUMMARY

New-product planning is an increasingly important activity in a modern economy because it is no longer very profitable just to sell imitative products in highly competitive markets. Markets, competition and product life cycles are changing at a fast pace. A product is new to a firm if it is new to it in any way or to any target market.

New products are so important to business survival that firms need some organized process for developing them. The process discussed here involves idea generation, screening, idea evaluation, development and commercialization. At each of these stages the company is looking to ensure that only viable ideas are progressed. New-product development requires a total-company effort to be successful—R&D, production, marketing and all the other functions must pull together if a successful product is to reach the market.

The failure rate of new products is high but it is lower for better-managed firms that recognize product development and management as vital processes. Some firms appoint product managers to manage individual products and new-product teams to ensure that the process is carried out successfully.

Branding and packaging can create new and more satisfying products. Packaging is concerned with protecting the product but also offers special opportunities to promote the product and inform customers. Variations in packaging can make a product attractive to different target markets. A specific package may have to be developed for each strategy.

Customers see brands as a guarantee of quality, and this leads to repeat purchasing. For marketers, such routine buying means lower promotion costs and higher sales. Should companies stress branding? The decision depends on whether the costs of brand promotion and honouring the brand guarantee can be more than covered by a higher price or more rapid turnover, or both. The cost of branding may reduce pressure on the other three Ps.

Branding gives marketing managers a choice. They can add brands and use individual or family brands. In the end, however, customers express their approval or disapproval of the whole Product (including the brand). The degree of brand familiarity is a measure of the marketing manager's ability to carve out a separate market. Brand familiarity affects Place, Price and Promotion decisions.

Guarantees are also important in strategy planning. A guarantee needs to be clearly stated. Strong warranties help to reassure consumers, especially if they are buying a product for the first time.

QUESTIONS AND PROBLEMS

1. What is a new product? Illustrate your answer.

2. Explain the importance of an organized new-product development process and illustrate how it might be used for (*a*) a new hair care product, (*b*) a new children's toy, (*c*) a new subscribers-only cable television channel.

3. Discuss how you might use the new-product development process if you were thinking about offering some kind of summer service to residents in a seaside resort.

4. Explain the role of product or brand managers. When would it make sense for one of a company's current brand managers to be in charge of the new-product development process? Explain your thinking.

5. If a firm offers one of its brands in a number of different countries, would it make sense for one brand manager to be in charge, or would each country require its own brand manager? Explain your thinking.

6. Discuss the social value of new-product development activities that seem to encourage people to discard products that are not all worn out. Is this an economic waste? How worn out is all worn out? Must a shirt have holes in it? How big?

7. Is a well-known brand valuable only to the owner of the brand?

8. Suggest an example of a product and a competitive situation where it would *not* be profitable for a firm to spend large sums of money to establish a brand.

9. List five brand names and indicate what product is associated with the brand name. Evaluate the strengths and weaknesses of the brand name.

10. Explain family brands. Should Toys "R" Us develop its own dealer brands to compete with some of the popular manufacturer brands it carries? Explain your reasons.

11. Is it more difficult to support a guarantee for a service than for a physical good? Explain your reasons.

SUGGESTED CASES

2. Pillsbury's Häagen-Dazs
11. Outdoor World

REFERENCES

1. 'Seems the only problem with new products is that they're new', *Brandweek*, 22 August 1994, pp. 36–40; 'Flops: Too many new products fail. Here's why—and how to do better', *Business Week*, 16 August 1993, pp. 76–82; G.D. Kortge and P.A. Okonkwo, 'Simultaneous new product development: Reducing the new product failure rate', *Industrial Marketing Management*, vol. 18, no. 4, 1989, pp. 301–6.

2. IPA Advertising Effectiveness Awards, *Annual Supplement to Marketing*, 1996, p. 14.

3. J.T. Vesey, 'Time-to-market: Put speed in product development', *Industrial Marketing Management*, May 1992, pp. 151–8.

4. 'Seeing the future first', *Fortune*, 5 September 1994, pp. 64–70; A. Griffin and J.R. Hauser, 'The voice of the customer', *Marketing Science*, Winter 1993, pp. 1–27.

5. BBA Mintex Don Ltd, Company documentation.

6. Adapted from F.R. Bacon, Jr. and T.W. Butler, Jr., *Planned Innovation*, rev. edn, Institute of Science and Technology, University of Michigan MI (Ann Arbor, 1980).

7. J. Surowiecki 'The billion dollar blade' *Management Today*, August 1998, pp. 32–6; Gillette Web site; 'Gillette succeeds as others fail by reinventing itself', *Brandweek*, 3 May 1993, p. 12; 'How a $4 razor ends up costing $300 million', *Business Week*, 29 January 1990, pp. 62–3.

8. R. Olins, 'Dyson aims to clean up new appliances', *The Sunday Times*, 10 May 1998, Business section, p. 8; R. Cooper, 'A clean sweep', *Marketing Business*, March 1998, p. 56.

9. D. Frey, 'Learning the ropes: My life as a product champion', *Harvard Business Review*, September–October 1991, pp. 46–57; M.F. Maute and W.B. Locander, 'Innovation as a socio-politial process: An empirical analysis of influence behavior among new product managers', *Journal of Business Research*, June 1994, pp. 161–74; V. Kasturi Rangan, R. Lal and E.P. Maier, 'Managing marginal new products', *Business Horizons*, September–October 1992, pp. 35–42; G.S. Low, R.A. Fullerton, 'Brands, brand management and the brand manager system', *Journal of Marketing Research*, vol. 3, no. 2, 1994, p. 173–90.

10. For more on brand extensions, see A. Rangaswamy, R.R. Burke and T.A. Oliva, 'Brand equity and the extendibility of brand names', *International Journal of Research in Marketing*, March 1993, pp. 61–76; B. Loken and D. Roedder John, 'Diluting brand beliefs: When do brand extensions have a negative impact?', *Journal of Marketing*, July 1993, pp. 71–84. For more on the importance of branding, see K. Lane Keller, 'Conceptualizing, measuring, and managing customer-based brand equity', *Journal of Marketing*, January 1993, pp. 1–22; J.A. Quelch and D. Kenny, 'Extend profits, not product lines', *Harvard Business Review*, September–October, vol. 72, no. 5, 199, pp. 153–60.

11. S. Creaton, 'Baileys remains the toast of the Irish drinks industry', *The Irish Times*, 24 July 1998, Business This Week section, p. 24.

12. IPA Advertising Effectiveness Awards, *Annual Supplement to Marketing*, 1996, p. 8.

13. 'More firms turn to translation experts to avoid costly embarrassing mistakes', *The Wall Street Journal*, 13 January 1977, p. 32.

14. 'The risks are rising in China', *Fortune*, 6 March 1995, pp. 179–80; 'Declaring War on the Pirates', *Business Week*, 24 October 1994, p. 56; J.E. Olsen and K.L. Granzin, 'Using channels constructs to explain dealers' willingness to help manufacturers combat counterfeiting', *Journal of Business Research*, June 1993, pp. 147–70; 'Copycats on a hot tin roof', *Business Week*, 19 September 1994, p. 43.

15. P. Fitzgerald, B. Corey, and R.J. Corey, 'Ethical dilemmas in packaging: Beliefs of packaging professionals', *Journal of Macromarketing*, Spring 1992, pp. 45–54.

CHAPTER 9
Place and Development of Channels of Distribution

When You Finish This Chapter, You Should

1 Understand how to determine place objectives.

2 Understand how and why marketing specialists develop to make distribution more effective.

3 Understand how to obtain cooperation and avoid conflict in channel systems.

4 Know how channel members in vertical marketing systems shift and share functions in order to meet customer needs.

5 Understand the differences between intensive, selective and exclusive distribution.

6 Understand the important new terms (shown in colour).

MOTION MEDIA TECHNOLOGY

Getting new products to commercialization is difficult enough but at that stage the challenge becomes actually getting the product to the market. This is precisely the dilemma facing Motion Media Technology, an English company that has developed reliable, low-cost video-phones and videoconferencing. The company specializes in the technological development side of the business with talented engineers and designers. It has two main products ready for sale—a stand-alone videophone and a video-conferencing system. Using high-speed ISDN telephone lines, these devices transmit at 15 frames per second, which the human eye will see as continuous motion. Both products are almost as convenient to use as the telephone.

As yet the market for such products is very limited and has not moved into the growth phase. Worldwide, only about 40 000 units of these types of products sell each year. These sales are mainly to big businesses, educational establishments and lawyers and bankers wishing to enhance their service by making their experts globally available through videoconferencing. Motion Media's systems will sell at about £2000, less than half the price of the closest competitor. It is expected that this lower price will help the market to grow but with new technology products and emerging markets, forecasting sales levels is notoriously difficult. As a very small company, Motion Media has difficulty servicing the whole market and making an impact in it.

It is hoping to reach the customers in a variety of ways. It has signed an Original Equipment Manufacturer (OEM) deal with Philips under which the Dutch electronics company will sell a system branded as its own. This allows Philips to help establish the market by its vast promotional resources being used to publicize the new performance levels yet lower price. Philips sees that this will create new market segments such as the small business owner or the home worker. Orders for the product will be made by Philips well in advance, thus saving Motion Media the financial burden of inventory.

In addition to the OEM deal, Motion Media wants to establish a presence in the market in its own right. It is trying to build relationships with worldwide distributors ranging from small entrepreneurial businesses to big companies with extensive sales networks. Motion Media is already supplying to very different markets in about 40 companies. It is also talking to a high-street electronics chain in an effort to get to the consumer market because the company believes that one day, videophones will be as popular as televisions. The market research confirms that consumers are keen on the idea of home videophones. As ISDN line rental prices fall, the home videophone market will grow.

Along with establishing the videophone market, the company needs to continue to pioneer technology so that it can maintain a number of generations of products. This will enable it to have credibility with the electronics companies, distributors, agents and retailers. After all, it is these groups who get the product to the customer.

PLACE DECISIONS ARE AN IMPORTANT PART OF MARKETING STRATEGY

Offering customers a good product at a reasonable price is important to a successful marketing strategy but it is not the whole story. Managers must also think about Place—making goods and services available in the right quantities and locations, and when customers want them. When different target markets have different needs, a number of Place variations may be required.

The next three chapters deal with the many important strategy decisions that a marketing manager must make concerning Place. Exhibit 9–1 gives an overview. This chapter starts with a discussion of the type of channel that is needed to meet customers' needs. We'll show why specialists are often involved and how they come together to form a channel of distribution—any series of firms or individuals who participate in the flow of products from producer to final user or consumer. We'll also consider how to manage relations among channel members to reduce conflict and improve cooperation.

Chapter 10 expands coverage of Place to include decisions that marketing managers make to decide what level of distribution service to offer and why they must coordinate storing and transporting activities to provide the desired service at a reasonable cost. Chapter 11 takes a closer look at the many different types of retailing and wholesaling firms and considers their role in channels as well as the strategy decisions they make to satisfy their own customers.

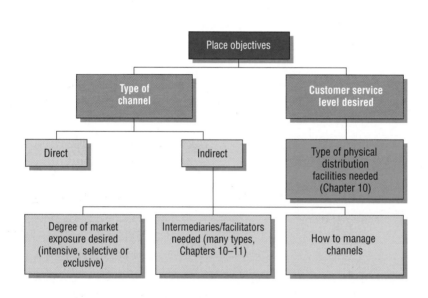

Exhibit 9–1 Strategy Decision Areas in Place

PLACE DECISIONS ARE GUIDED BY 'IDEAL' PLACE OBJECTIVES

All marketing managers want to be sure that their goods and services are available in the right quantities and locations when customers want them. But customers may have different needs with respect to time, place and possession utility as they make different purchases.

Product classes suggest place objectives

In Chapter 7 product classes were described. These summarize consumers' urgency to have needs satisfied and willingness to seek information, shop and compare for various classes of product. Each product class (conve-nience, shopping, speciality and unsought goods) is associated with certain forms of consumer behaviour. It follows that the class of product should guide marketing mix decisions. Here the concern is with using the product classes to handle Place decisions.

Exhibit 9–2 shows the relationship between consumer product classes and ideal Place objectives. Similarly, Exhibit 9–3 shows the business product classes and how they relate to customer needs. Study these exhibits carefully. They set the framework for making Place decisions. In particular, the product classes help us decide how much market exposure is needed in each geographic area.

Place and Development of Channels of Distribution

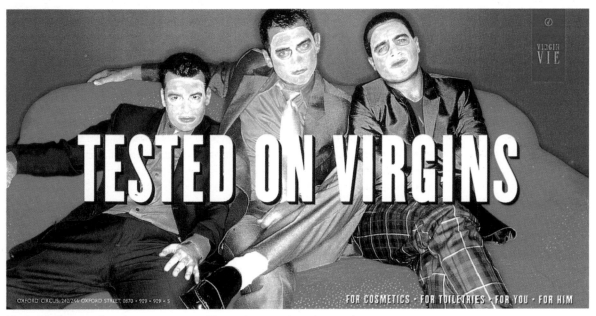

Virgin Vie is a retail outlet set up to provide products and services under an overal limage that is dynamic, challenging, energetic and fun

Consumer Product Class	Marketing Mix Considerations	Consumer Behaviour
Convenience products		
Staples	Maximum exposure with widespread, low-cost distribution; mass selling by producer; usually low price; branding is important.	Routinized (habitual), low effort, frequent purchases; low involvement.
Impulse	Widespread distribution with display at point of purchase.	Unplanned purchases bought quickly.
Emergency	Need widespread distribution near probable point of need; price sensitivity low.	Purchase made with time pressure when a need is great.
Shopping products		
Homogeneous	Need enough exposure to facilitate price comparison; price sensitivity high.	Customers see little difference among alternatives, seek lowest price.
Heterogeneous	Need distribution near similar products; promotion (including personal selling) to high-light product advantages; less price sensitivity.	Extensive problem solving; consumer may need help in making a decision.
Speciality products	Price sensitivity is likely to be low; limited distribution may be acceptable, but should be treated as a convenience or shopping product (in whichever category product would typically be included) to reach persons not yet sold on its speciality product status.	Willing to expend effort to get specific product, even if not necessary; strong preferences make it an important purchase.
Unsought products		
New unsought	Must be available in places where similar (or related) products are sought; needs attention-getting promotion.	Need for product not strongly felt; unaware of benefits or not yet gone through adoption process.
Regularly unsought	Requires very aggressive promotion, usually personal selling.	Aware of product but not interested; attitude towards product may even be negative.

Exhibit 9–2 Consumer Product Classes and Marketing Mix Planning

Business Product Classes	Marketing Mix Considerations	Buying Behaviour
Capitol Equipment	Usually requires skilful personal selling by producer, including technical contacts, and/or understanding of applications; leasing and specialized support services may be required.	Multiple buying influence (including top management) and new-task buying are common; infrequent purchase, long decision period, and boom-or-bust demand are typical.
Accessory equipment	Need fairly widespread distribution and numerous contacts by experienced and sometimes technically trained personnel; price competition is often intense, but quality is important.	Purchasing and operating personnel typically make decisions; shorter decision period than for installations.
Raw materials	Grading is important, and transportation and storing can be crucial because of seasonal production and/or perishable products; markets tend to be very competitive.	Long-term contract may be required to ensure supply.
Component parts and materials	Product quality and delivery reliability are usually extremely important; negotiation and technical selling typical on less standardized items; replacement after market may require different strategies.	Multiple buying influence is common; competitive bids used to encourage competitive pricing.
Maintenance, repair and operating (MRO) supplies	Typically require widespread distribution or fast delivery (repair items); arrangements with appropriate intermediaries may be crucial.	Often handled as straight rebuys, except important operating supplies may be treated much more seriously and involve multiple buying influence.
Professional services	Services customized to buyer's need; personal selling very important; inelastic demand often supports high prices.	Customer may compare outside service with what internal people could provide; needs may be very specialized.

Exhibit 9–3 Business Product Classes and Marketing Mix Planning

Place decisions are not automatic

A product may be sold both to final consumers and business customers, and each type of customer may want to purchase in different ways. Further, several different product classes may be involved if different market segments view a product in different ways. Thus, just as there is no automatic classification for a specific product, so there is not an automatic set of Place arrangements that is best. However, people in a particular target market should have similar attitudes and therefore should be satisfied with the same Place system. If different target segments view a product in different ways, marketing managers may need to develop several strategies, each with its own Place arrangements.

Place decisions have long-run effects

The marketing manager must also consider Place objectives in relation to the product life cycle; see Exhibit 7–6. Place decisions have long-run effects. They are usually harder to change than Product, Price and Promotion decisions. It can take years and a great deal of money to

develop effective working arrangements with others in the channel. Legal contracts with channel partners may also limit changes. And it's hard to move retail stores and wholesale facilities once leases are signed and customer movement patterns are settled. Yet as products mature, they typically need broader distribution to reach different target customers.

The distribution of premium pet foods followed this pattern. Most pet food producers reached consumers through supermarkets. Yet supermarkets were not willing to put much emphasis on specialized pet foods because there was not much demand. Marketing managers for Hill's Science Diet products concentrated on establishing distribution through non-grocery outlets, primarily pet shops and veterinary offices. These pet professionals have a lot of influence on what pet owners buy and they were reaching Science Diet's target market.

Technology is changing distribution

Developments in technology are changing the ways in which products can be made available and the ways in which consumers shop for products. Not that long ago, it seemed advanced to be able to order goods over the telephone and pay for them by credit card. Now that almost seems old-fashioned compared to the use of the Internet.

Electronic commerce (EC) is the term used to describe the use of electronic technologies in the marketing of goods. This covers marketing communications which, with the application of technology, can be precisely targeted and customized. EC also includes distribution and on-line shopping. On-line shopping is normally hosted on a WWW Internet server. Once connected to the server by their own PC, customers can interact with the system. This interaction usually takes the form of browsing and searching for products. The customer can select products and buy them without leaving their home. One of the benefits to the business is that it can gain information on the originator of the person contacting their site. Developments in software allow the customer's shopping behaviour to be tracked such as the customer's 'visits' to particular pages.

THE *IRISH TIMES* ON THE WEB

As a newspaper, the *Irish Times* could have regarded the Internet purely as a threat. After all, why should someone buy a newspaper when they can get all the information that they need from their PC and a modem? Instead, the *Irish Times* decided to concentrate on the opportunities that the World Wide Web offered. They researched best practice in the United States and Scandinavia in an effort to learn how to capitalize on the new electronic age. Research concluded that although the newspaper would remain its core product, on-line information products could be developed which would create added value for the paper's readers and advertisers, create alternative revenue sources and complement and enhance the newspaper.

The proposal was to develop a strategic position in the international 'Irish interest' marketplace while keeping pace with home market developments. The international market place is significant with 1.5 million Irish people living abroad and, more significantly, over 70 million people worldwide claiming Irish roots. Among the first papers in the world to be on the Internet, in the early days (1994) the site got 25 000 hits in the first month. It now gets in the order of 3.5 million per day and the number grows each month. The paper is now available on the Web from 4.a.m. local time with full colour, graphics, pictures and cartoons.

One of the prime sources of revenue for the *Irish Times* on the Web is from providing links to advertisers' sites and huge volumes of traffic. Once the reader clicks on the advertisement they are through to the advertiser's site. For example, Castle Rock Films wanted to promote the film *Some Mother's Sons* and they wanted to target an Irish interest audience in the United States. They chose the *Irish Times* on the Web and were astounded by the response. 'Click throughs' grew to 15 per cent—this is where the viewer sees the advertiser icon and clicks through to the advertiser's site—and the site developed its own discussion groups. Another example of effective advertising was the Sheen Falls Hotel, a beautiful hotel in the south west of Ireland. Their site, advertised on the *Irish Times* on the Web, managed to attract a conference from Australia. The virtual tour of the hotel was enough to attract the business!

The *Irish Times* on the Web has to continue to develop interesting products if it is to maintain its success. Anticipated new offerings include an archive service, bookselling, an ancestors/genealogy site and Irish horse racing information. In the meantime, the *Irish Times* on the Web offers the logical starting point to anyone looking for information about Ireland.[2]

Many ethical and security issues are raised by the use of the Internet. In particular, questions relating to the collection and use of information on consumers using on-line services need to be answered. Legislation will prescribe what is and is not legal but the ethics of individuals will continue to influence what is acceptable practice. The scale and pace of change indicates that these issues can only increase in importance.

It has been reckoned that each month sees about 1 million new users of the Internet. Put another way, 10 months has led to 10 million Internet users: by contrast, it took 7 years for the fax machine to get 10 million users. Projecting this rate leads to the staggering estimate of 500 million users by the end of the millennium. As businesses such as the *Irish Times* (see box) learn how to harness the Internet for marketing purposes, and as consumers ascend the Internet learning curve, the proportion of commerce conducted virtually can only increase. In doing business over the Internet, businesses can enjoy control over how their product is presented to the customer, cost advantages and the benefits that come from dealing 'directly' with customers.

The impact of technology is not confined to producers and consumers. Electronic communications mean that retailers and producers and retailers and customers can be linked to each other. When Marks and Spencer sells a particular item, its warehouse and the supplier also get that information. That enables the supplier to produce and replenish stock as it is needed.

CHANNEL SYSTEM MAY BE DIRECT OR INDIRECT

One of the most basic Place decisions producers must make is whether to handle the whole distribution themselves, or use wholesalers, retailers and other specialists (see Exhibit 9–1). Distributors, in turn, must select the producers with whom they will work.

Why a firm might want to use direct distribution

Many firms prefer to distribute directly to the final customer or consumer. One reason is that they want complete control over the marketing job. They may think that they can serve target customers at a lower cost or do the work more effectively than intermediaries. Further, working with independent intermediaries with different objectives can be troublesome.

Direct contact with customers

If a firm is in direct contact with its customers, it is more aware of changes in customer attitudes. It is in a better position to adjust its marketing mix quickly because there is no need to convince other channel members to help. If a product needs an aggressive selling effort or special technical service, the marketing manager can ensure that the salesforce receives the necessary training and motivation. In contrast, intermediaries often carry products of several competing producers. So they aren't willing to give any one item the special emphasis its producer wants.

Suitable intermediaries are not available

A firm may have to go direct if suitable intermediaries are not available or will not cooperate. This sometimes occurs with new products. Intermediaries who have the best contacts with the target market may be hesitant to add unproven products, especially really new products that don't fit well with their current business. Many new products die because the producer cannot find willing intermediaries and doesn't have the financial resources to handle direct distribution.

Finding details of the number of wholesalers, retailers and other types of distributor is sometimes easy.

In many European countries, specialist agencies such as Nielsen can provide data in detail of the flow of individual products (including the competition) through each of the major channels of distribution. A marketing manager can use this information to decide how to distribute its products. However, in some markets it is much more difficult to determine the number of each type of intermediary. Frequently it is necessary to conduct a detailed analysis of the distribution systems before making a choice about the best channel to use. This problem confronted many companies entering former Eastern European markets such as Hungary or Poland, where there was little or no centralized source of information about existing patterns of distribution. Later on in this chapter you will see how companies can conduct a distribution audit as part of the process of making choices about the best type of distribution system.

Common with business customers and services

Many business products are sold direct-to-customer. Norsk Hydro, a Norwegian chemicals manufacturer, sells much of its output directly to the end user, as does Novo Nordisk, a chemicals and pharmaceutical company in Denmark. This is understandable since in business markets there are fewer transactions and orders are larger. In addition, customers may be concentrated in a small geographic area, making distribution easier.

Many service firms also use direct channels. If the service must be produced in the presence of customers, there may be little need for intermediaries. An accounting firm like Arthur Andersen, for example, must deal directly with its customers. However, many firms that produce physical goods turn to distributors to help provide the services customers expect as part of the product. Siemens may hope that its authorized dealers don't get many repair calls, but the service is available when customers need it. Here the dealer produces the service.

Some consumer products are sold direct

Of course, some consumer products are sold direct. Farm shops that sell home-grown produce to customers are selling directly. Tupperware and Avon cosmetics are also familiar examples of direct distribution. Most of these firms rely on direct selling, which involves personal sales contact between a representative of the company and an individual consumer. However, most of these 'salespeople' are *not* company employees. Rather, they usually work as independent intermediaries, and the companies that they sell for refer to them as dealers, distributors, agents or some similar term. So, in a strict technical sense, this is not really direct producer-to-consumer distribution.

Don't be confused by the term *direct marketing*

An increasing number of firms now rely on *direct marketing*—direct communication between a seller and an individual customer using a promotion method other than face-to-face personal selling. Sometimes direct marketing promotion is coupled with direct distribution from a producer to consumers. However, many firms that use direct marketing promotion distribute their products through intermediaries. So the term *direct marketing* is primarily concerned with the Promotion area, not Place decisions. Direct marketing promotion is covered in more detail in Chapter 15.

When indirect channels are best

Even if a producer wants to handle the whole distribution job, sometimes it is simply not possible. Customers often have established buying patterns. For example, MK Electric, a producer of electrical supplies, might want to sell directly to big electrical contractors. But if contractors like to make all of their purchases in one convenient stop—at a local electrical wholesaler—the only practical way to reach them is through a wholesaler.

Similarly, consumers are spread throughout many geographic areas and often prefer to shop for certain products at specific places. For example, a consumer may see a Shell Store as *the* place to shop for emergency items, because it is conveniently located. The manufacturer will have to make sure that its products are available in the Shell outlets that have longer opening hours and are usually easier to access by car than most other outlets. This is one reason why most firms that produce consumer products use indirect channels as shown in Exhibit 9–4.

Direct distribution usually requires a significant investment in facilities and people. A new company or one that has limited financial resources may want to avoid that investment by working with established intermediaries. Further, some intermediaries play a critical role by providing credit to customers at the end of the channel. Even if the producer could afford to provide credit, a distributor who knows local customers can help reduce credit risks.

As these examples suggest, there may be a number of very specific reasons why a producer might want to work with a specific distributor. However, the most important reason for using indirect channels of distribution is that intermediaries can often help producers to serve customer needs better and at lower cost

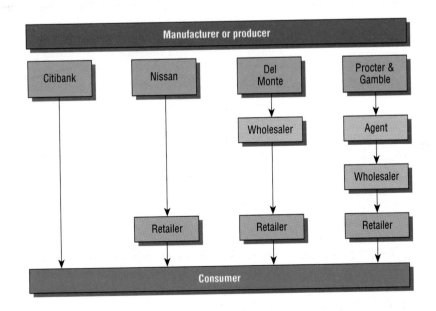

Exhibit 9–4 Four Examples of Basic Channels of Distribution for Consumer Products

DISCREPANCIES AND SEPARATIONS REQUIRE CHANNEL SPECIALISTS

The assortment and quantity of products customers want may be different from the assortment and quantity of products companies produce. Producers are often located far from their customers and may not know how best to reach them. Customers in turn may not know about their choices. Specialists develop to adjust these discrepancies and separations. This is the justification for the existence of intermediaries.

Intermediaries supply needed information

Economists often assume that customers have perfect information about all producers and that producers know which customers need what product, where, when and at what price. Yet, this assumption is rarely true. Therefore, specialists develop to help provide information to bring buyers and sellers together. For example, if you were building a house or having an extension put onto the house, you would probably not know where to find the best builders, plumbers and electricians. You would also probably feel a little uncomfortable in managing the project to ensure that the building work was done on time and to the right specification. A specialist surveyor or architect might be able to provide this knowledge and act on your behalf as an intermediary. In the same vein, a furniture retailer can help a customer find a producer who has a certain style chair with just the right combination of fabric and finish.

Most producers seek help from specialists when they first enter international markets. Specialists can provide crucial information about customer needs and insights into differences in the marketing environment. In some markets companies must operate through a local agent to meet legal requirements controlling any foreign management of local companies. A local specialist is therefore an obligatory partner.

Discrepancies of quantity and assortment

Discrepancy of quantity means the difference between the quantity of products it is economical for a producer to make and the quantity final users or consumers normally want. For example, most manufacturers of golf balls produce large quantities—perhaps 200 000 to 500 000 in a given time period. The average golfer, however, wants only a few balls at a time. Adjusting for this discrepancy usually requires intermediaries—wholesalers, retailers and the golf professional shop.

Producers typically specialize by product—and therefore another discrepancy develops. Discrepancy of assortment means the difference between the lines a typical producer makes and the assortment final consumers or users want. Most golfers, for example,

need more than golf balls. They want golf shoes, gloves, clubs, a bag and, of course, a golf course to play on. And they usually don't want to shop for each item separately. So, again, the distribution channels play a major role in making sure that the variety is available at the right time and place.

In actual practice, bringing products to customers is not as simple as the golf example. The golf professional's shop at the golf course usually carries even wider assortments, including clothing, confectionery products and soft drinks. And the professional buys from a variety of wholesalers who specialize by product line. Some of these wholesalers supply other wholesalers. These complications will be discussed later. The important thing to remember is that discrepancies in quantity and assortment cause distribution problems for producers and explain why many specialists develop.

Channel specialists adjust discrepancies with regrouping activities

Regrouping activities adjust the quantities and/or assortments of products handled at each level in a channel of distribution. There are four regrouping activities: accumulating, bulk-breaking, sorting and assorting. When one or more of these activities is needed, a marketing specialist may develop to fill this need.

Adjusting quantity discrepancies by accumulating and bulk-breaking

Accumulating involves collecting products from many small producers. Much of the coffee that comes from Colombia is grown on small farms in the mountains. Accumulating the small crops into larger quantities is a way of getting the lowest transporting rate—and making it more convenient for distant food processing companies to buy and handle it. Accumulating is especially important in less developed countries and in other situations, like agricultural markets, where there are many small producers.

Accumulating is also important with professional services because they often involve the combined work of a number of individuals, each of whom is a specialized producer. A hospital makes it easier for patients by accumulating the services of a number of healthcare specialists.

Bulk-breaking involves dividing larger quantities into smaller quantities as products get closer to the final market. Sometimes this even starts at the producer's level. A golf ball producer may need 25 wholesalers to help sell its output. And the bulk-breaking may involve several levels of intermediaries. Wholesalers may sell smaller quantities to other wholesalers—or directly to retailers. Retailers continue breaking bulk as they sell individual items to their customers.

Adjusting assortment discrepancies by sorting and assorting

Different types of specialists adjust assortment discrepancies. They perform two types of regrouping activities: sorting and assorting. Sorting means separating products into grades and qualities desired by different target markets. For example, an investment firm might offer its customers a chance to buy shares in a mutual fund made up only of stocks for certain types of companies—high-growth firms, ones that pay regular dividends, or ones that have good environmental track records. Similarly, a wholesaler that specializes in serving convenience stores may focus on smaller packages of frequently used products, whereas a wholesaler working with restaurants and hotels might handle only very large institutional packs of tea, coffee, milk powder, etc. Sorting is also a very important process for raw materials. Nature produces what it will and then the products must be sorted to meet the needs of different target markets.

Assorting means putting together a variety of products to give a target market what it wants. This is usually done by those closest to the final consumer or user-retailers or wholesalers who try to supply a wide assortment of products for the convenience of their customers. A grocery store is a good example. But some assortments involve very different products. A wholesaler selling tractors and mowers to golf courses might also carry grass seed, fertilizer and even golf ball washers or irrigation systems—for its customers' convenience.

To summarize: the rationale for intermediaries is that they overcome discrepancies in quantity and assortment. Discrepancies are overcome by accumulating, bulk-breaking, sorting and assorting products.

Watch for changes

Sometimes these discrepancies are adjusted badly, especially when consumer wants and attitudes shift rapidly. When videotapes became popular, an opportunity developed for a new specialist. Large numbers of consumers were suddenly interested in having an assortment of videos available, in one convenient place. Electronics stores focused only on selling the tape players and blank tapes. Videotape rental stores, such as Blockbuster, emerged to meet the new need. However, movie studios lowered the prices for tapes so more customers are buying rather than renting them. Because of that change, many types of retail stores now sell videos.

Specialists should develop to adjust discrepancies *if they must be adjusted.* That said, there is no point in having intermediaries just because that is the way it has always been done. Sometimes a breakthrough opportunity can come from finding a better way to reduce discrepancies, perhaps eliminating some steps in the channel. For example, Dell Computers found that it could sell computers direct to customers, at lower prices, by advertising in computer magazines and taking orders by mail or phone. With such an approach, Dell not only bypassed retail stores and the wholesalers who served them, it also avoided the expense of a large field salesforce. This cost advantage let Dell offer low prices and a marketing mix that appealed to some target segments.

CHANNELS MUST BE MANAGED

The whole channel should have a product-market commitment

Ideally, all of the members of a channel system should have a shared *product-market commitment*—with all members focusing on the same target market at the end of the channel and sharing the various marketing functions in appropriate ways. When members of a channel do this, they are better able to compete effectively for the customer's business. This simple idea is very important. Unfortunately, many marketing managers overlook it because it is not the way their firms have traditionally handled relationships with others in the channel.

Traditional distribution channels are common

In traditional channels of distribution—the various channel members make little or no effort to cooperate with each other. They buy and sell from each other—but each acts independently. Each channel member operates in its own best interest without worrying about the effect of its policies on other members of the channel. This is shortsighted, but it is easy to see how it can happen. The objectives of the various channel members may be different. For example, Mira, a manufacturer of showers, wants a wholesaler of building supplies to sell Mira products. But a wholesaler who carries an assortment of products from different producers may not care whose products get sold. The wholesaler just wants happy customers and a good profit margin. Likewise, the producer brings out new products that require shelf space from the retailer. The retailer is concerned to optimize the use of shelf space to offer customers a satisfactory assortment. These two views do not always concur.

Traditional channel systems are still typical—and very important—in some industries. The members of these channels have their independence, but there are costs. As we will see, such channels are declining in importance—with good reason.

Conflict gets in the way of cooperation

Because members of traditional channel systems often have different objectives and different ideas about how things should be done, conflict is common. There are two basic types of conflict in channels of distribution. Vertical conflicts occur between firms at different levels of the channel of distribution. For example, a producer and a retailer may disagree about how much shelf space or promotion effort the retailer should give the producer's product. Or conflict may arise if a producer that wants to reduce its excess inventory pushes a wholesaler to carry more inventory than the wholesaler really needs.

Horizontal conflicts occur between firms at the same level in the channel of distribution. For example, a furni-

ture shop that keeps a complete line of furniture on display isn't happy to find out that a shop which is part of a chain of similar shops (multiple) is offering customers lower prices on special orders of the same items. The discounter is getting a free ride from the competing shop's investment in inventory. The independent retailer is likely to feel aggrieved when a multiple is selling a product for less than the wholesale price the independent pays.

Specialization has the potential to make a channel more efficient but not if the specialists are so independent that the channel does not work smoothly. Potential conflicts should be anticipated and, if possible, managed. Usually the best way to do that is to get everyone focused on the same basic objective of satisfying the customer at the end of the channel.

 Internet Exercise

Avon sells cosmetics and other products through independent sales representatives (agents) and also through catalogue (both on-line and printed). Review the Avon web site (www.avon.com). Do you think that Avon's independent sales representatives would view the web site as competing for their customers' purchases and a source of conflict, or would they think it helps them promote the product and identify new prospects? Explain your thinking.

VERTICAL MARKETING SYSTEMS FOCUS ON FINAL CUSTOMERS

Vertical marketing systems are channel systems in which the whole channel focuses on the same target market at the end of the channel. Such systems make sense, and are growing, because if the final customer doesn't buy the product, the whole channel suffers. There are three types of vertical marketing systems—corporate, administered and contractual. Exhibit 9-5 summarizes some characteristics of these systems and compares them with traditional systems.

Corporate channel systems shorten channels

Some corporations develop their own vertical marketing systems by internal expansion and/or by buying other firms. With corporate channel systems, corporate ownership all along the channel, we might say the firm is going 'direct'. Actually the firm may be handling manufacturing, wholesaling *and* retailing, so it is more accurate to think of the firm as a vertical marketing system.

Corporate channel systems develop by vertical integration

Corporate channel systems often develop by vertical integration, acquiring firms at different levels of channel activity. Specialist confectionery manufacturers, Thorntons, has integrated forward and owns a chain of retail outlets in the United Kingdom through which it sells its products. Time, the computer manufacturer, sells its products from its own dedicated retail outlets. Similarly, Sony operates its own dedicated retail shops. Nike has set up its own outlets which specialize in the sale of Nike branded sportswear. Levi's also operates its own specialized retail outlets.

Vertical integration has many possible advantages—stability of operations, assurance of materials and supplies, better control of distribution, better quality control, larger research facilities, greater buying power, and lower executive overhead. The economies of vertical integration benefit consumers through lower prices and better products.

Characteristics	Type of channel			
	Traditional	Vertical marketing systems		
		Administered	Contractual	Corporate
Amount of cooperation	Little or none	Some to good	Fairly good to good	Complete
Control maintained by	None	Economic power and leadership	Contracts	Ownership by one company
Examples	Typical channel of "independents"	Unilever Sainsbury Nestlé	Body Shop Benetton	BMW

Exhibit 9–5 Characteristics of Traditional and Vertical Marketing Systems

Provided that the discrepancies of quantity and assortment are not too great at each level in a channel—that is, that the firms fit together well—vertical integration can be extremely efficient and profitable.

Administered and contractual systems may work well

Firms can often gain the advantages of vertical integration without building an expensive corporate channel. A firm can develop administered or contractual channel systems instead. In administered channel systems the channel members informally agree to cooperate with each other. They can agree to routinize ordering, standardize accounting and coordinate promotion efforts. Much of the sales of fast-moving consumer goods pass through this type of channel.

In contractual channel systems the channel members agree by contract to cooperate with each other. Franchises such as Benetton are typical of this type of channel. Someone who wants to open a Benetton outlet in a particular location signs a contract to operate in a particular way. The contract controls prices, sales quotas for ranges of merchandise, promotional activity and other terms of trade, to ensure that all Benetton outlets operate in a consistent way around the world.

With both of these systems, the members achieve some of the advantages of corporate integration while retaining some of the flexibility of a traditional channel system.

A manufacturer of consumer domestic products such as vacuum cleaners and toasters has developed an informal arrangement with the independent wholesalers in its administered channel system. It has agreed to keep production and inventory levels in the system balanced—using sales data from the wholesalers. Every week, its managers do a thorough analysis of up to 130 000 major appliances located in the many warehouses operated by its 87 wholesalers. Because of this analysis, both the producer and the wholesalers can be sure that they have enough inventory but not the expense of too much. The producer has better information to plan its manufacturing and marketing efforts.

Channel members in the grocery, hardware and pharmaceutical industries develop and coordinate similar systems. Computerized checkout systems track sales. The information is sent to the wholesaler's or manufacturer's computer, which enters orders automatically when needed. This reduces buying and selling costs, inventory investment and customer frustration with out-of-stock items throughout the channel.

THE BEST CHANNEL SYSTEM SHOULD ACHIEVE IDEAL MARKET EXPOSURE

It is not always the case that marketing managers want their products to have maximum exposure to potential customers. Some product classes require much less market exposure than others. Ideal market exposure makes a product available widely enough to satisfy target customers' needs but not exceed them. Too much exposure only increases the total cost of marketing.

Ideal exposure may be intensive, selective or exclusive

Intensive distribution is selling a product through all responsible and suitable wholesalers or retailers who will stock and/or sell the product. Selective distribution is selling through only those distributors who will give the product special attention. Exclusive distribution is selling through only one distributor in a particular geographic area. As we move from intensive to exclusive distribution, we give up exposure in return for some other advantage, including, but not limited to, lower cost. In practice, this means that Wrigley's chewing gum is handled, through intensive distribution, by over 80 000 retail outlets in Germany. Rolls-Royces are handled, through exclusive distribution, by only a limited number of agents across the country.

Intensive distribution—sell it where they buy it

Intensive distribution is commonly needed for convenience products and business supplies—such as pencils, paper clips and copier or printer paper, used by all plants and offices. Customers want such products nearby. The seller's intent is important here. Intensive distribution refers to the *desire* to sell through *all* responsible and suitable outlets. What this means depends on customer habits and preferences. If target customers normally buy a certain product at a certain type of outlet, ideally, you would specify this type of outlet in your Place policies.

If customers prefer to buy Panasonic portable TVs only at specialist electrical goods outlets, you would try to sell to all of those outlets to achieve intensive distribution. Today, however, many customers would buy small portable TVs at a variety of outlets, including large department stores such as El Corte Ingles in Spain or through mail-order companies such as Otto in Germany. An intensive distribution policy requires use of all these outlets, and more than one channel, to reach one target market. The range and variety of outlets available across Europe means that planning an intensive distribution strategy for the whole of Europe is an extremely complex activity. Limited resources means that companies frequently have to make choices to restrict sales to specific markets, even for products that seem to be intensively sold within one market.

Selective distribution—sell it where it sells best

Selective distribution covers the broad area of market exposure between intensive and exclusive distribution. It may be suitable for all categories of products. Only the better intermediaries are used here. Companies usually use selective distribution to gain some of the advantages of exclusive distribution while still achieving fairly widespread market coverage. Nautica is a US sportswear company that is establishing selective distribution in Europe. The company uses 75 speciality stores in key cities in the United Kingdom, France, Germany and Scandinavia to cover the market.

A selective policy might be used to avoid selling to wholesalers or retailers who (1) have a poor credit rating, (2) have a reputation for making too many returns or requesting too much service, (3) place orders that are too small to justify making calls or providing service or (4) are not in a position to do a satisfactory job. Selective distribution is becoming more popular than intensive distribution as firms see that they don't need 100 per cent coverage of a market to justify or support national advertising. Often the majority of sales come from relatively few customers and the others buy too little compared to the cost of working with them. That is, they are unprofitable to serve. This is called the 80/20 rule—80 per cent of a company's sales often come from only 20 per cent of its customers *until it becomes more selective in choosing customers*. Esprit, a producer of colourful, trendy clothing, was selling through about 4000 department stores and speciality shops. Esprit found that about half of the stores generated most of the sales. Sales analysis also showed that sales in Esprit's own stores were about 400 per cent better than sales in other sales outlets. As a result, Esprit cut back to about 2000 outlets and opened more of its own stores and profits increased.

Selective distribution can produce greater profits not only for the producer but also for all channel members because of the closer cooperation among them. Transactions become more routine, requiring less negotiation in the buying and selling process. Wholesalers and retailers are more willing to promote products aggressively if they know they're going to obtain the majority of sales through their own efforts. They may carry more stock and wider lines, do more promotion and provide more service, all of which lead to more sales.

Selective distribution makes sense for shopping and speciality products and for those business products that need special efforts from channel members. It reduces competition between different channels and gives each distributor a greater opportunity for profit. When producers use selective distribution, fewer sales contacts have to be made and fewer wholesalers are needed. A producer may be able to contact selected retailers directly.

In the early part of the life cycle of a new unsought good, a producer's marketing manager may have to use selective distribution to encourage enough intermediaries to handle the product. The manager wants to get the product out of the unsought category as soon as possible but cannot if it lacks distribution. Well-known distributors may have the power to get such a product introduced but sometimes on their own terms which often include limiting the number of competing wholesalers and retailers. The producer may be happy with such an arrangement at first but dislike it later when more retailers want to carry the product.

Exclusive distribution sometimes makes sense

Exclusive distribution is just an extreme case of selective distribution—the firm selects only one distributor in each geographic area. Besides the various advantages of selective distribution, producers may want to use exclusive distribution to help control prices and the service offered in a channel. A rather macabre example is a Dutch firm of undertakers. They have appointed Green Undertakings as their sole agent in the United Kingdom for cartonboard coffins, 99 per cent biodegradable starch eye caps and bodybags.[3]

Retailers of shopping products and speciality products often try to get exclusive distribution rights in their territories. Fast-food franchises often have exclusive distribution and that is one reason for their popularity. Owners of McDonald's franchises willingly pay a share of sales and follow McDonald's strategy to the letter in order to keep the exclusive right to a market.

Unlike selective distribution, exclusive distribution usually involves a verbal or written agreement stating that channel members will buy all or most of a given product from the seller. In return, these intermediaries are granted the exclusive rights to that product in their territories. Some intermediaries are so anxious to get a producer's exclusive franchise that they will do practically anything to satisfy the producer's demands.

Horizontal arrangements among competitors are illegal

Horizontal arrangements—among *competing* retailers, wholesalers or producers—to limit sales by customer or territory have consistently been ruled illegal by courts in the EU. Courts consider such arrangements obvious collusion that reduces competition and harms customers.

CHANNEL SYSTEMS CAN BE COMPLEX

Trying to achieve the desired degree of market exposure can lead to complex channels of distribution. Firms may need different channels to reach different segments of a broad product market or to be sure they reach each segment. Sometimes this results in competition between different channels.

Exhibit 9–6 shows the many channels used by a company that produces roofing tiles. It also shows (roughly) what percentage of the sales go to different channel members. Tiles are both consumer products (sold to do-it-yourselfers) and business products (sold to building contractors and roofing contractors). This

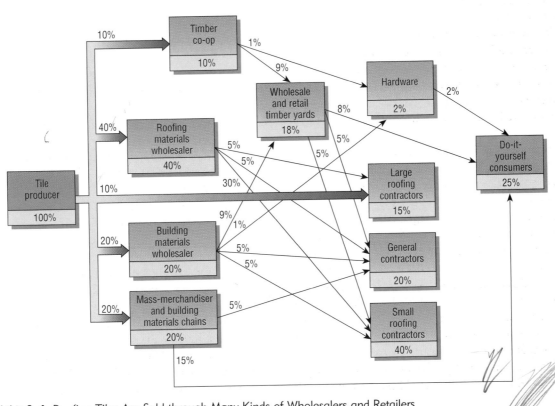

Exhibit 9–6 Roofing Tiles Are Sold through Many Kinds of Wholesalers and Retailers

helps explain why some channels develop. But note that the tiles go through different wholesalers and retailers—independents, and chains, hardware stores and mass-merchandisers. This can cause problems because different wholesalers and retailers want different markups. It also increases competition, including price competition. And the competition among different intermediaries may result in conflicts between the intermediaries and the producer.

Dual distribution channels may be needed

Dual distribution occurs when a producer uses several competing channels to reach the same target market, perhaps using several distributors in addition to selling directly. Dual distribution is becoming more common.

Big retail chains want to deal directly with producers. They want large quantities and low prices. The producer sells directly to retail chains, and relies on wholesalers to sell to smaller accounts. Some established intermediaries resent this because they don't appreciate *any* competition, especially price competition set up by their own suppliers.

On other occasions, producers are forced to use dual distribution because their present channels are doing a poor job or aren't reaching some potential customers. For example, Nike has now established its own retail outlets, which specialize solely on Nike brands to give itself better distribution. Its products will continue to sell through traditional sports shops, but this development allows it to control its own sales more effectively.

SUMMARY

In this chapter, we discussed the role of Place and noted that Place decisions are especially important because they may be difficult and expensive to change. An understanding of the market and how consumers behave should drive Place decisions. Product classes are useful starting points when making distribution decisions. Technology is changing aspects of marketing including distribution. Electronic Data Interchange and the Internet enable producers and intermediaries and customers to be closely linked to each other. On-line shopping and interactive marketing are increasing in popularity though many ethical and security issues remain unresolved.

Marketing specialists and channel systems develop to adjust discrepancies of quantity and assortment. Their regrouping activities are basic in any economic system. Adjusting discrepancies provides opportunities for creative marketers. The tasks involve accumulating, bulk-breaking, sorting and assorting products. The use of intermediaries is justified to the extent that intermediaries do these tasks more efficiently than producers.

Channel planning requires firms to decide on the degree of market exposure required. The ideal level of exposure may be intensive, selective or exclusive. The legality of limiting market exposure needs to be considered to avoid having to undo an expensively developed channel system or face the legal consequences.

The planning of distribution channels is important. We stressed that channel systems compete with each other and that vertical marketing systems seem to be winning. Vertical marketing systems operate on the basis of each member cooperating to ensure that the product is available when and where the customer wants it. Given these developments in the channel, producers are no longer automatically the most powerful member. Often intermediaries control or even dominate channels of distribution.

QUESTIONS AND PROBLEMS

1. Review the Motion Media case at the beginning of the chapter and discuss how its Place decisions relate to the product class concept. Explain your thinking.

2. Give two examples of service firms that work with other channel specialists to sell their products to final consumers. What marketing functions is the specialist providing in each case?

3. Discuss some reasons why a firm that produces capital equipment might use direct distribution in its domestic market, but use intermediaries to reach overseas customers.

4. Explain discrepancies of quantity and assortment using the clothing business as an example. How does the application of these concepts change when selling steel to the car industry? What impact does this have on the number and kinds of marketing specialists required?

5. Explain the four regrouping activities with an example from the building supply industry (nails, paint, flooring, plumbing fixtures, etc.). Do you think that many specialists develop in this industry, or do producers handle the job themselves? What kinds of marketing channels would you expect to find in this industry, and what functions would various channel members provide?

6. Insurance agents are distributors who help other members of the channel by providing information and handling the selling function. Does it make sense for an insurance agent to specialize and work exclusively with one insurance provider? Why or why not?

7. Discuss the Place objectives and distribution arrangements that are appropriate for the following products (indicate any special assumptions you have to make to obtain an answer):
   (a) A scale for products weighing up to two pounds which gives a direct readout of postage costs.
   (b) Children's toys: (i) radio-controlled model aeroplanes costing £80 or more, (ii) small rubber balls.
   (c) Heavy-duty, rechargeable, battery-powered wrenches for factory production lines.
   (d) Fibreglass fabric used in making roofing tiles.

8. Give an example of a producer that uses two or more different channels of distribution. Briefly discuss what problems this might cause.

9. Find an example of vertical integration. Are there any particular advantages to this vertical integration? If so, what are they? If there are no such advantages, how do you explain the integration?

10. What would happen if retailer-organized channels (either formally integrated or administered) dominated consumer product marketing?

11. How does the nature of the product relate to the degree of market exposure desired?

12. Why would distributors want exclusive distribution for a product? Why would producers want exclusive distribution? Would distributors be equally anxious to get exclusive distribution for any type of product? Why or why not? Explain with reference to the following products: confectionery, batteries, golf clubs, golf balls, steak knives, televisions and industrial woodworking machinery.

13. Discuss the promotion a new grocery product's producer would need in order to develop appropriate channels and move products through those channels. Would the nature of this job change for a new producer of dresses?

SUGGESTED CASE

7. Paper Supplies Corporation

REFERENCES

1. S. Gracie, 'Putting sales into motion', *The Sunday Times*, 2 September 1998, Business section, p. 12.

2. S. Conaty, 'The Irish Times on the Web', Key Note Address, Irish Marketing Teachers' Association, annual conference, Cork.

3. B. Butler, 'The one-stop coffin shop' *Management Today*, February 1997, pp. 58–60.

CHAPTER 10
Logistics and Distribution

When You Finish This Chapter, You Should

1 Understand why physical distribution (logistics) is such an important part of Place *and* marketing strategy planning.

2 Understand why the physical distribution customer service level is a key marketing strategy variable.

3 Understand the physical distribution concept and why it requires coordination of storage, transportation and related activities.

4 Know about the advantages and disadvantages of the various transportation methods.

5 Know how inventory decisions and storage affect marketing strategy.

6 Understand the distribution centre concept.

7 Appreciate how computers help to improve coordination of physical distribution in channel systems.

8 Understand the important new terms (shown in colour).

If you want a Coca-Cola, there's usually one close by, no matter where you might be in the world. And that's no accident. The top marketing executive for the best-known brand name in the world states the objective simply: 'Make Coca-Cola available within an arm's reach of desire.' To achieve that objective, Coke works with many different channels of distribution. But that's just the start. Think about what it takes for a bottle, can or glass of Coke to be there whenever you're ready. In warehouses and distribution centres, on trucks and at retail outlets, Coke handles, stores and transports over 250 billion servings of soft drink a year. Getting all that product to consumers could be a logistical nightmare, but Coke does it effectively and at a low cost.

Fast information about what the market needs helps keep Coke's distribution on target. In many European markets, computer systems show Coke managers exactly what's selling; that allows Coke to plan inventories and deliveries. Coke also operates a 24-hour-a-day communications centre to respond to the many requests it gets from channel members each year. Orders are processed instantly. This ensures that consumers at the end of the channel aren't lost because of stockouts. And Coke products move efficiently through the channel.

Coke's strategies in international markets rely on many of the ideas that have worked in the United States. But the stage of market development varies in different countries, so Coke's emphasis varies as well. To increase sales in France, for example, Coke must first make more product available at retail stores; so Coke is installing thousands of soft-drink coolers in French supermarkets. In Great Britain, Coke wants to have more inventory even closer to the point of consumption—in consumers' homes. So Coke is urging retailers to carry multipacks and larger packages. In Japan, by contrast, single-unit vending machine sales are very important so Coke uses a small army of truck drivers to constantly restock its 870 000 vending machines, more per capita than anywhere else in the world. In less developed areas, the Place system is not always so sophisticated. In the Philippines, for example, it's difficult for delivery trucks to reach some small shops in crowded areas. Instead, riders on bicycles equipped with side-cars make deliveries.

Coke is also working to increase sales on draft in international markets. As part of that effort, Coke equips restaurants and food outlets with Coke dispensers. Once a Coke dispenser is installed, the retailer usually doesn't have room for a competitor's dispenser. And when a consumer wants a fountain drink, Coke isn't just 'the real thing', it's the only thing.

Some people think Pepsi is beating Coke in the 'cola wars' because Pepsi's ads get so much attention. But as this case suggests, who wins the competition will depend on whole marketing strategies, including Place, not just promotion.[1]

QUESTIONS AND PROBLEMS

1. Explain how adjusting the customer service level could improve a marketing mix. Illustrate.

2. Briefly explain which aspects of customer service you think would be most important for a producer that sells fabric to a firm that manufactures furniture.

3. Briefly describe a purchase you made where the customer service level had an effect on the product you selected or where you purchased it.

4. Discuss the types of trade-offs involved in PD costs, service levels and sales.

5. Explain the total cost approach and why it may be controversial in some firms. Give examples of how conflicts might occur between different departments.

6. Discuss the relative advantages and disadvantages of rail, roads and air as transportation methods.

7. Discuss some of the ways that air transportation can change other aspects of a Place system.

8. Indicate the nearest location where you would expect to find large storage facilities. What kinds of products would be stored there? Why are they stored there instead of some other place?

9. When would a producer or intermediary find it desirable to use a public warehouse rather than a private warehouse? Illustrate, using a specific product or situation.

10. Discuss the distribution centre concept. Is this likely to eliminate the storage function of conventional wholesalers? Is it applicable to all products? If not, cite several examples.

11. Clearly differentiate between a warehouse and a distribution centre. Explain how a specific product would be handled differently by each.

12. Discuss some of the ways computers are being used to improve PD decisions.

13. Would a JIT delivery system require a supplier to pay attention to quality control? Give an example to illustrate your points.

14. Discuss the problems a supplier might encounter in using a JIT delivery system with a customer in a foreign country.

REFERENCES

1. 'Behemoth on a tear', *Business Week*, 3 October 1994, pp. 54–5; 'The Cola wars go to college', *Business Week*, 19 September 1994, p. 42; 'Coca-Cola still it in India despite fight from Pepsi', *Advertising Age International*, 18 July 1994, pp. I2ff; 'The World's Best Brand', *Fortune*, 31 May 1993, pp. 44–54.

2. A.C. Samli, L.W. Jacobs and J. Wills, 'What presale and postsale services do you need to be competitive', *Industrial Marketing Management*, February 1992, pp. 33–42; R.M. Pisharodi, 'Preference for supplier when supplier and customer perceptions of customer service levels differ', *The Logistics and Transportation Review*, March 1994, pp. 31–54; B.P. Shapiro, V.K. Rangan and J.J. Sviokla, 'Staple yourself to an order', *Harvard Business Review*, July–August, 1992, pp. 113–22; J.B. Fuller, J. O'Conor and R. Rawlinson, 'Tailored Logistics: The Next Advantage', *Harvard Business Review*, May–June 1993, pp. 87–98.

3. B.J. Gibson, H.L. Sink and R.A. Mundy, 'Shipper–carrier relationships and carrier selection criteria', *The Logistics and Transportation Review*, December 1993, pp. 371–82.

4. K. Raguraman and C. Chan, 'The development of sea–air intermodal transportation: An assessment of global trends', *The Logistics and Transportation Review*, December 1994, p. 379; 'Cargo that phones home', *Fortune*, 15 November 1993, p. 143; 'Grain processor improvises to stay afloat', *The Wall Street Journal*, 21 July 1993, p. B1ff.

5. K. Rao, R.R. Young and J.A. Novick, 'Third party services in the logistics of global firms', *The Logistics and Transportation Review*, December 1993, pp. 363–70.

6. P.A. Dion, L.M. Hasey, P.C. Dorin and J. Lundin, 'Consequences of inventory stockouts', *Industrial Marketing Management*, vol. 20, no. 1, 1991, pp. 23–8; R.D. White, 'Streamline inventory to better serve customers', *The Journal of Business Strategy*, March–April 1989, pp. 43–7.

7. A.B. Maltz, 'Outsourcing the warehousing function: Economics and strategic considerations', *The Logistics and Transportation Review*, September 1994, pp. 245–66; P.J. Daugherty, D.S. Rogers and T.P. Stank, 'Benchmarking: Strategic implications for warehousing firms', *The Logistics and Transportation Review*, March 1994, pp. 55–72.

8. M. Brown, 'The slow boat to Europe', *Management Today*, June 1997, p. 83–99.

9. *1993 Annual Report*, Tyson Foods; 'Holly Farms' marketing error: The chicken that laid an egg', *The Wall Street Journal*, 9 February 1988, p. 44.

10. *1997 Annual Report*, Clorox; *1993 Annual Report*, Clorox.

11. F.W. Gilbert, J.A. Young and C.R. O'Neal, 'Buyer–seller relationships in just-in-time purchasing environments', *Journal of Business Research*, February 1994, pp. 111–20; S. McDaniel, J.G. Ormsby and A.B. Gresham, 'The effect of JIT on distributors', *Industrial Marketing Management*, May 1992, pp. 145–50; S.J. Daniel and W.D. Reitsperger, 'Management control systems for JIT: An empirical comparison of Japan and the US', *Journal of International Business Studies*, Winter 1991, pp. 603–18.

12. B. Dearing, 'The strategic benefits of EDI', *The Journal of Business Strategy*, January–February 1990, pp. 4–6; R. O'Callaghan, P.J. Kaufmann and B.R. Konsynski, 'Adoption correlates and share effects of electronic data interchange systems in marketing channels', *Journal of Marketing*, April 1992, pp. 45–56; R. Germain, 'The adoption of logistics process technology by manufacturers', *Journal of Business Research*, May 1993, pp. 51–64; N.C. Hill and M.J. Swenson, 'Sales technology applications: The impact of electronic data interchange on the sales function', *Journal of Personal Selling & Sales Management*, Summer 1994, pp. 79–88.

CHAPTER 11
Retailers, Wholesalers and Their Strategy Planning

When You Finish This Chapter, You Should

1 Understand how retailers plan their marketing strategies.

2 Know about the many kinds of retailers that work with producers and wholesalers as members of channel systems.

3 Understand the differences among the conventional and non-conventional retailers, including those who accept the mass-merchandising concept.

4 Understand scrambled merchandising and the 'wheel of retailing'.

5 See why size or belonging to a chain can be important to a retailer.

6 Know the various kinds of wholesalers and the strategies that they use.

7 Know what progressive wholesalers are doing to modernize their operations and marketing strategies.

8 Understand why retailing and wholesaling have developed in different ways in different countries.

9 See how the Internet is having an impact on both retailing and wholesaling.

10 Understand the important new terms (shown in colour).

TESCO—RETAILING AT HOME AND ABROAD

Tesco is one of Britain's leading food retailers with 568 stores throughout England, Scotland, Wales and Northern Ireland. In an effort to expand its operations into Europe and to take advantage of opportunities for growth, Tesco now has 103 stores in France, 43 in Hungary, 31 in Poland and 13 in the Czech Republic and Slovakia. The company says it is committed to creating shareholder value through an innovative customer-focused strategy implemented by its people.

Tesco's marketing strategy has evolved over the years. In the 1970s it had a downmarket image of 'pile it high, sell it cheap'. The company decided to develop superstores and set about centralizing functions such as buying and distribution. Emphasis was put on giving customers greater choice, better quality products and more value for money in new and upgraded stores. Tesco enjoyed growth in the buoyant 1980s when consumers were happy to spend on value-added products.

By 1990 Tesco had improved its image dramatically. However, the end of the economic boom brought about recession and demand for premium products declined. A new form of competitor arrived in the market. Discount retailers such as Aldi and Netto from the continent set up much smaller stores with stock limited to two or three thousand product lines, compared to the average 15 000 of an average Tesco superstore. They provide very low prices on basic products and limited service. Market research showed Tesco that price was much more important to customers in the 1990s than the 1980s. Some customers were buying their basics at the discount stores and coming to Tesco for the quality goods that they needed.

Tesco devised a marketing strategy aimed at winning back customers on price, quality and customer service.

Tesco has managed to win back old customers and gain new ones. Its sales are the highest for any food retailer in the United Kingdom. The company uses market research to keep in touch with its customers and changes in the market. Qualitative and quantitative research is used to investigate customer loyalty and image. Customer panels tell store managers, along with retail and Head Office staff what they think of their local Tesco store. The database of Clubcard, their loyalty card, informs Tesco about customers' purchasing habits, promotion behaviour and the local catchment area. Research is also conducted with non-customers on the street and by telephone.

Tesco tries to have the same trading philosophy in central Europe as it does in the United Kingdom. Poland is an attractive market with a population of 40 million and a growing and promising economy. Its retail sector is unsophisticated with much trading taking place on the street, in kiosks or in small family-run shops. However, change is taking place at a rapid pace. In 1991 supermarkets and hypermarkets accounted for 6 per cent of food sales, a figure that had risen to 14 per cent in 1998. Within a few years it is expected that nearly half Poland's food sales will take place in supermarkets and hypermarkets. This is part of the reason why Tesco wants to have a significant presence in the market. It has already opened 1400 stores there, one of them is 10 000 square metres, much bigger than any of its UK stores.

Just as Poland is growing and its infrastructure improving, so too does Tesco. Polish customers and suppliers are different from those in Tesco's home market. In the United Kingdom, Tesco has a very close and commanding relationship with suppliers with many of the purchasing procedures conducted electronically. In Poland, suppliers have more power and use much less sophisticated techniques. For example, a tractor will turn up at a store with a load of turnips for sale. The development of relationships between suppliers, retailer and customers will be a learning process over the coming years.[1]

WHOLESALERS AND RETAILERS PLAN THEIR OWN STRATEGIES

Wholesalers and retailers are often a vital link in a channel of distribution and in the whole marketing process, helping both their suppliers and customers. The Tesco case shows that retailers, like other businesses, must select their target markets and marketing mixes carefully. Chapter 9 covered the functions that wholesalers and retailers perform as intermediaries in channel systems. In this chapter, the focus is on the major decision areas that retailers and wholesalers consider in developing their own strategies. The strategies used by different types of retailers and how they are evolving will be described. It is important to understand this evolution because the pace of change in retailing is accelerating. Then, the chapter considers the different types of wholesalers and how they adjust their strategies to meet the needs of both their suppliers and customers.

THE NATURE OF RETAILING

Retailing covers all the activities involved in the sale of products to final consumers. Retailers range from large, sophisticated chains of specialized shops such as Toys "R" Us, to individual merchants such as the woman who sells meat from an open stall in the central market in Kazakhstan. Because they serve individual consumers, even the largest retailers face the challenge of handling small transactions. The total number of transactions with consumers is much greater than at other channel levels.

Retailing is crucial to consumers in every macromarketing system. For example, in 1996, consumers spent US$ 727 009 million in the United Kingdom, US$ 1 363 219 million in Germany, US$ 930 875 million in France, US$ 34 352 million in Ireland and US$ 93 758 million in Denmark. Although figures vary, about one-third of this spending will have taken place through retailers. This indicates the importance of the retail function in marketing systems. If the retailing effort is not effective, other channel members suffer and some products do not get sold at all.[2]

The nature of retailing and its rate of change are generally related to the stage and speed of a country's economic development. In Western Europe, retailing tends to be more varied and more mature than in most other countries. By studying the European system and how it is changing you will better understand how retailing is evolving in other parts of the world.

PLANNING A RETAILER'S STRATEGY

Retailers interact directly with final consumers so strategy planning is critical to their survival. If a retailer loses a customer to a competitor, the retailer is the one who suffers. Producers and wholesalers still make *their* sale regardless of which retailer sells the product. Retailers must be guided by the old maxim 'Goods well bought are half sold'. Most retailers in developed nations sell more than one kind of product. The assortment of products they handle can be critical to their success. Yet it is best to think of the retailer's *whole offering*—assortment of goods and services, advice from sales assistants, convenience—as its 'Product'.

When you enter a Virgin Megastore, for example, you are primarily interested in purchasing a CD or cassette. However, the physical environment and atmosphere are different from other record shops. Prices may be more or less competitive than those in other shops, and the staff may be more or less knowledgeable and enthusiastic. The Virgin Megastore may provide you with headphones, which allow you to listen to recent releases. You will probably also find information about future concerts by featured bands. All of these aspects are part of the overall Megastore product.

 ## Internet Exercise

Tiffany & Co is widely recognised as one of the world's premiere jewellers. It commands high prices for what it offers. Go to the Tiffany web site (**www.tiffany.com**) and review the different sections. Do you think that the web site communicates superior value to the Tiffany target market? Explain your opinion and identify the specific aspects of the web site that support your view.

Consumers have reasons for buying from particular retailers

Different consumers prefer different kinds of retailers. The same retailer may appear to be relatively 'down-market' to one set of consumers with high levels of income. At the same time this retailer may appear to be exclusive to another set of low-income consumers. Visitors to affluent countries such as Switzerland and Sweden may have experienced this at first hand. Higher levels of income in Switzerland are associated with higher prices even for basic commodities.

The discussion of consumer behaviour and needs in Chapter 3 applies here. For example, some people enjoy shopping in prestige outlets such as Harrods or Burberry's. People on high incomes may still buy commodity products from 'budget' outlets such as Netto or Aldi, and at the same time buy a range of expensive products from more exclusive outlets. It is difficult to categorize outlets completely by the type of customers that they have.

The atmosphere in the outlet may also have an important emotional effect on how consumers view a retailer. How merchandise is displayed, what decorations, colours and finishes are used, and even the temperature, sounds and smell of a shop all contribute to its 'atmospherics' and shop image. The right combi-

nation of these factors may attract more target customers and encourage them to spend more. But interesting surroundings are usually costly, and the money is well spent only when the shopping atmosphere is consistent with the needs of the target market the retailer is trying to attract. Ultimately, the prices that consumers pay must cover the cost of the facilities where they shop. A shop's image may be a plus or a minus depending on the target market.[3]

As in other businesses, segmentation and positioning decisions are important to retailers. Ignoring emotional and social dimensions in those decisions can lead to serious errors in a retailer's strategy planning.

Economic needs—which shop has the best value?

Whatever the effect of other consumer needs, factors related to economic needs are usually very important when a consumer selects a retailer. Some of the most important factors include:

- *Price* (value offered, credit, special discounts).
- *Location* (convenience, parking, safety).
- *Product* selection (width and depth of assortment, quality).
- *Special* services (home delivery, special orders, gift wrap).
- *Helpful* salespeople (courteous, knowledgeable, fast checkout).
- *Fairness* in dealings (honesty, return privileges).

Retailers should consciously make decisions that set policies on all of these factors. After all, it is the combination of these factors that differentiate one retailer's offering and strategy from another. Later chapters go into more detail on the promotion and price strategy decisions that all firms, including retailers and wholesalers, make.

Different types of retailers emphasize different strategies

Retailers have an almost unlimited number of ways in which to alter their offerings, their marketing mixes, to appeal to a target market. Because of all the variations, it is oversimplistic to classify retailers and their strategies based on a single characteristic, such as merchandise, services or shop size. But a good place to start is by considering basic types of retailers and some differences in their strategies. Initially this chapter will look at conventional retailers and then see how others successfully modify conventional offerings to meet the needs of *some* consumers.

CONVENTIONAL RETAILERS—TRY TO AVOID PRICE COMPETITION

Single-line, limited-line retailers specialize by product

A hundred and fifty years ago, **general shops**—which carried anything they could sell in reasonable volume were the main retailers in Europe. With the growing number of consumer products, general shops could not offer enough variety in all their traditional lines. Some shops began specializing in dry goods, clothing, furniture or groceries. Now most conventional retailers are **single-line** or **limited-line shops**—shops that specialize in certain lines of related products rather than a wide assortment. Many shops specialize not only in a single line, such as clothing, but also in a *limited-line* within the broader line. Within the clothing line, a shop might carry *only* shoes, formal wear, men's casual wear or even ties, but offer depth in that limited line. For example, the Levi's chains of shops carries only leisure wear with the Levi's brand, and Sockshop carries a wide range of underwear, but little else.

The following statistics give some idea of the diversity of types and sizes of shops in one country. Norway has approximately 40 000 retail outlets. Of these the largest category is food, beverage and tobacco (11 000 outlets), followed by clothing and textiles (6500), furniture (3400), hardware, glass and sports (3000), watches and optical (3000) and cars and accessories (2700) (source: *Statistics Norway*, 1993). In 1993 476 outlets accounted for a turnover of Nkr 8255 in the Oslo region, whereas 852 outlets in northern Norway accounted for a turnover of Nkr 8150 in the same year.

Single-line, limited-line shops are being squeezed

The main advantage of such shops is that they can satisfy some target markets better. By adjusting to suit specific customers, they may even build a long-term relationship with their customers and earn a position as *the* place to shop for a certain type of product. Single-line and limited-line shops face the costly problem of having to stock some slow-moving items in order to satisfy the shop's target market. Many of these shops are small with high expenses relative to sales. They try to avoid competition on identical products so they can keep prices up. Examples of such shops include those selling knitting wool, photographic equipment, televisions and hi-fi equipment.

Conventional retailers such as this have been around for a long time and are still found in every community. They clearly satisfy many people's needs. In fact, in most countries conventional retailers still handle the vast majority of all retailing sales. However, this situation is changing fast. Nowhere is the change clearer than in Europe. Retailers who modify their mixes in the various ways suggested in Exhibit 11–1 are squeezing conventional retailers.

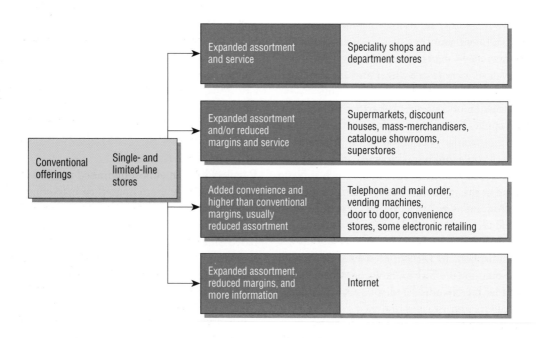

Exhibit 11–1 Types of Retailers and the Nature of Their Offerings

EXPAND ASSORTMENT AND SERVICE—TO COMPETE AT A HIGH PRICE

Speciality shops usually sell shopping products

A **speciality shop**—a type of conventional limited-line shop—is usually small and has a distinct 'personality.' Speciality shops often sell special types of shopping products, such as high-quality sporting goods, exclusive clothing, cameras or jewellery. They aim at a carefully defined target market by offering a unique product assortment, knowledgeable sales assistants and better service. The speciality shop's major advantage is that it caters for certain types of customers whom the management and sales assistants come to know well. This simplifies buying, speeds turnover and cuts costs due to obsolescence and style changes. Speciality shops will probably continue to be a part of the retailing scene as long as customers have varied tastes and the money to satisfy them.

Department stores combine many limited-line shops and speciality shops

Department stores are larger shops that are organized into many separate departments and offer many product lines. Each department is like a separate limited-line outlet and handles a wide variety of shopping products, such as men's wear or household goods. Typical examples of department stores include John Lewis in the United Kingdom, Karstadt in Germany, El Corte Ingles in Spain and Ahold in The Netherlands.

EVOLUTION OF MASS-MERCHANDISING RETAILERS

Mass-merchandising is different from conventional retailing

So far retailers have been decribed primarily in terms of their product *assortment*. This reflects traditional thinking about retailing. Supermarkets and discount houses could also be described in these terms but there are some important differences. Conventional retailers think that demand in their area is fixed and they have a 'buy low and sell high' philosophy. Many modern retailers reject these ideas. They accept the *mass-merchandising concept*, which says that retailers should offer low prices to get faster turnover and greater sales volumes, by appealing to larger markets. To understand mass-merchandising better, it is useful to look at its evolution from the development of supermarkets and discounters to modern mass-merchandisers, like Tengelman in Germany, Dansk Supermarked in Denmark and Tesco in the United Kingdom.

Supermarkets started the move to mass-merchandising

In terms of grocery distribution on a global basis, most food shops are still relatively small single-line or limited-line operations, a situation that makes shopping for food inconvenient and expensive. Many Italians, for example, still go to one shop for pasta, another for meat, and yet another for milk. Although this seems outdated, keep in mind that many of the world's consumers do not have access to **supermarkets**—large shops specializing in groceries with self-service and wide assortments.

The basic idea for supermarkets developed during the early 1930s. Some innovators felt they could increase sales by charging lower prices. They also introduced self-service and provided a broad product assortment in large shops. Success and profits came from large-volume sales, not from high traditional markups. In some countries the abolition of the manufacturer's right to insist on a fixed price at the retail outlet allowed retailers to begin to offer lower prices than their rivals. As such companies grew, so they were able to command even lower prices from their suppliers, thus accelerating their growth.

Modern supermarkets are planned for maximum efficiency. Scanners at checkout counters make it possible to carefully analyse the sales and profit of each item, and allocate more shelf space to faster-moving and higher-profit items. This helps sell more products, more efficiently. It also reduces the investment in inventory, makes stocking easier, and minimizes the cost of handling products. These issues are critical in modern supermarkets, such as Tesco that has 15 000 different product lines. *Survival* depends on such efficiency as net margins can often be very low.

Supermarkets have become very skilled at creating an environment where consumers are more likely to buy. Many factors are used to encourage purchase—music, lighting, distribution of basic essential items throughout the store, aisle width, end-of-aisle displays and even colour. Green is a commonly used colour in supermarket decor because of its associations with freshness and nature. In some countries, stores are also using aroma to create a shopping-conducive environment. For example, one store in the United Kingdom had the aroma of mulled wine pumped through the store at Christmas time in an effort to get customers into the shopping mood.

Scanning systems can also allow supermarkets to make choices about the best promotional deals to offer on individual products. Accurate information about product sales can be linked to different levels of promotional activity and the effects of the promotion in different shops can be monitored. Such systems can also be used to reward consumers when they are combined with membership or loyalty schemes. Customers who are members are rewarded with special targeted promotions, rebates on purchases and favourable banking facilities. This type of system is part of the effort of many retailers to build relationships with their customers so as to discourage consumers from switching shops.

Catalogue showroom retailers preceded discount houses

Catalogue showroom retailers such as Argos and Index sell products out of a catalogue and display showroom, with backup inventories. In the 1970s these operations expanded rapidly by aiming at final consumers and offering attractive catalogues and improved facilities. Catalogue showroom retailers offer price savings and deliver almost all the items in their catalogues from backroom warehouses. They emphasize well-known manufacturer brands of jewellery, gifts, luggage and small appliances but offer few services.

Mass-merchandisers have many departments

Mass-merchandisers are large, self-service shops with many departments that emphasize 'soft goods' (housewares, clothing and fabrics) and staples (like health and beauty aids) but still follow the emphasis on lower margins to get faster turnover. Mass-merchandisers, such as ITM-Intermarche (France), Dunnes Stores (Ireland) and Delhaize 'Le Lion' (Belgium), have checkout counters in the front of the shop and limited sales help on the floor. The average mass-merchandiser has nearly 5500

square metres of floor space, but many new shops are 9500 square metres or more. Mass-merchandisers grew rapidly and they have become the primary non-food place to shop for many frequently purchased consumer products. In fact, they have expanded so rapidly in many areas that they are no longer taking customers from conventional retailers but instead are locked in head-to-head competition with each other.

Superstores meet all routine needs

Some supermarkets and mass-merchandisers have moved towards becoming superstores—very large shops that carry not only foods, but all goods and services that the consumer purchases *routinely*. Such a store may look like a mass-merchandiser, but it is different in concept. A superstore is trying to meet *all* the customer's routine needs, usually at a price. Superstores carry about 50 000 items. In addition to foods, a superstore carries personal care products, medicine, some clothing, toys, some lawn and garden products, petrol and services such as dry cleaning, travel reservations, bill paying and banking. Typically just on the edge of a town or city, the superstores challenge the smaller more central shops and supermarkets by offering lower prices and, in many cases, extra services such as free car-parking. Hypermarkets are similar to superstores in terms of products offered and location, but have a larger floor space.

Single-line mass-merchandisers are also important

Since 1980 some retailers, focusing on single product lines, have adopted the mass-merchandisers' approach with great success. Toys "R" Us pioneered this trend. Similarly, Payless Drugshops, Ikea (furniture), Home Depot (home improvements) and JJB Sports (sports goods) attract large numbers of customers with their large assortment and low prices in a specific product category. These shops are called *category killers* because it is difficult for less specialized retailers to compete.

TOYS "R" US IS SERIOUS ABOUT RETAILING

Although toy sales have been flat for a number of years, sales for the Toys "R" Us chain have grown very rapidly. Yet Toys "R" Us didn't always enjoy this lofty success. In 1978 it nearly went bankrupt! Historically most toys were distributed through thousands of small, independent toy shops, although mass-merchandisers like Asda drew some customers by offering the fastest-selling toys at low prices. In this highly competitive market, Toys "R" Us pioneered a new retailing format and it was a real success.

Each shop, now more than 700 of them around the world, is conveniently located, and each offers low prices on a mind-boggling selection of over 18 000 toys. The company's buying clout helps it to get low prices from toy producers. In addition, it uses computers in each shop to spot fast-selling toys before they're hits. This allows the firm to buy early and avoid stockouts that trouble other toy retailers.

Toys "R" Us is aggressively opening shops in overseas markets such as Hong Kong and Japan. In these countries small shops and department stores still dominated toy distribution before Toys "R" Us entered the market.

To understand how it is affecting these markets, let's look at what happened when Toys "R" Us opened its first German shop in 1987. Small toy retailers pressed local governments to keep the chain out. They criticized the Toys "R" Us self-service approach and argued that there would be no expert to warn parents about dangerous toys. German toymakers were also hostile—and many initially refused to sell to the chain. They feared that its hard-nosed buying would eat into their profits. Consumers, on the other hand, liked Toys "R" Us, and sales grew fast. In fact, as other German retailers began to copy its approach, overall toy sales increased by 50 per cent. Toys "R" Us got one-quarter of that increase, but competitors also got more business and consumers got much better selections and prices.

SOME RETAILERS FOCUS ON ADDED CONVENIENCE

Supermarkets, discounters and mass-merchandisers provide many different products at low prices under one roof. However, sometimes consumers want more convenience even if the price is higher. Let's look at some retailers who meet this need.

Convenience (food) shops must have the right assortment

Convenience (food) shops are a convenience-oriented variation of the conventional limited-line food shops. Instead of expanding their assortment, however, convenience shops limit their stock to pickup or fill-in items like bread, milk, beer and snacks. They offer convenience, not assortment, and often charge prices 10 to 20 per cent higher than nearby supermarkets. However, as many petrol stations have been converted to convenience shops and other retailers have expanded their hours, intense competition is driving down convenience shop prices and profits.[4]

Vending machines are convenient

Automatic vending is selling and delivering products through vending machines. Although the growth in vending machine sales is impressive, such sales account for only a small percentage of sales. Yet for some target markets this retailing method can't be ignored. Vending machines provide an important way of reaching the market for many confectionery products and soft drinks. You will have seen the distinctive Coca-Cola and Mars vending machines in many public areas, particularly those where younger consumers are likely to frequent, e.g. in student unions, cinemas and railway and bus stations.

The major disadvantage to automatic vending is high cost. The machines are expensive to buy, stock, and repair relative to the volume they sell. They are also targets for theft. Marketers of similar non-vended products can operate profitably on a margin of about 20 per cent. The vending industry requires about 41 per cent to cover costs so they must charge higher prices.

Shop at home—with telephone, TV and direct-mail retailing

In-home shopping is becoming more popular—especially among time-pressured dual career families. **Telephone and direct-mail retailing** allow consumers to shop at home, usually placing orders by post or a phone call and charging the purchase to a credit card. Typically, catalogues and advertisements on TV let customers see the offerings, and purchases are delivered by carriers. Some consumers really like the convenience of this type of retailing, especially for products not available in local shops.

Mail-order companies such as Otto Versand in Germany and Great Universal Stores in the United Kingdom sell a wide range of products including clothing, furniture and electrical goods from a catalogue, which is changed regularly. Data about the purchases made can be used to target specific customers with offers that match their lifestyle and previous purchases. This approach reduces costs by using computer mailing lists to help target specific customers and by using warehouse-type buildings and limited sales help. Shoplifting, an expense for most retailers, is not a problem. After-tax profits for successful mail-order retailers average about 7 per cent of sales, more than twice the profit margins for most other types of retailers. However, with increasing competition and slower sales growth, these margins are eroding.

Door-to-door retailers—try to give personal attention

Door-to-door selling means going directly to the consumer's home. It accounts for only a small percentage of retail sales but meets some consumers' needs for convenience and personal attention. Door-to-door selling can also be useful with unsought products like encyclopaedias. It can also be useful for services such as dry cleaning where personal convenience may be a significant factor. With more adults working outside the home, it can be difficult to find someone at home during the day.

RETAILING ON THE INTERNET

The Internet has been described as the wild frontier of the information age. It offers marketers the opportunity to communicate with new and existing markets in a very integrated way. So, not only is the Internet a medium of communication, it is also a form of personal selling. Internet commerce is growing at a phenomenal rate. Goods and services sold on-line in Europe and the United States in 1998 came to more than US$5.1 billion, double the figure for 1997. If only the computer-literate are customers, there is still much growth ahead. However, with the arrival of TV sets that can be used to surf the Net, technology will become more user-friendly and the market grow yet more.

Although many people are unwilling to buy goods that they cannot physically touch, this is of little concern with items such as books, CDs and software all of which sell well on-line. Traditional high-street shops cannot compete with the prices offered by firms who enjoy some of the economies of retailing on-line. This means that Internet prices are usually at least 10 per cent less than those in conventional shops.

Conventional retailers are now establishing themselves on the Internet. Two Belgian chains, GIB and Delhaize, have set up their own Web sites, with the latter offering some customers free delivery to their own homes. Migros, the leading Spanish retailer, is offering Internet shopping, with customers able to choose from 39 500 food and non-food items, make payment on-line or within 10 days by post and have goods delivered quickly for a nominal fee. In Britain, Tesco are also offering electronic shopping and has also set itself up as an Internet Service Provider.

For manufacturers, the Internet offers a way to cut out the retailer altogether. Procter and Gamble, Coca-Cola, Kraft, Sara Lee, Nabisco and over 20 other lead-ing manufacturers have established the Consumer Direct Co-operative, which is testing the logistics of selling direct to customers in the United States. The ability to interact with their customers on the Net and build up a detailed database on them is a key incentive for manufacturers. The German market is a particularly receptive one for the Internet and companies such as Deutsche Telekom have made huge investments in technology so as to harness some of the market's potential.

For consumers, there are advantages to Internet shopping. For a start product assortments are not limited by location. Traditional thinking about retailing looks at product assortments from the perspective of location and shopping experience. On the Internet, by contrast, a consumer can get to a very wide assortment, perhaps from different sellers, by clicking from one Web site to the other. The assortment becomes much less limited.

On the Web, a customer cannot touch a product or really inspect it. Many consumers want to be able to do that and have been used to doing it. On the other hand, even when a consumer is in a retail outlet it is sometimes hard to get reliable information. At a Web site it is often possible to get much more information with just a click of a mouse, even though only the product and a brief description is presented on the initial page. It is also possible to access a much broader array of information such as product reviews, feature comparisons, performance tests and other data. More powerful computers are also opening up many possibilities for multimedia information, not just still pictures but full motion product demonstration videos and audio explanations. Internet customers can use 'intelligent shopping agents' to hunt down the goods they want and find the best prices.[5]

RETAILING TYPES ARE EXPLAINED BY CONSUMER NEEDS FILLED

Different types of retailers and how they evolved has been discussed. Earlier, we noted that no single characteristic provided a good basis for classifying all retailers. Now it helps to see the three-dimensional view of retailing presented in Exhibit 11–2. It positions different types of retailers in terms of three consumer-oriented dimensions: (1) width of assortment desired, (2) depth of assortment desired, and (3) a price/service combination. Price and service are combined because they are often indirectly related. Services are costly to provide. A retailer who wants to emphasize low prices usually has to cut some services. Shops with a lot of

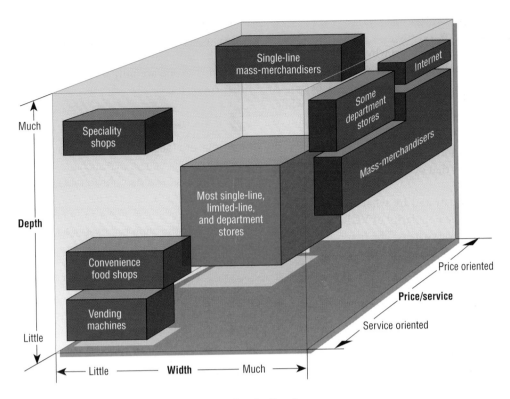

Exhibit 11–2 A Three-Dimensional View of the Market for Retail Facilities and the Probable Position of Some Present Offerings

service must charge prices that cover the added costs.

Most existing retailers can be positioned within this three-dimensional market diagram. Exhibit 11–2, for example, suggests the *why* of vending machines.

Some people, in the front upper left-hand corner, have a strong need for a specific item and are not interested in width of assortment, depth of assortment, or price.

WHY RETAILERS EVOLVE AND CHANGE

Exhibit 11–2 compares different types of *existing* shops. Retailing has changed over time and continues to change. Some of the ways in which these changes are happening are discussed next.

The wheel of retailing keeps rolling
The **wheel of retailing theory** says that new types of retailers enter the market as low-status, low-margin, low-price operators and then, if successful, evolve into more conventional retailers offering more services with higher operating costs and higher prices. Then they are threatened by new low-status, low-margin, low-price retailers, and the wheel turns again. Department stores, supermarkets and mass-merchandisers went through this cycle. The wheel of retailing theory, however, does not explain all major retailing developments. Vending

machines entered as high-cost, high-margin operations. Convenience food shops are high-priced. Suburban shopping centres do not always emphasize low price.

Scrambled merchandising—mixing product lines for higher profits
Conventional retailers tend to specialize by product line. However, most modern retailers are moving towards **scrambled merchandising**—carrying any product lines that will sell profitably. Supermarkets and smaller shops sell anything they can move in volume, such as magazines, one-hour photo processing, antifreeze and motor oil, potted plants and videotapes. Mass-merchandisers are not limited to everyday items, but also sell cameras, jewellery and even fax machines.

Product life-cycle concept applies to retailer types

Consumers' needs help explain why different kinds of retailers developed. In applying the product life-cycle concept this process can be understood better. A retailer with a new idea may have profits for a while. If it is a really good idea, imitation can be guaranteed and a squeeze on profits is also likely. Other retailers will copy the new format or 'scramble' their product mix to sell products that offer them higher margins or faster turnover.

The cycle is illustrated by what happened with video movies. As the popularity of VCRs grew, video shops cropped up everywhere. The first ones charged £5 a night for a tape. As more competitors entered, however, they drove prices (and profits) down. Competition heated up even more as supermarkets and other shops started to rent the most popular tapes, sometimes for as little as £1 a night. Other specialists, such as Blockbuster, increased the assortment to appeal to more consumers. In this heated competition, many video shops could not cover their costs and went out of business.

Although the cycle for video shops moved very quickly, retail life cycles can be much slower. But cycles do exist, and some conventional retailers are far along in their life cycles and may be declining. Recent innovators are still in the market growth stage. See Exhibit 11–3. Some retailing formats that are mature in Western Europe are only now beginning to grow in other countries.

Ethical issues

Most retailers face intense competitive pressure. The desperation that comes with such pressure has pushed some retailers towards questionable marketing practices. Critics argue, for example, that retailers too often advertise special sale items to bring price-sensitive shoppers into the shop but then don't stock enough to meet demand. Or a shop may sell bread at below cost to attract customers to the shop (in some European countries this is illegal). Special offers on other branded goods may be used for a similar purpose. Other shops are criticized for pushing consumers to trade up to more expensive items. The use of aroma marketing to stimulate customer buying has also been criticized. What is ethical and unethical in situations like these, however, is subject to debate. Retailers cannot always anticipate demand perfectly, and deliveries may not arrive on time. Similarly, trading up may be a sensible part of a strategy, if it is done honestly.

RETAILER SIZE AND PROFITS

A few large retailers do most of the business

A relatively small number of large retailers account for the majority of purchases in many European countries. Moreover, there is a trend towards even greater concentration over time. Exhibit 11–4 shows how increasingly fewer larger outlets account for the sales of goods to consumers in most European countries.

The larger retail shops, such as supermarkets, do most of the business. On the other hand, the many small retailers can't be ignored. They do reach many consumers and often are valuable channel members. From a manufacturer's point of view the drawback is that it is frequently costly to attempt to deal through all these outlets.

Chains are building market clout

One way for a retailer to achieve economies of scale is with a corporate chain. A **corporate chain shop** is one of several shops owned and managed by the same firm. Examples include Asda (United Kingdom), Hakon (Norway) and Sonae (Portugal). Chains account for a significant proportion of all retail sales. Most chains use central buying for their different shops. This allows them to take advantage of quantity discounts or opportunities for vertical integration, including developing their own efficient distribution centres. They can use EDI and other computer links to control inventory costs and stockouts. They may also spread promotion and management costs across many shops. Retail chains also have their own brands. Many of these chains are becoming powerful members in their channel systems. In fact, the most successful of these big chains control access to so many consumers that they have the economic power to dictate almost every detail of relationships with their suppliers.

Independents form chains

Competitive pressure from corporate chains encouraged the development of both cooperative chains and voluntary chains. **Cooperative chains** are retailer-sponsored groups, formed by independent retailers, that run their own buying organizations and conduct joint promotion efforts. Sales of cooperative chains are rising as they learn how to compete with corporate chains. Examples include Dagrofa (Denmark), Conad (Italy) and NISA (United Kingdom).

Voluntary chains are wholesaler-sponsored groups that work with 'independent' retailers. Some are linked

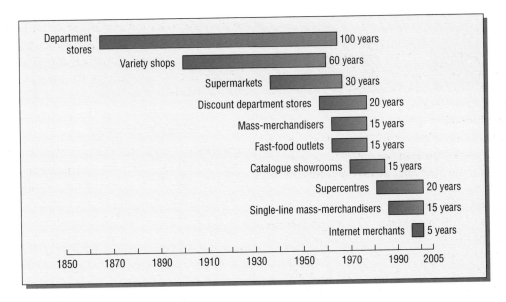

Exhibit 11–3 Retailer Life Cycles—Timing and Years to Market Maturity

by contracts stating common operating procedures and requiring the use of common shopfront designs, shop names and joint promotion efforts. Examples include Spar (United Kingdom) and Musgraves (Ireland).

Franchisers form chains

In a **franchise operation**, the franchiser develops a good marketing strategy, and the retail franchise holders (the franchisees) carry out the strategy in their own units. The franchisor acts like a voluntary chain operator—or a producer. Each franchise holder benefits from its relationship with the larger company and its experience, buying power, advertising and image. In return, the franchise holder usually signs a contract to pay fees and commission and agrees to follow franchise rules designed to continue the successful strategy. The franchiser gains entry to new markets as well as the fee and royalties that come from the franchisee. In addition, the franchiser has control over what products are sold, how they are displayed and generally how the business is run.

Voluntary chains tend to work with existing retailers, while some franchisers like to work with, and train, newcomers. For newcomers, a franchise often reduces the risk of starting a new business. There is some research to suggest that fewer franchise operations fail in the first few years than other new small businesses. Franchising has become popular. It is estimated that it accounts for 20 per cent of all retail trade in Britain, employs around 275 000 people with 92 per cent of the outlets trading profitably. One reason is that franchising is especially popular with service retailers, one of the fastest-growing sectors of the economy.[6]

LOCATION OF RETAIL FACILITIES

Location can spell success or failure for a retailer. A good location depends on target markets, competitors and costs. The decision about where to locate a business is therefore very much a marketing strategy decision. Some of the ideas a retailer should consider in selecting a location are discussed below. Remember that this is quite a detailed and specialized area and that only a brief overview is presented here.

Town centre shopping

Most cities have a central shopping area with many retail shops. At first, it may seem that such a district developed according to some plan. Actually, the location of individual shops is often more an accident of time and available space. However, it is possible to see patterns in the types of shops that locate in various areas. The *high street* is the area that attracts most shopper traffic. Because of this, the rents in the high street will be higher than elsewhere in the town or city. Most of the retail premises in the high street are occupied by multiples who can afford the higher rent better than the small local retailers. The types of products sold by the multiples in the high street typically include shopping products such as clothes, jewellery, shoes, cameras and financial services.

	Austria	Belgium	Czech Rep.	Denmark	Finland	France	Germany	Greece	Hungary	Ireland	Italy	Netherlands	Norway	Poland	Portugal	Spain	Sweden	Switzerland	UK	Turnover share (%)
Metro	✓						✓													3.2
Edeka				✓			✓													2.4
Rewe							✓													2.3
Aldi	✓	✓		✓	✓	✓	✓			✓	✓								✓	2.3
Spar	✓	✓	✓	✓	✓	✓	✓	✓			✓	✓	✓		✓	✓	✓	✓	✓	2.2
Carrefour						✓					✓				✓	✓				2.2
Intermarché		✓				✓									✓	✓				2.0
Promodes						✓	✓	✓			✓				✓	✓				2.0
Leclerc						✓										✓				2.0
Sainsbury																			✓	1.8
Tengleman	✓		✓				✓		✓		✓	✓								1.5
Tesco						✓													✓	1.4
Auchan						✓					✓			✓						1.2
Casino						✓					✓									1.1
ICA													✓				✓			1.1
Argyil																			✓	1.0
Migros	✓					✓														1.0
ASDA																			✓	1.0
Coop Italia											✓									0.8
Ahold		✓										✓			✓					0.8
Coop Sweden																	✓			0.8
Systeme U						✓														0.8
Coop Switzerland						✓												✓		0.7
Dock de France						✓										✓				0.7
Cora		✓				✓														0.6
Somerfield																			✓	0.6
GIB		✓												✓						0.6
Kesko					✓															0.5
Kwik save																			✓	0.5
Comptoir Moderne						✓										✓				0.4

Exhibit 11–4 Retailer Group Concentration in Europe

Planned shopping centres

Many town centres also now contain a **planned shopping centre** which is a set of shops planned as a unit to satisfy market needs. The shops sometimes act together for promotion purposes and sometimes provide free parking. It is more common to find specialist shops in planned shopping centres.

Out of town shopping

On the edge of town **regional shopping centres** are located. These are large centres in which the emphasis is on shopping products. Most of these are enclosed areas, making shopping easier in bad weather. They are usually anchored by one or more large department stores and include as many as 200 smaller shops. Shops that feature convenience products are often located at the edge of the centre so they do not get in the way of customers primarily interested in shopping.

Regional centres usually serve large populations and are typically found near populated suburban areas. They can draw customers from a radius of 50 to 60 kilometres or even farther from rural areas where shopping facilities are poor. These centres are enormous facilities in terms of geographic size and the mix of retailing and leisure facilities provided. The Metro Centre in the North of England is one of Europe's largest at 150 000 square metres.

DIFFERENCES IN RETAILING IN DIFFERENT COUNTRIES

New ideas spread across countries

New retailing approaches that succeed in one part of the world are often quickly adapted to other countries. As the former Eastern European countries begin to develop so retailing concepts from developed economies are increasingly applied. The learning curve in such countries is frequently much shorter and new entrants such as Tengelman, a major German retailer, are applying the approaches which they have developed in the West as fully as possible. As a result retailing is developing far more rapidly and at high levels of sophistication.

Mass-merchandising requires mass markets

The low prices, selections and efficient operations offered by mass-merchandisers and other large chains might be attractive to consumers everywhere. But consumers in less developed nations often don't have the income to support mass distribution. The small shops that survive in these economies sell in very small quantities, often to a small number of consumers.

Some countries block change

The political and legal environment severely limits the evolution of retailing in some nations. Japan is a prime example. For years its Large Shop Law, aimed at protecting the country's politically powerful small shopkeepers, has been a real barrier to retail change. The law restricts development of large shops by requiring special permits, which are routinely denied.

Japan says that it is taking steps to change the Large Shop Law; in fact, that is why Toys "R" Us was able to enter the Japanese market. Even so, most experts believe that it will be many years before Japan moves away from its system of small, limited-line shops. To put this in perspective, a typical family-run grocery shop in Japan is only about 23 square metres. The inefficiency of that retail distribution system is an important reason why Japanese consumers pay very high prices for consumer products. Many countries in other parts of Europe, Asia and South America impose similar restrictions.

Consumer cooperatives are popular in some countries

Retailing across Europe can take a wide variety of forms. Switzerland's Migros provides an example of diversity in just one retail operation. Migros runs a variety of different types of shop, ranging from supermarkets to appliance and electronics centres. Migros accounts for about 22 per cent of food sales in Switzerland and nearly 16 per cent of all retail sales. Consumer cooperatives probably won't become popular in markets where other types of retailers are already established and meeting customers' needs. However, some experts think consumer cooperatives like Migros could become a dominant form of retailing in central and eastern Europe.

WHAT IS THE FUTURE OF RETAILING?

Retailing has changed rapidly in the last 30 years and the changes are expected to continue. Innovative retailers are investing heavily in information technology and in supply chain relationships. It has been argued that retailers are moving responsibility for ensuring product availability to suppliers. Thus, sales are monitored by suppliers through computerized links and stocks are then automatically replenished. The invoicing and payment for the goods can also be done electronically. Given that it is the retailer who provides access to the market and to customers, the retailer has a powerful role in the supply chain. As retail trade concentrates and consolidates, large retailers become increasingly powerful.

Technology helps retailers to do their existing jobs more efficiently. It also brings about new forms of retailing such as electronic commerce and Internet shopping. This represents an opportunity for retailers to offer their wares electronically to the consumer. However, manufacturers can also avail themselves of the same opportunity. By offering their merchandise directly, the manufacturer is engaging in a process called 'disintermediation'. This may be a threat to the retailer who traditionally carried that product.

Many consumers simply do not have as much time to shop as they once did and a growing number are willing to pay for convenience. Shops will probably continue to make shopping more convenient by staying open later, carrying assortments that make one-stop shopping possible, and being sure stocks do not run out. This interest in convenience and time savings should also contribute to the growth of in-home shopping, including interactive shopping using the new generation of cable-TV and computer network services.[7]

WHAT IS A WHOLESALER?

Wholesalers perform a range of tasks for many different types of customer. For this reason, it is difficult to satisfactorily define the terms wholesaler and wholesaling. Some of their activities may even seem like manufacturing. As a result, some wholesalers describe themselves as 'manufacturer and dealer'. Some like to identify themselves with such general terms as merchant, jobber, dealer or distributor. Exhibit 11–5 outlines the different types of wholesaler.

In a narrow sense **wholesalers** can be defined as firms whose main function is to provide services to retailers. The core service is the sale of goods which the retailer sells on to the final consumer. However, wholesalers provide a much greater range of services including holding stock, providing a variety of choice for retailers, providing credit and advice, and assisting in joint promotions with retailers. Wholesalers also sell to all of the different types of organizational customers shown in Exhibit 4–1.

DIFFERENT KINDS OF WHOLESALERS HAVE DIFFERENT COSTS AND BENEFITS

It is easier to understand wholesalers—and their strategies—by seeing them as members of channels. We discussed the general functions that a channel intermediary might provide in Chapter 9 when it was explained why a producer might use an indirect channel of distribution. Moreover, wholesaling functions are just variations on the basic marketing functions—buying, selling, grading, storing, transporting, financing, risk taking and information gathering—as discussed in Chapter 1. Now these ideas are developed in more

detail. Different types of wholesalers perform different functions for their suppliers and customers.

Manufacturer's sales branches are considered wholesalers

Manufacturers who just take over some wholesaling activities are not considered wholesalers. However, when they set up **manufacturers' sales branches**—warehouses that producers set up at separate locations away from their factories—these establishments basically operate as wholesalers.

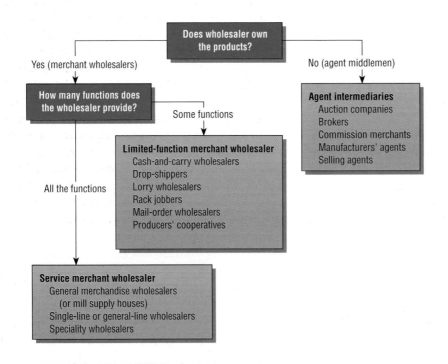

Exhibit 11–5 Types of Wholesaler

Traditional channels of distribution for banking have changed dramatically with the introduction of new technology. Today many customers use online connections from their homes to their banks.

MERCHANT WHOLESALERS ARE THE MOST NUMEROUS

Merchant wholesalers own (take title to) the products they sell. They often specialize in certain types of product or customer.

Full service wholesalers provide all the functions

Service wholesalers are merchant wholesalers who provide all the wholesaling functions. Within this basic group are three types: (1) general merchandise, (2) single-line and (3) speciality.

General merchandise wholesalers are service wholesalers who carry a wide variety of non-perishable items such as hardware, electrical supplies, plumbing supplies, furniture, pharmaceutical products, cosmetics and car equipment. With their broad line of convenience and shopping products, they serve hardware shops, pharmacies and small department stores.

Single-line (or general-line) wholesalers are service wholesalers who carry a narrower line of merchandise than general merchandise wholesalers. For example, they might carry only food, clothing or certain types of industrial tools or supplies. In consumer products, they serve the single-line and limited-line shops. In business products, they cover a wider geographic area and offer more specialized service.

Speciality wholesalers are service wholesalers who carry a very narrow range of products—and offer more information and service than other service wholesalers. A consumer products speciality wholesaler might carry only health foods or oriental foods instead of a full line of groceries. A speciality wholesaler of business products might limit itself to fields requiring special technical knowledge or service. Richardson Electronics is an interesting example. It specializes in distributing replacement parts, such as electron tubes, for old equipment that many manufacturers still use on the factory floor. Richardson describes itself as 'on the trailing edge of technology', but its unique products, expertise and service are valuable to its target customers, many of whom operate in countries where new technologies are not yet common.[8]

Pharmaceutical companies have many different types of customers. For most end customers, pharmaceutical products are bought from local retail outlets that are authorized to sell such products. It is typical that a manufacturer will use a wholesaler as a means to service the many retail outlets that carry its products.

Even in a relatively small country like Ireland, the number of retailers is over 1000. This causes logistical problems that are best overcome by using a wholesaler who specializes in servicing local retailers. Each retailer may well have accounts with more than one wholesaler so as to ensure continuity of supply. In Ireland there are no exclusive supply or purchase agreements. The pharmacy retailer is therefore free to move custom from one wholesaler to another and back again without penalty.

A retailer chooses a wholesaler on the basis of the product range stocked, service level, discounts and price. Many retailers receive deliveries once or twice per day from wholesalers. Once established, the business relationship between retailer and wholesaler can develop and lead to increased business. Typical services that the wholesaler provides to the pharmacy retailer include merchandising, shop layout advice, market and product information, training for shop sales staff, extended credit agreements for new owners, advice and assistance in securing finance, and loyalty schemes. In a market characterized by a huge diversity of products with low value and small order quantities, wholesalers provide a vital link in the distribution chain from production line to pharmacy shelf and hospital ward.

The environment for pharmacy wholesalers in Ireland is changing. Although the pharmaceutical market is growing, competitive pressures have reduced the profit margin for wholesalers. Large multiple retail chains, such as Boots, have become established in the market and FMCG retailers have also started retailing pharmacy products. In the United Kingdom, in-store pharmacies are common in supermarkets. These companies have their own distribution logistics and their growth would reduce the business available to independent wholesalers. Another trend is for independent retailers to consolidate their buying by being part of a group. This gives the retailers stronger bargaining power to secure better terms and discounts. At the other end of the supply chain, manufacturers are increasing their product portfolios and their products have shorter patent rights. The trend of smaller and lower value original dispensing packs increases the storage requirements for wholesalers who carry stock.

In such an environment the role of wholesalers in connecting manufacturers and retailers is important. However, changes in the marketing environment mean that wholesalers need to examine their efficiency levels. The retailer–customer base will show that there are different types of retailer and not all of them will be profitable customers for the wholesale. The 80:20 rule will be found to apply here, suggesting that the bulk of the wholesaler's business will come from a relatively small group of customers. The levels of service that the wholesaler gives to retailers should be determined by the profitability of the relationship. Thus, those retailers who put the bulk of their business with one wholesaler ought to receive more and better services than those retailers who do not place much business with the wholesaler. Thus, it should be clear that just as the manufacturer needs to develop an appropriate marketing mix, so too must the pharmaceutical wholesaler develop an attractive marketing mix for its target market of pharmacy retailers.

Limited-function wholesalers provide some functions

In contrast to full service merchant wholesalers, **limited-function wholesalers** provide only *some* wholesaling functions. Exhibit 11–6 shows the functions typically provided and those not provided. The following paragraphs discuss the main features of these wholesalers. Although less numerous in some countries, these wholesalers are very important for some products.

Cash-and-carry wholesalers want cash

Cash-and-carry wholesalers operate like service wholesalers, except that, as the term suggests, the customer must pay cash and is responsible for the delivery of the goods. Some retailers, such as small car repairers or restaurants, are too small to be served profitably by a service wholesaler. So service wholesalers set a minimum charge or just refuse to grant credit to a small business that may have trouble paying its bills. The cash-and-carry wholesaler can operate at lower cost because the retailers take over many wholesaling functions. Cash and carries are an effective way to meet the needs of small retailers and other organizational buyers. Makro, a Dutch company, is an example of a large, progressive cash-and-carry wholesaler.

Drop-shipper does not handle the products

Drop-shippers own (take title to) the products they sell—but they do *not* actually handle, stock or deliver them. Sometimes also called *desk-jobbers*, these wholesalers are mainly involved in selling. They get orders and pass them onto producers. Then the producer ships the order directly to the customer. Drop-shippers commonly sell bulky products (such as timber) for which additional handling would be expensive and possibly damaging.

Mail-order wholesalers reach outlying areas

Mail-order wholesalers sell out of catalogues that may be distributed widely to smaller industrial customers or retailers who might not be called on by other middlemen. These wholesalers operate in the hardware, jewellery, sporting goods and general merchandise lines. For example, Inmac uses a cata-

Functions	Cash-and-Carry	Drop-Shipper	Lorry	Mail Order	Cooperative	Rack Jobbers
For customers						
Anticipates needs	X		X	X	X	X
'Regroups' products (one or more of four steps)	X		X	X	X	X
Carries stocks	X		X	X	X	X
Delivers products			X		X	X
Grants credit		X	Maybe	Maybe	Maybe	Consignment (in some cases)
Provides information and advisory services		X	Some	Some	X	
Provides buying function		X	X	X	Some	X
Owns and transfers title to products	X	X	X	X	X	X
For producers						
Provides producers' selling function	X	X	X	X	X	X
Stores inventory	X		X	X	X	X
Helps finance by owning stocks	X		X	X	X	X
Reduces credit risk	X	X	X	X	X	X
Provides market information	X	X	Some	X	X	Some

Exhibit 11–6 Limited-Function Merchant Wholesalers

logue to sell a complete line of computer accessories. Inmac's catalogues are printed in six languages and distributed to business customers in Europe, the United States and Canada. Many of these customers do not have a local wholesaler.

Producers' cooperatives do sorting

Producers' cooperatives operate almost as full-service wholesalers with the profits going to the cooperative's customer-members. Cooperatives develop in agricultural markets where there are many small producers. Cooperatives usually emphasize sorting in order to improve the quality of farm products offered to the market. Some also brand these improved products and then promote the brands. Sunkist (citrus fruits) is one of the best known of these types of cooperative.

Rack jobbers sell hard-to-handle assortments

Rack jobbers specialize in hard-to-handle assortments of products that a retailer does not want to manage. Rack jobbers usually display the products on their own wire racks. For example, a grocery shop or mass-merchandiser might rely on a rack jobber to decide which paperback books or magazines it sells. The wholesaler knows which titles sell and applies that knowledge. Rack jobbers are usually paid cash for what is sold or delivered.

AGENTS ARE STRONG ON SELLING

Agents do not own the products

Agents are wholesalers who do not own the products they sell. Their main purpose is to help in buying and selling. They usually provide even fewer functions than the limited-function wholesalers, so they may operate at relatively low cost—sometimes 2 to 6 per cent of their selling price.

They are important in international trade

Agents are common in international trade. Many markets have only a few well-financed merchant wholesalers. The best that many producers can do is get local representation through agents and then arrange financing through banks that specialize in international trade. Agents are usually experts on local business customs and rules concerning imported products in their respective countries. Sometimes a marketing manager can't work through a foreign government's procedures without the help of a local agent. In some markets companies are obliged by law to work through a local agent.

Agents are usually specialists

Agents, like merchant wholesalers, normally specialize by customer type and by product or product line. So it is important to determine exactly what each one does. In the following sections, only the most important points about each type will be mentioned. Study Exhibit 11–7 for details on the functions provided by each.

One of the biggest growth markets in the 1990s has been the health and fitness industry. Fitness clubs are increasingly popular. Most hotel chains have installed fitness suites and chains of dedicated health and fitness clubs are springing up in many large towns. The larger chains have developed gyms that are large, include crèches, saunas, bars and restaurants under one roof. The average cost to kit out one of these gyms is £400 000 pounds. Where do the gym owners buy the equipment? How do the manufacturers make sure that their product is known and available to these customers?

Initially, many of the manufacturers used agents and distributors. The market size was small and did not justify dedicated sales staff from the manufacturer. The agents would carry the manufacturer's products as well as those of competitors'. As the market has grown, however, the manufacturers have switched to direct distribution. This gives the company control over how their product is marketed. As the manufacturers achieve critical mass in the market, they have sought to increase their service levels, get closer to their customers and to recapture distribution margin. By keeping a good margin on the product (rather than giving it to a distributor) the manufacturers have more leeway in dealing with customers and can give better discounted prices.

Price has become an especially important factor in the market. With many clubs consolidating and becoming part of chains, their bargaining power increases. A customer who is equipping a number of clubs will expect a heavily discounted price from the manufacturer. Just as price is under pressure, so too is service. Gym equipment is used heavily by energetic enthusiasts and problems are common. After-sales care, and staff dedicated to it, is a vital part of the marketing mix.

Some distributors have survived in the market. They do so by negotiating exclusive rights to serve certain markets. For example, Forza Fitness has an exclusive contract for distribution of Cybex equipment from America's second biggest manufacturer. The contract applies to the United Kingdom, Germany, Austria and Switzerland and the former Soviet Union. Reebok has also decided to join up with Forza to service these markets (plus Ireland) with retail and commercial fitness equipment. In order for Forza to survive it has had to develop a wide range of services and added-value elements. Forza offers turnkey products and provides an extensive range of products. That makes purchasing easier for the customer, strengthens the brand and simplifies servicing and maintenance arrangements.

Distributors such as Forza have two sets of customers. There are the end clients and the manufacturers. The end clients receive the products and service such as training of club staff to reduce the 35 per cent attrition in membership that is common in health and fitness clubs. The manufacturers gain from having their product sold despite being too small or specialized to distribute it directly to customers. In addition, they need to be reassured that their product is receiving the distributor's attention and is not being undersold because the distributor is working harder for a competitor's brand.[9]

Manufacturers' agents

A **manufacturers' agent** sells similar products for several non-competing producers for a commission on what is actually sold. Such agents work almost as members of each company's salesforce but they are really independent intermediaries. More than half of all agents are manufacturers' agents. A sports goods agent may call on small sports retailers offering them a range of tennis equipment from one manufacturer and judo equipment from another. Their main advantage is that they already call on some customers and can add another product line at relatively low cost, and at no cost to the producer until something sells. If an area's

Functions	Manufacturers' Agents	Brokers	Commission Merchants	Selling Agents	Auction Companies
For customers					
Anticipates needs	Sometimes	Some			
'Regroup' products (one or more of four steps)	Some		X		X
Carries stocks	Sometimes		X		Sometimes
Delivers products	Sometimes		X		
Grants credit			Sometimes	X	Some
Provides information and advisory services	X	X	X	X	
Provides buying function	X	Some	X	X	X
Owns and transfers title to products		Transfers only	Transfers only		
For producers					
Provides selling function	X	Some	X	X	X
Stores inventory	Sometimes		X		X
Helps finance by owning stocks					
Reduces credit risk				X	Some
Provides market information	X	X	X	X	

Exhibit 11–7 Functions Provided by Different Types of Agents

sales potential is low, a company may use a manufacturers' agent because the agent can do the job at low cost. Small producers often use agents everywhere because their sales volume is too small to justify their own salesforce.

Agents can be especially useful for introducing new products. For this service, they may earn 10 to 15 per cent commission. (In contrast, their commission on large-volume established products may be quite low—perhaps only 2 per cent.) A 10 to 15 per cent commission rate may seem small for a new product with low sales. Once a product sells well, however, a producer may think the rate is high and begin using its own sales representatives. Agents are well aware of this possibility. That's why most try to work for many producers and avoid being dependent on only one line.

Manufacturers' agents are very useful in fields where there are many small manufacturers who need to contact customers. They may cover a very narrow geographic area, such as a city or region. However, they are also important in international marketing, and an agent may take on responsibility for a whole country.

Import and export agents specialize in international trade

While manufacturers' agents operate in every country, **export or import agents** are basically manufacturers' agents who specialize in international trade. These agents help international firms to adjust to unfamiliar market conditions in foreign markets. The role of such agents can vary considerably. Frequently such agents can be used to identify the number and distribution of retailers in the market. They can frequently become involved in the recruitment and management of wholesalers and other intermediaries. They are very often used to collect market and competitive information.[11]

Brokers provide information

Brokers bring buyers and sellers together. Brokers usually have a *temporary* relationship with the buyer and seller while a particular deal is negotiated. They are especially useful when buyers and sellers don't come into the market very often. The broker's product is information about what buyers need and the availability of supplies. They may also aid in buyer–seller negotiation. If the transaction is completed, they earn a commission from whichever party hired them. **Export and import brokers** operate like other brokers, but they specialize in bringing together buyers and sellers from different countries.

Selling agents

Selling agents take over the whole marketing job of producers, not just the selling function. A selling agent may handle the entire output of one or more producers, even competing producers, with almost complete control of pricing, selling and advertising. In effect, the agent becomes each producer's marketing manager. Financial trouble is one of the main reasons a producer calls in a selling agent. The selling agent may provide working capital but may also take over the affairs of the business. A **combination export manager** is a blend of manufacturers' agent and selling agent—handling the entire export function for several producers of similar but non-competing lines.

Commission merchants handle and sell products in distant markets

Commission merchants and **export or import commission houses** handle products shipped to them by sellers, complete the sale and send the money, minus their commission, to each seller. Commission agents are common in agricultural markets where farmers must ship to big-city central markets. They need someone to handle the products there, as well as to sell them, because the farmer cannot go with each shipment. Commission agents are sometimes used in other trades, such as textiles. Here many small producers want to reach buyers in a central market, perhaps one in a distant country, without having to maintain their own sales force.

Auction companies

Auction companies provide a place where buyers and sellers can come together and complete a transaction. There are not many auction companies, but they are important in certain lines, such as livestock, fur, tobacco and used cars. For these products, demand and supply conditions change rapidly and the product must be seen to be evaluated. The auction company brings buyers and sellers together. Buyers inspect the products and then demand and supply interact to determine the price.

COMEBACK AND FUTURE OF WHOLESALERS

In earlier days, wholesalers dominated distribution. The many small producers and small retailers needed their services. This situation still exists in many countries, especially those with less developed economies. However, in the developed nations, as producers became larger some bypassed the wholesalers. Similarly, large retail chains often took control of functions that had been handled by wholesalers. In the light of these changes, many people predicted a gloomy future for wholesalers.

Producing profits, not chasing orders

Partly due to new management and new strategies, wholesalers have held their own, and many are enjoying significant growth. To be sure, many still operate in the old ways and wholesaling changes less rapidly than retailing. However, progressive wholesalers are becoming more concerned with their customers and with channel systems. Some offer more services. Others develop voluntary chains that bind them more closely to their customers. There is evidence that concentration is taking place in wholesaling with mergers and acquisitions among wholesalers. Modern wholesalers no longer require all customers to pay for all the services they offer simply because certain customers use them. Now some wholesalers offer basic service at minimum cost and then charge additional fees for any special services required.

Most modern wholesalers streamlined their operations to cut unnecessary costs and improve profits. To cut costs, they use computers to keep track of inventory and to order new stock only when it is really needed.

Computerized sales analysis helps them identify and drop unprofitable products. Wholesalers are also more selective in picking customers. They use a selective distribution policy when cost analysis shows that many of their smaller customers are unprofitable. With these less desirable customers gone, wholesalers give more attention to more profitable customers.

Progress to prosper

Many wholesalers are also modernizing their warehouses and physical handling facilities. They mark products with barcodes that can be read with hand-held scanners—so inventory, shipping and sales records can be easily and instantly updated. Computerized order-picking systems speed the job of assembling orders. New storing facilities are carefully located to minimize the costs of both incoming freight and deliveries. Delivery vehicles travel to customers in a computer-selected sequence that reduces the number of miles travelled. Wholesalers who serve manufacturers are rising to the challenge of JIT delivery systems and making renewed efforts to add value in the distribution channel.

Survival of the fit

Not all wholesalers are progressive, and some of the smaller, less efficient ones may fail. Efficiency and low cost, however, are not all that's needed for success. Some wholesalers will disappear as the functions they provided in the past are shifted and shared in different ways in the channel. Cost-conscious buyers for Sainsbury, Migros and other chains are refusing to deal with some of the intermediaries who represent small producers. They want to negotiate directly with the producer rather than just accept the price traditionally available from a wholesaler. Similarly, more producers see advantages in having closer direct relationships with fewer suppliers and they are paring the vendor roles to exclude wholesalers who do a poor job of meeting their needs. Efficient delivery services such as DHL are also making it easy and inexpensive for many producers to ship directly to their customers, even ones in foreign markets.[11]

 Is it an ethical issue?

There is no doubt that some wholesalers are being squeezed out of business. Some critics, including many of the wholesalers affected by these changes, argue that it is unethical for powerful suppliers or customers to simply cut out wholesalers who spend money and time, perhaps decades, developing markets. Contracts between channel members and laws sometimes define what changes are or are not legal. Ultimately however, ethical situations are the responsibility of individuals.

Survivors will need effective strategies

To survive, each wholesaler must develop a good marketing strategy. Profit margins are not large in wholesaling: typically they range from less than 1 per cent to 2 per cent. They have declined in recent years as the competitive squeeze has tightened. The wholesalers who do survive will need to be efficient, but that does not necessarily mean they all have low costs. Some wholesalers' higher operating expenses result from the strategies they select, including the special services they offer to *some* customers.

SUMMARY

Retailers must plan their marketing mixes with their target customers' needs in mind, while at the same time becoming part of an effective channel system. Many types of retailer have been described, each with its advantages and disadvantages. Modern retailers have discarded conventional practices and the old 'buy low and sell high' philosophy is no longer a safe guide. Lower margins with faster turnover is the modern philosophy as more retailers move into mass-merchandising. Even this is no guarantee of success as retailers' life cycles move on.

Scrambled merchandising will continue as retailing evolves to meet changing consumer demands. But important breakthroughs are still possible because consumers probably will continue to move away from conventional retailers. Electronic commerce can make a larger assortment of products available to more people—to better meet their particular needs.

Wholesalers can provide functions for those both above and below them in a channel of distribution. These services are closely related to the basic marketing functions. There are many types of wholesalers. Some provide all the wholesaling functions—while others specialize in only a few. Eliminating wholesalers would not eliminate the need for the functions they provide. It cannot be assumed that direct channels are more efficient.

Merchant wholesalers are the most numerous and account for the majority of wholesale trade. Their distinguishing characteristic is that they take title to (own) products. Agents, on the other hand, act more like sales representatives for sellers or buyers and they do not take title.

Despite various predictions, wholesalers continue to exist. The more progressive ones adapt to a changing environment. Wholesaling may not have experienced the scale and pace of change observed in retailing but change is affecting it. Inevitably, some smaller, and less progressive, wholesalers will fail, while larger, more efficient, and more market-oriented ones will survive and prosper by adapting to new opportunities.

CHAPTER 12

Promotion—Introduction to Integrated Marketing Communications

When You Finish This Chapter, You Should

1 Know the advantages and disadvantages of the promotion methods a marketing manager can use in strategy planning.

2 Understand the integrated marketing communications concept and why most firms use a mix of different promotion methods.

3 Understand the importance of promotion objectives.

4 Know how the communication process should affect promotion planning.

5 Know how the adoption processes can guide promotion planning.

6 Know how typical promotion plans are blended to get an extra push from intermediaries and help from customers in pulling products through the channel.

7 Understand how direct-response promotion is helping marketers to develop more targeted promotions.

8 Understand how to determine how much to spend on promotion efforts.

9 Understand the important new terms (shown in colour).

ALLIED IRISH BANK CHANGES ITS IDENTITY

Allied Irish Banks Limited was formed in 1966 by the coming together of three provincial Irish banks. By 1990 the company had surpassed the humble origins to which its name referred. The company had expanded to employ 14 000 people; it operated in Ireland, but also in the United Kingdom and the USA, and it had assets of £15 billion.

A reorientation of the company had been ongoing from the late 1980s and a new business mission had been developed. It stated: Value and service are at the heart of our business. We aim to provide real value to every one of our customers and to deliver the highest standards of service in banking and financial services. Having changed internally, the company began to examine its external image.

Marketing research revealed that there were problems with the company's identity and its communications. The name 'Allied Irish Banks plc' was meaningful in personal markets, though most people referred to it as AIB. In the non-Irish markets, the name suggested that the company was primarily Irish, thus overshadowing its international presence. The corporate logo had been designed to represent the coming together of three banks. It was a three-spoked roundel, rather like that used by Mercedes-Benz. The corporate colour was blue and did not provide distinctiveness in an industry where blue is de rigeur. The brand name 'Allied Irish Bank' appeared on all permanent media such as signs and stationery. All advertising copy included the end-line 'Allied Irish Bank: You bring out the best in us'.

Overall, the old identity and communications were found to have been useful when the message to be communicated was that the company was, indeed, an allied Irish bank. A new identity was required.

Early in 1990 the new identity was unveiled to the public in a blaze of advertising. Staff were informed of the new identity one week before the launch and were given watches, featuring the new logo, to commemorate the event. Promotional literature was widely distributed to increase awareness and understanding of the new identity. Media briefings were held for key journalists. The corporate identity consultants also briefed advertising and design agencies. Guidelines were developed to ensure consistency and coherence in the use of the new identity.

The new corporate name was AIB Group and AIB prefixes the specialist areas of the business such as AIB Bank, AIB Investment Managers, AIB Group Treasury and so on. The corporate symbol is inspired by one of the earliest known Celtic images of the Ark. Corporate colours, which feature on flags outside branches and on uniforms and stationery, are purple, red, gold and green. The company explained the changes as follows: The Ark is a symbol of our heritage, of security, and of the many communities we serve. Our new corporate colours express the warmth and friendliness of the Irish which is an integral part of AIB's character. These three elements—name, symbol and colour—sit within the framework of an overall style which expresses how we wish to serve and communicate with all our customers, with clarity, warmth and professionalism.

The company researched the impact of the changes with customers and staff. The company managed to arouse some unfavourable publicity in the changes. The main criticism is that the company used to design the new identity is non-Irish. AIB Group responded that it is no longer a purely Irish company. This illustrates a difference in perception, ironically one that the new identity seeks to overcome.

The scale of changes that the company has undertaken internally is reflected in the range of changes in its communications. The sheer volume of detail that needs to be managed to ensure that an appropriate corporate image is formed points to the need for integration of marketing communications.[1]

COMMUNICATIONS ARE A CORPORATE ISSUE

As the case illustrates, all organizations communicate. This may be done in a deliberate way through promotional campaigns or in a much more subtle manner, using the signals of corporate identity such as logos, slogans, letterheads, staff uniforms and the like. The important concern is that these communications should be managed. The organization needs to ensure that its identity 'fits'— that it is a genuine reflection of the organization's values, operations and ambitions. All the means by which the identity is communicated need to be planned and controlled to achieve consistency. Research is required to monitor the image that is conjured up in the mind of the various publics to which the organization relates. These publics include shareholders, employees, present and potential customers, and the local community.

Managing communications is a key marketing task. As Chapters 12 to 15 will show there are many methods of communication and they achieve a variety of outcomes. It is therefore important that communications are integrated. Through integration, communication can meet chosen objectives and address target markets.

The focus of these chapters is on communications that are designed to promote the organization and its products to target markets and the trade. The reader should take into account, however, that promotion is part of the overall communications engaged in by the organization.

SEVERAL PROMOTION METHODS ARE AVAILABLE

Promotion is communicating information between seller and potential buyer or others in the channel to influence attitudes and behaviour. The marketing manager's main promotion job is to inform target customers that the right Product is available at the right Place at the right Price. For example, car companies use a variety of methods to promote their brands. In the United Kingdom, 46 car manufacturers spent £500 million on 487 campaigns in 1995. That translated into 15 830 press pages, 3000 radio advertisements and extensive TV advertising. Indeed, such was the use of TV, that, on average, people in the United Kingdom watched 702 commercials in 1995, almost two per day!

It is reckoned that Alfa Romeo spent £1629 on advertising for each car sold while Volvo spent £583, Volkswagen £259 and BMW £149.[2]

What the marketing manager communicates is determined by target customers' needs and attitudes. *How* the messages are delivered depends on what mix of the various promotion methods the marketing manager chooses. A marketing manager can choose from several promotion methods—personal selling, mass selling, (otherwise known as mass communication) and sales promotion (see Exhibit 12–1). Further, because the different promotion methods have different strengths and limitations, a marketing manager usually uses them

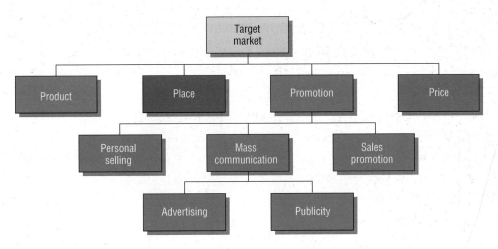

Exhibit 12–1 Basic Promotion Methods and Strategy Planning

in combination, that is the manager creates a promotions mix. As with other marketing mix decisions, it is critical that the marketer manager coordinates the different promotion methods as an integrated 'whole'—not as separate and unrelated parts.

Personal selling: flexibility is its strength

Personal selling involves direct spoken communication between sellers and potential customers. Face-to-face selling provides immediate feedback, which helps salespeople to adapt. Although salespeople are included in most marketing mixes, personal selling can be very expensive. It is often desirable to combine personal selling with mass communication and sales promotion.

Mass communication involves advertising and publicity

Mass communication is communicating with large numbers of potential customers at the same time. It is less flexible than personal selling, but when the target market is large and scattered, mass communication can be less expensive. Advertising and publicity are discussed in more detail in Chapter 13.

Advertising is the main form of mass communication. **Advertising** is any *paid* form of non-personal presentation of ideas, goods or services by an identified sponsor. It includes the use of such media as magazines, newspapers, radio and TV, and signs and posters. While advertising must be paid for, another form of mass communication—publicity—does not incur media fees.

Publicity avoids media costs

Publicity is any *unpaid* form of non-personal presentation of ideas, goods or services. Publicity people are paid to attract attention to the firm and its offerings *without having to pay media costs*. For example, book publishers try to get authors on TV chat shows because this generates a lot of interest and book sales, without the publisher paying for TV time. When Pepsi launched its new blue can it used many promotional devices that, in turn, gained a lot of publicity—for example, having Concorde painted blue for just 20 days! If a firm has a really new message, publicity may be more effective than advertising. Trade magazines, for example, may carry articles featuring the newsworthy products of regular advertisers—in part because they *are* regular advertisers. The firm's publicity department writes the basic copy and then magazine editors are encouraged to print it. Each year, magazines print photographs and stories about new cars: often the source of the information is the car producers. A consumer might not pay any attention to an advertisement, but carefully read a long magazine story containing the same information.

Sales promotion tries to spark immediate interest

Sales promotion refers to promotion activities, other than advertising, publicity and personal selling, that stimulate interest, trial or purchase by final customers or others in the channel. Sales promotion may be aimed at consumers, at intermediaries or even at a firm's own employees. Examples are listed in Exhibit 12–2.

Relative to other promotion methods, sales promotion can usually be implemented quickly and get results sooner. In fact, most sales promotion efforts are designed to produce immediate results. The topic of sales promotions is covered in more detail in Chapter 15.

Aimed at final consumers or users	Aimed at middlemen	Aimed at company's own salesforce
Contests Coupons Aisle displays Samples Trade shows Point-of-sale materials Banners and streamers Loyalty points Sponsored events	Price deals Promotion allowances Sales contests Calendars Gifts Trade shows Meetings Catalogues Merchandising aids	Contests Bonuses Meetings Portfolios Displays Sales aids Training materials

Exhibit 12–2 Examples of Sales Promotion Activities

Emphasizing advertising or personal selling or sales promotion

Many people think that promotion money gets spent primarily on advertising simply because advertising is all around them. The many advertisements in magazines and newspapers and on TV are impressive and costly. However, all the special sales promotions, such as coupons, free draws, trade shows, sporting events sponsored by firms and the like, add up to even more money. Similarly, sales assistants complete most retail sales. Behind the scenes, much personal selling goes on in the channels and in other business markets. In total, firms spend less money on advertising than on personal selling or sales promotion.

The amount of emphasis on each promotion method usually varies with each specific marketing strategy, depending on the target market and other elements of the marketing mix. The reason is that different promotion methods have different strengths and limitations. Because the different promotion methods complement each other, some communication tasks can be handled better or more economically with one method than with another. To get the whole promotion job done most firms use a mix of the three promotion methods.

The individual promotion methods are discussed in more detail in the next three chapters. First, however, it is important to understand the role of the whole promotions mix, personal selling, mass communication and sales promotion combined, so as to see how promotion fits into the rest of the marketing mix.

PLAN, INTEGRATE AND MANAGE THE PROMOTIONS MIX

Each promotion method has its own strengths and weaknesses—and in combination they provide a comprehensive set of tools for marketing communications. For example, Volvo advertising helps to build an image of the car to attract potential customers to the car showroom. Then the salesperson can build on this and engage in individual communication. The consumer may test drive the car, read more brochures, discuss with the salesperson their preferences and concerns. Ultimately, the sale may be closed with a special deal or sales promotion such as attractive credit terms or extended warranty. The role of promotion does not end here. Many car advertisements are read or noticed by recent customers who gain reinforcement for their choice from the advertisement.

Each promotional method involves its own distinct activities and requires different types of expertise. As a result, it is usually the responsibility of specialists, such as sales managers, advertising managers and promotion managers, to develop and implement the detailed plans for the various parts of the overall promotions mix.

Sales managers manage salespeople

Sales managers are concerned with managing the personal selling function in the organization. Often the sales manager is responsible for building good distribution channels and implementing Place policies. In smaller companies, the sales manager may also act as the marketing manager and be responsible for advertising and sales promotion.

Advertising managers work with advertisements and agencies

Advertising managers manage their company's mass communication effort in television, newspapers, magazines and other media. Their job is choosing the right media and developing the advertising campaigns.

Advertising departments within their own firms may help in these efforts or they may use outside advertising agencies. The advertising manager may also handle publicity. Alternatively, publicity may be handled by an outside agency or by whoever handles **public relations**—communication with non-customers, including employees, public interest groups, shareholders and the government.

 Internet Exercise

For many years, Saatchi and Saatchi have been thought of as an advertising Agency. With the growth in all forms of communication, the company has re-styled itself as an 'ideas company'. Explore what this means by visiting their web site **(www.saatchi.com)**.

Sales promotion managers need many talents

Sales promotion managers manage their company's sales promotion effort. In some companies, a sales promotion manager has independent status and reports directly to the marketing manager. If a firm's sales promotion spending is substantial, it probably *should* have a specific sales promotion manager. Sometimes, however, the sales or advertising departments handle sales promotion efforts—or sales promotion is left as a responsibility of individual brand managers. Regardless of who the manager is, sales promotion activities vary so much that many firms use both inside and outside specialists.

The marketing manager manages the marketing mix

Although many specialists may be involved in planning for and implementing specific promotion methods, determining the mix of promotion methods is a strategy decision and the responsibility of the marketing manager. The various promotion specialists tend to focus on what they know best and their own areas of responsibility. A creative advertising copywriter, even a very good one, may have no idea what a salesperson does during a call on a wholesale distributor. In addition, because of differences in outlook and experience, the advertising, sales and sales promotion managers often have trouble working with each other as partners or equals. Too often they just view other promotion methods as using up budget money they want. The marketing manager must weigh the advantages and disadvantages of the various promotion methods, then devise an effective promotion mix, fitting in the various departments and personalities and coordinating their efforts. Then, the advertising, sales and sales promotion managers should develop the details consistent with what the marketing manager wants to accomplish.

Send a consistent and complete message with integrated marketing communications

An effective blending of all of the firm's promotion efforts should produce integrated marketing communications—the intentional coordination of every communication from a firm to a target customer to convey a consistent and complete message. It seems obvious that all a firm's different communications to a target market should be consistent. However, when a number of different people are working on different promotion elements, they are likely to see the same big picture only if a marketing manager ensures that it happens. The challenge of consistency is usually greater when different aspects of the promotion effort are handled by different firms at different levels in the distribution channel. As already discussed, different channel members may have conflicting objectives, especially if they do not have a common focus on the consumer or business user at the end of the channel.[3]

Tango is a brand owned by Britvic, competing in the soft drinks market. The brand is marketed in Britain, Ireland, Germany, the Netherlands and Hungary. It has enjoyed a phased re-launch in the UK in the nineties. Investment in the brand is £124 million (from 1996–2001). The overall aim is to make Tango the biggest selling soft drinks brand outside the cola sector. The sales target for 2001 is 688 million litres (for comparison, Pepsi's target for 2001 is 700 million litres).

As part of the relaunch the Tango brand has adopted a zany, extrovert, irreverent image. Much of this was achieved through redesign of the packaging of Tango cans and through mass communications, in particular using outlandish advertising. The company wanted to extend the success of the relaunch of the Orange variety to its other flavours—Apple, Blackcurrant and Lemon. To do so, it needed to convince not just consumers but also the trade.

Trade objectives required Tango to get more shelf space from retailers and to ensure an equal emphasis on all four brands. The company needed to communicate that the other flavours are not just extensions to Orange but also brands in their own right. All of this meant that Britvic needed to communicate with retail customers. The particular emphasis was to inform the trade of the rationale of the relaunch and how retailers could benefit from the strategy.

The chosen method was to conduct presentations to selected retailers in a specially prepared Tango-branded caravan. Thus, the message was literally taken to the customers. The presentation addressed future marketing trends with a ten-minute video on branding issues. Britvic's broader objectives were presented, along with explanations of the 'reengineering' of the Tango brand, the strategy for each of the four flavours including details of each of the new advertising campaigns and marketing support.

Presentations were scheduled to last for 45 minutes but frequently lasted longer, such was the interest generated. More shelf space has been gained and retailers are stocking flavours that they did not previously take. Combined with the advertising campaign aimed at ultimate consumers, this trade campaign has helped the Tango brand to become more established in the market place.[4]

As a starting point, to get effective coordination and consistency, everyone involved with the promotion effort (in the company and channels) must clearly understand the plan for the overall marketing strategy. They all need to understand the role of each of the different promotion methods and how they will work together to achieve specific promotion objectives.

METHODS DEPEND ON PROMOTION OBJECTIVES

Overall objective is to affect behaviour

The different promotion methods are all different forms of communication. However, good marketing managers are not interested in just communicating. They want to communicate information that will encourage customers to choose a *specific* product. They know that if they have a better offering, informed customers are more likely to buy. Therefore, effective communications (1) reinforce present attitudes or relationships that might lead to favourable behaviour or (2) actually change the attitudes and behaviour of the firm's target market.

In terms of demand curves, promotion may help the firm make its present demand curve more inelastic, or shift the demand curve to the right, or both. These possibilities are shown in Exhibit 12–3. The buyer behaviour model introduced in Chapter 3 showed the many influences on buying behaviour. Affecting buyer behaviour is a challenging job, but that is the objective of Promotion.

Informing, persuading and reminding are basic promotion objectives

For a firm's promotion to be effective, its promotion objectives must be clearly defined because the right

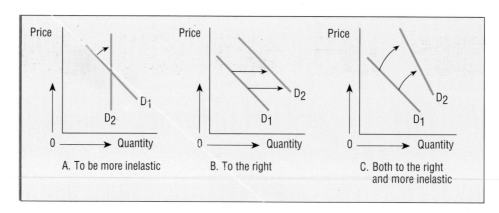

Exhibit 12–3 Promotion Seeks to Shift the Demand Curve

promotion mix depends on what the firm wants to accomplish. It is helpful to think of three basic promotion objectives: *informing*, *persuading* and *reminding* target customers about the company and its marketing mix. All try to affect buyer behaviour by providing more information. Even more useful is a more specific set of promotion objectives that states *exactly who* you want to inform, persuade or remind, and *why*. This is unique to each company's strategy and specific objectives vary by promotion method. Promotion objectives are outlined below and discussed in more detail in the next three chapters.

Informing is educating

Potential customers must know something about a product if they are to buy at all. A firm with a really new product may not have to do anything but inform consumers about it and show that it meets consumer needs better than other products. The promotional activities surrounding the introduction of Microsoft's Windows 95 and Windows 98 were very much concerned with informing customers of the product's availability.

Persuading usually becomes necessary

When competitors offer similar products, the firm must not only inform customers that its product is available but also persuade them to buy it. A *persuading* objective means the firm will try to develop a favourable set of attitudes so customers will buy, and keep buying, its product. Promotion with a persuading objective often focuses on reasons why one brand is better than competing brands. Consider, for example, the advertisements for cola that feature blind taste tests such as the Pepsi Challenge.

Reminding may be enough, sometimes

If target customers already have positive attitudes about a firm's marketing mix—or a good relationship with a firm—a reminding objective might be suitable. This objective can be extremely important in some cases. Even though customers have been attracted and have bought once, they are still targets for competitors' appeals. Reminding them of their past satisfaction may keep them from shifting to a competitor. Campbell realizes that most people know about its soups, so much of its advertising is intended to remind.

PROMOTION REQUIRES EFFECTIVE COMMUNICATION

Communication as a process

Promotion is wasted if it does not communicate effectively. There are many reasons why a promotion message can be misunderstood or not heard at all. One way of looking at communication is from the perspective of the receiver. The concern is to understand how the receiver deals with the message and how they derive meaning from it. It has been found that meaning derives from more than just the words. It includes objects, events and symbols in advertisements making connection with the individual's life.

Communication can also be seen as a process where a source tries to reach a receiver with a message. Exhibit 12–4 shows the elements of the **communication process**. This understanding of communication emphasizes the sender—their wish to be effective in communicating something to an audience. Here we see that a **source**, the sender of a message, is trying to deliver a message to a **receiver**—a potential customer. Research shows that customers evaluate not only the message, but also the source of the message in terms of trustworthiness and credibility. This is part of

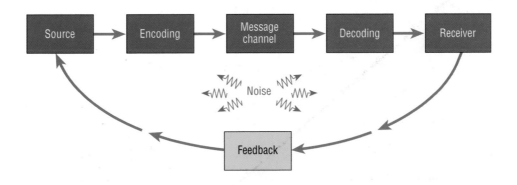

Exhibit 12–4 The Communication Process

the reason why celebrities, such as famous sports people, are used to endorse companies and brands (for example, Nike). A source can use many message channels to deliver a message. The salesperson does it in person with voice and action. Advertising must do it with magazines, newspapers, radio, TV and other media.

A major advantage of personal selling is that the source, the seller, can get immediate feedback from the receiver. It is easier to judge how the message is being received and change it if necessary. Mass sellers must usually depend on marketing research or total sales figures for feedback and that can take too long. This has prompted some marketers to include free telephone numbers and other ways of building direct-response feedback from consumers into their mass communication efforts.

The noise—shown in Exhibit 12–4—is any distraction that reduces the effectiveness of the communication process. Conversations and getting snacks during TV advertising are noise. The clutter of competing advertisements in a newspaper is noise. Advertisers planning messages must recognize that many possible distractions can interfere with communications.

The lessons of both views of communications (the receiver's and the sender's) are that marketers must consider many variables when using marketing communications. They must take into account not just their own intentions but also the mindset of the chosen audience if communication is to effective and the appropriate message, coding and medium used.

Encoding and decoding depend on a common frame of reference

The basic difficulty in the communication process occurs during encoding and decoding. Encoding is the source deciding what it wants to say and translating it into words or symbols that will have the same meaning to the receiver. Decoding is the receiver translating the message. This process can be very tricky. The meanings of various words and symbols may differ depending on the attitudes and experiences of the two groups. People need a common frame of reference to communicate effectively. See Exhibit 12–5.

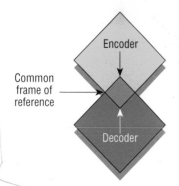

Exhibit 12–5 This Same Message May Be Interpreted Differently

The same message may be interpreted differently

Different audiences may see the same message in different ways, or interpret the same words differently. Such differences are common in international marketing when cultural differences or translation are problems. The American beer company Coors encouraged its English-speaking customers to 'turn it loose', but in Spanish the phrase meant 'to suffer from diarrhoea'. When American food producer Frank Perdue said, 'It takes a tough man to make a tender chicken', Spanish speakers heard, 'It takes a sexually stimulated man to make a chicken affectionate'. Many firms run into problems like this.[5]

Problems occur even without translation problems. For example, a new children's cough syrup was advertised as extra strength. The advertising people thought they were assuring parents that the product worked well. Cautious parents, however, avoided the product because they feared that it might be too strong for their children.

Message channel is important too

The communication process is complicated even more because the receiver knows the message is not only coming from a source, but also through some message channel—the carrier of the message. A particular message channel may enhance or detract from a message. A TV advertisement, for example, can *show* the effectiveness of a brand of dishwashing detergent in taking the grease away; the same claim in a newspaper advertisement might not be very convincing. On the other hand, a receiver may attach value to a product if the message comes in a well-respected newspaper or magazine. Some consumers buy products advertised in *Good Housekeeping* magazine, for example, because they have faith in its seal of approval. It has been found that the same advertisement placed in different magazines gets interpreted differently. Advertisements for the same product in *Cosmopolitan* were seen to be more extroverted, sophisticated, modern and stylish than those placed in *Woman's Own* magazine.[6]

 ## Ethical issues in marketing communications

Promotion is one of the most often criticized areas of marketing, and many of the criticisms focus on whether communications are honest and fair. Marketers must sometimes make ethical judgements in considering these charges and in planning their promotion.

Video publicity releases provide an interesting example. When a TV news programme broadcasts a video publicity release, consumers do not know it was prepared to achieve marketing objectives and believe the news staff to be the source. That may make the message more credible, but is it fair? As long as the publicity information is truthful, there is no problem. But grey areas still remain. Consider, for example, SmithKline Beecham's video about its new prescription heart attack drug. An estimated 27 million consumers saw the video on various TV news programmes in the United States. The video included a laundry list of possible side-effects and other warnings, just as is required for normal drug advertising. There is never any guarantee, however, that the warnings will not be edited out by local TV stations.

Critics raise similar concerns about the use of celebrities in advertisements. A person who plays the role of an honest and trustworthy person on a popular TV series may be a credible message source in an advertisement, but is it misleading to consumers? Some critics believe it is. Others argue that consumers recognize advertising when they see it and know celebrities are paid for their endorsements.

The most common criticisms of promotion relate to promotional messages that make exaggerated claims. What does it mean for an advertisement or a salesperson to claim that a product is the 'best available'? Is that the personal opinion of people in the firm, or should every statement, even very general ones, be backed up by objective proof. What type of proof should be required? Some promotional messages do misrepresent the benefits of a product. However, most marketing managers want to develop ongoing relationships with—and repeat purchases from—their customers. They realize that customers will not come back if the marketing mix does not deliver what the promotion promises. Further, consumers are becoming more sceptical about all the claims they hear and see. As a result, most marketing managers work to make promotion claims specific and believable.[7]

ADOPTION PROCESSES CAN GUIDE PROMOTION PLANNING

When planning communications and promotions, marketers may also take into account the process by which consumers adopt products. The steps in this process have been described under a variety of headings such as awareness, interest, evaluation, trial, decision and confirmation or awareness, interest, desire and action. Consumer buying is a problem-solving process in which buyers go through steps on the way to adopting (or rejecting) an idea or product. By appreciating the stage at which the consumer is, the marketer can tailor the form of promotion so that it is more appropriate.

The three basic promotion objectives can be related to these steps—see Exhibit 12–6. *Informing* and *persuading* may be needed to affect the potential customer's knowledge and attitudes about a product, and then bring about its adoption. Later promotion can simply *remind* the customer about that favourable experience and confirm the adoption decision.

The AIDA model is a practical approach

The action-oriented model, called *AIDA*, will be used in this and the next two chapters to guide some of the discussion. This model sees action/sale as the ultimate intention of marketing communications.[8]

The **AIDA model** consists of four promotion jobs: (1) to get *Attention*, (2) to hold *Interest*, (3) to arouse *Desire* and (4) to obtain *Action*. Exhibit 12–6 shows the relationship of the adoption process to the AIDA jobs. Getting attention is necessary to make consumers aware of the company's offering. Holding interest gives the communication a chance to build the consumer's interest in the product. Arousing desire affects the evaluation process, perhaps building preference. Obtaining action includes gaining trial, which may lead to a purchase decision. Continuing promotion is needed to confirm the decision and to encourage an ongoing relationship and additional purchases.

Promotion Objectives	Adoption Process (Chapter 6)	AIDA Model
Informing	Awareness	Attention
	Interest	Interest
Persuading	Evaluation	Desire
	Trial	
Reminding	Decision	Action
	Confirmation	

Exhibit 12–6 Relation of Promotion Objectives, Adoption Process and AIDA model

The AIDA and adoption processes look at individuals. This emphasis on individuals helps to develop an understanding of how people behave. It is also useful to look at markets as a whole. Different segments of customers within a market may behave differently, with some taking the lead in trying new products and, in turn, influencing others. Remember, however, that knowledge of how people use communications in their behaviour as consumers is still developing. The AIDA model is not a perfect representation. It is used here as a device to help to categorize the intention and appeals of marketing communications.

Promotion varies for different adopter groups

Research on how markets accept new ideas has led to the adoption curve model. The *adoption curve* shows when different groups accept ideas. It shows the need to change the promotion effort as time passes. It also emphasizes the relations among groups and shows that some groups act as leaders in accepting a new idea. Exhibit 12–7 shows the adoption curve for a typical successful product. Some of the important characteristics of each of these customer groups are discussed below.

Innovators are not adverse to risks

The innovators are the first to adopt. They are eager to try a new idea—and willing to take risks. Innovators tend to be young and well educated. They are likely to be mobile and have many contacts outside their local social group and community. Business firms in the innovator group usually are large and rather specialized, but aggressive small companies with an entrepreneurial view are often willing to take the risk of doing something new and different. An important characteristic of innovators is that they rely on impersonal and scientific information sources, or other innovators, rather than salespeople. They often search for information. For example, they might read articles in technical publications or informative advertisements in special-interest magazines or newspapers.

Early adopters are often opinion leaders

Early adopters are well respected by their peers—and are often opinion leaders. They tend to be younger, more mobile, and more creative than later adopters. Unlike innovators, they have fewer contacts outside their own social group or community. Business firms in this category also tend to be specialized. Of all the groups, this one tends to have the greatest contact with salespeople. Mass media are also important information sources. Marketers should be very concerned with attracting and selling the early adopter group. Their acceptance is really important in reaching the next group because the early majority look to the early adopters for guidance. The early adopters can help the promotion effort by spreading *word-of-mouth* information and advice among other consumers.

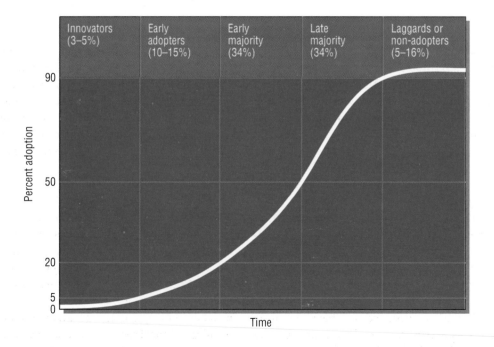

Exhibit 12–7 The Adoption Curve

Opinion leaders help spread the word

Marketers know the importance of personal conversations and recommendations by opinion leaders. If early groups reject the product, it may never get off the ground. For example, some cinema goers are the first to see new films. If they think a film is dull, they quickly tell their friends not to waste their time and money. Consumers are even more likely to talk about a negative experience than a positive experience. If opinion leaders accept a product, what they say about it can be very important. Such word-of-mouth publicity can be very effective in selling a product, long before the customer ever walks into the retail store. Some companies try to target promotion to encourage opinion leadership. When Canon introduced a new high-quality automatic 35 mm camera, it prepared special advertisements designed to help opinion leaders explain to others how the camera worked. The power of word-of-mouth communications should not be underestimated.[9]

Early majority group is deliberate

The early majority avoid risk and wait to consider a new idea after many early adopters have tried it—and liked it. Average-sized business firms that are less specialized often fit in this category. If successful companies in their industry adopt the new idea, so will they. The early majority have a great deal of contact with mass media, salespeople and early adopter opinion leaders. Members usually are not opinion leaders themselves.

Late majority is cautious

The late majority are cautious about new ideas. Often they are older than the early majority group and more set in their ways. They are less likely to follow opinion leaders and early adopters. In fact, strong social pressure from their own peer group may be needed before they adopt a new product. Business firms in this group tend to be conservative, smaller-sized firms with little specialization. The late majority make little use of marketing sources of information such as mass media and salespeople. They tend to be oriented more towards other late adopters rather than outside sources they don't trust.

Laggards or non-adopters hang on to tradition

Laggards or non-adopters prefer to do things the way they have been done in the past and are very suspicious of new ideas. They tend to be older and less well educated. They may also be low in social status and income. The smallest businesses with the least specialization often fit this category. They cling to the *status quo* and think it is the safe way. The main source of information for laggards is other laggards. This certainly is bad news for marketers who are trying to reach a whole market quickly or who want to use only one promotion method. In fact, it may not pay to bother with this group.[10]

HOW TYPICAL PROMOTION PLANS ARE MIXED AND INTEGRATED

There is no one right mix

Most marketing managers try to integrate and mix the different promotion methods. Each of the elements of the promotions mix has its specific advantages and limitations and some promotion jobs can be done more economically one way than another. Pepsi spent £700 000 in an integrated campaign for its Pepsi Max brand in Scotland. Television advertising featured the adventurous exploits of a number of sporty, exuberant young men (just like the target market for Pepsi Max). This was followed by poster and radio advertising. In addition, on-trade promotions and sampling campaigns were undertaken, featuring the characters from the TV advertising.[11]

There is no one *right* promotions mix for all situations. Each one must be developed as part of a marketing mix and should be designed to achieve the firm's promotion objectives in each marketing strategy. For example, if the channel of distribution for a firm's product involves intermediaries, the marketing manager must consider the promotions mix that is appropriate in the channel as well as what type of promotion should be targeted at customers at the end of the channel. Similarly, the emphasis among the three types of promotion typically varies depending on whether the customers at the end of the channel are business users or final consumers. Typical promotion mixes in these different situations are now discussed in more detail.

Promotion to intermediaries

When a channel of distribution involves intermediaries, their cooperation can be crucial to the success of the overall marketing strategy. Pushing (a product through a channel) means using normal promotion effort—personal selling, advertising and sales promotion—to help sell the whole marketing mix to possible channel members. This approach emphasizes the importance of building a channel and securing the wholehearted cooperation of channel members to push the product down the channel to the final user.

Producers usually take on much of the responsibility for the pushing effort in the channel. However, most wholesalers also handle at least some of the promotion to retailers or other wholesalers further down the channel. Similarly, retailers often handle at least some of the promotion in their local markets. When different firms in the channel handle different aspects of communicating to final consumers or business users, the overall promotion effort is most likely to be effective when all the individual messages are carefully integrated, that is, coordinated, consistent, and complete.

Promotion to intermediaries emphasizes personal selling

Salespeople handle most of the important communication with intermediaries. Intermediaries do not want empty promises. They want to know what they can expect in return for their cooperation and help. A salesperson can answer questions about what promotion will be directed towards the final consumer, each channel member's part in marketing the product, and important details on pricing, mark-ups, promotion assistance and allowances. A salesperson can help the firm determine when it should adjust its marketing mix from one channel member to another. In highly competitive urban areas, for example, mixes may emphasize price.

When a number of suppliers offer similar products and compete for attention and shelf space, the wholesaler or retailer usually pays attention to the one with the best profit potential. In these situations, the salesperson must convince the channel member that demand for the product exists—and that making a profit will be easy. A firm can make the salesperson's job easier by also targeting special sales promotion at intermediaries.

Sales promotions targeted at intermediaries usually focus on short-term arrangements that will improve the intermediaries' profits. For example, a soft-drink bottler might offer a convenience store a free case of drinks with each two cases it buys. The free case improves the store's profit margin on the whole purchase. Or a supplier might offer a price discount if the retailer uses a special point-of-purchase display. Other types of sales promotion, such as competitions that offer exotic holiday trips for high-volume intermediaries, are also common. It is important to appreciate that retailers operate on the basis of sales and profit per square metre. Shelf space is a premium asset that needs to be negotiated.

Firms run advertisements in trade magazines to recruit new channel members or to inform existing channel members about a new offering. Trade advertisements usually encourage intermediaries to contact the supplier for more information, and then a salesperson takes over.

Promotion to employees

Some firms emphasize promotion to their own employees, especially salespeople or others in contact with customers. This type of *internal marketing* effort is basically a variation on the pushing approach. One objective is to inform employees about important elements of the marketing strategy so that they work together as a team to implement it. Some firms use promotion to motivate employees to work harder at specific jobs, such as providing customer service or achieving higher sales. For example, many firms use sales contests and award free trips to high performing sales staff. Some companies design the advertising they target at customers so that the advertising also communicates to employees and boosts the employees' image. This is typical in service-oriented industries where the quality of the employees' efforts is a big part of the product.

Pulling policy—customer demand pulls the product through the channel

Regardless of what promotion a firm uses to get help from channel members or employees in pushing a product, most producers focus a significant amount of promotion on customers at the end of the channel. This helps to stimulate demand for the firm's offering and can help pull the product through the channel of distribution. *Pulling* means getting customers to ask the intermediary for the product.

Pulling and pushing are usually used in combination—see Exhibit 12–8. However, if intermediaries will not work with a producer, perhaps because they are already carrying a competing brand, a producer may try to use a pulling approach by itself. This involves highly aggressive and expensive promotion to final consumers or users, sometimes using coupons or samples, temporarily bypassing the intermediary. If the promotion works, the intermediaries are forced to carry the product to satisfy customer requests. However, this approach is risky. Companies can waste an expensive promotion effort if customers lose interest before reluctant intermediaries make the product available. At minimum, intermediaries should be told about the planned pulling effort, so they could be ready if the promotion succeeds.

Who handles promotion to final customers at the end of the channel varies in different channel systems, depending on the mix of pushing and pulling. Further, the promotion mix typically varies depending on whether customers are final consumers or business users.

Promotion to final consumers

The large number of consumers almost forces producers of consumer products and retailers to emphasize mass communication and sales promotion. Sales

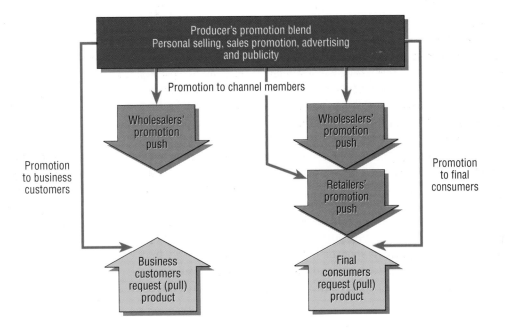

Exhibit 12–8 Promotion May Encourage Pushing in the Channel, Pulling by Customers or Both

promotions, such as competitions or free samples, may build consumer interest and short-term sales of a product. Effective mass communication may build enough brand familiarity so that little personal selling is needed, as in self-service and discount operations. If a product has already won brand preference, aggressive personal selling may not be needed. Reminder-type advertising may be all that is necessary to maintain a positive relationship.

Personal selling can also be effective. Some retailers, specialist shops in particular, rely heavily on well-informed salespeople. Technical products (such as camcorders or computers) and personal services (such as private healthcare and financial planning) may also require personal selling. Direct-selling firms like Avon and Amway also rely on personal selling. Personal selling to final consumers is usually found in relatively expensive channel systems, such as those for fashionable clothing, furniture, consumer electronics and cars.

Promotion to business customers

Producers and wholesalers who target business customers usually emphasize personal selling. This is practical because these customers are much less numerous than final consumers and their purchases are typically larger. Moreover, business customers may have technical questions or need adjustments in the marketing mix. An extremely technical business product may require a heavy emphasis on personal selling, using technically trained salespeople. This is the only sure way to make the prod-

uct understood and get feedback on how customers use it. The technical sales representative meets with engineers, production managers, purchasing agents and top managers and can adjust the sales message to the needs of these various influences.

Sales representatives can be more flexible in adjusting their companies' appeals to suit each customer and personal contact is usually required to close a sale. A salesperson is also able to call back later to follow up with additional information, resolve any problems and nurture the relationship with the customer.

While personal selling dominates in business markets, mass communication is also necessary. A typical sales call on a business customer is expensive because salespeople spend only a small proportion of their time actually selling. The rest is consumed by such tasks as travelling, paperwork, sales meetings and strictly service calls. It is seldom practical for salespeople to carry the whole promotion load. A firm invests too much in its salespeople to use their time and skill for jobs that could be handled in less costly ways. Advertisements in trade magazines, for instance, can inform potential customers that a product is available; and most trade advertisements give a toll-free telephone or fax number to stimulate direct enquiries. Domestic and international trade shows also help identify prospects. Even so, sellers who target business customers usually spend only a small percentage of their promotion budget on mass communication and sales promotion.

The professional services sector has a relatively poor history of marketing communications. Indeed, in some traditional professional services companies, marketing itself has not been adopted. More enlightened companies have adopted marketing and are developing a more sophisticated understanding of marketing and communications. An example of such a company in the business-to-business sector is Andersen Consulting which operates in high technology management consultancy, competing with IBM, EDS and Cap Gemeni. The company undertook extensive customer and market research when it split from the main Arthur Andersen accounting group in 1989. Since then it has used some very high-profile initiatives including poster and TV advertising campaigns, and sports sponsorship of the Williams Renault Formula One team and a top golfing tournament. By spending about twice as much as their nearest rival on marketing communications, Andersen Consulting has achieved a new identity and 93 per cent name recognition.[12]

Each market segment may need a unique mix

Knowing what type of promotion is typically emphasized with different targets is useful in planning the promotion mix. However, each unique market segment may need a separate marketing mix and a different promotion mix. Some mass-selling specialists miss this point. They think mainly in mass marketing, rather than target marketing, terms. Aiming at large markets may be desirable in some situations, but promotion aimed at everyone can end up hitting no one. In developing the promotion mix, care should be taken to avoid a shotgun approach when what is needed is a rifle approach, with a more careful aim.

INTEGRATED DIRECT-RESPONSE PROMOTION IS VERY TARGETED

The challenge of developing promotions that reach specific target customers has prompted many firms to turn to direct marketing, that is, direct communication between a seller and an individual customer using a promotion method other than face-to-face personal selling. Most direct marketing communications are designed to prompt immediate feedback—a direct response—by customers. That's why this type of communication is often called *direct-response promotion*.

Early efforts in the direct-response area focused on direct-mail advertising. A carefully selected mailing list, from the many available, allows advertisers to reach a specific target audience with specific interests. Direct-mail advertising proved to be very effective when the objective is to get a direct response by the customer.

Now it's more than direct-mail advertising

Achieving a measurable, direct response from specific target customers is still the heart of direct marketing. However, the promotion medium is evolving to include not just mail but telephone, print, computer networks, broadcast and even interactive video. The customer's response may be a purchase (or donation), a question, or a request for more information. More often than not, the customer responds by calling a free telephone number, or—in the case of business markets—by sending a fax. A knowledgeable salesperson talks with the customer on the phone and follows up. That might involve filling an order and having it shipped to the customer or putting an interested prospect in touch with a salesperson who makes a personal visit. There are, however, many variations on this approach. For example, some firms route incoming information-request calls to a computerized answering system. The caller indicates what information is required by pushing a few buttons on the telephone keypad, and then the computer instantly sends requested information to the caller's fax machine.

Direct-response promotion is often an important component of integrated marketing communications programmes and is closely tied to other elements of the marketing mix. However, what distinguishes this general approach is that the marketer targets more of the promotional effort at specific individuals who respond directly. Direct marketing is discussed in more detail in Chapter 15.

THE CUSTOMER MAY INITIATE THE COMMUNICATION PROCESS

Traditional thinking about promotion and the communication process has usually been based on the idea that it is the seller who initiates communication. The buyer is thought of as a somewhat passive receiver in the communication process, at least until attention, desire or action is stimulated. For this reason, targeting is especially important, helping to avoid wasting communications on those who are not interested in the message. Even with highly targeted direct-response promotion, the marketer typically takes the first step to get the interaction started.

Electronic media enable interactive communication

In the information age, it is much easier for customers to search for information on their own. In fact, it is possible for the buyer to access information and place an order without the direct involvement of the vendor. Interactive information technologies include the World Wide Web and e-mail servers on the Internet, caller-controlled fax-on-demand, computerized telephone voice-messaging systems, video kiosks in shopping areas, CD-ROM and Web TV.

The customer-initiated information search represents a change that will become more prevalent for more types of purchases in the future. There are significant differences between the traditional communications model and one that is customer-initiated as shown in Exhibit 12–9.

Customer initiates communication with a search process

In the model in Exhibit 12–9, the customer initiates the communication process with a decision to search for information in a particular message channel. The Internet gives access to archives of messages on many topics. In the next text step, the consumer selects a specific topic about which to receive information. The most typical approaches involve using a mouse, remote control device or a keypad to highlight a selection from an initial list or index. In the case of the Internet, a key word or phrase may be entered and then a search is made for topics that include it.

The consumer decides how much information to get

Once the specific topic is selected, the message for that topic is displayed. It may include a simple way to get more information, select another related topic, return to the original selection process or quit the search. After each message the consumer decides whether to search further. This interactive approach makes it easy for the consumer to get information conveniently and spend as much time searching, as he or she needs. However, noise may still be a problem, for example time may be wasted if the desired information is not available or is not easy to find. This can be frustrating for the consumer and constitutes a lost opportunity for the marketer.

Before placing information on the Web, a company needs to consider the content it wants users to see. Clean and accurate black-and-white text is preferable to colourful graphics with no information. However, graphics and colour should be used as they help to keep the reader interested and emphasize the information the company is trying to relay. The information should be organized to make sense to the user. The home page should use clear, descriptive titles, have well-organized menus and make it easy for the user to find the information for which he or she is

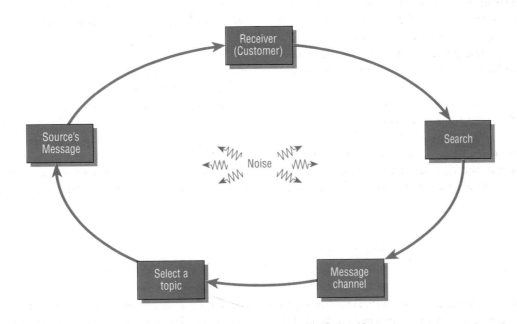

Exhibit 12–9 A Model of the Customer-Initiated Interactive Communication

searching. It should be clear from the home page what the company does and what information is available. In all of this, the user has control and decides when to receive information and advertising. Advertisements must be 'pull-through', meaning that the user comes to the advertisement instead of the advertisement being pushed to the user.

The 'action' element of the communications process can be immediate. At many Internet sites, the consumer can click on the selected item, charge it to a credit card and have it delivered. The traditional principles of communication are still important in customer-initiated interactive communication. At the same time, technology is enabling the customization of messages according to the needs of the consumer. New electronic media allow many types of information—pictures, text, video and sound—to be used. As a result, all the different promotional materials that a company develops can be available in one place. This allows for more integration of the communications mix.[13]

PROMOTION MIXES VARY OVER THE LIFE CYCLE

The particular promotion mix a firm selects depends on the target of the promotion, but it may be influenced by many other factors, including the stage in the product life cycle and the nature of the competition. Promotion can be blended in many ways. Typical ways in which firms spread their promotion budgets across the three promotion methods in these different stages are discussed next.

Stage of product in its life cycle

A new product seldom becomes a spectacular success overnight. The adoption curve helps explain why. Further, the product will probably go through the product life-cycle stages described earlier—market introduction, market growth, market maturity and sales decline. During these stages, promotion mixes may have to change to achieve different promotion objectives.

Market introduction stage

During market introduction, the basic promotion objective is to inform. If the product is a really new idea, the promotion must build **primary demand**—demand for the general product idea—not just for the company's own brand. Multimedia computers, electronic personal information managers and electric cars are good examples of product concepts where primary demand is just beginning to grow. There may be few potential innovators during the introduction stage, and personal selling can help find them. Firms also need salespeople to find good channel members and persuade them to carry the new product. Sales promotion may be targeted at salespeople or channel members to get them interested in selling the new product. Sales promotion may also encourage customers to try it.

LEVI'S PROMOTION OF CASUAL WEAR

Three-quarters of all firms now allow employees to dress casually at least once a week. Sales of men's suits have dropped by over a third in less than 10 years, while sales of casual business wear have skyrocketed. Levi-Strauss hopes to capitalize from these trends. They are not just advertising to increase selective demand for their Dockers and Slate brands of casual wear. They are also promoting the basic idea of casual wear at work

How does this work? Marketers at Levi's found that people often do not know what to wear to work when given the opportunity not to wear a formal suit. Levi's is trying to reach these customers through their employ-ers. Levi's has promoted itself to human resource managers as an expert on what is appropriate casual wear for business.

Levi's 'dress-down' campaign started in 1992. Levi's sent a letter with advice about the casual wear trend to 65 000 human resource managers. Since then Levi's has visited or advised more than 20 000 corporations. It suggests dress codes, arranges fashion shows for employees and offers free telephone numbers for enquiries. Its Internet web site (www.levi.com) provides information about casual wear and offers videotape with guidelines about casual wear. The videotape has been sent to human resource directors in over 7 000 firms.

There are two versions of the video guidelines—one that includes jeans and one that excludes them.

Levi's is also creating an extensive database of the people whom it advises for targeting direct-response promotions. For example, Levi's used the database to send letters to 12 500 human resource managers inviting them to visit Dockers shops for in-store fashion shows and advice. Those who responded receive a free Dockers outfit.

Levi's is pursuing casual business wear opportunities internationally. Its efforts include a 32-page advertisement that was run in newspapers and handed out on street corners in 14 major cities including London, Manila and Milan. Even in Japan, where formal blue suits are the norm, a newspaper advertisement offering information on casual business wear generated 1000 enquiries. Efforts such as these are helping Levi's to achieve its objective of being leader in casual business wear around the world.

All this promotional activity helps to increase Levi's sales, but it also helps customers and employers know what is good practice in business dress. As a marketing manager at Levi's put it, 'We did not create casual business wear, what we did was identify a trend and see a business opportunity'. By catching the trend at an early stage, Levi's has given it more momentum.[14]

Market growth stage

In the market growth stage, more competitors enter the market, and promotion emphasis shifts from building primary demand to stimulating **selective demand**—demand for a company's own brand. The main job is to persuade customers to buy, and continue to buy, the company's product. Now that more potential customers are trying and adopting the product, mass communication may become more economical. Salespeople and personal selling must still work in the channels, expanding the number of outlets and cementing relationships with current channel members.

Market maturity stage

In the market maturity stage, even more competitors have entered the market. Promotion becomes more persuasive. At this stage, mass communication and sales promotion may dominate the promotion mixes of consumer products firms. Business products may require more aggressive personal selling, perhaps supplemented by more advertising. The total budget allocated to promotion may rise as competition increases.

If a firm already has high sales relative to competitors, it may have a real advantage in promotion at this stage. If, for example, in a particular market Smirnoff has twice the sales for its premium vodka as Finlandia, its competitor, and they both spend the same *percentage* of total sales on promotion, Smirnoff will be spending twice as much and will probably communicate to more people. Smirnoff may get even more than twice as much promotion because of economies of scale.

Firms that have strong brands can use reminder-type advertising at this stage to ensure that customers remember the product name. Similarly, many firms turn to various types of frequent-buyer promotions or newsletters and other communications targeted at current customers to strengthen the buyer–seller relationship and keep customers loyal. This may be much less expensive—and more effective—than persuasive efforts to win customers away from competitors in a stagnant market.

Sales decline stage

During the sales decline stage, the total amount spent on promotion usually decreases as firms try to cut costs to remain profitable. Because some people may still want the product, firms need more targeted promotion to reach these customers. On the other hand, some firms may increase promotion to try to slow the cycle, at least temporarily. Crayola had almost all of the market for children's crayons, but sales were slowly declining as new kinds of markers came along. Crayola slowed the cycle with more promotion spending and a message to parents to buy their kids a 'fresh box'.

Nature of competition requires different promotion

Firms in monopolistic competition may favour mass communication because they have differentiated their marketing mixes and have something to talk about. As a market tends towards pure competition or oligopoly it is difficult to predict what will happen. Competitors in some markets try to out-promote each other. The only way for a competitor to stay in this kind of market is to match rivals' promotion efforts, unless the whole marketing mix can be improved in some other way. Competitive advertising is a common feature in our daily newspapers.

Some brands such as Mars are recognized in every international market because of the quality and consistency of their promotional messages

In markets that are drifting towards pure competition, some companies resort to price cutting. Lower prices may be offered to the trade, customers, or both. This *may* increase the number of units sold temporarily, but it may also reduce total revenue and the amount available for promotion *per unit*. Competitive retaliation, perhaps in the form of short-term sales promotions, may reduce the temporary sales gains and drag price levels down faster. The cash flowing into the business may decline and promotion spending may have to be cut back.

The focus here has been on promotion. However, changes in the product life cycle and competitive situation may require new marketing objectives, target markets and marketing mixes. All the strategy decisions—including those related to promotion spending and the promotions mix—should work together to achieve the objectives.[15]

SETTING THE PROMOTION BUDGET

Size of promotion budget affects promotion efficiency and mix

There are some economies of scale in promotion. An advertisement on national TV might cost less *per person* reached than an advertisement on local TV. Similarly, local radio and newspapers may be cheaper than neighbourhood newspapers or direct personal contact. But the *total cost* for some mass media may force small firms or those with small promotion budgets to use promotion alternatives that are more expensive per contact. For example, a small retailer might want to use local television but find that there is only enough money for an advertisement in the *Yellow Pages* and occasional newspaper advertising.

Smaller producers and firms that offer relatively undifferentiated consumer products emphasize personal selling first and rely mainly on sales promotion for the balance. The objective is to build good channel relations and encourage channel members to recommend and push the product. Note that here we are referring to percentages in the promotion mix, not the level of expenditure. Setting the overall level of promotion spending—and how much to spend on each type of promotion—is an important but difficult decision.

Budgeting for promotion—percentage of sales

The most common method of budgeting for promotion expenditures is to compute a percentage of either past sales or sales expected in the future. The virtue of this method is its simplicity. A similar percentage can be used automatically each year, eliminating the need to keep evaluating the kind and amount of promotion effort needed and its probable cost. It allows executives who are not too enthusiastic about the marketing concept to write off a certain percentage or amount of money while controlling the total amount spent. However, this method may not achieve the best results.

Find the task, budget for it

Just because budgeting a certain percentage of past or forecast sales is common doesn't mean that it is the best way. This mechanical approach leads to expanding marketing expenditure when business is good and cutting back when business is poor. It may be desirable to increase marketing expenditure when business is good. But when business is poor, this approach may just make the problem worse, if weak promotion is the reason for declining sales. The most sensible approach may be to be *more*, not less, aggressive!

Other methods of budgeting for marketing expenditures are:

1. Match expenditures with competitors.
2. Set the budget as a certain financial amount per sales unit (by case, by thousand, or by tonne) using the past year or estimated year ahead as a base.
3. Base the budget on any uncommitted revenue, perhaps including budgeted profits. Companies with limited resources may use this approach. Or a firm may be willing to sacrifice some or all of its current profits for future sales—that is, it looks at promotion spending as an *investment* in future growth.
4. Base the budget on the job to be done. For example, the spending level might be based on the number of new customers desired and the percentage of current customers that the firm must retain to leverage investments in already established relationships. This is called the **task method**—basing the budget on the job to be done.

Task method can lead to budgeting without agony

In the light of our continuing discussion about planning marketing strategies to reach objectives, the most sensible approach to budgeting promotion expenditure is the task method. In fact, this approach makes sense for *any* marketing expenditure, but the focus is on promotion.

A practical approach is to determine which promotion objectives are most important to the overall strategy and which promotion methods are most economical and effective for the communication tasks relevant to each objective. There is never enough money to do all the promotion that a company may wish to do. However, this approach helps to set priorities so that the money spent produces specific results.

The amount budgeted using the task method can be stated as a percentage of sales. Calculating the right amount is much more involved than picking up a past percentage. It requires careful review of the specific promotion (and marketing) tasks to be accomplished and how each task fits with others to achieve the overall objectives. The costs of these tasks are then totalled to determine how much should be budgeted for promotion (just as money is allocated for other marketing activities required by the strategy). In other words, the firm can assemble its total promotion budget directly from detailed plans rather than by simply relying on historical patterns or ratios.

This method also helps to eliminate budget fights between different promotion areas. Such conflicts may occur if managers and specialists responsible for different promotion methods see themselves as pitted against each other for a limited budget. However, the task method of budgeting encourages everyone—the marketing manager and the specialists—to focus on the overall strategy and what promotion objectives need to be achieved. The specialists may still make their own proposals and suggestions about how best to perform tasks and achieve the objectives. The task method means that the budget allocations are based on the most effective ways of getting things done—not on what the firm did last year, what some competitor does or even on internal 'politics'. With this approach, different promotion specialists are also more likely to recognize that different tasks and objectives are best served with different methods—and that they must all work together to achieve truly integrated marketing communications.[16]

The focus in this chapter has been on mixing the different promotion methods into an integrated whole. The different methods—publicity, personal selling, advertising and sales promotion—are complementary. In different situations they must be combined in different ways to achieve an effective and integrated overall promotion mix. The concepts discussed apply to all types of marketing communication. Yet, to be more skilled in matching specific promotion methods to specific tasks and objectives, it will help to know more about the strategy decisions involved in managing the major promotion areas. That is the focus of the next three chapters.

SUMMARY

Promotion is an important part of any marketing mix. Most consumers and intermediate customers can choose from among many products. To be successful, a producer must not only offer a good product at a reasonable price, but also inform potential customers about the product and where they can buy it. Further, producers must tell wholesalers and retailers in the channel about their product and their marketing mix. These intermediaries, in turn, must use promotion to reach their customers.

The promotions mix should fit logically into the strategy being developed to satisfy a particular target market. Strategy planning needs to state what should be communicated to them—and how. The overall promotion objective is to affect buying behaviour, but the basic promotion objectives relate to communications and are informing, persuading and reminding.

Three basic promotion methods can be used to reach these objectives. Behavioural science findings can help firms to combine various promotion methods for effective communication. In particular, what is known about the communication process and how individuals derive meaning from communications is useful in planning promotion mixes.

An action-oriented framework called AIDA was used to help to categorize various promotional intentions and appeals. The marketing managers plan promotion mixes. The marketing manager has the final responsibility for combining the promotion methods into one integrated promotion mix for each marketing mix.

In this chapter, some basic concepts that apply to all areas of promotion have been considered. In the next three chapters, advertising and publicity, personal selling, and sales promotion and direct marketing are discussed in more detail.

QUESTIONS AND PROBLEMS

1. Briefly explain the nature of the three basic promotion methods available to a marketing manager. What are the main strengths and limitations of each?

2. In your own words, discuss the integrated marketing communications concept. Explain what its emphasis on 'consistent' and 'complete' messages implies with respect to promotion mixes.

3. Relate the three basic promotion objectives to the four jobs (AIDA) of promotion using a specific example.

4. Discuss the communication process in relation to a producer's promotion of an accessory product—say, a new electronic security system businesses use to limit access to areas where they store confidential records.

5. Explain how an understanding of the adoption process would help you develop a promotion mix for digital tape recorders, a new consumer electronics product that produces high-quality recordings. Explain why you might change the promotion mix during the course of the adoption process.

6. Explain how opinion leaders affect a firm's promotion planning.

7. Discuss how the adoption curve should be used to plan the promotions mix(es) for a new car accessory—an electronic radar system that alerts a driver if he or she is about to change lanes into the path of a car that is passing through a 'blind spot' in the driver's mirrors.

8. A small company has developed an innovative new spray-on glass cleaner that prevents the build-up of electrostatic dust on computer screens and TVs. Give examples of some low-cost ways the firm might effectively promote its product. Be certain to consider both push and pull approaches.

9. Promotion has been the target of considerable criticism. What specific types of promotion are probably the object of this criticism? Give a specific example that illustrates your thinking.

10. With direct-response promotion, customers provide feedback to marketing communications. How can a marketing manager use this feedback to improve the effectiveness of the overall promotion mix?

11. Would promotion be successful in expanding the general demand for: (a) raisins, (b) air travel, (c) tennis rackets, (d) athletic shoes, (e) high-octane unleaded petrol, (f) single-serving, frozen gourmet dinners, (g) cement? Explain why or why not in each case.

12. What promotions mix would be most appropriate for producers of the following established products? Assume average- to large-sized firms in each case and support your answer.
   a. Chewing gum.
   b. Hosiery.
   c. Castings for car engines.
   d. Car tyres.
   e. A special computer used by manufacturers for computer-aided design of new products.
   f. Inexpensive plastic raincoats.
   g. A camcorder that has achieved speciality-product status.

14. If a marketing manager uses the task method to budget for marketing promotions, are competitors' promotion spending levels ignored? Explain your thinking and give an example that supports your point of view.

14. Discuss the potential conflict among the various promotion managers. How could this be reduced?

SUGGESTED CASE

10. WeddingWorld.com.

REFERENCES

1. K. Stewart, 'Corporate identity: a strategic marketing issue', *International Journal of Bank Marketing*, vol. 9, no. 1, 1991, pp. 32–9; K. Bourke, 'Corporate change: the convergence of internal and external communications strategies' *in* T. Meenaghan and P. O'Sullivan (eds), *Marketing Communications in Ireland*, Oak Press, Dublin, 1995, pp. 361–81.

2. 'Are the car advertisers wasting money?' *Campaign*, 10 May 1996, pp. 34–5. 'Advertising value cannot be judged by the cost alone', *Marketing*, 30 May 1996, p. 25.

3. P. Kitchen and D. Schultz, 'IMC: A UK as agency perspective', *Journal of Marketing Management*, vol. 14, no. 5, 1998, pp. 465–88.

4. 'Tango's £124m for global goal', *Marketing*, 16 May 1996, p. 1; 'Tango hits the road', *Marketing*, 30 May 1996, p. 29.

5. I. Doole and C. Asif Yaqub (1997) 'Developing an integrated advertising communications strategy: the challenge of Saudi Arabia' *in* R. Ashford *et al.* (eds), *Marketing Without Borders*, Academy of Marketing Conference Proceedings, Manchester, pp. 329–42.

6. M. Brennan, 'Establishing the existence of the media vehicle effect in women's magazines' *quoted in* T. Meenaghan and P. O'Sullivan (eds), *Marketing Communications in Ireland*, Oak Press, Dublin, 1995, pp. 331–2.

7. T.H. Bivins, 'Public relations, professionalism, and the public interest,' *Journal of Business Ethics*, February 1993, pp. 117–26; S.K. Balasubramanian, 'Beyond advertising and publicity: Hybrid messages and public policy issues', *Journal of Advertising*, December 1994, pp. 47–58.

8. For a useful review of the literature and bibliography on communications models see: K. Lawlor 'Advertising as communication' *in* T. Meenaghan and P. O'Sullivan (eds), *Marketing Communications in Ireland*, Oak Press, Dublin, 1995, pp. 29–48.

9. J. Singh, 'Voice, exit, and negative word-of-mouth behaviors: An investigation across three service categories', *Journal of the Academy of Marketing Science*, Winter 1990, pp. 1–16; J.G. Blodgett, D.H. Granbois and R.G. Walters, 'The effects of perceived justice on complainants' negative word-of-mouth behavior and repatronage intentions', *Journal of Retailing*, Winter 1993, pp. 399–428; P. Fitzgerald Bone, 'Word-of-mouth effects on short-term and long-term product judgments', *Journal of Business Research*, March 1995, pp. 213–24.

10. S. Ram and H.S. Jung, 'Innovativeness in product usage: A comparison of early adopters and early majority', *Psychology & Marketing*, January–February 1994, pp. 57–68; R.J. Fisher and L.L. Price, 'An Investigation into the Social Context of Early Adoption Behavior,' *Journal of Consumer Research*, December 1992, p. 477.

11. 'Pepsi Push Reaches Max,' *Marketing*, 6 June 1996, p. 4.

12. 'Nobody Mention The M-word', *Marketing*, Supplement, 30 May 1996, pp. III–V.

13. G. Hamel and J. Sampler, 'The e-corporation', *Fortune*, 7 December 1998, pp. 52–63; M.D. Anderson and J. Choobineh, 'Marketing on the Internet: Information strategy', *The Executive's Journal*, Summer 1996, pp. 22–29.

14. W. Perreault and E.J. McCarthy, *Basic Marketing*, 13th edn, McGraw-Hill, Boston, MA, 1999.

15. K.L. Ailawadi, P.W. Farris and M.E. Parry, 'Share and growth are not good predictors of the advertising and promotion/sales ratio,' *Journal of Marketing*, January 1994, pp. 86–97.

16. K.P. Corfman and D.R. Lehmann, 'The Prisoner's Dilemma and the role of information in setting advertising budgets', *Journal of Advertising*, June 1994, pp. 35–48; D.Y. Lee, 'The impact of firms' risk-taking attitudes on advertising budgets', *Journal of Business Research*, October–November 1994, pp. 247–56; P.J. Danaher and R.T. Rust, 'Determining the optimal level of media spending', *Journal of Advertising Research*, January–February 1994, pp. 28–34.

CHAPTER 13

Advertising and
Public Relations

When You Finish This Chapter, You Should

1 Understand why a marketing manager sets specific objectives to guide the advertising effort.

2 Understand when the various kinds of advertising are needed.

3 Understand how to choose the 'best' medium.

4 Understand how to plan the 'best' message—that is, the copy platform.

5 Understand what advertising agencies do and how they are paid.

6 Understand how to advertise legally.

7 Appreciate the role of public relations and publicity in the promotional mix.

8 Understand the advantages and disadvantages of public relations and publicity and their role in addressing an organization's publics.

9 Understand the issues involved in managing and securing publicity.

10 Understand the important new terms (shown in colour).

BORDEAUX WINE

Not that many years ago, for wine buyers Bordeaux wine was automatically associated with quality and was internationally recognized by discerning palates. With the arrival of wines from all over the world, particularly the New World, the Bordeaux brand was losing its position in the mind of the consumer. New World wines offered the consumer such a variety that consumers were beginning to question the quality of Bordeaux.

The Bordeaux Wine Trade Council (Le Conseil Interprofessionel du Vins de Bordeaux) is the organization that represents the wine companies of the Bordeaux region. It set itself the communications task of letting consumers know that Bordeaux wines are as interesting, dynamic, relevant, accessible and youthful as American and Australian wines. A Paris-based advertising agency was appointed, with a budget of £7 million for a pan-European advertising campaign. The target market comprised 25–40 year olds; the message—Bordeaux is an affordable wine that anyone can drink. The advertisements used and reinforced the existing Bordeaux wine logo of two bow-tied glasses of red and white wine.

The logo is used in a variety of formats and is associated with food. Press and poster advertisements feature the bow-tie shape made up with chips: the copy reads 'Fries: With a dash of Bordeaux'. Pasta and pizza toppings have also been used to represent the bow-tie shape. These advertisements were carried on poster sites and in magazines read by the target market such as *Elle*, *Marie Claire*, *Vanity Fair* and some trendy food magazines.

Having established the campaign, the Bordeaux Wine Trade Council took the decision to strengthen its efforts by using a promotion aimed at both consumers and retailers. The newly integrated campaign featured point of sale material including free recipe cards and a competition to win a free weekend to Bordeaux. Retailers were supplied with carrier bags, window display material and tissue wrap. Competitions for retailers were designed to reward retailers who knew the brand well and displayed it well. Although a pan-European campaign, this additional promotional effort was launched in the UK because it was felt to be more receptive to promotional activity than other countries such as Germany.

The benefits of the campaign take time to develop. The Bordeaux campaign represents integrated communications—advertising, point of sale promotion and competitions. In addition, it integrates the channel of distribution (the retailers) with the aim of taking the mystery out of Bordeaux for the retail trade and consumers. An added benefit is that a data base has been developed of Bordeaux retailers. This will be used for on-going communications with the trade and future marketing drives.[1]

ADVERTISING AND MARKETING STRATEGY DECISIONS

Mass selling makes widespread distribution possible and requires mass communication. Although a marketing manager might prefer to use personal selling to communicate with customers, it can be expensive on a per-contact or per-sale basis. Advertising is a potential solution to this problem. While not as flexible as personal selling, it can often reach large numbers of potential customers at the same time. It can inform and persuade customers as well as help to position a firm's marketing mix as the one that meets customers' needs. Similarly, sales promotion aimed at final customers, channel members or a firm's own employees is often important in swaying the target to immediate action. In the past decade, spending on sales promotion has grown at a rapid rate—especially in mature consumer-products markets where marketing managers rely heavily on sales promotion to get more attention from intermediaries

and to battle with rival firms for a larger share of consumers' purchases. Today, most promotional mixes contain advertising and sales promotion as well as personal selling and publicity.

Advertising contacts vary in cost and results. This means marketing managers, and the advertising managers who work with them, have important strategy decisions to make. They must decide: (1) who their target audience is, (2) what kind of advertising to use, (3) how to reach customers (via which types of media), (4) what to say to them (the copy platform), and (5) who will do the work. Exhibit 13–1 shows the initial discussion areas in this chapter. Measuring advertising effectiveness and some of the legal limits on advertising are also covered. Given the powerful role of company communications in all forms, the chapter also addresses public relations and publicity issues.

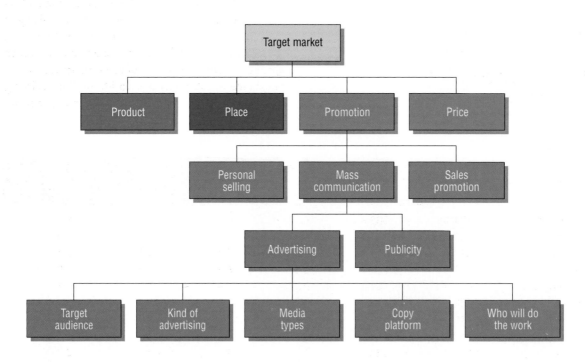

Exhibit 13–1 Strategy Planning for Advertising

THE IMPORTANCE OF ADVERTISING

Total spending is high—and growing internationally

As an economy grows, advertising becomes more important because more consumers have income and advertising can get results. Spending on advertising is

significant. Exhibit 13–2 shows the expenditure on advertising in Western European countries and the United States.[2] This is expressed in absolute terms and as a per capita spend. It is clear that advertising spending per capita in other countries is typically much lower than in the United States. Although exact and up-to-date figures are not available, all other nations combined spend only about 25 per cent more than the United States alone, and roughly half of that spending takes place in Europe. Lower media costs account for part of the difference in spending.

Individual advertisers do not spend that much

While total spending on advertising seems high, especially in the United States, it represents a small portion of what people pay for the goods and services they buy. US corporations spend an average of only about 2.5 per cent of their revenue on advertising. Worldwide, the percentage is even smaller. Advertising spending as a percentage of sales varies significantly across product categories. Producers of consumer products generally spend a larger percentage than firms that produce business products. For example, beverage companies spend 7.5 per cent, and companies that make toys and games spend 16.4 per cent. At the other extreme, companies that sell plastics to manufacturers spend only about 0.8 per cent on advertising. Some business products companies, those that depend on personal selling, may spend less than $1/10$ of 1 per cent.

Individual firms may spend more or less than others in the industry, depending on the role of advertising in their promotional mix and marketing mix. Of course, percentages do not tell the whole story. Nissan, which spends less than 1 per cent of sales on advertising, is among the top 50 advertisers worldwide. The really big spenders are very important to the advertising industry

Country	Total
Germany	21 410.4
UK	13 654.8
France	10 187.7
Italy	5 996.3
Spain	4 799.4
Netherlands	3 521.6
Switzerland	2 721.7
Sweden	1 958.4
Belgium	1 703.5
Austria	1 665.2
Denmark	1 509.2
Portugal	1 221.0
Norway[1]	1 140.0
Finland	1 086.9
Greece	970.8
Ireland	601.7

Exhibit 13–2(a) Advertising Expenditure by country (US$m)—1996

Notes: Data are net of discounts, they include agency commission and press classified advertising but exclude production costs. Data are ranked on total adspend.
[1] Data for Norway are estimates.

Country	Adspend per Capita		Index Europe–100	Real Year on Year Change (%)		
	Local Currency	US$		93/94	94/95	95/96
Switzerland	474.4	383.9	199.0	5.7	5.8	−3.5
Denmark	1 663.8	286.9	148.7	7.3	9.4	2.3
Germany	393.5	261.5	135.5	2.8	5.4	0.7
Norway[1]	1 671.0	259.1	134.3	6.6	10.0	7.8
United Kingdom	150.3	234.9	121.7	7.9	4.8	5.1
Netherlands	382.5	226.9	117.6	7.2	5.1	5.2
Sweden	1 480.6	220.8	114.4	13.5	4.2	−0.2
Finland	973.2	211.9	109.8	8.1	10.6	1.9
Austria	1 945.7	183.8	95.3	0.5	−0.7	2.7
France	896.1	175.2	90.8	3.3	2.3	0.9
Belgium	5 271.7	170.3	88.3	−2.0	9.9	2.3
Ireland	104.7	167.6	86.9	1.1	6.4	9.7
Portugal	19 060.6	123.6	64.1	10.8	12.8	14.7
Spain	15 491.7	122.3	63.4	−3.1	−1.2	−0.2
Italy	161 799.9	104.9	54.4	−0.8	−0.5	5.4
Greece	22 277.0	92.5	47.9	24.2	28.0	−35.2

Notes: Growth rates are based on total advertising expenditure at constant (1990) prices. Data are net of discounts, they include agency commission and press classified advertising but exclude production costs. Data are ranked by adspend per capita (US$).
[1] Data for Norway for 1995 and 1996 are estimates.

Exhibit 13–2(b) Per Capita Advertising & Advertising Growth—1996

because they account for a very large share of total advertising spending.

Advertising is important in certain markets, especially final consumer markets. Nevertheless, in total, advertising costs much less than personal selling and sales promotion.

Advertising does not employ that many people

While total advertising expenditures are large, the advertising industry itself employs relatively few people. The major expense is for media time and space. Many students hope for a glamorous job in advertising, but there are fewer jobs in advertising than you might think. Even in the United States, with the highest advertising spending of any nation, only about 500 000 people work directly in the advertising industry. This includes all people who help create or sell advertising or advertising media—advertising people in radio and television stations, newspapers and magazines; those in advertising agencies; and those working for retailers, wholesalers and producers. Advertising agencies employ only about half of all these people.

The versatility and variety of advertising

The choices available to advertisers nowadays are bewildering compared to the basic newspaper version that spawned the advertising industry. The most obvious media are TV, radio, newspapers, magazines, posters and cinema. After that many other media exist. Some are relatively mundane such as milk cartons and supermarket carrier bags. Others rely heavily on developing technology such as the Internet and interactive TV. Even screen savers are now recognized to be an advertising medium. For example, a very popular Guinness advertisement was downloaded 40 000 times from the Internet and passed on from one computer user to another. Yet other media forms are less remote than one might think. Pepsi have a seven-figure deal with the Mir space station and have a giant inflatable blue can 200 miles above earth. The can and cosmonauts feature in one of Pepsi's advertisements. Incidentally, any Pepsi delivered to the space station will be warm and flat—the rights to a new machine specially designed for the purpose, and which dispenses a sparkling cold drink are owned exclusively by Coke![3]

These advertising media are just some of the wide range available. The list is not exhaustive, indeed such a list would be almost impossible to compile with sheer pace of media development. It is useful to remember the scale of media choice, even if the most obvious ones are TV, radio, press, posters and cinema.

Remember also that advertising can be directed at many different groups. These may be large diverse targets such as all housewives in the country or very specialized such as postgraduate business students specializing in computer applications. Nor is all advertising geared to final consumers—channel members, the financial community, employees and other businesses are sometimes targeted by advertising. Finally, it is worth noting that advertising is not limited to commercial situations. Governments spend vast amounts of advertising money encouraging safer driving, health promotion, recruitment to defence forces, education for school leavers and so on.

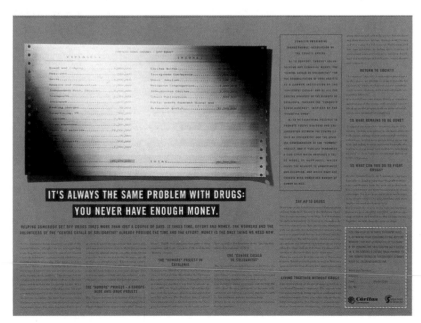

Effective advertising strategies can also help charitable foundations to raise money.

ADVERTISING OBJECTIVES ARE A STRATEGY DECISION

Advertising objectives must be specific

Every advertisement and every advertising campaign should have clearly defined objectives. These should grow out of the firm's overall marketing strategy and the jobs assigned to advertising. It is not enough for the marketing manager to say: 'Promote the product.' The marketing manager must decide exactly what advertising is expected to achieve. Advertising objectives should be more specific than personal selling objectives. One of the advantages of personal selling is that salespeople can shift their presentations to meet customers' needs. Each advertisement, however, is a specific communication. It must be effective not just for one customer but for thousands or millions of them.

The marketing manager sets the overall direction

The marketing manager might give the advertising manager one or more of the following specific objectives, along with the budget to accomplish them:

1. Help to introduce new products to specific target markets.
2. Help to position the firm's brand or marketing mix by informing and persuading target customers or intermediaries about its benefits.
3. Help to obtain desirable outlets and tell customers where they can buy a product.
4. Provide ongoing contact with target customers, even when a salesperson is not available.
5. Prepare the way for salespeople by presenting the company's name and the merits of its products.
6. Get immediate buying action.
7. Help to maintain relationships with satisfied customers and confirm their purchase decisions.

If you want half the market, say so!

The objectives listed above are not as specific and therefore not as meaningful as they could be. If a marketing manager really wants specific results, they should be clearly stated. A general objective: 'To help to expand market share', could be rephrased more specifically: 'To increase shelf space in our cooperating retail outlets by 25 per cent during the next three months'.

Once the marketing manager sets the overall objectives, the advertising manager should set specific objectives for each advertisement, as well as a whole advertising campaign. Without specific objectives, the creative specialists who develop individual advertisements may pursue their own objectives. They might set a vague objective, such as promote the product, and then create advertisements that win advertising industry artistic awards but fail to achieve the desired results.

Of course it is possible to do both—win advertising industry awards and achieve objectives. One company that has managed to do this is the Dutch insurance company Centraal Beheer, based in a small town called Apeldoorn. Over a 10-year period the company has used humour and stunning visuals to create a distinctive brand. The advertising is famous for 'the sting in the tail'. One advertisement opens with a grainy black and white sequence showing a ship being loaded. Various accidents are waiting to happen, such as a chain breaking, but never do. In the closing sequence, however, the viewer sees the ship's name—Titanic—painted on the bows. 'Just call us' then flashes on the screen. Centraal Beeher's slogan 'Insurance claim? Just ring Apeldoorn!' is practically a household saying in The Netherlands, with 9 out of 10 people able to identify what it stands for. In addition, over the period of the advertising, the company has jumped from twelfth to fourth place in the pecking order of Dutch insurance companies.[4]

Objectives guide implementation

The specific objectives obviously affect implementation. Advertising that might be right for encouraging consumers to switch from a competing brand might be all wrong for appealing to established customers with whom a firm already has a good relationship. Similarly, an advertisement that appeals to opinion leaders might not be what is needed to get repeat customers back into a retail outlet. As Exhibit 13–3 shows, the type of advertising that achieves objectives for one stage of the adoption process may be inappropriate for another. For example, most advertising for cameras in the United States, Germany and Japan focuses on foolproof pictures or state-of-the-art design because most consumers in these countries already own *some* camera. In Africa, where only about 20 per cent of the population owns a camera, advertisements must sell the whole concept of picture-taking.

With new products, most of the target market may have to be brought through the early stages of the adoption process. The advertising manager may use teaser campaigns along with informative advertisements. For more established products, advertising's job might be to build brand preference as well as help purchasers confirm their decisions. The Irish Tourist Board has a £10 million plus budget to help to communicate the emotional experience of Ireland. The aim is to develop a position for Ireland as a brand that is common across

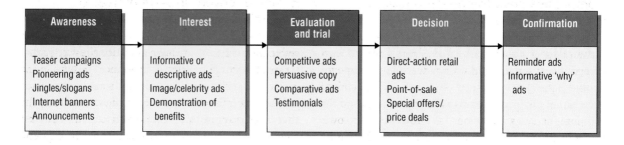

Awareness	Interest	Evaluation and trial	Decision	Confirmation
Teaser campaigns Pioneering ads Jingles/slogans Internet banners Announcements	Informative or descriptive ads Image/celebrity ads Demonstration of benefits	Competitive ads Persuasive copy Comparative ads Testimonials	Direct-action retail ads Point-of-sale Special offers/ price deals	Reminder ads Informative 'why' ads

Exhibit 13–3 Examples of Different Types of Advertising over Adoption Process Stages

the world. Research showed that various nationalities perceived the brand differently: Germans are interested in the outdoors, British in food and pubs, while clean hotels are the French preference. The advertising campaign is designed to achieve a consistent global brand for the Irish tourism product.[5]

OBJECTIVES DETERMINE THE KINDS OF ADVERTISING NEEDED

The advertising objectives largely determine which of two basic types of advertising to use—product or institutional. **Product advertising** tries to sell a product. It may be aimed at final users or channel members. **Institutional advertising** (also called *corporate advertising*) tries to promote an organization's image, reputation or ideas, rather than a specific product. Its basic objective is to develop goodwill or improve an organization's relations with various groups, not only with customers, but also current and prospective channel members, suppliers, shareholders, employees and the general public. The UK government, one of the top 50 advertisers in the world, uses institutional advertising to promote the United Kingdom as a place to do business.

Product advertising

Product advertising falls into three categories: pioneering, competitive and reminder advertising. This is depicted in Exhibit 13–4.

Pioneering advertising builds primary demand

Pioneering advertising tries to develop primary demand for a product category rather than demand for a specific brand. Pioneering advertising is usually done in the early stages of the product life cycle; it informs potential customers about the new product and helps to turn them into adopters.

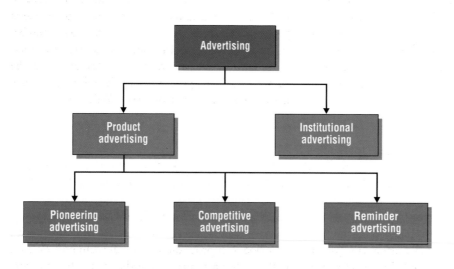

Exhibit 13–4
Product and Institutional Advertising

Competitive advertising—emphasizes selective demand

Competitive advertising tries to develop selective demand for a specific brand. A firm is forced into competitive advertising as the product life cycle moves along—to hold its own against competitors. The United Fruit Company gave up a 20-year pioneering effort to promote bananas in favour of promoting its own Chiquita brand. The reason was simple. While United Fruit was single-handedly promoting bananas, it slowly lost market share to competitors. It launched its competitive advertising campaign to avoid further losses.

Competitive advertising may be either direct or indirect. The **direct type advertising** aims for immediate buying action. The **indirect type advertising** points out product advantages to affect future buying decisions. Some of British Airways' advertising is of the competitive variety. In an effort to get immediate sales the advertisements are of the direct type with prices, timetables and telephone numbers to call for reservations, while others are of the indirect type. The latter focus on the quality of service and number of cities served and suggest you ask your travel agent about British Airways.

Comparative advertising is even rougher. **Comparative advertising** means making specific brand comparisons using actual product names. Many countries forbid comparative advertising, but that situation is changing. For example, Japan banned comparative advertising until some years ago, when the restrictions were relaxed. Japan's move followed an earlier change in the United States. This approach has led to legal as well as ethical problems and some advertisers and their agencies now back away from comparative advertising even in countries where it is allowed.

Some comparative advertisements leave consumers confused or even angry if the product they are using is criticized. Comparative advertisements can also backfire by calling attention to competing products that consumers had not previously considered. Comparative advertising seems to attract attention, so some advertisers will probably continue to use this approach, at least in countries that allow it.[6]

Reminder advertising—reinforces a favourable relationship

Reminder advertising tries to keep the product's name before the public. It may be useful when the product has achieved brand preference or insistence, perhaps in the market maturity or sales decline stages. It is used primarily to reinforce previous promotion. Here, the advertiser may use soft-sell advertisements that just mention or show the name as a reminder. The cigarette brand Silk Cut, for example, has relied on reminder advertisements because most consumers already know the brand name and—after years of promotion—associate the colour purple with the brand and with high product quality.[7]

Institutional advertising

Institutional advertising usually focuses on the name and prestige of an organization or industry. It may seek to inform, persuade or remind. Large companies with several divisions sometimes use a persuading kind of institutional advertising to link the divisions in customers' minds. Many Japanese firms such as Hitachi emphasize institutional advertising, in part because they often use the company name as a brand name. Likewise, many European banks use institutional advertising in addition to more specific product advertising. Companies sometimes rely on institutional advertising to present the company in a favourable light, perhaps to overcome image problems. Advertisements for an oil company, for example, might highlight its concern for the environment.

Some organizations use institutional advertising to advocate a specific cause or idea. Insurance companies, government health promotion agencies and some drinks companies, for example, use these advocacy advertisements to encourage people not to drink and drive. Glaxo Wellcome developed institutional advertising to help to fix its name firmly in consumer's minds after a series of takeovers in the pharmaceutical industry. The campaign promotes the company's research programmes to combat AIDS, tuberculosis and asthma. The advertisement has targeted politicians and healthcare professionals with the copy: 'Man has no greater enemy than disease. Disease has no greater enemy than Glaxo Wellcome'.[8]

COORDINATING ADVERTISING EFFORTS WITH COOPERATIVE RELATIONSHIPS

Vertical cooperation—advertising allowances, cooperative advertising

Sometimes a producer knows that a promotion job or advertising job should be done but finds that it can be done more effectively or more economically by someone further along in the channel. Alternatively, a large retail chain may approach manufacturers with a catalogue or programme and tell them how much it will cost to participate. In either case, the producer may offer **advertising allowances**—price reductions to firms further along in the channel to encourage them to advertise or otherwise promote the firm's products locally.

The objectives of cooperative advertising include both the stimulation of demand for the brand and the creation of sales at trade and consumer levels. Cooperative advertising tends to form part of a **push promotional strategy**. This is where the manufacturer or producer *pushes* the product through the channel and the channel, in turn, pushes the product to the ultimate customer. This contrasts with a **pull promotional strategy** which emphasizes promotion to the final customer so that their demand *pulls* the product through the channel to them.

Cooperative advertising involves channel members and producers sharing in the cost of advertisements. This helps wholesalers and retailers to compete in their local markets. It also helps the producer to get more promotion for the advertising spend because media usually give local advertisers lower rates than national or international firms. In addition, a retailer or wholesaler who is paying a share of the cost is more likely to follow through.

Integrated communications from cooperative relationships

Coordination and integration of advertising messages in the channel is another reason for cooperative advertising. One big, well-planned, integrated advertising effort is often better than many different, perhaps inconsistent, local efforts. Many franchise operations like the idea of communicating with one voice. For example, KFC encourages its franchisees to use a common advertising programme. Before, many developed their own local advertising that did not fit with the company's overall marketing strategy. Producers often get this coordination, and reduce local intermediary costs, by providing a master of an advertisement on videotape, cassette tape, or printed sheets. The intermediaries add their identification before turning the advertisement over to local media.

Allowances and support materials alone do not ensure cooperation. When channel members do not agree with the advertising strategy, it can be a serious source of conflict. For example, Benetton, the Italian sportswear company, wanted its 'United Colours' advertising campaign to be controversial. Pictures showed a dying AIDS victim and the torn, bloody uniform from the war in Bosnia. Most Europeans—including many of Benetton's retailers-franchisees—saw the advertisements as a tasteless attempt to exploit suffering. As a protest against the advertisements, a

group of German franchisees stopped paying their franchise fees and sued Benetton for damages. This is an extreme example, but even in routine situations a marketing manager should consider the likely reaction of other channel members before implementing any advertising programme.[9]

 Internet Excercise

Visit the Benetton web site (**www.benetton.com**). Scroll through to the pages on their advertising. Based on what you have read, how do you view their advertising campaigns. In what ways are they effective? Also, are there aspects of the web site that could be described as Public Relations?

 Ethical concerns may arise

Ethical issues sometimes arise concerning advertising allowance programmes. For example, a retailer may run one producer's advertisement to draw customers to the store but then sell them another brand. Is this unethical? Some producers think it is—that the retailer is intentionally misusing the money and switching customers to brands that pay the retailer a higher profit margin. A different view is that retailers are obligated to the producer to run the advertisement but obligated to consumers to sell them what they want, no matter whose brand it may be. A producer can often avoid the problem with a strategy decision by setting the allowance amount as a percentage of the retailer's actual purchases. That way, a retailer who doesn't produce sales doesn't get the allowance.

Horizontal cooperation—promotes different firms

Sometimes two or more firms with complementary products join together in a common advertising effort. Joint advertising encourages travellers to stay at a Hyatt Hotel and handle the expenses with an American Express card. Retailers in the same shopping centre often share the costs of promotion efforts. They might buy full-page newspaper advertisements listing the individual stores or promoting sales. Generally, the objective is the same as in vertical cooperation—to get more for the advertising spend.

Once it is known what the organization wants to achieve through advertising (objectives) and what kind of advertising is appropriate (pioneer/competitive/reminder) and who is involved in the channel, the concern is to decide how the advertising is to be delivered. This raises the complex issue of advertising media.

CHOOSING THE 'BEST' MEDIUM—HOW TO DELIVER THE MESSAGE

The choices surrounding which media to use come under the heading of media planning. This is more than buying advertising space. Decisions made about media have far-reaching consequences and need to reflect the advertiser's advertising objectives. Effectiveness depends on how well the medium fits with the rest of a marketing strategy, that is, it depends on (1) the promotion objectives, (2) what target markets are to be reached, (3) the funds available for advertising, and (4) the nature of the media, including *reach*, *frequency*, *impact* and *cost*.

Exhibit 13–5 shows some advantages and disadvantages of major kinds of media. However, some of the advantages noted in this table may not apply in all markets. In less developed countries, for example, newspapers may *not* be timely. Placing advertising may require a long lead-time if only a limited number of pages are available for advertisements. Direct mail may not be a flexible choice in a country with a weak postal system or high rate of illiteracy. Similarly, TV audiences are often less selective and targeted, but a special-interest cable TV show may reach a very specific audience.

Specify promotion objectives

Promotion objectives determine media decisions. If the objective is to increase interest and that requires demonstrating product benefits, TV may be the best alternative. If the objective is to inform—telling a long story with precise detail—and if pictures are needed, then print media—including magazines and newspapers—may be better. For example, Jockey switched its advertising to magazines from television when it decided to show the variety of colours, patterns and styles of its men's briefs. Jockey felt that it was too difficult to show this in a 30-second TV spot. Further, Jockey felt that there were problems with modelling men's underwear on television. However, Jockey might have stayed with TV if it had been targeting consumers in France or Brazil—where nudity in TV advertisements is common.[10]

Match the market with the media

To guarantee good media selection, the advertiser first must *clearly* specify its target market—a necessary step for all marketing strategy planning. Then the advertiser can choose media that are heard, read or seen by those target customers. The media available in a country may limit the choices. In less developed countries, for example, radio is often the only way to reach a broad-based market of poor consumers who cannot read or afford television. In most cases, however, the major problem is to select media that effectively reach the target audience. Most of the major media use marketing research to develop profiles of the people who buy their publications, or live in their broadcasting area. Generally, media research focuses on demographic characteristics. Such research seldom includes information on the segmenting dimensions specific to the product-markets that are important to *each* different advertiser. Research also cannot be definite about who actually reads each page or sees or hears each show.

A survey that has been developed relatively recently helps to overcome some of the information problems of

Kinds of Media	Advantages	Disadvantages
Newspaper	Flexible, timely, local market	May be expensive, short life, no 'pass-along'
Television	Demonstrations, good attention, wide reach	Expensive in total, 'clutter', less selective audience
Direct mail	Selected audience, flexible, can personalize	Relatively expensive per contact, junk mail—hard to retain attention
Radio	Wide reach, segmented audience, inexpensive	Weak attention, many different rates, short exposure
Yellow Pages	Reaches local customers seeking purchase information	Many other competitors listed in same place, hard to differentiate
Magazine	Very targeted, good detail, good 'pass-along'	
Outdoor	Flexible, repeat exposure, inexpensive	Inflexible, long lead times
Internet	Interactive, flexible, customer pull	'Mass market', very short exposure
		Narrow cost

Exhibit 13–5 Relative Advantages and Disadvantages of Major Kinds of Media

advertising across Europe. The European Media and Marketing Survey (EMS) contains data (160 megabytes worth) on the media consumption habits of citizens throughout Europe. This data can be combined with other consumption figures to yield rich data on 'who buys what and reads/views what'. For example, the EMS reports that the profile of portable computer users is changing. The bias in 1994 was towards men in the 25–49 age category, who were light TV viewers. The 1995–96 survey showed a more pronounced female bias, with a greater proportion of 25–40-year-olds. The media viewing habits of these groups are different. This is precisely the sort of detailed information that media planners require if they use the best media for their target market.[11]

Exhibit 13–6 shows how advertising spend is distributed across the traditional media in Europe. Although this varies by country, the majority of advertising in most countries is carried in the press.

In some countries media planning is very problematic because the media do not provide any information, or they provide audience profiles that make the media seem more attractive than it is. Where reliable data are not available (as is the case in some Eastern European countries) the advertisers or the agencies may do their own audience research.

Another problem is that the audience for media that *do* reach your target market may also include people who are *not* in the target group. But *you pay for the whole audience the particular medium delivers*—including those who are not potential customers. The cost of reaching the real target market escalates when the irrelevant audience is very large. Advertising during the Olympics, for example, may seem very attractive but it is also very expensive. The TV networks pay a high price to televise the Olympic Games. The European Broadcasting Union paid $250 million and NBC paid $456 million to the International Olympic Committees to be allowed to televise the Atlanta Olympics in 1996. The Olympics reach a very large audience—85 per cent of the world's viewing population—but it is also very diverse. Research suggests that many of the firms that sponsor advertisements on these big-audience shows would get better value for money by advertising during TV slots that reach more targeted audiences.[12]

Because it is so difficult to evaluate alternative media, some media analysts focus on objective measures such as cost per thousand of audience size or circulation. Advertisers preoccupied with keeping these costs down may ignore the relevant segmenting dimensions and slip into mass marketing. The media buyer may look only at the relatively low cost of mass media when a more specialized medium might be a much better buy. Its audience might have more interest in the product, or more money to spend, or more willingness to buy.

GILLETTE'S MEDIUM-CLOSE SHAVE IN IRAN

Gillette faces sharp competition from other razor producers in most parts of the world. But the situation it faced in Iran was even more prickly. Gillette wanted to introduce its Contour razor with a series of TV advertisements. Gillette used TV in other countries because it was the best medium for demonstrating the advantages of the Contour razor. And the cost was right; a one-minute advertisement on Iranian TV cost only $1 000. But TV advertisements turned out to be impossible as a first step. Since the 1980 Iranian revolution, the Ministry of Guidance, which controls advertising in Iran, prohibited Iran's two TV channels from advertising foreign products. In fact, until 1990 the ministry did not allow any TV advertising, even for local products.

The Ministry of Guidance wasn't Gillette's only obstacle. The Islamic religion discourages its followers from shaving. On the other hand, many Iranians *do* shave and Gillette figured that people who shave need razors.

Gillette turned to Mormohamad Fathi, head of an Iranian advertising agency, for help. He thought a practical first step would be to try to find a medium that would accept advertising for Gillette's Blue II, a less expensive razor than the Contour. Fathi took a Blue II advertisement from one Tehran newspaper to another, but they repeatedly turned him down. Fathi thought it was a good omen when he finally found a newspaper advertising manager without a beard but the man still needed persuading. Fathi explained to him: 'Shaving is not just for your face. If you have a car accident and someone has to shave your head, Gillette Blue II is the best.' Using this argument, the newspaper's advertising manager consulted his clergyman, who gave him permission to take the advertisement.

Once over that hurdle, other papers followed, and before long Gillette advertisements appeared regularly in Iranian print media. That helped pave the way for Fathi to plaster Gillette posters on buses all over Tehran. He also handed out hundreds of free samples to encourage consumers to try the razor and to build repeat sales. Fathi is persistent. With sales momentum building, you can bet it won't be long before Gillette's demonstration advertisements are showing in Iran's movie theatres.[13]

Country	Total	News-papers	Magazines	TV	Radio	Cinema	Outdoor/ Transport
Germany	21 410.4	10 308.7	4145.0	5 092.5	876.2	221.4	766.6
UK	13 654.8	5 579.7	2501.6	4 464.1	483.4	93.5	532.5
France	10 187.7	2 487.5	2326.5	3 412.2	710.6	64.9	1 186.0
Italy	5 996.3	1 256.9	985.0	3 402.5	198.6	–	153.3
Spain	4 799.4	1 511.8	747.4	1 809.6	472.4	39.6	218.7
Netherlands	3 521.6	1 755.1	786.5	664.3	172.6	13.0	129.9
Switzerland	2 721.7	1 496.8	502.4	254.9	75.2	29.9	362.5
Sweden	1 958.4	1 209.2	242.4	360.1	46.2	14.3	86.0
Belgium	1 703.5	449.3	397.5	548.6	137.6	23.0	147.6
Austria	1 665.2	758.8	290.7	347.4	161.4	–	106.9
Denmark	1 509.2	934.1	208.0	294.9	29.1	10.9	32.2
Portugal	1 221.0	170.8	209.3	649.0	85.1	2.6	104.1
Norway[1]	1 140.0	684.8	129.3	199.8	99.3	5.1	21.7
Finland	1 086.9	636.8	159.5	221.2	35.5	1.2	32.6
Greece	970.8	180.5	206.3	505.1	55.9	0.0	23.0
Ireland	601.7	351.5	23.5	146.6	44.3	4.7	31.1

Notes: Data are net of discounts, they include agency commission and press classified advertising but exclude production costs. Data are ranked on total adspend.
[1] Data for Norway are estimates.

Exhibit 13–6 (a) Advertising Expenditure by Country and Medium (US$m)—1996

Country	Total	News-papers	Magazines	TV	Radio	Cinema	Outdoor/ Transport
Austria	100.0	45.6	17.5	20.9	9.7	0.0	6.4
Belgium	100.0	26.4	23.3	32.2	8.1	1.4	8.7
Denmark	100.0	61.9	13.8	19.5	1.9	0.7	2.1
Finland	100.0	58.6	14.7	20.4	3.3	0.1	3.0
France	100.0	24.4	22.8	33.5	7.0	0.6	11.6
Germany	100.0	48.1	19.4	23.8	4.1	1.0	3.6
Greece	100.0	18.6	21.3	52.0	5.8	0.0	2.4
Ireland	100.0	58.4	3.9	24.4	7.4	0.8	5.2
Italy	100.0	21.0	16.4	56.7	3.3	0.0	2.6
Netherlands	100.0	49.8	22.3	18.9	4.9	0.4	3.7
Norway[1]	100.0	60.1	11.3	17.5	8.7	0.4	1.9
Portugal	100.0	14.0	17.1	53.2	7.0	0.2	8.5
Spain	100.0	31.5	15.6	37.7	9.8	0.8	4.6
Sweden	100.0	61.7	12.4	18.4	2.4	0.7	4.4
Switzerland	100.0	55.0	18.5	9.4	2.8	1.1	13.3
UK	100.0	40.9	18.3	32.7	3.5	0.7	3.9

Notes: Data are net of discounts, they include agency commission and press classified advertising but exclude production costs. Data are ranked on total adspend.
[1] Data for Norway are estimates.

Exhibit 13–6 (b) Distribution of Advertising Expenditure

Some media focus on specific target markets

Today the major media direct more attention to reaching smaller, more defined target markets. The most obvious evidence of this is in the growth of spending on direct-mail advertising to consumers listed in a database. However, other major media are becoming more targeted as well.

National print media may offer specialized editions. *Time* magazine, for example, offers not only several regional and metropolitan editions but also special editions for college students, educators, doctors and business managers. Magazines such as *Newsweek*, France's *Paris Match International* and Germany's *Wirtschaftwoche* provide international editions. Large city newspapers often have several editions to cater for city and suburban areas. Where these outlying areas are not adequately covered, however, suburban newspapers prosper, catering for the desire for local news.

Many magazines serve only special-interest groups—such as fishermen, soap opera fans, new parents, professional groups and personal computer users. In fact, the most profitable magazines seem to be the ones aimed at clearly defined markets. Many specialist magazines also have international editions that help marketers reach consumers with similar interests in different parts of the world. *PC Magazine*, for example, offers European and Japanese editions. There are trade magazines in many fields—such as chemical engineering, furniture retailing, electrical wholesaling, farming and the aerospace market. Guides to the thousands of magazines now available throughout Europe are available at country level.

Radio has become a more specialized medium. Some stations cater for particular regions. Others also aim at specific target markets interested particularly in sports or particular types of music such as rock, country or classical.

Cable TV channels—such as MTV, Cable News Network, Nickelodeon and ESPN—also target specific audiences. ESPN, for example, has an audience heavily weighted towards affluent male viewers. MTV appeals most strongly to affluent 25–34-year-old viewers. Fruit of the Loom buys advertising time on cable TV, especially MTV, to increase its market penetration with teenagers and young adults, who are more willing to buy leisure wear.

Infomercials—long commercials that are broadcast with a TV show format—give a glimpse of how targeted cable TV will become when consumers have access to hundreds of TV channels. With so many alternative channels competing for consumer attention, most channels will succeed only if they offer programmes and commercials that are very specific to the interests and needs of smaller, more homogeneous target markets. Consumers will be able to select channels that offer information about products that interest them.

Specialized media are small—but growing

The *major* advertising media listed in Exhibit 13–5 attract the vast majority of advertising media budgets. Advertising specialists always look for cost-effective new media that will help advertisers reach their target markets. In Eastern Europe, where major media are still limited, companies like Campbell's pay to put advertisements on bus shelters. Hotels and car rental companies buy space on advertising boards placed in the restrooms on aircraft. There are too many specialized media to go into all of them in detail here. They all require the same type of strategy decisions as the more typical mass media.

In recent years, these specialized media gained in popularity. One reason is that they get the mass-selling message to the target market close to the point of purchase. They also offer the advantage of making an advertiser's message stand out from the usual advertising clutter in the mass media. For example, in Amsterdam, the hub caps on a fleet of buses are used as a medium. The plastic hub caps have been designed to look like bottle tops and carry the brand name for Bavaria Malt Bier. The launch of this alcohol free beer coincided with heavy investment by the Dutch government in anti-drink-driving advertising.[14]

'Must buys' may use up available funds

Selecting which media to use is still akin to an art. The media buyer may start with a budgeted amount and try to buy the best mix to reach the target audience. Some media are obvious essential purchases, such as the local newspaper for a retailer in a small- or medium-sized town or region. Most firms serving local markets view a *Yellow Pages* listing as essential. These advertisements may even use up the available funds. If not, the media buyer must compare the relative advantages and disadvantages of alternatives and select a media *blend* that helps achieve the promotion objectives, given the available budget.

Although TV advertisements have a relatively low cost per thousand, the overall high cost of television may eliminate it from the media blend of many firms. Because TV advertising costs so much, many firms are moving away from television and experimenting with combinations of other media. Very targeted media, like direct-mail advertising, are growing rapidly as a result of this shift. An even bigger media revolution is brewing—and it has the potential to radically change the nature and role of advertising.

Interactive media and the information highway

Advances in information technology have an impact on every aspect of communication—and advertising communication is no exception. Satellite feeds instantly send radio and TV advertisements around the world. Computerized systems print individual consumer's names in the middle of magazine advertisements. New switching systems allow a cable TV company to route different advertisements to different households.

Customer databases target direct-mail advertising. As significant as such advances are, they mainly make it more efficient for advertisers to do what they have always done: send one-way communications to some target customers. More radical changes—based on interactive media that allow each different customer to get very different messages and to respond in different ways—are coming.

For years, advertisers have eagerly anticipated the widespread availability of interactive cable systems. Interactive cable will let consumers instantly respond to TV advertisements, perhaps by pushing a button on a special box that connects the TV set, phone and computer to incoming cable TV or telephone lines. One button might signal a request for more detailed information, or perhaps places an order for the product. These systems are beginning to come on-line in some areas. Some companies aren't waiting for interactive cable. They are experimenting with interactive advertising using multimedia computer networks that offer the same basic capabilities.

Many companies are also experimenting with the use the Internet as a medium. This allows companies to reach key market segments and to increase brand awareness. For example, Levi's have a home page. It features very little text but has a grid of icons each dedicated to different subjects such as company history, products and commercials. Others are designed to draw in Levi's target audience of 15–24-year-olds with 'e-zines' on youth culture and street fashion. Snickers use the Internet to target 13–24-year-old males with a site dedicated mainly to football.[15]

Apart from the targeting capability of the Internet, the other main advantage is that it allows two-way communication. This enables advertisers to gain feedback from those who read their pages. However, different organizations will have different marketing objectives for establishing and maintaining a Web presence. The Web can be used to introduce the company and its products to a wide and international audience thus gaining awareness and informing the market. Similarly, a firm that has well-known products may use the Web to solicit feedback from current customers as well as informing new customers. Web sites can be used to move customers and prospects through successive phases of the buying process, first attracting Net surfers, making contact with interested surfers (among those attracted), qualifying and converting some of these into interactive customers. Thus, the Internet is something of a mix between advertising and personal selling.

As a medium, the Internet has a particular audience. The majority of Web users are male, in their twenties and thirties, well-educated, with higher income levels than the population as a whole. While this may constitute a very attractive audience for some companies, it may well not be the precise segment that another company wishes to target.[16]

PLANNING THE 'BEST' MESSAGE—WHAT TO COMMUNICATE

Specifying the copy platform

As well as making decisions about *how* the messages will reach the target audience, it is necessary to decide on the copy platform—what the words and illustrations should communicate. This decision should flow from the promotion objectives and the specific jobs assigned to advertising.

Developing the copy platform is the job of advertising specialists. The advertising manager and the marketing manager need to understand the process to be sure that the job is done well. There are few tried-and-true rules in message construction, but behavioural research can help. Recall the discussion of the communication process and common frames of reference in Chapter 12. The concepts of needs, learning and perception discussed earlier also apply here. It is known, for example, that consumers have the ability to tune out messages or ideas that do not interest them. How much of the daily newspaper do you actually see as you leaf through it? An audience does not see everything the advertisers want them to see. How can an advertiser be more effective?

AIDA can guide message planning

Basically, the overall marketing strategy should determine *what* the message should say. Then management judgement, perhaps aided by marketing research, can help decide how to encode this content so it will be decoded as intended. As a guide to message planning, the AIDA concept is useful: getting Attention, holding Interest, arousing Desire and obtaining Action.

Getting attention

Getting attention is an advertisement's first job. If an advertisement fails to get attention, it does not matter how many people see or hear it. Many readers leaf through magazines and newspapers without paying attention to any of the advertisements. Many listeners or viewers do odd jobs or get snacks during radio and TV commercials. When watching a programme on videotape, they may zap past the commercial with a flick of the fast-forward button.

Many attention-getting devices are available. A large headline, very topical or shocking statements, attractive models, babies, animals, special effects, anything different or eye-catching, may do the trick. However, the attention-getting device should not detract from, and hopefully should lead to the next step, holding interest.

Holding interest

Holding interest is more difficult. A humorous advertisement, an unusual video effect, or a clever photo may get your attention, but once it has been noticed, then what? The viewer may pause to appreciate it, but if there is no relation between what got their attention and the marketing mix, they will move on. For example a young adult may take some notice when an advertisement features a sporty or dramatic scene but if the product being advertised is life insurance then it is unlikely to hold his or her attention.

The behavioural sciences give advertisers some insight about how to hold interest. The tone and language of the advertisement must fit with the experiences and attitudes of the target customers and their reference groups. As a result, many advertisers develop advertisements that relate to specific moods and emotions. They hope that the good feeling about the advertisement (and the whole marketing mix) will stick, even if the specific details of the copy platform are forgotten.

To hold interest, informative advertisements need to speak the target customer's language. Persuasive advertisements must provide evidence that convinces the customer. Celebrity endorsements may help. TV advertisements often demonstrate a product's benefits. Layouts for print advertisements should look right to the customer. Print illustrations and copy should be arranged to encourage the eye to move smoothly through the advertisement, perhaps from a headline that starts in the upper left-hand corner to the illustration or body copy in the middle and finally to the company or brand name ('signature') at the lower right-hand corner. If all of the elements of the advertisement work together as a whole, they will help to hold interest and build recall.[17]

Arousing desire

Arousing desire to own or use a particular product is one of an advertisement's most difficult jobs. The advertiser must communicate with the customer. To do this effectively, the advertiser must understand how target customers think, behave and make decisions. Then the advertisement must convince customers that the product can meet their needs. Testimonials may persuade a consumer that other people with similar needs have purchased the product and liked it. Product comparisons may highlight the advantages of a particular brand.

Some experts feel that an advertisement should focus on one *unique selling proposition* that aims at an important unsatisfied need. They discourage the approach of trying to tell the whole story in a single advertisement. Telling the whole story is the job of the whole promotional mix over time, not one advertisement. A good example of focusing on one product attribute in advertising is a recent Guinness campaign. The slogan used is 'Good things come to those who wait' and the 60-second TV advertisement cuts between a raging sea and a pouring pint. The emphasis is on a unique product feature —the length of time it takes to pour a pint of Guinness.[18]

If consumers see many different competing brands as essentially the same, focusing on a unique selling proposition may be particularly important. This can help set the brand apart and position it as especially effective in meeting the needs of the target market. Focusing on a unique selling proposition makes the most sense when a brand really does have a comparative advantage on an *important* benefit. That reduces the likelihood of competitors imitating the same idea.

An advertisement may also have the objective, especially during the market growth and market maturity stages, of supplying words customers can use to rationalize their desire to buy. Although products may satisfy certain emotional needs, many consumers find it necessary to justify their purchases on some economic or rational basis. Snickers chocolate bar advertisements helped to ease the guilt of calorie-conscious snackers by assuring them that 'Snickers satisfies you when you need an afternoon energy break'.

Obtaining action

Getting action is the final requirement and not an easy one. From communication research, we now know that prospective customers must be led beyond considering how the product *might* fit into their lives to actually trying it or letting a member of the company's sales staff come in and demonstrate it.

Direct-response advertisements can sometimes help promote action by encouraging interested consumers to do *something* that is less risky or demanding than actually making a purchase. For example, an advertisement that includes a free telephone number or a returnable coupon might prompt some consumers who are not yet ready to buy at least to call or write for more information. Then follow-up brochures or a telephone salesperson can provide additional information and attempt to prompt another action—perhaps a visit to a store or a 'no obligations' trial period. This approach seeks to get action one step at a time, where the first action suggested

Global Message Constraints	Global Media Constraints	**Exhibit 13–7** Message and Media Constraints for Global Advertisers
Social/cultural differences as to what is acceptable Literacy rates Legal restrictions on content Advertising freedom Credibility of source Language (translation of message, slang, non-verbal communication) Style of advertising (hard sell/soft sell, informative, entertaining)	General media availability Specific restrictions are imposed on particular media Legality of advertising particular products through such media Media costs	

provides a 'foot in the door' for subsequent communication efforts.

Whether or not some direct-response approach is used, to communicate more effectively advertisements might emphasize strongly felt customer needs. Careful research on attitudes in the target market may help uncover such strongly felt *unsatisfied* needs. Appealing to important needs can get more action and also provide the kind of information that buyers need to confirm their decisions. Post-purchase dissonance may set in and obtaining confirmation may be one of the important advertising objectives. Some customers seem to read more advertising *after* a purchase than before. The advertisement may reassure them about the correctness of their decision, as well as supply the words they use to tell others about the product.

Can global messages work?

During the 1980s, many international consumer products firms tried to use one global advertising message all around the world. Of course, they translated the message or made other minor adjustments but the focus was one global copy platform. Some did it because it looked as if it would save the cost of developing different advertisements for different countries. Others did it because they felt their customers' basic needs were the same, even if they lived in different countries. Some just did it because it was fashionable to 'go global'. The supposed benefits of global advertising include a reduction in production costs (but not media costs), consistency of image and exploitation of creative ideas.

This approach worked for some firms. Coca-Cola and Gillette, for example, feel that the needs their products serve are very similar for all consumers. They focus on the similarities among consumers who make up their target market rather than the differences. However, most firms who use this approach experience terrible results. They may save money by developing fewer advertisements, but they lose sales because they do not develop advertising messages, and whole marketing mixes, aimed at specific target markets. They are just trying to appeal to a global 'mass market'.

The limitations to global advertising relate to message and media constraints as shown in Exhibit 13–7.

Combining smaller market segments into a single, large target market makes sense if the different segments can be served with a single marketing mix. When that is not the case, the marketing manager should treat them as different target markets and develop different marketing mixes for each target.[19]

PIZZA HUT'S PAN-EUROPEAN PUSH

PepsiCo spent £13 million to produce and screen across 32 countries a global advertisement for Pizza Hut, one of its companies. The aim of the advertisement was to relaunch the Pizza Hut brand in Europe and, at the same time, to announce the arrival of a new product. Until the campaign, the company conceded that its restaurants in the UK looked a 'little tired', while in the rest of Europe they were brand new but not enough people were going into them. Europeans had the view that Pizza Hut was just another American fast food chain.

The company and their advertising agency (Abbott Mead Vickers BBDO) began to search for an appropriate celebrity to convey the brand personality of Pizza

Hut to the target market of 20–30-year-old Europeans. Rock stars, movie stars and sports personalities were all too expensive. Eventually supermodels Cindy Crawford and Linda Evangelista were recruited at a cost of £350 000 each.

The advertisement needed to convey Pizza Hut's young personality and that it meant eating quality pizzas in a relaxed environment. The advertisement also had to deliver the information that the company had a new product—the Stuffed Crust Pizza. This gave the advertising a news angle. The advertisement was rolled out across Europe. More mature markets with larger advertising budgets such as the UK and Spain had local executions.

The advertisement was deemed to have been successful on a number of counts. Footfall (number of patrons visiting Pizza Hut) increased and the percep-

tion of the brand was also enhanced. It is reckoned that Pizza Hut managed to turn around its performance in the European market from a 5 per cent decline into a mean average growth of 30 per cent from the date the advertising was launched.

The global campaign was made possible by all of the countries pooling their budgets, creating one sufficiently big budget to pay for production and screening. In effect, the advertisement represented over half the Pizza Hut total advertising budget for the year. The company was impressed by the value of a single campaign for a single message—even without the support of other promotional activities. Even so, it has to take account of the pitfalls of such a strategy—get a global advertisement wrong and the whole business can be put in jeopardy.[20]

ADVERTISING AGENCIES OFTEN DO THE WORK

An advertising manager manages a company's advertising effort. Some advertising managers, especially those working for large retailers, have their own advertising departments that plan specific advertising campaigns and carry out the details. Many others turn over much of the advertising work to specialists—the advertising agencies.

Advertising agencies are specialists

Advertising agencies are specialists in planning and handling the details of mass-communication for advertisers. Agencies play a useful role because they are independent of the advertiser and have an outside viewpoint. They bring experience to an individual client's problems because they work for many other clients. Further, as specialists they can often do the job more economically than a company's own department.

Some full-service agencies handle any activities related to advertising. They may even handle overall marketing strategy planning, as well as marketing research, product and package development and sales promotion. Some agencies make good marketing partners and almost assume the role of the firm's marketing department. In these situations, the relationship between the agency and the company is very close.

A full-service agency usually has three key departments—the creative department, the media department and the client-service department. The creative department create the advertisement using *copywriters and art directors* who often work in teams. The media depart-

ment develops the media plan determining how the advertising budget will be spent. Media schedulers or buyers place the advertising and monitor campaign effectiveness. The client-service department acts as the interface between the client and the agency. Most importantly they write the *advertising brief* which attempts to answer the 'who, why, when, where and how much?' questions. The *account director* helps to bring the advertising brief to fruition, presents the agencies ideas to the client and makes sure the work is faithful to the brief, is on time and within budget.[21]

Some agencies do not offer a full line of services. *Media buying services* specialize in selecting media to fit a firm's marketing strategy. They are used when a firm wants to schedule a number of advertisements, perhaps in different media, and needs help finding the blend that will deliver what it needs at the lowest cost. Similarly, creative specialists just create advertisements. These agencies handle the artistic elements of advertising but leave media planning, research and related services to others.

Creating advertising involves many activities

Once the advertising brief is agreed between the client and the agency, the work of developing the advertising campaign starts. The *traffic manager* oversees the campaign through the agency, dealing with costs, timetables and administration issues. Copywriters and art directors work together to produce ideas. These are often made up in the form of *storyboards*—strip cartoons describing a TV commercial. Before ideas are fully produced the client has an input and the concept may also be tested among consumers. When the concept is approved, the radio, TV and/or print production of the advertisement takes place. At this stage outside specialists may work with the creative team. Exhibit 13–8 illustrates the flow of work in developing an advertising campaign.

The biggest agencies handle much of the advertising

The vast majority of advertising agencies are small, with not more than 10 employees. The largest agencies account for most of the industry revenue. Some big agencies have merged, creating mega-agencies with worldwide networks. Although their headquarters are located in different countries, they have offices throughout the world. The move towards international marketing is a key reason behind the mergers. Before the mergers, marketers in one country often had difficulty finding a capable, full-service agency in the country where they wanted to advertise. The mergers combined the strengths of the individual agencies. The mega-agency can offer varied services wherever in the world a marketing manager needs them. This may be especially important for managers in large corporations like Toyota, Renault, Unilever, NEC, Philips, Procter & Gamble, Nestlé and Coca-Cola, who advertise internationally.

Some brands have been developed to sell across several countries. Kellogg's Frosties is promoted in the same commercial across Europe.

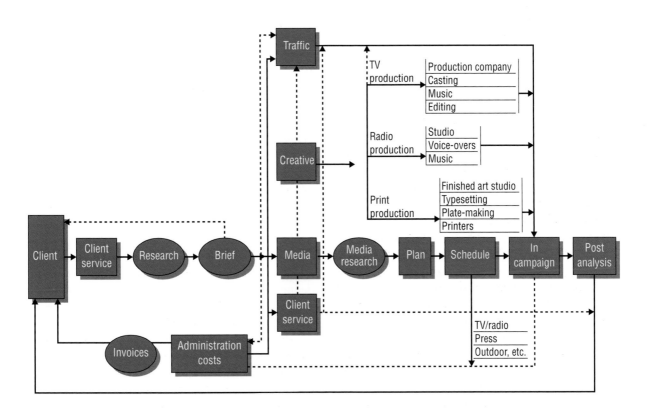

Exhibit 13–8 Activity Flow Chart for Advertising Campaign

In spite of the growth of these very large agencies, smaller agencies will continue to play an important role because the really big agencies are less interested in smaller accounts. Moreover, smaller agencies will continue to appeal to customers who want more personal attention and a close relationship that is more attuned to their marketing needs.

Advertising agency payment methods

Traditionally, advertising agencies are paid by the *commission system*. When agencies first emerged they acted as space brokers, buying newspaper space and selling it on to clients. In return, the media companies paid them a commission of 15 per cent of the official rate card value of the same space. Thus, on £100 worth of space, the agent would get a commission of £15, the media owner would earn £85 and the price to the advertiser would be £100. Today media owners usually have two prices: one for national advertisers and a lower rate for local advertisers, such as local retailers. The advertising agency gets a 15 per cent commission on national rates, but not on local rates. This makes it worthwhile for producers and national intermediaries to use agencies. National advertisers have to pay the full media rate anyway, so it makes sense to let the agency experts do the work and earn their commission. Local retailers, allowed the lower media rate, seldom use agencies. Even large retail chains may do most of their advertising in local markets where they have stores; Toys "R" Us, for example, uses local newspapers for most of its advertisements.

There is growing resistance to the idea of paying agencies the same way regardless of the work performed or *the results achieved*. The commission system also makes it hard for agencies to be completely objective about inexpensive media—or promotion campaigns that use little space or time. Much of the opposition to the traditional commission system comes from very large consumer products advertisers. They spend the most on media advertisements, and they think a 15 per cent fee is often too high, especially when an expensive advertising campaign doesn't produce the desired results. Not all agencies are satisfied with the present arrangement either. Some would like to charge additional fees as their costs rise and advertisers demand more services.

Firms that need a lot of service but spend relatively little on media, including most producers of business products, favour a fixed commission system. These are the firms the agencies would like to charge additional fees. As yet the commission system remains the dominant source of agency income but fee systems are becoming much more common. One recent UK survey found that 41 per cent of agencies were being paid on the basis of results.[22]

Some firms pay the agency based on results

A number of advertisers now 'grade' the work done by their agencies and the agencies' pay depends on the grade. For example, General Foods lowered its basic commission to about 13 per cent. However, the company pays the agency a bonus of about 3 per cent on campaigns that earn an A rating. If the agency only earns a B, it loses the bonus. If it earns a C, it must improve quickly or GF removes the account.

Variations on this approach are becoming common. For example, Carnation directly links its agency's compensation with how well its advertisements score in market research tests. Gillette and Lorillard use a sliding scale, and the percentage compensation declines with increased advertising volume. And some agencies develop their own plans in which they guarantee to achieve the results expected or give the advertiser a partial refund. These agencies realize that the advertising service they provide for their business customers is *their* product—and providing a guarantee helps to differentiate the quality of the service. An advantage of this approach is that it forces the advertiser and agency to agree on very specific objectives for their advertisements and what they expect to achieve. Yet many advertising agencies dislike the idea of being so closely scrutinized by clients or having to negotiate what they're paid. If the current trends continue, they may have to get used to it.

The advertising brief

A key task that has to be undertaken early in the relationship between client and agency is to develop and agree an **advertising brief**. In essence, this a working document that covers what is to be communicated to whom and to what end. Development of the brief is the responsibility of the agency, working closely with the client. If necessary, market research may be commissioned to build a better understanding of the particular marketing issues involved.

The advertising brief reviews the nature of the marketing problem that the advertising is to address— why the advertising is necessary. The target market will be described in terms of demographics and media consumption. It is also important to document the target market's attitudes and behaviour with regard to the product market and their behaviour in relation to the brand. Such profiles enable the client and agency to define and refine appropriate communications objectives. These form a key part of the advertising brief. Once it has been agreed, it forms the basis on which the creative specialists develop the advertisements.

The brief should emerge as a result of deliberations between the client and the agency, with an injection of market research. A well-developed advertising brief should contribute to a healthy client–agency relationship. In some cases, however, conflict emerges in the relationship.

Conflicts between advertising agencies and clients

The creative people in advertising agencies and their more business-oriented clients often disagree. Some creative people are production-oriented. They create an advertisement they like themselves or that will win artistic approval within their industry, and are less concerned about how well it fits into the rest of the client's marketing mix. This will inevitably create conflict. The advertiser's product managers or brand managers may be personally responsible for the success of particular products and feel that they have some right to direct and even veto the work of the creative agency people. Because the advertiser is paying the bills, the agency often loses these confrontations.

Severing the relationship

An advertiser is usually free to cancel the relationship at any time. This gives the advertiser extreme flexibility. If an agency is not doing a good job, the client can shop around for a new one. However, a decision to terminate the relationship with an agency should not be taken lightly. Too many marketing managers just use their advertising agency as a scapegoat. Whenever anything goes wrong, they blame the agency. While agency-swapping is common, in some countries, like Brazil, it is more difficult for a firm to dump its agency. Some industries are characterized by frequent account movements. One survey, for example, reckoned that the average amount of time that agencies held onto computer accounts was just 42 weeks. It is also possible for an agency to fire its client if they decide that for some reason they no longer wish to be associated with them.[23]

 ## Ethical conflicts may arise

Advertising agencies usually work closely with their clients, and they often have access to confidential information. This can create ethical conflicts if an agency is working with two or more competing clients. Most agencies are very sensitive to the potential problems and work hard to keep people and information from competing accounts completely separated. Many advertisers do not think that is enough and they do not want to risk a problem. They refuse to work with an agency that handles any competing accounts, even when they are handled in different offices. For example, a top executive for the Budweiser brand ended a 79-year relationship with an agency when one of the agency's subsidiaries accepted an assignment to buy media space for a competing brand of beer. Such a potential conflict of interest in handling competing products is more likely to emerge as a problem for the large international agencies.

MEASURING ADVERTISING EFFECTIVENESS IS NOT EASY

Success depends on the total marketing mix

It would be convenient if advertising results could be measured just by looking at sales. Certainly some breakthrough advertisements do have a very direct effect on a company's sales and the advertising literature is filled with success stories that 'prove' advertising increases sales. Similarly, market research firms can sometimes compare sales levels before and after—or during—the period of an advertising campaign. Yet, advertising success usually cannot be measured by just looking at sales. The total marketing mix, not just promotion generally or advertising specifically, is responsible for the sales result. Sales results are also affected by what competitors do and by other changes in the external marketing environment. Only with direct-response advertising can a company make a direct link between advertising and sales results. Then, if an advertisement does not produce immediate results, it is considered a failure.

To start to measure advertising effectiveness, it is necessary to examine the communication process again.

As noted earlier, one view sees advertising working in a progressive way from awareness to interest to desire to action (the AIDA model). Under this 'linear' model the consumer is the passive receiver of advertising, processing it in a rational needs-based manner. The other view of communications presents a more active, intuitive consumer who interacts with the communication, interprets it and forms meaning from it. In combination, these models suggest that advertising works at both levels—the rational and overt practical level and the symbolic, emotional and covert level. Effective advertising is advertising that has impact, integrates the brand and communicates the desired message. It follows from this that any measure of the effect of advertising ought to include examination of these dimensions.

Research and testing can improve the odds

Ideally, advertisers should pre-test advertising before it runs—rather than rely solely on their own impressions about how good an advertisement will be. The judgement of creative specialists or advertising experts may not help much. They often judge more on the basis of originality—or cleverness—of the copy and illustrations. Teamwork between the advertising agency, the client-company management and marketing research can help to ensure effectiveness. A good example of this is a popular advertising campaign for Guinness beer in Ireland. After the TV airing of the campaign entitled 'Anticipation', more than nine out of ten beer drinkers could recall the execution. On top of this, there was very strong association between details from the advertisement and the brand itself, implying that the brand had been successfully integrated into the creative heart of the campaign. The audience were also more aware that the well-known brand was of high quality and was becoming more popular and more in demand socially.[24]

Many progressive advertisers now demand laboratory or market tests to evaluate an advertisement's effectiveness. Sometimes laboratory-type devices that measure skin moisture or eye reaction are used to gauge consumer responses. In addition, before advertisements run generally, attitude research is sometimes used. Researchers often try to evaluate consumers' reaction to particular advertisements or parts of advertisements. For example, American Express used focus group interviews to get reactions to a series of possible TV advertisements. The company wanted the advertisements to convey the idea that younger people could qualify for its credit cards but it still wanted to present a prestige image. The agency prepared picture boards presenting different approaches, as well as specific copy. Four out of six possible advertisements failed to communicate the message to the focus groups. One idea that seemed to be effective became the basis for an advertisement that was tested again before being launched on TV.[25]

In addition, split runs on cable TV systems in test markets are proving to be an important approach for testing advertisements in a normal viewing environment. Retail audit data from outlets in those test markets can provide an estimate of how an advertisement is likely to affect sales. This approach provides marketing managers with a powerful new tool and it will become even more powerful in the future as more cable systems and telephone companies add new interactive technology that allows viewers to provide immediate feedback to an advertisement as it appears on the TV.

Hindsight may lead to foresight

After an advertisement has run, researchers may try to measure how much consumers recall about specific products or advertisements. Enquiries from customers may be used to measure the effectiveness of particular advertisements. The response to radio or television commercials—or magazine readership—can be estimated using various survey methods to check the size and composition of audiences. Further specific research is required if the advertiser wants to know more than who comprised the audience. Advertising tracking is research aimed at discovering the target audience's brand awareness, advertising awareness, what has been taken out from the advertisement and what shifts have occurred in the audience's thinking about the product.

While advertising research methods are not foolproof, they are superior to relying on judgement by advertising 'experts'. Until more effective advertising research tools are developed, the present methods of carefully defining specific advertising objectives, choosing media and messages to accomplish these objectives, testing the plans, and then evaluating the results of actual advertisements, seem to be most productive.

HOW TO AVOID UNFAIR ADVERTISING

Government agencies may say what is fair

In most countries the government takes an active role in deciding what kinds of advertising are allowable, fair and appropriate. For example, France and Japan limit the use of cartoon characters in advertising to children, and Sweden and Canada ban *any* advertising targeted directly at children. In Switzerland, an advertiser cannot use an actor to represent a consumer. New Zealand and Switzerland limit political advertisements on TV. In the United States, print advertisements must be identified so they are not confused with editorial matter; in other countries advertisements and editorial copy can be intermixed.

Most countries limit the number and length of commercials on broadcast media. Until recently, an Italian TV advertisement could be shown only 10 times a year.

What is seen as positioning in one country may be viewed as unfair or deceptive in another. For example, in many countries Pepsi advertises its cola as 'the choice of the new generation'. Japan's Fair Trade Committee does not allow it because right now Pepsi is not 'the choice'. Similarly, Hungary's Economic Competition Council fined Unilever $25 000 for running an advertisement that claimed that its OMO detergent removed stains better than ordinary detergent. The

Council said the advertisement was unfair because Hungarian consumers would interpret the phrase 'ordinary detergent' as a reference to a locally-produced detergent.

Differences in rules mean that a marketing manager may face very specific limits in different countries, and local experts may be required to ensure that a firm does not waste money developing advertising programmes that will never be shown, or which consumers will think are deceptive. In many cases the regulations require interpretation and some companies push the boundaries. While, for example, it may be illegal to target children, how does the advertiser or regulator determine whether or not an advertisement is doing so?

 ## What is unfair or deceptive is changing

What constitutes unfair and deceptive advertising is a difficult question and one marketing managers will have to wrestle with for years. Sometimes the law provides guidelines, but in most cases the marketing manager must make personal judgements as well. The social and political environment is changing worldwide. Practices considered acceptable some years ago are now considered deceptive or otherwise questionable.[26]

One company that fell foul of 'good taste' was Beamish and Crawford, an Irish drinks company that ran a poster advertisement for their Scrumpy Jack cider. It showed an apple with a teardrop and the caption saying: 'She was sweet, tender and juicy so we flattened her'. The Advertising Standards Authority for Ireland upheld complaints that the advertisement was offensive and appeared to condone violence against women. The company had argued, in defence, that apples are technically female and that many other people had enjoyed the humour of the advertisement. Nevertheless, the advertisement had to be withdrawn.[27]

Advertising sophistication

As advertising has developed over time, it has become a much more complex and sophisticated communication form. Knowledge has grown about marketing, markets and consumer behaviour. Nevertheless, it is impossible to fully appreciate the subtleties involved. The main reason for less than full understanding is, of course, that advertising is designed by people and directed to people. While some of the processes involved are known, many relating to how consumers process communication and develop meaning from messages are not well understood.

Just as advertising has developed, so too have consumers increased in sophistication. It is reckoned that by the age of 21, the average American has seen 800 000 advertisements and that is just on TV! This advertising-literate consumer is more aware that marketing messages are targeting him or her. As a consequence, audiences screen out many of these messages. Even those that are not screened out may be perceived in a very sceptical light because the advertiser is obviously an 'interested party'. Messages are not automatically credible when the source is an advertiser.

Because of the credibility issue, many marketers also use publicity as part of their promotional mix. With publicity, the credibility of the source of the message is greatly enhanced. This chapter will now explore publicity and public relations.

PUBLIC RELATIONS AND PUBLICITY

Public relations is a broad term that covers how an organization relates to and communicates with the various groups with whom it interacts. Public relations has also been described as the discipline responsible for the management of the corporate reputation. This section explores public relations and one of its main tools—publicity.

Public relations relates to the corporation and its publics

Public relations, usually referred to as PR, tends to relate to the organization as a whole rather than to a specific brand or product. Thus, while advertising and sales promotions emphasize the brand in a particular market, PR reflects the corporation. Essentially the objective is to build good relationships between the corporation and the groups with whom it comes into contact. Well-managed public relations help to present the organization in an attractive light and to foster goodwill. Unfortunately, PR is overlooked in many organizations until a problem emerges and then PR is expected to solve it—to make the best of a bad job.

Public relations is distinctive in the promotional mix in that it addresses a wider array of audiences than the other promotional mix elements. Usually advertising, sales promotions and personal selling are directed to buyers and those with buying influence. By contrast, PR communicates with many groups that have a bearing on the organization. These groups are called *publics* and they include customers, suppliers, distributors, employees, the financial community, shareholders, government, media, opinion formers and special interest groups.

All of these publics can facilitate and/or impede the organization in its operations. Publics form opinions about the organization—does it produce good-quality products, does it treat its suppliers and distributors fairly, is it a good employer, is it financially sound and a good investment, is it efficient and competitive, are its operations and products environmentally safe? Consider high-profile ventures such as Euro Tunnel and Disneyland Paris. Both have been the subject of media attention and the financial community has had a rather sceptical view of both projects, employees another view and customers yet another view.

It makes sense for an organization to cultivate its relationships with its public rather than just reacting to them. The media are a particular public that may be used to carry publicity about the organization and for this reason media relations are particularly important.

The tools of public relations

In order to build good relationships with its publics, the organization can use the tools of public relations. These include sponsorship, attending exhibitions, corporate communications, community activities, special events and publicity. It should be remembered that an organization could have very good public relations without any publicity. It is the case, however, that publicity is regarded as the most widely used of the PR tools. Many of the other tools are also used extensively by some companies. For example, the tobacco companies are quite restricted by legislation as to where they can advertise: they have therefore used sponsorship of sports events to present a positive image. In the main, the advantages and disadvantages of public relations apply to publicity and they are therefore considered under the publicity heading.

Publicity—part of PR and the promotional mix.

Publicity and public relations are part of the promotional mix of the company. As such, they need to be integrated with the other promotional elements. Integration is necessary to avoid sending conflicting messages but integration can also help to secure more impact. For example, some companies deliberately use controversial advertising in order to get media attention. Advertising-led PR has been used by Benetton, Calvin Klein, Gossard and other well-known companies. Such integration means that more coverage and impact is extracted from the advertising spend.

Publicity is any *unpaid* form of non-personal presentation of ideas, goods or services. One only has to take a quality newspaper to see that publicity is prevalent. The newspaper will carry stories about new products, innovations, personnel changes, financial activities and special events—anything that is newsworthy. Publicity is similar to advertising in that it uses the media to communicate with others. The difference lies in the fact that a media fee is charged for advertising but not for publicity. For this reason, publicity is sometimes called 'free advertising' but this is a little misleading. In order to secure publicity, other nonmedia expenses are incurred.

The advantages and disadvantages of PR and publicity

As with all promotion, the overall aim of publicity is to show the company and its products in an attractive light. Compared to other forms of promotion, public relations and publicity have some advantages and disadvantages. The main advantages relate to cost and credibility.

PR and publicity are relatively inexpensive. Costs are confined to the time and expertise required to write press releases, target the right media, deliver the material and handle any press enquiries. Publicity also enjoys higher credibility among its audience. Readers perceive the material to come from the editor and media journalists and therefore assume that it is more objective than advertising that sets out to sell something. Editorial coverage is thought to have a credibility factor of three or four times that of advertising. As consumers, we display less resistance to editorial messages than to advertising one.

The disadvantages of publicity concern the issue of control of the message. In some cases, the organization may prefer no publicity (especially if it is a 'bad news' item). In other cases, the organization may seek publicity in an effort to achieve specific objectives with specific publics. Meanwhile, the media wants stories that will interest readers and it is the editor who decides if and how a story is covered. The editorial decision may be at odds with what the organization wants. It is reckoned that up to 95 per cent of press releases get thrown out. This situation contrasts with advertising where the advertiser can dictate exactly how and where an advertisement is shown.

ADVERTISING-LED PUBLICITY

Advertising is an integral part of our lives and an embedded component of our cultures. Advertising is topical and, most importantly in media terms, advertising itself may also be newsworthy. Increasingly, the press cover stories about advertising, especially where the advertising features sex, celebrities or controversy. It is wrong to assume that publicity about controversial advertising is something that has happened accidentally, that somehow the advertising agency has misjudged public opinion. On the contrary, some advertising deliberately uses material that may shock or offend people. In doing so, they ensure that the advertising gets noticed by the audience. Given that we are subject to a massive quantity of promotional messages (1300 per day by one estimate) getting our attention as consumers is a major challenge. The more shocking the advertisement, the more likely it also is that the media will give editorial space to it.

Controversial advertising is designed to be attention seeking and to get publicity. Perhaps the best known of this genre is the Benetton advertising. The images captured by Benetton in-house photographer Oliviero Toscani include new-born babies, exploding cars, dying AIDS patients, nuns and priests, black and white men handcuffed together, and human hearts. These advertisements have gained a lot of public attention and publicity. However, this has not been positive. In Germany, Benetton retailers have sued the company, stating that the advertising has been so offensive that it has lost sales. In the UK, the advertisements have led the industry regulator—The Advertising Standards Authority—to strengthen its code of practice. This code covers offensive advertising in relation to religion, sex, sexual orientation and disability.

One company that has successfully used advertising-led publicity is lingerie company Gossard with its Wonderbra (brassiere) campaign in Britain and Ireland. Wonderbra developed a series of poster advertisements with the emphasis on the cleavage enhancing properties of the Wonderbra. The copy or text along with the poster used unsubtle straplines such as: 'Pleased to see me boys?' The poster campaign had a budget of £130 000 but it is reckoned that it generated media coverage that would have cost £4.4 million to buy. If one accepts that editorial is four times more credible than advertising, this means that the £130 000 campaign became £17.6 million worth of advertising! This is an example of an advertising campaign that had a very definite objective to secure media attention.

Companies are clearly tempted by the opportunity to stretch their advertising budgets further. They need to engage in the publicity-seeking business with caution. Bad publicity can irrevocably damage the brand and the company. The chairman of the largest high street jewellers in the United Kingdom described his company's products as 'crap' in a luncheon speech to a City audience. Despite a change of name for the company and his resignation, the company has not recovered from the damage of that flippant, but widely publicized, remark.[28]

Managing the image of the organization

It is worth remembering that an organization has an image in the mind of the various publics whether that image is actively managed or not. The image may be positive or negative, accurate or inaccurate when compared to the reality of the company. It is important that the company or organization understands the attitudes of the various publics to it. From there, the company can communicate more appropriately in order to ensure awareness and a corporate image that reflects reality. If an organization sends out conflicting messages the result is a confused image. This is another reason for the communications of the organization to be integrated.

Securing publicity

One of the main PR tools is publicity and within publicity the news or press release is the main form. Other forms include letters to the editor, feature stories and press conferences. To secure publicity, to make sure that the press release or news story is actually picked up by the media, it needs to be of interest to them. Editors need a constant supply of newsworthy stories for their publications. The press release has to be written for the interest of the editor and the reader. The issues that interest the reader and editor are not necessarily the same as company interests.

It is good practice to work with journalists—to employ them on a freelance basis— in preparing press releases. They do not necessarily see the organization as it sees itself. Journalists also have a feel for what makes a good story and how it should be written. Getting a good story and writing it well are only two of the tasks. The press release also needs to be targeted at the right people and at the right publications. Again the help of publicity professionals may be useful in this task.

The chances of getting the company press release published are enhanced by having a well-written, well-targeted, newsworthy story. Timing also plays a key role. If the press release lands on the editor's desk on a light day during which there is little news, it has more chance of being taken up than if there is a major news story breaking. The publicity process is facilitated if the company has generally good relations with the media.

Measuring publicity

Since publicity is something that should be *managed*, it follows that some measure of publicity is necessary. The easiest measure is *column inches*—how many columns of press coverage refer to the organization and/or its products or purpose. This is very much a quantity-based measure and gives no indication of whether the publicity was positive or negative. Indeed, with a negative story, lack of column inches would be a more appropriate measure! Both the quantity and the quality of publicity matter and both should therefore be monitored.

SUMMARY

An effective advertising campaign depends on using the 'best' available medium and the 'best' message considering: (1) promotion objectives, (2) the target markets and (3) the funds available for advertising.

Specific advertising objectives determine what kind of advertising to use—product or institutional. If product advertising is needed, then the particular type must be decided—pioneering, competitive (direct or indirect), or reminder. Advertising allowances and cooperative advertising may be helpful.

Many technical details are involved in mass communications, and advertising agencies handle many of these jobs. The advertising brief must develop specific objectives otherwise the advertising may have little direction and be almost impossible to evaluate.

Advertising, through effective communication, should ultimately affect sales by creating awareness, interest, desire and action. However, it is the whole marketing mix that affects sales and the results of advertising usually cannot be measured by sales changes alone.

Public relations and publicity are also promotional tools. They require integration with the other promotional variables to ensure that the organization presents a consistent identity. Integration also gives the opportunity for synergy or better impact by the promotional variables working together.

In many cases public relations and publicity relate more to the corporate level than the brand. They also are directed to a wider array of publics than customers and distributors. These publics can facilitate or impede the organization in its operations and purpose. Publicity is relatively inexpensive and has more credibility among its audience than advertising. However, publicity can be difficult to control because the decision to publish a story (or not) is taken by the editor, not the company.

It is important that public relations and publicity are managed. This means that the organization should monitor its image among the various publics and ensure that communications consistently reflect the reality of the organization. Press releases are one of the main tools of publicity. These need to be carefully prepared if they are to be taken up by the media.

QUESTIONS AND PROBLEMS

1. Identify the strategy decisions a marketing manager must make in the advertising area.

2. Discuss the relation of advertising objectives to marketing strategy planning and the kinds of advertising actually needed. Illustrate.

3. List several media that might be effective for reaching consumers in a developing nation with low per capita income and a high level of illiteracy. Briefly discuss the limitations and advantages of each media you suggest.

4. Give three examples where advertising to intermediaries might be necessary. What are the objective(s) of such advertising?

5. What does it mean to say that 'money is invested in advertising?' Is all advertising an investment? Illustrate.

6. Find advertisements to final consumers that illustrate the following types of advertising: (*a*) institutional, (*b*) pioneering, (*c*) competitive, (*d*) reminder. What objective(s) does each of these advertisements have? List the needs each advertisement appeals to.

7. Describe the type of media that might be most suitable for promoting: (*a*) tomato soup, (*b*) greeting cards, (*c*) a business component material, (*d*) playground equipment. Specify any assumptions necessary to obtain a definite answer.

8. Discuss the use of testimonials in advertising. Which of the four AIDA steps might testimonials accomplish? Are they suitable for all types of products? If not, for which types are they most suitable?

9. Find a magazine advertisement that you think does a particularly good job of communicating to the target audience. Would the advertisement communicate well to an audience in another country? Explain your thinking.

10. Johnson & Johnson sells its baby shampoo in many different countries. Do you think baby shampoo would be a good product for Johnson & Johnson to advertise with a single global message? Explain your thinking.

11. Discuss the future of smaller advertising agencies now that many of the largest are merging to form mega-agencies.

12. Does advertising cost too much? How can this be measured?

13. How would your local newspaper be affected if local supermarkets switched their weekly advertising and instead used a service that delivered weekly, free-standing advertisements directly to each home?

14. Is it unfair to advertise to children? Is it unfair to advertise to less educated or less experienced people of any age? Is it unfair to advertise for 'unnecessary' products? Is it unfair to criticize a competitor's product in an advertisement?

15. Discuss some ways that a firm can link its sales promotion activities to its advertising and personal selling efforts—so that all of its promotion efforts result in an integrated effort.

16. Take a copy of a quality newspaper and identify the stories in it that are publicity for organizations and their products or purpose. Evaluate whether they constitute good publicity or bad publicity.

17. Identify examples of publicity about advertising. Why have companies used advertising that is clearly controversial?

18. Using your university as an example, compile a list of typical items that it could use to generate newsworthy stories. What media would you target with these stories.

SUGGESTED CASE

11. Outdoor World

REFERENCES

1. 'How TWBA Direct is tackling the problem of Bordeaux Wine', *Campaign*, 7 June 1996, p. 30.
2. 'Advertising Expenditure in Western European Countries', The European Advertising and Media Forecast *in Retail Marketing Pocket Book 1998*, The Advertising Association with NTC Publications, Henley-on-Thames; 'International special report: Top global markets,' *Advertising Age International*, 21 March 1994, pp. I11–20.
3. 'Screen saver success is not what you do, it's how you do it', *Campaign*, 14 June 1996, p. 29.
4. 'Centraal Beheer revitalises financial ads', *Campaign*, 21 June 1996, p. 27.
5. 'Branding The island of Ireland', *Campaign*, 7 June 1996, p. 16.
6. T.E. Barry, 'Comparative advertising: What have we learned in two decades?', *Journal of Advertising Research*, March–April 1993, pp. 19–29; N. Donthu, 'Comparative advertising intensity', *Journal of Advertising Research*, November–December 1992, pp. 53–8; W.T. Neese and R.D. Taylor, 'Verbal Strategies for Indirect Comparative Advertising', *Journal of Advertising Research*, March–April 1994, pp. 56–69; S. Putrevu and K.R. Lord, 'Comparative and noncomparative advertising: Attitudinal effects under cognitive and affective involvement conditions', *Journal of Advertising*, June 1994, p. 77.
7. D. Hill, 'Can they stop us wearing silk cut socks?', *The Observer*, 20 July 1997, p. 5.
8. 'First ads for Glaxo Wellcome', *Campaign*, 7 June 1996, p. 7; J.K. Ross III, L.T. Patterson, and M.A. Stutts, 'Consumer perceptions of organizations that use cause-related marketing', *Journal of the Academy of Marketing Science*, Winter 1992, pp. 93–8.
9. 'Store owners rip into Benetton', *Advertising Age*, 6 February 1995, p. 1; 'Benetton, German Retailers squabble', *Advertising Age*, 6 February 1995, p. 46; 'Benetton brouhaha', *Advertising Age*, 17 February 1992, p. 62.
10. 'Klein jeans' sexy insert didn't spur sales', *The Wall Street Journal*, 5 May 1992, p. B1ff.; 'No sexy sales ads, please—we're Brits and Swedes', *Fortune*, 21 October 1991, p. 13; 'Why Jockey switched its ads from TV to print', *Business Week*, 26 July 1976, pp. 140–2.
11. 'Euro media and marketing survey fills info gap', *Campaign*, 26 April 1996, p 27.
12. 'Going for gold', *The Times Magazine*, 15 June 1996, pp. 18–25.
13. 'Smooth talk wins Gillette ad space in Iran', *Advertising Age International*, 27 April 1992, p. I-40; C.L. Bovee and W.F. Arens, *Contemporary Advertising*, pp. 671–2; J. Levine, 'Global lather,' *Forbes*, 5 February 1990, pp. 146, 148; A. Fahey, 'International ad effort to back Gillette Sensor', *Advertising Age*, 16 October 1989, p. 34; 'Multinationals tread softly while advertising in Iran', *Advertising Age International*, 8 November 1993, p. 121.
14. 'Bus hub caps', *Marketing*, 25 January, 1996, p. 9.
15. 'Levi's Invests In Getting Into The Market With A Surf-Friendly, World-Wide Site', *Campaign*, 23 February 1996, p. 32; 'Mars takes a walk on the wild side as Snickers gets wacky on the Net', *Campaign*, 19, April 1996, p. 34.
16. L. Pitt and R. Watson 'From surfer to buyer on the WWW: What marketing managers might want to know', *Journal of General Management*, vol. 22, no. 1 Autumn 1996, pp. 1–13; M. Anderson and J. Choobineh, 'Marketing on the Internet', *Information Strategy: The Executive's Journal*, Summer 1996, pp 22–9.
17. S. O'Donohoe, 'Advertising uses and gratifications', *European Journal of Marketing*, vol. 28, no. 8/9, pp. 52–75; M. Rogers and K.H. Smith, 'Public perceptions of subliminal advertising: Why practitioners shouldn't ignore this issue', *Journal of Advertising Research*, March–April 1993, pp. 10–18; K.T. Theus, 'Subliminal advertising and the psychology of processing unconscious stimuli:

A review of research,' *Psychology & Marketing*, May–June 1994, pp. 271–90.

18. A. Marcantonio, 'Guinness goes Italian?' *The Express*, 30 May 1998, p. 60.

19. F. Zandpour *et al.*, 'Global reach and local touch: Achieving cultural fitness in TV advertising', *Journal of Advertising Research*, September–October 1994, pp. 35–63; M.G. Harvey, 'A model to determine standardization of the advertising process in international markets', *Journal of Advertising Research*, July–August 1993, pp. 57–64; 'International special report: Global Media', *Advertising Age International*, 18 July 1994, pp. 111–16; A. Kanso, 'International advertising strategies: Global commitment to local vision', *Journal of Advertising Research*, January–February 1992, pp. 10–14.

20. 'Pizza Hut fattens up a European ad strategy', *Marketing*, 6 June 1996, p. 7.

21. A. Lee and B. Sternthal 'Putting copy-testers to the test', Mastering Marketing, *The Financial Times*, Supplement, 2 November 1998, pp. 6–8.

22. 'Contract of the decade up for grabs', *The Times*, 4 September 1996, p. 22.

23. 'Will ads be the key to winning the computer war?', *Campaign*, 7 June 1996, p. 14.

24. P. Nash, 'Advertising effectivness—The Holy Grail?' *in* T. Meenaghan and P. O'Sullivan, *Marketing Communications In Ireland*, Oak Tree Press, Dublin, 1996, ch. 29, pp. 567–84.

25. 'Behind the scenes at an American Express commercial', *Business Week*, 20 May 1985, pp. 84–88.

27. L. Jury , 'Illegal, indecent, dishonest, untruthful. How much has the message from Adland hanged?', *The Independent*, London, 17 July 1997, p. 3.

27. 'Cider Advert Dropped After Complaints', *Irish Times*, 19 June 1996, p. 3.

28. 'Nasty, brutish and short-lived', *The Sunday Times*, 29 January 1995, p. 10,18; 'Playing with fire', *Marketing*, 23 November 1995, pp. 47–49; 'Do they have to debase women to sell cars?', *Daily Mail*, 30 March 1993, p. 14.

CHAPTER 14
Personal Selling

When You Finish This Chapter, You Should

1 Understand the importance and nature of personal selling.

2 Know the three basic sales tasks—order getting, order taking and sales support and what the various kinds of salespeople can be expected to do.

3 Know what the sales manager must do, including selecting, training and organizing salespeople to carry out the personal selling job.

4 Understand how the right compensation plan can help motivate and control salespeople.

5 Understand when and where to use the three types of sales presentations.

6 Understand the important new terms (shown in colour).

HOUSE OF HARDY

All over the world there are people who love to fish and in the universal language of the sport, one name reigns supreme—that of Hardy. For over a century the House of Hardy has been renowned as the manufacturer of the finest game fishing tackle in the world. The brand name is synonymous with quality and excellence. Throughout its history the company has been responsible for advances in fishing tackle design.

Hardy products are sold in over 50 different countries and on every continent. The company has won design awards in Japan and is recognized as a very successful British exporter. The US marketing subsidiary is based in Evergreen, Colorado, the heart of American fishing country. In London, the House of Hardy's Pall Mall retail shop has been a mecca for fishing enthusiasts for over 100 years. Celebrities such as Eric Clapton, Nick Faldo and the late King Hussein of Jordan and members of the British royal family are all customers. House of Hardy staff regularly fish with these customers, and learn to appreciate the elite positioning of the brand and enhance their pride in the company.

During the 1980s, however, the company was, in dire circumstances. Sales were less than £3 million and production was down to a three-day week. Large batch sizes forced resentful dealers to keep excessively high stocks. There were over twenty packaging styles and there was little innovation in the product range. A turnaround programme was put in place. A museum was created at the factory to emphasize the historic credentials of the company. The retail distribution network was transformed with a dedicated marketing division for the company in the United States. Production systems were transformed to ensure greater responsiveness to demand, and greater effort was invested in new technologies. By 1997, sales had nearly doubled and the business had again achieved profitability.

One of the reasons for the successful turnaround was a dedication to understanding customers. House of Hardy salespeople are all previous customers of the business. The company owns fishing tackle shops in London and Perth. These provide the setting for product test marketing initiatives. More shops are planned for America, Paris, Tokyo and Osaka. The retail outlets host three seminars a year where customer perceptions can be gauged of the products, services, retail environment and pricing, as well as attitudes to competitors' offerings. Other retail outlets have an inventory commitment of at least £10 000 and, under the terms of their contract, House of Hardy products must be on display within the shop.

Representatives from all UK and European sales outlets are invited to attend a one and a half day conference every year. This includes presentations from the PR and advertising agencies on the coming year's strategy as well as a fashion show of House of Hardy leisure goods. Staff from the US headquarters attend an annual conference lasting five days. This includes time spent at the factory and fishing in rivers in Scotland and England. In addition, full-day product knowledge seminars are provided for the most enthusiastic customers. These events are customized for the clientele. They provide an opportunity to explain product differences to people who subsequently become sales ambassadors for the brand and offers a chance to sell the most expensive products.

Sharing and collecting marketing information is a hallmark of the revitalized House of Hardy. Sales figures are circulated to House of Hardy's 150 staff every day. The figures are broken down by product and geographical market. All wholly owned retail outlets are equipped with till-top sets that keep track of stock movements on a sale-by-sale basis. Other sales outlets are given incentives to also use the sets. The information gathered helps the company to keep track of sales patterns and emerging market trends, adjusting production schedules accordingly. The House of Hardy also receives inventory statements each month from dealers.

Retailers are offered support to sell House of Hardy products. They are given training in effective window dressing. At annual conferences they are encouraged to exchange information on best practice. Fishing tackle retailers typically pay 3.4 per cent commission on credit card sales. The House of Hardy discussed the issue directly with banks on behalf of retailers handling House of Hardy merchandise and by using collective bargaining power was able to reduce the commission to 1.5 per cent. Retailers' partnerships with the House of Hardy were also strengthened by the company helping to negotiate preferential rates on business and property insurance.

The US market has its own set-up. A national team of nine sales staff works exclusively on House of Hardy products to ensure total product knowledge. The Colorado base is much better than the original system, which used a warehouse in New Jersey, and an import agent (who went bankrupt). Product literature is produced exclusively for the American market, as there are differences in how Americans and Europeans cast for fish.

The company tends to focus on the opinions of the end user, rather than dealers and agents. Anglers from 16 different countries sit with distributors and sales agents. The fishing equipment manager spends half of his time coordinating input from different members on future rods, reels and other products. An example of the value put on feedback is how the company handled a query from Japan. A Japanese distributor identified the need for a new design of fishing rod to meet the needs of Japanese anglers. He was introduced to a production team of five who worked with him. Together they decided on the specification, design and production requirements of the new product. The entire process took just three hours and is testament to the company's dedication to innovation in response to the market.[1]

THE IMPORTANCE AND ROLE OF PERSONAL SELLING

Salespeople are communicators who build relationships

The job of reaching the marketplace is diverse. The House of Hardy case contains examples of many ways used by one company—distributors, agents, wholly owned retail outlets and direct sales staff. Promotion involves communicating with potential customers and sometimes personal selling is the best way to do it.

Almost every company can benefit from personal selling. While face-to-face with prospects, salespeople can be more effective than an advertisement or a display. They can adjust what they say or do to take into consideration culture and other behavioural influences on the customer. They can ask questions to find out about a customer's specific interests. They can also stay in tune with the prospect's feedback and adjust the presentation as they move along. If, when, the prospect is ready to buy, the salesperson is there to ask for the order. Afterwards, the salesperson is there to be certain that the customer is satisfied and that the relationship between the customer and firm continues to be mutually beneficial.

The salesperson is valuable to the company in *selling* its products. The salesperson is also of value in helping the customer to *buy* products. Too often, the salesperson is viewed as someone whose job it is to persuade a customer to buy. While this may be part of their job, in many cases their main task is to inform and advise customers. Consider trying to buy food, clothes, footwear, white goods, holidays, insurance or jewellery without the help of a salesperson. Likewise, the retailer needs help to buy in a suitable, timely assortment of merchandise to resell. Going further back into the supply chain, the producer or manufacturer needs the help of salespeople to buy equipment, materials and services. The salesperson should therefore be thought of as a vital part of the marketing system.

Personal selling requires strategy decisions

Marketing managers must decide how much, and what kind of, personal selling effort each marketing mix needs. As part of their strategy planning, they must determine the role of personal selling in the promotions mix. Thereafter they must specify (1) how many salespeople they need, (2) what kind of salespeople they need, (3) what kind of sales presentation to use, (4) how to select and train salespeople and (5) how to supervise and motivate them. The sales manager provides inputs into these strategy decisions. Once made, it is the sales manager's job to implement the personal selling part of a marketing strategy.

In this chapter, the importance and nature of personal selling are discussed as are the strategy decisions faced by sales and marketing managers. These strategy decisions are shown in Exhibit 14–1.

This chapter uses a number of frameworks and 'how-to' approaches that guide sales strategy decisions. Because these approaches apply equally to domestic and international markets, that distinction is not emphasized in this chapter. This does not mean, however, that personal selling techniques do not vary from one country to another. To the contrary, in dealing with *any* customer, the salesperson must be very sensitive to cultural influences and other factors that might affect the communication process. For example, a Japanese customer and an Arab customer might respond differently to subtle aspects of a salesperson's behaviour. The Arab customer might expect to be very close to a salesperson, perhaps only 70 centimetres away, while they talk. The Japanese customer might consider that distance rude. Similarly, what topics of discussion are considered sensitive, how messages are interpreted and which negotiating styles are used vary from one country to another. A salesperson must know

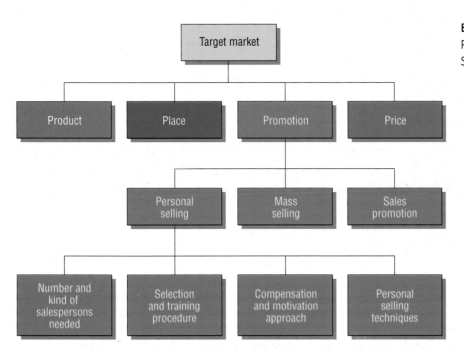

Exhibit 14–1 Strategy Planning for Personal Selling

295

how to communicate effectively with each customer, wherever and whoever that customer is. Those details are beyond the strategy planning focus of this text.[2]

Personal selling in the promotions mix

Personal selling is important in some promotion mixes and absolutely essential in others. Some feel that personal selling is the dynamic element that keeps the economy going. The salespeople bring in the orders that are essential to business survival and growth. Personal selling is often a company's largest single operating expense. This is another reason why it is important to understand the decisions in this area. Bad sales management decisions can be costly not only in lost sales, but also in actual out-of-pocket expenses.

The extent to which a promotions mix relies on the personal selling component, relative to the other promotional methods, is quite different between consumer markets and industrial markets. Research suggests that the promotions mix for industrial markets spends 70 per cent of the budget on personal selling compared to 32 per cent of the budget of consumer markets. Exhibit 14–2 shows the breakdown in spending.

Personal selling tends to be a major part of the promotions mix when one or more of the following conditions are present: there is high level of product complexity; the product is of significance to the buyer; other forms of communication would be relatively ineffective; and, where there is a 'push' element to the marketing strategy.

Even when a firm relies more heavily on personal selling it is still important that promotional efforts are integrated. Personal selling cannot work in isolation from other promotional methods. Advertising complements personal selling by creating awareness and interest that the salesperson can use as a basis from which to induce trial and purchase. Likewise, direct marketing can create leads for the salesperson to follow up. In other cases, the salesforce can be responsible for distributing sales promotion literature and merchandising material. All these situations reflect an integrated approach and benefit from the complementary role of each of the promotional variables.

	% of Marketing Budget	
	Consumer	Industrial
Advertising	25	3
Sales promotion	33	7
Other	10	20
Salesforce	32	70

Exhibit 14–2 Average Promotions Mix for Consumer and Industrial Markets[3]

Old-fashioned stereotypes vs. new professionals

You may think of personal selling in terms of an old-fashioned stereotype: someone with no more to offer than a funny story, a big expense account and an engaging grin. The modern salesforce is made up of professionals—problem solvers—who have something definite to contribute to their employers *and* their customers. As methods of doing business have changed, so has the selling function. Increasingly, businesses may be seen as part of cooperative networks, with suppliers and customers working in a close, possibly long-term, relationship. In these circumstances the salesperson has a strategic role as a manager of customers. This requires effective personal interaction and a perspective that views the customer's problem as the seller's problem.

The salesperson as representative

The salesperson may also be thought of, and is sometimes called, a 'representative'. They act as a representative of the whole company, responsible for explaining its total effort to target customers rather than just pushing products. The salesperson may provide information about products, explain and interpret company policies, negotiate prices or diagnose the technical problems that sometimes affect products.

The sales representative is often the only link between the firm and its customers, especially if the customers are far removed from the company's base. When a number of people from the firm are involved with the customer organization—which is increasingly common as more suppliers and customers form closer relationships—it is usually the sales representative who coordinates the relationship for his or her firm.

As this suggests, salespeople also represent their *customers* back inside their own firm. Recall that feedback is an essential part of both the communication process *and* the basic management process of planning, implementing and control. For example, the sales representative is likely to be the one to explain to the production manager why a customer is unhappy with product performance or quality—or to the physical distribution manager why slow dispatch causes problems.

Salesforce aids in market information function

The salesforce can aid in the marketing information function. The sales representative may be the first to hear about a new competitor or a competitor's new product or strategy. Sales representatives who are well attuned to customers' needs can be a key source of ideas for new products. In working with customers, understanding their problems and how they use products, the salesperson is at the cutting edge of marketing.

Salespeople can also be strategy planners

In effect, some salespeople are expected to be marketing managers in their own territories. Others become marketing managers by default because top management has not provided detailed strategy guidelines. Either way, salespeople may take the initiative to fill the gap. They may develop their own marketing mixes or even their own strategies. Some firms fail to give their salespeople a clear idea of their target customers. Although the salespeople are assigned a territory, they may have to start from scratch with strategy planning. The salesperson may have choices about (1) what potential customers to target, (2) which relationships to develop, (3) which particular products to emphasize, (4) which intermediaries to call on or to work with the hardest, (5) how to use promotion money and (6) how to adjust prices.

A salesperson who can devise profitable strategies, and implement them well, can be very successful. The opportunity is there for those prepared and willing to work. Even a starting job may offer great opportunities. Recently-appointed salespeople—especially those working for producers or wholesalers—are responsible for larger sales volumes than many small companies. Sales jobs are often viewed as entry-level positions and used to evaluate candidates for promotion. Success in this job can lead to rapid promotion to higher-level sales and marketing jobs.

WHAT KINDS OF PERSONAL SELLING ARE NEEDED?

If a firm has too few salespeople, or the wrong kind, important personal selling tasks may not be completed and money may be wasted. A sales manager needs to find a good balance—the right number and the right kind of salespeople. This balance may change over time with other changes in strategy or the market environment.

One of the difficulties of determining the right number and kind of salespeople is that every sales job is different. While an engineer or accountant can look forward to fairly specific duties, the salesperson's job changes constantly. However, there are three basic types of sales tasks. This gives a starting point for understanding what selling tasks need to be done and how many people are needed to do them.

Personal selling is divided into three tasks

The three **basic sales tasks** are order getting, order taking and supporting. These terms refer to their primary task—*although one person may do all three tasks in some situations.* Exhibit 14–3 shows these three forms of personal selling. It also depicts that producers, wholesalers and retailers can undertake the three forms. This chapter considers order getting, order taking and sales support.

As the names imply, order getters and order takers obtain orders for their company. Every marketing mix must have someone or some way to obtain orders. In contrast, supporting salespeople are not directly interested in orders. Their function is to help the order-oriented salespeople.

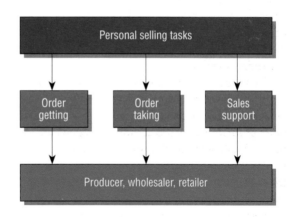

Exhibit 14–3 Personal Selling and the Channels of Distribution

SALES SITUATIONS

It is easy to underestimate the extent to which many everyday situations give rise to the need for selling activities. All the following situations involve selling in some guise.

- Your company is expanding its marketing effort to a new region. Retail outlets have yet to be recruited to carry your brand.

- A new office park is being built and your firm is competing to supply office furniture and equipment.
- Your event management business has just heard that the local Chamber of Commerce intends to hold a series of conferences to increase awareness of European Union initiatives.

- Legal changes mean that all restaurants have to install facilities for the disabled. Your firm specializes in sanitary-ware for the disabled but has previously only dealt in the institutional market.
- The camera given to you by your parents for your sixteenth birthday has been stolen. The latest 35 mm auto focus cameras seem the best replacement so you visit a few outlets to evaluate the alternatives available.

- A cheque has arrived in the post and you visit your bank branch to lodge it.
- The weekly grocery shopping is due so you go to the local supermarket, select your goods and go to the checkout.
- Your company has launched a new product in their range and it needs to be placed in retail outlets.
- As a wholesaler you supply the on-trade (pubs and restaurants) and off-trade (off-licences and liquor stores) with a range of spirits and wines. The deals

and bonuses change frequently and each outlet requires a sales visit each week.

- You are an enthusiastic runner but find that you have been suffering a little from sore shins. Someone at your athletics club suggests that this can be caused by wearing incorrect running shoes. You visit the sports shop and ask for advice.
- As a retailer you are attracted by the special price deal on a range of Mexican snack foods. You know that the range will be popular with your customers but just don't have time to rearrange the shelf displays to promote the range. You contact the wholesaler to see if it can help.

These situations all require a sales effort. The nature of the sales effort varies in each case though there are obviously similarities. In the first set of cases the salesperson is acting as an order getter, in the second set of cases the salesperson is an order taker, and, finally, the sales person is there to support the sale.

ORDER GETTERS—DEVELOP NEW BUSINESS RELATIONSHIPS

Order getters are concerned with establishing relationships with new customers and developing new business. **Order getting** means seeking possible buyers with a well-organized sales presentation designed to sell a product, service or idea. The emphasis here is on getting results—orders. A good order getter may appear very low-key if that is what the target customer seems to want. Order getters must know what they are talking about—not just be a personal contact. Order-getting salespeople work for producers, wholesalers and retailers and are normally are well paid.

Producers' order getters— find new opportunities

Producers of all kinds of products, especially business products, have a great need for order getters. They use order getters to locate new prospects, open new accounts, see new opportunities and help establish and build channel relationships. High-calibre order getters are essential to sell installations and accessory equipment where large sums are involved and where top-level management participates in the buying decision.

Top-level customers are more interested in ways to save or make more money than in technical details.

Good order getters cater for this interest. They help the customer to identify ways to solve problems, and then sell concepts, ideas and benefits, not just physical products. The goods and services they supply are merely the means of achieving the customer's end.

Order getters are also necessary to sell raw materials, components, supplies and services—but mainly for initial contacts. Since many competitors offer nearly the same product, the order getter's crucial selling job is to establish the relationship and get the company's name on the approved suppliers list. Keeping it there requires constant attention to the customer's needs and doing whatever is necessary to maintain a mutually beneficial relationship between the supplier and customer firms.

Order getters for professional services, and other products where service is a crucial element of the marketing mix, face a special challenge. The customer usually cannot inspect a service before deciding to buy. The order getter's communication and relationship with the customer may be the only basis on which to evaluate the quality of the supplier.

An order getter in business markets needs the know-how to help solve customers' problems. Often the order getter needs to understand a customer's whole business as well as technical details about the product and its applications. This is especially important for salespeople whose customers are producers. To have technically competent order getters, firms often give special training to university graduates. Such salespeople can then work intelligently with their specialist customers. In fact, they may be more technically competent in their narrow specialism than anyone they encounter—so they provide a unique service. For example, a salesperson for automated manufacturing equipment must understand everything about a prospect's production process as well as the technical details of converting to computer-controlled equipment.

One industry where product knowledge is absolutely crucial is the pharmaceutical industry. When Zantac 75 remedy for indigestion was launched as an over-the-counter medicine (no doctor's prescription necessary), Warner Wellcome sales staff had to wade through seven training manuals to present the product competently to pharmacists. To reduce the chore of learning, an e-mail game was designed to last throughout the five-week campaign. Product learning was reinforced by questions from world leader personae adopted for the game.[4]

Wholesalers' order getters—almost hand it to the customer

The sales representatives of merchant wholesalers who are progressive are developing into consultants and store advisors rather than just order takers. Such order getters may become retailers' partners in the job of moving goods from the wholesale warehouse through the retail store to consumers. These order getters almost become a part of the retailer's staff, helping to check stock, write orders, conduct demonstrations and plan advertising, special promotions and other retailing activities.

Agents often are order getters, particularly the more aggressive manufacturers' agents and brokers. They face the same tasks as producers' order getters. Unfortunately for them, once the order getting is done and the customers become established and loyal, producers may try to eliminate the agents and save money with their own order takers.

Retail order getters influence consumer behaviour

Convincing consumers about the value of products they have not seriously considered takes a high level of personal selling ability. Order getters for unsought products must help customers see how a new product can satisfy needs now being filled by something else. Early order getters for microwave ovens, for example, faced a tough job. They had to convince sceptical customers that this new kind of cooking was safe and that it would be more convenient than traditional approaches, once the customer got used to it. Without order getters, many of the products relied on today, ranging from mortgages to air-conditioners, might have died in the market introduction stage. The order getter helps to bring products out of the introduction stage into the market growth stage. Without sales and profits in the early stages, the product may fail and not be offered again.

Order getters are helpful for selling *heterogeneous* shopping products. Consumers shop for many of these items on the basis of price and quality. They welcome useful information. Cars, furniture and furnishings, cameras, jewellery and fashion items can be sold effectively by an enthusiastic, helpful order getter. Thoughtful advice, based on and understanding of the consumer and thorough knowledge of the product and its alternatives, may really help consumers and bring profits to the salesperson and retailer.

ORDER TAKERS—MAINTAIN AND NURTURE RELATIONSHIPS

Order takers sell to the regular or established customers, complete most sales transactions, and maintain relationships with their customers. After a customer becomes interested in a firm's products through an order getter or supporting salesperson or through advertising or sales promotion, an order taker usually answers any final questions and completes the sale. **Order taking** is the routine completion of sales made regularly to the target customers. The routine completion of sales usually requires ongoing follow-up with the customer to make certain that the customer is totally satisfied and to be certain that the relationship will continue in the future.

Sometimes sales managers or customers use the term *order taker* as a put-down when referring to salespeople who do not take any initiative. While a particular salesperson may perform poorly enough to justify criticism, it is a mistake to downgrade the function of order taking. Order taking is extremely important. Many firms lose sales just because no one ever asks for the order—and closes the sale. Moreover, the order taker's job is not just limited to placing orders. Even in business markets where customers place routine orders with computerized order systems and EDI, order takers do a variety of important jobs that are essential to the business relationship.

Producers' order takers—train, explain, and collaborate

Once industrial, wholesale or retail accounts are established, regular follow-up is necessary. Order takers work on improving the whole relationship with the customer, not just on completing a single transaction. Even if computers handle routine reorders, someone has to explain details, make adjustments, handle complaints, explain or negotiate new prices and terms, place sales promotion materials, and keep customers informed of new developments. Someone may have to train customers' employees to use machines or products. In sales to channels, someone may have to train wholesalers' or retailers' salespeople. All these activities are part of the order taker's job. A failure in meeting a customer's expectations on any of these activities might jeopardize the relationship and future sales.

Producers' order takers often have a regular route with many calls. To handle these calls well, they must have energy, persistence, enthusiasm and a friendly personality that wears well over time. They sometimes have to take the blame when something goes wrong with some other element of the marketing mix.

Firms sometimes use order-taking jobs to train potential order getters and managers. Such jobs give them an opportunity to meet key customers and to understand their needs better. And frequently they run into some order-getting opportunities. Order takers who are alert to order-getting opportunities can make the big difference in generating new sales. At most banks, tellers are basically order takers and service providers. When a customer comes in to make a deposit or cash a cheque, the teller provides the needed service and that is it. In contrast, some banks now encourage tellers to help get new business. Tellers are trained to ask customers if they have ever considered investing in one of the bank's special savings accounts, or if they would like to learn more about the bank's credit cards. They give the interested customers sales literature about the bank's various financial services and ask if the customer would like to speak with a customer service representative. This selling effort needs to be carefully managed otherwise customers will dislike being sold to every time they visit the branch.

Wholesalers' order takers—not getting orders but keeping them

While producers' order takers usually handle relatively few items, and sometimes even a single item, wholesalers' order takers may sell 125 000 items or more. Most wholesale order takers just sell out of their catalogue. They have so many items that they cannot possibly emphasize them all, except perhaps newer or more profitable items. There are just too many items to single any out for special attention. The order taker's strength is a wide assortment, rather than detailed knowledge of individual products.

The wholesale order taker's main job is to maintain close contact with customers, perhaps once a week, and fill any needs that develop. Sometimes such order takers almost become part of the organization of the producer or retailer customers they serve. Some retailers leave it to the salesperson to take inventory, and then write up the order. Obviously, this relationship of trust cannot be abused. After writing up the order, the order taker normally checks that the company fills the order promptly and accurately. The order taker also handles any adjustments or complaints and generally acts as a liaison between the company and its customers.

Such salespeople are usually the low-pressure type—friendly and easygoing. Usually these jobs are not as well paid as the order-getting variety but they attract many because they are not as taxing. They require relatively less travel, and there is little or no pressure to get new accounts. There can also be a social aspect with the salesperson sometimes becoming good friends with customers.

Retail order takers

Retail order takers play a vital role in a retailer's marketing mix. Customers expect prompt and friendly service. They will find a new place to shop—or to do their banking or have their car serviced—rather than deal with a salesperson who is rude or appears to be inconvenienced by having to complete a sale. Retail order takers should also have product knowledge, though with so many product lines this is not always easy.

It may require a special effort to motivate these staff. One company that made such an effort is Unipath. The company realized that pharmacy sales staff are often the first contact for women wanting to buy pregnancy tests. For such a product the advice given must be sensitive and accurate. Unipath had a database compiled of pharmacy assistants whom it could later target with an education programme about its products, using promotions to encourage them to enrol. A quarterly magazine was also developed containing articles about women's health issues, promotions, competitions and details about Unipath's diagnostic products. Pharmacy staff were encouraged to use its information to win prizes and compete to become Assistant of the Year.[4]

Unfortunately, order taking may be almost mechanical at the retail level—for example, at the supermarket checkout counter. Some retail salespeople are poor order takers because they are not paid much—often only the minimum wage. In any case, order taking at the retail level appears to be declining in quality. There may be fewer such jobs in the future as more marketers make adjustments in their mixes and turn to self-service selling. Checkout counters now have automated electronic scanning equipment that reads price codes directly from packages. Some supermarkets use systems where customers do their own scanning, and the salesperson simply accepts the money.

SUPPORTING SALESFORCE—INFORMS AND PROMOTES IN THE CHANNEL

Supporting salespeople help the order-oriented salespeople—but they do not try to get orders themselves. Their activities are aimed at enhancing the relationship with the customer and getting sales in the long run. For the short run, however, they are ambassadors of goodwill who may provide specialized services and information. Almost all supporting salespeople work for producers or intermediaries who do this supporting work for producers. There are two types of supporting salespeople: missionary salespeople and technical specialists.

Missionary salespeople can increase sales
Missionary salespeople are supporting salespeople who work for producers—calling on channel members and their customers. They try to develop goodwill and stimulate demand, help the intermediary to train their salespeople, and often take orders for delivery by the intermediary. Missionary salespeople are sometimes called *merchandisers* or *detailers*.

Producers who rely on merchant wholesalers to obtain widespread distribution often use missionary salespeople. The sales representative can give a promotion boost to a product that otherwise would not get much attention from the intermediaries because it is just one of many they sell. A missionary salesperson for Vicks' cold remedy products, for example, might visit pharmacies during the cold season and encourage them to use a special end-of-aisle display for Vicks' cough syrup—and then help to set it up. The wholesaler that supplies the store would benefit from any increased sales, but might not take the time to urge use of the special display.

An imaginative missionary salesperson can double or triple sales. Naturally, this doesn't go unnoticed. Missionary sales jobs are often a route to order-oriented jobs. In fact, this position is often used as a training ground for new salespeople. Recent graduates are often recruited for these positions.

Technical specialists are experts who know product applications
Technical specialists are supporting salespeople who provide technical assistance to order-oriented salespeople. Technical specialists usually are science or engineering graduates with the know-how to understand the customer's applications and explain the advantages of the company's product. They are usually more skilled in showing the technical details of their product than in trying to persuade customers to buy it. For example, Nike offer technical support to their sales efforts. The Nike technical specialist is called an 'ekin'—because they have to know the product backwards!

Before the specialist's visit, an order getter probably has stimulated interest. The technical specialist provides the details. The order getter usually completes the sale, but only after the customer's technical people give at least tentative approval.

Today many of the decision makers who influence organizational purchases have more technical knowledge than they did in the past. As a result, firms need more technical specialists. Many companies train their technical specialists in presentation skills to help them to be not only technically accurate, but also persuasive. Technical specialists who are also good communicators often become highly paid order getters.

Three tasks may have to be blended
A particular salesperson might be given two—or all three—of the selling tasks. Ten per cent of a particular job may be order getting, 80 per cent order taking, and the remaining 10 per cent supporting. Another company might have many different people handling the different sales tasks. This can lead to **team selling**—when different sales representatives work together on a specific account. Sometimes one or more of the 'sales representatives' on a team may not be from the sales department at all. If improving the relationship with the customer calls for technical support from the quality control manager, then that person becomes a part of the team, at least temporarily. Information technology companies such as Hewlett-Packard, IBM and Digital use team selling to provide customized solutions in hardware, software, technical support and so on. The team selling approach is costly and requires much coordination to be effective.[5]

Strategy planners need to specify what types of selling tasks the salesforce will handle. Once the tasks are specified, the sales manager needs to assign responsibility for individual sales jobs so that the tasks are completed and the personal selling objectives achieved.

Exhibitions—a specialized selling venue and task

Exhibitions and trade fairs represent a specialized venue for selling and a particular selling challenge. The advantages of exhibitions are that suppliers can meet and strengthen relationships with their customers. The audience at these events are tightly targeted, interested visitors. They may be from the trade and be buyers or in some way influential in the buying process. The exhibition also allows sales staff the opportunity to collect information on customers and competitors. Company and product image can be enhanced and staff morale boosted by exhibitions and trade shows.

As always with the promotions mix, exhibitions offer the opportunity for integration with other elements, to produce a more powerful impact. Knorr managed to mix a number of promotional elements to good effect. Research showed that its product—soup—

was perceived as 'boring' and that the most popular place to eat soup was as a starter in pubs. The company salesforce was not targeting pubs and was underperforming in this sector. The solution was to send publicans ideas for tasty soups. The company sent them free 'Soups of the World' packs containing a recipe guide, point-of-sale material and product samples. After this, the salesforce 'blitzed' a National Pub Trade Exhibition, and it carried out demonstrations and inserted advertisements in the trade press.[4]

While there many advantages to exhibiting, it is an expensive process—a small regional show can cost £2000-£50 000 to take part in, but the more prestigious exhibitions such as Cologne, Milan and Chicago can be as much as £250 000. The sales objectives and non-sales objectives need to be carefully specified before a company commits itself and its sales staff to such an expense. Sales staff need to be trained for attendance—some salespeople who are very effective in the field have difficulty adapting to the exhibition environment. Contacts made at the exhibition should be registered and followed up after the event.[6]

THE RIGHT STRUCTURE HELPS ASSIGN RESPONSIBILITY

A sales manager must organize the salesforce so that all the necessary tasks are done well. A large organization might have different salespeople specializing by different selling tasks *and* by the target markets they serve.

Different target markets need different selling tasks

The target market will influence the size and organization of the salesforce. Each target market will have a certain number of accounts, call frequency, geographic coverage and profitability. Sales managers often divide salesforce responsibilities based on the type of customer involved. For example, Bigelow—a company that makes quality carpet for homes and office buildings—divided its salesforce into two groups of specialists. Some Bigelow salespeople call only on architects to help them choose the best type of carpet for new office buildings. These representatives know all the technical details, such as how well a certain carpet fibre will wear or its effectiveness in reducing noise from office equipment. Often no selling is involved because the architect only suggests specifications and does not actually buy the carpet.

Other Bigelow salespeople call on retail carpet stores. These representatives identify stores that do not carry

Bigelow carpets—and work to establish a relationship and get that crucial first order. Once a store has bought, these representatives encourage the store manager to keep a variety of Bigelow carpets in stock. They also take orders, help to train the store's salespeople and try to solve any problems that occur.

Big accounts get special treatment

As industrial concentration has taken place and as purchasing has become centralized, there is greater likelihood that a few accounts may be of central importance to an organization. Very large customers require special selling effort and relationships with them are treated differently. These customers need to be very well serviced and the account well managed. The customer will expect high levels of expertise and professionalism. For example, a producer selling to a chain of supermarkets or department stores is likely to treat that chain as a key account and to dedicate a salesperson, or even a sales team, exclusively to it.

Telephone selling

Some firms have a group of salespeople who specialize in **telemarketing**—using the telephone to 'call' on customers or prospects. A 'phone call has many of the benefits of a personal visit—including the ability to modify the message as feedback is received. The big advantage of telemarketing is that it saves time and money. Telemarketing is especially useful when customers are small or in hard-to-reach places. Many firms are finding that a telemarketing salesforce can build profitable relationships with customers it might otherwise have to ignore altogether. Telemarketing is also important when many prospects have to be contacted to reach one actually interested in buying. In these situations, telemarketing may be the only economical approach. Telemarketing has grown in popularity. Large and small firms alike find that it allows them to extend their personal selling efforts to new target markets, and it increases the frequency of contact between the firm and its customers. Convenient incoming free telephone lines also make it fast and easy for customers to place orders or to get assistance. In the United Kingdom, the Automobile Association (AA) has found that customers prefer to buy car insurance and rescue cover using the Internet or telephone. The result is that the AA has closed their 142 high street shops.

Sales tasks are done in sales territories

Often companies organize selling tasks on the basis of a **sales territory**—a geographic area that is the responsibility of one salesperson or several working together. A territory might be a region of a country, a country, city or part of a city, depending on the market potential. Companies like Lockheed Aircraft Corporation often consider a whole country as *part* of a sales territory for one salesperson.

Carefully set territories can reduce travel time and the cost of sales calls. Assigning territories can also help reduce confusion about who has responsibility for a set of selling tasks. Consider the case of the Hyatt Hotel chain. Until recently, each hotel had its own salespeople to get bookings for big conferences and business meetings. That meant that professional associations and other prospects who had responsibility for selecting meeting locations might be called on by sales representatives from 20 or 30 different Hyatt hotels in different parts of the world. Now, the Hyatt central office divides up responsibility for working with specific accounts; one representative calls on an account and then tries to sell space in the Hyatt facility that best meets the customer's needs.

Sometimes simple geographic division is not straightforward. A company may have different products that require very different knowledge or selling skills, even if products sell in the same territory or to the same customer. For example, Du Pont makes special films for hospital X-ray departments as well as chemicals used in laboratory blood tests. A salesperson who can talk to a radiologist about the best film for a complex X-ray probably can't be expected to know everything about blood chemistry!

Size of the salesforce

Once the important selling tasks are specified and the responsibilities divided, the sales manager must decide how many salespeople are needed. This requires information and judgement. An increase in the number of sales staff will lead to an increase in revenue, but it also adds to costs. A number of factors need to be taken into the equation. These include the number of customers, sales potential of customers, their geographic concentration and the availability of financial resources. *How* the size of the salesforce is computed varies. Although software is available to help, the more basic methods are still popular.

The logic of the workload method is that to service the market requires a certain workload that can be divided evenly across sales staff. A number of tasks are involved:

- Customers are classified into categories according to their potential;
- the frequency and duration of sales calls for each category of account is determined; and
- the workload to service the market is calculated.
- The total time available per salesperson and the contact time per salesperson is computed; and,
- using these figures the requisite number of salespeople is determined.

The workload method can be quantitative, but it can also be based on the sales manager's educated guess about how many people are required in total. Clearly, it ought to be important to take account of the varying types of customers, profitability and sales territories.

Although the selling task can be translated into the number of visits each customer needs per week, month, quarter or year, this varies according to the industry concerned. One study found that the average number of sales calls made per week by a salesperson was 28—but in agriculture the call rate was 56 per week and in computers and information technology the average was 8 per week.[7]

Over time the right number of salespeople may change, as selling tasks change. Consideration of what type of salespeople and how many should be ongoing. If the salesforce needs to be reduced, it does not make sense to let a lot of people go all at once—especially when it could be avoided with some planning. Conversely, finding and training effective salespeople takes time and it is also an ongoing job.

INFORMATION TECHNOLOGY PROVIDES HELP

Software and hardware

Personal selling involves communication and, just like every other aspect of communication, rapid developments in information technology are having a profound impact on personal selling. The sales manager, with help from specialists in information technology, needs to decide what types of tool are needed and how they will be used.

The software available enables spreadsheet analysis, electronic presentations, time management, sales forecasting, customer contact and shelf-management. Hardware includes mobile telephones, fax machines, laptop computers, pagers and video-conferencing systems. These technologies enhance the sales representative's ability to meet customer needs and achieve the objectives of the job. They do not, however, change the basic nature of the job and the sales tasks that need to be accomplished.

SOUND SELECTION AND TRAINING TO BUILD A SALESFORCE

Selecting good salespeople takes judgement

Despite the importance of hiring *good, well-qualified* salespeople, the selection in many companies is a hit-or-miss affair, done without serious thought about exactly what kind of person the firm needs. Managers may hire friends and relations, or whoever is available—because they feel that the only qualifications for sales jobs are a friendly personality and nice appearance. This approach leads to poor sales—and costly salesforce turnover. Progressive companies are more careful. They constantly update a list of possible job candidates. They schedule candidates for multiple interviews with various executives, do thorough background checks and even use psychological tests. Although such techniques cannot guarantee success, a systematic approach based on several different inputs results in a better salesforce.

One problem in selecting salespeople is that two different sales jobs with identical titles may involve very different selling tasks—and require different skills. A carefully prepared job description helps to avoid this problem.

Job descriptions should be in writing and specific

A **job description** is a written statement of what a salesperson is expected to do. It might list 10 to 20 specific tasks—as well as routine prospecting and sales report writing. Each company must write its own job specifications. They should provide clear guidelines about what selling tasks the job involves. This is critical to determine the kind of salespeople who should be selected and later it provides a basis for seeing how they should be trained, how well they are performing, and how they should be paid.

Good salespeople are trained, not born

The idea that good salespeople are born may have some truth—but it is not the whole story. A *born* salesperson—if that term refers to an outgoing, enthusiastic kind of individual—may not do nearly as well when the going gets rough as a less extroverted person who has had solid, specialized training.

It is a good idea to talk to customers in order to find out what qualities they value in a salesperson. Generally, they will emphasize the importance of good product knowledge, especially for the manufacturing and processing industries. After that, personal qualities become important—honesty, reliability, courtesy, professionalism, punctuality and communication skills. A salesperson needs to be taught—about the company and its products, about giving effective sales presentations and about building strong relationships with the firm's customers. Firms often hire new salespeople and immediately send them out on the road, or the retail sales floor, with no grounding in the basic selling steps and no information about the product or the customer. They just get a price list and a pat on the back. This is totally inadequate.

All salespeople need some training

It is up to sales and marketing management to be sure that the salespeople know what they are supposed to do—and how to do it. A job description is helpful in telling them what they are expected to do, but showing them how to get the job done is harder, because people may be hired with different backgrounds, skills and levels of intelligence. Some trainees are hired with no knowledge of the company or its products—and little knowledge of selling. Others may come in with a lot of industry knowledge and much selling experience—including some bad habits developed at another company.

In other situations, salespeople may have some relevant selling experience but need to know more about the firm's customers and their needs. Even a firm's own sales veterans may get set in their ways and profit greatly by—and often welcome the chance for—additional training.

The kind of initial sales training should be modified based on the experience and skills of the group involved. The company's sales training programme should cover at least the following areas: (1) company policies and practices, (2) product information, (3) building relationships with customer firms and (4) professional selling skills.

Selling skills can be learned

Many companies spend the bulk of their training time on product information and company policy. They neglect training in selling techniques because they think selling is something anyone can do. More progressive companies know that training in selling skills can pay off. For example, training can help salespeople learn how to be more effective in cold calls on new prospects, in listening carefully to identify a customer's real objections and in closing the sale. Training can also help a salesperson to better analyse why present customers buy from the company, why

former customers now buy from competitors and why some prospects remain only prospects.

 Internet Excercise

The Motivating Tape Company sells various training videos. Go to the firm's web site at **www.achievement.com** and then scroll down and select Sales Training. Review the list of sales training videos. In terms of training for people just starting in a sales career, what areas are covered by the videos? What areas are not covered by the videos?

Training is ongoing

The duration of the initial training period depends on the job. Some training programmes go on for many months. For example, some new IBM sales representatives don't call on an account by themselves for the first six months or more. Some form of sales training should go on indefinitely. Many companies use weekly sales meetings or work sessions, annual or semiannual conventions or conferences, and regular newsletters, as well as normal sales supervision, to keep salespeople up to date.[8]

COMPENSATING AND MOTIVATING SALESPEOPLE

To recruit and retain good salespeople, a firm has to develop an attractive compensation plan designed to motivate. Ideally, sales representatives should be paid in such a way that what they want to do, for personal interest and gain, is also in the company's interest. Most companies focus on financial motivation, but public recognition, sales contests and simple personal recognition for a job well done can be highly effective in encouraging greater sales effort. The main emphasis here, however, will be on financial motivation.[9]

Two basic decisions must be made in developing a compensation plan: (1) the level of compensation and (2) the method of payment.

Compensation varies with job and needed skills

To attract good salespeople, a company must pay at least the going rate in the market for different kinds of salespeople. Order getters are paid more than order takers, for example. The job description explains the salesperson's role in the marketing mix. It should show whether the salesperson needs any special skills or has any special responsibilities that require higher pay levels. To be sure it can afford a specific type of salesperson, the company should estimate—when the job description is written—how valu-

able such a salesperson will be. A good order getter may be worth £30 000 to £70 000 to one company but only £10 000 to £20 000 to another—just because the second firm doesn't have enough to sell! In such a case, the second company should rethink its job specifications—or completely change its promotion plans—because the going rate for order getters is much higher than £10 000 a year.

If a job requires extensive travel, aggressive pioneering, or contacts with difficult customers, the remuneration may have to be higher. The salesperson's compensation level should compare—at least roughly—with the pay scale of the rest of the firm. Normally, salespeople earn more than the office or production force but less than top management.

Payment methods vary

Once a firm decides on the general level of compensation, it has to set the method of payment. There are three basic methods of payment: (1) *straight salary*, (2) *straight commission* or (3) a *combination plan*. Straight salary normally supplies the most security for the salesperson—and straight commission the most incentive. These two represent extremes. Most companies want to offer their salespeople some balance between incentive and security, so the most popular method of payment is a combination plan that includes some salary and some commission. Bonuses, profit sharing, pensions, stocks and shares, insurance, company car and expense accounts may also be included. Still, some blend of salary and commission provides the basis for most combination plans.

The appropriate method of payment is the one that optimizes the degree of control, incentive, flexibility, and simplicity. These issues are summarized in Exhibit 14-4.

Sales costs and sales investment

Bear in mind that the salesforce compensation, however it is organized, is an investment in the sales effort. It is also a very real and substantial cost. One Irish survey found that the total per annum cost of a field salesperson was £43 000, of which £18 000 was salary.[7] This represents a significant investment, deserving of sound management.

	Salary (%100)	Commission (100%)
Control	Control gained only through close supervision	Control gained through linking task and commission. Need to guard against unethical selling
Incentive	If link between effort and outcome not obvious (as with support sales staff), salary emphasis appropriate	Motivation comes where direct link between reward and effort
Flexibility	Straight salary gives same reward regardless of effort or results	Commission systems can be tailored to task and sales results
Simplicity	Straight salary is most simple for company and sales staff	Can be complex, especially where different commission levels apply for products/customers

Exhibit 14–4 Payment Methods and Associated Issues

SALESPEOPLE WORK SMARTER—WITH THEIR FINGERTIPS

Laptop computers help salespeople to work more efficiently, not just harder. Salespeople use computers in many different ways.

Without a laptop, it was impossible for a wholesaler's salespeople to master Cincinnati Milacron's product line. Now a computer asks a series of questions and then helps the salesperson figure out which of 65 000 grinding wheels and hundreds of cutting fluids to sell to each metal shop. After adding this system, Milacron doubled its market share—without adding new salespeople.

Laptops help to keep salespeople for London Fog clothing up to date when they are on the road calling on accounts. Early each morning before leaving the hotel, the sales representatives call into the company's central computer. It downloads to the laptops all the latest information about product availability, prices, customers' accounts and the like. Later in the day, when a customer has a question about product delivery, the sales representative can answer it instantly—without scheduling another appointment or even calling the home office.

Salespeople for Metropolitan Life Insurance company use laptops to help to analyse the financial implications of different customer investments. For example, when the manager of a pension fund wanted to see what would happen if she switched money from one investment to another, the salesperson used spreadsheet software on the laptop to do the analysis—on the spot. The customer was convinced, and the sales representative closed a £422 000 sale.

When Hewlett-Packard equipped a group of salespeople with laptops, the machines helped to improve communications and reduced the amount of time in meetings at the head office. As a result, salespeople were able to spend 27 per cent more time with customers—and sales rose by 10 per cent.

Results like these explain why the number of companies equipping their salespeople with laptops is growing so rapidly. Laptops that include built-in cellular phones that can send and receive faxes are attracting even more companies.[10]

Sales managers must plan, implement and control

There are no easy answers to the compensation problem. It is up to the sales manager—together with the marketing manager—to develop a good compensation plan. The sales manager's efforts must be coordinated with the whole marketing mix because personal selling objectives can be accomplished only if enough money is allocated for this job. Further, managers must regularly evaluate each salesperson's performance and ensure that all the necessary tasks are being done well. The compensation plan may have to be changed if remuneration and work are out of line. By evaluating performance, firms can also identify areas that need more attention, by the salesperson or management. In Chapter 19, the issue of controlling marketing activities is addressed.

PERSONAL SELLING TECHNIQUES—PROSPECTING AND PRESENTING

Sales training programmes stress the importance of training in selling techniques. The basic steps each salesperson should follow include prospecting and selecting target customers, planning sales presentations, making sales presentations and following up after the sale. Exhibit 14–5 shows these steps. The salesperson is just carrying out a planned communication process.

Prospecting—narrowing down to the right target

Although a marketing strategy should specify the segmenting dimensions for a target market, that does not mean that each target customer is individually identified! Narrowing the personal selling effort down to the right target requires constant, detailed analysis of markets and much prospecting. Basically, **prospecting**

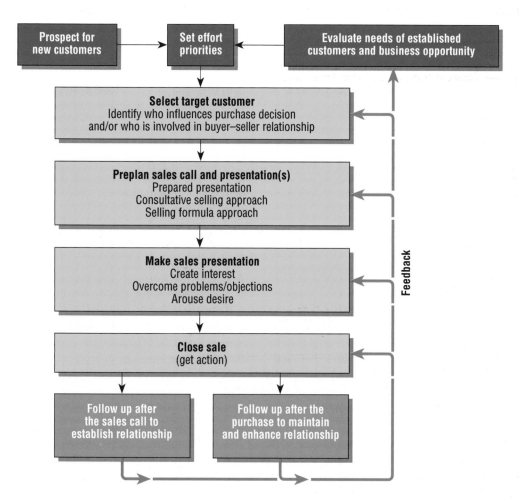

Exhibit 14–5 Key Steps in the Personal Selling Process

involves following all the leads in the target market to identify potential customers.

Finding prospects who will help to make the buying decision is not as easy as it sounds. In business markets, for example, the salesperson may need to do some detective work to find the real purchase decision makers. Multiple buying influence is common, and companies regularly rearrange their organization structures and buying responsibilities. Most salespeople use the telephone for much of their detective work. A phone call often saves the wasted expense of personal visits to prospects who are not interested—or it can provide much useful information for planning a follow-up sales visit. Keen prospects may even place an order over the phone.

Some companies provide prospect lists to make this part of the selling job easier. For example, one insurance company checks the local newspaper for marriage announcements—then a salesperson calls to see if the new couple is interested in finding out more about life insurance.

All customers are not equal

While prospecting focuses on identifying new customers, established customers also require attention. It is often time consuming and expensive to establish a relationship with a customer, so once established it makes sense to keep the relationship healthy. That requires the representative to routinely review active accounts, rethink customers' needs and reevaluate each customer's long-term business potential. Relationship-building skills are required. Some small accounts may have the potential to become big accounts, and some accounts that previously required a lot of costly attention may no longer warrant it. The sales representative may therefore need to set priorities both for new prospects and existing customers.

How long to spend with whom?

Once a set of possible prospects—and customers who need attention—have been identified, the salesperson must decide how much time to spend with each one. A sales representative must qualify prospects and existing accounts to see if they deserve more effort. The salesperson usually makes these decisions by weighing the potential sales volume as well as the likelihood of a sale. This requires judgement. Well-organized salespeople usually develop some system because they have too many demands on their time. They cannot wine and dine every prospect or customer.

Some firms provide their representatives with personal computers, and specially developed computer software, to help with this process. Most of them use some grading scheme. A sales representative might estimate how much each prospect or customer is likely to

purchase—and the probability of getting and keeping the business given the competition. The computer then combines this information and grades each prospect. Attractive accounts may be labelled A—and the salesperson may plan to call on them weekly until the sale is made, the relationship is in good shape or the customer is moved into a lower category. B customers might offer somewhat lower potential—and be called on monthly. C accounts might be called on only once a year—unless they happen to contact the salesperson. And D accounts might be transferred to a telemarketing group or even ignored—unless the customer takes the initiative.

Three kinds of sales presentations may be useful

Once the salesperson selects a target customer, it is necessary to plan for the sales call. This pre-call planning usually involves preparing a **sales presentation**—a salesperson's effort to make a sale or address a customer's problem. Which kind of sales presentation to make is a strategy decision. The kind of presentation should be decided before the sales representative goes calling. In situations where the customer comes to the salesperson, in a retail store for instance, planners have to make sure that prospects and customers are brought together with salespeople.

A marketing manager can choose two basically different approaches to making sales presentations: the prepared approach or the consultative selling approach. Another approach, the selling formula approach, is a combination of the two. Each of these has its place.

The prepared sales presentation

The **prepared sales presentation** approach uses a memorized presentation that is not adapted to each individual customer. A prepared (canned) presentation builds on the stimulus–response model. This model says that a customer faced with a particular stimulus will give the desired response—in this case, a yes answer to the salesperson's prepared statement, which includes a **close**, the salesperson's request for an order.

If one trial close does not work, the sales representative tries another prepared presentation—and attempts another closing. This can go on for some time—until the salesperson runs out of material or the customer either buys or decides to leave. Exhibit 14–6 shows the relative participation of the salesperson and customer in the prepared approach. Note that the salesperson does most of the talking.

In modern selling, firms commonly use the canned approach when the prospective sale is low in value and only a short presentation is practical. It is appropriate when salespeople are not very skilled. The company can control what they say and in what order. The canned approach is clearly very limited. It treats all potential customers alike. It may work for some and not for others and the salespeople probably will not know why or learn from experience. A prepared approach may be suitable for simple order taking, but it is no longer considered good selling for complicated situations.

Consultative selling—builds on the marketing concept

The **consultative selling approach** involves developing a good understanding of the individual customer's needs before trying to close the sale. This name is used because the salesperson is almost acting as a consultant to help identify and solve the customer's problem. With this approach, the sales representative makes some general benefit statements to get the customer's attention and interest. Then the salesperson asks questions and *listens carefully* to understand the customer's needs. The customer does most of the talking at this stage. Once they agree on needs, the seller tries to show the customer how the product fills those needs—and to close the sale. This is a problem-solving approach—in which the customer and salesperson work together to satisfy the customer's needs. That is why it is sometimes called the need-satisfaction approach. Exhibit 14–7 shows the participation of the customer and the salesperson during such a sales presentation.

The consultative selling approach is most useful if there are many subtle differences among the customers in one target market. In the extreme, each customer may be thought of as a separate target market—with the salesperson trying to adapt to each one's needs and attitudes. This kind of selling takes more skill—and time. The salesperson must be able to analyse what motivates a particular customer—and show how the company's offering would help the customer satisfy those needs. The salesperson may even conclude that the customer's problem is really better solved with someone else's product. That might result in one lost sale, but it also is likely to build real trust and more sales opportunities over the life of the relationship with the customer. As you might expect, this is the kind of selling that is typical in business markets when a salesperson already has established a close relationship with a customer. It also applies for some consumer products. The role of the person selling financial services or travel products has a strong consultative dimension.

Selling formula approach—some of both

The **selling formula approach** starts with a prepared presentation outline, much like the prepared approach, and leads the customer through some logical steps to a final close. The prepared steps are logical because it is assumed that the target customer's needs and attitudes are understood.

Exhibit 14–8 shows the selling formula approach. The salesperson does most of the talking at the beginning of the presentation to communicate key points early. This part of the presentation may even have been prepared as part of the marketing strategy. As the sales presentation moves along, however, the salesperson brings the customer into the discussion to help clarify just what needs this customer has. The salesperson's job is to discover the needs of a particular customer to know how to proceed. Once it is clear what kind of customer this is, the salesperson comes back to show how the product satisfies this specific customer's needs and to close the sale.

This approach can be useful for both order-getting and order-taking situations where potential customers are similar and firms must use relatively untrained salespeople. Some office equipment and computer producers use this approach. They know the kinds of situations their salespeople meet and roughly what they want them to say. Using this approach speeds training and makes the sales force productive sooner.

AIDA helps plan sales presentations

AIDA—Attention, Interest, Desire, Action: each sales presentation, except for some very simple canned types,

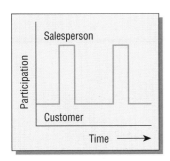

Exhibit 14–6 Prepared Approach to Sales Presentation

Exhibit 14–7 Consultative Selling Approach to Sales Presentation

Exhibit 14–8 Selling Formula Approach to Sales Presentation

may follow this AIDA sequence. The time a sales representative spends on each of the steps might vary depending on the situation and the selling approach being used. It is still necessary to begin a presentation by getting the prospect's *attention*, and hopefully, to move the customer to *action* through a close.

Each sales manager and salesperson needs to think about this sequence in deciding what sales approach to use and in evaluating a possible presentation. Does the presentation get the prospect's attention quickly? Will the presentation be interesting? Will the benefits be clear so that the prospect is moved to buy the product? Does the presentation consider likely objections and anticipate problems so the sales representative can act to close the sale when the time is right? Although these may seem like simple things, too frequently they are neglected and a sale is lost.

On the other hand, most sales representatives sooner or later face a sales situation in which they must make more difficult ethical decisions about how to balance company interests, customer interests and personal interests. Conflicts are less likely to arise if the firm's market-ing mix really meets the needs of its target market. Similarly, they are less likely to arise when the firm sees the value of developing a longer term relationship with the customer. Then, the salesperson is arranging a happy marriage. By contrast, ethical conflicts are more likely when the sales representative's personal outcomes (such as commission income) or the selling firm's profits hinge on making sales to customers whose needs are only partially met by the firm's offering. The question is: how close must the fit be between the firm's products and the customer's needs before it is appropriate for the sales-person to push for a sale?

Ethical issues may arise

As in every other area of marketing communications, ethical issues arise in the personal selling area. The most basic issue is simply whether a salesperson's presentation is honest and truthful. This is a straightforward issue. A company is not served well by a salesperson who lies or manipulates customers to get their business.

BAD SELLING IN THE UK FINANCIAL SERVICES SECTOR

Sometimes we buy certain products because we are obliged to, not because we want to. Many financial services purchases fall into this category. We buy financial services in order to satisfy the law, conduct the business of day-to-day living and have shelter now and security in the future. The products that satisfy these requirements are insurance, cheque accounts, mortgages and investments. The financial services industry in the UK has been the subject of much negative publicity over the eighties and nineties—it is the industry we love to hate!

The industry has undergone the process of de-regulation. This means that banks, building societies, insurance companies, intermediaries and the like are all competing against each other for the customer's business. From having been a sleepy industry with set boundaries and each of the players with their special-ist business, the financial service industry is coming to terms with the realities of an increasingly competitive marketplace.

Rising consumer demand has coincided with an increasing variety of financial products on offer. The problem is that these products can be quite complex. Under these circumstances it becomes very difficult for the potential customer to evaluate the options. How does one work out the price—set up fees, maintenance fees, commissions, charges and interest rates? Or, how does one establish the quality of the proposed purchase? Even after having bought the financial product, the customer may well have difficulty working out if it is good value, better or worse than any of the alternatives. Understandably, many customers buy on the basis of trusting the seller rather than a detailed appreciation of the product.

Given the complexity of financial products and the role of trust, the sales function in the financial services industry is critical. Unfortunately, unscrupulous practice and unethical selling have been widespread and have led to a lack of consumer confidence in the industry. Surveys show that as many as three-quarters of respondents are not confident that a financial sales-person would be totally honest. Customers believe that financial salespeople put their own interests ahead of the customer.

The high point of the negative publicity concerns 500 000 customers who were advised to opt out of occu-pational pension schemes to private pension plans. One investigation by the regulators reckoned that 83 per cent may have been wrongly advised! Salespeople encour-aged the sale of endowment plans. These have insurance policies associated with them and the seller earns a large commission for their sale.

As a result of such bad selling practices, the industry is now subject to new regulations. Financial services salespeople are now legally obliged to declare who they represent, to know their customers' needs, give best advise and to disclose fees and commissions. Companies are also obliged to ensure that their staff are trained and qualified to sell financial products.

This case illustrates the power of the customer, through publicity, to bring about change for the better. Financial service companies are learning that they must treat their customers as partners in a process.[11]

Ideally, companies can avoid the whole problem by supporting their salespeople with a marketing mix that really offers target customers unique benefits. However, marketing managers and salespeople alike should recognize that the ideal may not exist in every sales call. Top executives, marketing managers and sales managers set the tone for the ethical climate in which a salesperson operates. If they set impossible goals or project a 'do-what-you-need-to-do' attitude, a desperate salesperson may yield to the pressure of the moment. When a firm clearly advocates ethical selling behaviour, and makes it clear that manipulative selling techniques are not acceptable, the salesperson has a clear code of conduct by which to work.[12]

SUMMARY

Selling is not a question of getting rid of the product. In fact, a salesperson who is not given strategy guidelines may have to become the strategy planner for the market he or she serves. Ideally, however, the sales manager and marketing manager work together to set some strategy guidelines: the kind and number of salespersons needed, the kind of sales presentation desired, and selection, training and motivation approaches.

Three basic sales tasks were discussed: (1) order getting, (2) order taking and (3) supporting. Most sales jobs combine at least two of these three tasks. Once a firm specifies the important tasks, it can decide on the structure of its sales organization and the number of salespeople it needs. The nature of the job—and the level and method of compensation—also depend on the blend of these tasks. Firms should develop a job description for each sales job. This, in turn, provides guidelines for selecting, training, and compensating salespeople.

Once the marketing manager agrees to the basic plan and sets the budget, the sales manager must implement the plan—including directing and controlling the salesforce. This includes assigning sales territories and controlling performance. A sales manager is deeply involved with the basic management tasks of planning and control—as well as ongoing implementation of the personal selling effort.

Some basic selling techniques and three kinds of sales presentations were identified and reviewed. Each has its place—but the consultative selling approach seems best for higher-level sales jobs. In these kinds of jobs, personal selling is achieving a new, professional status because of the competence and level of personal responsibility required of the salesperson. The day of the old-time glad-hander is passing in favour of the specialist who is creative, industrious, persuasive, knowledgeable, highly trained—and therefore able to build a relationship with the buyer.

QUESTIONS AND PROBLEMS

1. What strategy decisions are needed in the personal selling area? Why should the marketing manager make these strategy decisions?

2. What kind of salesperson (or what blend of the basic sales tasks) is required to sell the following products? If there are several selling jobs in the channel for each product, indicate the kinds of salespeople required. Specify any assumptions necessary to give definite answers.
   a. Laundry detergent.
   b. Costume jewellery.
   c. Office furniture.
   d. Men's underwear.
   e. Mattresses.
   f. Corn.
   g. Life insurance.

3. Distinguish among the jobs of producers', wholesalers', and retailers' order-getting salespeople. If one order getter is needed, must all the salespeople in a channel be order getters? Illustrate.

4. Discuss the role of the manufacturers' agent in a marketing manager's promotion plans. What kind of salesperson is a manufacturers' agent? What type of compensation plan is used for a manufacturers' agent?

5. Discuss the future of the speciality shop if producers place greater emphasis on mass selling because of the inadequacy of retail order taking.

6. Compare and contrast missionary salespeople and technical specialists.

7. How would a straight commission plan provide flexibility in the sale of a line of women's clothing products that continually vary in profitability?

8. Explain how a compensation plan could be developed to provide incentives for experienced salespeople and yet make some provision for trainees who have not yet learned the job.

9. Cite an actual local example of each of the three kinds of sales presentations discussed in the chapter. Explain for each situation whether a different type of presentation would have been better.

10. Describe a consultative selling sales presentation that you experienced recently. How could it have been improved by fuller use of the AIDA framework?

11. How would our economy operate if personal salespeople were outlawed? Could the economy work? If so, how? If not, what is the minimum personal selling effort necessary? Could this minimum personal selling effort be controlled by law?

SUGGESTED CASE

12. Furniture To Go

REFERENCES

1. House of Hardy brochures 1998; *Sunday Times Enterprise Network*.

2. A. Zoltners, 'Creating a sales force to be reckoned with: 'Mastering marketing', *The Financial Times*, 2 November 1998, pp. 2–3; M. Besson, D. Rouzies and M. Segalla (1997) 'Cultural typology and managers' preferences: A European study of sales force compensation structure in the banking sector' in D. Arnott *et al.* (eds), *Marketing: Progress, Prospects and Perspectives*, Proceedings of 26th EMAC Conference, Warwick, 1997, pp. 1464–70; P. A. Herbig and H. E. Kramer, 'Do's and don'ts

of cross-cultural negotiations', *Industrial Marketing Management*, November 1992, pp. 287–98; J.S. Hill and R.R. Still, 'Organizing the overseas sales force—How multinationals do it', *Journal of Personal Selling and Sales Management*, Spring 1990, pp. 57–66.

3. 'Average promotions mix for consumer and industrial markets', PIMS Newsletter no. 50, quoted in P.R. Smith, *Marketing Communications – An Integrated Approach*, Kogan Page, London, 1993.

4. 'Trade promotions', Sales Promotions Supplement, *Marketing*, 9 May 1996, p. xv.

5. S. J. Puri and P. Korgaonkar, 'Couple the buying and selling teams', *Industrial Marketing Management*, vol. 20, no. 4, 1991, pp. 311–18; 'P&G rolls out retailer sales teams', *Advertising Age*, 21 May 1990, p. 18; F.C. Cespedes, S.X. Doyle and R.J. Freedman, 'Teamwork for today's selling', *Harvard Business Review*, March–April, 1989, pp. 44–59; M.A. Moon and G.M. Armstrong, 'Selling teams: A conceptual framework and research agenda', *Journal of Personal Selling & Sales Management*, Winter 1994, pp. 17–30.

6. R. Pfeiffer *et al.*, 'A comparative survey of trade fairs in UK and Germany in three industry sectors' *in* D. Arnott *et al.* (eds), Marketing: *Progress, Prospects and Perspectives*, Proceedings of 26th EMAC Conference, Warwick, 1997, pp. 1934–43; D. Bello, 'Improving trade show effectiveness by analysing attendees', *Industrial Marketing Management*, vol. 22, pp. 311–18; P. Herbig, B. O'Hara and F. Palumbo, 'Measuring trade show effectiveness: An effective exercise', *Industrial Marketing Management*, vol. 23, pp. 165–70; D. Shipley and K. Wong, 'Exhibiting Strategy and Implementation', *International Journal of Advertising*, vol. 12, pp. 117–30; D. Shipley, 'Exhibiting planning and practice', *in* T. Meenaghan and P. O'Sullivan (eds), *Marketing Communications in Ireland*, Oak Tree Press, Dublin, 1996, Ch. 26, pp. 516–31.

7. S. de Burca and M. Lambkin, 'Sales force management in Ireland', *in* M. Lambkin and T. Meenaghan (eds) *Perspectives on Marketing Management in Ireland*, Oak Tree Press, Dublin, 1994, Ch. 19, pp. 295–317.

8. E.D. Honeycutt, Jr., J.B. Ford and J.F. Tanner, Jr., 'Who trains salespeople? The role of sales train-ers and sales managers', *Industrial Marketing Management*, February 1994, pp. 65–70; R.C. Eriffmeyer, K.R. Russ and J.F. Hair, Jr., 'Traditional and high-tech sales training methods', *Industrial Marketing Management*, May 1992, pp. 125–32.

9. R. Darmon, 'Optimal quota-reward plans for sales force motivation and satisfaction measure-ment' *in* D. Arnott *et al.* (eds), *Marketing: Progress, Prospects and Perspectives*, Proceedings of 26th EMAC Conference, Warwick, 1997, pp. 329–41; B.S. O'Hara, J.S. Boles and M.W. Johnston, 'The influence of personal vari-ables on salesperson selling orientation', *Journal of Personal Selling and Sales Management*, Winter 1991, pp. 61–8.

10. 'Companies sold on the latest technology for the sales force,' *Chicago Tribune*, 8 November 1992, Sect. 19, p. 5; 'New software is helping reps fill custom orders without glitches', *The Wall Street Journal*, 11 August 1992, p. B6; 'Salespeople on road use laptops to keep in touch,' *The Wall Street Journal*, 25 April 1991, p. B1; 'If only Willy Loman had used a laptop,' *Business Week*, 12 October 1987, p. 137.

11. M. Bennett, 'Money Matters', *Marketing Business*, January–February, 1994–95, pp. 12–16; N. Gardner (1997) 'Get tough with pension rogues, Labour urged', *The Sunday Times*, Money section, p. 1; C. Merrell, 'Simple, low cost plans come too late for victims of an industry's abuses', *The Times*, 16 July 1997, p. 29; M. Woolf (1997) 'Number of complaints hits new record high', *The Observer*, Business section, p. 1.

12. For more on selling and ethics, see J.B. Deconinck, 'How sales managers control unethical sales force behavior', *Journal of Business Ethics*, October 1992, pp. 789–98; R.W. Clark and A. Darnell Lattal, 'The ethics of sales: Finding an appropriate balance', *Business Horizons*, July–August 1993, pp. 66–9; A.J. Dubinsky, M.A. Jolson, M. Kotabe and C. Un Lim, 'A cross-national investigation of indus-trial salespeople's ethical perceptions', *Journal of International Business Studies*, Winter 1991, pp. 651–70; A. Singhapakdi and S.J. Vitell, 'Analyzing the ethical decision making of sales professionals', *Journal of Personal Selling and Sales Management*, Fall 1991, pp. 1–12.

CHAPTER 15
Sales Promotion and Direct Marketing

When You Finish This Chapter, You Should

1 Understand the importance and nature of sales promotion.

2 Know the advantages and limitations of different types of sales promotion.

3 Understand the nature of direct marketing and its distinguishing characteristics.

4 Have an appreciation of the development of direct marketing and its role in the promotional mix.

5 Know the importance of customer data for effectiveness in direct marketing.

6 Understand the important new terms (shown in colour).

COTTON COUNCIL INTERNATIONAL

Cotton Council International (CCI) is an organization funded by the US cotton industry. The industry is made up of many different sectors from cotton growers to ginners, warehousers, oilseed crushers, textile mills and merchants. In Europe, well-known brands such as Lee and Wrangler jeans, Fruit of the Loom T-shirts, Russell Athletic Sportswear, Schiesser underwear, Bossi and 'Fleuresse' bed linen as well as Pringle of Scotland and Bensimon clothing have used the COTTON USA Mark to identify their pure cotton products to consumers.

Part of CCI's task is to stimulate and develop demand for US cotton. Europe represents a large market for cotton-based products with the world's highest concentration of affluent consumers—ideal textile consumers—and is therefore a target for CCI promotions.

For Spring 1996, CCI dedicated $1.5 million to its European marketing programme, the overall objective being to build awareness and appreciation of the COTTON USA Mark and to strengthen its quality position. To this end, advertising was placed in the trade press and consumer press and, in particular, in women's magazines.

The 1996 initiative illustrates the integrative and complementary role of sales promotions. CCI designed a retail promotion for COTTON USA featuring a consumer competition. The objective was to help build retail traffic and increase sales of COTTON USA licensee's labelled merchandise in Germany, Italy and the United Kingdom. Purchasers of a COTTON USA labelled product (such as Fruit of the Loom T-shirt or Pringle of Scotland knitwear) were eligible to enter a competition draw. The grand prize in each country was a limited edition COTTON USA VW Golf car.

The competition was promoted through point-of-sale merchandising display units, supplied free by CCI to licensees for distribution throughout their retail network. The unit drew attention to the promotion, contained entry forms and had space for the licensee to add their brand name. A consumer advertising campaign preceded the competition, relying heavily on European women's magazines such as *Elle*, *Marie-Claire*, *Cosmopolitan*, *Freunden* (Germany), *Vogue Italia*, *Amica*, *Anna* (Italy) and *Biba* (France).

CCI have therefore used both advertising and sales promotion in order to encourage sales of other organizations' goods by retailers to the final consumer. Demand for branded cotton goods is being used to stimulate demand for the primary product—cotton. This helps CCI to fulfil their mission to represent the interests of the US cotton industry.[1]

SALES PROMOTION—STIMULATING CHANGE

The nature of sales promotion

Sales promotion refers to those promotion activities that stimulate interest, trial or purchase by final customers or others in the channel by offering added value, usually on a temporary basis. Exhibit 15–1 shows examples of typical sales promotions targeted at final customers, channel members or a firm's own employees. Sales promotions are sometimes referred to as non-media activity or as 'below-the-line' activity. This differentiates sales promotions from advertising and publicity and also includes them as part of the overall promotions mix.

Sales promotions are generally used to complement the other promotion methods. While advertising campaigns and salesforce strategy decisions tend to have longer term effects, a particular sales promotion activity usually lasts for only a limited time period. Sales promotion can often be implemented quickly—and get sales results sooner than advertising. Further, sales promotion objectives usually focus on prompting some short-term action. For an intermediary, such an action might be a decision to stock a product, provide a special display space, to pay an invoice early, or give the product special emphasis in selling efforts to final customers. For a consumer, the desired action might be to try a new product, switch from another brand, buy more of a product, or perhaps buy earlier than would otherwise be the case. The desired action by an employee might be a special effort to satisfy customers or more emphasis on selling a certain product.

Because of the immediate nature of the impact, sales promotions have, in the past, been thought of as merely *tactical*. This view is changing and the strategic role of sales promotions and their integral role in the promotional mix are being recognized. One only has to consider how sales promotions can be used effectively throughout the product life cycle to appreciate the strategic role of sales promotion. This is discussed a little later in the chapter.

Sales promotion spending is growing

Sales promotion involves so many different types of activity that it is difficult to estimate accurately how much is spent on them in total. There is general consensus, however, that the total spending on sales promotion now exceeds spending on advertising. This is a new balance of expenditure. It used to be the case that the bulk of the promotional budget was allocated to advertising.

Spending on sales promotion has grown rapidly. Companies that sell frequently purchased consumer products—especially staples such as food products, health and beauty aids, and household cleaning products—have been the source of much of that increased spending. There are several reasons why these firms have been shifting their promotion mixes to put more emphasis on sales promotion.

One basic reason for increased use of sales promotion by consumer products firms is that they are generally competing in mature markets. There is only so much soap, cereal and deodorant that consumers want to buy—regardless of how many different brands there are vying for their attention and money. There is also only so much shelf space that retailers will allocate to a particular product category.

The competitive situation is intensified by the growth of large, powerful retail chains. They have put more emphasis on their own dealer brands and have also demanded more sales promotion support for the manufacturer brands they do carry. Perhaps in part because of this competition, many consumers have become more price sensitive. Many sales promotions have the effect of lowering the prices consumers pay. So sales promotion has been effective as a tool to overcome consumer price resistance.

Aimed at final consumers or users	Aimed at middlemen	Aimed at company's own sales force
Contests	Price deals	Contests
Coupons	Promotion allowances	Bonuses
Aisle displays	Sales contests	Meetings
Samples	Calendars	Portfolios
Trade shows	Gifts	Displays
Point-of-sale materials	Trade shows	Sales aids
Banners and streamers	Meetings	Training materials
Loyalty points	Catalogues	
Sponsored events	Merchandising aids	

Exhibit 15–1 Examples of Sales Promotion Activities

Traditional view	Current view	Future direction of sales promotion
• Techniques driven	• Greater integration with other communication elements	• Sales promotion has a strategic role in data capture and transactional data management
• Instant results-sales	• More strategic orientation with longer lead time in developing campaigns and a broadening of the view of the role of SP in brand and product management	• Sales promotions becoming more addressable as part of the marketer's ongoing dialogue with the consumer
• Tactical with short lead time and evaluation only in terms of sales	• Sales promotion follows the lead of advertising—extends and develops the themes created by advertising campaign • Greater spend on sales promotions as proportion of the overall communications budget	• Greater involvement of senior management in the sales promotion • Brand value benefits not just sales and short-term stocking objectives
• Delegated to most junior marketing staff	• Powerful retailers dictating and managing sales promotion and consumer data	• Sales promotion becoming more sophisticated, controlled and accountable
• Reactive to market conditions	• Clients expect strategic input from their agencies	• Continuing integration of marketing communication methods, particularly sales promotion and direct marketing

Exhibit 15–2 Changing Views of Sales Promotion[2]

Changes in technology have also made sales promotion more efficient. For example, with scanners at retail checkout counters, it is possible to instantly pinpoint a customer who is the target for a particular coupon. If a customer buys a bottle of Kraft salad dressing, Kraft can have the retailer's computerized cash register print out a coupon—on the spot—to encourage the customer to buy Kraft again the next time. Alternatively, a competitor might target that customer with a coupon to encourage brand switching.

Because the impact and effect of sales promotions is more easily measured, marketers can more easily justify such expenditure. Sales promotions can therefore attract resources that long-term efforts may not. The growth of sales promotion has also been fostered by the availability of more consultants, advertising agencies and specialists who help plan and implement sales promotion programmes. Ultimately, the basic reason for the growth of spending on sales promotion is that it now understood can be a very effective marketing activity.

Changing views of sales promotion

As the use of sales promotions has increased, marketers have changed their view of its role. Where sales promotions used to be thought of as purely short-term tactics, they now are perceived as part of the integrated marketing communications, discussed in Chapter 12. Indeed, as technology increases the ability to tailor and target sales promotions, their role in the promotions mix and overall marketing strategy will further evolve. These changing views of sales promotion are represented in Exhibit 15–2. There are, however, particular management challenges in the sales promotion area.

CHALLENGES IN MANAGING SALES PROMOTION

Does sales promotion erode brand loyalty?

Some experts think that marketing managers—especially those who deal with consumer package goods—put too much emphasis on sales promotions. They argue that the effect of most sales promotion is temporary and that money spent on advertising and personal selling helps the firm more over the long term. Their view is that most sales promotions do not help develop close relationships with consumers and instead erode brand loyalty.

There *is* heavy use of sales promotion in mature markets where competition for customers and attention from channel members is fierce. Moreover, if the total market is not growing, sales promotions may just encourage 'deal-prone' customers (and intermediaries) to switch back and forth among brands. Here, all the expense of the sales promotions and the swapping around of customers simply contributes to lower profits for everyone. It also increases the prices that consumers pay because it increases selling costs—and ultimately it is consumers who pay for those selling costs.

However, it is important to see that once a marketing manager is in this situation there may be little choice other than to continue. At the mature stage of the product life cycle, frequent sales promotions may be needed just to offset the effects of competitors' promotions. The only escape from this competitive rat race is for the marketing manager to seek new opportunities—with a strategy that does not rely solely on short-term sales promotions for competitive advantage.

There are alternatives

Firms are also experimenting with other approaches. For example, some reimburse intermediaries for promotion effort in proportion to their sales to final consumers. Thus, their focus is on supporting those intermediaries who actually increase sales to final consumers—which can be quite different to just directing sales promotion expenditure to intermediaries who simply make the product available. Making the product available is a means to an end, but if making it available—without producing sales—is all that is accomplished, the sales promotion effort does not make sense.[3]

Costly mistakes

Sales promotions require careful management of all the details so as to avoid making costly mistakes. Because sales promotion includes a wide variety of activities, each of which may be custom-designed and used only once, a wide range of skills is required. Mistakes caused by lack of experience can be very costly. One promotion sponsored by Hoover proved to be a disaster. The promotion offered free flights with the purchase of a Hoover appliance. Although Hoover was able to bulk buy flights at a discount, the value of the promotion was much greater than the value of the purchase. Very few restrictions were placed on the promotion so that those who bought even the cheapest Hoover appliance were eligible to enter. Retailers were in the position of pre-selling the goods before they had even arrived in the store. When consumer demand was extremely high, the company realized that it had a very expensive promotion on its hands. Consumers who did not receive their flights have successfully sued Hoover. The bill is well over £50 million and continues to rise as the Hoover Holiday Pressure Group pursues the company. Untold damage has also been wreaked on the brand. The promotion has become a notorious marketing mistake.[4]

Not a sideline for amateurs

Sales promotion mistakes are likely to be worse when a company has no sales promotion adviser. If the personal selling or advertising managers are responsible for sales promotion, they often treat it as a 'stepchild'. They allocate money to sales promotion if there is any 'left over', or if a crisis develops. Many companies, even some large ones, do not have a separate budget for sales promotion or even know what it costs in total.

Making sales promotion work is a learned skill, not a sideline for amateurs. That is why specialists in sales promotion have developed, both inside larger firms and as outside consultants. Although these people are experts, and are willing to take over the whole sales promotion job it is still the marketing manager's responsibility to set sales promotion objectives and policies that will fit in with the rest of each marketing strategy.

Planning, implementing and controlling a sales promotion

As stated earlier, sales promotions should not be run as an *ad hoc* activity but should be planned, implemented and controlled as part of the marketing strategy for the brand. Each sales promotion should be designed to achieve specific, quantified, time-bound objectives. Setting these objectives is the first task in managing the sales promotion.

Whether using an agency or running its own sales promotion, the company needs to establish a budget to cover all costs. Costs are incurred for artwork, copy, print, prizes/gifts, personnel, agency fees, post and packaging, and merchandising, plus the consequent costs that arise in the other marketing mix elements. These include product costs, promotional packaging, price discounts and advertising/PR support. Costs can be manipulated by using alternatives such as different prizes or reducing/increasing the coverage of the sales promotion (geographically, or through the number of intermediaries involved).

One of the attractive features of sales promotion is that the impact or effect can be more easily measured than that of advertising or public relations. An effective sales promotion is one that achieves the objectives set for it, within budget. Basic data relate to the number of respondents, redemption rates and increased sales. More in-depth analysis of effectiveness requires measures of trade-distribution changes, cost/benefit analysis and rate-of-sale changes. These measures help to control the particular sales promotion and to assess what worked or did not work well. In addition, this information is useful for the planning of future sales promotions.

SALES PROMOTION IN AN INTERNATIONAL CONTEXT

International dimensions may also have a significant impact on sales promotion alternatives. For example, in countries with a large number of very small retailers some types of trade promotion are difficult, or even impossible, to manage. A typical Japanese grocery retailer with only 19 square metres of space, for example, does not have room for *any* special end-of-aisle displays. Consumer promotions may be affected too. Polish consumers, for example, are sceptical about product samples; they do not have a lot of experience with sampling and they figure that if it is free something's amiss. In some developing nations samples cannot be distributed through the mail because they are routinely stolen from mailboxes before they ever get to the target customer. Similarly, coupons will not work unless

consumers can redeem them, and in some regions there are no handling agents to help with that effort. In some countries consumer free draws or sweepstakes are banned because they are seen as a form of gambling.

Within the European Union efforts are being made to harmonize the regulations and legal situation of sales promotions. Some countries, such as Germany and Norway, have a restrictive legal environment while others, such as the United Kingdom and Ireland, have more permissive legislation. The latter are lobbying strongly to ensure that their relatively permissive regulations become the standard. Exhibit 15–3 summarizes the sales promotions that are permitted in each EU member state. It shows that what is a legal sales promotion method in one country may be illegal in another.

Promotional techniques	UK	NL	B	SP	IR	IT	F	G	DK
On pack promotions	✔	✔	?	✔	✔	✔	?	✔	✔
Banded offers	✔	?	?	✔	✔	✔	?	✔	✔
In pack premiums	✔	?	?	✔	✔	✔	?	?	?
Multi purchase offers	✔	?	?	✔	✔	✔	?	✘	✔
Extra product	✔	✔	✔	✔	✔	✔	?	✘	✔
Free product	✔	?	✔	✔	✔	✔	✔	✘	?
Reusable/other use pack	✔	✔	✔	✔	✔	✔	✔	?	✔
Free mail-ins	✔	✔	?	✔	✔	✔	?	✔	✔
Which purchase premiums	✔	?	✔	✔	✔	✔	?	✘	?
Cross-product offers	✔	✔	✘	✔	✔	✔	?	✔	✔
Collector devices	✔	✔	✔	✔	✔	✔	✔	✔	✔
Competitions	✔	?	?	✔	✔	?	✔	✔	?
Self-liquidating premiums	✔	✔	✔	✔	✔	✔	✔	✔	✔
Free draws	✔	✘	?	✔	✔	✔	?	✔	?
Share-outs	✔	✔	?	✔	✔	?	?	✔	?
Sweepstake/lottery	?	✘	?	✔	✘	?	?	✔	✘
Money-off vouchers	✔	✔	✔	✔	✔	✔	✔	?	✔
Money-off next purchases	✔	✔	✔	✔	✔	✔	✔	✘	✔
Cash-backs	✔	✔	✔	✔	✔	✘	✔	✘	✔
In-store demos	✔	✔	✔	✔	✔	✔	✔	✔	✔

Key: ✔ Permitted ✘ Not permitted ? May be permitted

Exhibit 15–3 Permitted Promotional Techniques Across Europe[5]

SALES PROMOTION FOR DIFFERENT TARGETS AT DIFFERENT TIMES

Promotion throughout the product life cycle
Sales promotions are extremely versatile. The different forms of sales promotions are capable of being used with various groups and designed to achieve different effects.

Given this versatility, sales promotions can be useful throughout the product life cycle. Exhibit 15–4 shows that various product objectives can be achieved by the use of sales promotion methods at the various life-cycle stages.

Life-cycle stage	Product objectives	Sales-promotion methods
Introduction	• Consumer trial • Distribution	• Product sampling • In-store demonstrations • Banded offers • Coupons
Growth	• Stimulate demand for product/brand • Continued brand preference	• Sampling • Coupons • Premiums
Maturity	• Encourage dealer loyalty • Encourage switching to the brand • Increased usage • Encourage retrial by lapsed users	• Competitions • Money off next purchase • Self-liquidating offers • Companion brand offers
Decline	• To maintain distribution	• Trade promotion • Allowances and discounts

Exhibit 15–4 Sales Promotion and the Product Life Cycle[6]

The fact that sales promotions can be effective throughout the life of a brand shows their strategic role. Clearly, sales promotion activities should therefore be planned and not just used in an *ad hoc* manner.

Sales promotion for final consumers or users

Earlier, it was noted that sales promotion can be aimed at final consumers or users, channel members and company employees. Each of these groups may be reached by sales promotions and a variety of outcomes is possible.

Much of the sales promotion aimed at final consumers or users tries to increase demand—perhaps temporarily—or speed up the time of purchase, or to engender repeat purchasing. Such promotion might involve developing materials to be displayed in retailers' stores, including banners, sample packages, calendars and various point-of-sale materials. The sales promotion people also might develop special displays for supermarkets. They might be responsible for 'sweepstakes' contests as well as for coupons designed to get customers to buy a product by a certain date. As noted earlier the type of sales promotion activity that is legal and popular varies by region. For example, in Australia, coupons are seldom used in the grocery market, yet are very popular in New Zealand. In Europe, coupons are extensively (but not universally) used but as Exhibit 15–3 shows the legality of sales promotion activities is not yet standardized.

All these sales promotion efforts will achieve specific objectives. For example, if customers already have a preferred brand, it may be hard to get them to try anything new. Or it may take a while for them to become accustomed to a different product. A free trial-sized bottle of mouthwash might be just what it takes

to get cautious consumers to try—and like—the new product. Such samples might be distributed house to house, by mail, at stores or attached to other products sold by the firm. In this type of situation, sales of the product might start to pick up as soon as customers try the product and find out that they like it. Sales may continue at the higher level after the promotion is over if satisfied customers make repeat purchases. Thus, the cost of the sales promotion in this situation might be viewed as a long-term investment.

Many markets are in the maturity stage of the life cycle. This is characterized by companies competing for existing customers, rather than new customers entering the market. In this environment it is especially important for companies, once they have got customers, to keep them. Sales promotions can help in this customer retention task. Under loyalty programmes, each time the customer buys from the company their purchases are recorded on a database and accumulate to earn some sort of privileges. This may be in the form of discount or points that contribute towards gifts or travel (such as the Air Miles scheme). A 'loyalty card' is used to electronically record purchases. The marketing information recorded by this form of sales promotion has other marketing uses such as customer analysis and direct marketing.

Typical examples of loyalty schemes include IKEA's family card and the Shell Smart card. In the business market the highest profile loyalty schemes are those run by airlines. It is argued that these have been almost too successful. A survey in the *Official Airlines Guide* found that 90 per cent of business travellers belonged to a scheme (rising to 99 per cent in the United States). Over 80 per cent said that the scheme did influence their choice of airline. The question is: What do the airlines do next?

The schemes are expensive to run but cannot be abandoned without losing customers and market share.

When a product is already established, consumer sales promotion usually focuses on stimulating sales in the short term. For example, after a price-off coupon for a soft drink is distributed sales might temporarily pick up as customers take advantage of buying at a lower price. They may even consume more of the soft drink than would have otherwise been the case. However, once the coupon period is over, sales would return to the original level or they might even decline for a while. This is what happens if customers use a coupon to 'stock up' on a product at the low price. Then it takes them longer than usual to buy the product again.

When the objective of the promotion is focused primarily on producing a short-term increase in sales, it is sensible for the marketing manager to evaluate the cost of the promotion relative to the extra sales expected. If the increase in sales will not at least cover the cost of the promotion, it probably does not make sense to do it. Otherwise, the firm is 'buying sales' at the cost of reduced profit.

Sales promotion directed at industrial customers might use the same kinds of ideas. In addition, the sales promotion people might set up and staff trade show exhibitions. These exhibitions are valuable because the audience is comprised of interested parties—possibly buyers, influencers or other members of the decision-making unit. Some industrial sellers give promotional items, pen sets, cigarette lighters, watches or more expensive items (perhaps with the firm's brand name on them)—to 'remind' industrial customers of their products. This is common practice in many industries but it can also be a sensitive area. Some companies do not allow buyers to take any gift of any kind from a supplier, fearing that it could compromise the buyer's judgement.

The ethical issue concerning such gift giving is particularly acute in the pharmaceutical industry where the customer is the medical doctor buying on behalf of patients. Clearly this is a position of trust and the patient would like to be assured that the medical doctor makes professional judgements, not influenced by the free gifts from drugs companies.

Sales promotion for intermediaries

Sales promotion aimed at intermediaries, sometimes called *trade promotion*, stresses price-related matters. The objective may be to encourage channel members to stock new items, buy in larger quantity, buy early, pay early or stress a product in their own promotion efforts. The tools used here include price and/or merchandise allowances, promotion allowances and perhaps sales contests to encourage retailers or wholesalers to sell specific items, or the company's whole line. Offering to send contest winners to Paris, for example, may increase sales.

Motorsports were chosen as the most effective way to motivate Cellnet's dealer staff into making more mobile phone connections and beating the threat of competitors. Cellnet were already sponsoring Formula One driver, Damon Hill. The company had packs, signed by Damon Hill, sent to dealer staff, containing lap sheets on which sales staff could record their connections. Promotional gifts of clothes and record vouchers were used to reward sales as was a competition to win one of three Renault Clio Williams cars.[7]

Much of the sales promotion spending targeted at intermediaries has the effect of reducing the price that they pay for merchandise from a supplier. In this respect, it is useful to consider trade promotions in the context of other price-related matters. For this reason, more detail is given on different types of trade discounts and allowances in Chapter 16.

GOODFELLAS PIZZA LAUNCH

As Ireland has a strong retailer concentration, suppliers need the cooperation of the trade, particularly in terms of stocking, display space and adequate facings for their products. Promotions aimed at the trade to achieve these objectives are therefore commonplace. One such trade promotion was the recent launch of Goodfellas Pizza, a classic example of a creative and well-executed promotion. The *target audience* was the managing directors, marketing/commercial directors and buyers of Ireland's top multiple and symbol group stores. This audience accounts for 90 per cent of total frozen pizza sales. The *objective* was the attendance of these key decision makers and buyers at a themed launch of Goodfellas Pizza. This is a much solicited group, as on average one new product is launched daily on the Irish market.

The *strategy* was the use of a high-impact invitation, which would create excitement and awareness of the launch event. This invitation/package was hand delivered to the key decision makers for each of the eight target retailing groups. The package contained a personalized director's chair and, using the 'A Star is Born' theme, had teasing graphics and copy to whet the appetite of the recipient.

The company used a Call-Mail-Call strategy, the initial call confirming the availability of the target to receive the package prior to the sending of the mailing itself; the hand delivering of the mailing package; and a follow-up call organizing the time and pick-up location for a limousine drive to the launch. At the launch venue, Windmill Lane Studios in Dublin, a 'premiere' effect had been created. Each attendee had a personalized director's chair awaiting them on arrival and was lavishly entertained. The event climaxed with the presentation of the new product.

A *budget* of £16 000 had been allocated to the campaign and a cost of £103 was incurred per response. Subsequent evaluation showed this launch to have been the most successful ever in Ireland, with each company asking to bring several executives. Goodfellas captured 60 per cent market share of this intensely competitive and crowded market in the first six months.[8]

Sales promotion for own employees

Sales promotion aimed at the company's own salesforce might try to encourage getting new customers, selling a new product or selling the company's whole line. Depending on the objectives, the tools might be competitions, bonuses on sales or number of new accounts, and holding sales meetings at attractive venues to raise everyone's spirits.

Ongoing sales promotion work might also be aimed at the salesforce—to help sales management. Sales promotion might be responsible for preparing sales portfolios, videotapes on new products, displays and other sales aids. Sales promotion people might develop the sales training material that the salesforce uses in working with customers and other channel members. They might develop special racks for product displays that the sales representative sells or gives to retailers. In other words, rather than expecting each individual salesperson or the sales manager to develop these sales aids, sales promotion might be given this responsibility. This has the added value of letting the salesperson know that the company supports them in their efforts to secure new business.

Service-oriented firms, such as hotels or restaurants, now use sales promotions targeted at their employees. Some, for example, give a monthly cash prize for the employee who provides the 'best service'. The employee's picture is displayed to give recognition.

Sales promotions can be summarized as follows. Sales promotions are versatile, coming in many forms and being used with employees, the trade and consumers. Likewise, sales promotions have a role over the life cycle of a brand. The management of sales promotions poses particular challenges. Care needs to be taken to ensure that sales promotions are integrated with the other promotional variables.

DIRECT MARKETING

The modern promotions mix usually contains some form *of direct marketing*. The term direct marketing covers many activities such as direct mail and telemarketing which create and exploit direct relationships with customers; it also includes some forms of advertising, sales promotion and personal selling. Direct marketing may be used as part of an integrated campaign or it may be used on its own.

When Land Rover was launching its first new model Range Rover in 25 years, the company decided to rely solely on direct marketing. The total cost of the UK campaign was £34 000, much less than motor manufacturers usually spend on new model launches. The database used contained 7000 Range Rover owners, past and present, and a further 5000 prospects who were owners of other luxury cars. They were invited to a series of launch events, staged by Range Rover dealers over two days. As part of the launch, the Range Rover was to be sent on three epic expeditions—to Vermont, Patagonia and Japan. Three teaser postcards from the three locations were sent to ensure that recipients remembered the date of the launch. Local dealers followed up with personal invitations. The campaign clearly worked: attendance averaged over 95 per cent and sales were also reported to be high. One dealer even managed to sell three months' allocation on the spot.[9]

At its broadest, *direct marketing* can be thought of as any activity that creates and exploits a direct relationship with the customer. A more focused definition sees direct marketing primarily as a media-based path to the customer. The question really is 'what is direct'? The selling of the product, in other words its distribution, may be direct. The early forms of direct marketing were used to sell seeds and garden nursery products by mail order. Increasingly, direct marketing is about direct promotion or communication with customers.

The evolution of direct marketing

Direct marketing has developed from two main sources—direct mail and mail order. It is interesting to note that direct mail is a medium for advertising whereas mail order is a form of distribution. This relates to the two perspectives that exist today, reflected in the two definitions of direct marketing mentioned earlier.[7] Although direct marketing may seem to be very modern, it has quite a long history. One of the first mail-order catalogues was issued in 1667 by an English gardener called William Lucas. The origins of direct mail can be traced to the 1770s when a 'circular letter' was used to keep informed the key participants in the movement that preceded the American Civil War. From this period onwards, trade and mail catalogues flourished selling in particular seeds and nursery materials. Medicines, musical instruments and sewing machines featured in the catalogues of the nineteenth century. In 1905 the first catalogue to give credit terms was issued. The development of credit cards in the 1950s gave further impetus to the evolution of direct marketing. Latterly, technology has maintained the development of direct marketing. This has given rise to new media (other than direct mail), free telephone numbers, electronic databases, direct-response television and so on. Exhibit 15–5 illustrates a selected chronology of the evolution of direct marketing.

The growth of direct marketing has been influenced by a number of factors. As media costs have increased, advertisers have been trying to get better value for money. In this respect, direct-response advertising is sometimes thought of as 'double duty' advertising, giving more immediate and measurable results. Another factor fuelling the growth of direct marketing is the fragmentation of markets. There are those who argue that mass markets are dead and that marketing needs to cater for much smaller segments. Direct marketing opens up the possibility of one-to-one marketing. The development and application of computer technology is evident in practically every aspect of direct marketing. This has led to cost-effectiveness in the storage, analysis and retrieval of large volumes of data. It is now relatively easy, for example, to customize a publication or mailshot for particular groups or individuals.

Just as these factors have contributed to the development of direct marketing, so has the variety of forms of direct marketing increased.

1667	First gardening catalogue
1775	Circular letter pre-American Civil War
1780s	Trade and mail catalogues
1890s	First Sears catalogue
1905	Spiegel's catalogue offers credit terms
1920s	First catalogue offering books
1950s	Development of the credit card
1960s	Other media (non-mail) develop
1970s	Free telephone numbers; computer technology
1980s	Databases and lists for sale
1990s	Increasing adoption of interactive technologies

Exhibit 15–5 Evolution of Direct Marketing[10]

The characteristics of direct marketing

A number of factors distinguish direct marketing from general marketing. Firstly, direct marketing emphasizes control and is extremely *measurable*. Direct marketing activity normally invites the customer to respond immediately by completing a coupon, returning an order, agreeing to see a salesperson, making a telephone call or some other immediate response. It is therefore relatively easy to establish responses to the direct marketing activity. For example, when the Tango soft drink company wanted to revitalize its Apple Tango brand, it used direct-response television advertising, followed by direct-response cinema and radio advertising. The audience was invited to telephone the company if they were 'having problems with the seductive properties of Apple Tango'. Half a million calls were received and the company's volume share increased by 22 per cent. Compared to other forms of promotional effort, it is therefore much easier to measure the response to direct marketing.[11]

Direct marketing also makes greater use of *targeting*. Given the direct nature of the relationship with the customer, the company is able to gain and use targeting information. Initially the information helps the company to attract and acquire customers. Thereafter, information gained helps to provide and promote appropriate products to that customer. For example, geographic information systems enable the marketer to know what sort of house and area in which the person lives—whether rural or urban, detached house or high-rise flat. If someone lives in a city apartment, there is not much point in sending a gardening catalogue to them. Apart from geodemographics, the customer's purchase behaviour and response to offers can be added to the customer profile. As this builds over time, much more precise targeting is possible.

Direct marketing is also characterized by relying heavily on *lists* and *databases*. These may develop from the company's own record of its customers and ex-customers.

Call centres are now widely used by companies to handle their day-to-day contact directly with their customers.

These lists are extremely valuable because it is reckoned that an existing customer is three to eight times more responsive than a non-customer. Increasingly, however, lists of specialized target groups are available for purchase from list brokers and list owners. These lists vary in price according to how up-to-date they are and how precisely targeted they are. The more basic lists cost around £100 per thousand names/addresses, while others can cost £300 per thousand. Examples of lists available in the United Kingdom are shown in Exhibit 15-6.

Direct marketing is characterized by *interaction and feedback*. The customer or prospect should receive and be engaged by the communication, leading to a response. A more personalized and targeted communication is clearly more likely to get the recipient's attention (and a response) than one that is part of a general promotional drive. As interactive media develop, they offer a more developed direct communications capability. This should enhance the nature of interaction and feedback between company and customer.

The final distinguishing characteristic of direct marketing relates to the strategic aspect. Direct marketing may be used over time and this *continuity* allows the company to build lifetime relationships rather than occasional transactions. The form of direct marketing where continuity and the relationship aspect are most manifest is in loyalty programmes. For example, the Swedish company IKEA runs a family club that enables them to keep track of their customers. In the UK, Tesco (a retail store) launched a loyalty scheme where shoppers collect points each time they make a purchase. Only six months after its introduction, the Tesco Clubcard had allowed the company to build a database of more than five million customers. This is

Prominent People

25 000 Rolls-Royce, Lamborghini
  and Jaguar owners
2 500 UK millionaires
10 000 rich ladies
7 000 tennis court owners
13 000 private plane owners

Entertainment Seekers

19 000 theatre goers
27 000 Shaftesbury Theatre goers
186 000 club goers

Improvers

47 000 named clergy
26 000 buyers of self-improvement books
106 000 home improvers
1 000 000 home movers
Owners of Black 'n' Decker drills

Miscellaneous

100 000 aerial home photograph owners
49 000 tall ladies
43 700 librarians
4 100 management consultants
160 prisons and detention centres

Exhibit 15–6 Examples of Target Customer Lists[12]

now used as a driving force for communicating with the company's customers, and competitors have followed suit. Market segments can be identified and communications targeted to increase frequency of use or to thank better customers.

Direct marketing is distinctive in a number of ways. These can be summarized under the headings of measurability, targeting, reliance on lists and databases, interaction and feedback, and continuity.

The various forms of direct marketing

Direct marketing comes in many forms—direct mail, telemarketing, door-to-door marketing (including pyramid and network selling), direct-response television advertising, computerized home shopping, leaflet drops and so on. Exhibit 15–7 shows the forms of direct marketing available by media type. It is interesting to note the prevalence of electronic media. This indicates that direct marketing will continue to grow.

As a measure of how widespread direct marketing is, it is now reckoned that 97 per cent of all financial services companies in the UK use it, that a third of all TV advertisements have a response telephone number, that three-quarters of all US advertising carries some direct-response mechanism. Exhibit 15–8 shows the amount of direct mail received per capita each year. Clearly the amount of direct mail activity varies by country to quite a degree, the highest rate being nearly ten times the lowest rate. This indicates the various stages of development of direct marketing and its associated infrastructure throughout Europe. The laws affecting direct marketing are not harmonized. While in the United Kingdom it is permissive, in Denmark the law surrounding how much customer information can be kept and for how long is very sensitive.

When one considers the volume of addressed direct mail across Europe, a very clear upward trend emerges. Over a 10-year period, the total volume has very nearly doubled, as Exhibit 15–9 shows. This raises the problem

Print Media
Direct mail (addressed and unaddressed)
Press (direct response advertising)
Leaflets/Inserts/Flyers
Posters
Catalogues
On-Pack

Electronic Media
Telephone (and associated technologies)
Facsimile
Television
Radio
Electronic Catalogues
Computer diskettes/CD-ROM
Computer on-line marketplaces
Electronic kiosks

Distribution Media*
Lists
Door-to-door
Referral systems
Electronic networks
On-pack or via physical products

* The traditional dichotomy of print and electronic leads to the exclusion of other 'media', which may essentially be described as 'distribution' media.

Exhibit 15–7 Direct Marketing by Media Type[13]

Market	Volume Per Capita
Switzerland	105
Belgium	86
Germany	67
France	64
Sweden	62
Denmark	51
Norway	49
Finland	44
United Kingdom	42
Spain	34
Ireland	16
Portugal	11

Exhibit 15–8 Address Direct Mail Volume Per Head of Population 1994.[14]

Year	Addressed Direct Mail (millions)
1983	8 466
1986	9 447
1987	10 446
1988	11 997
1989	13 282
1990	13 959
1991	14 568
1992	15 579
1993	16 708

Exhibit 15–9 European Volume of Addressed Direct Mail 1983–93

REFERENCES

1. Information supplied by Cotton Council International.

2. L. Cuddihy, K. UiGhallachoir and F. Hayden 'Sales Promotion – An Irish Perspective', In: T. Meenaghan and P. O'Sullivan (eds) 1996, *Marketing Communications in Ireland*, Oak Tree Press, Dublin, Ch. 22, p. 443.

3. S. Derrick, 'Just rewards,' *Marketing Business*, January 1999, pp. 37–9; D.R. Glover, 'Distributor attitudes toward manufacturer-sponsored promotions', *Industrial Marketing Management*, vol. 20, no. 3, 1991, pp. 241–50; A.S.C. Ehrenberg, K. Hammond and G.J. Goodhardt, 'The after-effects of price-related consumer promotions,' *Journal of Advertising Research*, July/August 1994, pp. 11–2.

4. H. Acland, 'Playing by the rules', *Marketing Business*, January 1999, pp. 39–40; 'The sins of over-redemption', *Marketing*, 23 May 1996, p. 12.

5. European Federation For Sales Promotions, *Newsletter*, Brussels, Issue 1, p. 2.

6. L. Cuddihy, K. UiGhallachoir and F. Hayden 'Sales promotion—An Irish perspective', *in*: T. Meenaghan and P. O'Sullivan (1996), *Marketing Communications in Ireland*, Dublin, Oak Tree Press, Ch. 22, pp. 437–58.

7. 'Trade promotions', *Marketing*, 9 May 1996, Supplement, p. xiv.

8. 'The 1995 Royal Mail Direct Marketing Awards—Gold Award', *Marketing*, 14 December 1995, p. 9.

9. K. Fletcher, C. Wheeler and J. Wright, 'Database marketing: A channel, a medium or a strategic approach?' *International Journal of Advertising*, vol. 10, no. 2, 1991, pp. 117–28.

10. M. Baier, *Elements of direct marketing*, McGraw Hill, New York, 1983.

11. 'The 1995 Royal Mail Direct Marketing Awards—Integrated campaign', *Marketing*, vol. 14 December 1995, p. 28.

12. P.R. Smith *Marketing Communications: An Integrated Approach*, Kogan-Page, London, 1993.

13. M. McGowan 'Direct Marketing – Irish perspectives', in T. Meenaghan and P. O'Sullivan (eds) 1996, *Marketing Communications in Ireland*, Oak Tree Press, Dublin, Ch. 27, pp. 532–45.

14. Association of European Postal Administrators, 'Useage trends in the european direct mail market, 1994, Report, Postal Directory Marketing Services Survey, AEPA, Brussels, 1994.

15. K. Sengupta and A. Severin, '£1.4 bn pile of junk through the letter box', *The Independent*, 17 July 1997, p. 5.

16. 'Reading your mind', *Marketing*, 22 February 1996, pp. 33–4.

CHAPTER 16
Pricing Objectives and Policies

When You Finish This Chapter, You Should

1 Understand how pricing objectives should guide planning for pricing decisions.

2 Understand choices the marketing manager must make about price flexibility and price levels over the product life cycle.

3 Understand the legality of price level and price flexibility policies.

4 Understand the many possible variations of a price structure including discounts, allowances and who pays transportation costs.

5 Understand the important new terms (shown in colour).

PROCTER AND GAMBLE'S 'EVERY DAY LOW PRICES'

Procter and Gamble (P&G) is a market leader in the market for household products. Its brand names are famous throughout the world—Fairy Liquid, Pampers and Ariel. In the mid-1990s, P&G introduced to the United Kingdom, a new pricing strategy called 'every day low prices'. The strategy cut the price of many P&G brands by about 10 per cent. The aim is to keep these low prices permanently.

Clearly, such a price cut is costly to the company. In this case P&G is financing the lower prices by cutting down on advertising. P&G annually spend £5.4 billion on marketing throughout the world and £1 billion on advertising for sales of £21 billion. The 'every day low prices' strategy means that P&G intend to spend one-fifth of net sales, rather than the original one-quarter, on marketing support.

The reasoning behind this dramatic move by P&G is quite clear. In the United States, United Kingdom and the rest of the world, P&G's biggest competitors are retailer own-label brands. These own-labels have been growing in popularity and are said to account for up to 60 per cent of the market in some categories. This gives power to the retailer in the channel of distribution. With finite shelf space, decisions about allocating shelf facings are the prerogative of the retailer. The retailer is clearly going to allocate more space to the own-label brand over that of the manufacturer.

By cutting prices P&G has made a first move. The choice for retailers in responding to the P&G price cut would be either to oppose the price cuts or to cut their own prices. Consumers would be unimpressed by retailers that were not in favour of price reductions. The retailers have therefore been forced to reduce their prices. This means that they have a narrower profit margin on which to operate and less resources to spend on heavy sales promotions. The effects of these price cuts are wide-ranging and still working their way out. Consumers are better off with lower priced products. The advertising and media industry are coming to terms with losing the big spend of a major client.[1]

PRICE HAS MANY STRATEGY DIMENSIONS

As the Procter and Gamble case shows, decisions about prices have a wide-ranging impact—on the business, its competitors, customers and the channel of distribution. Price is one of the four major variables in the marketing mix. Pricing decisions are especially important because they affect both the number of sales a firm makes and how much money it earns.

Guided by the company's objectives, marketing managers must develop a set of pricing objectives and policies. They must spell out what price situations the firm will face and how it will handle them. These policies should explain: (1) how flexible prices will be, (2) at what level they will be set over the product life cycle, (3) to whom and when discounts and allowances will be given and (4) how transportation costs will be handled. See Exhibit 16-1. These price-related decision areas are the focus of this chapter. In the next chapter, we will discuss how specific prices are set, consistent with the firm's pricing objectives and policies and its whole marketing strategy.

Pricing decisions are more complex than they may initially seem. For example, you may see a package holiday which is attractive because it includes a 'free' car for your use during your holiday. However, when you land at your holiday destination, you may find that you are still obliged to take out extra insurance to cover you against basic risks. This is a hidden price that you did not originally know about. When you get to the hotel you might find that you have only paid for a basic room with a view over the hotel car park. An upgrade fee allows you to move to the front of the hotel with a view over the beach. As you turn up for breakfast the next morning you find that your room rate covers only continental breakfast, rather than the full buffet. A supplementary payment then allows you to take full advantage of the appetising range of food. During the day you buy soft drinks at the pool-side, but realize that you are paying very high charges because the hotel regards you as a captive market that can be overcharged. You make a call home and then find that the hotel has added its supplement to the call that you made from your room.

Each of these different elements is part of the overall price that you have paid for your holiday. Given the range of needs of individual holiday makers, you can see how difficult it can then seem to determine prices. There is not one single pricing decision. All of these prices influence your view as a consumer of the value for money that you experienced on your holiday.

The price equation

This example emphasizes that when a seller quotes a price, it is related to *some* assortment of goods and services. So **Price** is what is charged for 'something'. Of course, price may be called different things in different settings. Golf professionals charge for tuition. Landlords collect rent. Hotels display a room rate. Banks ask for interest when they lend money. Bus and train companies charge fares. Doctors, lawyers and consultants set fees. Employees want a wage. People may call it different things, but *any business transaction in our modern economy*

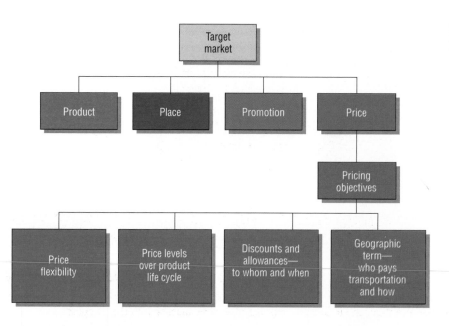

Exhibit 16–1 Strategy Planning for Price

can be thought of as an exchange of money, the money being the Price, for something. The something can be a physical product in various stages of completion, with or without supporting services, with or without quality guarantees and so on. Or it could be a pure service, such as dry cleaning, legal advice or car insurance.

The nature and extent of this something determines the amount of money exchanged. Some customers pay list price. For example, some hotel customers are prepared

to pay the price shown at reception, while others realize that it is frequently possible to bargain prices down, particularly at quiet times or later on in the day. Others obtain large discounts or allowances because something is *not* provided. Exhibit 16–2 summarizes some possible variations for consumers or users and Exhibit 16–3 for channel members. These variations are discussed more fully below. But here it should be clear that Price has many dimensions.[2]

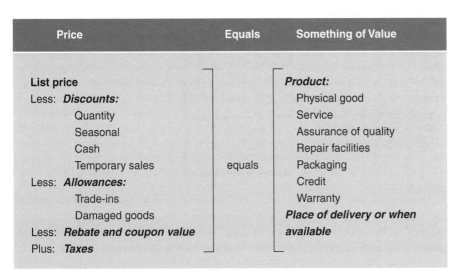

Exhibit 16–2 Price as Seen by Consumers or Uses

Price	Equals	Something of Value
List price		**Product:**
Less: *Discounts:*		Physical good
Quantity		Service
Seasonal		Assurance of quality
Cash		Repair facilities
Temporary sales	equals	Packaging
Less: *Allowances:*		Credit
Trade-ins		Warranty
Damaged goods		**Place of delivery or when**
Less: *Rebate and coupon value*		**available**
Plus: *Taxes*		

Exhibit 16–3 Price as Seen by Channel Members

Price	Equals	Something of Value
List price		**Product:**
Less: *Discounts:*		Branded—well known
Quantity		Guaranteed
Seasonal		Warranted
Cash		Service—repair facilities
Trade or functional		Convenient packaging for handling
Temporary 'deals'	equals	**Place:**
Less: *Allowances*		Availability—when and where
Damaged goods		**Price:**
Advertising		Price-level guarantee
Push money		Sufficient margin to allow chance for profit
Stocking		**Promotion:**
Plus: *Taxes and tariffs*		Promotion aimed at customers

OBJECTIVES SHOULD GUIDE STRATEGY PLANNING FOR PRICE

Pricing objectives should flow from, and fit in with, company-level and marketing objectives. Pricing objectives should be *explicitly stated* because they have a direct

effect on pricing policies as well as the methods used to set prices.[3] Exhibit 16–4 shows the various types of pricing objectives discussed in this chapter.

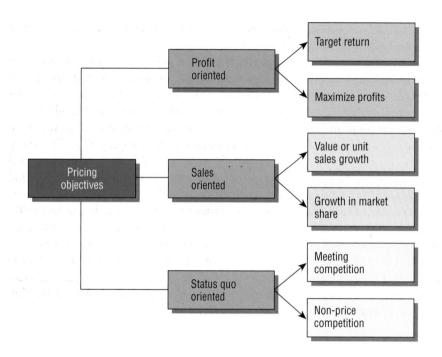

Exhibit 16–4 Possible Pricing Objectives

PROFIT-ORIENTED OBJECTIVES

Target returns provide specific guidelines

A **target return objective** sets a specific level of profit as an objective. Often this amount is stated as a percentage of sales or of capital investment. A large manufacturer like Philips might aim for a 15 per cent return on investment. The target for grocery chains might be a 5 per cent return on sales. A target return objective has administrative advantages in a large company. Performance can be compared against the target. Some companies eliminate divisions, or drop products, that do not yield the target rate of return.

Satisfactory profits may be the objective

Some managers aim for only satisfactory returns. They just want returns that ensure the firm's survival and convince shareholders they are doing a good job. Similarly, some small family-run businesses aim for a profit that will provide a comfortable lifestyle.[4]

Many private and public non-profit organizations set a price level that will just recover costs. In other words, their target return figure is zero. For example, a government agency may charge motorists a toll for using a bridge, but then drop the toll when the bridge is paid for. In many European countries the prices charged by utilities such as water, gas and electricity for their services are subject to government control and regulation. Such services are seen as meeting general consumer requirements and control is

deemed to be in the public interest to ensure that society as a whole can afford the basic service.

Healthcare organizations are frequently subject to control in terms of the prices that they are allowed to charge for operations on patients. In some member countries within the EU, the government regulates the prices for specific operations and will only fund a certain number of such procedures each year. Because funding is limited this may mean that people have to wait considerable periods of time before they are able to have their operation. This is designed to create equality in the distribution of relatively limited funds for meeting health care needs, but may lead to long waiting lists.

In many of these same countries private healthcare organizations are often able to offer similar operations to patients who have private healthcare policies. Such patients have decided to use a proportion of their income to allow them to 'pay' more for healthcare and not wait for operations. There is considerable debate about the ethics of allowing a pricing system to determine the standards of healthcare which are available to different members of the population.

Profit maximization can be socially responsible

A **profit maximization objective** seeks to get as much profit as possible. It might be stated as a desire to earn a rapid return on investment. Put more bluntly profit maximization seeks to charge as much as the market will bear.

It is often assumed that anyone seeking a profit maximization objective will charge high prices—prices that are not in the public interest. However, this point of view is not correct. Pricing to achieve profit maximization does not always lead to high prices. Demand and supply *may* bring extremely high prices if competition cannot offer good substitutes. But this happens if and only if demand is highly inelastic. If demand is very elastic, profit maximizers may charge relatively low prices. Low prices may expand the size of the market and result in greater sales and profits. For example, when prices of VCRs were very high, only innovators and wealthy people bought them. When Philips and its competitors lowered prices, nearly everyone bought a VCR. In other words, when demand is elastic, profit maximization may occur at a *lower* price.

Profit maximization objectives can also produce desirable results indirectly. Consumers vote with their money for firms that do the right thing. The results of this voting guide other firms in deciding what they should do. If a firm is earning a very large profit, other firms will try to copy or improve on what the company offers. Frequently, this leads to lower prices. IBM sold its original personal computer for about £2500 in 1981. As Compaq, Dell and other competitors started to copy IBM, it added more power and features and cut prices. By the late 1990s customers could buy a personal computer with much more power, speed and data storage for about £500.[5]

We saw this process at work in Chapter 7—in the rise and fall of profits during the product life cycle. Contrary to popular belief, a profit maximization objective is often socially desirable.

SALES-ORIENTED OBJECTIVES

A **sales-oriented objective** seeks some level of unit sales, monetary sales or share of market—*without referring to profit*.

Sales and profit are not the same

Some managers are more concerned about sales growth than profits. They think sales growth always leads to more profits. This kind of thinking causes problems when a firm's costs are growing faster than sales or when managers do not keep track of their costs. Recently, many major companies have had declining profits in spite of growth in sales. Generally, however, business managers now pay more attention to profits, not just sales.

Market share objectives are popular

Many firms seek to gain a specified share (percentage) of a market. A benefit of a market share objective is that it forces a manager to pay attention to what competitors are doing in the market. In addition, it's usually easier to measure a firm's market share than to determine if profits are being maximized. Large consumer packaged goods firms, such as Unilever, Cadbury's and Nestlé, often use market share objectives.

Aggressive companies often aim to increase market share or even to control a market. Sometimes this makes sense. If a company has a large market share, it may have better economies of scale than its competitors. Therefore, if it sells at about the same price as its competitors, it gets more profit from each sale. Or lower costs may allow it to sell at a lower price and still make a profit. The Procter and Gamble case at the start of this chapter shows how price was used to try to gain back market share from retailer brands. This is also evidence of the conflicts that can emerge within the channel of distribution.

Universal Studios very successfully gained market share in 1996 from Walt Disney World in Florida through pricing. Universal's five-day pass was about £66 compared with Disney's £124 five-day pass. Disney responded not by cutting its prices but by banning some hotels in Florida from selling tickets for Disney theme parks. The hotels in question were also selling tickets for Universal.[6]

A company with a long-run view may decide that increasing market share is a sensible objective when the overall market is growing. The hope is that larger future volume will justify sacrificing some profit in the short run. Companies as diverse as Sony, Coca-Cola and IBM look at opportunities in Eastern Europe this way. Of course, objectives aimed at increasing market share have the same limitations as straight sales growth objectives. A larger market share, if gained at too low a price, may lead to profitless success. The key point regarding sales-oriented objectives is that larger sales volume, by itself, does not necessarily lead to higher profits.

The German digital telephone market started in 1992. Since then it has grown rapidly and some estimates suggest that by the year 2005, every second German over the age of 14 will be carrying a mobile phone. Already, in 1999, there are approximately 12.5 million users. As the market has become established and grown, new companies have entered and competition has intensified. Increased competition has led to prices being cut. All suppliers offer reduced prices and special offers to try to secure their share of the market.

One company, DeutscheTelekom, offered a 60 per cent reduction in rates to one particular area code selected by customers. Its main competitor, Mannesmann, then matched this offer and slashed rates for calls made to numbers in the same area code as the caller. The smaller companies have also used price in an effort to attract new customers to them. Some offer reduced rates for calls after 6 p.m. (rates during the day are double), while others cut their basic service charges.

Having endured the costly initial 24-month contracts, existing customers are also price-sensitive and are prepared to move to a new supplier for a better deal. Some customers are so concerned about price that they prefer to buy pre-paid cards. This means that these users pay no basic charges; when the card runs out, they buy another or switch to a company offering a better deal.

Continuing price cuts and extra service means that customers are better off. The market also grows, with new customers attracted into it. Consolidated sales for mobile 'phones rose 34 per cent to DM14 billion in 1997, DM12 billion of which came from voice traffic. By 2005, consolidated sales are expected to reach DM40 billion. However, higher sales do not necessarily mean more profit. Because of the price war, it is expected that some of the smaller service providers will have to merge, be bought-out or go bankrupt. Thus, customers may be better off but suppliers face a leaner future.

STATUS QUO PRICING OBJECTIVES

Stable price objectives

Managers satisfied with their current market share and profits sometimes adopt **status quo objectives**—don't-rock-the-*pricing*-boat objectives. Managers may say that they want to stabilize prices, or meet competition, or even avoid competition. This thinking is most common when the total market is not growing. Maintaining stable prices may discourage price competition and avoid the need for hard decisions.

Or stress non-price competition instead

A *status quo* pricing objective may be part of an aggressive overall marketing strategy focusing on **non-price competition**—aggressive action on one or more of the Ps other than Price. Fast-food chains like McDonald's and Burger King experienced very profitable growth by sticking to non-price competition for many years. However, when others started to take away customers with price-cutting, the other chains also turned to price competition.

MOST FIRMS SET SPECIFIC PRICING POLICIES—TO REACH OBJECTIVES

Specific pricing policies are vital for any firm. Otherwise, the marketing manager has to rethink the marketing strategy every time a customer asks for a price.

Administered prices help achieve objectives

Price policies usually lead to **administered prices**—consciously set prices. In other words, instead of letting daily market forces decide their prices, most firms (including *all* of those in monopolistic competition) set their own prices. They may hold prices steady for long periods of time or change them more frequently if that is what's required to meet objectives.

If a firm does not sell directly to final customers, it usually wants to administer both the price it receives from intermediaries and the price final customers pay. After all, the final price that customers pay will ultimately affect the quantity it sells. Yet it is often difficult to administer prices throughout the channel. Other channel members may also wish to administer prices to achieve their own objectives. This is what happened to Alcoa, one of the largest aluminium producers. To reduce its excess inventory, Alcoa offered its wholesalers a 30 per cent discount off its normal price. Alcoa expected the wholesalers to pass most of the discount along to their customers to stimulate sales throughout the channel. Instead, wholesalers bought *their* aluminium at the lower price but passed on only a small part of the discount to customers. As a result, the quantity Alcoa sold did not increase much, and it still had excess inventories, while the wholesalers made more profit on the aluminium they did sell.

In the United Kingdom, Esso used to compete using tokens as a promotional device. Consumers received these 'Esso Tiger Tokens' each time they made a purchase. The tokens could then be redeemed against various products. Research showed, however, that customers reacted more favourably to lower prices. Esso therefore abandoned the use of tokens and competes on

the basis of Pricewatch, which guarantees to match local prices at 2100 stations. While Esso has made a deliberate choice to price this way, some firms just follow the general competitive price level and do not even try to administer prices. They just meet competition, or worse, mark up their costs with little thought to demand. They act as if they have no choice in selecting a price policy.

Remember that Price has many dimensions. Managers *do* have many choices. They *should* administer their prices. And they should do it carefully because, ultimately, customers must be willing to pay these prices before a whole marketing mix succeeds. In the rest of this chapter, we'll talk about policies a marketing manager must set to do an effective job of administering Price.[8]

PRICE FLEXIBILITY POLICIES

One of the first decisions a marketing manager has to make is about price flexibility. Should the firm use a one-price or a flexible-price policy?

One-price policy—the same price for everyone

A **one-price policy** means offering the same price to all customers who purchase products under essentially the same conditions and in the same quantities. The majority of companies use a one-price policy, mainly for administrative convenience and to maintain goodwill among customers. A one-price policy makes pricing easier. The marketing manager must be careful to avoid a rigid one-price policy. This can amount to broadcasting a price that competitors can undercut, especially if the price is somewhat high. One reason for the growth of discount outlets is that conventional retailers rigidly applied traditional margins and stuck to them.

Flexible-price policy—different prices for different customers

A **flexible-price policy** means offering the same product and quantities to different customers at different prices. Flexible-price policies often specify a *range* in which the actual price charged must fall.

Flexible pricing is most common in the channels, in direct sales of business products and at retail for expensive items and homogeneous shopping products. Retail shopkeepers in less-developed economies typically use flexible pricing. These situations usually involve personal selling, not mass selling. The advantage of flexible pricing is that the salesperson can make price adjustments, considering prices charged by competitors, the relationship with the customer, and the customer's bargaining ability.[9]

Most car dealers use flexible pricing. The producer suggests a list price, but the dealers bargain for what they

can get. Their salespeople negotiate prices every day. Inexperienced consumers, reluctant to bargain, could pay hundreds of pounds more than the dealer is willing to accept. By contrast, however, Daewoo dealers have earned high customer-satisfaction ratings by offering haggle-weary consumers a one-price policy.

Flexible pricing does have disadvantages. A customer who finds that others paid lower prices for the same marketing mix will be unhappy. This can cause real conflict in channels. One of the most obvious ways round this is to offer to beat the price that the consumer may be able to find for the same item anywhere else. In some cases the retailer may offer to rebate double the difference, making a powerful incentive for the price to be set competitively in the first place.

If buyers learn that negotiating can be in their interest, the time needed for bargaining will increase. This can increase selling costs and reduce profits. In addition, some sales staff let price cutting become a habit. This reduces the role of price as a competitive tool—and leads to a lower price level. It can also have a major effect on profit. A small price cut may not seem like much; but keep in mind that all of the revenue that is lost would go to profit. For example, if salespeople for a producer that usually earns profits equal to 15 per cent of its sales cut prices by an average of about 5 per cent, profits would drop by a third!

Air travel within Europe also illustrates flexibility in pricing and how price can be changed in response to the market. On any given flight in Europe, there can be up to 30 different air fares operating. These fares are constantly changing as airlines match or cut fares charged by competitors. These can be monitored in real time through global computer reservation systems. One of these—Galileo—posts thousands of changes each day.

PRICE-LEVEL POLICIES—OVER THE PRODUCT LIFE CYCLE

When marketing managers administer prices—as most do—they must consciously set a price level policy. As they enter the market, they have to set introductory prices that may have long-run effects. They must consider where the product life cycle is—and how fast it's moving. They must also decide if their prices should be above, below or somewhere in between relative to the market.

Let's look for a moment at a new product in the market introduction stage of its product life cycle. The price-level decision should focus first on the nature of market demand. There are few (or no) direct substitute marketing mixes. Given the demand curve for this product, a high price may lead to higher profit from each sale, but also to fewer units sold. A lower price might appeal to more potential customers. With this in mind, should the firm set a high or low price?

Skimming pricing—feeling out demand at a high price

A **skimming price policy** tries to sell to the upper end of a market—the top of the demand curve—at a high price before aiming at more price-sensitive customers. (The term 'skimming' is derived from the analogy of skimming the cream off the top of the milk.) A skimming policy is more attractive if demand is quite inelastic, at least at the upper price ranges. Skimming may maximize profits in the market introduction stage for an innovation, especially if there is little competition. Competitor analysis may help to clarify whether barriers will prevent or discourage competitors from entering.

 Skimming has critics

Some critics argue that firms should not try to maximize profits by using a skimming policy on new products that have important social consequences. A patent-protected life-saving drug or a genetic technique that increases crop yields, for example, is likely to have an inelastic demand curve. Yet many of those who need the product may not have the money to buy it. This is a serious concern. However, it is also a serious problem if firms don't have any incentive to take the risks required to develop breakthroughs in the first place.

Price moves down the demand curve

A skimming policy usually involves a slow reduction in price over time. See Exhibit 16–5. Note that as price is reduced, new target markets are probably being sought and attracted. As the price level steps-down the demand curve, new Place, Product and Promotion policies may be also be required.

When Hewlett-Packard (HP) introduced its laser printer for personal computers, it initially set a high price, around £2200. HP had a good head start on competitors and a close substitute was not available. HP sold the high-priced printer mainly to computer professionals and business users with serious desktop publishing needs. They were distributed through a select group of authorized HP computer dealers whose salespeople could explain the printer. When other firms entered the market with similar printers, HP added features and lowered its price. It

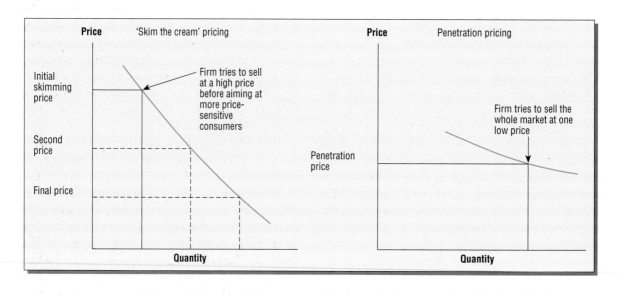

Exhibit 16–5 Alternative Introductory Pricing Policies

also did more advertising and added mail-order intermediaries to reach new target markets. Then, just as competitors were entering the market to go after budget-oriented buyers, HP introduced a new model at a lower price and added office-supply warehouse stores, like PC World, to the distribution channel. This is very typical of skimming. It involves dropping prices through a series of marketing strategy changes over the course of the product life cycle.

In the mid-1990s the price of personal computers (PCs) started to fall dramatically. Consumers can buy much more speed and capacity at no extra cost, or even at lesser prices than a few years previously. The reason for the fall in prices was the producers' view that the market was beginning to reach saturation levels. While innovation will continue, lower prices can be effective in bringing new customers into the market and encouraging owners of PCs to upgrade.

Skimming is also useful when little is known about the shape of the demand curve. It is usually safer to start with a high price that customers can refuse and then reduce it if necessary.

Penetration pricing—get volume at a low price

A **penetration pricing policy** tries to sell to the whole market at one low price. Such an approach might be wise when the elite market, those willing to pay a high price, is small. This is the case when the whole demand curve is fairly elastic. See Exhibit 16–5. A penetration policy is even more attractive if selling larger quantities results in lower costs because of economies of scale. Penetration pricing may be wise if the firm expects strong competition very soon after introduction. A low penetration price may be called a stay-out price. It discourages competitors from entering the market.

When PCs became popular, Borland International came out with a complete programming language, including a textbook, for under £30. Business customers had paid thousands of pounds for similar systems for mainframe computers. But Borland felt it could sell to hundreds of thousands of customers, and earn large total profits, by offering a really low price that would attract individual users as well as business firms. A low price helped Borland penetrate the market early. For several years, IBM, Microsoft and other big companies were not able—or willing—to compete directly with Borland at that price. When they finally did match Borland's price, Borland already had a large base of very loyal customers who weren't interested in switching to something new.

Introductory price dealing— temporary price cuts

Low prices do attract customers. Therefore, marketers often use **introductory price dealing**—temporary price cuts—to speed new products into a market. Introductory price dealing may be used to get customers to try a new product concept as part of the pioneering effort or to attract customers to a new brand entry later in the life cycle. However, don't confuse these *temporary* price cuts with low penetration prices. The plan here is to raise prices as soon as the introductory offer is over. By then, hopefully, target customers will have tried the product and decided it was worth buying again at the regular price.

Established competitors often choose not to meet introductory price dealing, as long as the introductory period is not too long or too successful. However, some competitors quickly match introductory price deals with their own short-term sale prices; they want to discourage their established customers from 'shopping around'.

Meeting competition may be necessary

Regardless of their introductory pricing policy, most firms face competition sooner or later in the product life cycle. When that happens, how high or low a price is may be relative not only to the market demand curve, but also to the prices charged by competitors. The nature of competition usually affects whether companies set their prices below, at or above competition. The clearest case is pure competition. The market really makes the decision. To offer products above or below the market price is foolish.

Meeting competitors' prices may also be the practical choice in mature markets that are moving towards pure competition. Here, firms typically face downward pressure on both prices and profits. Profit margins are already thin—and for many firms they would disappear or turn into losses at a lower price. A higher price would simply prompt competitors to promote their price advantage.

Similarly, there is little choice in oligopoly situations. Pricing at the market, that is, meeting competition, may be the only sensible policy. To raise prices might lead to a large loss in sales, unless competitors also adopt the higher price. Likewise, cutting prices would probably lead to similar reductions by competitors, downwards along an inelastic industry demand curve. This can only lead to a decrease in total revenue for the industry and probably for each firm. This situation faces the major European airlines today.

To avoid these problems, each oligopolist may choose a *status quo* pricing objective and set its price at the competitive level. Some critics call this pricing behaviour conscious parallel action, implying it is unethical and the same as intentional conspiracy among firms. As a practical matter, however, that criticism may be overly harsh. Firms ought not to ignore their competitors. If firms do collude on artificially high prices, they can leave the industry vulnerable to new entrants who undercut their prices. This is what airlines such as Virgin, Ryan Air and Easy Jet have done.

There are alternatives in monopolistic competition

In monopolistic competition, there are more pricing options. At one extreme, some firms clearly price above the market—and may even promote the fact. Harrods has a reputation as one of the most expensive stores in the world. Other firms emphasize below-the-market prices in their marketing mixes. Prices offered by discounters and mass-merchandisers, such as Aldi and Netto, illustrate this approach. They may even promote their pricing policy with catchy slogans such as 'guaranteed lowest prices' or 'we'll beat any advertised price'.

Above or below what market?

These examples raise an important question. Do these various strategies promote prices that are above or below the market, or are they really different prices for different target markets or different marketing mixes? In setting price-level policies, it is important to clearly define the *relevant target market* and *competitors* when making price comparisons. Perhaps some target customers do see important differences in the product, or in the convenience of location, or in the whole marketing mix. In such a case the marketing strategy is different, not just the price levels.

Dixons is a major UK retailer of electrical and electronic goods. It concentrates on a price-sensitive end of the market. Consider Dixons' prices again from this view. Dixons may have lower camera prices than conventional camera retailers, but it offers less help in the shop, less selection, and it will not take old cameras in trade. Dixons may be appealing to budget-oriented shoppers who compare prices among different mass-merchandisers. A speciality camera shop, appealing to different customers, may not be a direct competitor! Thus, it may be better to think of Dixons' price as part of a different marketing mix for a different target market, not as a below-the-market price.

A camera producer with this point of view might develop a different strategy for the Dixons' channel and the speciality store channel. In particular, the producer might offer the speciality shop one or more models that are not available to Dixons—to ensure that customers don't view the two shops as direct competitors with price the only difference.

Different price-level policies through the channel

When a product is sold to channel members instead of final consumers, the price should be set so that the channel members can cover costs and make a profit. To achieve its objectives, a manufacturer may set different price-level policies for different levels in the channel. For example, a producer of a slightly better product might set a price level that is low relative to competitors when selling to retailers, while suggesting an above-the-market retail price. This encourages retailers to carry the product and to emphasize it in their marketing mix because it yields higher profits.

The price of money may affect the price level

So far the discussion has focused on the price level of a firm's product. A nation's money also has a price level—what it is worth in some other currency. For example, on 1 October 1998 one pound sterling was worth 2.80 German marks. In other words, the exchange rate for the German mark against the pound was 2.80. Exhibit 16–6 lists exchange rates for money from several countries over a number of years, against the ECU. From this exhibit you can see that exchange rates change over time and sometimes the changes are significant.[10]

Within Europe there have been major changes in the role of exchange rates during the 1990s. In the early 1990s a major crisis hit the European monetary system (EMS). The EMS was designed to produce a regular and predictable relationship between European currencies. Member countries undertook to maintain the exchange rates between currencies within agreed limits largely through changing interest rates. In theory this would lead to enhanced opportunities for international trade between members of the system. In reality this led to considerable problems, particularly in countries such as Ireland, when the system effectively collapsed in 1993. The key events leading to the collapse were the reunification of Germany, the entry of the United Kingdom into the system, and uncertainty about the Maastricht Treaty. These three factors combined with other pressures led to a virtual abandonment of the system with currencies free to vary against each other within a broad band of plus or minus 15 per cent.

With the introduction of the euro in 1999, exchange rates have been fixed for the 11 EU members who have joined the euro. The 11 countries making up Euroland are Austria, Belgium, Finland, France, Germany, Ireland, Italy, the Netherlands, Luxembourg, Portugal and Spain. These countries will use the euro as a paper and electronic currency until 2002, when new notes and coins will come into circulation. The old national currencies in Euroland are fixed to the euro at a rate specified to six decimal places. At the time of the launch of the euro, it was worth £0.704 sterling but that rate fluctuates because the United Kingdom is not a member.

There are many implications for businesses whether or not their countries are members of the euro. This is because most businesses trade with other businesses

National currency units per ECU							
	1985	1986	1987	1988	1989	1990	1991
EU							
Austria	20.70	14.98	14.55	14.59	14.57	14.46	14.43
Belgium	44.91	43.78	43.04	43.43	43.38	42.50	42.26
Denmark	8.02	7.94	7.88	7.95	8.05	7.88	7.91
Finland	6.20	4.98	5.07	4.94	4.72	4.87	5.01
France	6.80	6.80	6.93	7.04	7.02	6.93	6.98
Germany	2.23	2.13	2.07	2.07	2.07	2.06	2.05
Germany, East	2.23	2.13	2.07	2.07	2.07	2.06	2.05
Germany, West	2.23	2.13	2.07	2.07	2.07	2.06	2.05
Greece	105.74	137.43	156.22	162.55	178.88	201.93	225.17
Ireland	0.72	0.73	0.78	0.78	0.78	0.77	0.77
Italy	1448.00	1461.87	1494.71	1537.33	1510.20	1526.11	1534.18
Luxembourg	44.91	43.78	43.04	43.43	43.38	42.50	42.26
The Netherlands	2.51	2.40	2.33	2.33	2.34	2.32	2.31
Portugal	130.25	147.09	162.58	169.19	173.32	181.46	178.74
Spain	129.13	137.46	142.19	137.60	130.41	129.58	128.43
Sweden	8.60	6.70	7.31	7.24	7.10	7.54	7.48
United Kingdom	0.59	0.67	0.70	0.66	0.67	0.72	0.70

National currency units per ECU							
	1992	1993	1994	1995	1996	October 1997	Unit of currency
EU							
Austria	14.20	13.60	13.50	13.03	13.26		Schilling
Belgium	41.55	40.40	39.55	38.10	38.78	40.45	Belgian franc
Denmark	7.81	7.58	7.52	7.24	7.26	7.46	Danish kroner
Finland	5.78	6.68	6.17	5.64	5.64		Markka
France	6.85	6.62	6.57	6.45	6.41	6.59	French franc
Germany	2.02	1.93	1.92	1.85	1.88	1.96	Deutsche Mark
Germany, East	2.02	1.93	1.92	1.85			Deutsche Mark
Germany, West	2.02	1.93	1.92	1.85			Deutsche Mark
Greece	246.11	267.85	287.15	299.41	301.44		Drachma
Ireland	0.76	0.80	0.79	0.81	0.78	0.76	Irish pound (punt)
Italy	1587.85	1836.96	1908.21	2106.66	1931.39	1921.00	Lira
Luxembourg	41.55	40.40	39.55	38.10	38.79	40.45	Luxembourg franc
The Netherlands	2.28	2.17	2.15	2.07	2.11	2.21	Netherlands guilder
Portugal	174.36	188.02	196.41	193.88	193.16	199.80	Portuguese escudo
Spain	131.95	148.81	158.48	161.16	158.64	165.60	Peseta
Sweden	7.51	9.10	9.13	9.23	8.40	8.39	Swedish kronor
United Kingdom	0.73	0.78	0.77	0.82	0.80	0.68	Pound sterling

Note: Annual average market rates.

Exhibit 16–6 Exchange Rages against ECU 1985–97.[10]

outside their own country so, at some level, there is importing and exporting and the likelihood of dealing with businesses who trade in the euro. From an accounting point of view, systems need to be capable of dealing with the euro. In marketing terms, it may mean being able to convert prices to the euro (there is complex formula for doing this) or adopting it as the company's base currency.[11]

Internet Excercise

Xenon Laboratories has set up a web site with a system that uses current exchange rates to convert one country's currency to another. Go to the web site (**www.ausmall.com.au**), scroll down to the reference section, and click on International Currency Converter. How much is your currency worth in $US today?

Foxfield Mushrooms is managed by the Kiernan Bros and is based in Kilnaleck, Co. Cavan. Like many of the other companies operating in the flourishing mushroom industry, it mainly manufactures compost which is sold to satellite growers, who, in turn, produce mushrooms to order for Foxfield which are then exported. The company employs approximately 100 people including full-time staff and part-time mushroom pickers.

Most of its raw materials are sourced locally. For example the company spends about £0.5 million per annum on straw. Its exports go exclusively to the United Kingdom, with 50 per cent going to retail outlets like Tesco's and Sainsbury's, 30 per cent to the wholesale trade and the remainder to processing companies. Sales in the UK rose from £2 million in 1986 to £8 million in 1992. Like most mushroom producers, the company operates on the basis of fixed contracts with its British customers. These contracts are based in sterling rather than in Irish punts. Therefore any devaluation of the pound sterling effectively reduced the company's margins.

During the currency crisis sterling's value was devalued and the company's margins were reduced by 12–14 per cent. It was unable to renegotiate its contract prices. Furthermore Foxfield faced competition on the domestic market from cheaper British imports. Interest rates on the company's loans increased and it shelved investment plans.

Foxfield mushrooms is exactly the sort of company that is most vulnerable to fluctuations in foreign currency values. It sourced virtually all its inputs in a country with a strengthening currency, namely Ireland, and sold most of its outputs to the UK where the currency had weakened.

To assist companies which found themselves in this position the Irish Government introduced The Market Development Fund. This fund was designed to provide short term funding to support companies like Foxfield which had found themselves in this situation. The fund proved successful in helping companies through this problem period.[12]

Consumers want value pricing

Sooner or later there is competition in most product markets and, in today's competitive markets, more and more customers are demanding real value. **Value pricing** means setting a fair price level for a marketing mix that really gives customers what they need. Value pricing does not necessarily mean cheap in the sense of low-grade. Nor does it mean high prestige if the right quality of goods and services do not accompany the prestige. Rather the focus is on the customer's requirements and the whole strategy.

Daewoo is a good example of a company that has built its profile in European markets through value pricing. Many elements of the car purchase such as number plates and delivery, are provided as part of an inclusive price, whereas most competitors would charge extra. Direct Line insurance company provides a full insurance broker service over the telephone, and is able to offer significantly cheaper quotations for many kinds of driver.

Value pricing builds relationships— and repeat purchases

These companies deliver on their promises. They try to give the consumer pleasant surprises, such as an unexpected service or a useful new feature or environmentally sound packaging, because it builds customer loyalty. They guarantee what they offer and they return the price if the customer is not completely satisfied. They avoid unrealistic price levels—prices that are high only because consumers already know the brand name. They build relationships with customers so the customers will be loyal and come back the next time they purchase.

Value pricing is simply the best pricing decision for the type of market-oriented strategy planning discussed throughout this whole text. To build profits and customer satisfaction, the whole marketing mix, including the price level, must meet target customers' needs.

MOST PRICE STRUCTURES ARE BUILT AROUND LIST PRICES

Prices start with a list price

Most price structures are built around a base price schedule or price list. **Basic list prices** are the prices final customers or users are normally asked to pay for products. In this book, unless noted otherwise, list price refers to basic list price.

In the next chapter, we discuss how firms set these list prices. For now, however, we'll consider variations from list price and why they are made.

DISCOUNT POLICIES—REDUCTIONS FROM LIST PRICES

Discounts are reductions from list price given by a seller to buyers who either give up some marketing function or provide the function themselves. Discounts can be useful in marketing strategy planning. In the following discussion, think about what function the buyers are giving up, or providing, when they get each of these discounts.

Quantity discounts encourage volume buying

Quantity discounts are discounts offered to encourage customers to buy in larger amounts. This lets a seller get more of a buyer's business or shifts some of the storing function to the buyer, or reduces shipping and selling costs, or all of these. Such discounts are of two kinds: cumulative and non-cumulative.

Cumulative quantity discounts apply to purchases over a given period, such as a year, and the discount usually increases as the amount purchased increases. Cumulative discounts are intended to encourage *repeat* buying by a single customer by reducing the customer's cost for additional purchases. This is a way to develop closer, ongoing relationships with customers. For example, a builder's merchant might give a cumulative quantity discount to a building contractor who is not able to buy all of the needed materials at once. The merchant wants to reward the contractor's patronage and discourage shopping around. The merchant knows that its market is very competitive. So the cumulative discount is just part of an effort to build loyalty with existing customers. The discount is small relative to the cost of constantly trying to attract new customers to replace departures.

The major supermarket chains in the United Kingdom, such as Sainsbury, Tesco and Safeway have developed similar loyalty schemes to encourage regular customers at their shops. Members are given a card that records purchases. Periodically shoppers can claim rebates on their shopping bills as a result of the cumulative value of purchases. An additional benefit for the company is the customer information that the use of the card provides.

Non-cumulative quantity discounts apply only to individual orders. Such discounts encourage larger orders but do not tie a buyer to the seller after that one purchase. These discounts may be used to discourage small orders, which are expensive to handle. For the most part they are mainly used to encourage bigger orders. The builder's merchant may purchase and resell insulation products made by several competing producers. One of these producers might try to encourage the merchant to stock

Price comparisons are frequently made for telephone services. Phone companies such as Tele2 are increasingly stressing their price competitiveness

CHAPTER 17

Price Setting in the Business World

When You Finish This Chapter, You Should

1 Understand how most wholesalers and retailers set their prices, using mark-ups.

2 Understand why turnover is so important in pricing.

3 Understand the advantages and disadvantages of average cost pricing.

4 Know how to use break-even analysis to evaluate possible prices.

5 Know how to find the most profitable price and quantity, using marginal analysis, total revenue and total cost.

6 Know the many ways that price setters use demand estimates in their pricing.

7 Understand the important new terms (shown in colour).

MAGIC OF SPAIN

Package holidays have revolutionized the way people take their holidays. It is hard to believe that such holidays are a relatively new innovation in travel and leisure. Introduced in the late 1960s such holidays have introduced many people to the delights of a holiday abroad in a wide range of increasingly exotic locations from Bali to Bermuda and Moscow to Madrid.

The growth in popularity of the package holiday stems from a basic economic principle, namely economies of scale. As more people travelled to the same destinations tour operators were able to get better deals from airlines and hotels allowing them to pass lower prices and better value on to customers. Lower prices made holidays to destinations such as Spain, Greece and Italy more attractive, thus making it possible to reduce prices still further. Growth was also encouraged by the development of new generations of aircraft, capable of transporting large numbers of passengers safely and reliably to their destination. It was also linked to greater consumer awareness and desire to sample new destinations.

Spain has always been a popular destination for the international tourist. A combination of predictably good weather, culture and heritage, and relatively good value accommodation and food persuaded many travellers to take their annual holiday in destinations such as the Costa Brava, the Costa Blanca and the Costa del Sol. Each year millions of tourists fly from Germany, the United Kingdom, the Netherlands, Sweden and other European departure points.

Magic of Spain is one travel company that specializes in Spain as a tourist destination. Each year Magic of Spain brochures are distributed, largely through travel agents, typically well ahead of the travelling season. Wide ranges of packages are included in the brochure, designed to meet the varied needs of many different tourists.

Many other tour companies offer holidays to Spain. The typical brochure offers a range of different destinations, hotel grades and levels of accommodation from full board to self-catering. Some stress the use of scheduled flights that allow the passenger to travel at conventional times. Others offer lower prices but involve travelling late at night or early in the morning at times that do not suit the needs of individual travellers. Some operators offer the option of upgrading flights to business class. Such upgrades make checking in easier and provide a range of extra services for passengers on the aircraft.

One page of the Magic of Spain brochure detailing holidays to Andalucia in southern Spain illustrates the complex range of pricing decisions that a tour operator has to make. The page is typical of many such pages. It describes a particular destination, Frigiliana, a village close to Nerja, some 60 kilometres from Malaga. There are several self-catering alternatives for holiday makers, ranging from a converted mill with its own swimming pool and barbecue area, to smaller cottages, each with their own self-catering facilities.

Prices are shown per person. There are 10 different price ranges depending on departure dates. There are also different prices for different lengths of stay. Each of these variations is shown for each of the different types of accommodation on offer. Supplementary prices are shown for a range of different departure points and departure times. A simple calculation shows that there are over 4000 alternative prices for a holiday to this particular destination on this page alone! This particular brochure has 145 pages each with similar levels of detailed price information.

It is obvious that pricing decisions for tour operators are complex. The operator will only make a profit if it is fully aware of its costs. This will depend on the deals which it has made with travel and hotel companies. Profit will depend on levels of occupancy. The company will have to have a minimum number of customers, just to break even. Profit will also depend on getting the prices in the brochures right. Customers are increasingly price conscious and will shop around for the best deal. Many hotels sell room space to different tour operators, who are free to set lower prices for the same basic two weeks in the sun. Prices need to be related to costs, but they must also be competitive, because the consumer can quickly compare the offers in two competing brochures. Significant price differences for the same package can be detected very quickly.

Magic of Spain attempts to add extra value through negotiating special bonuses for customers. These bonuses include celebration bonuses for honeymooners and all couples celebrating a wedding anniversary or birthday during their holidays, first night's stay free and reductions on airport parking fees.

PRICE SETTING IS A KEY STRATEGY DECISION

In the last chapter, we discussed the idea that pricing objectives and policies should guide pricing decisions. We accepted the idea of a list price and went on to discuss variations from list. Setting the right prices is critical to the success of a tour operator such as Magic of Spain, as shown in the case. Now, we'll see how the basic list price is set in the first place—based on information about costs, demand and profit margins. See Exhibit 17–1.

Many firms set a price by just adding a standard mark-up to the average cost of the products they sell. This is changing. More managers are realizing that they should set prices by evaluating the effect of a price decision not only on profit margin for a given item, but also on demand and therefore on sales volume and costs. In very competitive markets such as grocery retailing, this approach often leads to low prices that increase profits *and* at the same time reduce customers' costs. For other firms in different market situations, careful price setting leads to a premium price for a marketing mix that offers customers something unique. These firms commonly focus on setting prices that earn attractive profits, as part of an overall marketing strategy that meets customers' needs.

There are many ways to set list prices. For simplicity they can be reduced to two basic approaches: *cost-oriented* and *demand-oriented* price setting. We will discuss cost-oriented approaches first because they are most common. Also, understanding the problems of relying only on a cost-oriented approach shows why a marketing manager must also consider demand to make good price decisions. Let's begin by looking at how most retailers and wholesalers set cost-oriented prices.

SOME FIRMS JUST USE MARK-UPS

Mark-ups guide pricing by intermediaries
Some firms, including most retailers and wholesalers, set prices by using a **mark-up**—an amount added to the cost of products to get the selling price. For example, suppose that a grocery chain such as Aldi buys a packet of coffee. To make a profit, the chain obviously must sell

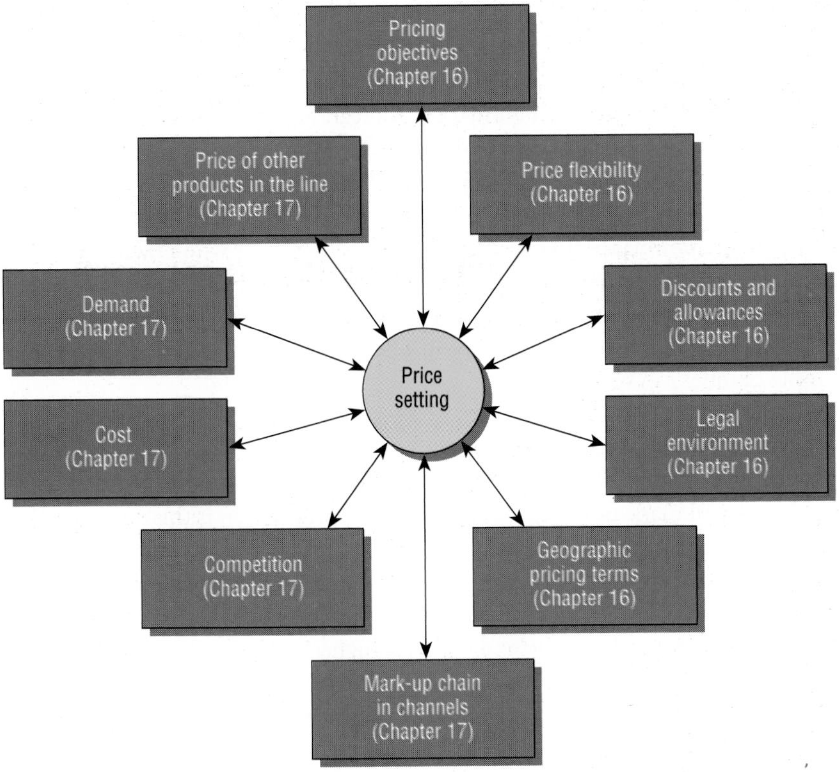

Exhibit 17–1 Key Factors That Influence Price Setting

the coffee for more than it paid. If it adds £1 to cover operating expenses and provide a profit, we say that the store is marking up the item £1.

Mark-ups, however, usually are stated as percentages rather than amounts of money. And this is where confusion sometimes arises. Is a mark-up of £1 on a cost of £2 a mark-up of 50 per cent? Or should the mark-up be figured as a percentage of the selling price—£3—and therefore be 33 per cent? A clear definition is necessary.

Mark-up per cent is based on selling price—a convenient rule

Unless otherwise stated, mark-up (per cent) means the percentage of selling price that is added to the cost to get the selling price. So the £1 mark-up on the £3 selling price is a mark-up of 33 per cent. Mark-ups are related to selling price for convenience. There is nothing wrong with the idea of mark-up on cost. However, to avoid confusion, it's important to state clearly which mark-up per cent you're using. Managers often want to change a mark-up on cost to one based on selling price—or vice versa. The calculations used to do this are simple (see the section on mark-up conversion in Appendix B, on Marketing Arithmetic).[1]

Many use a 'standard' mark-up per cent

Many intermediaries select a standard mark-up per cent and then apply it to all their products. This makes pric-

ing easier. When you think of the large number of items the average retailer and wholesaler carry—and the small sales volume of any one item—this approach may make sense. Spending the time to find the best price to charge on every item in stock (day-to-day or week-to-week) might not pay.

Moreover, different companies in the same line of business often use the same mark-up per cent. There is a reason for this: their operating expenses are usually similar. So a standard mark-up is acceptable as long as it's large enough to cover the firm's operating expenses—and provide a reasonable profit.

Mark-ups are related to gross margins

How does a manager decide on a standard mark-up in the first place? A standard mark-up is often set close to the firm's *gross margin*. Managers regularly see gross margins on their operating (profit and loss) statements. The gross margin is the amount left—after subtracting the cost of sales (cost of goods sold) from net sales—to cover the expenses of selling products and operating the business. (See Appendix B, Marketing Arithmetic, if you are unfamiliar with these ideas.) Aldi knows that there will not be any profit if the gross margin is not large enough. For this reason, Aldi might accept a mark-up per cent on the brand of coffee that is close to the store's usual gross margin per cent.

Smart producers pay attention to the gross margins and standard mark-ups of intermediaries in their channel. They usually allow trade (functional) discounts similar to the standard mark-ups these intermediaries expect.

Mark-up chain may be used in channel pricing

Different firms in a channel often use different mark-ups. A **mark-up chain**—the sequence of mark-ups firms use at different levels in a channel—determines the price structure in the whole channel. The mark-up is figured on the *selling price* at each level of the channel.

For example, Black & Decker's selling price for an electric drill becomes the cost the hardware wholesaler pays. The wholesaler's selling price becomes the hardware retailer's cost. And this cost plus a retail mark-up becomes the retail selling price. Each mark-up should cover the costs of running the business and leave a profit.

Exhibit 17–2 illustrates the mark-up chain for an electric drill at each level of the channel system. The production (factory) cost of the drill is £21.60. In this case, the producer takes a 10 per cent mark-up and sells the product for £24.00. The mark-up is 10 per cent of £24.00 or £2.40. The producer's selling price now becomes the wholesaler's cost—£24.00. If the wholesaler is used to taking a 20 per cent mark-up on selling price, the mark-up is £6.00 —and the wholesaler's selling price becomes £30.00. £30.00 now becomes the cost for the hardware retailer. And a retailer who is used to a 40 per cent mark-up adds £20.00, and the retail selling price becomes £50.00.

High mark-ups do not always mean big profits

Some people, including many traditional retailers, think high mark-ups mean big profits. Often this is not the case. A high mark-up may result in a price that's too high, a price at which few customers will buy. If little is sold, then little is earned, regardless of how high the mark-up. Many retailers and wholesalers seem more concerned with the size of their mark-up on a single item than with their total profit. Ultimately, their high mark-ups may lead to low profits.

Lower mark-ups can speed turnover and the stockturn rate

Some retailers and wholesalers, however, try to speed turnover to increase profit, even if this means reducing their mark-ups. They realize that a business runs up costs over time. If they can sell a much greater amount in the same time period, they may be able to take a lower mark-up and still earn higher profits at the end of the period. An important idea here is the **stockturn rate**—the number of times the average stock is sold in a year. Various methods of figuring stockturn rates can be used (see the section 'Computing the Stockturn Rate' in Appendix B). A low stockturn rate may be bad for profits.

At the very least, a low stockturn increases inventory carrying cost and ties up working capital. If a firm with a stockturn of 1 (once per year) sells products that cost it £100 000, it has that much tied up in inventory all the time. A stockturn of 5 requires only £20 000 worth of inventory (£100 000 cost   5 turnovers a year).

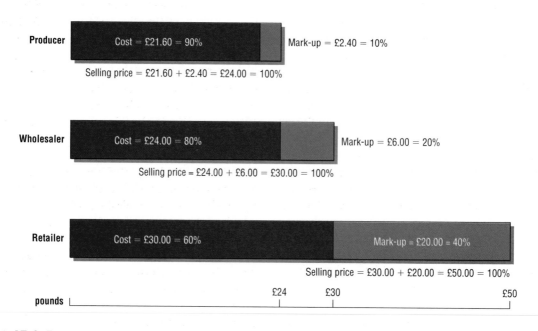

Exhibit 17–2 Examples of Mark-up Chain and Channel Pricing

Whether a stockturn rate is high or low depends on the industry and the product involved. A car parts wholesaler may expect an annual rate of 1—while a grocery store might expect 10 to 12 stockturns for soaps and detergents and 50 to 60 stockturns for fresh fruits and vegetables.

Mass-merchandisers run in fast company

Although some intermediaries use the same standard mark-up per cent on all their products, this policy ignores the importance of fast turnover. Mass-merchandisers know this. They put low mark-ups on fast-selling items and higher mark-ups on items that sell less frequently. For example, Asda (a major UK multi-sector retailer) may put a small mark-up on fast-selling health and beauty aids (like toothpaste or shampoo) but higher mark-ups on appliances and clothing. Similarly, it may put low mark-ups on fast-selling items such as milk, eggs and detergents. The mark-up on these items may be less than half the average mark-up for all grocery items, but this does not mean they are unprofitable. The store earns the small profit per unit more often.

Where does the mark-up chain start?

Mark-ups may eventually become standard in a trade. Most channel members tend to follow a similar process, adding a certain percentage to the previous price. The question is: Who sets price in the first place? The firm that brands a product is usually the one that sets its basic list price. It may be a large retailer, a large wholesaler, or, most often, the producer.

Some producers just start with a cost per unit figure and add a mark-up—perhaps a standard mark-up—to obtain their selling price. Or they may use some rule-of-thumb formula such as:

Selling price = Average production cost per unit   3

A producer who uses this approach might develop rules and mark-ups related to its own costs and objectives. Yet even the first step, selecting the appropriate cost per unit to build on, is not straightforward. Cost-oriented price setting can take a number of approaches and these are now discussed.

AVERAGE-COST PRICING IS COMMON AND CAN BE DANGEROUS

Average-cost pricing means adding a reasonable mark-up to the average cost of a product. A manager usually finds the average cost per unit by studying past records. Dividing the total cost for the last year by all the units produced and sold in that period gives an estimate of the average cost per unit for the next year. If the cost was £32 000 for all labour and materials and £30 000 for fixed overhead expenses, such as selling expenses, rent and manager salaries, then the total cost is £62 000. If the company produced 40 000 items in that time period, the average cost is £62 000 divided by 40 000 units, or £1.55 per unit. To get the price, the producer decides how much profit per unit to add to the average cost per unit. If the company considers 45 pence a reasonable profit for each unit, it sets the new price at £2.00. Exhibit 17–3A shows that this approach produces the desired profit, if the company sells 40 000 units.

It does not make allowances for cost variations as output changes

Average-cost pricing is simple but it can also be dangerous. It is easy to lose money with average-cost pricing.

To see why, follow this example further.

First, remember that the average cost of £2.00 per unit was based on output of 40 000 units. However, if the firm is only able to produce and sell 20 000 units in the next year, it may be in trouble. Twenty thousand units sold at £2.00 each (£1.55 cost plus 45 pence for expected profit) yield a total revenue of only £40 000. The overhead is still fixed at £30 000, and the variable material and labour cost drops by half to £16 000—for a total cost of £46 000. This means a loss of £6000, or 30 pence a unit. The method that was supposed to allow a profit of 45 pence a unit actually causes a loss of 30 pence a unit! See Exhibit 17–3B.

The basic problem with the average cost approach is that it does not consider cost variations at different levels of output. In a typical situation, costs are high with low output, and then economies of scale set in—the average cost per unit drops as the quantity produced increases. This is why mass production and mass distribution often make sense. It shows the importance of developing a better understanding of the different types of costs a marketing manager should consider when setting a price.

A. Calculation of Planned Profit if 40 000 Items Are Sold		B. Calculation of Actual Profit if Only 20 000 Items Are Sold	
Calculation of costs:		**Calculation of costs:**	
Fixed overhead expenses	£30 000	Fixed overhead expenses	£30 000
Labour and materials (£.80 a unit)	32 000	Labour and materials (£.80 a unit)	16 000
Total costs	£62 000	Total costs	£46 000
'Planned' profit	18 000		
Total costs and planned profit	£80 000		
Calculation of profit (or loss):		**Calculation of profit (or Loss):**	
Actual unit sales price (£2.00*)	£80 000	Actual unit sales price (£2.00*)	£40 000
Minus: total costs	62 000	Minus: total costs	46 000
Profit (loss)	£18 000	Profit (loss)	(£6 000)
Result:		**Result:**	
Planned profit of £18 000 is earned if 40 000 items are sold at £2.00 each		Planned profit of £18 000 is not earned. Instead, £6 000 loss results if 20 000 items are sold at £2.00 each.	

*Calculation of 'reasonable' price:	Expected total costs and planned profit	£80 000	£2.00
	Planned number of items to be sold	40 000	

Exhibit 17–3 Results of Average-Cost Pricing

MARKETING MANAGER MUST CONSIDER VARIOUS KINDS OF COSTS

Average-cost pricing may lead to losses because there are a variety of costs—and each changes in a *different* way as output changes. Any pricing method that uses cost must consider these changes. To understand why, we need to define six types of costs.

There are three kinds of total cost:

1. **Total fixed cost** is the sum of those costs that are fixed in total, no matter how much is produced. Among these fixed costs are rent, depreciation, managers' salaries, property taxes and insurance. Such costs stay the same even if production stops temporarily.
2. **Total variable cost**, on the other hand, is the sum of those changing expenses that are closely related to output such as expenses for parts, wages, packaging materials, outgoing freight and sales commissions. At zero output, total variable cost is zero. As output increases, so do variable costs. If Lee doubles its output of jeans in a year, its total cost for denim cloth also (roughly) doubles.
3. **Total cost** is the sum of total fixed and total variable costs. Changes in total cost depend on variations in total variable cost since total fixed cost stays the same.

There are three kinds of average cost

The pricing manager usually is more interested in cost per unit than total cost because prices are usually quoted per unit.

1. **Average cost** (per unit) is obtained by dividing total cost by the related quantity (that is, the total quantity that causes the total cost).
2. **Average fixed cost** (per unit) is obtained by dividing total fixed cost by the related quantity.
3. **Average variable cost** (per unit) is obtained by dividing total variable cost by the related quantity.

An example shows cost relations

A good way to get a feel for these different types of costs is to extend our average-cost pricing example (Exhibit 17–3A). Exhibit 17–4 shows the six types of cost and how they vary at different levels of output. The line for 40 000 units is highlighted because that was the expected level of sales in our average-cost pricing example. For simplicity, we assume that average variable cost is the same for each unit. Notice, however, that total variable cost increases when quantity increases.

Exhibit 17–5 shows the three average cost curves from Exhibit 17–4. Notice that average fixed cost goes down steadily as the quantity increases. Although the average variable cost remains the same, average cost decreases continually too. This is because average fixed cost is decreasing. With these relations in mind, let's reconsider the problem with average-cost pricing.

Quantity (Q)	Total Fixed Costs (TFC)	Average Fixed Costs (AFC)	Average Variable Costs (AVC)	Total Variable Costs (TVC)	Total Cost (TC)	Average Cost (AC)
0	£30 000	—	—	—	£30 000	—
10 000	30 000	£3.00	£0.80	£8 000	38 000	£3.80
20 000	30 000	1.50	0.80	16 000	46 000	2.30
30 000	30 000	1.00	0.80	24 000	54 000	1.80
40 000	30 000	0.75	0.80	32 000	62 000	1.55
50 000	30 000	0.60	0.80	40 000	70 000	1.40
60 000	30 000	0.50	0.80	48 000	78 000	1.30
70 000	30 000	0.43	0.80	56 000	86 000	1.23
80 000	30 000	0.38	0.80	64 000	94 000	1.18
90 000	30 000	0.33	0.80	72 000	102 000	1.13
100 000	30 000	0.30	0.80	80 000	110 000	1.10

$$\begin{bmatrix} 110\,000\ \text{(TC)} \\ 80\,000\ \text{(TVC)} \\ 30\,000\ \text{(TFC)} \end{bmatrix} \quad \text{(Q) } 100\,000 \begin{bmatrix} 0.30\ \text{(AFC)} \\ 30\,000\ \text{(TFC)} \\ 0.80\ \text{(AVC)} \end{bmatrix} \quad \begin{bmatrix} 100\,000\ \text{(Q)} \\ 0.80\ \text{(AVC)} \\ 80\,000\ \text{(TVC)} \end{bmatrix} \quad \begin{bmatrix} 30\,000\ \text{(TFC)} \\ 80\,000\ \text{(TVC)} \\ 110\,000\ \text{(TC)} \end{bmatrix} \quad \text{(Q) } 100\,000 \begin{bmatrix} 1.10\ \text{(AC)} \\ 110\,000\ \text{(TC)} \end{bmatrix}$$

Exhibit 17–4 Cost Structures of a Firm

 Internet Exercise

Easyjet is one of Europe's new breed of airlines, specialising in a no-frills air service and cut prices. Visit their web-site **(www.easyjet.com)**. How much discount is offered for on-line bookings? Why are Easyjet offering the discount? What costs do Easyjet avoid that other, more traditional airlines, have to incur?

Ignoring demand is the major weakness of average-cost pricing

Average-cost pricing works well if the firm actually sells the quantity it used to set the average cost price. Losses may result, however, if actual sales are much lower than

expected. On the other hand, if sales are much higher than expected, then profits may be very good but this will only happen by luck, because the firm's demand is much larger than expected.

To use average-cost pricing, a marketing manager must make *some* estimate of the quantity to be sold in the coming period. Without a quantity estimate, it is not possible to compute average cost. Unless this quantity is related to price, that is, unless the firm's demand curve is considered, the marketing manager may set a price that doesn't even cover a firm's total cost! You saw this happen in Exhibit 17–3B, when the firm's price of £2.00 resulted in demand for only 20 000 units and a loss of £6 000. The demand curve is still important even if

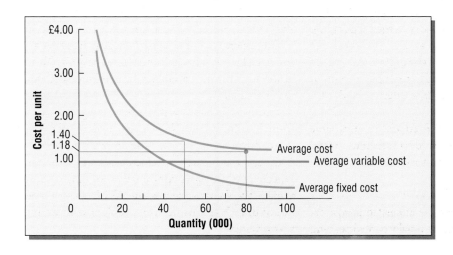

Exhibit 17–5 Typical Shape of Cost (per unit) Curves when AVC Is Assumed Constant Per Unit

management does not take time to think about it. For example, Exhibit 17–6 shows the demand curve for the firm we're discussing. This demand curve shows *why* the firm lost money when it tried to use average-cost pricing. At the £2.00 price, quantity demanded is only 20 000. With this demand curve and the costs in Exhibit 17–4, the firm will incur a loss whether management sets the price at a high £3 or a low £1.20. At £3, the firm will sell only 10 000 units for total revenue of £30 000. Total cost will be £38 000—for a loss of £8000. At the £1.20 price, it will sell 60 000 units, at a loss of £6000. However, the curve suggests that at a price of £1.65 consumers will demand about 40 000 units, producing a profit of about £4000.

In short, average-cost pricing is simple in theory, but often fails in practice. In stable situations, prices set by this method may yield profits but not necessarily *maximum* profits. And note that such cost-based prices may be higher than a price that would be more profitable for the firm, as shown in Exhibit 17–6. When demand conditions are changing, average-cost pricing is even more risky.

Exhibit 17–7 summarizes the relationships discussed above. Cost-oriented pricing requires an estimate of the total number of units to be sold. That estimate determines the *average* fixed cost per unit and thus the average total cost. Then the firm adds the desired profit per unit to the average total cost to get the cost-oriented selling price. How customers react to that price determines the actual quantity the firm will be able to sell. That quantity may not be the quantity used to compute the average cost! Further, the quantity the firm actually sells (times price) determines total revenue (and total profit or loss). A deci-

sion made in one area affects each of the others, directly or indirectly. Average-cost pricing does not consider these effects. A manager who forgets this can make serious pricing mistakes.

Experience curve pricing is even riskier

In recent years, some aggressive firms have used a variation of average-cost pricing called experience curve pricing. **Experience curve pricing** is average-cost pricing using an estimate of *future* average costs. This approach is based on the observation that over time, as an industry gains experience in certain kinds of production, managers learn new ways to reduce costs. The effect of such learning on costs varies in different businesses. Studies suggest that costs decrease about 15 to 20 per cent each time cumulative production volume (experience) doubles, at least in some industries. So some firms set average-cost prices where they expect costs to be when products are sold in the future, not where costs actually are when the strategy is set. This approach is more common in rapidly growing markets (such as in the electronics business) because cumulative production volume (experience) grows faster.

If costs drop as expected, this approach can work fairly well. However, it has the same risks as regular average-cost pricing unless demand is included in the price setting. This means the price setter has to estimate what quantity will be sold to be able to read the right price from the experience-based average-cost curve.[2]

Another danger of average-cost pricing is that it ignores competitors' costs and prices. Just as the price of a firm's own product influences demand, the price of available substitutes may impact demand.

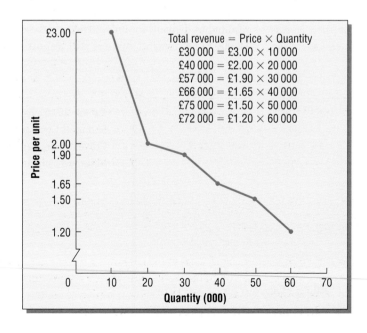

Exhibit 17–6 Evaluation of Various Prices along a Firm's Demand Curve

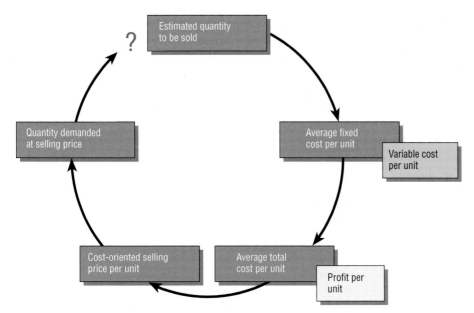

Exhibit 17–7 Summary of Relationships among Quantity, Cost and Price Using Cost-Oriented Pricing

SOME FIRMS ADD A TARGET RETURN TO COST

Target return pricing scores sometimes

Target return pricing—adding a target return to the cost of a product—has become popular in recent years. With this approach, the price setter seeks to earn (1) a percentage return (say 10 per cent per year) on the investment or (2) a specific total monetary return.

This method is a variation of the average-cost method since the desired target return is added into total cost. As a simple example, if a company had £180 000 invested and wanted to make a 10 per cent return on investment, it would add £18 000 to its annual total costs in setting prices. This approach has the same weakness as other average-cost pricing methods. If the quantity actually sold is less than the quantity used to set the price, then the company doesn't earn its target return—even though the target return seems to be part of the price structure. In fact, we already saw this in Exhibit 17–3. Remember that we added £18 000 as an expected profit—or target return. The return was much lower when the expected quantity was not sold. (It could be higher too—but only if the quantity sold is much larger than expected.) Target return pricing clearly does not guarantee that a firm will hit the target.

Hitting the target in the long run

Managers in some larger firms, who want to achieve a long-run target return objective, use another cost-oriented pricing approach—**long-run target return pricing**—adding a long-run average target return to the cost of a product. Instead of estimating the quantity they expect to produce in any one year, they assume that during several years' time their plants will produce at, say, 80 per cent of capacity. They use this quantity when setting their prices.

Companies that take this longer-run view assume that there will be recession years when sales drop below 80 per cent of capacity. For example, a company may sell roof insulation materials. In years when there is little construction, output is low and the firm does not earn the target return. However, the company also has good years when it sells more insulation and exceeds the target return. Over the long run, managers expect to achieve the target return. Sometimes they are right, depending on how accurately they estimate demand!

BREAK-EVEN ANALYSIS CAN EVALUATE POSSIBLE PRICES

Some price setters use break-even analysis in their pricing. **Break-even analysis** evaluates whether the firm will be able to break even, that is, cover all its costs, with a particular price. This is important because a firm must cover all costs in the long run or there is not much point being in business. This method focuses on **the break-even point** (BEP)—the quantity where the firm's total cost will just equal its total revenue.

Break-even charts help find the BEP

To help understand how break-even analysis works, look at Exhibit 17–8, an example of the typical break-even chart. *The chart is based on a particular selling price*—in this case £1.20 a unit. The chart has lines that show total costs (total variable plus total fixed costs) and total revenues at different levels of production. The BEP on the chart is at 75 000 units—where the total cost and total revenue lines intersect. At that production level, total cost and total revenue are the same—£90 000.

This chart also shows some typical assumptions made to simplify break-even analysis. Note that the total revenue curve is assumed to be a straight line. This means that each extra unit sold adds the same amount to total revenue. Stated differently, this assumes that *any quantity can be sold at the same price*. For this chart, a selling price of £1.20 a unit has been assumed. You can see that if the firm sells the break-even quantity of 75 000 at £1.20 each, it will earn a total revenue of £90 000.

In addition, the total cost curve in the chart is assumed to be a straight line. This means that average variable cost (AVC) is the same at different levels of output. For Exhibit 17–8, the AVC is 80 pence per unit.

The difference between the total revenue and total cost at a given quantity is the profit—or loss! The chart shows that below the break-even point, total cost is higher than total revenue—and the firm incurs a loss. The firm would make a profit above the break-even point. However, the firm would only reach the break-even point, or get beyond it into the profit area, *if* it could sell at least 75 000 units at the £1.20 price.

How to compute a break-even point

A break-even chart is an easy-to-understand visual aid, but it's also useful to be able to compute the break-even point.

The BEP, in units, can be found by dividing total fixed costs (TFC) by **the fixed-cost (FC) contribution per unit**—the assumed selling price per unit minus the variable cost per unit. This can be stated as a simple formula:

$$\text{BEP (in units)} = \frac{\text{Total fixed cost}}{\text{Fixed cost contribution per unit}}$$

This formula makes sense when we think about it. To break even, we must cover total fixed costs. Therefore, we must figure the contribution each unit will make to covering the total fixed costs (after paying for the variable costs to produce the item). When we divide this per-unit contribution into the total fixed costs that must be covered, we have the BEP (in units).

To illustrate the formula, let's use the cost and price information in Exhibit 17–8. The price per unit is £1.20. The average variable cost per unit is 80 pence. So the FC contribution per unit is 40 pence (£1.20; 80 pence). The total fixed cost is £30 000 (see Exhibit 17–8). Substituting in the formula:

$$\text{BEP} = \frac{£30\,000}{0.40} = 75\,000 \text{ units}$$

From this, if this firm sells 75 000 units, it will exactly cover all its fixed and variable costs. If it sells even one more unit, it will begin to show a profit, in this case, 40 pence per unit. Note that once the fixed costs are covered, the part of revenue formerly going to cover fixed costs is now *all profit*.

BEP can be stated in monetary terms

The BEP can also be figured in monetary terms. The easiest way is to compute the BEP in units and then multiply by the assumed per-unit price. If you multiply

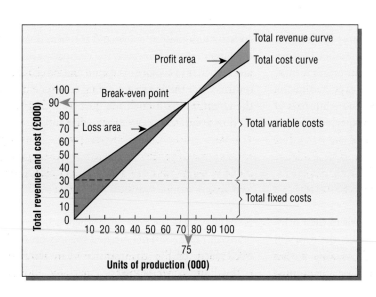

Exhibit 17–8 Break-Even Chart for a Particular Situation

the selling price (£1.20) by the BEP in units (75 000) you get £90 000—the BEP in sterling.

Each possible price has its own break-even point

Often it's useful to compute the break-even point for each of several possible prices and then compare the BEP for each price to likely demand at that price. The marketing manager can quickly reject some price possibilities when the expected quantity demanded at a given price is way below the BEP for that price.

A target profit can be included

So far in the discussion of BEP the focus has been on the quantity at which total revenue equals total cost, that is, where profit is zero. We can also vary this approach to see what quantity is required to earn a certain level of profit. The analysis is the same as described above for the BEP in units, but the amount of target profit is added to the total fixed cost. Then, when we divide the total fixed cost plus profit figure by the contribution from each unit, we get the quantity that will earn the target profit.

Break-even analysis shows the effect of cutting costs

Break-even analysis makes it clear why managers must constantly look for effective new ways to get jobs done at lower costs. For example, if a manager can reduce the firm's total fixed costs—perhaps by using computer systems to cut out excess inventory carrying costs—the BEP will be lower and profits will start to build sooner. Similarly, if the variable cost to produce and sell an item can be reduced, the fixed-cost contribution per unit increases; that too lowers the BEP and profit accumulates faster for each product sold beyond the break-even point.

Break-even analysis is helpful, but not a pricing solution

Break-even analysis is helpful for evaluating alternatives. It is also popular because it's easy to use. Yet break-even analysis is too often misunderstood. Beyond the BEP, profits seem to be growing continually. And the graph, with its straight-line total revenue curve, makes it seem that any quantity can be sold at the assumed price. This usually is not true. It is the same as assuming a perfectly horizontal demand curve at that price. In fact, most managers face down-sloping demand situations. And their total revenue curves do *not* keep going up.

The firm and costs discussed in the average cost pricing example earlier in this chapter illustrate this point. Exhibit 17–4 confirms that the total fixed cost (£30 000) and average variable cost (80 pence) for that firm are the same ones shown in the break-even chart (Exhibit 17–8). So this break-even chart is the one that would be drawn for that firm assuming a price of £1.20 a unit. However, the demand curve for that case showed that the firm could only sell 60 000 units at a price of £1.20. So that firm would never reach the 75 000-unit break-even point at a £1.20 price. It would only sell 60 000 units, and it would lose £ 6000! A firm with a different demand curve, say one where the firm could sell 80 000 units at a price of £1.20, would in fact break even at 75 000 units.

Break-even analysis is a useful tool for analysing costs but it is a cost-oriented approach and suffers the same limitation as other cost-oriented approaches. Specifically, it does not consider the effect of price on the quantity that consumers will want, that is, the demand curve. So to really zero in on the most profitable price, marketers are better off estimating the demand curve itself and then using marginal analysis, which will be discussed next.

MARGINAL ANALYSIS CONSIDERS BOTH COSTS AND DEMAND

Our examples of cost-oriented pricing approaches show that a marketing manager and anyone else involved in setting a price must really understand how costs vary at different sales quantities. However, the examples also show that it is not enough just to understand costs. The price setter should also consider demand. The challenge is to consider both demand and costs at the same time because the price decision usually affects both costs and revenue, and they determine profit.

Marginal analysis—helps find the best price

The best pricing tool marketers have for looking at costs and revenue (demand) at the same time is marginal

analysis. **Marginal analysis** focuses on the change in total revenue and total cost from selling one more unit to find the most profitable price and quantity. Marginal analysis doesn't just seek a price that will result in *some* profit. It seeks the price that *maximizes* profits. This objective makes sense. If you know how to make the biggest profit, you can always adjust to pursue other objectives—while knowing how much profit is being given up!

Marginal analysis when demand curves slope down

We'll focus on the many situations in which demand curves are down-sloping, especially monopolistic competition. In these situations, the firm has carved out a market niche for itself and does have a pricing decision to make. The special case of oligopoly will be discussed briefly. Pure or nearly pure competition will not be covered as in that situation marketing managers have little difficulty with the pricing decision. They do not have much choice except to use the market price.

In monopolistic competition, the firm faces a down-sloping demand curve. The price setter must pick a specific price on that curve and generally will offer that price to all potential buyers. The marketer can hope to increase sales volume by lowering the price. However, all customers, even those who might be willing to pay more, pay this lower price. Even though the quantity has increased, the total revenue may decrease. Therefore, a manager should consider the effect of alternative prices on total revenue (and profit). The way to do this is to look at marginal revenue.

Marginal revenue can be negative

Marginal revenue is the change in total revenue that results from the sale of one more unit of a product. When the demand curve is down-sloping, this extra unit can be sold only by reducing the price of *all* items.

Exhibit 17–9 shows the relationship between price, quantity, total revenue and marginal revenue in a situation with a straight-line, down-sloping demand curve.

The firm in this example can sell four units for a total revenue of £420 or five units for £460. Thus the marginal revenue for the fifth unit is £460 – £420 or £40. Considering only revenue, it would be desirable to sell this extra unit. Will revenue continue to rise if the firm sells more units at lower prices? No! Exhibit 17–9 shows that negative marginal revenues occur at lower price levels. Obviously, this is not good for the firm! (Note: the

(1) Quantity (Q)	(2) Price (P)	(3) Total Revenue (1) (2) TR	(4) Marginal Revenue MR
0	£150	£ 0	
1	140	140	£140
2	130	260	120
3	117	351	91
4	105	420	69
5	92	460	40
6	79	474	14
7	66	462	12
8	53	424	38
9	42	378	46
10	31	310	68

Exhibit 17–9 Marginal Revenue and Price

total revenue obtained if price is cut may still be positive, but the marginal revenue—the extra revenue gained—may be positive or negative.)

Marginal revenue curve and demand curve are different

The marginal revenue curve is always below a down-sloping demand curve because the price of each last unit must be lower to sell more. This is shown in Exhibit 17–10, which uses the data from Exhibit 17–9. The fact that the demand curve and the marginal revenue curves are different in monopolistic competition is very important. Both curves will be used to find the best price and quantity.

Marginal cost—the cost of one more unit

As shown already, various kinds of costs behave differently. Further, there is an important kind of cost similar

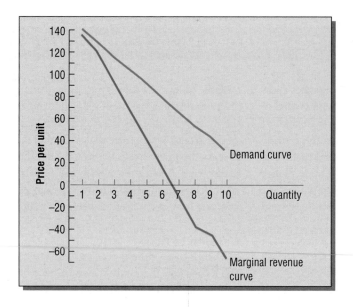

Exhibit 17–10 A Plotting of the Demand and Marginal Revenue Data in Exhibit 17–9

to marginal revenue: marginal cost. This cost is vital to marginal analysis. **Marginal cost** is the change in total cost that results from producing one more unit. If it costs £275 to produce 9 units of a product and £280 to produce 10 units, then marginal cost is £5 for the 10th unit. In other words, marginal cost, contrasted to average cost per unit, is the additional cost of producing one more *specific unit*; average cost is the average for *all units*.

Cost structure example

Exhibit 17–11 shows how these costs can vary for a typical firm. *Fill in the missing numbers in this exhibit.* Notice that variable cost is no longer assumed constant per unit in Exhibit 17–11. Here we use the more realistic assumption that variable costs will go down for a while and then rise.

Exhibit 17–11 illustrates three important points.

First, total fixed costs do not change over the entire range of output—but total variable costs increase continually as more and more units are produced. Therefore, total costs—the sum of total fixed costs and total variable costs—will increase as total quantity increases.

Second, average costs will decrease—for a while—as quantity produced increases. Remember that average costs are the sum of average fixed costs and average variable costs—and here average fixed costs are going down because total fixed costs are divided by more and more units as output increases. For example, given a total fixed cost of £200, at a production level of four units, the average fixed cost is £50. At a production level of five units, the average fixed cost is £40.

Third, average costs in this table start rising for the last two units because average variable costs are increasing faster than average fixed costs are decreasing. The firm may be forced to use less efficient facilities and workers, go into overtime work, or pay higher prices for the materials it needs. This turn-up of the average cost curve is common after economies of scale run out.

The marginal cost of just one more is important

The marginal cost column in Exhibit 17–11 is the most important cost column for our purposes. It shows what each extra unit costs. This suggests the *minimum* extra revenue we would like to get for that additional unit. Like average cost, marginal cost drops but it begins to rise again at a lower level of output than average cost does.

Marginal cost starts to increase at five units. This can be seen in Exhibit 17–12—which shows the behaviour of the average cost, average variable cost and marginal cost curves. Note that the marginal cost curve intersects the average variable cost and average cost curves from below *at their low points*, and then rises rapidly. This is typically how this curve behaves.

How to find the most profitable price and the quantity to produce

Since a manager must choose only *one* price level (for a time period), the question is which price to choose. This price determines the quantity that will be sold. To maximize profit, a manager should be willing to sell more units if the marginal revenue from selling them is at least equal to the marginal cost of the extra units. From this we get the following *rule for maximizing profit*: the highest profit is earned at the price where marginal cost is just less than or equal to marginal revenue.*

---

* This rule applies in the typical situations where the curves are shaped similarly to those discussed here. Technically, however, we should add the following to the rule for maximizing profit: the marginal cost must be increasing or decreasing at a lesser rate than marginal revenue.

(1) Quantity Q	(2) Total Fixed Cost TFC	(3) Average Fixed Cost AFC	(4) Total Variable Cost TVC	(5) Average Variable Cost AVC	(6) Total Cost (TFC TVC TC) TC	(7) Average Cost (AC TC Q) AC	(8) Marginal Cost (per unit) MC
0	£200	£ 0	£ 0	£0	£200	Infinity	
1	200	20	96	96	296	296	£96
2	200	100	116	58	316	—	20
3	200	—	—	—	331	110.33	—
4	200	50	—	—	344	—	—
5	200	40	155	31	—	71	11
6	200	—	168	—	—	61.33	13
7	—	—	183	—	—	—	15
8	—	—	223	—	—	—	—
9	—	—	307	—	507	56.33	—
10	—	20	510	51	710	71	£203

Exhibit 17–11 Cost Structure for Individual Firm (fill in missing numbers)

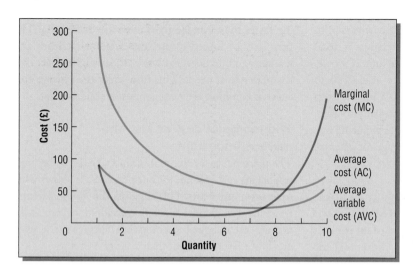

Exhibit 17–12 Per-Unit Cost Curves (for data in Exhibit 17–11)

This optimal price is *not* found on the marginal revenue curve. This profit-maximizing selling price is found by referring to the demand curve, which shows what price customers are willing to pay for the optimum quantity.

To make sure you understand the method for finding this optimal price, study the following example carefully. To make doubly sure that this approach is fully explained, we will calculate the most profitable price and quantity using total revenue and total cost curves first, and then show that you will get the same answer with marginal curves. This will give you a check on the method, as well as help you see how the marginal revenue–marginal cost method works.

Profit maximization with total revenue and total cost curves

Exhibit 17–13 provides data on total revenue, total cost, and total profit for a firm. Exhibit 17–14 graphs the

total revenue, total cost and total profit relationships. The highest point on the total profit curve is at a quantity of six units. This is also the quantity where we find the greatest vertical distance between the TR curve and the TC curve. Exhibit 17–13 shows that a price of £79 will result in selling six units, so £79 is the price that leads to the highest profit.

A price lower than £79 would result in a higher sales volume but the total profit curve declines beyond a quantity of six units. So a profit-maximizing marketing manager would not be interested in setting a lower price.

Profit maximization using marginal curves

Now we can apply the rule for maximizing profit using marginal curves. We again find that £79 is the best price and that 6 is the best quantity. See Exhibit 17–15, which graphs the marginal revenue and marginal cost data from Exhibit 17–13.

(1) Quantity (Q)	(2) Price (P)	(3) Total Revenue (TR)	(4) Total Variable Cost (TVC)	(5) Total Cost (TC)	(6) Profit (TR − TC)	(7) Marginal Revenue (MR)	(8) Marginal Cost (MC)	(9) Marginal Profit (MR − MC)
0	£150	£ 0	£ 0	£200	£ 200			
1	140	140	96	296	156	£140	£ 96	£ 44
2	130	260	116	316	56	120	20	100
3	117	351	131	331	20	91	15	76
4	105	420	144	344	76	69	13	56
5	92	460	155	355	105	40	11	29
6	79	474	168	368	106	14	13	1
7	66	462	183	383	79	12	15	27
8	53	424	223	423	1	38	40	78
9	42	378	307	507	129	46	84	130
10	31	310	510	710	400	68	203	271

Exhibit 17–13 Revenue, Cost and Profit for an Individual Firm

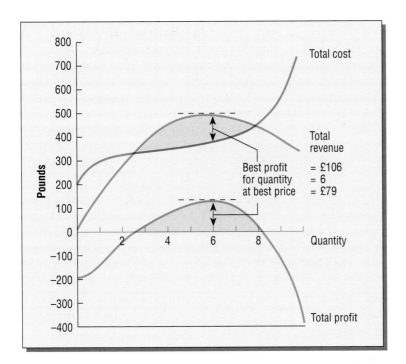

Exhibit 17–14 Graphic Determination of the Output Giving the Greatest Total Profit for a Firm

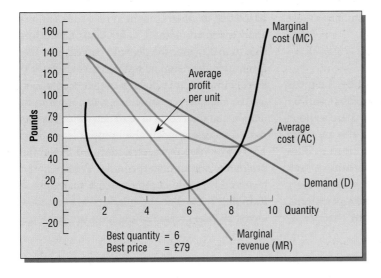

Exhibit 17–15 Alternative Determination of the Most Profitable Output and Price for a Firm

In Exhibit 17–15, the intersection of the marginal cost and marginal revenue curves occurs at a quantity of six. This is the most profitable quantity. The best price must be obtained by going up to the demand curve and then over to the vertical axis—*not* by going from the intersection of MR and MC over to the vertical axis. Again, the best price is £79.

The graphic solution is supported by the data in Exhibit 17–13. At a price of £79 and a quantity of six, marginal revenue equals £14 and marginal cost is £13. There is a profit margin of £1—suggesting that it might be profitable to offer seven rather than six units. This is not the case, however. The marginal cost of the seventh unit is £15, while its marginal revenue is actu-

ally negative. Lowering the price to £66 to sell seven units (instead of only six) will reduce total profit by £27.

It is important to realize that *total* profit is *not* near zero when marginal revenue (MR) equals marginal cost (MC). **Marginal profit**—the extra profit on the last unit—is near zero. That is exactly why the quantity obtained at the MR/MC intersection is the most profitable. Marginal analysis shows that when the firm is finding the best price to charge, it should lower the price—to increase the quantity it will sell—as long as the last unit it sells will yield *extra* profits.

Again, the marketing manager must choose only *one* price. Marginal analysis is useful in helping to set the best price to charge for all that will be sold. It might help to think of the demand curve as an if-then curve—*if* a price is selected, *then* its related quantity will be sold. Before the marketing manager sets the actual price, all these *if-then* combinations can be evaluated for profitability. Once the price level is set, the results will follow—that is, the related quantity will be sold.

A profit range is reassuring

We've been trying to find the most profitable price and quantity. In a changing world, this is difficult. Fortunately, this best point is surrounded by a profitable range. Note that in Exhibit 17–14, there are two break-even points rather than a single point, which was the case when we were discussing break-even analysis. The second break-even point falls farther to the right because total costs turn up and total revenue turns down. These two break-even points are important. They show the range of profitable operations. Although marginal analysis seeks the price that gives the *maximum* profit, we know that this point is an ideal rather than a realistic possibility. So it's essential that you know there is a *range of profit* around the optimum—it isn't just a single point. This means that pursuing the most profitable price is a wise approach.

Operating at a loss

The marginal analysis approach to finding the most profitable price will also find the price that will be *least unprofitable* when market conditions are so poor that the firm must operate at a loss. If sales are slow, the firm may even have to consider closing. The marketing manager might have something to say about that. A key point here is that most fixed costs will continue even if the firm stops its operations. Some fixed costs may even involve items that are so 'sunk' in the business that they cannot be sold for anything near the cost shown on the company's records. An unsuccessful company's special-purpose buildings and machines may be worthless to anyone else. So fixed costs may be irrelevant to a decision about closing the business.

Marginal costs are another matter. If the firm can recover the marginal cost of the last unit (or, more generally, the variable cost of the units being considered), it may want to continue operating. The extra income would help pay the fixed costs and reduce the firm's losses. If it can't meet marginal costs, it should stop operations temporarily or go out of business. The exceptions involve social or humanitarian considerations, or the fact that the marginal costs of closing temporarily are high and stronger demand is expected *soon*. However, if marginal costs can be covered in the short run, even though all fixed costs cannot, the firm should stay in operation.

Marginal analysis helps get the most in pure competition

Marketing managers caught in pure competition can also apply marginal methods. They don't have a price decision to make since the demand curve is flat. (Note: this means that the marginal revenue curve is flat at the same level.) However, they do have output decisions. They can use the marginal revenue curve, therefore, with their own unique marginal cost curve to determine the most profitable (or least unprofitable) output level. See Exhibit 17–16. And this approach leads to a different (and more profitable) output than the lowest average-cost decision favoured by some common-sense managers. Note in Exhibit 17–16 that the quantity associated with the lowest average cost is not the most profitable quantity.

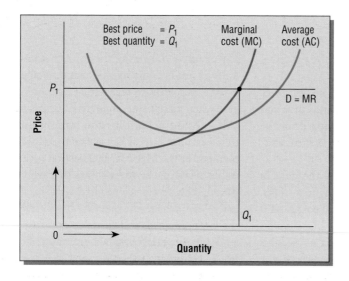

Exhibit 17–16 Finding the Most Profitable (or least unprofitable) Price and Quantity in Pure Competition (in the short run)

Marginal analysis applies in oligopoly too

Chapter 17 noted that marketing managers who compete in oligopoly situations often just set a price that meets what competitors charge. Marginal analysis helps to explain this situation better. Exhibit 17–17 shows a demand curve and marginal revenue curve typical of what a marketing manager in an oligopoly situation faces. The demand curve is kinked, and the current market price is at the kink. The dashed part of the marginal revenue line in Exhibit 17–17 shows that marginal revenue drops sharply at the kinked point. This is a technical but important matter. It helps explain why prices are relatively 'sticky' at the kinked point.

Even if costs change (and each firm's supply curve moves up or down), the marginal cost curve is still likely to cross the marginal revenue curve somewhere along the drop in the marginal revenue curve. In this case, even though costs are changing, and there may seem to be a reason for changing the price. Setting the price at the level of the kink maximizes profit!

A price leader usually sets the price

Most of the firms in an oligopoly are aware of the economics of their situation, at least intuitively. Usually, a **price leader** sets a price for all to follow, perhaps to maximize profits or to get a certain target return on investment and (without any collusion) other members of the industry follow. The price leader is usually the firm with the lowest costs. That may give it more flexibility than competitors. This price may be maintained for a long time or at least as long as all members of the industry continue to make a reasonable profit. Sometimes, however, a price leader tries to lower the price, and a competitor lowers it even further. This can lead to price wars, at least temporarily. This sometimes happens in

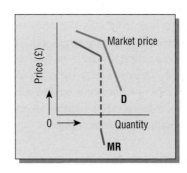

Exhibit 17–17
Marginal Revenue Drops Fast in an Oligopoly

competition between major airlines. Price wars in oligopoly tend to be very unprofitable for each firm and the whole industry so they usually pass fairly quickly.

A rough demand estimate is better than none

Marginal analysis is a flexible and useful tool for marketing managers. Some managers do not take advantage of it because they think it is just not practical to try to determine the exact shape of the demand curve. Such a view misses the point of marginal analysis. Marginal analysis encourages managers to think very carefully about what they *do know* about costs and demand. Only rarely is either type of information exact. So in practical applications the focus of marginal analysis is not on finding the precise price that will maximize profit. Rather, the focus is on getting an estimate of how profit might vary across a *range of relevant prices*. Further, a number of practical demand-oriented approaches can help a marketing manager do a better job of understanding the likely shape of the demand curve for a target market. We'll discuss these approaches next.

DEMAND-ORIENTED APPROACHES FOR SETTING PRICES

Value in use pricing— how much will the customer save?

Organizational buyers think about how a purchase will affect their total costs. Many marketers who aim at business markets keep this in mind when estimating demand and setting prices. They use **value in use pricing**—which means setting prices that will capture some of what customers will save by substituting the firm's product for the one currently being used.

For example, a producer of computer-controlled machines used to assemble cars knows that his machine doesn't just replace a standard machine. It also reduces labour costs, quality control costs, and—after the car is sold—costs of warranty repairs. The potential savings

(value in use) might be different for different customers—because they have different operations, costs and the like. The marketer can estimate what each car producer will save by using the machine—and then set a price that makes it less expensive for the car producer to buy the computerized machine than to stick with the old methods. The number of customers who have different levels of potential savings also provides some idea about the shape of the demand curve.[3]

Customers may have reference prices

Some people do not devote much thought to what they pay for the products they buy, including some frequently purchased goods and services. But most consumers have a **reference price**—the price they expect to pay—for many of the products they purchase. And different customers may have different reference prices for the same basic type of purchase. For example, a person who really enjoys reading might have a higher reference price for a popular paperback book than another person who is only an occasional reader. Marketing research can sometimes identify different segments with different reference prices.[4]

Leader pricing—make it low to attract customers

Leader pricing means setting some very low prices—real bargains—to get customers into retail stores. The idea is not to sell large quantities of the leader items but to get customers into the store to buy other products. Certain products are picked for their promotion value and priced low—but above cost. In food stores, the leader prices are the 'specials' that are advertised regularly to give an image of low prices. Leader items are usually well-known, widely used items that customers don't stock heavily—milk, butter, eggs or coffee—but on which they will recognize a real price cut. In other words, leader pricing is normally used with products for which consumers do have a specific reference price.

Leader pricing may try to appeal to customers who normally shop elsewhere. But it can backfire if customers buy only the low-price leaders. To avoid hurting profits, managers often select leader items that aren't directly competitive with major lines—as when bargain-priced cassettes is the leader for a stereo equipment store.

Psychological pricing—some prices just seem right

Psychological pricing means setting prices that have special appeal to target customers. Some people think there are whole ranges of prices that potential customers see as the same. So price cuts in these ranges do not increase the quantity sold. However, just below this range, customers may buy more. Then, at even lower prices, the quantity demanded stays the same again—and so on. Exhibit 17–18 shows the kind of demand curve that leads to psychological pricing. Vertical drops mark the price ranges that customers see as the same. Pricing research shows that there *are* such demand curves.

Odd-even pricing is setting prices that end in certain numbers. For example, products selling below £50 often end in the number 5 or the number 9—such as 49 pence or £24.95. Prices for higher-priced products are often £1 or £2 below the next even figure, such as £99 rather than £100. Some marketers use odd-even pricing because they think consumers react better to these prices, perhaps seeing them as 'substantially' lower than the next highest even price. Marketers using these prices

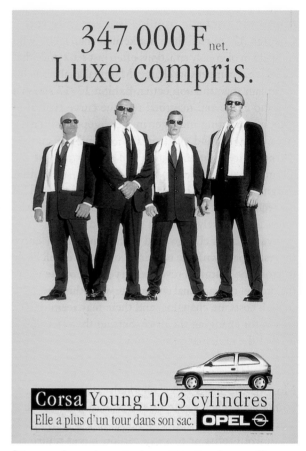

Price can be an important consideration for specific market segments. Opel stresses the value for money of its Corsa range

seem to assume that they have a rather jagged demand curve, that slightly higher prices will substantially reduce the quantity demanded. Long ago, some retailers used odd-even prices to force their clerks to give change. Then the clerks had to record the sale and could not pocket the money. Today, however, it's not always clear why firms use these prices or whether they really work.[5]

Prestige pricing indicates quality

Prestige pricing is setting a rather high price to suggest high quality or high status. Some target customers want

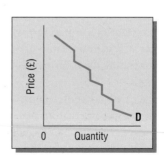

Exhibit 17–18
Demand Curve when Psychological Pricing is Appropriate

the best, so they will buy at a high price. On the other hand, if the price seems cheap, they worry about quality and don't buy. Prestige pricing is most common for luxury products—such as furs, jewellery and perfume. It is also common in service industries. Here the customer cannot see the product in advance and relies on price to judge its quality. Target customers who respond to prestige pricing give the marketing manager an unusual demand curve. Instead of a normal down-sloping curve, the curve goes down for a while and then bends back to the left again. See Exhibit 17–19.

Price lining

Price lining is setting a few price levels for a product line and then marking all items at these prices. This approach assumes that customers have a certain reference price in mind that they expect to pay for a product. For example, most ties are priced between £20 and £80. In price lining, there are only a few prices within this range. Ties will not be priced at £20.00, £22.50, £27.80 and so on. They might be priced at four levels—£20, £30 and £50.

Price lining has advantages other than just matching prices to what consumers expect to pay. The main advantage is simplicity, for both sales assistants and customers. It is less confusing than having many prices. Some customers may consider items in only one price class. Their big decision, then, is which item(s) to choose at that price.

A British example of both price lining and odd-even pricing is found in the football boot market. Companies such as Adidas, Diadora and Mitre have many different football boots yet practically all of them fall into retail price points of £29.99, £39.99, £49.99 and so on. This makes the purchase process easier for the retailer and the customer.

For retailers, price lining has several advantages. Sales may increase because (1) they can offer a bigger variety in each price class and (2) it's easier to get customers to make decisions within one price class. Stock planning is simpler because demand is larger at the relatively few prices. Price lining can also reduce costs because inventory needs are lower.

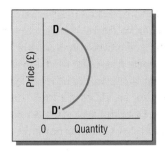

Exhibit 17–19
Demand Curve Showing a Prestige Pricing Situation

Demand-backward pricing

Demand-backward pricing is setting an acceptable final consumer price and working backwards to what a producer can charge. Producers of final consumer products, especially shopping products, such as women's and children's clothing and shoes commonly use it. It is also used for toys or gifts for which customers will spend a specific amount because they are seeking a £10 or a £15 gift. Here a reverse cost-plus pricing process is used. This method has been called *market-minus pricing*.

The producer starts with the retail (reference) price for a particular item and then works backward—subtracting the typical margins that channel members expect. This gives the approximate price the producer can charge. Then, the average or planned marketing expenses can be subtracted from this price to find how much can be spent producing the item. Chocolate bar manufacturers do this. They alter the size of the bar to keep the bar at the expected price.

Demand estimates are needed for demand-backward pricing to be successful. The quantity that will be demanded affects production costs—that is, where the firm will be on its average cost curve. Also, because competitors can be expected to make the best product possible, it is important to know customer needs to set the best amount to spend on manufacturing costs. By increasing costs a little, the product may be so improved in consumers' eyes that the firm will sell many more units. If consumers only want novelty, additional quality may not increase the quantity demanded and should not be offered.

PRICING A FULL LINE

Our emphasis has been—and will continue to be—on the problem of pricing an individual product mainly because this makes our discussion clearer. In reality, most marketing managers are responsible for more than one product. In fact, their 'product' may be the whole company line! So we'll discuss this matter briefly.

Full-line pricing—market- or firm-oriented?

Full-line pricing is setting prices for a whole line of products. How to do this depends on which of two basic situations a firm is facing.

In one case, all products in the company's line are aimed at the same general target market, which makes it important for all prices to be related. For example, a producer of TV sets can offer several price and quality levels to give its target customers some choice. The different prices should appear reasonable when the target customers are evaluating them. In the other case, the different products in the line are aimed at entirely different target markets so there doesn't have to be any relation between the various prices. A chemical producer of a wide variety of products with several target markets, for example, probably should price each product separately.[6]

Cost is not much help in full-line pricing

The marketing manager must try to recover all costs on the whole line—perhaps by pricing quite low on competitive items and much higher on less competitive items. Estimating costs for each product is a big problem because there is no single right way to assign a company's fixed costs to each of the products. Further, if any cost-oriented pricing method is carried through without considering demand, it can lead to very unrealistic prices. To avoid mistakes, the marketing manager should judge demand for the whole line as well as demand for each individual product in each target market.

As an aid to full-line pricing, marketing managers can assemble directly variable costs on the many items in the line to calculate a price floor. To this floor they can add a reasonable mark-up based on the quality of the product, the strength of the demand for the product and the degree of competition. Finally, the image projected by the full line must be evaluated.

Complementary product pricing

Complementary product pricing is setting prices on several products as a group. This may lead to one product being priced very low so that the profits from another product will increase—and increase the product group's total profits. A new Gillette razor, for example, may be priced low to sell the blades, which must be replaced regularly.

Complementary product pricing differs from full-line pricing because different production facilities may be involved so there is no cost allocation problem. Instead, the problem is really understanding the target market and the demand curves for each of the complementary products. Then, various combinations of prices can be tried to see what set will be best for reaching the company's pricing objectives.

Product-bundle pricing—one price for several products

A firm that offers its target market several different products may use **product-bundle pricing**—setting one price for a set of products. Firms that use product-bundle pricing usually set the overall price so that it's cheaper for the customer to buy the products at the same time than separately. Film processors sometimes bundle the cost of a roll of film and the cost of the processing. Restaurants will sometimes include several different courses as part of a set menu that would cost less than the cost of each item bought separately. Bundling encourages customers to spend more and buy products that they might not otherwise buy, because the 'added cost' of the extras is not as high as it would normally be.

An example of bundle pricing can be found in the British funeral market. This is oligopolistic with the vast amount of the market being accounted for by three firms. Their practice is to quote for a whole funeral package, rather than individual items. One lady was so incensed that she could not buy just a coffin that she has opened her own business—Green Undertakings—selling items such as coffins, body bags, shrouds and 'do it yourself' funeral advice.[7]

Most firms that use product-bundle pricing also set individual prices for the unbundled products. This may increase demand by attracting customers who want one item in a product assortment but don't want the extras. Many firms treat services this way. A software company may have a product-bundle price for its software and access to a freephone telephone assistance service. However, customers who don't need help can pay a lower price and get just the software.[8]

BID PRICING AND NEGOTIATED PRICING DEPEND HEAVILY ON COSTS

A new price for every job

Bid pricing means offering a specific price for each possible job rather than setting a price that applies for all customers. Building contractors, for example, must bid on possible projects. And many companies selling services (like cleaning or data processing) must submit bids for jobs they would like to have. The big problem in bid pricing is estimating all the costs that will apply to each job. This may sound easy, but a complicated bid may involve thousands of cost components. Further, management must include an overhead charge and a charge for profit. Sometimes it isn't even possible to figure out costs in advance. This may lead to a contract where the customer agrees to pay the supplier's total cost plus an agreed-on profit figure (say, 10 per cent of costs or a fixed amount)—after the job is finished.

Demand must be considered

Competition must be considered when adding in overhead and profit for a bid-price. Usually, the customer will get several bids and accept the lowest one. So unthinking addition of typical overhead and profit rates should be avoided. Some bidders use the same overhead and profit rates on all jobs—regardless of competition—and then are surprised when they don't get some jobs.

Because bidding can be expensive, a marketing manager may want to be selective about which jobs to bid on and choose those which have the greatest chance of success. Firms can spend thousands—or even millions—just developing bids for large business or government customers.[9]

Negotiated bids

Some buying situations (including much government buying) require the use of bids—and the purchasing agent must take the lowest bid. In other cases, however, the customer asks for bids and then singles out the company that submits the *most attractive* bid—not necessarily the lowest—for further bargaining.

Negotiated prices—what will a specific customer pay?

The list price or bidding price the seller would like to charge is sometimes only the *starting point* for discussions with individual customers. What a customer will buy—if the customer buys at all—depends on the **nego-**

tiated price, a price set based on bargaining between the buyer and seller.

As with simple bid pricing, negotiated pricing is most common in situations where the marketing mix is adjusted for each customer—so bargaining may involve the whole marketing mix, not just the price level. For example, a firm that produces machine tools used by other manufacturers to make their products might use this approach. Each customer may need custom-designed machines and different types of installation service. Through the bargaining process, the seller tries to determine what aspects of the marketing mix are most important to the customer. For one customer, selling price may be most important. There the seller might try to find ways to reduce costs of other elements of the marketing mix, consistent with the customer's needs, in order to earn a profit. Another customer might want more of some other element of the marketing mix, such as more technical help after the sale, and be less sensitive to price.

Sellers must know their costs to negotiate prices effectively. However, negotiated pricing *is* a demand-oriented approach. Here, the seller is very carefully analysing a particular customer's position on a demand curve, or on different possible demand curves based on different offerings, rather than the overall demand curve for a group of customers. This is a challenging job, and the details are beyond the scope of this book. However, the techniques for supply and demand analysis we've been discussing apply here as they do with other price-setting approaches.

SUMMARY

In this chapter, we discussed various approaches to price setting. Generally, retailers and wholesalers use mark-ups. Some just use the same mark-ups for all their items. Others find that varying the mark-ups increases turnover and profit. In other words, they consider demand and competition!

Many firms use average-cost pricing to help set their prices but this approach sometimes ignores demand completely. A more realistic approach to average-cost pricing requires a sales forecast—maybe just assuming that sales in the next period will be roughly the same as in the last period. This approach does enable the marketing manager to set a price—but the price may or may not cover all costs and earn the desired profit.

Break-even analysis is useful for evaluating possible prices. It provides a rough-and-ready tool for eliminating unworkable prices but management must estimate demand to evaluate the chance of reaching these possible break-even points.

Marginal analysis is a useful tool for finding the most profitable price—and the quantity to produce. The most profitable quantity is found at the intersection of the marginal revenue and marginal cost curves. To determine the most profitable price, a manager takes the most profitable quantity to the firm's demand curve to find the price target customers will be willing to pay for this quantity.

The major difficulty with demand-oriented pricing is estimating the demand curve. Experienced managers, aided perhaps by marketing research, can estimate the nature of demand for their products. Such estimates are useful, even if they are not exact. Sometimes, when all that is needed is a decision about raising or lowering price, even rough demand estimates can be very revealing. Further, a firm's demand curve does not cease to exist simply because it is ignored. Some information is better than none at all. And it appears that some marketers do consider demand in their pricing as when using value in use pricing, leader pricing, odd-even pricing, prestige pricing, full-line pricing and even bid pricing.

Throughout the book it has been stressed that firms must consider the customer before they do anything. This certainly applies to pricing. It means that when managers are setting a price, they have to consider what customers will be willing to pay. This is not necessarily easy but it is useful to know that there is a profit range around the best price. Therefore, even rough estimates about what potential customers will buy at various prices will probably lead to a better price than mechanical use of traditional mark-ups or cost-oriented formulas.

While the focus in this chapter is on price setting, it's clear that pricing decisions must consider the cost of offering the whole marketing mix. Costs should not be accepted as a given. Target marketers always look for ways to be more efficient—to reduce costs while improving what they offer customers. Improved coordination of physical distribution, for example, may improve customer service and reduce costs. Carefully defined target markets may make promotion spending more efficient. Products that really meet customers' needs reduce costly new-product failures. Channel members can shift and share functions—so that the cost of performing needed marketing activities is as low as possible. Marketers should set prices based on demand as well as on costs. In addition, creative marketers look for ways to reduce costs—because costs affect profit.

QUESTIONS AND PROBLEMS

1. Why do many department stores seek a mark-up of about 40 per cent when some discount houses operate on a 20 per cent mark-up?

2. A producer distributed its riding lawnmowers through wholesalers and retailers. The retail selling price was £800, and the manufacturing cost to the company was £312. The retail mark-up was 35 per cent and the wholesale mark-up 20 per cent. (*a*) What was the cost to the wholesaler? To the retailer? (*b*) What percentage mark-up did the producer take?

3. Relate the concept of stock turnover to the growth of mass-merchandising. Use a simple example in your answer.

4. If total fixed costs are £200 000 and total variable costs are £100 000 at the output of 20 000 units, what are the probable total fixed costs and total variable costs at an output of 10 000 units? What are the average fixed costs, average variable costs, and average costs at these two output levels? Explain what additional information you would want to determine what price should be charged.

5. Explain how experience curve pricing differs from average-cost pricing.

6. Construct an example showing that mechanical use of a very large or a very small mark-up might still lead to unprofitable operation while some intermediate price would be profitable. Draw a graph and show the break-even point(s).

` 7. The Davis Company's fixed costs for the year are estimated at £200 000. Its product sells for £250. The variable cost per unit is £200. Sales for the coming year are expected to reach £1 250 000. What is the break-even point? Expected profit? If sales are forecast at only £875 000, should the Davis Company shut down operations? Why?

8. Distinguish among price, marginal revenue and average revenue (where average revenue is total revenue divided by the quantity sold).

9. Draw a graph showing a demand and supply situation where marginal analysis correctly indicates that the firm should continue producing even though the profit and loss statement shows a loss.

10. Discuss the idea of drawing separate demand curves for different market segments. It seems logical because each target market should have its own marketing mix. On the other hand, won't this lead to many demand curves and possible prices? And what will this mean with respect to functional discounts and varying prices in the marketplace? Will it be legal? Will it be practical?

11. Nicor Company is having a profitable year. Its only product sells to wholesalers for 80 pence a can. Its managers feel that a 60 per cent gross margin should be maintained. Its manufacturing costs consist of: material, 50 per cent of cost; labour, 40 per cent of cost; and overhead, 10 per cent of cost. Both material and labour costs increased 10 per

cent since last year. Determine the new price per can based on its present pricing method. Is it wise to stick with a 60 per cent margin if a price increase would mean lost customers? Answer using graphs and MC–MR analysis. Show a situation where it would be most profitable to (*a*) raise price, (*b*) leave price alone, (*c*) reduce price.

12. How does a prestige pricing policy fit into a marketing mix? Would exclusive distribution be necessary?

13. Cite a local example of odd-even pricing and evaluate whether it makes sense.

14. Cite a local example of psychological pricing and evaluate whether it makes sense.

15. Is a full-line pricing policy available only to producers? Cite local examples of full-line pricing. Why is full-line pricing important?

SUGGESTED CASES

4. Lilybank Lodge
13. Wire Solutions
14. Plastic Master

REFERENCES

1. M.A. Jolson, 'A diagrammatic model for merchandising calculations', *Journal of Retailing*, Summer 1975, pp. 3–9.

2. W.W. Alberts, 'The experience curve doctrine reconsidered', *Journal of Marketing*, July 1989, pp. 36–49; G.S. Day and D.B. Montgomery, 'Diagnosing the experience curve', *Journal of Marketing*, Spring 1983, pp. 44–58; G.D. Kortge *et al.*, 'Linking experience, product life cycle, and learning curves: Calculating the perceived value price range', *Industrial Marketing Management*, July 1994, pp. 221–8.

3. L. Krishnamurthi, 'Pricing: Part art, part science', Mastering Marketing, Part 3, *The Financial Times*, 19 October 1998, pp. 7–8; Benson, P. Shapiro and Barbara P. Jackson, 'Industrial pricing to meet customer needs', *Harvard Business Review*, November–December 1978, pp. 119–27; M.H. Morris and D.A. Fuller, 'Pricing an industrial service', *Industrial Marketing Management*, May 1989, pp. 139–46.

4. H. Kristiaan and B. Hardie, 'A re-examination of reference price models: Is any single specification correct?' *in* D. Arnott *et al.* (eds) *Marketing: Progress, Prospects and Perspectives*, Proceedings of 26th EMAC Conference, Warwick Business School, 1997, pp. 1717–24; D.S. Putler, 'Incorporating reference price effects into a theory of consumer choice', *Marketing Science*, Summer 1992, pp. 287–309; K.D. Frankenberger and Ruiming Liu, 'Does consumer knowledge affect consumer responses to advertised reference price claims?', *Psychology & Marketing*, May–June 1994, pp. 235–52; A. Biswas, 'The moderating role of brand familiarity in reference price perceptions', *Journal of Business Research*, November 1992, pp. 251–62.

5. P. Gendell, M. Fox and P. Wilton, 'Estimating the effect of odd-pricing' *in* D. Arnott *et al.* (eds) *Marketing: Progress, Prospects and Perspectives*, Proceedings of 26th EMAC Conference, Warwick Business School, 1997, pp 1684–97; R.M. Schindler and A.R. Wiman, 'Effects of odd pricing on price recall', *Journal of Business Research*, November 1989, pp. 165–78; 'Strategic mix of odd, even prices can

lead to increased retail profits', *Marketing News*, 7 March 1980, p. 24.

6. F. Feinberg, 'Product line pricing with variable consumer cross-elasticities' *in* D. Arnott *et al.* (eds) *Marketing: Progress, Prospects and Perspectives*, Proceedings of 26th EMAC Conference, Warwick Business School, 1997, pp. 1655–73.

7. C. Derwent, 'The one-stop coffin shop', *Management Today*, February 1997, pp 58–60.

8. M.S. Yadav and K.B. Monroe, 'How buyers perceive savings in a bundle price: An examination of a bundle's transaction value,' *Journal of Marketing Research*, August 1993, pp. 350–8; D. Paun, 'When to bundle or unbundle products', *Industrial Marketing Management*, February 1993, pp. 29–34.

9. T. Mandják and J. Simon, 'Some aspects of Hungarian bidding: First results of an empirical study' *in* D. Arnott *et al.* (eds) *Marketing: Progress, Prospects and Perspectives*, Proceedings of 26th EMAC Conference, Warwick Business School, 1997, pp. 1844–54; D.T. Ostas, 'Ethics of Contract Pricing', *Journal of Business Ethics*, February 1992, pp. 137–46; D.T. Levy, 'Guaranteed pricing in industrial purchases: Making use of markets in contractual relations', *Industrial Marketing Management*, October 1994, pp. 307–14; A. Akintoye and M. Skitmore, 'Pricing approaches in the Construction Industry', *Industrial Marketing Management*, November 1992, pp. 311–18.

CHAPTER 18
Developing Innovative Marketing Plans

When You Finish This Chapter, You Should

1 Know the content of, and differences among, strategies, marketing plans and a marketing programme.

2 Know how to use SWOT analysis and other planning approaches to help to develop a marketing strategy that fits the firm's objectives and resources and meets customers' needs.

3 Understand why product classes and typical mixes is a good starting point for planning.

4 Understand the basic forecasting approaches and why they are used to evaluate the profitability of potential strategies.

5 Know what is involved in preparing a marketing plan, including estimates of costs and revenue and specification of other time-related details.

6 Understand the different ways a firm can plan to become involved in international marketing.

7 Understand the important new terms (shown in colour).

DISNEYLAND PARIS

Euro Disney has had mixed fortunes since it opened in Paris, but a new marketing plan has been implemented to successfully relaunch it. The plan brings together a number of key actions with the express objective of increasing the number of visitors to the theme park.

More attention is now paid to segmenting the market, rather than treating it as a single European market. The target market contains about 110 million customers coming from France and countries bordering it. Within this target, the emphasis is now on attracting families and new visitors. New visitors are particularly valuable. Research has shown that each new visitor, having enjoyed the Disney experience, intends to return and recommends the park to 18 people.

In order to increase visitor numbers, changes have been planned across the marketing mix. From the summer of 1994, research was conducted with visitors to the park (or 'guests' as they are known in Disney jargon). The results were a huge vote in favour of the name Disneyland Paris. The initial choice of Euro Disney was led more by politics than marketing. The Americans were keen to attract support from the French and to protect themselves from accusations of cultural imperialism. 'Euro' was thought to be a useful alibi. In reality, the park has nothing that is European in it and visitors came expecting a Disneyland experience like that found in American parks but located in France. The name change was staged—first Euro Disney became Euro Disneyland; then the size of 'Euro' was reduced on the logo, before disappearing completely in October 1995. The official name is now Disneyland Paris.

The other main change to the product has been the addition of the Space Mountain attraction, opened in June 1995. This helped to bring about an increase in visitors—numbers went up by 21 per cent in 1995. Increasing visitor numbers can also be credited to the reduction in prices. With the primary objective of increasing volume, the pricing variable is critical.

Prices were reduced across the board—entrance fees, shop merchandise, restaurant meals and hotel rates—for example, the price of an adult entrance ticket dropped by 22 per cent in one go. Economy-level hotels dropped prices by 30 per cent and enjoyed increased occupancy. In addition the use of seasonal pricing has been simplified with the move from three seasons to two (April to September and October to March).

The use of channels of distribution was also changed in the new marketing plan. Initially, Disney used a 'pull' policy, believing in the power of the brand to attract visitors. Disney did not make any great efforts to train agents or to organize their visits to the park. Today, travel agents account for more than half of hotel sales and a much closer relationship has been built between Disney and their agents. The commission system has also changed and agents earn commission not just on set-price tickets but on promotional prices as well.

At the same time, Disney has been building a computer database to enable it to engage in direct marketing activities such as direct mailings. Likewise the reservation phone number appears on all Disneyland Paris advertisements. The more independence they can get from the travel trade, the more they can save on commissions.

On the promotional front, Disneyland Paris have the advantage of twelve exclusive partnerships signed at the opening of the park (Coca-Cola, IBM, Renault, American Express...). As confidence in the park has returned, these partners have been becoming more proactive in using the association. Investments by the partners contribute to publicizing Disneyland Paris. In the past the partnerships were not exploited, perhaps because they were negotiated at very senior levels between companies without consultation with marketing teams. Now, Disneyland Paris is being used by these companies in a myriad of ways. Renault christened its Espace, The Space Mountain; Coca-Cola and Carrefour jointly ran a competition on more than 200 million cans with Disneyland prizes; and American Express has offered cardholders the opportunity to win trips as part of its loyalty awards. These are all promotions that help Disneyland Paris to achieve its marketing relaunch and to increase visitor numbers.

The results of the marketing plan are already evident. The turnover of hotels increased by 16 per cent and the number of visitors to the park increased by 21 per cent and the company was able to announce its first profits in 1995. However, much still needs to be done if the company is to meet its obligations to creditors. The marketing plan must continue to be informed by an understanding of the marketplace and to employ its marketing activities to meet the challenges of that market.[1]

MARKETING PLANNING PROCESS IS MORE THAN ASSEMBLING THE FOUR PS

The Disneyland Paris case shows that developing a successful marketing strategy is a creative process. It is also a logical process. The logic that leads to a sound strategy may need to change as both the market environment and target customers change and knowledge of them increases. Strategy planning is guided by basic principles. The marketing concept emphasizes that all a firm's activities should focus on its target markets. Further, a firm should try to find a competitive advantage in meeting the needs of some target market(s) that it can satisfy very well. The target market(s) should be large enough to support the firm's efforts and it should yield a profit. Ideally, the strategy should take advantage of trends in the external market, rather than try to go against them. This process, based on target marketing, has been discussed in Chapter 3, and forms the basic structure of this book.

A marketing *strategy* consists of a target market and a marketing mix; it is a 'big picture' of what a firm will do in a target market. A marketing *plan* includes the time-related details—including expected costs and revenues—for that strategy. In most firms, the marketing manager must ultimately combine the different marketing plans into an overall marketing *programme*.

This chapter starts with a review of the many variables that must be considered in the marketing strategy planning process, and highlights some of the key ways a marketing manager can identify the right blend of the marketing mix for an innovative strategy. The process by which these ideas come together in a marketing plan is discussed.

Forecasting target market potential and sales is important not only in evaluating opportunities but also in developing the time-related details for a plan. Plans must ultimately be blended into an overall programme and these tasks are described. The chapter includes a special inset on some of the challenges of planning strategies for international markets.

 Internet Exercise

Visit the Disneyland Paris web site (**www.disneyland-paris.com**). What developments have taken place in relation to the product offering and other aspects of the marketing strategy since the case study was written?

BLENDING THE FOUR PS REQUIRES UNDERSTANDING OF A TARGET MARKET

Marketing strategy planning process brings focus

Developing a good marketing strategy and turning the strategy into a marketing plan requires blending the ideas discussed throughout this text. Exhibit 18–1 provides a broad overview of the major areas. These different areas are integrated in order to develop logical marketing mixes, marketing strategies, marketing plans and a marketing programme.

As suggested in Exhibit 18–1, developing an effective marketing strategy involves a process of narrowing down to a specific target market and marketing mix that represents a real opportunity. This narrowing-down process requires a thorough understanding of the market. Careful analysis of customers' needs, current or prospective competitors and the firm's own objectives and resources enhance that understanding. Similarly, favourable or unfavourable factors and trends in the external market environment may make a potential opportunity more or less attractive.

There are usually more strategy possibilities than a firm can pursue. Each possible strategy usually has a number of different potential advantages and disadvantages. This can make it difficult to select the best target market and marketing mix. However, developing a set of specific qualitative and quantitative screening criteria—to define what business and markets the firm wants to compete in—can help to eliminate potential strategies that are not well suited to the firm.

Another useful aid for helping to identify a feasible strategy is **SWOT analysis**—which identifies and lists the firm's strengths and weaknesses and its opportunities and threats. The name SWOT is simply an abbreviation for the words Strengths, Weaknesses, Opportunities and Threats. Ideally, the firm is looking to convert weaknesses into strengths and threats into opportunities, at the same time matching the strengths to the opportunities. In practice, a good SWOT analysis helps the manager to focus on a strategy that takes advantage of the firm's opportunities and strengths while avoiding its weaknesses and threats to its success. These can be compared with the advantages and disadvantage of strategies that are considered. For example, if a firm is considering a strategy that focuses on a target market that is already being served by several strong competitors, success will usually hinge on some sort of competitive advantage. Such a competitive advantage might be based on a better marketing mix—perhaps an innovative new product, improved distribution, more effective promotion or a better price. Just offering a marketing mix that is similar to competitors' usually does not provide a competitive advantage—nor any real basis for the firm to position or differentiate its marketing mix as better for customers.

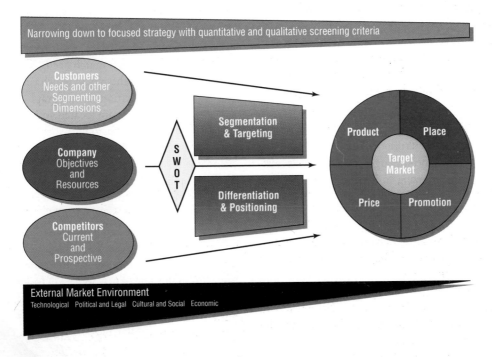

Exhibit 18–1 Overview of Marketing Strategy Planning Process

FAIRLY PRICKLY. **FAIRY SOFT.**

Some products have developed consistently successful marketing programmes. The marketing strategy for Fairy has been modified in a variety of different ways over many years.

Marketing mix flows from target market dimensions

Ideally, the ingredients of a good marketing mix flow logically from all the relevant dimensions of a target market. The market definition and segmenting approaches discussed in Chapter 6 help the marketing manager to identify which dimensions are qualifying and which are determining in customers' choices.

Waterford Crystal is the world's leading brand in the premium tabletop crystal market (vases, glasses, bowls, etc.). It had to develop a new marketing mix when the recession began to affect its principal market—the United States. There, its high income target customers were starting to trade down, moving to lower price purchasing points and modifying their tastes in the crystal market. The company responded by launching a new brand— Marquis—designed in a more contemporary way and positioned in a lower price tier of the premium crystal market. The Marquis brand had distinctive advertising and did not share shelf space with the existing Waterford Crystal brand. By targeting a specific segment with a specially devised marketing mix, the company managed to successfully create a new brand, capturing additional business and avoiding cannibalizing the Waterford Crystal brand. It capitalized on strengths (its skills, reputation and distribution penetration) and managed to match these with the opportunity that existed at the slightly lower end of the market. This helped the company to spread its risk in not relying exclusively on the premium market. Within the parent company of Waterford Wedgwood, it is the crystal division that is the best performer.[2]

Product benefits must match needs. The promotions mix is determined by the way in which customers search for, and use, information. Demographic dimensions reveal where customers are located and if they have the income to buy. Where customers shop for or buy products helps to define channel alternatives. The value of the whole marketing mix and the urgency of customer needs, combined with an understanding of what customers see as substitute ways of meeting needs, help companies to estimate price sensitivity.

It would seem that a full understanding of the needs and attitudes of a target market would make the task of combining the four Ps easy. Yet there are three important gaps in this line of reasoning. (1) Insufficient information may be available about the needs and attitudes of our target markets. (2) Competitors are also trying to satisfy these or similar needs—and their efforts may force a firm to shift its marketing mix. (3) The other dimensions of the marketing environment may be changing—which may require more changes in marketing mixes. These points warrant further consideration.

Product classes suggest typical marketing mixes

While complete knowledge of a potential target market is not possible, it is usually relatively straightforward to decide whether the product is a consumer product or a business product and which product class is most relevant. Identifying the proper product class helps because it suggests how a typical product should be distributed and promoted. Knowing how potential customers would view the company's product can give a head start on developing a marketing mix. A convenience product, for example, usually needs more intensive distribution and the producer usually takes on more responsibility for promotion. A speciality product needs a clear brand identity, which may require a positioning effort. A new unsought product will need a mix that leads customers through the adoption process.

QUICK METAL STRATEGY PLANNING FASTENS ON CUSTOMER NEEDS—AND PROFITS

Loctite Corporation, a producer of industrial supplies, used careful strategy planning to launch Quick Metal—a putty-like adhesive for repairing worn machine parts. Loctite chemists had developed similar products in the past. But managers paid little attention to developing a complete marketing strategy—and sales had been poor.

Before creating Quick Metal, Loctite identified some attractive target customers. Research showed that production people were eager to try any product that helped get broken machines back into production. Quick Metal was developed to meet the needs of this target market. Advertisements appealed to such needs with copy promising that Quick Metal 'keeps machinery running until the new parts arrive'. Channel members also received attention. During the introduction stage, sales representatives made frequent phone calls and sales visits to the nearly 700 wholesalers who handle Loctite products. Loctite awarded cash prices to those selling the most Quick Metal.

A tube of Quick Metal was priced at £12.00—about twice the price (and profit margin) of competing products but Loctite's customers weren't concerned about price. They responded to a quality product that could keep their production lines operating.

Based on past experience, some estimated that a typical product for this market might reach sales of £200 000 a year. Loctite didn't rely on a typical strategy. Instead the company offered a carefully targeted marketing mix to meet the needs of a specific target market. It sold 100 000 tubes the first week—and within seven months sales exceeded £1.5 million. Loctite's careful planning paid off in an immediate market success—and high profits.[3]

Typical versus atypical

The typical marketing mix for a given product class is not necessarily right for all situations. Some very profitable marketing mixes depart from the typical—to satisfy some target markets better. A marketing manager may have to develop a mix that is *not* typical because of various market realities, including special characteristics of the product or target market, the competitive environment and each firm's capabilities and limitations. In fact, it is often through differentiation of the firm's product and/or other elements of the marketing mix that the marketing manager can offer unique value to target customers.

Superior mixes may be breakthrough opportunities

When marketing managers fully understand their target markets, they may be able to develop marketing mixes that are superior to competitors' mixes. Such understanding may enable the firm to take advantage of opportunities. Taking advantage of these opportunities can lead to large sales and profitable growth. This is why it is important to look for breakthrough opportunities rather than just trying to imitate competitors' offerings.

NutraSweet built its original success on an innovative product that met consumers' needs. The strategy NutraSweet's marketing managers planned involved more than a good product. The typical marketing strategy for firms that supply ingredients to food and soft-drink companies emphasized personal selling to producers. In contrast, NutraSweet's marketing managers used mass selling to promote their brand name and red swirl logo directly to consumers.

They also persuaded producers who used the ingredient to feature the NutraSweet brand name prominently on containers and in advertisements. In addition, because there was little direct competition, they used a profitable skimming approach to pricing—and charged different producer-customers different prices depending on the value NutraSweet added to their product. Now that NutraSweet's patent is expired, competitors will face a challenge entering the market because it will take a huge marketing effort—and a high promotion budget—to offset consumers' familiarity with the NutraSweet name.

Just as some mixes are superior, some mixes are clearly inferior or unsuitable. For example, a national TV advertising campaign might make sense for a large company but it might be completely out of the question for a small manufacturer that only has the resources to start offering a new product in a limited geographic area.

The marketing manager blends the four Ps

Exhibit 18–2 reviews the major marketing strategy decision areas organized by the four Ps. Each of these requires careful decision making. Yet, marketing planning involves much more than just independent decisions and assembling the parts into a marketing mix. The four Ps must be creatively *blended*—so the firm develops the best mix for its target market. In other words, each decision must fit well as part of a logical whole, working well with all the others.

The job of integrating the four Ps strategy decisions is that of the marketing manager. This integration is essential. It is easy for specialists to focus on their own areas and expect the rest of the company to work for, or around, them. This is especially true in larger firms, where specialists are needed, because the size of the whole marketing job is too big for one person. Yet, the ideas of the product manager, advertising manager, sales manager and physical distribution manager may have to be adjusted to improve the whole mix. It is critical that each marketing mix decision work well with all of the others. A breakdown in any one decision area may doom the whole strategy to failure.

Product life cycle guides planning

Careful consideration of where a firm's offering fits in the product life cycle can also be a big help in evaluating the best marketing mix. Exhibit 18–3 summarizes how marketing mix variables typically change over the product life cycle. This exhibit is a good review of many topics that have been discussed throughout the text. Certainly, the pioneering effort that is required for a really new product concept is different to the job of taking market share away from an established competitor late in the market growth stage.

The lesson from the product life cycle is that markets change continually. For example, the sportswear company Adidas lost its way in the market in the 1980s. The

Product

Physical good
Service
Features Quality
 level
Accessories
Installation
Instructions
Warranty
Product lines
Packaging
Branding

Place

Objectives
Channel type
Market exposure
Kinds of
 intermediaries
Kinds and
 locations of
 stores
How to handle
 transporting
 and storing
Service levels
Recruiting
 intermediaries
Managing
 channels

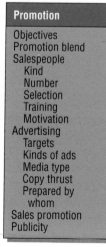

Promotion

Objectives
Promotion blend
Salespeople
 Kind
 Number
 Selection
 Training
 Motivation
Advertising
 Targets
 Kinds of ads
 Media type
 Copy thrust
 Prepared by
 whom
Sales promotion
Publicity

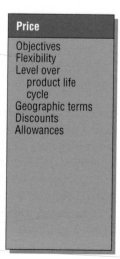

Price

Objectives
Flexibility
Level over
 product life
 cycle
Geographic terms
Discounts
Allowances

Exhibit 18–2 Strategy Decision Organized by the Four Ps

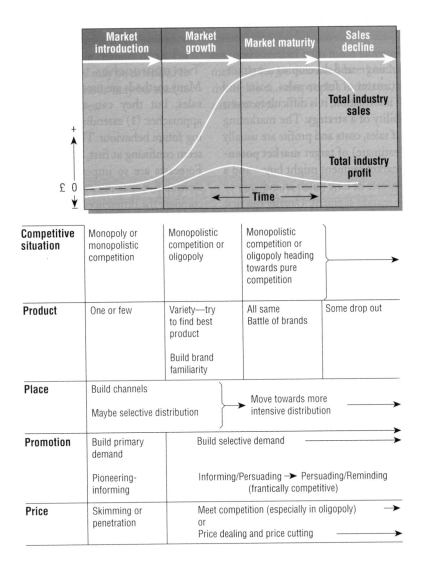

Exhibit 18–3 Typical Changes in Marketing Variables over the Product Life Cycle

company did not keep up with trends and allowed quality to deteriorate. In the meantime Nike and Reebok, who targeted specific segments such as football and womenswear, dominated the market. As part of a radical set of changes the company moved production to low-wage factories in the Far East, greater emphasis was put on design and the advertising budget was doubled.

During the 1990s Adidas has enjoyed an upturn in its fortunes. The Adidas three-stripe logo became part of the 'retro' look and models such as Cindy Crawford and Claudia Schiffer and rock idols sported Adidas gear on television and in film and music videos, giving the company a publicity bonanza. The company emphasizes its history of celebrity wearers from 1928 and spends

more on communications than ever before. Although the company advertises its sporting heritage, it is worth remembering that about 90 per cent of Adidas products are purchased for wear on the streets instead of sports fields. The fashion cycle will continue to change and Adidas will have to change its marketing mix to keep in tune with the times.[4]

As the Adidas example shows, because markets change continually, strategies must be planned that can adjust to changing conditions. The original marketing plan for a new marketing strategy may even include details about what adjustments in the marketing mix or target market will be required as the nature of competition and the adoption process evolve.[5]

Compare the profitability of alternative strategies

Once costs and revenue for possible strategies are estimated, it makes sense to compare them with respect to overall profitability. Exhibit 18–6 shows such a comparison for a small appliance currently selling for £15—Mix A in the example. Here, the marketing manager simply estimates the costs and likely results of four reasonable alternatives. Assuming profit is the objective *and* there are adequate resources to consider each of the alternatives, marketing Mix C is obviously the best alternative.

Spreadsheet analysis speeds through calculations

Comparing the alternatives in Exhibit 18–6 is quite simple. Sometimes, however, marketing managers need much more detail to evaluate a plan. Hundreds of calculations may be required to see how specific marketing resources relate to expected outcomes such as total costs, expected sales and profit. To make that part of the planning job simpler and faster, marketing managers often use spreadsheet analysis. With **spreadsheet analysis**, costs, sales and other information related to a problem are organized into a data table—a spreadsheet—to show how changing the value of one or more of the numbers affects the other numbers. This is possible because the relationships among the variables are programmed in the computer software. Lotus 1-2-3, Excel, Supercalc and Appleworks are examples of well-known spreadsheet programs.

A spreadsheet helps to answer 'what if' questions

Spreadsheet analysis allows the marketing manager to evaluate what-if type questions. For example, a marketing manager might be interested in the question 'What if I charge a higher price and the number of units sold stays the same? What will happen to profit?' To look at how a spreadsheet program might be used to help answer this 'what if' question, consider Mix C in Exhibit 18–6.

The manager might set up the data in this table as a computer spreadsheet. The table involves a number of relationships. For example, price times total units equals sales; and total cost equals selling cost plus advertising cost plus overhead cost plus total product costs (7 000 units   £5 per unit). If these relationships are programmed into the spreadsheet, a marketing manager can ask questions like: 'What if I raise the price to £20.20 and still sell 7 000 units? What will happen to profit?' To get the answer, all the manager needs to do is type the new price in the spreadsheet and the program computes the new profit—£26 400.

In addition, the manager may also want to do many 'what if' analyses, for example, to see how sales and profit change over a range of prices. Computerized spreadsheet analysis does this quickly and easily. For example, if the manager wants to see what happens to total revenue as the price varies between some minimum (say £19.80) and a maximum (say £20.20), the program can show the total revenue and profit for a number of price levels in the range from £19.80 to £20.20. See Exhibit 18–7.

In a problem like this, the marketing manager might be able to do the same calculations quickly by hand. With more complicated problems the spreadsheet program can be extremely helpful—making it very convenient to analyse different alternatives more carefully.

THE MARKETING PLAN BRINGS ALL THE DETAILS TOGETHER

Marketing plan provides a blueprint for implementation

The marketing plan documents the selected target market, the (integrated) marketing mix to meet that target market's needs, and estimates the costs and expected results for that strategy. The plan serves as a blueprint for the firm's marketing activities.

Marketing plans vary by company and circumstance. In general, however, the plan should contain the type of information outlined in Exhibit 18–8. This outline is basically an overview of the topics covered throughout this text. In essence, the plan documents: the situation in relation to market segments, competitors and the marketing environment; the product issues associated with the targeted segment(s); the subsequent objectives and strategies associated with the other marketing mix variables (place, promotion and price); information requirements; expected costs and sales; and the timing of actions and expected results.

Exhibit 18–8 provides a summary outline of the different sections of a complete marketing plan. You can see that this outline is basically an abridged overview of the topics covered throughout the text—and highlighted in this chapter.

Marketing Mix	Price	Selling Price	Advertising Cost	Total Units	Sales	Total Cost	Total Profit
A	£15	£20 000	£ 5 000	£5 000	£ 75 000	£70 000	£ 5 000
B	15	20 000	20 000	7 000	105 000	95 000	10 000
C	20	30 000	30 000	7 000	140 000	115 000	25 000
D	25	40 000	40 000	5 000	125 000	125 000	0

*For the same target market, assuming product costs per unit are £5 and fixed (overhead) costs are £20 000

Exhibit 18–6 Comparing the Estimated Sales, Costs and Profits of Four 'Reasonable' Alternative Marketing Mixes*

Price	Selling Price	Advertising Cost	Total Units	Sales	Total Cost	Total Profit
£19.80	£30 000	£30 000	£7 000	£138 600	£115 000	£23 600
19.90	30 000	30 000	7 000	139 300	115 000	24 300
20.00	30 000	30 000	7 000	140 000	115 000	25 000
20.10	30 000	30 000	7 000	140 700	115 000	25 700
20.20	30 000	30 000	7 000	141 400	115 000	26 400

Exhibit 18–7 A Spreadsheet Analysis Showing How a Change in Price Affects Sales and Profit (based on Marketing Mix C from Exhibit 18–6)

Name of Product Market
Major screening criteria relevant to product-market
  opportunity selected
  Quantitative (ROI, profitability, risk level, etc.)
  Qualitative (nature of business preferred, social
  responsibility, etc.)
  Major constraints

Customer Analysis (organizational or final consumer)
Possible segmenting dimensions (customer needs,
  other characteristics)
  Identification of qualifying dimensions and deter-
  mining dimensions
Identification of target market(s) (one or more specific
  segments)
  Operational characteristics (demographics,
  geographic locations, etc.)
  Potential size (number of people,
  cash purchase potential, etc.)
  and likely growth
Key psychological and social influences on
  buying purchase
Type of buying situation
Nature of relationship with customers

Competitor Analysis
Nature of current/likely competition
Current and prospective competitors (and/or rivals)
  Current strategies and likely responses to plan
Competitive barriers to overcome and sources of
  potential competitive advantage

Analysis of Other Aspects of External Market Environment (favourable and unfavourable factors and trends)
  Economic environment
  Technological environment
  Political and legal environment
  Cultural and social environment

Company Analysis
Company objectives and overall marketing objectives
Company resources
SWOT: Identification of major Strengths, Weaknesses,
  Opportunities and Threats (based on above analyses
  of company resources, customers, competitors, and
  other aspects of external market environment)

Marketing Information Requirements
Marketing research needs (with respect to customers,
  marketing mix effectiveness, external environment, etc.)

Exhibit 18–8 Summary Outline of Different Sections of Marketing Plan

Secondary data and primary data needs
Marketing information system needs, models to be
used, etc.

Product
Product class (type of consumer or business product)
Current product life-cycle stage
New-product development requirements (people, funds,
time, etc.)
  Product liability, safety and social responsibility
  considerations
Specification of core physical good and/or service
  Features, quality, etc.
Supporting customer service(s) needed
Warranty (what is covered, timing, who will support, etc.)
Branding (manufacturer versus dealer, family brand
  versus individual brand, etc.)
Packaging
  Promotion and labelling needs
  Protection needs
Cultural sensitivity of product
Fit with product line

Place
Objectives
  Degree of market exposure required
  Distribution customer service level required
Type of channel (direct, indirect)
  Other channel members and/or facilitators required
    Type/number of wholesalers (agent, merchant, etc.)
    Type/number of retailers
  How discrepancies and separations will be handled
  How marketing functions are to be shared
Coordination needed in company, channel,
and supply chain
  Information requirements (EDI, the Internet, e-mail,
  etc.)
Transportation requirements
Inventory product-handling requirements
Facilities required (warehousing,
  distribution centres, etc.)
Reverse channels (for returns, recalls, etc.)

Promotion
Objectives
Major message theme(s) for integrated marketing
  communications ('desired positioning')
Promotion mix
  Advertising (type, media, copy thrust, etc.)
  Personal selling (type and number of salespeople,
    how compensated, how effort will be allocated, etc.)
  Sales promotion (for channel members, customers,
    employees)
  Publicity
  Interactive media
Mix of push and pull required
Who will do the work

Price
Nature of demand (price sensitivity, price of substitutes)
Demand and cost analyses (marginal analysis)
Markup chain in channel
Price flexibility
Price level(s) (under what conditions) and impact on
customer value
Adjustments to list price (geographic terms, discounts,
allowances, etc.)

Special Implementation Problems to Be Overcome
People required
Manufacturing, financial, and other resources needed

Control
Marketing information system needs
Criterion measures comparison with objectives
  (customer satisfaction, sales, cost, performance
  analysis, etc.)

Forecasts and Estimates
Costs (all elements in plan, over time)
Sales (by market, over time, etc.)
Estimated operating statement (*pro forma*)

Timing
Specific sequence of activities and events, etc.
Likely changes over the product life cycle

Exhibit 18–8 contd.

Marketing plan spells out the timing of the strategy

Some time schedule is implicit in any strategy. A marketing plan simply spells out this time period and the time-related details. Usually, a reasonable length of time is used, such as six months, a year or a few years. However, it might be only a month or two in some cases, especially when rapid changes in fashion or tech-

nology are important. Or a strategy might be implemented over several years, perhaps the length of a product life cycle or at least the early stages of the product's life.

Although the outline in Exhibit 18–8 does not explicitly show a place for the time frame for the plan or the specific costs for each decision area, they should be included in the plan—along with expected estimates of sales and profit—so that the plan can be compared with *actual performance* in the future. In other words, the plan not only makes it clear to everyone what is to be accomplished and how—but it also provides a basis for the control process after the plan is implemented.

Flowcharts help set time-related details for the plan

Figuring out and planning the time-related details and schedules for all the activities in the marketing plan can be a challenge—especially if the plan involves a substantial initiative. To do a better job in this area, many managers have turned to flowcharting techniques such as CPM (critical path method) or PERT (programme evaluation and review technique). These methods were originally developed as part of the US space programme (NASA) to ensure that the various contractors and subcontractors stayed on schedule and reached their goals as planned. PERT, CPM and other similar project management approaches are even more popular now because inexpensive programs for personal computers make them easier and faster to use. Updating is also easier.

The computer programs develop detailed flowcharts to show which marketing activities must be done in sequence and which can be done concurrently. These charts also show the time needed for various activities. The total of the time allotments along the various chart paths shows the most critical (the longest) path—as well as the best starting and ending dates for the various activities. Flowcharting basically requires that all the activities, which have to be performed anyway, be identified ahead of time and their probable duration and sequence shown on one diagram. (It uses nothing more than addition and subtraction.) Working with such information should be part of the planning function anyway. The chart can be used later to guide implementation and control.[7]

A complete plan spells out the reasons for decisions

The plan outline shown in Exhibit 18–8 is quite complete. It does not just provide information about marketing mix decisions, it also includes information about customers (including segmenting dimensions), competitors' strategies, other aspects of the marketing environment and the company's objectives and resources. This material provides important background relevant to the 'why' of the marketing mix and target market decisions. Too often managers do not include this information; their plans just lay out the details of the target market and the marketing mix strategy decisions. This short-cut approach is more common when the plan is really simply an update of a strategy that has been in place for some time. However, that approach may involve some risks.

Managers too often make the mistake of casually updating plans in minor ways—perhaps only changing some costs or sales forecasts—but otherwise following what was done in the past. A risk with this approach is that it is easy to lose sight of why those strategy decisions were made in the first place. When the market situation changes, the original reasons may no longer apply. Yet, if the logic for those strategy decisions is not retained, it is easy to miss changes taking place that should result in a plan being reconsidered. For example, a plan that was established in the growth stage of the product life cycle may have been very successful for a number of years. A marketing manager cannot be complacent and assume that success will continue forever. When market maturity is reached the firm may encounter difficulties, unless the basic strategy and plan are modified. If a plan spells out the details of the market analysis and logic for the marketing mix and target market selected, then it is a simple matter to routinely check and update it. Remember: the idea is for all the analysis and strategy decisions to fit together as an integrated whole. Thus, as some of the elements of the plan or marketing environment change the whole plan may need a fresh approach.

COMPANIES PLAN AND IMPLEMENT WHOLE MARKETING PROGRAMMES

Several plans make a programme

Most companies implement more than one marketing plan at the same time. A *marketing programme* blends all a firm's marketing plans into one big plan. When the various plans in the company's programme are different, managers may be less concerned with how well the plans fit together—except when they compete for the firm's usually limited financial resources.

When the plans are more similar, however, the same salesforce may be expected to carry out several plans. Or the firm's advertising department may develop the publicity and advertising for several plans. In these cases, product managers try to get enough of the common resources, say, salespeople's time, for their own plans. Because a company's resources are usually limited, the marketing manager must make difficult choices. Not every opportunity can be pursued. Instead, limited resources force a choice among alternative plans while the programme is developed.

Finding the best programme requires judgement

There is no one best way to compare various plans. Managers sometimes rely on evaluation tools such as portfolio analysis. Inevitably, the process is a combination of calculations and judgement. Assuming the company has a profit-oriented objective, managers can evaluate the more profitable plans first, in terms of both potential profit and resources required. A plan's impact on the entire programme also needs to be evaluated. One profitable-looking alternative might be a poor first choice if it consumes all the company's resources and side-tracks several plans that together would be more profitable and spread the risks.

Some juggling among the various plans, comparing profitability versus resources needed and available, moves the company towards the most profitable programme. This is another area where spreadsheet analysis can help the manager to evaluate a large number of alternatives.

PLANNING FOR INVOLVEMENT IN INTERNATIONAL MARKETING

When developing a plan for international markets, marketing managers must decide the extent to which the firm will be involved. Six basic kinds of involvement will be overviewed: exporting, licensing, contract manufacturing, management contracting, joint venturing and wholly owned subsidiaries. These options are described in the box on pages 395–396. A useful example of the challenges of international involvement is provided by Procter and Gamble's experience in China.

PROCTER AND GAMBLE'S CHINESE SUCCESS STORY

For many years it has been felt that the Chinese market was virtually impenetrable for Western companies. It was claimed that only the very wealthy would have the means to buy foreign products and that distribution on a national scale would only be practicable with the rebuilding of infrastructure some time in the 21st century. In addition, it was reckoned that the Chinese government would act to protect local businesses against foreign rivals.

The success of Procter and Gamble in China refutes many of these suspicions and has provided evidence of the market's attractiveness for other foreign companies. In terms of market size, it is simplest to consider that one-fifth of the world's population live in China.

Procter and Gamble has become one of the leading producers of consumer products in China and their turnover is increasing by 50 per cent each year. The first Western company to have a presence in China, the Procter and Gamble subsidiary broke even in 1994 and recorded its first profits in 1995. The company acts as a multinational and operates a number of joint ventures, (one of which is a production centre in Guangzhou) and employs 4500 people. Management is made up of 100 expatriates who try to teach the company's American methods to the employees. Local recruitment takes place from the 25 best universities in China. In addition, Procter and Gamble has a research and development centre in Beijing in a joint effort with Qinghua University. Apart from its human resource management policy, the reasons for Procter and Gamble's success are attributed to adapting the product to the local market and establishing an effective distribution network.

Somewhat ironically, dandruff has been a key ingredient in this success story! Few Chinese shampoos were any use against dandruff. Aware of the potential, the firm first launched an advertising campaign to make the public aware of the problem (which is particularly evident in a population with black hair). Head and Shoulders shampoo became the market leader inside three years of its introduction to the market. When Rejoice and Pantene were introduced, they came with an anti-dandruff enriched formula. These brands sell at three times the price of local brands, yet have managed to take the largest share of the market. This is helped by the extensive use of advertising—in one month Procter and Gamble buys more TV advertising than their nearest Chinese rivals do in one year.

Distribution has also been a particular strength for Procter and Gamble. Its approach is akin to a military campaign. In order to gain intensive distribution it started by drawing up maps and marking the location of corner shops and larger shops in 228 towns with over 200 000 inhabitants. Following an advertising campaign, a salesforce in corporate uniform of white polo shirt with 'Winning Team' printed on the back, tackle the towns giving away free samples of Tide and Ariel.

Thus far, the Chinese government has allowed foreign competitors to invade the mass consumer market. This enabled Procter and Gamble to develop by taking over other firms without too many bureaucratic obstacles. However, the government does recognize that these consumer goods sections of the economy are in danger of being swallowed up. Procter and Gamble has taken over three of the largest eight local washing powder producers as well as having their own popular brands of Tide and Ariel. This means that it now controls nearly one half of this production in China. The Chinese government has stated that it is going to watch Procter and Gamble closely. With eleven joint ventures and solely funded enterprises in China and a combined investment of $300 million, the company's commitment to China is substantial.[8]

Planning for international markets

Usually marketing managers must plan the firm's overall marketing programme so it is flexible enough to be adapted for differences in different countries. When the differences are significant, top management should delegate a great deal of responsibility for strategy planning to local managers (or even distributors). In many cases, it is not possible to develop a detailed plan without a 'local feel'. In extreme cases, local managers may not even be able to fully explain some parts of their plans because they are based on subtle cultural differences. Then plans must be judged only by their results. The organizational structure should give these managers a great deal of freedom in their planning, but ensure tight control against the plans they develop. Top management can simply insist that managers stick to their budgets and meet the plans that they themselves create. When a firm reaches this stage, it is being managed like a well-organized domestic corporation, which insists that its managers (of divisions and territories) meet their own plans so that the whole company's programme works as intended.

EXPORTING

Some companies get into international marketing just by **exporting**—selling some of what the firm produces to foreign markets. Some firms start exporting just to get rid of surplus output. For others, exporting comes from a real effort to look for new opportunities.

Some firms try exporting without doing much planning. They do not change the product—or even the service or instruction manuals! As a result, some early efforts are not very satisfying—to buyers or sellers. This is the case for the Irish company that exported canned vegetables to France. Having found that Irish customers liked the fact that their products came without preservatives, the company decided to make this more obvious on the exports to France. Accordingly, the French labels declared 'Sans preservatifs'. In France, this, of course, means 'without condoms'.

Exporting facilitators

Exporting does require knowledge about the foreign market. Managers who do not have enough knowledge to plan the details of a programme can often get expert help from distribution specialists. Export agents can handle the paperwork as products are shipped outside the country. Then agents or merchant wholesalers can handle the importing details. Even large producers with many foreign operations turn to international intermediaries for some products or markets. Such intermediaries know how to handle the sometimes-confusing formalities and specialized functions. A manager trying to develop a plan alone can make a small mistake that ties products up at national borders for days or months.

Exporting does not have to involve permanent relationships. Channel relationships do, however, take time to build and should not be treated lightly—sales representatives' contacts in foreign countries are investments. It is relatively easy to cut back on these relationships— or even drop them—if the plan does not work.[9]

Some firms, on the other hand, plan more formal and permanent relationships with nationals in foreign countries. The relationships might involve licensing, contract manufacturing, management contracting or joint venturing.

Licensing
Licensing is a relatively easy way to enter foreign markets. **Licensing** means selling the right to use some process, trademark, patent, or other right for a fee or royalty. The licensee takes most of the risk because it must invest some capital to use the right. Further, the licensee usually does most of the planning for the markets it is licensed to serve. If good partners are available, this can be an effective way to enter a market. Gerber entered the Japanese baby food market this way but still exports to other countries.[10]

Contract manufacturing
Contract manufacturing means turning over production to others while retaining the marketing process. Sears used this approach when it opened stores in Latin America and Spain. This approach does not make it any easier to plan the marketing programme, but it may facilitate implementation. For example, this approach can be especially desirable where labour relations are difficult or where there are problems obtaining supplies or government cooperation. Growing nationalistic feelings may make this approach more attractive in the future.

Management contracting
Management contracting means the seller provides only management skills—others own the production and distribution facilities. Some mines and oil refineries are operated this way—and Hilton operates hotels all over the world for local owners. This is a relatively low-risk approach to international marketing. The company makes no commitment to fixed facilities, which can be

vulnerable, if political situations develop, to being taken over or damaged in riots. If conditions deteriorate, key management people can leave the nationals to manage the operation.[11]

Joint venturing
Joint venturing means a domestic firm entering into a partnership with a foreign firm. As with any partnership, there can be honest disagreements over objectives, for example, how much profit is desired and how fast it should be paid, as well as operating policies. Where a close working relationship can be developed, perhaps based on one firm's technical and marketing know-how and the foreign partner's knowledge of the market and political connections, this approach can be very attractive to both parties.

In some situations, a joint venture is the only type of involvement possible. A joint venture usually requires a substantial commitment from both parties and they both must agree on a joint plan. When the relationship does not work out well, the ensuing nightmare can make the manager wish that the venture had been planned as a wholly-owned operation. The terms of the joint venture may block this for years.

Wholly-owned subsidiaries
When a firm thinks a foreign market looks really promising, it may want to take the final step. A wholly-owned **subsidiary** is a separate firm, owned by a parent company. This gives the firm complete control of the marketing plan and operations, and also helps a foreign branch work more easily with the rest of the company. If a firm has too much capacity in a country with low production costs, for example, it can move some production there from other plants and then export to countries with higher production costs.

Multinational corporations
As firms become more involved in international marketing, some begin to see themselves as worldwide businesses that transcend national boundaries. These **multinational corporations** have a direct investment in several countries and run their businesses depending on the choices available anywhere in the world. Multinationals, such as Nestlé, Shell (Royal Dutch Shell), Unilever, Sony and Honda, have well-accepted brands all around the world. These multinational operations no longer just export or import. They hire local workers and build local plants. They have relationships with local businesses and politicians. These powerful organizations learn to plan marketing strategies that deal with nationalistic feelings and typical border barriers, treating them simply as part of the marketing environment.[12]

SUMMARY

In this chapter, the importance of developing whole marketing mixes has been stressed, not just developing policies for the individual four Ps and hoping they will fit together into some logical whole. The marketing manager is responsible for developing a workable blend, integrating all of the efforts of the firm into a coordinated whole that makes effective use of the firm's resources and guides it toward its objectives.

As a starting place for developing new marketing mixes, a marketing manager can use the product classes that have served as a thread through this text. Even if the manager cannot fully describe the needs and attitudes of target markets, it is usually possible to select the appropriate product class for a particular product. This, in turn, will help set Place and Promotion policies. It may also clarify what type of marketing mix is typical for the product. However, just doing what is typical may not give a firm any competitive advantage. Creative strategies are often the ones that identify new and better ways of uniquely giving the target customers what they want or need. Similarly, seeing where a particular offering fits in the product life cycle helps to clarify how current marketing mixes are likely to change in the future.

Developing and evaluating marketing strategies and plans usually requires that the manager use some approach to forecasting. Two basic approaches to forecasting market potential and sales were covered: (1) extending past behaviour and (2) predicting future behaviour. The most common approach is to extend past behaviour into the future. This gives reasonably good results if market conditions are fairly stable. Methods here include extension of past sales data and the factor method. Projecting the past into the future is risky when big market changes are likely. To make up for this possible weakness, marketers predict future behaviour using their own experience and judgement. They also bring in the judgement of others, using the jury of executive opinion method and salespeople's estimates. They may also use surveys, panels, and market tests. Any sales forecast depends on the marketing mix the firm actually selects.

Once forecasts of the expected sales—and estimated of the associated costs—for possible strategies are available, alternatives can be compared regarding potential profitability. Spreadsheet analysis software is an important tool for such comparisons. In the same vein, project planning approaches, such as CPM and PERT, can help the marketing manager do a better job in planning the time-related details for the strategy that is selected.

The marketing manager must develop a marketing plan for carrying out each strategy and then merge a set of plans into a marketing programme. Finally, different approaches that are helpful in planning strategies to enter international markets were described. The different approaches have different strengths and weaknesses.

So far, the emphasis has been on planning. The next chapter considers the management jobs of implementation and control. The focus will be on implementation that continuously improves and does a better job of meeting customers' needs—and on timely control that results in improved implementation and strategies while there's still time to do something about it.

QUESTIONS AND PROBLEMS

1. Distinguish clearly between a marketing strategy, a marketing plan and a marketing programme.

2. Discuss how a marketing manager could go about choosing among several possible marketing plans, given that choices must be made because of limited resources. Would the job be easier in the consumer product or in the business product area? Why?

3. Explain how understanding the product classes can help a marketing manager develop a marketing strategy for a really new product that is unlike anything currently available.

4. Distinguish between competitive marketing mixes and superior mixes that lead to breakthrough opportunities.

5. Explain the difference between a forecast of market potential and a sales forecast.

6. Suggest a plausible explanation for sales fluctuations for (*a*) bicycles, (*b*) ice cream, (*c*) lawnmowers, (*d*) tennis rackets, (*e*) oats, (*f*) disposable nappies and (*g*) latex for rubber-based paint.

7. Explain the factor method of forecasting. Illustrate your answer.

8. Why is spreadsheet analysis a popular tool for marketing strategy planning?

9. In your own words, explain how a flowcharting technique such as PERT or CPM can help a marketing manager develop a better marketing plan.

10. Why should a complete marketing plan include details concerning the reasons for the marketing strategy decisions and not just the marketing activities central to the four Ps?

11. Consider how the marketing manager's job becomes more complex when it's necessary to develop and plan *several* strategies as part of a marketing programme. Be sure to discuss how the manager might have to handle different strategies at different stages in the product life cycle. To make your discussion more concrete, consider the job of a marketing manager for a sporting product manufacturer.

12. How would marketing planning be different for a firm that has entered foreign marketing with a joint venture and a firm that has set up a wholly-owned subsidiary?

13. How can a firm set the details of its marketing plan when it has little information about a foreign market it wants to enter?

SUGGESTED CASES

9. Enviro Pure Water

14. Plastic Master

16 Aluminium Basics Co.

REFERENCES

1. 'Disneyland Paris: Le plan marketing qui a sauvé Le Parc', *L'Essential du Management*, vol. 12, Fevrier 1996, pp. 42–7; 'Euro Disney Revenue Up', *The Sunday Times*, 24 July 1997, p. 26.

2. F. McHugh, 'Waterford to cut English production after sluggish sales', *The Sunday Times*, Business section, 24 January 1999, p. 1; D. White, 'Waterford: Stretching the Brand', *Business and Finance*, 10 April 1997, pp. 28–31; P. Galvin, 'The turnaround at Waterford Crystal' *in Marketing Through Turbulent Times*, Proceedings of Business and Finance National Marketing Conference, Cork, Ireland, 1993, pp. 2–4; R. O'Donoghue, 'Marquis by Waterford: Creating A New International Brand', *Irish Marketing Review*, vol. 7, 1994, pp. 31–7.

3. *1993 Annual Report*, Loctite; 'Companies to watch: Loctite Corporation', *Fortune*, 19 June 1989, p. 148; 'Loctite: Home is where the customers are,' *Business Week*, 13 April 1987, p. 63; *1987 Annual Report*, Loctite Corporation; 'Loctite listens to the marketplace', *in* R. Alsop and B. Abrams, *The Wall Street Journal on Marketing*, Dow Jones & Co., New York, 1986, pp. 281–3.

4. C. Wallace, 'Adidas goes for gold', *Time*, 20 January 1997, p. 3; 'The revival of Adidas', *Campaign*, 22 March 1996, pp. 32–3.

5. T. Meenaghan and P. O'Sullivan (1986) 'The shape and length of the product life cycle', *Irish Marketing Review*, vol. 1, Spring, pp. 83–102; P.F. Kaminski and D.R. Rink, 'PLC: The missing link between physical distribution and marketing planning,' *International Journal of Physical Distribution and Materials Management*, vol. 14, no. 6, 1984, pp. 77–92.

6. Checking the accuracy of forecasts is a difficult subject. See R.H. Evans, 'Analyzing the potential of a new market', *Industrial Marketing Management*, February 1993, pp. 35–40; H. Winklhofer and A. Diamantopoulos, 'The impact of firm and export characteristics on the accuracy of export sales forecasts: An empirical study' *in* D. Arnott *et al.* (eds) *Marketing: Progress, Prospects and Perspectives*, Proceedings of 26th EMAC Conference, Warwick Business School, 1997, pp. 1349–69; S.H. McIntyre, D.D. Achabal and C.M. Miller, 'Applying case-based reasoning to forecasting retail sales', *Journal of Retailing*, Winter 1993, pp. 372–98; P.A. Berbig, J. Milewicz and J.E. Golden, 'The do's and don'ts of sales forecasting', *Industrial Marketing Management*, February 1993, pp. 49–58; D.L. Kendall and M.T. French, 'Forecasting the potential for new industrial products', *Industrial Marketing Management*, vol. 20, no. 3, 1991, pp. 177–84.

7. W. Sandy, 'Avoid the breakdowns between planning and implementation', *The Journal of Business Strategy*, September–October 1991, pp. 30–3; M. MacInnis and L.A. Heslop, 'Market planning in a high-tech environment', *Industrial Marketing Management*, May 1990, pp. 107–16; B. Arinze, 'Market planning with computer models: A case study in the software industry', *Industrial Marketing Management*, May 1990, pp. 117–30.

8. A. Cantin, 'Comment Procter a imposé ses marques en Chine', *L'Essential du Management*, February 1996, pp. 54–8; *Xinhua Business Weekly*, 9 August 1997, as in www.chinavista.com/ business/news/archive/sep/sep15-05.html.

9. R. McNaughton, 'The foreign market entry mode and channel change decision processes of small computer software firms' *in* D. Arnott *et al.* (eds) *Marketing: Progress, Prospects and Perspectives* Proceedings of 26th EMAC Conference, Warwick Business School, 1997, pp. 1349–69; A. Petrou, 'Selection of foreign entry modes in banking: An issue of control and resources' *in* D. Arnott *et al.*, ibid; J. Whitelock and D. Jobber, 'An investigation into the determinants of initial market entry into an international market' *in* R. Ashford *et al.* (eds) *Marketing Without Borders*, Proceedings of the Academy of Marketing Conference, Manchester Metropolitan University, 1997, pp. 1065–79; S.C. Okoroafo, 'Modes of entering foreign markets', *Industrial Marketing Management*, vol. 20, no. 4, 1991, pp. 341–6; S. Tamer Cavusgil, S. Zou, and G.M. Naidu, 'Product and promotion adaptation in export ventures: An empirical investigation,' *Journal of International Business Studies*, Third Quarter 1993, pp. 479–506.

10. J.A. Quelch, 'How to build a product licensing program', *Harvard Business Review*, May–June 1985, p. 186ff.

11. R. Porter Lynch, 'Building alliances to penetrate European markets', *Journal of Business Strategy*, March–April 1990, pp. 4–9; K. Ohmae, 'The global logic of strategic alliances', *Harvard Business Review*, March–April 1989, pp. 143–54; P. Lawrence and C. Vlachoutsicos, 'Joint ventures in Russia: Put the locals in charge', *Harvard Business Review*, January–February 1993, pp. 44–55.

12. C. Chan and N.B. Holbert, 'Whose empire is this, anyway? Reflections on the Empire State of multi-national corporations', *Business Horizons*, July–August 1994, pp. 51–4; S.H. Akhter and Y.A. Choudhry, 'Forced withdrawal from a country market: Managing political risk,' *Business Horizons*, May–June 1993, pp. 47–54; M. Krishna Erramilli and C.P. Rao, 'Service Firms' international entry-mode choice: A modified transaction-cost analysis approach', *Journal of Marketing*, July 1993, pp. 19–38; M. Krishna Erramilli, 'Influence of some external and internal environmental factors on foreign market entry mode choice in service firms', *Journal of Business Research*, December 1992, pp. 263–76; T. Ohbora, A. Parsons and H. Riesenbeck, 'Alternative routes to global marketing', *The McKinsey Quarterly*, vol. 3, pp. 53–74.

CHAPTER 19

Implementing and Controlling Marketing Plans

When You Finish This Chapter, You Should

1 Understand how information technology is speeding up feedback for better implementation and control.

2 Know why effective implementation is critical to customer satisfaction and profits.

3 Understand how sales analysis can aid marketing strategy planning.

4 Understand performance analysis, and its emphasis on exceptions in performance.

5 Understand the difference between the full-cost approach and the contribution-margin approach.

6 Understand how planning and control can be combined to improve the marketing management process.

7 Understand the marketing audit and when and where it should be used.

8 Understand the important new terms (shown in colour).

L'ORÉAL: CONSTANT PLANNING, IMPLEMENTATION AND CONTROL

L'Oréal is the world's biggest cosmetics manufacturer and has more than eighty years experience in the development and management of premium brands. It groups its product portfolio under four main headings: professional hairdressing products; mainstream consumer brands (which with salon products make up 49 per cent of sales; the luxury perfumes and beauty division (22.6 per cent of sales); the specialist 'active cosmetics' division of skin products sold only at pharmacies and specialist beauty shops (9.8 per cent of sales). Remaining sales come from the company's pharmaceuticals subsidiary (16.8 per cent of sales) and women's magazines such as *Marie Claire* (1.8 per cent).

L'Oréal invests heavily in innovation, which is seen as an effective way to defend a premium brand. The cosmetics market is special because loyalty to brands runs deeper than it does in many other sectors. L'Oréal concentrates on higher-value added products, cosmetics for example, rather than bulk commodities (such as soap) which are more vulnerable to own-label competitors. Research carried out in Spain by McKinsey management consultants has shown that cosmetics fall outside the top 10 sectors for own-label goods in the United Kingdom, France, the Netherlands and Spain.

The company constantly manages the brands with plans and strategies developed and implemented in accordance with the market. The company tries to be proactive in brand management, believing that it is preferable to adjust strategy early, rather than worrying about performance after months of poor sales performance.

Management activity is underpinned by constant monitoring of the market, through market research. This enables L'Oréal to adapt to new patterns in consumer habits and the growing number of increasingly demanding consumers. Selective distribution is used to reach the discerning and discriminating customers. Market research is used to find gaps in markets and to discover what customers want. The company's research and development programme accounts for 2.6 per cent of sales. It searches continuously for new, potentially market-leading products. Advertising and marketing costs (33 per cet of sales) work to introduce new products and to win and maintain market position. Costs are constantly tightened so as to improve the margins on established products.

An example of L'Oréal's proactive management is Dop, a shampoo well known in France. The brand was well established but unexciting and beginning to look a bit vulnerable. It was the sort of brand that could have been overtaken by own-label shampoos in the climate of recession. L'Oréal took the brand and relaunched it. With an effective marketing plan, the brand was repositioned and manages to retain a leading position in the French market in spite of its higher price.

This is similar to how L'Oréal treated its Helena Rubenstein perfume and beauty range. The range was under-performing, so much research and planning effort went into deciding on the level at which Helena Rubenstein should be positioned. Three or four years were spent considering all the detailed elements that would position the brand as a modern luxury product—packaging, pricing, retailing and so on.

Other stories of L'Oréal's active management include the revival of the Lanvin luxury range. The Diparco group of mass-market cosmetics has also been relaunched under a new name and image (Gemey-Paris). This has been done to coordinate a formerly disparate range of products and enable them to be marketed more effectively. This change was planned over several years.

L'Oréal invest massive research and marketing expenditure to reinforce a leading position. Integral to these investments is the constant management of brands—developing and implementing plans that are based on a thorough understanding of the marketplace. As the marketplace changes, L'Oréal has new plans and strategies in place.[1]

GOOD PLANS SET THE FRAMEWORK FOR IMPLEMENTATION AND CONTROL

The primary emphasis in this book is on the strategy planning part of the marketing manager's job. There is a good reason for this focus. Strategy decisions, those that decide what business the company is in and the strategies it will follow, either set the firm on a course towards profitable opportunities or, alternatively, towards costly failure. If a marketing manager makes an error with these basic decisions, there may never be a second chance to set things straight. In contrast, if good strategies and plans are developed, the marketing manager—and everyone else in the organization—knows *what* needs to be done. Thus, good marketing plans set the framework for effective implementation and control.

Although planning was considered in a separate chapter to this one, it is important to appreciate that planning, implementation and control are part of a process that is circular. Thus, for example, information on how well plans are working—control information—gets fed back into the system and helps to form new plans. Likewise, the plan itself sets the groundwork for what needs to be measured and controlled.

Implementation puts plans into operation—and control provides feedback

Developing a potentially profitable plan does not automatically ensure either satisfied customers or profit for the firm. Achieving the outcomes envisioned in the plan requires that the whole marketing management process to work well. The marketing management process includes not only marketing strategy planning but also implementation and control. In fact, in today's highly competitive markets customer satis-

faction often hinges on skilful implementation. Further, the ongoing success of the firm is often dependent on control—the feedback process that helps the marketing manager learn (1) how ongoing plans and implementation are working and (2) how to plan for the future.

Some specific opportunities and challenges with respect to implementation and control have been discussed as each of the marketing strategy decision areas was introduced. In this chapter, more detail will be given on concepts and approaches for making implementation and control more effective. This chapter starts with a discussion of how dramatic improvements in information technology are resulting in changes in implementation and control—and in the whole strategy planning process. For many firms, these changes are critically important, offering new ways to meet customer needs. The role of control-related tools will be explained—such as sales and performance analysis—in improving the quality of planning and implementation decisions. One form of control of a more strategic nature, the marketing audit, is discussed at the end of this chapter.

 Internet Exercise

Visit the L'Oreal web site (**www.loreal.com**). Select one of L'Oreal's brands and investigate how it is marketed. Try to build up the information so that you can infer the marketing strategy and plan for that brand. Does this match the information you have already? For example is the brand available in a store near you? How does its pricing (and other elements of the marketing mix) compare with competing products?

THE ROLE OF INFORMATION IN IMPLEMENTATION AND CONTROL

Feedback improves the marketing management process

In the past, strategies were planned and implemented but it then usually took a long time before feedback was available as to whether the strategy and implementation were really working as intended. For example, a marketing manager might not have much feedback on what was happening with sales, expenses and profits until financial summaries were available—and that sometimes took months or even longer. Further, summary data was not very useful in pinpointing which specific aspects of the plan were working and which were not. In that environment, the feedback was so general and took so long that often there was not anything the manager could do about a problem except start over again.

That situation has now changed dramatically in many types of business. As discussed previously, firms use marketing information systems to track sales and cost details day-by-day and week-by-week. Throughout the book examples have been given of how marketers get more information faster and use it quickly to improve a strategy or its implementation. For example, scanner data from a retail audit can provide a marketing manager with almost immediate feedback on whether or not a new consumer product is selling at the expected level in each specific retail outlet and whether or not it is actually selling to the intended target market rather than some other group. For example, managers at Pepsi are able to observe virtually immediately how sales and market shares change as they roll out the 'blue' can in each region.

Fast feedback can be a competitive advantage

Faster feedback on decisions can often help the marketing manager to develop a competitive advantage. More immediate information enhances the implementation capabilities. Potential problems can be identified early and be prevented from developing into big problems. For example, a manager who gets detailed daily reports that compare actual sales results in different regions with sales forecasts in the plan is able to see very quickly if there is a problem in a specific region. Then the cause of the problem can be traced. If sales are going slowly because the new salesperson in that region is inexperienced, the sales manager might immediately spend more time working with that representative. On the other hand, if the problem is that a chain of retail outlets in that particular region is not willing to allocate much shelf space for the firm's product, then the salesperson might need to develop a special analysis to show the buyers for that specific chain how the product could improve the chain's profit.

The basic strategy planning concepts emphasized throughout the text are enduring and will always be at the heart of marketing. Yet, the fast pace that is now possible in getting information for control is resulting in fundamental changes in how many managers work, make decisions, plan and implement their plans. Managers who can quickly adjust the details of their efforts to solve customer problems better or respond to changes in the market can do a more satisfactory job for their firms—because they can make certain that their plans are really performing as expected. In other words, information enables the marketing manager to be effective.

The marketing manager is responsible

Fast feedback can improve implementation and control. Computers now take the drudgery out of analysing data. This kind of analysis is not possible unless the data is in machine-processible form, so it can be sorted and analysed quickly. Here, the creative marketing manager plays a crucial role by insisting that the necessary data be collected. If the necessary data is not captured, information will be difficult, if not impossible, to get later.

A marketing manager may need many different types of information to improve implementation efforts or develop new strategies. In the past, this has often caused delays, even if the information was in a machine-processible form. In a large company, for example, it could take days or even weeks for a marketing manager to find out how to get needed information from another department. Imagine how long it could take for a marketing manager to get sales data from sales offices in different countries around the world.

New information technologies offer speed and detail

New approaches for electronic communication help to solve these problems. For example, the use of fibre optic telephone lines or satellite transmission systems allows the *immediate* transfer of data from a computer at one location to another. A sales manager with a portable computer can access the firm's mainframe computer via telephone. Marketing managers working at different locations on different aspects of a strategy can use electronic mail to communicate through networks that link their computers for easy data transfer. The Internet makes distance-working possible.

This type of electronic pipeline makes data available instantly. A report, such as one that summarizes sales by product, salesperson or type of customer, that in the past was done once a month now might be done weekly or even daily. Computer software can be programmed to search for and 'flag' results that indicate a problem of some sort. Then the manager can allocate more time to resolv-ing that particular problem. Effective use of information technology is becoming much more common, especially as more marketing managers find that they are losing out to competitors who get information more quickly and adjust their implementation and strategies more often.[2]

EFFECTIVE IMPLEMENTATION MEANS THAT PLANS WORK AS INTENDED

When a marketing manager has developed a good marketing plan, the challenge of implementing it often involves hundreds—or thousands—of opera-tional decisions and activities. In a small company, these may all be handled by a few people or even by a single person. In a large corporation, literally hundreds of different people may be involved in implementa-tion. That may require a massive amount of careful coordination and communication. Either way, opera-tional decisions and activities need to be well-executed if customers are to get what is intended. However, even a good plan can leave customers dissatisfied—and switching to someone else's offering—if imple-mentation is poor.

Good implementation builds relationships with customers

Implementation is especially critical in mature and highly competitive markets. When several firms are all following basically the same strategy—quickly imitat-ing competitors' ideas—customers are often won or lost based on differences in the quality of implementation. Consider the rental car business. Hertz has a strategy that targets business travellers with a choice of quality cars, convenient reservations, first pick-up and drop-off, availability at most major airports and a premium price. Hertz is extremely successful with that strategy even though there is little to prevent other companies from trying the same approach. A major part of Hertz's success is due to implementation. Customers keep coming back because the Hertz service is both reliable and painless.

When a Hertz 'Gold' customer calls to make a reservation, the company already has the standard information about that customer in a computer data-base. At the airport, the customer avoids the queues at the Hertz counter and instead picks up an already-completed rental contract and goes straight to the Hertz bus. The driver gets the customer's name and radios ahead to have someone start the specific car that customer will drive. That way the air-condition-ing or heating is already on when the bus driver deliv-ers the customer to his or her car. The customer is certain that he or she is at the right place because there is an electronic sign beside each car with the customer's name on it. Systems have been set up by Hertz to ensure that all of this works—day in and day out, customer after customer. The systems are required to implement its plan—and to keep customers loyal.[3]

Implementation deals with internal or external matters

As the Hertz example illustrates, marketing imple-mentation usually involves decisions and activities related to both internal and external matters. Determining how the correct car will end up in the right parking slot, how the Hertz bus driver will contact the office and who will coordinate getting the message to the person who starts the car are all inter-nal matters. They are invisible to the customer—as long as they work as planned. On the other hand, some implementation issues are external and involve the customer. For example, the contract must be completed correctly and be available when and where the rental customer comes to pick it up, and someone needs to have filled the car with fuel and cleaned it.

Implementation has its own objectives

Whether implementation decisions and activities are internal or external, they all must be consistent with the objectives of the overall strategy and with the other details of the plan. However, there are also three general objectives that apply to all implementation efforts. Other things being equal, the manager wants to get each implementation job done better, faster and at lower cost. The ideal of doing things better, faster and at lower cost is easy to accept. In practice, however, implementation is often complicated by trade-offs among the three objectives. For example, doing a job better may take longer or cost more.

Just as a marketing manager should constantly look for new strategy opportunities, it is important to be creative in looking for better solutions to implemen-tation problems. That may require finding ways to better coordinate the efforts of the different people involved, setting up standard operating procedures to deal with recurring problems or juggling priorities to deal with the unexpected. When the Hertz bus driver is sick, someone still has to be there to pick up the customers and deliver them to their cars.

Implementation requires innovation

Sometimes the implementation effort can be improved by approaching the task in a new or different way. Exhibit 19–1 shows some of the ways that firms are using information technology to improve specific implementation jobs. Note that some of the examples in Exhibit 19–1 focus on internal matters and some on external, customer-oriented matters.

Structure and skills for effective implementation

Implementation covers many tasks, a breadth of details and involves many other parties. For implementation to be effective, the organization must have appropriate systems, policies and actions. If a salesperson, for example, negotiates payment and delivery terms with customers, these terms must be in keeping with company policies. Likewise, the organization's systems must monitor and support sales activities. In addition to these structural requirements, effective implementation is also due to the skills of the people involved.

Marketing people need to be able to work with others within the marketing function, but also with other functional areas such as production, inventory, personnel and so on. This calls for interaction skills and, in particular, the ability to communicate and work as part of a team. Effective planning and implementation also require initiative, creativity and the ability to think strategically as well as deal with day-to-day detail.

In common with all managers, the marketing manager is faced with choices about how to allocate scarce resources. The marketing manager needs to ensure that each area has the budget to carry out its part of the plan. In addition, the degree of efficiency in using those resources must be measured. As already mentioned (and will be taken up later in this chapter) implementation of plans must be monitored to ensure that the firm is being effective. The manager must have access to timely and appropriate information for this task. Monitoring skills also include being logical, analytical and numerate. Implementation requires the effective harnessing of many parts of the organization. The manager must negotiate and work with the other functions, their decisions, practices and so on. It is important to recognize where power, authority and responsibilities lie. Political skills are necessary therefore to deal with the organization in its formal and informal guises.[4]

Marketing Mix Decision Area	Operational Problem	Implementation Approach
Product	Develop design of a new product as rapidly as possible without errors	Use 3-D computer-aided design software
	Pre-test consumer response to different versions of a label	Prepare sample labels with PC graphics software
Place	Coordinate inventory levels with middlemen to avoid stockouts	Use bar code scanner, EDI, and computerized reorder system
	Get franchisee's inputs and cooperation on a new programme	Set up a televideo conference
	Quickly distribute TV ad to local stations in many different markets	Distribute final video version of the ad via satellite link
Promotion	Answer final consumers' questions about how to use a product	Put a free telephone number and web site address on product label
	Identify frequent customers for a quantity discount	Create a 'favoured customer' club with an ID card
Price	Figure out if price sensitivity impacts demand for a product; make it easier for customers to compare prices	Show unit prices (for example, per ml) on shelf markers; set different prices in similar markets and track sales, including sales of competing products

Exhibit 19–1 Examples of Approaches to Overcome Specific Marketing Implementation Problems

CONTROL PROVIDES FEEDBACK TO IMPROVE PLANS AND IMPLEMENTATION

Keeping a firmer hand on the controls

Control is the process whereby feedback is used to monitor the ongoing implementation of plans and to inform future plans. Computers and other types of information technology are speeding up the flow of feedback and prompting a revolution by allowing managers to improve plans and implementation quickly and continuously. On the other hand, the basic marketing management issues surrounding better implementation and strategy decisions remain unchanged.

A good manager wants to know: which products' sales are highest and why, which products are profitable, what is selling where and the costs of the marketing process. Managers need to know what is happening, in detail, if profits and profitability are to be improved. Unfortunately, traditional accounting reports are usually too general to be much help in answering these questions. A company may be showing a profit, while 80 per cent of its business comes from only 20 per cent of its products or customers. The other 80 per cent may be unprofitable. Without special analyses, managers will not know the source of profits. This 80/20 relationship is fairly common and is often referred to as the *80/20 rule*.

What happened with Ben and Jerry's Peace Pops premium ice-cream bars is a good example. The initial plan called for intensive distribution of boxes of Peace Pops in supermarket freezers to compete with competitors like Dove Bar and Häagen-Dazs. After six months, total sales were 50 per cent lower than expected. However, detailed sales analysis by package and channel revealed a bright spot: individual Peace Pops were selling very well in local delicatessens. After further work to better understand the reasons for this focused success, Ben and Jerry's marketing people realized that most of their target customers saw the premium-price Peace Pop as an impulse product, rather than as a staple purchase made during the weekly grocery shopping. Ben and Jerry's revised the strategy to reach impulse buyers at convenience stores better. Within a year, the revised strategy worked. Sales increased 60 per cent, and the sales analysis showed that 70 per cent of the sales were at convenience stores.[5]

As the Ben and Jerry's example shows, it *is* possible for marketing managers to get detailed information about how marketing plans are working, but only if the necessary data is generated. In this section, the kinds of information that can be available and how such information is used will be discussed. The techniques are not complicated, requiring only simple arithmetic. A computer can quickly and easily take care of the more detailed calculations.

SALES ANALYSIS

Sales analysis—a detailed breakdown of a company's sales records—can be very informative, especially the first time it is done. Detailed data can keep marketing executives in touch with what is happening in the market. In addition, routine sales analyses prepared each week, month or year may show trends thus enabling planning assumptions to be checked.

To ignore sales analysis risks not only poor sales forecasting but poor decisions in general. One manufacturer did much national advertising on the assumption that the firm was selling all over the country. However, a simple sales analysis showed that most current customers were located within 150 miles of the factory! In other words, the firm did not know who and where its customers were and it wasted most of the money it spent on national advertising.

Detailed sales analysis is possible only if a manager asks for the data. Valuable sales information is often buried, perhaps on sales invoices or in accounting records. It could even be argued that the extent to which the firm uses this accounting data for marketing purposes is an indication of the extent to which it is truly marketing oriented.

Types of marketing data

There is no one best way to analyse sales data. Several breakdowns may be useful, depending on the nature of the company and product and what dimensions are relevant. Typical breakdowns include:

1. Geographic region—country, region, city or sales representative's territory.
2. Product, package size, grade or colour.
3. Customer size.
4. Customer type or class of trade.
5. Price or discount class.
6. Method of sale—mail, telephone or direct sales.
7. Financial arrangement—cash or credit.
8. Size of order.
9. Commission class.

Data Overload

While some sales analysis is better than none—or better than getting data too late for action—sales breakdowns that are too detailed can lead to data overload. It is good practice to ask only for those breakdowns that will help in decision making. The use of graphs and figures make it easier to see patterns that otherwise might be hidden in a computer printout. To avoid coping with mountains of data, much of which may be irrelevant, *performance analysis* may be used.

PERFORMANCE ANALYSIS LOOKS FOR DIFFERENCES

Numbers are compared

Performance analysis looks for exceptions or variations from planned performance. In simple sales analysis, the figures are merely listed or graphed, but are not compared against standards. In performance analysis, comparisons are drawn. For example, one territory may be compared against another, against the same territory's performance last year or against expected performance. The purpose of performance analysis is to improve operations. The salesperson, territory or other factors showing poor performance can be identified and singled out for detailed analysis and corrective action. Alternatively, outstanding performances can be analysed to see if the successes can be explained and made the general rule. Performance analysis does not have to be limited to sales. Other data can be analysed; this data may include miles travelled, number of calls made, number of orders or the cost of various tasks.

A performance analysis can be quite revealing, as shown in the following example.

Straight performance analysis— an illustration

A manufacturer of business products sells to wholesalers through five sales representatives, each serving a separate territory. Total net sales for the year amount to £2 386 000. Salesforce compensation and expenses come to £198 000, yielding a direct-selling expense ratio of 8.3 per cent—that is, £198 000   £2 386 000   100.

This information—taken from a profit and loss statement—is interesting, but it doesn't explain what is happening from one territory to another. To get a clearer picture, the manager compares the sales results with other data *from each territory*. See Exhibits 19–2 and 19–3. Keep in mind that exhibits like these and others

Sales Area	Total Calls	Total Orders	Order–Call Ratio	Sales by Sales Rep	Average Sales Rep Order	Total
A	1 900	1 140	60.0%	£912 000	£800	195
B	1 500	1 000	66.7	720 000	720	160
C	1 400	700	50.0	560 000	800	140
D	1 030	279	27.1	132 000	478	60
E	820	165	20.1	62 000	374	50
Total	6 650	3 284	49.3%	£2 386 000	£634	605

Exhibit 19–2 Comparative Performance of Sales Reps

Sales Area	Annual Compensation	Expense Payments	Total Sales Rep Cost	Sales Produced	Cost–Sales Ratio
A	£22 800	£11 200	£34 000	£912 000	3.7%
B	21 600	14 400	36 000	720 000	5.0
C	20 400	11 600	32 000	560 000	5.7
D	19 200	24 800	44 000	132 000	33.3
E	20 000	32 000	52 000	62 000	83.8
Total	£104 000	£94 000	£198 000	£2 386 000	8.3%

Exhibit 19–3 Comparative Cost of Sales Reps

that follow in this chapter are now very easy to generate. Popular computer programs like Lotus 1-2-3 and dBASE IV make it easy to apply the ideas discussed here, even on inexpensive desktop computers.

The representatives in sales areas D and E are not doing well. Sales are low and marketing costs are high. Perhaps more aggressive sales representatives could do a better job,

but the number of customers suggests that sales potential might be low. Perhaps the whole plan needs revision.

The figures themselves do not provide the answers, but they do reveal the areas that need improvement. This is the main value of performance analysis. It is up to management to find the remedy, either by revising or changing the marketing plan.

A SERIES OF PERFORMANCE ANALYSES MAY FIND THE REAL PROBLEM

Performance analysis helps to monitor whether the firm's marketing plans are working properly and can facilitate diagnosis of problems, as shown in the following example. To appreciate how performance analysis can be part of a problem-solving process, follow this example carefully, one exhibit at a time. Try to anticipate the marketing manager's decision.

The case of The Stereo Company Ltd

Stereo's sales manager finds that sales for Britain and Ireland are £130 000 below the quota of £4 500 000 (that is, actual sales are £14 370 000) for the January to June period. The quota is based on forecast sales of the various types of stereo equipment the company sells. Specifically, the quota is based on forecasts for each product type in each store in each sales representative's territory.

Pam Dexter, the sales manager, thinks this difference is not too large (1.52 per cent) and is inclined to overlook the matter, especially since forecasts usually err to some extent. She considers sending a letter to all the Britain and Ireland sales representatives and district supervisors—a letter aimed at stimulating sales effort. Exhibit 19–4

shows the overall picture of Stereo's sales in Britain and Ireland. What do you think the manager should do?

Scotland has the poorest performance, but it is not too bad. Rather than write a stern letter to Scotland, the sales manager decides to analyse the performance of the four sales reps in Scotland. Exhibit 19–5 shows a breakdown of the Scotland figures by sales representative. What conclusion or action do you suggest now?

Since Shanna Smith previously was the top sales representative, the sales manager wonders if Smith is having trouble with some of her larger customers. Before making a drastic move, she obtains an analysis of Smith's sales to the five largest customers. See Exhibit 19–6. What action could the sales manager take now? Should Smith be fired?

Smith's sales in all the large retail outlets are down significantly although her sales in many small outlets are holding up well. Smith's problem seems to be general and may indicate a lack of effort. Before calling her, the sales manager decides to look at Smith's sales of the four major products. Exhibit 19–7 shows Smith's sales. What action is indicated now?

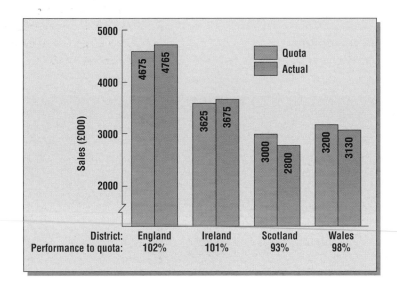

Exhibit 19–4 Sales Performance—Britain and Ireland, January–June (£000)

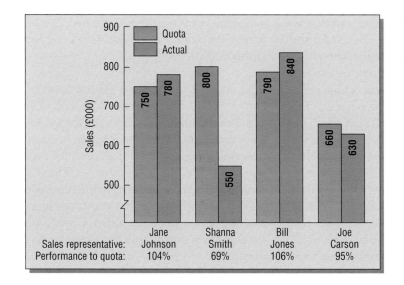

Exhibit 19–5 Sales Performance—Scotland, January–June (£000)

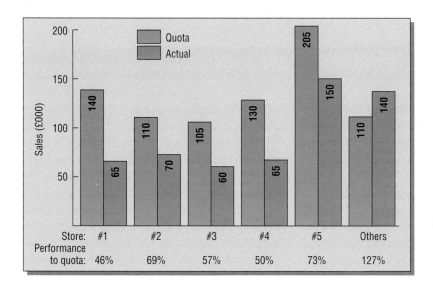

Exhibit 19–6 Sales Performance—Selected Stores of Shanna Smith in Scotland, January–June (£000)

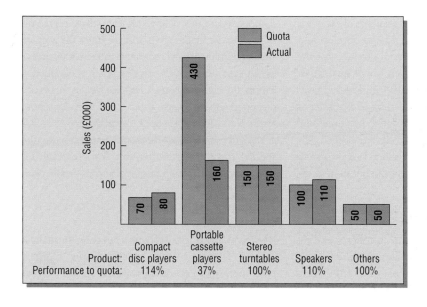

Exhibit 19–7 Sales Performance by Product for Shanna Smith in Scotland, January–June (£000)

Smith is having trouble with portable cassette players. Was the problem Smith or the players? Further analysis by product for the whole region shows that everyone in Britain and Ireland is having trouble with portable players because a competitor is cutting prices. However, higher sales on other products hid this fact. Since portable player sales are doing all right overall, the problem is only now showing up. The series of performance analyses indicates that this is the *major* problem.

Since overall company sales are fairly good, many sales managers would not bother with this analysis. Some might trace the problem to Smith. Without detailed sales records and performance analysis, they might assume that Smith, rather than business conditions or aggressive competition, is at fault. Even Smith herself might not be able to pinpoint the problem.

This case shows that total figures can be deceiving. Marketing managers should not make rash decisions or judgements until they have all the facts. Some students want to fire Smith after they see the store-by-store data (Exhibit 19–6).

The iceberg principle—90 per cent is below the surface

The Stereo Company also illustrates the **iceberg principle**—much good information is hidden in summary data. Icebergs show only about 10 per cent of their mass above water level. The other 90 per cent is it. The same is true of much business and marketing data. Since total sales may be large and company activities varied, problems in one area may operate below the surface. Closer analysis may reveal problems that can have the potential to cause severe damage. The 90:10 ratio, or the 80/20 rule mentioned earlier, must not be ignored. Averages and summaries are helpful, but they require close inspection and analysis to ensure that they do not hide more than they reveal.

MARKETING COST ANALYSIS

So far sales analysis has been emphasized but costs can and should be analysed and controlled. The case of Watanake Packaging, Ltd (WPL) illustrates the point. WPL developed a new strategy to target the packaging needs of producers of high-tech electronic equipment. WPL designed unique polystyrene inserts to protect electronic equipment during transportation. It assigned order getters to develop new accounts and recruited agents to develop international markets. The whole marketing mix was well received and the firm's skimming price led to good profits. Over time, however, competing suppliers entered the market. When marketing managers at WPL analysed costs, it realized that its once-successful strategy was slipping. Personal selling expense as a percentage of sales had doubled because it took longer to find and develop new accounts. It was costly to design special products for the many customers who purchased only small quantities. Profit margins were also falling because of increased price competition. In contrast, the analysis showed that sales of ordinary cardboard boxes for transportation of agricultural products were very profitable. WPL therefore stopped calling on *small* electronics firms and developed a new plan to build the firm's share of the less glamorous, but more profitable, cardboard box business.

Marketing costs have a purpose

Detailed cost analysis is very useful in understanding production costs, but much less is done with *marketing cost analysis*. Careful analysis of most marketing costs shows that the money is spent for a specific purpose, for example to develop or promote a particular product or to serve particular customers.[6]

Reconsider Exhibit 19–3 from this perspective. It shows that the company's spending on sales compensation and sales expenses varies by salesperson and market area. By further breaking down, and comparing, the costs of different sales representatives, the marketing manager has a much better idea of what it is costing to implement the strategy in each sales area. In this example, it is clear that the sales representatives in sales areas D and especially E are not only falling short in sales, but also that their costs are high relative to other representatives who are getting more results. The table shows that the difference is not due to annual compensation; that is lower. Rather, these representatives have expenses that are two or three times the average. The smaller number of total customers in these sales areas might explain the lower levels of sales, but it probably does not explain the higher expenses. Perhaps the customers are more dispersed and it requires more travel to reach them. Here again, the cost analysis doesn't explain *why* the results are as they are—but it does direct the manager's attention to a specific area that needs attention. A more detailed breakdown of costs may help to pinpoint the specific cause.

Allocate costs to specific customers and products

Because marketing costs have a purpose, it usually makes sense to allocate costs to specific market segments, or customers, or to specific products. In some situations, companies allocate costs directly to the various geographical market segments they serve. This may let managers directly analyse the profitability of the firm's target markets. In other cases, companies allocate costs to specific customers or specific products and then add these costs for market segments depending on how much of which products each customer buys.

Should all costs be allocated?

The allocation of costs is a problematic area. Some costs are likely to be fixed for the near future, regardless of what decision is made. In addition, some costs are likely to be *common* to several products or customers, making allocation difficult. Two basic approaches to handling this allocating problem are possible—the full-cost approach and the contribution-margin approach.

Full-cost approach

In the **full-cost approach**, all costs are allocated to products, customers or other categories. Even fixed costs and common costs are allocated in some way. Because all costs are allocated, costs can be subtracted from sales to find the profitability of various customers, products and so on. This *is* of interest to some managers.

The full-cost approach requires that difficult-to-allocate costs be split on some basis. Here the managers assume that the work done for those costs is equally beneficial to customers, to products, or to whatever group they are allocated. Sometimes this allocation is done mechanically. Often, however, logic can support the allocation, if it is accepted that marketing costs are incurred for a purpose. For example, advertising costs not directly related to specific customers or products might be allocated to *all* customers based on their purchases—on the theory that advertising helps to bring in the sales.

Contribution-margin approach

With the **contribution-margin approach**, all functional costs are not allocated in *all* situations. In considering various alternatives, it may be more meaningful to consider only the costs directly related to specific alternatives. Variable costs are relevant in this instance.

The contribution-margin approach focuses attention on variable costs, rather than on total costs. Total costs may include some fixed costs that do not change in the short run and can safely be ignored or some common costs that are more difficult to allocate.[7]

The two approaches can lead to different decisions

The difference between the full-cost approach and the contribution-margin approach is important. The two approaches may suggest different decisions, as the following example shows.

Full-cost example

Exhibit 19–8 shows a profit and loss statement—using the full-cost approach—for a department store with three operating departments. (These could be market segments or customers or products.)

The administrative expenses that are the only fixed costs in this case have been allocated to departments based on the sales volume of each department. This is a typical method of allocation. In this case, some managers argued that Department 1 was clearly unprofitable—and should be eliminated—because it showed a net loss of £500. Were they right?

To find out, see Exhibit 19–9, which shows what would happen if Department 1 were eliminated.

Several facts become clear right away. The overall profit of the store would be reduced if Department 1 were dropped. Fixed costs of £39 000—now being charged to Department 1—would have to be allocated to the other departments. This would reduce net profit by £2500, because Department 1 previously covered £2500 of the £3000 in fixed costs. Such shifting of costs would then make Department 2 unprofitable.

	Totals	Dept. 1	Dept. 2	Dept. 3
Sales	£100 000	£50 000	£30 000	£20,000
Cost of sales	80 000	45 000	25 000	10 000
Gross margin	20 000	5 000	5 000	10 000
Other expenses:				
Selling expenses	5 000	2 500	1 500	1 000
Administrative expenses	6 000	3 000	1 800	1 200
Total other expenses	11 000	5 500	3 300	2 200
Net profit or (loss)	£9 000	£(500)	£1 700	£7 800

Exhibit 19–8 Profit and Loss Statement by Department

Contribution-margin example

Exhibit 19–10 shows a contribution-margin income statement for the same department store. Note that each department has a positive contribution margin. Here the Department 1 contribution of £2500 stands out better. This actually is the amount that would be lost if Department 1 were dropped. (The example assumes that the fixed administrative expenses are *truly* fixed—that none of them would be eliminated if this department were dropped.)

A contribution-margin income statement shows the contribution of each department more clearly, including its contribution to both fixed costs and profit. As long as a department has some contribution-margin, and as long as there is no better use for the resources it uses, the department should be retained.

Contribution-margin versus full-cost approach

Using the full-cost approach often leads to conflicts within a company. Any method of allocation can make some products or customers appear less profitable. For example, it is logical to assign all common advertising costs to customers based on their purchases. This approach can be criticized on the grounds that it may make large-volume customers appear less profitable than they really are—especially if the marketing mix aimed at the larger customers emphasizes price more than advertising.

Those in the company who want the smaller customers to look more profitable usually argue *for* this allocation method on the grounds that general advertising helps build good customers because it affects the overall image of the company and its products. The allocation method used may reflect on the performance of various managers and it may affect their salaries and bonuses. Product managers, for example, are especially interested in how the various fixed and common costs are allocated to their products. Each, in turn, might prefer to have costs shifted to someone else's products. Arbitrary allocation of costs also may have a direct impact on the morale of the salesforce. If they see their variable costs loaded with additional common or fixed costs over which they have no control, they may question whether it is worth while to make the effort.

To avoid these problems, firms often use the contribution-margin approach. It is especially useful for evaluating alternatives and for showing operating managers and salespeople how they are performing. The contribution-margin approach shows what they have actually contributed to covering general overhead and profit. Top management, on the other hand, often finds full-cost analysis more useful. In the long run, some products, departments or customers must pay for the fixed costs.

PLANNING AND CONTROL COMBINED

Thus far, sales and cost analyses have been treated separately. A combination of sales analysis and cost analysis enables management to monitor the effectiveness of plans and to see when and where new strategies are needed.

Cindy's Fashions, a typical clothing retailer, is a useful example. This firm made a net profit of £155 000 last

year. Cindy Reve, the owner, expects no basic change in competition and slightly better local business conditions. Therefore, she sets this year's profit objective at £163 000—an increase of about 5 per cent.

Next she develops tentative plans to show how she can make this higher profit. She estimates the sales volumes, gross margins and expenses, broken down by

	Totals	Dept. 2	Dept.
Sales	£50 000	£30 000	£20 000
Cost of sales	35 000	25 000	10 000
Gross margin	15 000	5 000	10 000
Other expenses:			
Selling expenses	2 500	1 500	1 000
Administrative expenses	6 000	3 600	2 400
Total other expenses	8 500	5 100	3 400
Net profit or (loss)	£6 500	£(100)	£6 600

Exhibit 19–9 Profit and Loss Statement by Department If Department 1 Were Eliminated

months and by departments in her store, that she would need to net £163 000.

Exhibit 19–11 is a planning and control chart Reve developed to show the contribution each department should make each month. At the bottom of Exhibit 19–11, the plan for the year is summarized. Inserting the actual performance and a measure of variation means that this chart can be used to do both planning and control.

Exhibit 19–11 shows that Reve is focusing on the monthly contribution to overhead and profit by each

	Totals	Dept. 1	Dept. 2	Dept. 3
Sales	£100 000	£50 000	£30 000	£20 000
Variable costs:				
Cost of sales	80 000	45 000	25 000	10 000
Selling expenses	5 000	2 500	1 500	1 000
Total variable costs	85 000	47 500	26 500	11 000
Contribution margin	15 000	£ 2 500	£ 3 500	£ 9 000
Fixed costs				
Administrative expenses	6 000			
Net profit	£ 9 000			

Exhibit 19–10 Contribution–Margin Statement by Departments

	Contribution to Store					Store Expense	Operating Profit	Cumulative Operating Profit
	Dept. A	Dept. B	Dept. C	Dept. D*	Total			
January								
Planned	27 000	9 000	4 000	1 000	39 000	24 000	15 000	15 000
Actual								
Variation								
February								
Planned	20 000	6 500	2 500	1 000	28 000	24 000	4 000	19 000
Actual								
Variation								
November								
Planned	32 000	7 500	2 500	0	42 000	24 000	18 000	106 500
Actual								
Variation								
December								
Planned	63 000	12 500	4 000	9 000	88 500	32 000	56 500	163 000
Actual								
Variation								
Total								
Planned	316 000	70 000	69 000	4 000	453 000	288 000	163 000	163 000
Actual								
Variation								

*The objective of minus £4000 for this department was established on the same basis as the objectives for the other departments—that is, it represents the same percentage gain over last year when Department D's loss was £4200. Plans call for discontinuance of the department unless it shows marked improvement by the end of the year.

Exhibit 19–11 Planning and Control Chart for Cindy's Fashions

department. The purpose of monthly estimates is to get more frequent feedback and allow faster adjustment of plans. Generally, the shorter the planning and control period, the easier it is to correct problems before they become critical.

In this example, Reve uses a modified contribution-margin approach—some of the fixed costs can be allocated logically to particular departments. On this chart, the balance left after direct fixed and variable costs are charged to departments is called *contribution to store*. The idea is that each department will contribute to covering *general* store expenses, such as

top-management salaries and holiday decorations, and to net profits.

In Exhibit 19–11, the whole operation is brought together when Reve computes the monthly operating profit. The operating profit for each month is computed as the total of the contributions from each of the four departments less general store expenses.

As time passes, Reve can compare actual sales with what is projected. If actual sales were less than projected, corrective action could take either of two courses: improving implementation efforts or developing new, more realistic strategies.

THE MARKETING AUDIT

The analyses discussed so far are designed to help a firm to plan and control its operations. This type of control focuses on the operational performance of marketing plans. Such control confines itself to the assessment of already-decided plans. As such, the emphasis is on periodic performance—by week, month and quarter. By necessity, only a few critical elements are monitored—such as sales variations by product in different territories. Responsibility for day-to-day implementing, controlling and planning of the marketing function usually rests with the marketing manager.

The marketing audit provides strategic control

As well as operation-level control, it is appropriate to have control at a strategic marketing level. Unfortunately, this is often left until some crisis emerges that forces management to more comprehensively evaluate its marketing activities. Crisis management usually does not allow much time for reflection and is concerned with adjusting marketing mixes or shifting strategies in the short run. Strategic marketing control should evaluate the effectiveness of the firm's marketing efforts. So that such control is undertaken regularly, not just in times of crisis, marketing specialists have developed the marketing audit. A marketing audit is similar to an accounting audit or a personnel audit, which businesses have used for some time.

The **marketing audit** is a systematic, critical and unbiased review and appraisal of the basic objectives and policies of the marketing function. It also addresses the way in which marketing is organized, its methods, procedures and people employed to implement the policies. The marketing audit forces the organization to question what it is doing and why it is doing it (for example in which markets it operates and the methods

used to service those markets). This contrasts with operational control, which concerns itself with performance against standards set in the plan (for example, sales per region, outlet, salesperson).[8]

An extensive and exhaustive process

A marketing audit takes an overview of the business and it evaluates the whole marketing function. It requires a detailed assessment of the company's marketing efforts to see if they are the most appropriate for the firm and market conditions. Customers' needs and attitudes change and competitors continually develop new and better plans. Indeed, practically every aspect of the marketing environment is variable. This means that policies, plans, systems and methods can become dated, or even obsolete. It is therefore good practice to audit marketing activities.

One company that audited its advertising practices found that it was not relating well to its audience. Colgate-Palmolive had been running a campaign for its deodorant 'soft and gentle' for three years. When it carried out research it realized that the advertisement was 'not hitting the mark'. Consumers were not remembering the advertising, nor were they associating with it. Further research on other toiletry products found that much of the advertising irritated rather than persuaded the female market. During the 1980s, female consumers were bombarded with lots of glamour images of shoulder-padded women who had it all and always wooed the perfect man. In the 1990s, fashion became more relaxed and the natural look more popular and women are not considered freaks if they choose to be single. New advertising was therefore developed that reflected the modern woman's priorities. The focus changed from the glamorous career woman to feature real women in familiar situations. Without such a strategic review, the company could have continued with the previous, inappropriate campaign.[9]

Sometimes, marketing managers are so involved in the detail that it is difficult for them to be entirely objective. For this reason it can be useful to get an outside perspective. The outsider can help the firm to see whether it really focuses on some unsatisfied needs and offers appropriate marketing mixes. The audit may be performed by a separate department within the company—perhaps by a marketing controller. In order to get both expert and objective evaluation, it may be better to use an outside organization such as a marketing consulting firm.

The auditor also evaluates the quality of the effort—looking at who is doing what and how well. Many issues are considered in the marketing audit, including:

- The marketing environment—changes and trends giving rise to opportunities and threats.
- Company marketing operations—effectiveness of procedures.
- Company structures, interdepartmental relationships and relationships with outside agencies.
- Marketing information systems—adequacy, accuracy, timeliness of information.
- Marketing strategies—for example are product lines efficient? Is the marketing mix(es) balanced and cohesive?
- Profitability—which activities and product markets are profitable or not profitable?)
- People and staffing—are the right people in the right jobs?

A marketing audit can be a large undertaking with quite exhaustive information requirements. The marketing audit requires the identification, measurement, collection and analysis of relevant facts. In many cases, customers, competitors, channel members and employees will be interviewed. For example, a bank with the objective of delivering quality service would need to conduct extensive customer research to assess its performance. Such research would identify the factors that customers see as important and then measure how the bank is performing on those dimensions. It might also do research to see how other banks are rated and to ascertain staff opinions. Results may lead the organization to reconsider whether it ought to compete on the service issue or if sales staff are sufficiently well trained to deliver quality service or if it might be appropriate to operate a telephone banking operation. One bank found that most of its customers were satisfied with its quality of service. However, a proportion of customers reported experiencing problems. While problems are inevitable, especially in a service business, the research showed that the bank was handling these problems badly. A large proportion of customers who had problems had to call the bank a number of times and wait over two weeks to have the problem dealt with. Even then, only half the problems seemed to be resolved to the customer's satisfaction. These results forced the bank to look at service problems and to develop skills in identifying and handling customer problems.[10]

As with other forms of control, management judgement needs to be brought to bear on the *interpretation* of audit information. In practically every area of marketing there exist many ways of doing the job. For example, how marketing performance is measured differs between organizations. Therefore evaluation is, in some respects, partially subjective. The information generated by the marketing audit has strategic control purposes, but it is also an input to the planning process. Thus, the audit has both a planning and control function.[11]

Ideally, a marketing audit should not uncover problems. Good management, in terms of analysis, planning, implementing and control, means continually evaluating the effectiveness of the operation. In practice, however, managers often become identified with certain strategies and pursue them blindly—when other strategies might be more effective. Since an outside view can give needed perspective, marketing audits are a useful process.

SUMMARY

In this chapter, the focus has been on the important role of implementation and control in satisfying customers and the firm's ongoing success. Although planning, implementation and control have been treated in two separate chapters, it is important to appreciate that the whole process is a cycle with data from control (strategic and operational) feeding into planning decisions.

Improvements in information technology are playing a critical role in revolutionizing these areas. Managers need to develop new and creative ways to improve implementation. It can often give a firm a competitive advantage in building stronger relationships with customers, even in highly competitive mature markets.

A marketing programme must be controlled. Good control helps to locate and correct weaknesses, as well as finding strengths that may be applied throughout the marketing programme. Control works hand in hand with planning.

Simple sales analysis just gives a picture of what happened. When sales forecasts or other data showing expected results are also brought into the analysis, performance can be evaluated. Cost analysis also can be useful. There are two basic approaches to cost analysis—full-cost and contribution-margin. Using the full-cost approach, all costs are allocated in some way. Using the contribution-margin approach, only the variable costs are allocated. Both methods have their advantages and special uses.

Ideally, the marketing manager should arrange for a constant flow of data that can be analysed routinely, preferably by computer, to help control present plans and plan new strategies.

A marketing audit can help to provide strategic control. It evaluates the company's marketing efforts to ensure that the company is pursuing appropriate objectives and strategies. The audit also investigates marketing structures, systems, procedures and people. Either a separate department within the company or an outside organization may conduct this audit.

While finding new approaches helps with some implementation problems, getting better implementation often depends on being vigilant in improving what the firm and its people are already doing.

QUESTIONS AND PROBLEMS

1. Give an example of how a firm has used information technology to improve its marketing implementation and do a better job of meeting your needs.
2. Should marketing managers leave it to the computer experts to develop reports that the marketing manager will use to improve implementation and control. Why or why not?
3. Give an example of a firm that has a competitive advantage because of the excellent job it does with implementation activities that directly impact customer satisfaction. Explain why you think your example is a good one.
4. Various breakdowns can be used for sales analysis depending on the nature of the company and its products. Describe a situation (one for each) where each of the following breakdowns would yield useful information. Explain why.
   a. By geographic region.
   b. By product.
   c. By customer.
   d. By size of order.
   e. By size of salesforce commission on each product or product group.
5. Distinguish between a sales analysis and a performance analysis.
6. Carefully explain what the iceberg principle should mean to the marketing manager.
7. Explain the meaning of the comparative performance and comparative cost data in Exhibits 19–2 and 19–3. Why does it appear that eliminating sales areas D and E would be profitable?
8. Most sales forecasting is subject to some error (perhaps 5 to 10 per cent). Should we then expect variations in sales performance of 5 to 10 per cent above or below quota? If so, how should we treat such variations in evaluating performance?

9. Why is there controversy between the advocates of the full-cost and the contribution-margin approaches to cost analysis?
10. The June profit and loss statement for the Browning Company is shown. If competitive conditions make price increases impossible—and management has cut costs as much as possible—should the Browning Company stop selling to hospitals and schools? Why?

Browning	Company	Statement
Retailers	Hospitals and Schools	Total
Sales:		
80 000 units at		
£0.70....................... £56 000		£56 000
20000 units at		
£.60.........................	£12 000	£12 000
Total........................ 56 000	12 000	68 000
Cost of sales................... 40 000	10 000	50 000
Gross margin.................. 16 000	2 000	18 000
Sales and administrative expenses:		
Variable...................... 6 000	1 500	7 500
Fixed......................... 5 600	900	6 500
Total........................ 11 600	2 400	14 000
Net profit (loss)................ £ 4 400	£(400)	£ 4 000

11. Explain why a marketing audit might be necessary—even in a well-run company. Who or what kind of an organization would be best to conduct a marketing audit? Would a marketing research firm be good? Why?

SUGGESTED CASE

17. Romano's Take-Away

REFERENCES

1. www.loreal,com); S. Stern, 'Counter offensive', *International Management*, October 1993, pp. 54–5.

2. F. Leverick, D. Littler, M. Bruce and D. Wilson, 'Using information technology effectively: a study of marketing installations', *Journal of Marketing Management*, vol. 14, no. 8, pp. 927–62; D. Soberman, 'Information overload and the new dealers in data', *Mastering Marketing, The Financial Times*, 23 November 1998; R. Charan, 'How networks reshape organizations—For results', *Harvard Business Review*, September–October 1991, pp. 104–15; W.J. Bruns, Jr. and W.W McFarlan, 'Information technology puts power in control systems', *Harvard Business Review*, September–October 1987, pp. 89–94.

3. 'How market leaders keep their edge', *Fortune*, 6 February 1995, pp. 88–98.

4. T.V. Bonoma, 'Making your marketing strategy work', *Harvard Business Review*, March–April 1984, pp. 68–76; B.J. Coe, 'Key differentiating factors and problems associated with implementation of strategic market planning', *in 1985 American Marketing Association Educators' Proceedings*, R.F. Lusch *et al.* (eds) American Marketing Association, Chicago, 1985, pp. 275–81.

5. *1993 Annual Report*, Ben & Jerry's; 'Ben & Jerry's: Surviving the big squeeze', *Food Business*, 6 May 1991, pp. 10–12; 'The peace pop puzzle,' *INC.*, March 1990, p. 25; *1990 Annual Report*, Ben & Jerry's. See also W.C. Taylor, 'Control in an age of chaos', *Harvard Business Review*, November–December 1994, pp. 64–90; B.J. Jaworski, V. Stathakopoulos and H.S. Krishnan, 'Control combinations in marketing: Conceptual framework and empirical evidence', *Journal of Marketing*, January 1993, pp. 57–69.

6. R. Cooper and R.S. Kaplan, 'Profit priorities from activity-based costing', *Harvard Business Review*, May–June 1991, pp. 130–7; D.M. Lambert and J.U. Sterling, 'What types of profitability reports do marketing managers receive?' *Industrial Marketing Management*, November 1987, pp. 295–304; N.F. Piercy, 'The marketing budgeting process: Marketing management implications', *Journal of Marketing*, October 1987, pp. 45–59; M.J. Sandretto, 'What kind of cost system do you need?' *Harvard Business Review*, January–February 1985, pp. 110–18.

7. Technically, a distinction should be made between variable and direct costs, but we will use these terms interchangeably. Similarly, not all costs that are common to several products are fixed costs, and vice versa. But the important point here is to recognize that some costs are fairly easy to allocate, and other costs are not. See S.A. Washburn, 'Establishing strategy and determining costs in the pricing decision', *Business Marketing*, July 1985, pp. 64–78.

8. D. Brownlie, 'Marketing Audits and Auditing: Diagnosis Through Intervention', *Journal of Marketing Management*, vol. 12, 1996, pp. 4–12; L.L. Berry, J.S. Conant and A. Parasuraman, 'A framework for conducting a services marketing audit', *Journal of the Academy of Marketing Science*, Summer 1991, pp. 255–68; J.F. Grashof, 'Conducting and using a marketing audit', *in* E.J. McCarthy *et al.* (eds) *Readings in Basic Marketing*, I.L. Irwin, Homewood, 1984; A.M. Tybout and J.R. Hauser, 'A marketing audit using a conceptual model of consumer behavior: Application and evaluation', *Journal of Marketing*, Summer 1981, pp. 82–101.

9. 'Soft and Gentle', *Marketing*, 7 April 1996, p. 5.

10. K.M. Stewart (1996) 'An exploration of customer exit, with empirical findings from the retail banking sector in Northern Ireland', PhD Thesis (unpublished), National University of Ireland.

11. T. Ambler and F. Kokkinaki (1997) 'Measures of marketing success' *in* R. Ashford *et al.* (eds) *Marketing Without Borders*, Proceedings of The Academy of Marketing Conference, Manchester Metropolitan University, 1997, pp. 13–28; M. Thomas (1997) 'Measures of marketing performance' *in* R. Ashford *et al.* (eds), ibid., pp. 1529–44.

CHAPTER 20
Managing Marketing's Link with other Functional Areas

When You Finish This Chapter, You Should

1 Understand why turning a marketing plan into a profitable business requires money, information, people, and a way to get or produce goods and services.

2 Understand the ways that marketing strategy decisions may need to be adjusted in light of available financing.

3 Understand how a firm can implement and expand a marketing plan using internally generated cash flow.

4 Understand how different aspects of production capacity and flexibility should be coordinated with marketing strategy planning.

5 Understand the ways that the location and cost of production affect marketing strategy planning.

6 Know how marketing managers and accountants can work together to improve analysis of the costs and profitability of specific products and customers.

7 Know some of the human resource issues that a marketer should consider when planning a strategy and implementing a plan.

8 Understand the important new terms (shown in colour).

BENETTON

The term 'Italian family business' tends to conjure up the image of a small, local entrepreneurial effort. The reality of Benetton—a family owned and run business—could not be further from such an image. In 1965, the teenage Luciano Benetton was bicycling deliveries of his sister Giuliana's handknitted sweaters. The first Benetton store opened in 1969 in Belluno and the next year saw the Paris store opened.

Now Benetton is a brand recognized throughout the world. It has more than 7 000 stores in 120 countries and sales of over £1.1 billion. It remains a family business with the three brothers and a sister running the business. Luciano Benetton is the chairman (and creative mind) of the Benetton Group, Giuliana is in charge of design, finance is taken care of by Gilberto and Carlo takes care of production.

From starting out with classic colours of sweaters, the company developed its markets through creating brighter more youthful colours. The company is very responsive to the market and demand. Benetton has pioneered a system whereby the sweater is first produced without a colour. Feedback from the marketplace is used to then decide what colours to use—if the market says yellow, then production turns out yellow sweaters. The combination of shorter production times and responsiveness to the market give Benetton an advantage over competitors.

Nor has the company confined itself to woollen garments. It also produces cotton and denim casual wear for men, women and children. Such is the success of the brand that it is now used on watches, bags, shoes, gloves, hats and other accessories. The Benetton brand is also promoted by advertising that has used shocking images. This has added to the brand's fame.

Having achieved such a successful business, the company is very wealthy. In order to grow, it is developing an interest in the sports market. The Benetton portfolio now includes Nordica ski boots, Kastle skis and bicycles, Rollerlade skates and sportswear, Asolo mountain boots, Killer Loop snowboard equipment and Prince tennis and golf equipment. These will be sold in a separate chain of retail outlets. The Benetton skills in efficient sourcing, and distribution, production and marketing as well as its knowledge of international markets are being applied to the whole portfolio of brands in the Benetton 'family'.[1]

MARKETING IN THE BROADER CONTEXT

The Benetton case is an example of the marketing concept in action—everyone in the firm working together to satisfy customer needs at a profit. Once a marketing strategy has been developed—and turned into a marketing plan—the blueprint for what needs to be done is in place. This text has developed concepts and approaches relevant to marketing strategy planning, implementation and control.

From the outset, it has been emphasized that a good marketing strategy—selection of a target market and a marketing mix to meet target customers' needs—depends on the fit with the specific firm and its market environment. In Chapter 6 we discussed how a firm's resources and objectives might allow it to pursue some opportunities and not others. Given an understanding of how marketing decisions fit together into an integrated strategy, it is appropriate to take a closer look at some of the most important ways that marketing links to other functional areas. How companies create and sustain excellent marketing programmes will also be discussed.

In this chapter the perspective is still that of a marketing manager. Thus the emphasis is not on the technical details of other functional areas, but rather on the most important ways that relationships with other areas influence choices among the strategy decisions discussed throughout the text. Implementing a marketing plan usually requires a financial investment so this chapter starts with a discussion of financial issues required to start up a new plan and the ongoing money that may be needed to meet expenses. Then production and operations are discussed. We've already explained how marketing can make economies of scale in production possible, but here more detail is presented on how available production capacity, production flexibility and operating issues influence marketing planning. We'll also take a closer look at how accountants and marketing managers work together to understand and manage marketing costs. The chapter concludes with a discussion of human resource issues. New marketing strategies often upset the standard ways of doing things, and without wholehearted cooperation change is difficult.

The importance of the linkages with production, finance, accounting and human resources for the marketing manager depends on the situation. In an entrepreneurial start up, the same person may be making all of the decisions and handling everything. In a small but established company that is trying to expand, the challenges may be different. In a large company with many different specialists, it may be much more complicated.

The emphasis will be on new efforts. When a new strategy involves only a minor modification to a plan that the firm is already implementing successfully, specialists in different areas usually have a good idea of how their activities link to other areas. However, when a potential strategy involves a more significant change—such as the development and introduction of a totally new product idea or a big reorganization of the firm's salesforce or channel systems—understanding the links between the different functional areas is usually much more critical.

A business cannot expand, add new capabilities or bring in people to handle new marketing activities if it does not have the resources. A product cannot be marketed unless it can be produced. A plan cannot be implemented if there are not enough people with the right skills available.

FINANCIAL RESOURCES TO IMPLEMENT MARKETING PLANS

Bright marketing ideas for new ways to satisfy customer needs do not go very far if there is not enough money to put a plan into operation. Finding and allocating capital—the money invested in a firm—is usually handled by a firm's chief financial manager. Entrepreneurs and others who own their own companies may handle this job themselves or may get help from outside financial specialists and consultants. In most firms, however, there is a separate manager who handles financial matters and works with the chief executive to make major finance decisions.

Good communication between a marketing manager and the firm's finance manager is critical. They must work together to ensure that marketing plans are realistic and that the firm can successfully implement them with the money that is or will be available. Further, a successful strategy should ultimately generate profit—and the financial manager needs to know how much money to expect—and when to expect it—to be able to plan for how it will be used.[2]

Within an organization, different potential opportunities compete for capital. There is usually not enough money to do everything, so strategies that are inconsistent with the firm's financial objectives and resources are not likely to be funded. It is often best for the marketing manager to use relevant financial measures as quantitative screening criteria when evaluating various alternatives in the first place.

Marketing plans that *are* funded usually must work within a budget constraint. Ideally, the marketing manager should have some input to decisions on that budget in order to get the marketing tasks done. It is not practical to develop a plan and budget that requires money that simply is not available. As a result, at least some important marketing strategy decisions may need to be adjusted, either in the short or long term, to work within the available budget. For example, a marketing manager might prefer to have control over sales for a new product by hiring new people for a separate sales force. However, if enough money is not available for salesforce salaries and benefits as well as for travel and other selling expenses, then the best alternative might be to start with manufacturers' agents. They work for a commission and are not paid until after they generate a sale—and some sales revenue. Then, as the market develops and the plan becomes profitable there may be both the money and a good reason—perhaps lower cost or better control—to expand the firm's own salesforce.

Finance managers usually think about two different uses of capital. First, capital may be required to pay for investments in facilities, equipment and other fixed assets. These installations are usually purchased and then used, and depreciated, over a number of years. In addition, a firm needs working capital, money to pay for short-term expenses such as employee salaries, advertising, marketing research, inventory storing costs and suppliers' invoices. A firm must usually pay for these ongoing expenses as they occur, and often that is before it gets revenue for the goods and services it sells. As a result there is usually a continuing need for working capital.

It is also useful for a marketing manager who is developing a plan to think about likely capital needs in this same way. In general, the more ambitious the plan, the greater the amount of capital that is needed. Capital is usually a critical resource when a plan calls for rapid growth—especially if the growth calls for expensive new facilities. Clearly, a plan to build a chain of 15 hotels requires more money for buildings and equipment—as well as more money for salaries, food and supplies—than a plan for a single hotel. Such a plan might require that the firm borrow money from a commercial lender. In contrast, a plan that simply calls for improving the service in an existing hotel, perhaps by adding several people to handle room-service, would require much less

money. In fact, increased food sales from room service might quickly generate more than enough earnings to pay for the added people.

As these examples imply, there are a number of different possible sources of capital. However, it is useful to reduce them down to two categories: *external sources*, such as loans or sales of shares, and *internal sources*, such as cash accumulated from the firm's profits. A firm usually seeks outside funding in advance of when it is needed to invest in a new strategy. Internally generated profits may be accumulated and used in the same way, but often internal money is used as it becomes available. In other words, with internally generated funding a firm's marketing programme may be expected to 'pay its own way'.

The timing of when financing is available has an important effect on marketing strategy planning, so this topic is addressed in more detail. External sources of funds are discussed first.

External funding—investors expect a return

While a firm might like to fund its marketing programme from rapid growth in its own profits, that is not always possible. New companies often do not have enough money to start that way. An established company with some capital may not have as much as it needs to make long-term investments in factories or other facilities and still have enough working capital for the routine expenses of implementing a plan. Getting started may also involve losses—perhaps for several years—before earnings come in. In these circumstances, the firm may need to turn to one of several sources of external capital.

A firm may be able to raise money by a share issue. Share sales may be public or private, and the buyers may be individuals, including a firm's own employees, or institutional investors (such as a pension fund or venture capital firm). Shareholders want a good return on their investment. That can happen if the company pays owners of its shares a regular dividend. It also happens if the value of the shares goes up over time. Neither is likely if the firm is not consistently earning profits. Further, the value of a firm's shares typically does not increase unless its profits are *growing*. This is one reason that marketing managers are always looking for profitable new growth opportunities. Profits can also improve by being more efficient—getting the marketing jobs done at lower cost, doing a better job holding onto customers, and the like—but continued growth in profits usually requires that a firm pursue new market opportunities. Ultimately, a firm that does not have a successful (or at least promising) marketing strategy cannot attract and keep investors.

BCO Technologies is a small electronics company based in Belfast, Northern Ireland. The company deliberately chose Northern Ireland as the best location because of the availability of financial support from a consortium including Northern Ireland's Industrial Development Board, the International Fund for Ireland and other financial organizations that specialize in supplying start up capital to new high-technology companies. Finance of over £32 million was secured from a range of sources to set up a mass production facility for a process which will lead to dramatic savings in the production of components for telephones and other users of electronics components.

The company's chief executive Scott Blackstone invented a novel way of processing silicon wafers. He had a successful career with some of the largest semiconductor manufacturers before seeking to set up his own business. It was difficult to find sources of funding for new high technology ventures in the United States, so Blackstone looked for funding in Europe, initially in Scotland and the Republic of Ireland. However, Northern Ireland had natural advantages, not least the availability of government grants which could cover up to 50 per cent of the capital required. The incentive structure for companies choosing to locate in Northern Ireland is seen as tailormade for high-volume, capital-intensive and technology-intensive manufacturing projects, because of its emphasis on capital costs and research and development.

Northern Ireland also offered BCO the possibility of linking with local universities that have an excellent reputation in microelectronics research. 'We were able immediately to hire people who actually did their PhDs in the fields in which we were working', says Blackstone.

The challenge the company now faces is to move from development to full-scale production. Orders are coming in rapidly. BCO has supply agreements in the pipeline with British Aerospace, Siemens and smaller specialist firms that supply the electronics industry. As the company makes the factories operational, the slow down in the global semiconductor demand has come as something of a relief, allowing the company to meet all its customers' demands.[3]

The time horizon for profit and growth that investors have in mind can be very important to the marketing manager. If investors are patient and willing to wait for a new strategy to become profitable, a marketing manager may have the luxury of developing a plan that will be very profitable in the long run even if it has short-term losses. BCO will be loss making for at least two years until its volumes build up. Its shareholders recognize this and this has been built into the company's financial plans. Many Japanese firms also take this approach. However, most marketing managers face intense pressure to develop plans that will generate profits quickly; there's more risk for investors if potential profits are distant in the future. This sometimes means that companies are unwilling to invest in projects which may give them greater advantage in the market.

Trying to develop a plan that produces profit in the short term and also positions the firm for long-run success is challenging. For example, a low penetration price for a new product may help to both prevent competition and build a large, loyal base of customers who will be repeat purchasers long into the future. Yet, a skimming price may be better for profits in the short term. Even so, the marketing manager's plans and programme must take the investors' time horizon into consideration. Unhappy investors can, and often do, demand new management or put their money somewhere else. In that situation a firm, or a marketing manager, that fails in the short term may find out that there is no long-run!

 ## Forecasts may become an ethical issue

Both individual and institutional investors usually want detailed information about a firm and its plans before they invest money in the firm's shares. This information is usually provided by an accountant, but financial estimates do not mean much unless they are based on realistic estimates of demand, revenue and marketing expenses. The marketing manager is usually the one who must provide that information. A marketing manager who is optimistic about the potential of a marketing plan may be hesitant to lay out the potential limitations of a plan or its forecasts—especially if the full story might scare off needed investors. However, this is an important ethical issue. While investors know that there is always some uncertainty in forecasts, they have a right to information that is as accurate as possible. Put another way, just as a marketing manager should not mislead a buyer of the firm's products, it is not appropriate to mislead investors who are 'buying into' the firm's marketing plan.

These issues are particularly critical in large-scale ventures, such as the Channel Tunnel and Disneyland Paris, where investors were invited for long-term projects that require considerable financing long before the projects were completed and earning money. The shares of some pharmaceutical drugs companies are also frequently bought long before new drugs have been given approval, on the basis of anticipated sales and profit potential. To some extent this is a gamble for investors, but there is an ethical issue for marketing managers in providing accurate forecasts of future levels of sales and profitability.

Debt financing involves an interest cost

Rather than sell shares, some firms prefer **debt financing**—borrowing money based on a promise to repay the loan, usually within a fixed time period and with a specific interest charge. This might involve a loan from a commercial bank. People or institutions that lend the money typically do not get an ownership share in the company, and they are usually even less willing to take a risk than are investors who buy stock. Cultural differences apply to banking. In some countries bankers are very conservative and not that familiar with the different industrial sectors. In other countries, bankers who deal with business customers are required to build up an understanding of their particular industrial sectors.

When a firm needs to borrow a large amount of money to fund its plans the cost of borrowing the money can be a real financial burden—especially if the money is to be repaid over time rather than in a lump sum after a plan is already profitable. Just as a firm's selling price must cover all of the marketing expenses and the other costs of doing business before profits begin to accumulate, it must also cover the interest charge on borrowed money. The impact of interest charges on prices can be significant. For example, the gap between the prices charged by fast-growing, efficient supermarket chains such as Carrefour in France and individual grocery stores would be even greater if the chains were not paying big interest charges on loans to fund new facilities.

While the cost of borrowing money can be high, it may still make sense if the money is used to implement a marketing plan that earns an even greater return. In that way, the firm 'leverages' the borrowed money to make a profit. Even so, there are often advantages if a firm can pay for its plans with internally generated capital.[4]

Winning strategies generate capital

A company with a successful marketing strategy has its own internal source of funds—profits that become

cash in the bank! Reinvesting cash generated from operations is usually less expensive than borrowing money because no interest expense is involved. Internal financing often helps a firm to earn more profit than a competitor that is operating on borrowed money—even if the internally financed company is selling at a lower price.

Firms that do not want the expense of borrowed money or that cannot get external funding often start with a less costly strategy and a plan to expand it as quickly as is allowed by earnings. A firm with limited resources can sometimes develop a plan that allows for growth through internally generated money. On the other hand, a company with a mature product that has limited growth potential can invest the earnings from that product in developing a new opportunity that is more profitable. Lotus Development, the software company, is a good example. It used profits from its Lotus 1-2-3 spreadsheet, which faced tough competition from Microsoft's Excel, to fund the development of Lotus Notes, an innovative product for the fast-growing segment of computer users who want an easy way to communicate with other members of their work group.

A marketing manager who wants to plan strategies based on the expected flow of internal funding needs a good idea of how much cash will be available. A **cash flow statement** is a financial report that forecasts how much cash will be available after paying expenses. The amount that is available is not always just the 'bottom line' or net profit figure shown on the firm's operating statement. Some expenses, such as depreciation of facilities and equipment, are subtracted from revenues for tax and accounting purposes but do not actually involve writing a cheque. In other words, depreciation is a 'noncash' expense. So, in determining cash flow, marketing managers and their finance manager colleagues often look at a company's earnings *before* subtracting out these expenses. Similarly, they may look at earnings before taxes as certain types of reinvestment result in a reduction in taxes.[5]

Adjusting the strategy to fit the budget

Most firms rely on a combination of internal and external capital. An adequate overall amount of capital makes it possible to expand more rapidly or to implement a more ambitious plan from the outset. However, when a marketing manager must rely—at least in part—on internally generated funds to make a strategy self-supporting, that may need to be considered in selecting between alternative strategies or in specific marketing mix decisions for a given strategy.

When finances are tight, it is sensible to look for strategy alternatives that might get a better return on money that is already invested. A firm that sells diagnostic equipment to hospitals might look for another related product for its current salespeople to sell while calling on the same customers. Similarly, a firm that has a successful domestic product might look for new international markets where little or no modification of the product would be required. A firm that is constantly fighting to rewin customers might be better off with a programme that offers loyal customers a discount; the increase in the number of customers served might more than offset the lost revenue per sale. Any increase in revenue and profit contribution that the strategy generates, without increasing fixed costs and capital invested, increases profit and the firm's return on investment.

Strategy decisions within each of the marketing mix areas often have significantly different capital requirements. In the product area, for example, new product development for a product that is closely related to a firm's existing line is usually less costly than venturing into a totally new area. A brand extension or product that uses a family brand name may require less up-front advertising and promotion expense to establish consumer awareness. On the other hand, offering more models, package sizes, flavours or colours of a product will also certainly increase front-end capital needs and increase costs.

Place decisions often have significant financial implications—depending on how responsibilities are shifted and shared in the channel. Indirect distribution usually requires less investment capital than direct approaches. Merchant wholesalers and retailers who pay for products when they purchase them—and who

pay the costs of carrying inventory—help a producer's cash flow. Similarly, agents may take on much of the selling effort with a lower investment than would be required were the firm to do it alone. Working with intermediaries and facilitators, such as storage and transportation firms, may help to reduce the capital requirements for logistics facilities. Expanding into new market areas that can be served from an existing distribution centre may result in greater economies of scale without increased investment.

Similarly, capital requirements are less when intermediaries take on much of the responsibility for promotion in the channel. Wholesalers and retailers have less incentive to do promotion when the firm uses intensive distribution; intensive distribution is also likely to require a bigger initial investment in personal selling.

Promotional mixes that focus on stimulating consumer pull usually require a big front-end investment in advertising and consumer promotions. For example, it is not unusual for a consumer packaged goods producer to spend half of a new product's first year sales revenue on advertising. Thus, it may be less risky for a firm with limited capital to put more emphasis on a strategy that relies on push rather than pull.

Of course, when a marketing manager is looking at how different strategy decisions relate to the firm's financial situation, they can't be considered separately. It is the financial impact of the whole strategy that must be considered. However, a strategy that might potentially produce the greatest profit or the fastest return on investment may not be best—or even sensible—if it is not feasible given the firm's financial situation.

PRODUCTION MUST BE COORDINATED WITH THE MARKETING PLAN

Production capacity takes many forms

Being able to produce a product does not necessarily mean there is a market for it—or that it can be sold at a profit. On the other hand, if a firm is going to sell a product—whether it is a good or a service or combination of the two—*somebody* has to be able to produce it. In screening product-market opportunities, a marketing manager needs to have a realistic understanding of what is involved in turning a product concept into something the firm can really deliver. If a firm is going to pursue an opportunity, it is also critical that there be effective coordination between marketing planning and **production capacity**—the

ability to produce a certain quantity and quality of specific goods or services.

Different aspects of production capacity may be important in different situations. A firm may have the ability to easily or quickly produce some types of products but not others. For those it can currently produce, it may only be able to handle limited quantities without a major investment in new facilities, equipment, or people. Alternatively, it may have—and be paying for—more capacity than it can use. It may be able to produce only one product at a time—or it may be able to produce many different products. These variations are now discussed in more depth because different aspects of production capacity have varying impact on marketing planning.[6]

NAVICO LTD

Navico Ltd is an English company that specializes in marine communication and instrumentation equipment. Its customers are boat owners of all types: weekend sailors, racing yachts, boat builders and fleet owners in over 50 different markets worldwide. Navico's mission statement reads as follows:

Our goal for the period leading up to the next millennium is to position Navico in the perception of the market as a true world class manufacturer of high quality products representing excellent value. To achieve this objective we will continuously:

Introduce innovation in design, quality and service into the marine electronics market;

Bring to market by our own research and development or through forming strategic alliances a complete range of marine electronics for the marine leisure industry;

Make substantial gains into the commercial market in the field of communications equipment;

Drive down manufacturing costs through the use of modern manufacturing techniques and wherever possible through economies of scale.

Navico spends time and effort finding out what is happening in its markets and to its customers. The company brings sales agents from world-wide together to discuss product ideas, technical opportunities and the potential of new products. Sales agents also help to track customer needs and provide regular feedback to Navico. Competitor products are monitored and analysed to see if the company can improve on them. From their market research and intelligence it became clear that weekend sailors do not want to have to spend time installing equipment—they want to be on the water! Navico therefore trained its sales agents how to install the equipment and also how to do regular repairs and maintenance. These customers also prefer their boat's equipment to have a complementary look. This has led Navico to focus on getting boat builders to install Navico equipment as original in new boats.

In order to come up with attractive products, Navico not only works with customers and sales agents. It also works with outside designers and has formed strategic alliances with other companies so that it can offer a full product range to the market. The range includes radar, cartography and Global Positioning Systems, marine VHF, auto pilots and yacht instrumentation. For Navico, the process of developing new products is continuous. The marketing people get ideas from customers and agents. Research and development staff work on these ideas and their feasibility is regularly assessed. Thus, marketing, R&D and production engineers work together closely.

The same integrated effort also characterizes ongoing production. The production director, sales and marketing manager, the assembly manager and production team leaders meet monthly. Weekly production schedules are planned and the composition of each production team is determined according to the job in hand. An extremely flexible workforce and a flat management structure deal with variable production patterns. The use of a kanban system ensures that stock for 2–4 weeks production is at the factory. Wall-mounted boards let all staff know what sales orders are in the process of being completed. The team approach to the overall business, new product development and ongoing production means that the multi-skilled workforce feel responsible for the products made. There is an emphasis on 'taking ownership' and a greater degree of focus on the customer. Adopting an integrated effort has enabled Navico to grow. From 1993, the company has invested 18 per cent of its revenue in research and development, tooling and marketing. In return, its turnover has grown by an average of 17 per cent each year.[7]

Use excess capacity to improve profits

If a firm has unused production capacity, it is sensible for a marketing manager to try to identify new markets or new products that make more effective use of that investment. For example, a company that produces rubber floor mats for cars might be able to add a similar line of floor mats for domestic use. Expanded production might result in lower costs and better profits for the mats the firm was already producing—because of economies of scale. However, the marketing manager would have to consider the extra costs involved in selling to this new market. In addition, revenue and profit contribution from the new products could improve the return on investment the firm had already made.

If a firm's production capacity is flexible, many different marketing opportunities might be possible. For example, the marketing manager for the firm above might see even better profit potential further away from its current markets There might be better growth and profits in static-electricity-free mats for computer and telecommunications equipment than for car accessories.

Make best use of scarce capacity

The marketing manager's job is not simply to fill the capacity of the factory. It may be more profitable to operate the factory at half capacity, provided that the right mix of work is being handled. In an ideal world, marketing should attempt to fill the factory with the optimum mix of profitable business. In reality orders come in with unpredictable frequency, the levels of profitability per order are frequently difficult to establish, and the quantities required by customers can frequently vary considerably from the original forecast.

Design flexibility into operations

Because production flexibility can give a firm a competitive advantage in meeting a target market's needs better or faster, many firms are trying to design more flexibility into their operations. In fact, without flexible production systems it may not be possible for a firm to provide business customers with the just-in-time delivery service or rapid response replenishment of inventories that they want and expect. Similarly, a firm that uses EDI or some other type of computerized reorder system to find out immediately when a sale is made further down the channel of distribution, may not be able to take advantage of the information if it cannot do anything about it until weeks or months later.

Producing-to-order requires flexibility

Many companies have responded by trying to introduce flexible low cost production systems. Traditionally manufacturing would have preferred high volume orders of standardized products. This would lead to efficiencies in production and make the whole manufacturing job simpler. Today many companies have developed a strategic approach to manufacture, which allows them to produce greater variety at lower cost. Individual products or services can be supplied at lower costs and still meet individual customer requirements.

Banks and other finance companies have now seen the potential of this approach and set up telephone service systems which allow customers to access a wide range of service over the telephone at their own convenience, rather than at conventional bank opening times. Such service can be offered more cheaply because the financial institution does not need to operate the physical premises associated with traditional modes of operation.

Car manufacturers, producers of specialized machine tools and other types of manufacturers, as well as service firms, have been creating products based on specific orders from individual customers for a long time. However, a wide variety of companies are now looking for innovative ways to serve smaller segments of customers by using **mass customization**—tailoring the principles of mass production to meet the unique needs of individual

customers. Note that using the principles of mass production is not the same thing as trying to appeal to everyone in some mass market. With the mass-customization approach, a firm may still focus on certain market segments within a broad product market. However, in serving individuals within those target segments it tries to get a competitive advantage by finding a low cost way to give each customer more or better choices.

A new mass-customization programme for Levi's jeans illustrates the changes that are coming in this arena. With this programme, a customer goes to a participating retail outlet and a computerized video system prepares a precise set of measurements for that customer. Then, the computer transmits the measurements to a Levi's factory where they are automatically converted into a customized pattern for a pair of jeans. Computer-controlled cutting and sewing machines then make jeans from that pattern—and they are shipped directly to the customer.[8]

Of course, not every firm will be able to adjust its offering to each individual customer, but advances in communications and computer-controlled production may offer up a host of possibilities for marketing managers—and firms—who look for better ways to meet the unique needs of individual customers.

 Internet Exercise

CDuctive offers an on-line service in which the customer selects certain tracks of music and, for a fee, CDuctive will create a custom CD of those selections. Explore the CDuctive web site (**www.cductive.com**) and then list what you think are the major (1) strengths and (2) weaknesses of this approach.

Slow adjustments result in stockouts

Another aspect of flexibility concerns how quickly and easily a firm can adjust the quantity of a product it produces. This can be an especially important consideration when demand is uncertain—as is often the case when the marketing manager is planning a new strategy. If a new marketing mix is more successful than expected, demand can quickly outstrip supply. Waiting lists can then develop, sometimes to the frustration of customers who may switch to other suppliers, for example with new car launches.

Scarce supply wastes marketing effort

This kind of problem can be serious. Carefully planned promotion spending is wasted if advertising and other promotions cannot be put on hold until supply catches up with demand. Further, consumers and channel members may quickly become frustrated by stockouts. More nimble competitors may get a window of opportunity to introduce an imitation product. By the time the original innovator is able to increase production, consumers may already be loyal to the other brand.

Staged distribution may match capacity

Problems of matching supply and demand are likely to be greatest when a marketing plan calls for quick expansion into many different market areas all at once. That is one reason many marketing managers plan a regional roll-out of new product innovations. Similarly, initial distribution may focus on certain types of channel—say pharmacists alone rather than pharmacists and supermarkets. Experience with the early stages of the implementation effort can help the marketing manager determine how much promotion effort is required to keep distribution channels full—but not stocked out. Conversely, if sales from these initial efforts are developing more slowly than expected, it may be possible to speed up the move into market areas or new types of channels.

Some companies may not make anything at all

Just because a firm doesn't have the capability to produce a product itself does not mean that a potential opportunity should be ignored. A profitable concept may justify investment in new production capabilities. Alternatively, an increasing number of firms have found that they can satisfy customers and build profits without doing any production 'in house'. Instead, they look for capable suppliers to produce a product that meets the specifications laid out in the firm's marketing plan. (At the extreme, a firm may even act like a **virtual corporation**—where the firm is primarily a coordinator—with a good marketing concept). Nike, the US sportswear company, is one of many in the sports sector that out-sources production of its goods. Service companies also use this strategy. Debonair, a small 'no-frills' European airline, out-sources activities such as customer check-in.

The fashion industry is one where the product is seen as the most important aspect of the business. Creativity and design are highly regarded. The designer's ideas and concepts are brought to life in the custom-designed dresses that are worn by the rich and famous. This helps to develop the designer as a brand name that can be applied to other merchandise such as ready-to-wear (prêt-à-porter) clothes and perfume. These generate the major amount of revenue for the fashion houses. This tradition of designer-led fashion is well established.

Calvin Klein challenged this way of doing business. Using excellence in marketing he has taken his designer brand to the mass market, making the brand accessible much more widely. Instead of starting with catwalk dresses, Calvin Klein brought to the European market the cK line of merchandise in perfume, underwear and jeans. Rather than exclusivity in retailing with a small, London- or Paris-based boutique like other designers, Calvin Klein opened and 1 700 square metre store in Milan, followed by similar stores in Moscow, Barcelona,

Lisbon and London. Extensive promotions have been used with sponsorship, postcards, poster and magazine advertising. These have been effective in making the Calvin Klein brand known throughout the world. Sales in Europe for 1996 were $1 billion, twice that for the previous year.

Other fashion companies are now using similar strategies. Donna Karen has developed the DKNY brand for the needs of the larger part of the market and is setting up much more extensive retail network in Europe. The same holds for Ralph Lauren.

These companies in the fashion industry have discovered the benefits of focusing on the market and marketing rather than the creation of fashion that is bought by a few rich and famous people. The outsourcing of production for many of these designer brands allows the companies to concentrate on marketing activities. In many instances the companies are better at analysing markets, designing fashions, and marketing them than at production.[9]

While out-sourcing production may increase a firm's flexibility in some ways, it often has disadvantages. Costs are often higher and it may be difficult—or even impossible—to control quality. Similarly, product availability may be unpredictable. If several firms are involved in producing the final product, coordination and logistics problems may arise. A company with a line of accessories for cyclists faced this problem when it decided to introduce a plastic water bottle. Its other products were metal, so it turned to outside suppliers to produce the bottles. However, getting the job done required three suppliers. One made the plastic bottles, another printed the colourful designs on them, and the third attached a clip to hold the bottle to a bike.

Moving the product from one specialist to another added costs, and whenever one supplier hit a snag all of the others were affected. The firm was constantly struggling to fill orders on time—and too often was losing the battle. In the light of these problems, as soon as the bottle proved to be profitable, the firm decided to invest in its own production facilities. With its own production, it could be faster and more flexible in responding to special requests from the large retailers who handle its products.

Batched production requires inventories

If it is expensive for a firm to switch from producing one product (or product line) to another, it may have no alternative but to produce in large batches and maintain large inventories. Then it can supply demand from inventory while it is producing some other product. However, this approach requires careful planning of where in the channel inventories will be held. A firm that must pay the costs of carrying extra inventory to avoid stockouts may not be able to compete with a firm that has more flexible production.

Location of production

A marketing manager also needs to consider carefully the marketing implications of where products are produced. It often does make sense for a firm to produce where it can produce most economically, if the cost of transporting and storing products to match demand does not offset the savings. On the other hand, production in areas distant from customers can make the distribution job much more complicated.

Offshore production may complicate marketing

Of course, any changes in operational routines required to implement a firm's marketing plan can cause unexpected surprises. However, when overseas production is involved the ripple effect of any such problems is likely to be bigger.

 ## Some critics object to overseas production

Marketing managers must be aware of and sensitive to criticisms that may arise concerning overseas production. Some of these concerns relate to nationalism and the exporting of jobs. Other issues are sometimes at stake.

While low-cost overseas labour may reduce costs and prices for domestic consumers, some critics argue that the costs are only lower because the work is handled in countries with lower workplace safety standards and fewer employee protections. At the extreme, some firms have been boycotted for relying on low-cost Chinese labour; the boycotters charged that Chinese suppliers were using political prisoners as slave labour. In other instances, companies such as those in the sports shoe sector have received negative publicity for using child labour to have their goods produced.[10]

Marketing managers cannot ignore such concerns. Just as a firm has a social responsibility in the country where it sells products, it also has a social responsibility to the people who produce its products. It makes sense to consider the standard in that country. Pay or safety standards that seem low in developed countries may make it possible for workers in a less developed one to have a better, healthier life.

Service firms may transfer some tasks

Firms that produce services often must locate near their customers. However, some service firms are finding ways to reduce the cost of some of their production work with **task transfer**—using telecommunications to move service operations to places where there are pools of skilled workers. For example, Nylerin is a company based in County Kerry in the Republic of Ireland that does 'back office' work on medical claims on behalf of an American insurance company.

Sometimes the decision to expand into a distant market requires moving production closer to that location. For example, import or export tariffs and quotas may make it impossible for an internationally oriented firm to compete if it does not have local production facilities. Similarly, some products are very expensive to transport long distances. That may give local firms a big cost—and price—advantage.

Price must cover production costs

In Chapter 17, we introduced the behaviour of various cost curves and how they fit, along with demand curves, into the pricing puzzle. Production costs are usually an important component of the overall costs that must be considered in pricing, so a marketing manager needs to have a reasonable understanding of the costs associated with production, especially when product features called for in the marketing plan drive costs.

A marketing manager who is well informed in this area can play an important role in working with production people to decide which costs are necessary—to add value that meets customer needs—and which are just added expense with little real benefit. For example, a software firm was providing a very detailed instruction book along with the disks in its distribution package. The book was running up costs and causing delays because it needed to be changed and reprinted every time the firm came out with a new version of its software. The marketing manager realized that most of the detail in the book was not necessary. When users of the software had a problem, they did not want to search for the book but instead wanted the information on the computer screen. Providing the updated information on the disk was faster and cheaper than printing the books. Further, packaging costs were lower without the book. As an added bonus, customers were more satisfied with the online help than they had been with the book. In a situation like this, it is easy to identify specific costs associated with the production job. However, it's often difficult to get a good understanding all of the costs associated with a product without help from the firm's accountants.

ACCOUNTING DATA CAN HELP IN UNDERSTANDING COSTS AND PROFIT

Accounting data that helps managers track where costs and profits are coming from is an important aid for strategy decisions. Unfortunately, accounting statements that are prepared for tax purposes and for outside investors often are not helpful for managers who need to make decisions about marketing strategy.

Understanding profitability depends on being able to identify the specific costs of different goods and services. This was shown in the last chapter when two basic approaches to handling costs—the full-cost approach and the contribution-margin approach—resulted in different views of profitability. At that point, however, we didn't go into any detail about how marketing managers and accountants can work together to get a better understanding of costs—especially how to allocate costs that seem to be *common* to several products or customers, making allocation of costs difficult. In recent years, some accountants have devoted more attention to approaches to this problem and given it the name 'activity-based accounting'.[11]

Marketing cost analysis usually requires a new way of classifying accounting data. Instead of using the type of accounts typically used for financial analysis, we have to use functional accounts.

Natural versus functional accounts

Natural accounts are the categories to which various costs are charged in the normal financial accounting cycle. These accounts include salaries, wages, social security, taxes, supplies, raw materials, car petrol and oil expenses, advertising and others. These accounts are called natural because they have the names of their expense categories.

However, factories do not use this approach to cost analysis. In the factory, **functional accounts** show the *purpose* for which expenditures are made. Factory functional accounts include shearing, milling, grinding, floor cleaning, maintenance and so on. Factory cost accounting records are organized so that managers can determine the cost of particular products or jobs and their likely contribution to profit. Marketing jobs are done for specific purposes too. With some planning, the costs of marketing can also be assigned to specific categories, such as customers and products. Then their profitability can be calculated.

First, get costs into functional accounts

The first step in marketing cost analysis is to reclassify the entire cost entries in the natural accounts into functional cost accounts. For example, the many cost items in the natural *salary* account may be allocated to functional accounts with the following names: storing, inventory control, order assembly, packing and shipping, transporting, selling, advertising, order entry, invoicing, credit extension and accounts receivable. The same is true for rent, depreciation, heat, light, power and other natural accounts.

The way natural account amounts are shifted to functional accounts depends on the firm's method of operation. It may require time studies, space measurements, actual counts and managers' estimates.

Then reallocate to evaluate profitability of profit centres

The next step is to reallocate the functional costs to those items, or customers or market segments, for which the amounts were spent. The most common reallocation of functional costs is to products and customers. After these costs are allocated, the detailed totals can be combined in any way desired, for example, by product or customer class, region, and so on.

The costs allocated to the functional accounts equal, in total, those in the natural accounts. They're just organized differently. Instead of being used only to show *total* company profits, the costs can now be used to calculate the profitability of territories, products, customers, salespeople, price classes, order sizes, distribution methods, sales methods or any other breakdown desired. Each unit can be treated as a profit centre.

Cost analysis helps track down the loser

The following example illustrates these ideas. The case is simplified and the numbers are small. However, the same basic approach can be used in more complicated situations. In this case, the usual financial accounting approach, with natural accounts, shows that the company made a profit of £938 last month (Exhibit 20–1). However, such a profit and loss statement does not show the profitability of the company's three customers. So the managers decide to use marketing cost analysis because they want to know whether a change in the marketing mix will improve profit.

First, we distribute the costs in the five natural accounts to four functional accounts—sales, packaging, advertising, and billing and collection (see Exhibit 20–2)—according to the functional reason for the expenses. Specifically, £1 000 of the total salary cost is for sales reps who seldom even come into the office since their job is to call on customers; £900 of the salary cost is for packaging labour; and £600 is for office help. Assume that the office force split its time about evenly between addressing advertising material and billing and collection. So we split the £600 evenly into these two functional accounts.

The £500 for rent is for the entire building but the company uses 80 per cent of its floor space for packaging and 20 per cent for the office. Thus £400 is allocated to the packaging account. We divide the remaining £100 evenly between the advertising and billing accounts because these functions use the office space about equally. Stationery, stamps and office equipment charges are allocated equally to the latter two accounts for the same reason. Charges for wrapping supplies are allocated to the packaging account because these supplies are used in packaging. In another situation, different allocations and even different accounts may be sensible, but these work here.

Allocating functional cost to customers

Now we can calculate the profitability of the company's three customers. We need more information before we can allocate these functional accounts to customers or products. It is presented in Exhibit 20–3.

Exhibit 20–3 shows that the company's three products vary in cost, selling price and sales volume. The products also have different sizes, and the packaging costs aren't related to the selling price. So when packaging costs are allocated to products, size must be considered. We can do this by computing a new measure—a packaging unit—which is used to allocate the costs in the packaging account. Packaging units adjust for relative size and the number of each type of product sold. For example, Product C is six times larger than A. While the company sells only 10 units of Product C, it is bulky and requires 10 times 6, or 60 packaging units. So we must allocate more of the costs in the packaging account to each unit of Product C.

Exhibit 20–3 also shows that the three customers require different amounts of sales effort, place different numbers of orders and buy different product combinations.

Jones seems to require more sales calls. Smith places many orders that must be processed in the office—with increased billing expense. Brown placed only one order—for 70 per cent of the sales of high-valued Product C.

Sales		£17 000
Cost of sales		11 900
Gross margin		5 100
Expenses:		
Salaries	£2 500	
Rent	500	
Wrapping supplies	1 012	
Stationery and stamps	50	
Office equipment	100	
		4 162
Net profit		£ 938

Exhibit 20–1 Profit and Loss Statement, One Month

Natural Accounts		Sales	Packaging	Advertising	Billing and Collection
			Functional Accounts		
Salaries	£2 500	£1 000	£ 900	£300	£300
Rent	500		400	50	50
Wrapping supplies	1 012		1 012		
Stationery and stamps	50			25	25
Office equipment	100			50	50
Total	£4 162	£1 000	£2 312	£425	£425

Exhibit 20–2 Spreading Natural Accounts to Functional Accounts

Exhibit 20–4 shows the computations for allocating the functional amounts to the three customers. There were 100 sales calls in the period. Assuming that all calls took the same amount of time, we can calculate the average cost per call by dividing the £1 000 sales cost by 100 calls—giving an average cost of £10. We use similar reasoning to break down the invoicing and packaging account totals. Advertising during this period was for the benefit of Product C only—so we split this cost among the units of C sold.

Calculating profit and loss for each customer

Now we can compute a profit and loss statement for each customer. Exhibit 20–5 shows how each customer's purchases and costs are combined to prepare a statement for each customer. The sum of each of the four major components (sales, cost of sales,

expenses and profit) is the same as on the original statement (Exhibit 20–1)—all we've done is rearrange and rename the data.

For example, Smith bought 900 units of A at £10 each and 300 units of B at £5 each—for the respective sales totals (£9 000 and £1 500) shown in Exhibit 20–5. We compute cost of sales in the same way. Expenses require various calculations. Thirty sales calls cost £300—30 £10 each. Smith placed 30 orders at an average cost of £12.50 each for a total ordering cost of £375. Total packaging costs amounted to £1 530 for A (900 units purchased £1.70 per unit) and £153 for B (30 units purchased £5.10 per unit). There were no packaging costs for C because Smith didn't buy any of Product C. Neither were any advertising costs charged to Smith—all advertising costs were spent promoting Product C, which Smith didn't buy.

Products	Cost/Unit	Selling Price/Unit	Number of Units Sold in Period	Sales Volume in Period	Relative 'Bulk' per Unit	Packaging 'Units'
A	£ 7	£ 10	1 000	£10 000	1	1 000
B	35	50	100	5 000	3	300
C	140	200	10	2 000	6	60
			1 110	£17 000		1 360

Customers	Number of Sales Calls in Period	Number of Orders Placed in Period	Number of Each Product Ordered in Period		
			A	B	C
Smith	30	30	900	30	0
Jones	40	3	90	30	3
Brown	30	1	10	40	7
Total	100	34	1 000	100	10

Exhibit 20–3 Basic Data for Cost and Profit Analysis Example

Sales calls	£1 000/100 calls	£10/call
Billing	£425/34 orders	£12.50/order
Packaging units costs	£2 312/1 360 packaging units	£1.70/packaging unit or £1.70 for Product A £5.10 for Product B £10.20 for Product C
Advertising	£425/10 units of C	£42.50/unit of C

Exhibit 20–4 Functional Cost Account Allocations

business. The restaurant develops a strategy that targets local business people with an attractive luncheon buffet. The restaurant decides on a buffet because research shows that target customers want a choice of good healthy food and are willing to pay reasonable prices for it, as long as they can eat quickly and get back to work on time.

As the restaurant implements its new strategy, the manager wants a measure of how things are going. So she encourages customers to fill out comment cards that ask 'How did we do today?' After several months of operation, things seem to be going reasonably well, although business is not as brisk as it was at first. The manager reads the comment cards and divides the ones with complaints into categories to count up different reasons why customers were not satisfied.

Fix the main problems first

Then the manager creates a graph showing a frequency distribution for the different types of complaints. Quality people call this a **Pareto chart**—a graph that shows the number of times a problem cause occurs, with problem causes ordered from most frequent to least frequent. The manager's Pareto chart, shown in Exhibit 20–6, reveals that customers complain most frequently that they have to wait for a seat. There were other common complaints: the buffet was not well organized, the table was not clean, and so on. However, the first complaint is much more common than the next most frequent.

This type of pattern is typical. The worst problems often occur over and over again. This focuses the manager's attention on which implementation problem to fix first. A rule of quality management is to slay the dragons first, which simply means start with the biggest problem. After removing that problem, the battle moves onto the next most frequent problem. If this is done *continuously*, a lot of problems can be solved. In addition customers are better satisfied.

Identify the causes of problems

So far, our manager has only identified the problem. To solve it, she creates a **fishbone diagram**—a visual aid that helps organize cause-and-effect relationships for 'things gone wrong'. The restaurant manager, for example, discovers that customers wait to be seated because tables are not cleared soon enough. In fact, the Pareto chart (Exhibit 20–6) shows that customers also complain frequently about tables not being clean. So the two implementation problems may be related.

The manager's fishbone diagram (Exhibit 20–7) summarizes the various causes for tables not being cleaned quickly. There are different basic categories of causes— restaurant policy, procedures, people problems and the physical environment. With this overview of different ways the service operation is going wrong, the manager can decide what to fix. She establishes different formal measures. For example, she counts how frequently different causes delay customers from being seated. She finds that the cashier's faulty credit card machine holds up bill processing. The fishbone diagram shows that restaurant policy is to clear the table after the entire party leaves. Customers therefore have to wait at their tables while the staff deals with the jammed credit card machine, and cleaning is delayed. With the credit card machine replaced, the staff can clear the tables sooner and, because they are not so hurried, they do a better cleaning job. Two dragons are on the way to being slayed!

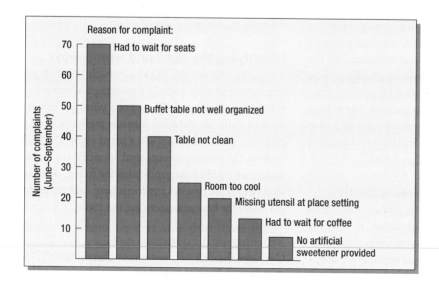

Exhibit 20–6 Pareto Chart Showing Frequency of Different Complaints

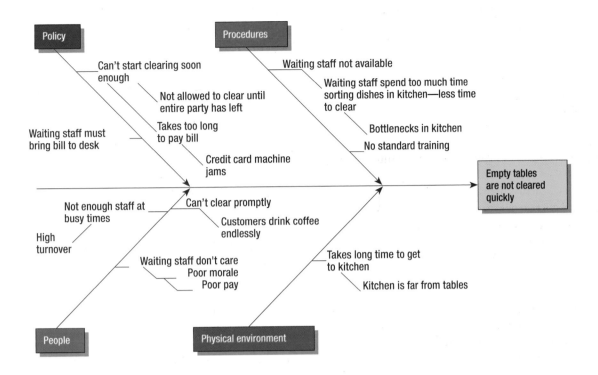

Exhibit 20–7 Fishbone Diagram Showing Cause and Effect for 'Why Tables Are Not Cleared Quickly'

Our case shows that people in different areas of the restaurant affect customer satisfaction. The waiting staff couldn't do what was needed to satisfy customers because the cashier had trouble with the credit card machine. The TQM approach helps everyone to see and understand how their job affects what others do and ultimately the customer's satisfaction.[12]

Building quality into services

The restaurant case illustrates how a firm can improve implementation with TQM approaches. We used a service example because providing customer service is often a difficult area of implementation. Recently, marketers in service businesses have been paying a lot of attention to improving service quality.

Some people seem to forget that almost every firm must implement service quality as part of its plan, whether its product is primarily a service, primarily a physical good or a blend of both. For example, a manufacturer of ball bearings is not just providing wholesalers or producers with round pieces of steel. Customers need information about deliveries, they need orders filled properly and they may have questions to ask the firm's accountant, receptionist or engineers. Because almost every firm must manage the service it provides to customers, let's focus on some of the special concerns of implementing quality service.[13]

Train people and empower them to serve

Quality gurus like to say that the firm has only one job: to give customers exactly what they want, when they want it and where they want it. Marketing managers have been saying that for some time too. Customer service is hard to implement because the server is inseparable from the service. A person doing a specific service job may perform one specific task correctly but still annoy the customer in a host of other ways. Customers will not be satisfied if employees are rude or inattentive, even if they 'solve the customer's problem'. There are two keys to improving how people implement quality service: (1) training and (2) empowerment.

Firms that commit to customer satisfaction realize that all employees who have any contact with customers need training: many firms see 40 hours a year of training as a minimum. Simply showing customer-contact employees around the rest of the business, so that they learn how their contribution fits in the total effort, can be very effective. Good training usually includes role playing on handling different types of customer requests and problems. This is not just sales training! A rental car attendant who is rude when a customer is trying to return a car may leave the customer dissatisfied even if the rental car was perfect. How employees treat a customer is as important as whether they perform the task correctly.

Companies cannot afford an army of managers to inspect how each employee implements a strategy and such a system usually does not work anyway. Quality cannot be 'inspected in'. It must come from the people who do the service jobs. Firms that are committed to service quality empower employees to satisfy customers' needs. **Empowerment** means giving employees the authority to correct a problem without first checking with management. At a Hilton hotel, an empowered room-service employee knows it is acceptable to run across the street to buy the specific mineral water a guest requests.

Manage expectations—with good communication

The implementation effort sometimes leaves customers dissatisfied because they expect much more than it is possible for the firm to deliver. Some firms react to this by shrugging their shoulders and faulting customers for being unreasonable. Research in the service quality area, however, suggests that the problems often go away if marketers clearly communicate what they are offering. Customers are satisfied when the service matches their expectations, and careful communication leads to reasonable expectations.

Separate the routine and plan for the special

Implementation usually involves some routine services and some that require special attention. Customer satisfaction increases when the two types of service encounters are separated. For example, banks set up special windows for commercial deposits and supermarkets have cash-only checkouts. In developing the marketing plan, it is important to analyse the types of service customers will need and plan for both types of situations. In some cases, completely different strategies may be required. Increasingly, firms try to use computers and other equipment to handle routine services. ATMs are quick and convenient for dispensing cash. Travellers on British Airways, domestic shuttle services can buy tickets at a ticket dispensing machine rather than queue at the ticket desk.

Firms that study special service requests can use training so that even unusual customer requests become routine to the staff. Every day, hotel guests lose their keys, bank customers run out of cheques and supermarket shoppers leave their wallets at home. A well-run service operation anticipates these special events so service providers can respond in a way that satisfies customers' needs.

Managers lead the quality effort

Quality implementation, whether in a service activity or in another activity, doesn't just happen by itself. Managers must show that they are committed to doing things right to satisfy customers and that quality is everyone's job. The top executive at American Express had his board of directors give him the title chief quality officer so that everyone in the company would know he was personally involved in the TQM effort.

Getting a return on quality is important

While the cost of poor quality is lost customers, keep in mind that the type of quality efforts we've been discussing also result in costs. It takes time and energy to keep records, analyse the details of implementation efforts, and search for ways to reduce whatever type of defects might appear. It's important to find the right balance between quality in the implementation effort and what it costs to achieve.

Marketing managers who lose sight of that balance have often created quality programmes that cost more than they are worth. It is easy to fall into the trap of running up *unnecessary costs* trying to improve some facet of implementation that really is not that important to customers, customer satisfaction or customer retention. When that happens, customers may still be satisfied, but the firm cannot make a profit because of the extra costs. In other words, there is not a financial return on the money spent to improve the quality of the implementation effort. Remember that getting everyone to work together to satisfy customers should be the route to profits. If the firm is spending money on quality efforts that don't really contribute to customer satisfaction—or that cost more to provide than customers will ultimately be willing to pay for—then someone has lost sight of the marketing concept.

As this suggests, TQM is not a 'cure all'. Further, it is not the only method for improving marketing implementation, but it is an important approach. Some firms don't yet use TQM; they may be missing an opportunity. Other firms apply some quality methods but act like they are the private property of a handful of 'quality specialists' who want to control things. That is not good either. Everyone must own a TQM effort—and keep a balanced view of how it improves customer satisfaction and what it costs.

As more marketing managers see the benefits of TQM, it will become a more important part of marketing thinking, especially marketing implementation. And when managers really understand implementation, they can do a better job developing strategies and plans in the first place.[14]

PEOPLE PUT PLANS INTO ACTION

People are an important resource

The best marketing strategy in the world may fail if the right people are not available to implement the plan. Large firms usually have a separate human resources department staffed by specialists who work with others in the firm to ensure that good people are available to do jobs that need to be done. A small firm may not have a separate department—but somebody (perhaps the owner or other managers) must deal with people-management matters such as recruiting and hiring new employees, deciding how people will be compensated and what to do when a job is not being performed well or is no longer necessary. Human resource issues are often critically important both in a marketing manager's choice among different possible marketing opportunities and in the actual implementation of marketing plans.

Some of the human resource issues that are important to a marketing manager have already been discussed. For example, Chapter 14 reviewed strategy decisions in the personal selling area and discussed a number of sales management issues—including selection, training, supervision, motivation and compensation. Similarly, the total quality management discussion in the previous section described why training and empowerment for service providers are often critical in achieving service quality and in satisfying customers.[15]

This section briefly reconsiders these issues, but from a broader perspective: how and why they need to be considered in planning new strategies and implementing plans—especially plans that involve change. For example, change is likely to occur when a firm's sales are growing and when it is expanding its marketing efforts—to go after new markets or to introduce and promote new products.

New strategies usually require people changes

New strategies often involve new and different ways of doing things. Even if such changes are required to ensure that the firm will survive and make a profit, changes often upset the *status quo* and long-established vested interests of its current employees. A production manager who has spent a career becoming an expert in producing fine wood furniture may not like the idea of switching to a build-it-yourself line—even if that is what customers want. A senior sales representative with a well-established territory may not want to work hard at developing new accounts for a new product. When the market maturity stage of the product life cycle hits, a finance manager needs to appreciate that profit growth will resume only if the firm takes some risk and invests in a new product concept.

As these examples suggest, many of the people affected by a new strategy may not be under the control of the marketing manager. In acting alone the marketing manager may not be the 'change agent' who can instantly turn everyone in the organization into an enthusiastic supporter of the plan. However, if the marketing manager doesn't think about how a new strategy will affect people—and how what people do will affect the success of the strategy—even the best strategy may fail.

Many small businesses rely on the skills of the owner. Marketing is only one responsibility alongside production, finance and staff relationships

Communication helps promote change

Communication is an important consideration here. The marketing manager must find ways to communicate with others in the organization so as to explain the new strategy, what needs to happen, and why. People cannot be expected to pull together in an organization-wide effort if they do not know what is going on. Such communication might be handled in meetings, memoranda, casual discussions, an internal newsletter or any number of other ways, depending on the situation. However, the communication should occur. At a minimum, the marketing manager needs to have clear communication with the human resources manager—or with other managers—who will participate in preparing the firm's personnel for a change.

Rapid growth strains human resources

When developing a marketing plan, a pragmatic marketing manager must take a realistic look at how quickly the firm's personnel can get geared up for the plan, or whether it will be possible to get people who can. Sometimes a firm simply cannot change or grow as fast from a people standpoint as the market might allow. Firms that are expecting or experiencing rapid growth face special challenges in getting enough qualified people to do what needs to be done. A fast-growing retail chain that opens many new stores doesn't just need money for new land and buildings and inventory, it also needs new store managers, assistant managers, sales staff, customer service people, advertising managers, computer operators and maintenance people. At least some of the 'new blood' have to learn about the culture of the company, its customers and its products at the same time as they are learning the nuts and bolts of performing their jobs well. Hiring people and getting them up to speed takes time and energy.

Allow time for training and other changes

Training may be especially important in situations like this, but training—like other organizational changes—takes time. A marketing manager who wants to re-organize the firm's saleforce so that salespeople are assigned to specific customers rather than by specific product line may have a great idea, but it cannot be implemented overnight. A salesperson who is supposed to be a specialist in meeting the needs for a certain customer won't be able to do a very good job if all he or she knows about is the specific product that was previously the focus. Even if nothing else were involved, the plan would need to include time for the training to take place.

Each change may result in several others

That may sound simple, but keep in mind that the changes may not stop there. A change in how sales territories and assignments are structured is likely to require changes in compensation. The specific details of the new compensation system need to be developed and accountants need time to adjust their computer programs to make certain that the salespeople actually get paid. Similarly, the changes in the salesforce are likely to require changes in who they report to—and the structure of sales management assignments.

The objective of this example is not just to list all of the specific changes that might be required for this specific strategy decision, but rather to highlight the more general point that changing people usually takes time—and only so much change can be absorbed effectively in a limited period.

Plan time for changes from the outset

A marketing manager who ignores the 'ripple effects' of a change in strategy may later expect everyone else in the organization to bend over backwards, work overtime, and otherwise do everything possible to meet a schedule that was put together with little, or no, forethought. Certainly there are cases of heroic efforts by people in organizations to turn someone's vision into a reality. Yet it is more typical for such a plan to fall behind schedule, to run up unnecessary costs or simply to fail. Marketing managers who work that way are likely to be criticized for 'not having the time to do it right the first time, but having the time to do it over again.'

Cut-backs need human resource plans

If rapidly expanding marketing efforts involve human resource challenges, decisions to drop products, channels of distribution or even certain types of customers can be even more traumatic. In these situations, people always worry that *someone* will lose his or her job—and that is stressful.

Dropping products or making other changes that would result in a cutback on people doing certain jobs must be planned very carefully—and with a good dose of humanity. To the extent possible, it is important to plan a phase-out period so that people can make other plans. During the last decade, too many firms downsized (or, as some people call it, 'rightsized' or 'dumbsized', so rapidly that long-time loyal employees who had made valuable contributions to the firm and its customers were simply left to their own devices. If a phase-out is carefully planned—considering not only the implications for production facilities and contracts with outside firms, but also the people inside—it may be possible to develop strategies that will create exciting new jobs for those who would otherwise be displaced.[16]

Marketing pumps life into an organization

This line of thinking highlights again that marketing is the heart that pumps the lifeblood through an organization. Marketing managers who create profitable marketing strategies and implement them well create a need for a firm's production workers, accountants, finance managers, lawyers and its human resources people. In this chapter we have talked about marketing links with those other functions, but ultimately organizations, and the various departments within them, consist of *individuals*. If the marketing manager makes good strategy decisions—ones that lead to satisfied customers and profits—each of the individuals in the organization has a chance to prosper and grow.[17]

SUMMARY

Even when everyone in an entire company embraces the marketing concept, coordinating marketing strategies and plans with other functional areas is a challenge. Yet, it is a challenge that marketing managers must address. It does not make sense to select a strategy that the firm cannot implement. Implementing new plans usually requires money, people, and a way to produce goods or services the firm will sell.

Cooperation between the marketing manager and the finance department helps to ensure that there is sufficient funding available for the initial one-time investments and ongoing working capital needed to implement a marketing plan. If funding comes from outside investors, the marketing manager may need to develop a strategy that satisfies them as well as customers. If the money available is limited, the strategy may need to be scaled back in various ways, or the marketing manager may need to find creative ways to phase in a strategy over time so that it generates enough cash flow to 'pay its own way'.

There also needs to be close coordination between a firm's production specialists and the marketing plan. To get that coordination, the marketing manager needs to consider the firm's production capacity when evaluating alternative strategies. Flexibility in production may allow the firm to pursue different strategies at the same time—or to switch strategies more easily when new opportunities develop.

Figuring out the profitability of a strategy, product or customer often requires a real understanding of costs—production costs, marketing costs and other costs that may accumulate. Traditional accounting reports are often not very useful in pinpointing these costs. However, marketing managers and accountants are now working together to get more accurate cost information—by developing functional accounts rather than just relying on natural accounts typically used for financial analysis.

Money, physical resources and information are all important in developing a successful strategy, but most strategies are implemented by people. Therefore a marketing manager must also be concerned with the availability and skills of the firm's people—its human resources. New marketing strategies may upset established ways of doing things. In that case, plans need to be clearly communicated so that everyone knows what to expect. Further, plans need to take into consider the time—and effort—that will be required to get people up to speed on the new jobs they will be expected to do.

Making the strategic planning decisions that concern how a firm is going to use its overall resources—from marketing, production, finance and other areas—is the responsibility of the managing director, not the marketing manager. Further, the marketing manager usually cannot dictate what a manager in some other department should do. However, it is sensible for the marketing manager to make recommendations on these matters. The marketing strategies and plans that the marketing manager recommends are more likely to be accepted—and then successfully implemented—if the links between marketing and other functional areas have been carefully considered from the outset.

QUESTIONS AND PROBLEMS

1. Identify some of the ways that a firm can raise money to support a new marketing plan. Give the advantages and limitations—from a marketing manager's perspective—of each approach.

2. An entrepreneur who started a chain of car service centres to do fast oil changes wants to expand quickly by building new facilities in new markets, but does not have enough capital. His financial advisor suggested that he might be able to get around the financial constraint—and still grow rapidly—if he franchised his idea. That way the franchisees would invest to build their own centres, but fees from the franchise agreement would also provide cash flow to build more company-owned outlets. Do you think this is a good idea? Why or why not?

3. Explain, in your own words, why investors in a firm's shares might be interested in a firm's marketing manager developing a new growth-oriented strategy? Would it be just as good, from the investors' standpoint, for the manager to just maintain the same level of profits? Why or why not?

4. A woman with extensive experience in home healthcare and a good marketing plan has approached a bank for a loan, most of which she has explained she intends to 'invest in advertising designed to recruit part-time nurses and to attract home-care patients for her firm's services'. Other than the furniture in her leased office space, she has few assets. Is the bank likely to loan her the money? Why?

5. Could the idea of mass customization be used by a publisher of textbooks to allow different lecturers to order customized teaching materials—perhaps even unique books made up of chapters from a number of different existing books? What do you think would be the major advantages and disadvantages of this approach?

6. Give examples of two different ways that a firm's production capacity might influence a marketing manager's choice of a marketing strategy.

7. Is a small company's flexibility increased or decreased by turning to outside suppliers to produce the products it sells. Explain your thinking.

8. Explain how a marketing manager's sales forecast for a new marketing plan might be used by:
   a. A financial manager.
   b. An accountant.
   c. A production manager.
   d. A human resources manager.

9. Explain the difference between natural accounts and functional accounts.

10. Could the approaches to cost allocation that we discussed in this chapter apply to a firm—such as a travel agency—that produces only services. Explain your thinking.

11. What are the major advantages of total quality management as an approach for improving implementation of marketing plans? What limitations can you think of?

12. What types of human resource issues does a marketing manager face when planning to expand sales operations from a branch office in a new overseas market? Are the problems any different than they would be in a new domestic market?

SUGGESTED CASES

9. Eviro Water Pure
17. Romano's Take-Away

REFERENCES

1. See www.benetton.com; R. Ollins, 'Benetton steps up its pace in sport', *The Sunday Times*, Business section, 27 July 1997, p. 8; J. Rossant, 'A cozy deal at Benetton', *Business Week*, 28 July 1997; R. Tredre, 'Hue and cry over blood-red Benetton', *The Observer*, 18 February 1996, p. 6; M. Brasier, 'Planners please Benetton', *Electronic Telegraph*, 25 September 1996; 'Made In Italy', Benetton Home Page, 1995.

2. S. Albers, 'Rules for The Allocation Of A Marketing Budget Across Products Or Market Segments' *in* D. Arnott *et al.* (eds), Proceedings of 26th EMAC Conference, Warwick Business School, 1997, pp. 1–17; J. Pennings *et al.*, 'The marketing-finance interface towards financial services' *in* D. Arnott *et al.* (eds) ibid, pp. 1915–24.

3. 'At £40m BCO proves its worth', *Belfast Telegraph*, 19 May 1998; 'Flotation raises £9.3m for BCO', *Belfast Telegraph*, 18 December 1997; J. Brown, 'BCO technologies', *Belfast Telegraph*, 30 July 1996, p. 8.

4. R.C. Pozen, 'Institutional investors: The reluctant activists', *Harvard Business Review*, January–February 1994, p. 140; W.K. Schilit, 'The globalization of venture capital', *Business Horizons*, January–February 1992, pp. 17–23; M.E. Porter, 'Capital disadvantage: America's failing capital investment system', *Harvard Business Review*, September–October 1992, pp. 65–83; B. Parks, 'Rate of Return – The poison apple?' *Business Horizons*, May–June 1993, pp. 55–58.

5. A. Bhide, 'Bootstrap finance: The art of start-ups', *Harvard Business Review*, November–December 1992, pp. 109–17; M. Rubinstein, 'Effective industrial marketing with a piggy bank budget', *Industrial Marketing Management*, August 1992, pp. 203–14; A. Bhide, 'How entrepreneurs craft strategies that work', *Harvard Business Review*, March–April 1994, pp. 150–63.

6. R.G. Schroeder and M.J. Pesch, 'Focusing the factory: Eight lessons', *Business Horizons*, September–October 1994, pp. 76–81; J.P. Womack and D.T. Jones, 'From lean production to the lean enterprise', *Harvard Business Review*, March–April 1994, pp. 93–105; A.D. Bartmess, 'The plant location puzzle', *Harvard Business Review*, March–April 1994, pp. 20–38; R.H. Hayes and G.P. Pisano, 'Beyond world-class: The new manufacturing strategy', *Harvard Business Review*, January–February 1994, pp. 77–87; V.L. Crittenden, L.R. Gardiner and A. Stam, 'Reducing conflict between marketing and manufacturing', *Industrial Marketing Management*, November 1993, pp. 299–310; P.A. Konijnendijk, 'Dependence and conflict between production and sales', *Industrial Marketing Management*, August 1993, pp. 161–8; K.B. Kahn and J.T. Mentzer, 'Norms that distinguish between marketing and manufacturing', *Journal of Business Research*, June 1994, pp. 111–18; W.B. Wagner, 'Establishing supply service strategy for shortage situations', *Industrial Marketing Management*, December 1994, pp. 393–402; R.W. Schmenner, 'So You Want to Lower Costs?', *Business Horizons*, July–August 1992, pp. 24–28.

7. D. Sumner Smith, 'The enterprise network', *The Sunday Times*, 15 February 1998, Business section, p. 11; Extended Case, *Sunday Times Enterprise Network*, www.enterprisenetwork.co.uk.

8. For more on Levi Strauss' custom-fit jeans for women, see 'One writer's hunt for the perfect jeans', *Fortune*, 17 April 1995, p. 30; 'Levi Strauss sizes the retail scene', *Advertising Age*, 23 January 1995, p. 4; B.J. Pine, II, B. Victor, and A.C. Boynton, 'Making mass customization work', *Harvard Business Review*, September–October 1993, pp. 108–21.

9. D. Thomas, 'The Calvin conquest,' *Newsweek*, 26 May 1997, p. 47; 'Calvin Klein Inc.: Definitive pact is reached on sale of jeans division', *The Wall Street Journal*, 15 July 1994, p. B4.

10. E. Malikn, 'Pangs of conscience over sweat-shops', *Business Week*, 29 July 1996; 'Managing by Values', *Business Week*, 1 August 1994, pp. 46–52; M. Nichols, 'Third-world families at work: Child labor or child care?' *Harvard Business Review*, January–February 1993, pp. 12–23.

11. J.K. Shim and J.G. Siegel, *Modern Cost Management and Analysis*, Barrons, Hauppauge, NY, 1992; J.K. Shank and V. Govindarajan, Strategic Cost Management: *The New Tool for Competitive Advantage*, The Free Press, New York, 1993; R. Cooper and R.S. Kaplan, 'Profit

priorities from activity-based costing', *Harvard Business Review*, May–June 1991, pp. 130–37; D.M. Lambert and J.U. Sterling, 'What types of profitability reports do marketing managers receive?' *Industrial Marketing Management*, November 1987, pp. 295–304.

12. The restaurant case is adapted from M. Gaudard, R. Coates and L. Freeman, 'Accelerating improvement', *Quality Progress*, October 1991, pp. 81–8. For more on quality management and control, see 'TQM: more than a dying fad?' *Fortune*, 18 October 1993, pp. 66–72; C.R. O'Neal and W.C. LaFief, 'Marketing's lead role in Total Quality', *Industrial Marketing Management*, May 1992, pp. 133–44; S. Aggarwal, 'A quick guide to Total Quality Management', *Business Horizons*, May–June 1993, pp. 66–8; D. Niven, 'When times get tough, what happens to TQM?' *Harvard Business Review*, May–June 1993, pp. 20–37; P. Mears, 'How to stop talking about, and begin progress toward, Total Quality Management', *Business Horizons*, May–June 1993, pp. 11–14; 'The Quality imperative', *Business Week* (special issue), 25 October 1991.

13. H. Kasper, 'Corporate culture and market orientation in services: A matter of definition and communication', *in* D. Arnott *et al.* (eds), op. cit., 1997, pp. 663–8; C. Boshoff and J. Gnoth, 'The what, how, when and who of service recovery', *in* D. Arnott *et al.* (eds), op. cit. , pp. 181–90.

14. R. Rust, A.J. Zahorik and T.L. Keiningham, *Return on Quality*, Probus, Chicago, 1994; K. Storbacka *et al.*, 'Managing customer relationships for profit: The dynamics of relationship quality', *International Journal of Service Industry Management*, vol. 5, 1994, no. 5, pp. 21–38; H.N. Shycon, 'Improved customer service: Measuring the payoff', *The Journal of Business Strategy*, January–February 1992, pp. 13–17; A.L. Daniel, 'Overcome the barriers to superior customer service', *The Journal of Business Strategy*, January–February 1992, pp. 18–24; L.A. Schlesinger and J.L. Heskett, 'The service-driven service company', *Harvard Business Review*, September–October 1991, pp. 71–81; J.S. Hensel, 'Service quality improvement and control: A customer-based approach', *Journal of Business Research*, January 1990, pp. 43–54; S.W. Kelley, 'Developing customer orientation among service employees', *Journal of the Academy of Marketing Science*, Winter 1992, pp. 27–36; W. George, 'Internal marketing and organizational behavior: A partnership in developing customer-conscious employees at every level', *Journal of Business Research*, January 1990, pp. 63–70; R. Frey, 'Empowerment or else', *Harvard Business Review*, September–October 1993, p. 80; F.K. Sonnenberg, 'Marketing: Service quality: Forethought, Not Afterthought', *The Journal of Business Strategy*, September–October 1989, pp. 54–8; C. Meyer, 'How the right measures help teams excel', *Harvard Business Review*, May–June 1994, pp. 95–104; S.W. Brown and T.A. Swartz, 'A gap analysis of professional service quality', *Journal of Marketing*, April 1989, pp. 92–8.

15. L. Pitt and D. Nel (1997) 'Service Quality To Internal Customers' *in* R. Ashford *et al.* (eds) *Marketing Without Borders*, Proceedings of the Academy of Marketing Annual Conference, Manchester Metropolitan University (1997), pp. 725–42; I. Papasolomou and T. Proctor, 'Internal marketing – Its relationship with an organisation's service climate and with the concepts of organisational behaviour, organisation development, and human resource management' *in* R. Ashford *et al.* (eds), ibid., pp. 769–80.

16. M. Glassman and B. McAfee, 'Integrating the personnel and marketing functions: The challenge of the 1990s', *Business Horizons*, May–June 1992, pp. 52–9; M. Viswanathan and E.M. Olson, 'The implementation of business strategies: Implications for the sales function', *Journal of Personal Selling & Sales Management*, Winter 1992, pp. 45–58; L. McTier Anderson and J.W. Fenton, Jr., 'The light at the end of the HRM tunnel: Window of opportunity or an oncoming train?' *Business Horizons*, January–February 1993, pp. 72–76; J. Daniel Duck, 'Managing change: The art of balancing', *Harvard Business Review*, November–December 1993, pp. 109–18; J.R. Emshoff, 'How to increase employee loyalty while you downsize', *Business Horizons*, March–April 1994, pp. 49–57.

17. N. Piercy, 'Partnership between marketing and human resource management for implementation effectiveness in services marketing' *in* R. Ashford *et al.* (eds), op. cit., 1997, pp. 865–78; G. Panigyrakis and C. Veloustou,' Interfaces of the product/brand manager – A cross sector analysis in consumer goods companies' *in* D. Arnott *et al.* (eds), op. cit., pp. 993–1012.

APPENDIX A
Economics Fundamentals

When You Finish This Appendix, You Should

1 Understand the 'law of diminishing demand.'

2 Understand demand and supply curves, and how they set the size of a market and its price level.

3 Know about elasticity of demand and supply.

4 Know why demand elasticity can be affected by availability of substitutes.

5 Know the different kinds of competitive situations and understand why they are important to marketing managers.

6 Recognize the important new terms (shown in colour).

A good marketing manager should be an expert on markets and the nature of competition in markets. The economist's traditional analysis of demand and supply is a useful tool for analysing markets. In particular, you should master the concepts of a demand curve and demand elasticity. A firm's demand curve shows how the target customers view the firm's Product, really its whole marketing mix. And the interaction of demand and supply curves helps set the size of a market and the market price. The interaction of supply and demand also determines the nature of the competitive environment, which has an important effect on strategy planning. These ideas are discussed more fully in the following sections.

PRODUCTS AND MARKETS AS SEEN BY CUSTOMERS AND POTENTIAL CUSTOMERS

Economists provide useful insights

How potential customers (not the firm) see a firm's product (marketing mix) affects how much they are willing to pay for it, where it should be made available, and how eager they are for it, if they want it at all. In other words, their view has a very direct bearing on marketing strategy planning.

Economists have been concerned with market behaviour for years. Their analytical tools can be quite helpful in summarizing how customers view products and how markets behave.

Economists see individual customers choosing among alternatives

Economics is sometimes called the 'dismal science', because it says that most customers have a limited income and simply cannot buy everything they want. They must balance their needs and the prices of various products. Economists usually assume that customers have a fairly definite set of preferences and that they evaluate alternatives in terms of whether the alternatives will make them feel better (or worse) or in some way improve (or change) their situation.

But what exactly is the nature of a customer's desire for a particular product? Usually economists answer this question in terms of the extra utility the customer can obtain by buying more of a particular product or how much utility would be lost if the customer had less of the product. (Students who wish further discussion of this approach should refer to indifference curve analysis in any standard economics text.)

It is easier to understand the idea of utility if we look at what happens when the price of one of the customer's usual purchases changes.

The law of diminishing demand

Suppose that consumers buy potatoes in 5 kg bags at the same time as they buy other foods such as bread and rice. If the consumers are mainly interested in buying a certain amount of food and the price of the potatoes drops, it seems reasonable to expect that they will switch some of their food money to potatoes and away from some other foods. But if the price of potatoes rises, you expect our consumers to buy fewer potatoes and more of other foods.

The general relationship between price and quantity demanded illustrated by this food example is called the **law of diminishing demand**. It says that if the price of a product is raised, a smaller quantity will be demanded and if the price of a product is lowered, a greater quantity will be demanded. Experience supports this relationship between prices and total demand in a market, especially for broad product categories or commodities such as potatoes.

Exhibit A-1 Demand Schedule for Potatoes (5 kilo bags)

The relationship between price and quantity demanded in a market is what economists call a 'demand schedule'. An example is shown in Exhibit A–1. For each row in the table, Column 2 shows the quantity consumers will want (demand) if they have to pay the price given in Column 1. The third column shows that the total revenue (sales) in the potato market is equal to the quantity demanded at a given price times that price. Note that as prices drop, the total unit quantity increases, yet the total revenue decreases. Fill in the blank lines in the third column and observe the behaviour of total revenue, which is of particular importance to the marketing manager. We will explain what you should have noticed, and why, a little later.

The demand curve—usually down-sloping

If your only interest is seeing at which price the company will earn the greatest total revenue, the demand schedule may be adequate. But a demand curve shows more. A **demand curve** is a graph of the relationship between price and quantity demanded in a market, assuming that all other things stay the same. Exhibit A–2 shows the demand curve for potatoes—really just a plotting of the demand schedule in Exhibit A–1. It shows how many potatoes potential customers will demand at various possible prices. This is a 'down-sloping demand curve'. Most demand curves are down-sloping. This just means that if prices are decreased, the quantity customers demand will increase.

Demand curves always show the price on the vertical axis and the quantity demanded on the horizontal axis. In Exhibit A–2, we have shown the price in pounds sterling. For consistency, we will use pounds sterling in other examples. However, keep in mind that these same ideas hold regardless of what money unit (dollars, yen, euro, kroner, etc.) is used to represent price. Even at this early point, you should keep in mind that markets are not necessarily limited by national boundaries or by currency.

Note that the demand curve shows only how customers will react to various possible prices. In a market, we see only one price at a time, not all these prices. The curve, however, shows what quantities will be demanded depending on what price is set. You probably think that most business people would like to set a price that would result in a large sales revenue. Before discussing this, however, we should consider the demand schedule and curve for another product to get a more complete picture of demand curve analysis.

Microwave oven demand curve looks different

A different demand schedule is the one for standard 32 litre microwave ovens shown in Exhibit A–3. Column (3) shows the total revenue that will be obtained at various possible prices and quantities. Again,

Point	(1) Price of Potatoes per Bag (P)	(2) Quantity Demanded (bags per month) (Q)	(3) Total Revenue per Month (P Q TR)
A	£1.60	8 000 000	£12 800 000
B	1.30	9 000 000	
C	1.00	11 000 000	11 000 000
D	0.70	14 000 000	
E	0.40	19 000 000	

Exhibit A–1 Demand Schedule for Potatoes (5 kg bags)

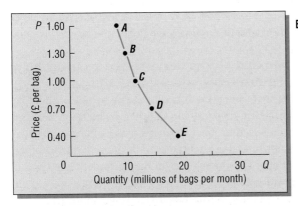

Exhibit A–2 Demand Curve for Potatoes (5 kg bags)

Point	(1) Price per Microwave Oven (P)	(2) Quantity Demanded per Year (Q)	(3) Total Revenue (TR) per Year (P Q TR)
A	£300	20 000	£6 000 000
B	250	70 000	15 500 000
C	200	130 000	26 000 000
D	150	210 000	31 500 000
E	100	310 000	31 000 000

Exhibit A–3 Demand Schedule for 32 litre Microwave Ovens

as the price goes down, the quantity demanded goes up. But here, unlike the potato example, total revenue increases as prices go down, at least until the price drops to £150. Every market has a demand curve for some time period

These general demand relationships are typical for all products. But each product has its own demand schedule and curve in each potential market, no matter how small the market. In other words, a particular demand curve has meaning only for a particular market. We can think of demand curves for individuals, groups of individuals who form a target market, regions and even countries. And the time period covered really should be specified although this is often neglected because we usually think of monthly or yearly periods.

The difference between elastic and inelastic

The demand curve for microwave ovens (see Exhibit A–4) is downsloping, but note that it is flatter than the curve for potatoes. It is important to understand what this flatness means. We will consider the flatness in terms of total revenue since this is what interests business managers.*

When you filled in the total revenue column for potatoes, you should have noticed that total revenue drops continually if the price is reduced. This looks undesirable for sellers and illustrates inelastic demand. **Inelastic demand** means that although the quantity demanded increases if the price is decreased, the quantity demanded will not 'stretch' enough, that is, it is not elastic enough to avoid a decrease in total revenue.

In contrast, elastic demand means that if prices are dropped, the quantity demanded will stretch (increase) enough to increase total revenue. The upper part of the microwave oven demand curve is an example of elastic demand. But note that if the microwave oven price is dropped from £150 to £100, total revenue will decrease. We can say, therefore, that between £150 and £100, demand is inelastic, that is, total revenue will decrease if price is lowered from £150 to £100. Thus, elasticity can be defined in terms of changes in total revenue. If total revenue will increase if price is lowered, then demand is elastic. If total revenue will decrease if price is lowered, then demand is inelastic. (Note: A special case known as 'unitary elasticity of demand' occurs if total revenue stays the same when prices change.)

Total revenue may increase if price is raised

A point often missed in discussions of demand is what happens when prices are raised instead of lowered. With elastic demand, total revenue will decrease if the price is raised. With inelastic demand, however, total revenue will increase if the price is raised.

The possibility of raising price and increasing total revenue at the same time is attractive to managers. This

occurs only if the demand curve is inelastic. Here total revenue will increase if price is raised, but total costs probably will not increase, and may actually go down, with smaller quantities. Keep in mind that profit is equal to total revenue minus total costs. So when demand is inelastic, profit will increase as price is increased!

The ways total revenue changes as prices are raised are shown in Exhibit A–5. Here total revenue is the rectangular area formed by a price and its related quantity. The larger the rectangular area, the greater the total revenue.

P_1 is the original price here, and the total potential revenue with this original price is shown by the area with blue shading. The area with red shading shows the total revenue with the new price, P_2. There is some overlap in the total revenue areas, so the important areas are those with only one colour. Note that in the left-hand figure, where demand is elastic, the revenue added (the red-only area) when the price is increased is less than the revenue lost (the blue-only area). Now, contrast this to the right-hand figure, when demand is inelastic. Only a small blue revenue area is given up for a much larger (red) one when price is raised.

An entire curve is not elastic or inelastic

It is important to see that it is wrong to refer to a whole *demand curve as elastic or inelastic*. Rather, elasticity for a particular demand curve refers to the change in total revenue between two points on the curve, not along the whole curve. You saw the change from elastic to inelastic in the microwave oven example. Generally, however, nearby points are either elastic or inelastic, so it is common to refer to a whole curve by the degree of elasticity in the price range that normally is of interest—the *relevant range*.

Demand elasticities affected by availability of substitutes and urgency of need

At first, it may be difficult to see why one product has an elastic demand and another an inelastic demand. Many factors affect elasticity, such as the availability of substitutes, the importance of the item in the customer's budget and the urgency of the customer's need and its relation to other needs. By looking more closely at one of these factors, the availability of substitutes, it is easier to understand why demand elasticities vary.

Substitutes are products that offer the buyer a choice. For example, many consumers see grapefruit as a substitute for oranges and hot dogs as a substitute for hamburgers. The greater the number of 'good' substitutes available, the greater will be the elasticity of demand. From the consumer's perspective, products are 'good' substitutes if they are very similar (homogeneous). If consumers see products as extremely different, or heterogeneous, then a particular need cannot easily be satisfied by substitutes. Demand for the most satisfactory product may be quite inelastic.

---

*Strictly speaking, two curves should not be compared for flatness if the graph scales are different, but for our purposes now, we will do so to illustrate the idea of 'elasticity of demand'. Actually, it would be more correct to compare two curves for one product, on the same graph. Then both the shape of the demand curve and its position on the graph would be important.

As an example, if the price of hamburgers is lowered (and other prices stay the same), the quantity demanded will increase a lot, as will total revenue. The reason is that not only will regular hamburger users buy more hamburgers, but also some consumers who formerly bought other snacks will probably buy hamburgers. But if the price of hamburgers is raised, the quantity demanded will decrease, perhaps sharply. Still consumers will buy some hamburgers, depending on how much the price has risen and their individual tastes. (see Exhibit A–6).

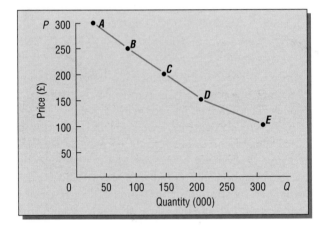

Exhibit A–4 Demand Curve for 32 litre Microwave Ovens

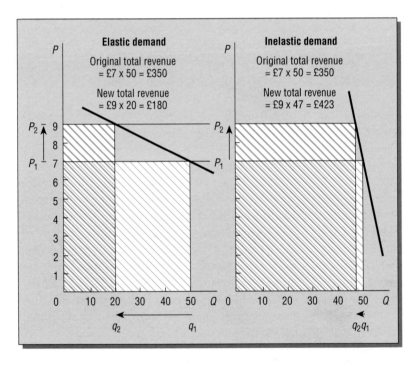

Exhibit A–5 Changes in Total Revenue as Price Increases

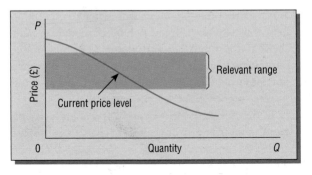

Exhibit A–6 Demand Curve for Hamburger (a product with many substitutes)

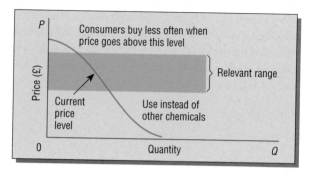

Exhibit A–7 Demand Curve for Motor Oil (a product with few substitutes)

In contrast to a product with many 'substitutes', such as a hamburger, consider a product with few or no substitutes. Its demand curve will tend to be inelastic. Motor oil is a good example. Motor oil is needed to keep cars running. Yet no one person or family uses great quantities of motor oil. So it is not likely that the quantity of motor oil purchased will change much as long as price changes are *within a reasonable range*. Of course, if the price is raised to a staggering figure, many people will buy less oil (change their oil less frequently). If the price is dropped to an extremely low level, manufacturers may buy more, say, as a lower-cost substitute for other chemicals typically used in making plastic (Exhibit A–7). But these extremes are outside the relevant range.

Demand curves are introduced here because the degree of elasticity of demand shows how potential customers feel about a product, and especially whether they see substitutes for the product. To get a better understanding of markets, we must extend this economic analysis.

MARKETS AS SEEN BY SUPPLIERS

Customers may want a product, but if suppliers are not willing to supply it, then there is no market. So we'll study the economist's analysis of supply. And then we'll bring supply and demand together for a more complete understanding of markets.

Economists often use this kind of analysis to explain pricing in the marketplace. But that is not our intention. Here the interest is in how and why markets work, and the interaction of customers and potential suppliers. Later in this appendix the competition affects prices, but our full discussion of how individual firms set prices, or should set prices, was discussed in Chapters 16 and 17.

Supply curves reflect supplier thinking

Generally speaking, suppliers' costs affect the quantity of products they are willing to offer in a market during any period. In other words, their costs affect their supply schedules and supply curves. While a demand curve shows the quantity of products customers will be willing to buy at various prices, a **supply curve** shows the quantity of products that will be supplied at various possible prices. Eventually, only one quantity will be offered and purchased. So a supply curve is really a hypothetical (what-if) description of what will be offered at various prices. It is, however, a very important curve. Together with a demand curve, it summarizes the attitudes and probable behaviour of buyers and sellers about a particular product in a particular market, that is, in a product market.

Some supply curves are vertical

We usually assume that supply curves tend to slope upwards, that is, suppliers will be willing to offer greater quantities at higher prices. If a product's market price is very high, it seems only reasonable that producers will be anxious to produce more of the product and even put workers on overtime or perhaps hire more workers to increase the quantity they can offer. Going further, it seems likely that producers of other products will switch their resources (farms, factories, labour or retail facilities) to the product that is in great demand.

On the other hand, if consumers are willing to pay only a very low price for a particular product, it's reasonable to expect that producers will switch to other products, thus reducing supply. A supply schedule (Exhibit A–8) and a supply curve (Exhibit A–9) for potatoes illustrate these ideas. This supply curve shows how many potatoes would be produced and offered for sale at each possible market price in a given month.

In the very short run (say, over a few hours, a day, or a week), a supplier may not be able to change the supply at all. In this situation, we would see a vertical supply curve. This situation is often relevant in the market for fresh

Point	Possible Market Price per 5 kg Bag	Number of Bags Sellers Will Supply per Month at Each Possible Market Price
A	£1.60	17 000 000
B	1.30	14 000 000
C	1.00	11 000 000
D	0.70	8 000 000
E	0.40	3 000 000

Exhibit A–8
Supply Schedule for Potatoes (5 kg bags)

Note: This supply curve is for a month to emphasize that farmers might have some control over when they deliver their potatoes. There would be a different curve for each month.

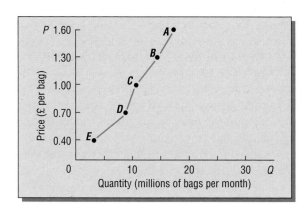

Exhibit A–9 Supply Curve for Potatoes (5 kg bags)

produce. Fresh strawberries, for example, continue to ripen, and a supplier wants to sell them quickly, preferably at a higher price but in any case they must be sold.

If the product is a service, it may not be easy to expand the supply in the short run. Additional hairdressers or medical doctors are not quickly trained and licensed, and they only have so much time to give each day. Further, the prospect of much higher prices in the near future cannot easily expand the supply of many services. For example, a hit play or an 'in' restaurant or nightclub is limited in the amount of 'product' it can offer at a particular time.

Elasticity of supply

The term *elasticity* is also used to describe supply curves. An extremely steep or almost vertical supply curve, often found in the short run, is called **inelastic supply** because the quantity supplied does not stretch much (if at all) if the price is raised. A flatter curve is called **elastic supply** because the quantity supplied does stretch more if the price is raised. A slightly upsloping supply curve is typical in longer-run market situations. Given more time, suppliers have a chance to adjust their offerings, and competitors may enter or leave the market.

DEMAND AND SUPPLY INTERACT TO DETERMINE THE SIZE OF THE MARKET AND PRICE LEVEL

Having treated market demand and supply forces separately, now we must bring them together to show their interaction. The *intersection* of these two forces determines the size of the market and the market price—at which point (price and quantity) the market is said to be in *equilibrium*.

The intersection of demand and supply is shown for the potato data discussed above. In Exhibit A–10, the demand curve for potatoes is now graphed against the supply curve in Exhibit A–9. In this potato market, demand is inelastic—the total revenue of all the potato producers would be greater at higher prices. But the market price is at the **equilibrium point**, where the quantity and the price sellers are willing to offer are equal to the quantity and price that buyers are willing to accept. The £1 equilibrium price for potatoes yields a smaller *total*

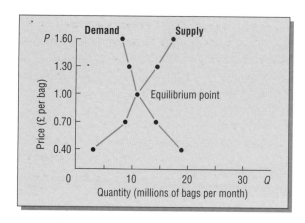

Exhibit A–10 Equilibrium of Supply and Demand for Potatoes (5 kg bags)

revenue to potato producers than a higher price would. This lower equilibrium price comes about because the many producers are willing to supply enough potatoes at the lower price. *Demand is not the only determiner of price level. Cost must also be considered—via the supply curve.*

Some consumers get a surplus

Presumably, a sale takes place only if both buyer and seller feel they will be better off after the sale. But sometimes the price a consumer pays in a sales transaction is less than what he or she would be willing to pay.

The reason for this is that demand curves are typically down-sloping, and some of the demand curve is above the equilibrium price. This is simply another way of showing that some customers would have been willing to pay more than the equilibrium price, if they had to. In effect, some of them are getting a bargain by being able to buy at the equilibrium price. Economists have traditionally called these bargains the **consumer surplus**, that is, the difference to consumers between the value of a purchase and the price they pay.

Some business critics assume that consumers do badly in any business transaction. In fact, sales take place only if consumers feel they are at least getting their money's worth. As we can see here, some are willing to pay much more than the market price.

DEMAND AND SUPPLY HELP US UNDERSTAND THE NATURE OF COMPETITION

The elasticity of demand and supply curves, and their interaction, help to predict the nature of competition a marketing manager is likely to face. For example, an extremely inelastic demand curve means that the manager will have much choice in strategy planning, and especially price setting. Apparently customers like the product and see few substitutes. They are willing to pay higher prices before cutting back much on their purchases.

Clearly, the elasticity of a firm's demand curves makes a big difference in strategy planning, but other factors also affect the nature of competition. Among these are the number and size of competitors and the uniqueness of each firm's marketing mix. Understanding these market situations is important because the freedom of a marketing manager, especially control over price, is greatly reduced in some situations.

A marketing manager operates in one of four kinds of market situations. We'll discuss three kinds: pure competition, oligopoly and monopolistic competition.

The fourth kind, monopoly, isn't found very often and is like monopolistic competition. The important dimensions of these situations are shown in Exhibit A–11.

When competition is pure
Many competitors offer about the same thing
Pure competition is a market situation that develops when a market has:

1. Homogeneous (similar) products.
2. Many buyers and sellers who have full knowledge of the market.
3. Ease of entry for buyers and sellers; that is, new firms have little difficulty starting in business and new customers can easily come into the market.

More or less pure competition is found in many agricultural markets. In the potato market, for example, there are thousands of small producers and they are in pure competition. Let's look more closely at these producers.

Although the potato market as a whole has a down-sloping demand curve, each of the many small producers in the industry is in pure competition, and each of them faces a flat demand curve at the equilibrium price. This is shown in Exhibit A–12. As shown at the right of Exhibit A–12, an individual producer can sell as many bags of potatoes as he chooses at £1—the market equilibrium price. The equilibrium price is determined by the quantity that all producers choose to sell given the demand curve they face. But a small producer has little effect on overall supply (or on the equilibrium price). If this individual farmer raises 1/10 000th of the quantity offered in the market, for example, you can see that there will be little effect if the farmer goes out of business, or doubles production.

The reason an individual producer's demand curve is flat is that the farmer probably couldn't sell any potatoes above the market price. And there is no point in selling below the market price! So, in effect, the individual producer has no control over price.

Markets tend to become more competitive

Not many markets are *purely* competitive. But many are close enough so we can talk about 'almost' pure competition situations—those in which the marketing manager has to accept the going price. Such highly competitive situations aren't limited to agriculture. Wherever *many* competitors sell *homogeneous* products, such as textiles, timber, coal, printing and laundry services, the demand curve seen by *each producer* tends to be flat.

| | Types of situations | | | |
Important dimensions	Pure competition	Oligopoly	Monopolistic competition	Monopoly
Uniqueness of each firm's product	None	None	Some	Unique
Number of competitors	Many	Few	Few to many	None
Size of competitors (compared to size of market)	Small	Large	Large to small	None
Elasticity of demand facing firm	Completely elastic	Kinked demand curve (elastic and inelastic)	Either	Either
Elasticity of industry demand	Either	Inelastic	Either	Either
Control of price by firm	None	Some (with care)	Some	Complete

Exhibit A–11 Some Important Dimensions Regarding Market Situations

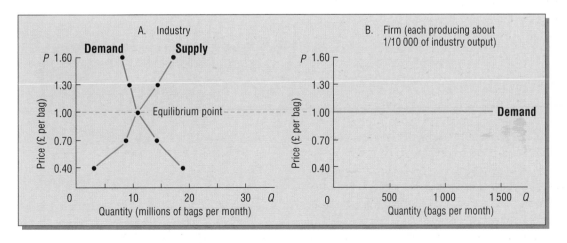

Exhibit A–12 Interaction of Demand and Supply in the Potato Industry and the Resulting Demand Curve Facing Individual Potato Producers

Markets tend to become more competitive, moving towards pure competition (except in oligopolies as shown below). On the way to pure competition, prices and profits are pushed down until some competitors are forced out of business. Eventually, in long-run equilibrium, the price level is only high enough to keep the survivors in business. No one makes any profit: they just cover costs.

When competition is oligopolistic
A few competitors offer similar things

Not all markets move towards pure competition. Some become oligopolies.

Oligopoly situations are special market situations that develop when a market has:

1. Essentially homogeneous products—such as basic industrial chemicals or petrol.
2. Relatively few sellers—or a few large firms and many smaller ones who follow the lead of the larger ones.
3. Fairly inelastic industry demand curves.

The demand curve facing each firm is unusual in an oligopoly situation. Although the industry demand curve is inelastic throughout the relevant range, the demand curve facing each competitor looks 'kinked.' See Exhibit A–13. The current market price is at the kink.

There is a market price because the competing firms watch each other carefully, and know it is wise to be at the kink. Each firm must expect that raising its own price above the market price will cause a big loss in sales. Few, if any, competitors will follow the price increase. So the firm's demand curve is relatively flat above the market price. If the firm lowers its price, it must expect competitors to follow. Given inelastic industry demand,

the firm's own demand curve is inelastic at lower prices, assuming it keeps 'its share' of this market at lower prices. Since lowering prices along such a curve will drop total revenue, the firm should leave its price at the kink, that is, the market price.

Actually, however, there are price fluctuations in oligopolistic markets. Sometimes this is caused by firms that don't understand the market situation and cut their prices to get business. In other cases, big increases in demand or supply change the basic nature of the situation and lead to price-cutting. Price cuts can be drastic, such as Du Pont's price cut of 25 per cent for Dacron. This happened when Du Pont decided that industry production capacity already exceeded demand, and more plants were due to start production.

It is important to keep in mind that oligopoly situations don't just apply to whole industries and national markets. Competitors who are focusing on the same local target market often face oligopoly situations. A suburban community might have several petrol stations, all of which provide essentially the same product. In this case, the 'industry' consists of the petrol stations competing with each other in the local product market.

As in pure competition, oligopolists face a long-run trend towards an equilibrium level, with profits driven towards zero. This may not happen immediately and a marketing manager may try to delay price competition by relying more on other elements in the marketing mix.

When competition is monopolistic
A price must be set

You can see why marketing managers want to avoid pure competition or oligopoly situations. They prefer a market in which they have more control. **Monopolistic**

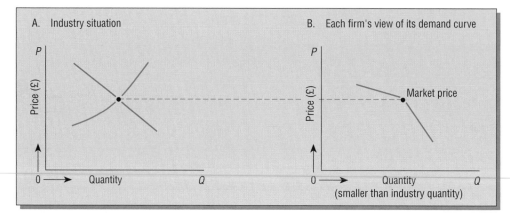

Exhibit A–13 Oligopoly—Kinked Demand Curve—Situation

competition is a market situation that develops when a market has:

1. Different (heterogeneous) products—in the eyes of some customers.
2. Sellers who feel they do have some competition in this market.

The word *monopolistic* means that each firm is trying to get control in its own little market. But the word *competition* means that there are still substitutes. The vigorous competition of a purely competitive market is reduced. Each firm has its own down-sloping demand curve. But the shape of the curve depends on the similarity of competitors' products and marketing mixes. Each monopolistic competitor has freedom—but not complete freedom—in its own market.

Judging elasticity will help set the price

Because a firm in monopolistic competition has its own down-sloping demand curve, it must make a decision about price level as part of its marketing strategy planning. Here, estimating the elasticity of the firm's own demand curve is helpful. If it is highly inelastic, the firm may decide to raise prices to increase total revenue. But if demand is highly elastic, this may mean many competitors with acceptable substitutes. Then the price may have to be set near that of the competition. And the marketing manager probably should try to develop a better marketing mix.

SUMMARY

The economist's traditional demand and supply analysis provides a useful tool for analysing the nature of demand and competition. It is especially important that you master the concepts of a demand curve and demand elasticity. How demand and supply interact helps to determine the size of a market and its price level. The interaction of supply and demand also helps to explain the nature of competition in different market situations. Three competitive situations were discussed: pure competition, oligopoly and monopolistic competition. The fourth kind, monopoly, isn't found very often and is like monopolistic competition.

The nature of supply and demand, and competition, is very important in marketing strategy planning. Careful study of this appendix will therefore build a good foundation for later work.

QUESTIONS AND PROBLEMS

1. Explain in your own words how economists look at markets and arrive at the 'law of diminishing demand.'
2. Explain what a demand curve is and why it is usually down-sloping. Then, give an example of a product for which the demand curve might not be down-sloping over some possible price ranges. Explain the reason for your choice.
3. What is the length of life of the typical demand curve? Illustrate your answer.
4. If the general market demand for men's shoes is fairly elastic, how does the demand for men's dress shoes compare to it? How does the demand curve for women's shoes compare to the demand curve for men's shoes?
5. If the demand for perfume is inelastic above and below the present price, should the price be raised? Why or why not?
6. If the demand for shrimp is highly elastic below the present price, should the price be lowered?

7. Discuss what factors lead to inelastic demand and supply curves. Are they likely to be found together in the same situation?
8. Why would a marketing manager prefer to sell a product that has no close substitutes? Are 'high profits' almost guaranteed?
9. If a manufacturer's well-known product is sold at the same price by many retailers in the same community, is this an example of pure competition? When a community has many small grocery stores, are they in pure competition? What characteristics are needed to have a purely competitive market?
10. List three products that are sold in purely competitive markets and three that are sold in monopolistically competitive markets. Do any of these products have anything in common? Can any generalizations be made about competitive situations and marketing mix planning?
11. Cite a local example of an oligopoly, explaining why it is an oligopoly.

APPENDIX B
Marketing Arithmetic

When You Finish This Appendix, You Should

1 Understand the components of an operating statement (profit and loss statement).

2 Know how to compute the stockturn rate.

3 Understand how operating ratios can help analyse a business.

4 Understand how to calculate mark-ups and mark-downs.

5 Understand how to calculate return on investment (ROI) and return on assets (ROA).

6 Understand the important new terms (shown in colour).

Marketing students must become familiar with the essentials of the language of business. Business people commonly use accounting terms when talking about costs, prices and profit. And using accounting data is a practical tool in analysing marketing problems.

THE OPERATING STATEMENT

An **operating statement** is a simple summary of the financial results of a company's operations over a specified period of time. *The main purpose of the operating statement is determining the net profit figure and presenting data to support that figure.* This is why the operating statement is often referred to as the *profit and loss statement.*

Exhibit B–1 shows an operating statement for a wholesale or retail business. The statement is complete and detailed so you will see the framework throughout the discussion, but the amount of detail on an operating statement is *not* standardized. Many companies use financial statements with much less detail than this one. They emphasize clarity and readability rather than detail. To really understand an operating statement, however, you must know about its components.

Exhibit B–1 An Operating Statement (profit and loss)

Smith Company
Operating Statement
For the Year Ended December 31, 199X

Gross sales			£540 000
Less Returns and allowances			40 000
Net sales			£500 000
Cost of sales			
Beginning inventory at cost		£80 000	
Purchases at billed cost	£310 000		
Less: Purchase discounts	40 000		
Purchases at net cost	270 000		
Plus freight-in	20 000		
Net cost of delivered purchase		290 000	
Cost of products available for sale		370 000	
Less: Ending inventory at cost		70 000	
Cost of sales			300 000
Gross margin (gross profit)			200 000
Expenses:			
Selling expenses:			
Sales salaries	60 000		
Advertising expenses	20 000		
Delivery expenses	20 000		
Total selling expenses	100 000		
Administrative expense:			
Office salaries	30 000		
Office supplies	10 000		
Miscellaneous administrative expense	5 000		
Total administrative expense		45 000	
General expense:			
Rent expense	10 000		
Miscellaneous general expenses	5 000		
Total general expense	15 000		
Total expenses			160 000
Net profit from operation			£ 40 000

Only three basic components

The basic components of an operating statement are *sales*—which come from the sale of goods and services; *costs*—which come from the making and selling process; and the balance, called *profit or loss*, which is just the difference between sales and costs. So there are only three basic components in the statement: sales, costs and profit (or loss). Other items on an operating statement are there only to provide supporting details.

Time period covered may vary

There is no one time period an operating statement covers. Rather, statements are prepared to satisfy the needs of a particular business. This may be at the end of each day or at the end of each week. Usually, however, an operating statement summarizes results for one month, three months, six months or a full year. Since the time period does vary, this information is included in the heading of the statement as follows:

SMITH COMPANY
Operating Statement
For the (Period) Ended (Date)

Also, see Exhibit B–1.

Management uses of operating statements

Before going on to a more detailed discussion of the components of our operating statement, let's think about some of the uses for such a statement. Exhibit B–1 shows that a lot of information is presented in a clear and concise manner. With this information, a manager can easily find the relation of net sales to the cost of sales, the gross margin, expenses and net profit. Opening and closing inventory figures are available, as is the amount spent during the period for the purchase of goods for resale. Total expenses are listed to make it easier to compare them with previous statements, and to help control these expenses.

All this information is important to a company's managers. Assume that a particular company prepares monthly operating statements. A series of these statements is a valuable tool for directing and controlling the business. By comparing results from one month to the next, managers can uncover unfavourable trends in the sales, costs or profit areas of the business and take any needed action.

A skeleton statement gets down to essential details

Refer to Exhibit B–1 and begin to analyse this seemingly detailed statement to get first-hand knowledge of the components of the operating statement.

As a first step, take all the items that have amounts extended to the third, or right-hand, column. Using these items only, the operating statement looks like this:

Gross sales	£540 000
Less: Returns and allowances	40 000
Net sales	500 000
Less: Cost of sales	300 000
Gross margin	200 000
Less: Total expenses	160 000
Net profits (loss)	£40 000

Is this a complete operating statement? The answer is yes. This skeleton statement differs from Exhibit B–1 only in supporting detail. All the basic components are included. In fact, the only items we must list to have a complete operating statement are:

Net sales	£500 000
Less: Costs	460 000
Net profit (loss)	£40 000

These three items are the essentials of an operating statement. All other subdivisions or details are just useful additions.

Meaning of sales

Now let's define the meaning of the terms in the skeleton statement.

The first item is sales. What do we mean by sales? The term gross sales is the total amount charged to all customers during some time period. However, there is always some customer dissatisfaction, or errors in ordering and shipping goods. This results in returns and allowances, which reduce gross sales. A return occurs when a customer sends back purchased products. The company either refunds the purchase price or allows the customer credit on other purchases. An allowance occurs when a customer is not satisfied with a purchase for some reason. The company gives a price reduction on the original invoice (bill), but the customer keeps the goods and services.

These refunds and price reductions must be considered when the firm computes its net sales figure for the period. Really, we're only interested in the revenue the company manages to keep. This is net sales—the actual sales the company receives. Therefore, all reductions, refunds, cancellations and so forth made because of returns and allowances, are deducted from the original total (gross sales) to get net sales. This is shown below:

Gross sales	£540 000
Less: Returns and allowances	40 000
Net sales	£500 000

Meaning of cost of sales

The next item in the operating statement—cost of sales—is the total value (at cost) of the sales during the period. We'll discuss this computation later. Meanwhile, note that after we obtain the cost of sales figure, we subtract it from the net sales figure to get the gross margin.

Meaning of gross margin and expenses

Gross margin (gross profit) is the money left to cover the expenses of selling the products and operating the business. Firms hope that a profit will be left after subtracting these expenses.

Selling expense is commonly the major expense below the gross margin. Note that in Exhibit B–1 expenses are all the remaining costs subtracted from the gross margin to get the net profit. The expenses in this case are the selling, administrative and general expenses. (Note that the cost of purchases and cost of sales are not included in this total expense figure—they were subtracted from net sales earlier to get the gross margin. Note also that some accountants refer to cost of sales as cost of goods sold.)

Net profit, at the bottom of the statement, is what the company earned from its operations during a particular period. It is the amount left after the cost of sales and the expenses are subtracted from net sales. Net sales and net profit are not the same. Many firms have large sales and no profits: they may even have losses. That is why understanding costs, and controlling them, is important.

DETAILED ANALYSIS OF SECTIONS OF THE OPERATING STATEMENT

Cost of sales for a wholesale or retail company

The cost of sales section includes details that are used to find the cost of sales (£300 000 in our example).

In Exhibit B–1, you can see that beginning and ending inventory, purchases, purchase discounts and freight-in are all necessary to calculate costs of sales. If we pull the cost of sales section from the operating statement, it looks like this:

Cost of sales:		
Beginning inventory at cost		£80 000
Purchases at billed cost	£310 000	
Less: Purchase discounts	40 000	
Purchases at net cost	270 000	
Plus: Freight-in	20 000	
Net cost of delivered purchases		290 000
Cost of goods available for sale		370 000
Less: Ending inventory at cost		70 000
Cost of sales		£300 000

Cost of sales is the cost value of what is *sold*—not the cost of goods on hand at any given time.

Inventory figures merely show the cost of goods on hand at the beginning and end of the period the statement covers. These figures may be obtained by physically counting goods on hand on these dates, or estimated from perpetual inventory records that show the inventory balance at any given time. The methods used to determine the inventory should be as accurate as possible because these figures affect the cost of sales during the period and net profit.

The net cost of delivered purchases must include freight charges and purchase discounts received because these items affect the money actually spent to buy goods and bring them to the place of business. A purchase discount is a reduction of the original invoice amount for some business reason. For example, a cash discount may be given for prompt payment of the amount due. We subtract the total of such discounts from the original invoice cost of purchases to get the *net* cost of purchases. To this figure we add the freight charges for bringing the goods to the place of business. This gives the net cost of *delivered* purchases. When we add the net cost of delivered purchases to the beginning inventory at cost, we have the total cost of goods available for sale during the period. If we now subtract the ending inventory at cost from the cost of the goods available for sale, we get the cost of sales.

One important point should be noted about cost of sales. The way the value of inventory is calculated varies from one company to another and can cause significant differences in the cost of sales and the operating statement. (See any basic accounting textbook for how the various inventory valuation methods work.)

Cost of sales for a manufacturing company

Exhibit B–1 shows the way the manager of a wholesale or retail business arrives at cost of sales. Such a business *purchases* finished products and resells them. In a manufacturing company, the purchases section of this operating statement is replaced by a section called cost of production. This section includes purchases of raw materials and parts, direct and indirect labour costs and factory overhead charges (such as heat, light and power) that are necessary to produce finished products. The cost of production is added to the beginning finished products inventory to arrive at the cost of products available for sale. Often, a separate cost of production statement is prepared, and only the total cost of production is shown in the operating statement. See Exhibit B–2 for an illustration of the cost of sales section of an operating statement for a manufacturing company.

Expenses

Expenses go below the gross margin. They usually include the costs of selling and the costs of administering the business. They do not include the cost of sales, either purchased or produced.

There is no right method for classifying the expense accounts or arranging them on the operating statement. They can just as easily be arranged alphabetically or according to amount, with the largest placed at the top and so on down the line. In a business of any size, though, it is clearer to group the expenses in some way and use subtotals by groups for analysis and control purposes. This was done in Exhibit B–1.

Summary on operating statements

The statement presented in Exhibit B–1 contains all the major categories in an operating statement, together with a normal amount of supporting detail. Further detail can be added to the statement under any of the major categories without changing the nature of the statement. The amount of detail is normally determined by how the statement will be used. A shareholder may be given a sketchy operating statement, while the one prepared for internal company use may have a lot of detail.

COMPUTING THE STOCKTURN RATE

A detailed operating statement can provide the data needed to compute the stockturn rate—a measure of the number of times the average inventory is sold during a year. Note that the stockturn rate is related to the *turnover during a year*—not the length of time covered by a particular operating statement.

Cost of sales		
Finished products inventory (beginning)	£ 20 000	
Cost of production (Schedule 1)	100 000	
Total cost of finished products available for sale	120 000	
Less: Finished products inventory (ending)	30 000	
Cost of sales	£90 000	
Schedule 1, Schedule of cost of production		
Beginning work in process inventory		15 000
Raw materials:		
Beginning raw materials inventory	10 000	
Net cost of delivered purchases	80 000	
Total cost of materials available for use	90 000	
Less: Ending raw materials inventory	15 000	
Cost of materials placed in production	75 000	
Direct labour	20 000	
Manufacturing expenses:		
Indirect labour	£4 000	
Maintenance and repairs	3 000	
Factory supplies	1 000	
Heat, light and power	2 000	
Total manufacturing expenses		10 000
Total manufacturing costs		105 000
Total work in process during period		120 000
Less: Ending work in process inventory		20 000
Cost of production		£100 000

Exhibit B–2 Cost of Sales Section of an Operating Statement for a Manufacturing Firm

CASES

1. McDonald's 'Seniors' Restaurant

Suzanne Drolet is manager of a McDonald's restaurant in a city with many 'seniors.' She has noticed that some senior citizens have become not just regular patrons—but patrons who come for breakfast and stay on until about 3 p.m. Many of these older customers were attracted initially by a monthly breakfast special for people aged 55 and older. The meal costs £1.99, and refills of coffee are free. Every fourth Monday, between 100 and 150 seniors jam Suzanne's McDonald's for the special offer. But now almost as many of them are coming every day—turning the fast-food restaurant into a meeting place. They sit for hours with a cup of coffee, chatting with friends. On most days, as many as 100 will stay from one to four hours.

Suzanne's employees have been very friendly to the seniors, calling them by their first names and visiting with them each day. In fact, Suzanne's McDonald's is a happy place—with her employees developing close relationships with the seniors. Some employees have even visited customers who have been hospitalized. 'You know,' Suzanne says, 'I really get attached to the customers. They're like my family. I really care about these people'. They are all 'friends' and it is part of McDonald's corporate philosophy (as reflected in its Web site, www.mcdonalds.com) to be friendly with its customers and to give back to the communities it serves.

These older customers are an orderly group—and very friendly to anyone who comes in. Further, they are neater than most customers, and carefully clean up their tables before they leave. Nevertheless, Suzanne is beginning to wonder if anything should be done about her growing 'non-fast-food' clientele. There's no crowding problem yet, during the time when the seniors like to come. But if the size of the senior citizen group continues to grow, crowding could become a problem. Further, Suzanne is concerned that her restaurant might come to be known as an 'old people's' restaurant—which might discourage some younger customers. And if customers felt the restaurant was crowded, some might feel that they wouldn't get fast service. On the other hand, a place that seems busy might be seen as 'a good place to go' and a 'friendly place.'

Suzanne also worries about the image she is projecting. McDonald's is a fast-food restaurant (there are over 23 000 of them in 109 countries), and normally customers are expected to eat and run. Will allowing people to stay and visit change the whole concept? In the extreme, Suzanne's McDonald's might become more like a café where the customers are never rushed—and feel very comfortable about lingering over coffee for an hour or two! Suzanne knows that the amount her senior customers spend is similar to the average customer's purchase—but the seniors do use the facilities for a much longer time. However, most of the older customers leave McDonald's by 11:30—before the noon crowd comes in.

Suzanne is also concerned about another possibility. If catering to seniors is OK, then should she do even more with this age group? In particular, she is considering offering bingo games during the slow morning hours—9 a.m. to 11 a.m. Bingo is popular with some seniors, and this could be a new revenue source—beyond the extra food and drink purchases that probably would result. She figures she could charge £5 per person for the two-hour period and run it with two under-utilized employees. The prizes would be coupons for purchases at her store (to keep it legal) and would amount to about two-thirds of the bingo receipts (at retail prices). The party room area of her McDonald's would be perfect for this use and could hold up to 150 persons.

Evaluate Suzanne Drolet's current strategy regarding senior citizens. Does this strategy improve this McDonald's image? What should she do about the senior citizen market—i.e., should she encourage, ignore or discourage her seniors? What should she do about the bingo idea? Explain.

2. Pillsbury's Häagen-Dazs

Jan Phillips is the newly hired ice cream product-market manager for the United States for Häagen-Dazs—the world's leading brand of super premium ice cream (now available in 28 countries) and the market leader in the US Pillsbury says Häagen-Dazs (www.pillsbury.com/main/brands/haagen) is profitable globally, with total sales in 1997 of more than $900 million. The company saw its sales grow rapidly during the 1990s, but now its markets are facing significant change and very aggressive competition. Phillips is responsible for Häagen-Dazs' ice cream strategy planning for the United States.

Other product-market managers are responsible for Europe, Japan and other global markets. Therefore, Phillips will be expected to focus only on the United States while 'everyone' will be watching her (and the United States) for clues about what may happen elsewhere.

Overall, ice cream sales in the US have been off 1 to 2 per cent in the last two years. Still, some new entries have made a big splash. Starbucks, the coffee king, is one such brand. Last year, in its first year in grocery-store freezer sections, its Frappuccino bars—in several flavours—were a big hit. In addition, the Starbucks brand quickly became the nation's top-selling premium coffee ice cream. Now it's expanding to other flavours. Häagen-Dazs, along with a few other super premium producers, is continuing to grow at rates of 2 to 3 per cent. But most other US super premium producers are reporting flat sales—and some are going out of business. The easy availability of super premium ice cream in supermarkets has hurt some of these producers who sell through ice-cream stores, which specialize in take-away cones, sundaes and small containers of ice cream. It is also thought that, at least in part, the decline in sales growth of super premium ice cream in the United States since the early 1990s is due to competition from other products such as lower-calorie yoghurts and low-fat ice cream.

Despite a real concern about healthy diets, Americans seem to swing back and forth in their yearnings for low fat and rich taste. There is some evidence that 'dessert junkies' who want to indulge without too much guilt are turning to low-fat frozen yoghurt and low-fat ice cream. This has encouraged a number of super premium ice cream competitors to offer these products too. Pillsbury's Häagen-Dazs, International Dairy Queen and Baskin Robbins are selling frozen yoghurt. And Kraft—which makes Frusen Glädjè, Edy's and Dreyer's Grand Ice Cream—is among many other ice-cream makers who are promoting gourmet versions of low-fat ice cream.

Because of the competition from low-fat products, Häagen-Dazs recently introduced a line of low-fat super premium ice cream. The new low-fat line contains no more than three grams of fat per serving. That compares with six times that or more grammes of fat in a half-cup serving of its full-fat versions. Häagen-Dazs believes that its low-fat super premium ice-cream is better tasting than other alternatives. Its belief is that 'people like to make every calorie count'. Having worked on the low-fat item for more than two years, it developed a process whereby a concentration of dairy proteins from lactose-reduced skim milk give a mouth-feel that approximates that of a higher-fat product. Häagen-Dazs sells its low-fat products in a variety of flavours.

Most ice-cream products are considered economy and regular brands—priced at $2 to $4 a half gallon. Super premium ice cream retails for $2.50 to $3.50 a pint, or $8 to $10 a half gallon. The suggested retail price for a pint of Häagen-Dazs is $3.09. The low-fat version is comparably priced to the full-fat product.

Many other US ice cream producers have turned to frozen yoghurt for growth. Frozen yoghurt sales were in a slump for a long time because many people didn't like the tart taste. But after the product was reformulated it started to win customers. The difference is that today's frozen yoghurt tastes more like ice cream.

The yoghurt market leader, TCBY Enterprises, Inc. (www.tcby.com), which had sales of only about $2 million in 1983, has risen to over $100 million in sales. It numbers 2800 stores worldwide and is franchised in over 60 countries. In the US, yoghurt makers are using aggressive promotion against ice cream. TCBY ads preach: 'Say goodbye to high calories—say goodbye to ice cream' and 'All the pleasure, none of the guilt'. And the ads for its non-fat frozen yoghurt emphasize: 'Say goodbye to fat and high calories with the great taste of TCBY Non-fat Frozen Yogurt.'

Baskin Robbins has introduced yoghurt in many of its US stores and has even changed its name to Baskin Robbins Ice Cream and Yoghurt. Häagen-Dazs also offers yoghurt in most of its stores.

Although the flurry of consumer interest in low-fat yoghurt and low-fat ice cream certainly created some new market opportunities, it is not clear how consumers will react to these products over the longer term. One reason is that many consumers who were initially excited about being able to buy a good tasting, low-fat frozen dessert have realized that low fat does not necessarily mean low calorie. In fact, Jan Phillips has been trying to identify a product that Häagen-Dazs could produce that would offer consumers great taste, low fat and low calories all at the same time. One possibility she is seriously considering is to introduce a line of sorbets based on exotic fruits like kiwi and mango and that use low-calorie sweeteners.

A sorbet is basically the same as sherbet, but European sorbets usually have an icy texture and include less milk. This is the sort of product that Jan Phillips has in mind. She thinks that it might have an upmarket appeal and also be different from what is already in the premium ice-cream case.

On the other hand, calling a product by a different name doesn't make it really new and different, and basic sherbet has been around for a long time and never been a big seller. Further, consumers don't think of sorbet in the same way that they think about a rich-tasting bowl of ice cream. You don't have to convince people that they might like premium ice cream. Sorbet, on the other hand, isn't something that consumers crave and make a special trip to buy.

Further, Phillips is very conscious that the Häagen-Dazs brand should stand for high quality and the best ingredients. Yet, it's not clear that consumers will think of sorbet as a premium product. Rather, they might just see it as ground-up ice with some flavouring thrown in. But, if sorbet isn't the right way to go with new-product development, how should Häagen-Dazs counter the competition from other low-fat ice-cream brands like Ben & Jerry's and other new entries to the super premium category like Starbucks?

Evaluate what is happening in the ice-cream market, especially regarding the apparent levelling off of super premium ice cream sales and the possibilities for growth of the sorbet market. Is Jan Phillips' idea about rolling out a low-cal fruit sorbet a good idea? Would it be better to use the Häagen-Dazs brand name or a different brand name? What else, if anything, would need to be different about the strategy? Why?

3. Republic Polymer Company

Gary Walden, a chemist in Republic Polymer's polymer resins laboratory, is trying to decide how hard to fight for the new product he has developed. Walden's job is to find new, more profitable applications for the company's present resin products—and his current efforts are running into unexpected problems.

During the last four years, Walden has been under heavy pressure from his managers to come up with an idea that will open up new markets for the company's foamed polystyrene.

Two years ago, Walden developed the 'foamed-dome concept'—a method of using foamed polystyrene to make dome-shaped roofs and other structures. He described the procedure for making domes as follows: The construction of a foamed dome involves the use of a specially designed machine that bends, places and bonds pieces of plastic foam together into a pre-determined dome shape. In forming a dome, the machine head is mounted on a boom, which swings around a pivot like the hands of a clock, laying and bonding layer upon layer of foam board in a rising spherical form.

According to Walden, polystyrene foamed boards have several advantages:

1. Foam board is stiff—but can be formed or bonded to itself by heat alone.
2. Foam board is extremely lightweight and easy to handle. It has good structural rigidity.
3. Foam board has excellent and permanent insulating characteristics. (In fact, the major use for foam board is as an insulator.)
4. Foam board provides an excellent base on which to apply a variety of surface finishes, such as a readily available concrete-based stucco that is durable and inexpensive.

Using his good selling abilities, Walden easily convinced his managers that his idea had potential.

According to a preliminary study by the marketing research department, the following were areas of construction that could be served by the domes:

1. Bulk storage.
2. Cold storage.
3. Educational construction.
4. Covers for industrial tanks.
5. Light commercial construction.
6. Planetariums.
7. Recreational construction (such as a golf-course driving range).

The marketing research study focused on uses for existing dome structures. Most of the existing domes are made of cement-based materials. The study showed that large savings would result from using foam boards—due to the reduction of construction time.

Because of the new technology involved, the company decided to do its own contracting (at least for the first four to five years). Walden thought this was necessary to make sure that no mistakes were made by inexperienced contractor crews. (For example, if not applied properly, the plastic may burn.)

After building a few domes in the United States to demonstrate the concept, Walden contacted some leading US architects. Reactions were as follows:

'It's very interesting, but we're not sure the fire marshall of Chicago would ever give his OK.'

'Your tests show that foamed domes can be protected against fires, but there are no *good* tests for unconventional building materials as far as I am concerned.'

'I like the idea, but foam board does not have the impact resistance of cement.'

'We design a lot of recreational facilities, and kids will find a way to poke holes in the foam.'

'Building codes in our area are written for wood and cement structures. Maybe we'd be interested if the codes change.'

After this unexpected reaction, management didn't know what to do. Walden still thinks they should go ahead with the project. He wants to build several more demonstration projects in the United States and at least three each in Europe and Japan to expose the concept in the global market. He thinks architects outside the United States may be more receptive to really new ideas. Further, he says, it takes time for potential users to 'see' and accept new ideas. He is sure that more exposure to more people will speed acceptance. And he is convinced that a few reports of well-constructed domes in leading trade papers and magazines will go a long way towards selling the idea. He is working on getting such reports right now. But his managers aren't sure they want to approve spending more money on 'his' project. His immediate boss is supportive, but the rest of the review board is less sure about more demonstration projects or going ahead at all—just in the United States or in global markets.

Evaluate how Republic Polymer got into the present situation. What should Gary Walden do? What should Walden's managers do? Explain.

4. Lilybank Lodge

Nestled in the high country of New Zealand's South Island is a getaway adventure playground aimed unashamedly at the world's very wealthy. Presidents, playboys and other such globe-trotters are the prime targets of this fledgling tourism business developed by Lilybank Lodge. The lodge offers this exclusive niche the opportunity of a secluded holiday in a little-known paradise. Guests, commonly under public scrutiny in their everyday lives, can escape such pressures at a hunting retreat designed specifically with their needs in mind.

A chance meeting between a New Zealand Department of Conservation investigator and the son of the former Indonesian president marked the beginning of this speciality tourist operation. Recognizing that 'filthy rich' public figures are constantly surrounded by security and seldom have the luxury of going anywhere incognito, the New Zealander, Gerard Olde-Olthof, suggested that he and his new friend purchase a high-country station and hunting-guide company that was for sale. Olde-Olthof believed that the facilities, and their secluded and peaceful environment, would make an ideal holiday haven for this elite group. His Indonesian partner concurred.

Olde-Olthof, who was by now the company's managing director, developed a carefully tailored package of goods and services for the property. Architecturally designed accommodations, including a game trophy room and eight guest rooms, were constructed using high-quality South Island furniture and fittings, to create the ambience necessary to attract and satisfy the demands of their special clientele.

Although New Zealand had an international reputation for being sparsely populated and green, Olde-Olthof knew that rich travellers frequently complained that local accommodations were below overseas standards. Since the price (NZ$700 a night) was not a significant variable for this target market, sumptuous guest facilities were built. These were designed to be twice the normal size of most hotel rooms, with double-glazed windows that revealed breathtaking views. Ten full-time staff and two seasonal guides were recruited to ensure that visitors received superior customized service, in fitting with the restrained opulence of the lodge.

The 28 000 hectares of original farmland that made up the retreat and backed on to the South Island's Mount Cook National Park, were converted into a big-game reserve. All merino sheep on the land were sold, and deer, elk, chamois and wapiti were brought in and released. This was a carefully considered plan. Olde-Olthof, the former conservationist, believed that financially and environmentally this was the correct decision. Not only do tourists, each staying for one week and taking part in safari shooting, inject as much cash into the business as the station's annual wool clip used to fetch, but the game does less harm to the environment than sheep. Cattle, however, once part of the original station, were left to graze on lower riverflat areas.

For those high-flying customers seeking less blood-thirsty leisure activities, Lilybank developed other product-line extensions. Horse-trekking, golfing on a nearby rural course (with no need for hordes of security forces), world-class photographic opportunities, helicopter trips around nearby Lake Tekapo, nature walks and other such activities formed part of the exclusive package.

While still in the early stages of operation, this retreat has already attracted a steady stream of visitors. To date the manager has relied solely on positive word of mouth, publicity, and public relations to draw in new customers. Given the social and business circles in which his potential target market moves, Olde-Olthof considers these to be the most appropriate forms of marketing communication. The only real concern for Lilybank Lodge has been the criticism of at least one New Zealand lobby group that the company is yet another example of local land passing into 'foreign' hands, and that New Zealanders are prevented from using the retreat and excluded from its financial returns. However, this unwelcome attention has been fairly short-lived.

Identify the likely characteristics of the market segment being targeted by the company. Why are most target customers likely to be foreigners rather than New Zealanders? Suggest what expectations target customers are likely to have regarding the quality, reliability and range of services. What are the implications for Lilybank Lodge? How difficult is it for Lilybank Lodge to undertake market research? Elaborate.

5. Sophia's Ristorante

Sophia Manderino, the owner and manager of Sophia's Ristorante, is reviewing the slow growth of her restaurant. She's also thinking about the future and wondering if she should change her strategy. In particular, she is wondering if she should join a fast-food or family restaurant franchise chain. Several are located near her, but there are many franchisors without local restaurants. After doing some research on the Internet, she has learned that with help from the franchisers, some of these places gross £500 000 to £1 million a year. Of course, she would have to follow someone else's strategy—and thereby lose her independence, which she doesn't like to think about. But those sales figures do sound good, and she has also heard that the return to the owner-manager (including salary) can be over £100 000 per year. She has also considered putting a web page for Sophia's Ristorante on the Internet but is not sure how that will help.

Sophia's Ristorante is a fairly large restaurant—about 2000 square feet—located in the centre of a small shopping centre completed early in 1997. Sophia's sells mainly full-course 'home-cooked' Italian-style dinners (no bar) at moderate prices. In addition to Sophia's restaurant, other businesses in the shopping mall include a supermarket, a hair salon, a drinks store, a video rental store and a vacant space that used to be a hardware store. The hardware store failed when a warehouse-style operation located nearby. Sophia has learned that a pizzeria is considering locating there soon. She wonders how that competition will affect her. Ample parking space is available in the shopping mall, which is located in a residential section of a growing suburb, along a heavily travelled major traffic route.

Sophia graduated from a nearby university and has lived in this town with her husband and two children for many years. She has been self-employed in the restaurant business since her graduation from university in 1976. Her most recent venture—before opening Sophia's—was a large restaurant that she operated successfully with her brother from 1987 to 1993. In 1993, Sophia sold out her share because of illness. Following her recovery, she was anxious for something to do and opened the present restaurant in April 1997. Sophia feels her plans for the business and her opening were well thought out. When she was ready to start her new restaurant, she looked at several possible locations before finally deciding on the present one. Sophia explained: 'I looked everywhere, but here I particularly noticed the heavy traffic when I first looked at it. So obviously the potential is here.'

Having decided on the location, Sophia signed a 10-year lease with option to renew for 10 more years, and then eagerly attacked the problem of outfitting the almost empty store space in the newly constructed building. She tiled the floor, put in walls of wood, installed plumbing and electrical fixtures and an extra cloakroom, and purchased the necessary restaurant equipment. All this cost £100 000—which came from her own cash savings. She then spent an additional £1500 for glassware, £2000 for an initial food stock, and £2125 to advertise Sophia's Ristorante's opening in the local newspaper. The paper serves the whole area, so the £2125 bought only three quarter-page ads. These expenditures also came from her own personal savings. Next she hired five waiting staff at £175 a week and one chef at £350 a week. Then, with £24 000 cash reserve for the business, she was ready to open. Reflecting her sound business sense, Sophia knew she would need a substantial cash reserve to fall back on until the business got on its feet. She expected this to take about one year. She had no expectations of getting rich overnight. (Her husband—a teacher—was willing to support the family until the restaurant caught on.)

The restaurant opened in April and by August had a weekly gross revenue of only £1800. Sophia was a little discouraged with this, but she was still able to meet all her operating expenses without investing any new money in the business. By September business was still slow, and Sophia had to invest an additional £2000 in the business just to survive.

Business had not improved in November, and Sophia stepped up her advertising—hoping this would help. In December, she spent £800 of her cash reserve for radio advertising—10 late-evening spots on a news programme at a local radio station. Sophia also spent $1 100 more during the next several weeks for some newspaper ads.

By April 1998, the situation had begun to improve, and by June her weekly gross was up to between £2100 and £2300. By March 1999, the weekly gross had risen to about £2800. Sophia increased the working hours of her staff six to seven hours a week—and added another cook to handle the increasing number of customers. Sophia was more optimistic for the future because she was finally doing a little better than breaking even. Her full-time involvement seemed to be paying off. She had not put any new money into the business since summer 1998 and expected business to continue to rise. She had not yet taken any salary for herself, even though she had built up a small surplus of about £6000. Instead, she planned to put in a bigger air-conditioning system at a cost of £4000—and was also planning to use what salary she might have taken for herself to hire two new waiting staff to handle the growing volume of business. And she saw that if business increased much more she would have to add another chef.

Evaluate Sophia's past and present marketing strategy. What should she do now? Should she seriously consider joining some franchise chain?

6. Runners World

Sue Koenig, owner of the Runners World, is trying to decide what she should do with her retail store and how committed she should be to her current target market.

Sue is 36 years old, and she started her Runners World retail store in 1987 when she was only 24 years old. She was a nationally ranked runner herself—and felt that the growing interest in jogging offered real potential for a store that provided serious runners with the shoes and advice they needed. The jogging boom quickly turned Runners World into a profitable business selling upmarket running shoes—and Sue made a very good return on her investment for the first 10 years. From 1987 until 1997, Sue emphasized Nike shoes, which were well accepted and seen as top quality. Nike's aggressive promotion and quality shoes resulted in a positive image that made it possible to get a $5 to $7 per pair premium for Nike shoes. Good volume and good margins resulted in attractive profits for Sue Koenig.

Committing so heavily to Nike seemed like a good idea when its marketing and engineering were the best available. In addition to running shoes, Nike also had other athletic shoes Sue could sell. So, even though they were not her primary focus, Sue did stock other Nike shoes including walking shoes, shoes for aerobic exercise, basketball shoes, tennis shoes and cross-trainers. However, recently sales have flattened out for a number of reasons.

One of those reasons is tied to the activity of running itself. More and more people have found that jogging isn't just hard work—it's hard on the body, especially the knees. So many runners have switched to other less demanding exercise programmes.

Another factor is consumer interest in fashion and style rather than the engineering in the shoes they buy. Many consumers who don't really do any serious exercise are still buying running shoes as their day-to-day casual shoes, but they are buying fashionable, instead of functional, ones. As a result, many department stores, discount stores, and regular shoe stores have put more and more emphasis on athletic shoes in their product assortment. Teenagers and young adults have extended their interest in shoes from athletic hightops like Air Jordan X111 to a wider range of styles including Vans, Airwalks, Etnies, Skechers, Lugz and Timberland. The outdoorsy appeal of Timberland has been particularly effective. It is estimated that 15 to 20 per cent of the shoe business 'went brown' in 1997.

But, in addition to Timberland's brown shoe phenomenon, is the popularity of new sports like boarding. Athletic footwear geared to boarders—such as Vans, Airwalks and Etnies—chalked up annual sales gains of 20 to 50 per cent in 1996 and 1997. The shoes are cheap: a pair of Vans costs £45 to £50 compared to Nike's retail average of £70 to £75. They have dimpled rubber soles instead of waffled ones, a discreet logo instead of a swoosh, along with simple colours and designs.

Increased competition is a basic problem. Although Nike continues to command 47 per cent of the athletic shoe business in the US, Reebok International has a 16 per cent share and Adidas is at 5 per cent. However, a rejuvenated Adidas has been coming on strong and could overtake Reebok. It is already regaining market share lost to LA Gear and Fila. Thus, the athletic shoe business has become very, very competitive. Even for serious runners, other brands besides Nike have cultivated a fine image. New Balance is one such brand that has made a lot of headway targeting baby boomers instead of teens and Generation X. So it may be advantageous for Sue to not be so predominantly tied to one brand.

There is also more competition from the proliferation of retail outlets carrying athletic shoes and clothing. In Sue's area, there are a number of local and on-line retail chains offering lower-cost and lower-quality versions of similar shoes as well as related fashion wear. Other chains, like Foot Locker, have focused their promotion and product lines on specific target markets. Still, all of them (including Sue's Runners World, the local chains and Foot Locker) are scrambling to catch up with rival category killers whose selections are immense.

Another problem is the backlash against Nike itself. Many people think the Nike brand has become too common to be cool. The over-hype seems to be turning off important core customers who are gravitating to other brands. Part of this turnoff is also based on Nike's 'bad boy' image. Nike has been accused of using paid endorsers to sell overpriced sneakers to underprivileged kids, and of operating sweatshops that exploit Asian workers. Nike has done a lot of good work, but its recent publicity has been mostly bad.

Sue is not certain what to do. Although sales have dropped, she is still making a reasonable profit and has a relatively good base of repeat customers—primarily serious runners. An important question that Sue is debating is whether there really is a big enough market in her area for serious athletic shoes. Further, is there a market for the Nike version of these shoes that tend to emphasize function over fashion? Sue's belief is that runners seldom switch brands after settling on something they like. Still, she is dismayed by Nike's recent strategy. Instead of responding with hotter products or lower prices when its sales started to decline, Nike tried to raise its prices ahead of inflation. Retailers, like Sue, stocked up but consumers weren't buying.

Still, Sue knows there is power behind the Nike hype and with Nike's recent push into sports equipment, it means that the brand has a commanding presence in the shoe, sportswear and sports-equipment markets. Would it be better for her to try to develop a plan that takes advantage of Nike's strength in all three markets?

She also worries that she'll lose the loyalty of her repeat customers if she shifts the store further away from her running 'niche' towards more fashionable athletic shoes or towards fashionable casual wear. Yet, athletic wear—women's, in particular—has come a long way in recent years. Designers like Donna Karan, Calvin Klein, Georgio Armani and Ralph Lauren are part of the fast-growing women's wear business. These days, young people—regardless of gender—have an obsession for sports and that carries over into athletic wear. Not only does athletic wear include designer and sports-licensed clothing, but also what is described as 'attitude wear'. Attitude wear includes T-shirts and other clothing that features in-your-face sports-inspired slogans. Marketers, large and small, are gearing up to tap this segment.

So, Sue is trying to decide if there is anything else she can do to better promote her current store and product line, or if she should think about changing her strategy in a more dramatic way. At a minimum, that would involve retraining her current salespeople and perhaps hiring more fashion-oriented salespeople. But a real shift in emphasis would require that Sue make some hard decisions about her target market and her whole marketing mix. She's got some flexibility—it's not like she's a manufacturer of shoes with a big investment in a factory that can't be changed. On the other hand, she's not certain she's ready for a big change—especially a change that would mean starting over again from scratch. She started Runners World because she was interested in running—and felt she had something special to offer. Now, she worries that she's just clutching at straws without a real focus—or any obvious competitive advantage. She also knows that she is already much more successful than she ever dreamed when she started her business—and in her heart she wonders if she wasn't just spoiled by growth that came fast and easy at the start.

Evaluate Sue Koenig's present strategy. Evaluate the alternative strategies she is considering. Is her primary problem her emphasis on running shoes, her emphasis on Nike products, or is it something else? What should she do? Why?

7. Paper Supplies Corporation*

Diane Chin, marketing manager for Paper Supplies Corporation, must decide whether she should permit her largest customer to buy some of Paper Supplies' commonly used file folders under the customer's brand rather than Paper Supplies' own FILEX brand. She is afraid that if she refuses, this customer—Office Centre—will go to another file folder producer and Paper Supplies will lose this business.

Office Centre is a major distributor of office supplies and has already managed to put its own brand on more than 45 high-sales-volume office supply products. It distributes these products—as well as the branded products of many manufacturers—through its nationwide distribution network, which includes 150 retail stores. Now Ken Sawyer, vice president of marketing for Office Centre, is seeking a line of file folders similar in quality to Paper Supplies' FILEX brand, which now has over 60 per cent of the market.

This is not the first time that Office Centre has asked Paper Supplies to produce a file folder line for Office Centre. On both previous occasions, Diane Chin turned down the requests and Office Centre continued to buy. In fact, Office Centre not only continued to buy the file folders but also the rest of Paper Supplies' lines. And total sales continued to grow as Office Centre built new stores. It accounts for about 30 per cent of Diane Chin's

business. And FILEX brand file folders account for about 35 per cent of this volume.

In the past Paper Supplies consistently refused such dealer-branding requests—as a matter of corporate policy. This policy was set some years ago because of a desire (1) to avoid excessive dependence on any one customer and (2) to sell its own brands so that its success is dependent on the quality of its products rather than just a low price. The policy developed from a concern that if it started making products under other customers' brands, those customers could shop around for a low price and the business would be very fickle. At the time the policy was set, Diane Chin realized that it might cost Paper Supplies some business. But it was felt wise, nevertheless, to be better able to control the firm's future.

Paper Supplies Corporation has been in business 28 years and now has a sales volume of $40 million. Its primary products are file folders, file markers and labels, and a variety of indexing systems. Paper Supplies offers such a wide range of size, colour and type that no competition can match it in its part of the market. About 40 per cent of Paper Supplies' file folder business is in specialized lines such as: files for oversized blueprint and engineering drawings; see-through files for medical markets; and greaseproof and waterproof files for marine, oilfield, and other hazardous environmental markets. Paper Supplies' competitors are mostly small paper converters. But excess capacity in the industry is substantial, and these converters are always hungry for orders and willing to cut price. Further, the raw materials for the FILEX line of file folders are readily available.

Paper Supplies' distribution system consists of 10 regional stationery suppliers (40 per cent of total sales), Office Centre (30 per cent), and more than 40 local stationers who have wholesale and retail operations (30 per cent). The 10 regional stationers each have about six branches, while the local stationers each have one wholesale and three or four retail locations. The regional suppliers sell directly to large corporations and to some retailers. In contrast, Office Centre's main volume comes from sales to local businesses and casual customers at its 150 retail stores.

Diane Chin has a real concern about the future of the local stationers' business. Some are seriously discussing the formation of buying groups to obtain volume discounts from vendors and thus compete more effectively with Office Centre's 50 retail stores, the large regionals and the superstore chains, which are spreading rapidly. These chains—for example, Staples, Office World, Office Max and Office Square—operate stores of 1500 to 1900 square metres (i.e. large stores compared to the usual office supply stores) and let customers wheel through high-stacked shelves to supermarketlike checkout counters. These chains generate £5 million to

*Adapted from a case study written by Professor Hardy, Universtity of Western Onatrio, Canda

£15 million in annual business—stressing convenience, wide selection, and much lower prices than the typical office supply retailers. They buy directly from manufacturers, such as Paper Supplies, bypassing wholesalers like Office Centre. It is likely that the growing pressure from these chains is causing Office Centre to renew its proposal to buy a file line with its own name.

None of Diane's other accounts is nearly as effective in retailing as Office Centre—which has developed a good reputation in every major city in the country. Office Centre's profits have been the highest in the industry. Further, its brands are almost as well known as those of some key producers—and its expansion plans are aggressive. And now, these plans are being pressured by the fast-growing superstores—which are already knocking out many local stationers.

Diane is sure that Paper Supplies' brands are well entrenched in the market, despite the fact that most available money has been devoted to new-product development rather than promotion of existing brands. But Diane is concerned that if Office Centre brands its own file folders it will sell them at a discount and may even bring the whole market price level down. Across all the lines of file folders, Diane is averaging a 35 per cent gross margin, but the commonly used file folders sought by Office Centre are averaging only a 20 per cent gross margin. And cutting this margin further does not look very attractive to Diane.

Diane is not sure whether Office Centre will continue to sell Paper Supplies' FILEX brand of folders along with Office Centre's own file folders if Office Centre is able to find a source of supply. Office Centre's history has been to sell its own brand and a major brand side by side, especially if the major brand offers high quality and has strong brand recognition.

Diane is having a really hard time deciding what to do about the existing branding policy. Paper Supplies has excess capacity and could easily handle the Office Centre business. And she fears that if she turns down this business, Office Centre will just go elsewhere and its own brand will cut into Paper Supplies' existing sales at Office Centre stores. Further, what makes Office Centre's offer especially attractive is that Paper Supplies' variable manufacturing costs would be quite low in relation to any price charged to Office Centre—i.e. there are substantial economies of scale, so the 'extra' business could be very profitable—if Diane doesn't consider the possible impact on the FILEX line. This Office Centre business will be easy to get, but it will require a major change in policy, which Diane will have to sell to Paul Jennings, Paper Supplies' president. This may not be easy. Paul is primarily interested in developing new and better products so the company can avoid the 'commodity end of the business'.

Evaluate Paper Supplies' current strategy. What should Diane Chin do about Office Centre's offer? Explain.

8. Mixed Media Technologies

Josh Sullivan, manager of Mixed Media Technologies, is looking for ways to increase profits. But he's turning cautious after the poor results of his last effort—during the previous Christmas season. Mixed Media Technologies (MMT), is located along a busy street about two miles from the centre of a city of 1 million and near a large university. It sells a wide variety of products used for its different types of multimedia presentations. Its lines include high-quality still, video and digital cameras, colour scanners for use with computers, and projection equipment—including 35-mm slide projectors, overhead projectors and electronic projectors that produce large-screen versions of computer output. Most of the sales of this specialized equipment are made to local schools for classroom use, to industry for use in research and sales, and to the university for use in research and instruction.

MMT also offers a good selection of production-quality video media (including hard-to-get betacam tapes and recordable CDs), specialized supplies (such as the acetates used with full-colour computer printers), video and audio editing equipment, and a specialized video editing service. Instead of just duplicating videos on a mass production basis, MMT gives each video editing job individual attention—to add an audio track or incorporate computer graphics as requested by a customer. This service is really appreciated by local firms that need help producing high-quality videos—for example, for training or sales applications.

To encourage the school and industrial trade, MMT offers a graphics consultation service. If a customer wants to create a video or computerized presentation, professional advice is readily available. In support of this free service, MMT carries a full line of computer software for multimedia presentations and graphics work.

MMT has four full-time shop assistants and two outside sales representatives. The sales representatives call on business firms, attend trade shows, make presentations for schools and help both present and potential customers in their use and choice of multimedia materials. Most purchases are delivered by the sales representatives or the store's delivery van. Many orders come in by phone or mail.

The people who make most of the over-the-counter purchases are (1) serious amateurs and (2) some professionals who prepare videos or computerized presentation materials on a fee basis. MMT gives price discounts of up to 25 per cent of the suggested retail price to customers who buy more than £2000 worth of goods per year. Most regular customers qualify for the discount.

In recent years, many amateur photographers have started to buy relatively inexpensive new digital cameras to capture family pictures. Frequently, the buyer is a computer user who wants to use the computer as a digital darkroom—and the cameras now available make this easy. MMT has not previously offered the lower-priced and lower-quality digital models such buyers commonly want. But Josh Sullivan knew that lots of such digital cameras were bought and felt that there ought to be a good opportunity to expand sales during the Christmas gift-giving season. Therefore, he planned a special pre-Christmas sale of two of the most popular brands of digital cameras and discounted the prices to competitive discount store levels—about £600 for one and £900 for the other. To promote the sale, he posted large signs in the shop windows and ran ads in a Christmas gift-suggestion edition of the local newspaper. This edition appeared each Wednesday during the four weeks before Christmas. At these prices and with this promotion, Josh hoped to sell at least 100 cameras. However, when the Christmas returns were in, total sales were five cameras. Josh was extremely disappointed with these results—especially because trade experts suggested that sales of digital cameras in these price and quality ranges were up 200 per cent over last year—during the Christmas selling season.

Evaluate what Mixed Media Technologies is doing and what happened with the special promotion. What should Josh Sullivan do to increase sales and profits?

9. Enviro Pure Water*

Manish (Manny) Krishna established his company, Enviro Pure Water (Enviro), to market a product designed to purify drinking water. The product, branded as the PURITY II Naturalizer Water Unit, is produced by Environmental Control, a corporation that focuses primarily on water purification and filtering products for industrial markets.

Enviro Pure Water is a small but growing business. Manny started the business with initial capital of only $20 000—which came from his savings and loans from several relatives. Manny manages the company himself. He has a secretary and six full-time salespeople. In addition, he employs two college students part-time; they make telephone calls to find prospective customers and set up appointments for a salesperson to demonstrate the unit in the customer's home. By holding spending to a minimum, Manny has kept the firm's monthly operating budget at only $4500—and most of that goes for rent, his secretary's salary, and other necessities like computer supplies and telephone bills.

The PURITY II system uses a reverse osmosis purification process. Reverse osmosis is the most effective technology known for improving drinking water. The device is certified by the Environmental Protection Agency to reduce levels of most foreign substances, including mercury, rust, sediment, arsenic, lead, phosphate, bacteria and most insecticides.

Each PURITY II unit consists of a high-quality 1-micron sediment removal cartridge, a carbon filter, a sediment filter, a housing, a tap and mounting hardware. The compact system fits under a kitchen sink or a drinks bar sink. An Enviro salesperson can typically install the PURITY II in about a half hour. Installation involves attaching the unit to the cold-water supply line, drilling a hole in the sink, and fastening the special tap. It works equally well with water from a municipal system or well water and it can purify up to 5 litres daily. Enviro sells the PURITY II to consumers for $395, which includes installation.

The system has no moveable parts or electrical connections and it has no internal metal parts that will corrode or rust. However, the system does use a set of filters that must be replaced after about two years. Enviro sells the replacement filters for $80. Taking into consideration the cost of the filters, the system provides water at a cost of approximately $0.19 per litre for the average family.

There are two major benefits from using the PURITY II system. First, water treated by this system tastes better. Blind taste tests confirm that most consumers can tell the difference between water treated with the PURITY II and ordinary tapwater. Consequently, the unit improves the taste of coffee, tea, frozen juices, ice cubes, mixed drinks, soup and vegetables cooked in water. Perhaps more important, the PURITY II's ability to remove potentially harmful foreign matter makes the product of special interest to people who are concerned about health and the safety of the water they consume.

The number of people with those concerns is growing. In spite of increased efforts to protect the environment and water supplies, there are many problems. Hundreds of new chemical compounds—ranging from insecticides to industrial chemicals to commercial cleaning agents—are put into use each year. Some of the residue from chemicals and toxic waste eventually enters water supply sources. Further, floods and hurricanes have damaged or completely shut down water treatment facilities in some cities. Problems like these have led to rumours of possible epidemics of such dread diseases as cholera and typhoid—and more than one city has recently experienced near-panic buying of bottled water.

Given these problems and the need for pure water, Manny believes that the market potential for the PURITY II system is very large. Residences, both single family and apartment, are one obvious target. The unit

---

*The original version of this case was developed by Professor Ben Emis of the University of Southern California, and is adapted for use here with his permission.

is also suitable for use in boats and recreational vehicles; in fact, the PURITY II is standard equipment on several upmarket RVs. And it can be used in pubs and restaurants, in institutions such as schools and hospitals, and in commercial and industrial buildings.

There are several competing ways for customers to solve the problem of getting pure water. Some purchase bottled water. Companies such as Ozarka deliver water monthly for an average price of $2.0 per litre. The best type of bottled water is distilled water; it is absolutely pure because it is produced by the process of evaporation. However, it may be *too pure*. The distilling process removes needed elements such as calcium and phosphate—and there is some evidence that removing these trace elements contributes to heart disease. In fact, some health-action groups recommend that consumers should not drink distilled water.

A second way to obtain pure water is to use some system to treat tapwater. PURITY II is one such system. Another system uses an ion exchange process that replaces ions of harmful substances like iron and mercury with ions that are not harmful. Ion exchange is somewhat less expensive than the PURITY II process, but it is not well suited for residential use because bacteria can build up before the water is used. In addition, there are a number of other filtering and softening systems. In general, these are less expensive and less reliable than the PURITY II. For example, water softeners remove minerals but do not remove bacteria or germs.

Manny's first year with his young company has gone quite well. Customers who have purchased the system like it, and there appear to be several ways to expand the business and increase profits. For example, so far he has had little time to make sales calls on potential commercial and institutional users or residential builders. He also sees other possibilities such as expanding his promotion effort or targeting consumers in a broader geographic area.

At present, Enviro distributes the PURITY II in the 13-county gulf coast region of Texas. Because of legislation, the manufacturer cannot grant an exclusive distributorship. However, Enviro is currently the only PURITY II distributor in this region. In addition, Enviro has the right of first refusal to set up distributorships in other areas of Texas. The manufacturer has indicated that it might even give Enviro distribution rights in a large section of northern Mexico.

The agreement with the manufacturer allows Enviro to distribute the product to retailers, including hardware stores, plumbing supply dealers, and the like. Manny has not yet pursued this channel, but a PURITY II distributor in Florida reported some limited success selling the system to retailers at a wholesale price of $275. Retailers for this type of product typically expect a markup of about 33 per cent of their selling price.

Environmental Control ships the PURITY II units directly from its warehouse to the Enviro office via UPS. The manufacturer's $200 per unit selling price includes the cost of shipping. Enviro only needs to keep a few units on hand because the manufacturer accepts faxed orders and then ships immediately—so delivery never takes more than a few days. Further, the units are small enough to inventory in the back room of the Enviro sales office. Several of the easy-to-handle units will fit in the trunk of a salesperson's car.

Manny is thinking about recruiting additional salespeople. Finding capable people has not been a problem so far. However, there has already been some turnover, and one of the current salespeople is complaining that the compensation is not high enough. Manny pays salespeople on a straight commission basis. A salesperson who develops his or her own prospects gets $100 per sale; the commission is $80 per unit on sales leads generated by the company's telemarketing people. For most salespeople, the mix of sales is about half and half. Enviro pays the students who make the telephone contacts $4 per appointment set up and $10 per unit sold from an appointment.

An average Enviro salesperson can easily sell 20 units per month. However, Manny believes that a really effective and well-prepared salesperson can sell much more, perhaps 40 units per month.

Enviro and its salespeople get good promotion support from Environmental Control. For example, Environmental Control supplies sales training manuals and sales presentation flip charts. The materials are also well done, in part because Environment Control's promotion manager previously worked for Electrolux vacuum cleaners, which are sold in a similar way. The company also supplies print copy for magazine and newspaper advertising and tapes of commercials for radio and television. Thus, all Enviro has to do is buy media space or time. In addition, Environmental Control furnishes each salesperson with a portable demonstration unit, and the company recently gave Enviro three units to be placed in models of apartment buildings.

Manny has worked long hours to get his company going, but he realizes that he has to find time to think about how his strategy is working and to plan for the future.

Evaluate Manish Krishna's current marketing strategy for Enviro Pure Water. How do you think he's doing so far, and what should he do next? Why?

10. WeddingWorld.com

Hazel Hunter is happy with her life, but she is disappointed that the idea she had for starting her own business hasn't taken off as expected. Within a few weeks she either has to renew the contract for her Internet

Web site or decide not to put any more time and money into her idea. She knows that it doesn't make sense to renew the contract if she doesn't come up with a plan to make her Web-site-based business profitable—and she doesn't like to plan. She's a 'doer,' not a planner.

Hazel's business, WeddingWorld.com, started as an idea 18 months ago as she was planning her own wedding. She attended a bridal exhibition to get ideas for a wedding dress, check out catering companies and florists, and in general learn more about the various services available to newlyweds. While there she and her fiancé went from one retailer's stand to another to sign up for their wedding gift registries. Almost every major retailer in the city offered a gift registry service. Being listed in all of the registries improved the odds that her wedding gifts would be items she wanted and could use—and it saved time and hassle for gift-givers. On the way back from the exhibition, Hazel and her fiancé discussed the idea that it would be a lot easier to register gift preferences once on a central Internet site than to provide lots of different stores with bits and pieces of information. A list at a Web site would also make it easier for gift-givers—at least those who were computer users.

The more they discussed the idea of a Web site offering wedding-related services, the more it looked like a good opportunity. Except for the annual bridal exhibition, there was no other obvious place for consumers to get information about planning a wedding and buying wedding-related services. And for retailers, banks, insurance companies, honeymoon resorts, home builders and many other types of firms, there was no other central place to target promotion at newlyweds. Further, the amount of money spent on weddings and wedding gifts is very substantial, and right before and after getting married many young couples make many important purchase decisions for everything from life insurance to pots and pans.

Hazel was no stranger to the Internet. She worked as a Web site designer for a small firm whose one and only client was IBM. That IBM was the only client was intentional rather than an accident. A year earlier IBM had decided that it wanted to 'outsource' certain aspects of its Web site development work and have it handled by an outside contractor. After negotiating a three-year contract to do IBM's work, several IBM employees left their jobs and started the business. IBM was a good client and all indications were that IBM could give the firm as much work as it could handle as it hired new people and prospected for additional accounts over the next few years. Hazel especially liked the creative aspects of designing the 'look' of a Web site, and technical specialists handled a lot of the subtle details.

Before joining this new company, Hazel had several marketing-related jobs. Her first job as a college graduate was with an advertising agency, but she was in a 'backroom' operation handling a lot of the arrangements for printing and mailing large-scale direct-mail promotions. In spite of promises that it was a path to other jobs at the agency, the pay was bad, the work was always pressured, and every aspect of what she had to do was boring. After six punishing months, she left and went looking for something else.

When a number of job applications didn't turn up something quickly, she took a part-time job doing telemarketing calls for a life insurance company. Hazel's boss told her that she was doing a great job reeling in prospects—but she hated disturbing people at night and just didn't like making sales pitches. Fortunately for her, that pain didn't last long. A neighbour in Hazel's apartment complex got Hazel an interview for a receptionist position at an advertising agency. That, at least, got her foot in the door. Her job description wasn't very interesting, but in a small agency she had the opportunity to learn a lot about all aspects of the business—ranging from working on client proposals and media plans to creative sessions for new campaigns. In fact, it was from a technician at that agency that she learned to work with the graphics software used to create advertising layouts—and Web site pages. When the Web site design job came open at the new firm, her boss gave her a glowing recommendation and in two days she was off on her new career.

Although Hazel's jobs had not been high profile positions, they did give her some experience in sales promotion, personal selling, and advertising. Those skills were complemented by the technical computer skills of her husband, who made a living as a database programmer for a large software consulting firm. Taking everything as a whole, they thought that they could get a wedding-related Web site up and running and make it profitable.

There were a number of different facets to the original plan for WeddingWorld.com. One part focused on recruiting advertisers and 'sponsors' who would pay to be listed at the Web site and be allocated a Web page (which Hazel would design) describing their services, giving contact information, and the like. Another facet focused on services for people who were planning to get married. In addition to an on-line wedding gift registry, sections of the Web site provided information about typical wedding costs, planning checklists, details about how to get a required marriage licence, advice on financial matters, and other helpful information. A man and woman could sign up for the service on-line and could pay the modest £20 'membership' fee for a year by credit card. Friends, family, and invited guests could visit the Web site at no charge and get information about wedding preferences, local hotels, discounts on car hire, and even printable maps to all of the churches in the area.

When Hazel told friends about her plan, they all thought it sounded like a great idea. In fact, each time she discussed it someone came up with another idea for a feature to add to the Web site. But generating more new ideas was not the problem. The problem was generating revenue. Hazel had already contracted for space from an Internet service provider and created some of the initial content for the Web site, but she only had one paying sponsor—who happened to be a family friend.

Hazel started by creating a colourful flyer describing the Web site and sent it to most of the firms that had participated in the bridal fair. When no one sent back the reply coupon for more information, she started to make calls (mainly during her lunch hour at her full-time job). Some stores seemed intrigued by the concept, but no one seemed ready to sign up. One reason was that they all seemed surprised at the cost to participate and get ad space at the web site—£2400 a year. Another problem was that no one wanted to be the first to sign up. As one florist shop owner put it, 'If you pull this off and other florists sign up, then come back and I will too.'

Getting couples to sign up went slowly too. Hazel paid for four display ads in local Sunday newspapers in the society section, sent information sheets about the Web site to clergy in the area, listed the Web site with about 25 Internet search engines, and sent carefully crafted press releases announcing the service to almost every publication in the area. One article that resulted from a press release got some attention, and for a few weeks there was a flurry of e-mail enquiries about her Web page. But, after that, it slowed to a trickle again.

Hazel's diagnosis of the problem was simple. Most people thought it was a great idea, but few couples knew to look on the Internet for such a service. Similarly, potential advertisers were not accustomed to the idea of paying for Internet advertising. They didn't know if the cost was reasonable or if the medium was effective.

Hazel's life as a married person was going well and her job as a Web page designer kept her very busy. Her free time outside work was always in short supply because the young crowd at her office always had some scheme for how to keep entertained. So, she wasn't about to leave her job to devote herself full time to her business idea. Further, she thought that once it got rolling she would only have to devote 10 hours a week to it to earn an extra £30 000 a year.

However, it still wasn't clear how to get it rolling. After a year of trying on and off, she only had four paying ad sponsors, and one of them had already notified her that he didn't plan to sign up again because it wasn't clear that the Web site had generated any direct leads or sales. Further, it looked like anything she could do to attract more 'members' would end up being expensive and inefficient.

Hazel thinks the idea has real potential, and she's willing to do the work, but she's not certain if she can make it pay off. She has to decide soon, because the bill for the Internet service provider is sitting on her desk.

What is Hazel's strategy? What should she do? If she were to move forward, what strategy would you recommend? Why?

11. Outdoor World

Jamie McCullough, owner of Outdoor World, is worried about his business' future. He has tried various strategies for two years now, and he's still barely breaking even.

Two years ago, Jamie McCullough bought the inventory, supplies, equipment and business of Outdoor World—located on the edge of a large city. The business is in an older building along a major road leading out of town—several miles from any body of water. The previous owner had sales of about £400 000 a year—but was just breaking even. For this reason—plus the desire to retire—the owner sold to Jamie for roughly the value of the inventory.

Outdoor World had been selling two well-known brands of small pleasure boats, a leading outboard motor, two brands of jet-skis, and a line of camping equipment. The total inventory was valued at £150 000—and Jamie used all of his own savings and borrowed some from two friends to buy the inventory and the business. At the same time, he took over the lease on the building—so he was able to begin operations immediately.

Jamie had never operated a business of his own before, but he was sure that he would be able to do well. He had worked in a variety of jobs—as a used-car salesman, car mechanic and a jack-of-all-trades in the maintenance departments of several local businesses.

Soon after starting his business, Jamie hired his friend, Omar, who had a similar background. Together, they handle all selling and setup work on new sales and do maintenance work as needed. Sometimes the two are extremely busy—at the peaks of each sport season. Then both sales and maintenance keep them going up to 16 hours a day. At these times it's difficult to have both new and repaired equipment available as soon as customers want it. At other times, however, Jamie and Omar have almost nothing to do.

Jamie usually charges the prices suggested by the various manufacturers—except at the end of a season when he is willing to make deals to clear the inventory. He is annoyed that some of his competitors sell mainly on a price basis—offering 10 to 30 per cent off a manufacturer's suggested list prices—even at the beginning of a season! Jamie doesn't want to get into that kind of business, however. He hopes to build a loyal following based on friendship and personal service. Further, he doesn't think he really has to cut price because all of his lines are exclusive for his store. No stores within a five-mile radius carry any of his brands, although nearby retailers offer many brands of similar products.

To try to build a favourable image for his company, Jamie occasionally places ads in local papers and buys some radio spots. The basic theme of this advertising is that Outdoor World is a friendly, service-oriented place to buy the equipment needed for the current season. Sometimes he mentions the brand names he carries, but generally Jamie tries to build an image for concerned, friendly service—both in new sales and repairs—stressing 'We do it right the first time.' He chose this approach because, although he has exclusives on the brands he carries, there are generally 10 to 15 different manufacturers' products being sold in the area in each product category—and most of the products are quite similar. Jamie feels that this similarity among competing products almost forces him to try to differentiate himself on the basis of his own store's services.

The first year's operation wasn't profitable. In fact, after paying minimal salaries to Omar and himself, the business just about broke even. Jamie made no return on his £150 000 investment.

In hopes of improving profitability, Jamie jumped at a chance to add a line of lawn mowers, tractors and trimmers as he was starting into his second year of business. This line was offered by a well-known equipment manufacturer who wanted to expand into the area. The equipment is similar to that offered by other lawn equipment manufacturers. The manufacturer's willingness to do some local advertising and to provide some point-of-purchase displays appealed to Jamie. And he also liked the idea that customers would probably want this equipment sometime earlier than boats and other summer items. So he thought he could handle this business without interfering with his other peak selling seasons.

It's two years since Jamie bought Outdoor World—and he's still only breaking even. Sales have increased a little, but costs have gone up too because he had to hire some part-time help. The lawn equipment helped to expand sales—as he had expected—but unfortunately, it did not increase profits as he had hoped. Jamie needed part-time helpers to handle this business—in part because the manufacturer's advertising had generated a lot of sales inquiries. Relatively few inquiries resulted in sales, however, because many people seemed to be shopping for deals. So Jamie may have even lost money handling the new line. But he hesitates to give it up because he doesn't want to lose that sales volume, and the manufacturer's sales rep has been most encouraging—assuring Jamie that things will get better and that his company will be glad to continue its promotion support during the coming year.

Jamie is now considering the offer of a mountain bike producer that has not been represented in the area. The bikes have become very popular with students and serious bikers in the last several years. The manufacturer's sales rep says industry sales are still growing (but not as fast as in the past) and probably will grow for many more years. The sales rep has praised Jamie's service orientation and says this could help him sell lots of bikes because many mountain bikers are serious about buying a quality bike and then keeping it serviced. He says Jamie's business approach would be a natural fit with bike customers' needs and attitudes. As a special inducement to get Jamie to take on the line, the sales rep says Jamie will not have to pay for the initial inventory of bikes, accessories and repair parts for 90 days. And, of course, the company will supply the usual promotion aids and a special advertising allowance of £10 000 to help introduce the line. Jamie likes the idea of carrying mountain bikes because he has one himself and knows that they do require some service year-round. But he also knows that the proposed bikes are very similar in price and quality to the ones now being offered by the bike shops in town. These bike shops are service rather than price-oriented, and Jamie feels that they are doing a good job on service—so, he is concerned with how he could be 'different.'

Evaluate Jamie McCullough's overall strategy(ies) and the mountain bike proposal. What should he do now?

12. Furniture to Go

Susan Kurczak, owner of Furniture to Go, is discouraged with her salespeople and is even thinking about hiring some new blood. Kurczak has been running Furniture to Go for 10 years and has slowly built the sales to £3.5 million a year. Her store is located on the outskirts of a growing city of 275 000 population. This is basically a factory city, and she has deliberately selected manual workers as her target market. She carries some higher-priced furniture lines but emphasizes budget combinations and easy credit terms.

Kurczak is concerned that she may have reached the limit of her sales growth—her sales have not been increasing during the last two years even though total furniture sales have been increasing in the city as new people move in. Her local radio spots and newspaper advertising seems to attract her target customers, but many of these people come in, shop around, and leave. Some of them come back—but most do not. She thinks her product selections are very suitable for her target market and is concerned that her salespeople don't close more sales with potential customers.

In Shopping for Furniture I Found (Find) that	Demographic Groups			
	Group A	Group B	Group C	Group D
I looked at furniture in many stores before I made a purchase.	78%	72%	52%	50%
I went (am going) to only one store and bought (buy) what I found (find) there.	2	5	10	11
To make my purchase I went (am going) back to one of the stores I shopped in previously.	63	59	27	20
I looked (am looking) at furniture in no more than three stores and made (will make) my purchase in one of these.	20	25	40	45
I like a lot of help in selecting the right furniture.	27	33	62	69
I like a very friendly salesperson.	23	28	69	67

Table 1

Several times, she has discussed this matter with her 10 salespeople. Her staff feel they should treat customers the way they personally want to be treated. They argue that their role is to answer questions and be helpful when asked—not to make suggestions or help customers make decisions. They think this would be too 'hard sell'.

Kurczak says their behaviour is interpreted as indifference by the customers attracted to the store by her advertising. She has tried to convince her salespeople that customers must be treated on an individual basis—and that some customers need more help in looking and deciding than others. Moreover, Kurczak is convinced that some customers would appreciate more help and suggestions than the salespeople themselves might want. To support her views, she showed her staff the data from a study of furniture store customers (see Tables 1 and 2) that she found on the Internet web site for a furniture trade association. She tried to explain the differences in demographic groups and pointed out that her store was definitely trying to aim at specific people. She argued that they (the salespeople) should cater to the needs and attitudes of their customers—and think less about how they would like to be treated themselves. Further, Kurczak announced that she is considering changing the sales compensation plan or hiring new blood if the present employees can't do a better job. Currently, the sales reps are paid £15 000 per year plus a 5 per cent commission on sales.

Contrast Kurczak's strategy and thoughts about her salespeople with their apparent view of her strategy and especially their role in it. What should she do now? Explain.

13. Wire Solutions

Myra Martinez, marketing manager of consumer products for Wire Solutions, is trying to set a price for her most promising new product—a space-saving shoe rack suitable for small homes or apartments.

Demographic Status

Upper class (Group A); 13% of sample
This group consists of managers, proprietors or executives of large businesses; professionals, including doctors, lawyers, engineers, college professors and school administrators and research personnel and sales personnel, including managers, executives and upper-income salespeople.
Family income over £25 000

Middle class (Group B); 37% of sample
Group B consists of white-collar workers, including clerical, secretarial, salesclerks, bookkeepers, etc. It also includes school teachers, social workers, semiprofessionals, proprietors or managers of small businesses, industrial foremen and other supervisory personnel.
Family income between £10 000 and £30 000

Lower middle class (Group C); 36% of sample
Skilled workers and semiskilled technicians are in this category, along with factory operatives, construction workers and some domestic and personal service employees.
Family income between £6000 and £25 000.
No one in this group has above a secondary school education.

Lower class (Group D); 14% of sample
Non-skilled employees, day labourers. It also includes some factory operatives and domestic and service people.
Family income under £10 000.

Table 2   The Sample Design

Wire Solutions is a custom producer of industrial wire products. The company has a lot of experience bending wire into many shapes—and also can chrome- or gold-plate finish products. The company was started 13 years ago and has slowly built its sales volume to £3.2 million a year. Just one year ago, Myra Martinez was appointed marketing manager of the consumer products division. It is her responsibility to develop this division as a producer and marketer of the company's own branded products—as distinguished from custom orders, which the industrial division produces for others.

Martinez has been working on a number of different product ideas for almost a year now and has developed several designs for CD holders, cassette holders, plate holders, doll stands, collapsible book ends and other such products. Her most promising product is a shoe rack for crowded homes and apartments. The wire rack attaches to the inside of a wardrobe door and holds eight pairs of shoes.

The rack is very similar to one the industrial division produced for a number of years for another company. That company sold the shoe rack and hundreds of other related items out of its 'products for organizing and storing' mail-order catalogue. Managers at Wire Solutions were surprised by the high sales volume the catalogue company achieved with the rack. In fact, that is what interested Wire Solutions in the consumer market—and led to the development of the separate consumer products division.

Martinez has sold hundreds of the shoe racks to various local hardware, grocery and general merchandise stores and wholesalers on a trial basis, but each time she has negotiated a price—and no firm policy has been set. Now she must determine what price to set on the shoe rack—which she plans to push aggressively wherever she can. Actually, she hasn't decided on exactly which channels of distribution to use. But trials in the local area have been encouraging, and, as noted above, the experience in the industrial division suggests that there is a large market for this type of product. Further, she noticed that a large discount store in her local area was selling a similar rack made of plastic. When she talked casually about her product with the store manager, he suggested that she contact the chain's houseware buyers at head office. The manufacturing cost on this product—when made in reasonable quantities—is approximately £1.40 if it is painted black and £1.80 if it is chromed. Similar products have been selling at retail in the £4.95 to £9.95 range. The sales and administrative overhead to be charged to the division will amount to £90 000 a year. This will include Martinez's salary and some office expenses. She expects that a number of other products will be developed in the near future. But for the coming year, she hopes the shoe rack will account for about half the consumer products division's sales volume.

Evaluate Myra Martinez's strategy planning so far. What should she do now? What price should she set for the shoe rack? Explain.

14. Plastic Master

Nora Hall is trying to decide whether to leave her present job to buy into another business and be part of top management.

Hall is now a sales representative for a plastics components manufacturer. She calls mostly on large industrial accounts—such as refrigerator manufacturers—who might need large quantities of custom-made products like door liners. She is on a straight salary of £35 000 per year, plus expenses and a company car. She expects some salary increases but doesn't see much long-run opportunity with this company.

As a result, she is seriously considering changing jobs and investing £40 000 in Plastic Master—an established thermoplastic moulder (manufacturer). Mr Hanson, the present owner, is nearing retirement and has not trained anyone to take over the business. He has agreed to sell the business to Steve Burton, a lawyer, who has invited Nora Hall to invest and become the sales manager. Steve Burton has agreed to match Hall's current salary plus expenses, plus a bonus of 2 per cent of profits. However, she must invest to become part of the new company. She will get a 5 per cent interest in the business for the necessary £40 000 investment—almost all of her savings.

Plastic Master is well established—and last year had sales of £2.2 million but zero profits (after paying Hanson a salary of £40 000). In terms of sales, cost of materials was 46 per cent; direct labour, 13 per cent; indirect factory labour, 15 per cent; factory overhead, 13 per cent; and sales overhead and general expenses, 13 per cent. The company has not been making any profit for several years—but has been continually adding new machines to replace those made obsolete by technological developments. The machinery is well maintained and modern, but most of it is similar to that used by its many competitors. Most of the machines in the industry are standard. Special products are made by using specially made dies with these machines.

Sales have been split about two-thirds custom-moulded products (that is, made to the specification of other producers or merchandising concerns) and the balance proprietary items (such as housewares and game items, like poker chips and cribbage sets). The housewares are copies of articles developed by others—and indicate neither originality nor style. Hanson is in charge of selling the proprietary items, which are distributed through any available wholesale channels. The custom-moulded products are sold through two full-time sales reps—who receive a 10 per cent commission on individual orders up to £20 000 and then 3 per cent above that level—and also by three manufacturers' reps who get the same commissions.

The company seems to be in fairly good financial condition—at least as far as book value is concerned. The £40 000 investment will buy almost £60 000 in assets—and ongoing operations should pay off the seven-year note (see Table 1). Steve Burton thinks that—with new management— the company has a good chance to make big profits. He expects to make some economies in the production process—because he feels most production operations can be improved. He plans to keep custom-moulding sales at approximately the present £1.4 million level. His new strategy will try to increase the proprietary sales volume from £800 000 to $2 million a year. Nora Hall is expected to be a big help here because of her sales experience. This will bring the firm up to about capacity level—but it will mean adding additional employees and costs. The major advantage of expanding sales will be spreading overhead.

Some of the products proposed by Steve Burton for expanding proprietary sales are listed below.

New products for consideration:
Safety helmets for cyclists.
Water bottles for cyclists and in-line skaters.
School lunch boxes.
Toolboxes.
Cupboard organizer/storage boxes for toys.
Short legs for furniture.
Outside house shutters.
Importing and distributing foreign housewares.

Plastic Master faces heavy competition from many other similar companies. Further, most retailers expect a wide margin—sometimes 50 to 60 per cent of retail selling price. Even so, manufacturing costs are low enough so Plastic Master can spend some money for promotion while still keeping the price competitive. Apparently, many customers are willing to pay for novel new products—if they see them in stores. And Hall isn't worried too much by tough competition. She sees plenty of that in her present job. And she does like the idea of being an 'owner and sales manager'.

Evaluate Plastic Master's situation and Steve Burton's strategy. What should Nora Hall do? Why?

15. Deluxe Foods, Ltd*

Jessica Walters, marketing manager of Deluxe Foods, Ltd—a Canadian company—is being urged to approve the creation of a separate marketing plan for Quebec. This would be a major policy change because Deluxe Foods' international parent is trying to move towards a global strategy for the whole firm and Jessica has been supporting Canada-wide planning.

Jessica Walters has been the marketing manager of Deluxe Foods for the last four years—since she arrived from international headquarters in Minneapolis. Deluxe Foods—headquartered in Toronto—is a subsidiary of a large US-based consumer packaged-food company with worldwide sales of more than $2 billion in 1994. Its Canadian sales are just over $350 million—with the Quebec and Ontario markets accounting for 69 per cent of the company's Canadian sales.

The company's product line includes such items as cake mixes, puddings, pie fillings, pancakes, prepared foods and frozen dinners. The company has successfully introduced at least six new products every year for the last five years. Products from Deluxe Foods are known for their high quality and enjoy much brand preference throughout Canada—including the Province of Quebec.

*This case was adapted from one written by Professor Roberta Tamilia, University of Windsor, Canada.

Assets			Liabilities and Net Worth	
Case		£ 13 000	Liabilities:	
Accounts receivable		55 000	Accounts payable	£ 70 000
Building	£225 000		Notes payable—7 years (machinery)	194 000
Less: depreciation	75 000			
		150 000		
Machinery	1 400 000		Net worth:	
Less: depreciation	450 000		Capital stock	900 000
		950 000	Retained earnings	4 000
Total assets		£1 168 000	Total liabilities and net worth	£1 168 000

Table 1   Plastic Master., Statement of Financial Conditions, December 31, 199x

Cake mixes	107	Soft drinks	126
Pancakes	87	Pie fillings	118
Puddings	114	Frozen dinners	79
Salad dressings	85	Prepared packaged foods	83
Molasses	132	Cookies	123

Table 1   Per Capita Consumption Index, Province of Quebec (Canada   100)

The company's sales have risen every year since Jessica Walters took over as marketing manager. In fact, the company's market share has increased steadily in each of the product categories in which it competes. The Quebec market has closely followed the national trend except that, in the past two years, total sales growth in that market began to lag.

According to Walters, a big advantage of Deluxe Foods over its competitors is the ability to coordinate all phases of the food business from Toronto. For this reason, Walters meets at least once a month with her product managers—to discuss developments in local markets that might affect marketing plans. While each manager is free to make suggestions—and even to suggest major changes—Jessica Walters has the responsiblity of giving final approval for all plans.

One of the product managers, Marie LeMans, expressed great concern at the last monthly meeting about the poor performance of some of the company's products in the Quebec market. While a broad range of possible reasons—ranging from inflation and the threat of job losses to politics—were reviewed to try to explain the situation, LeMans insisted that it was due to a basic lack of understanding of that market. She felt not enough managerial time and money had been spent on the Quebec market—in part because of the current emphasis on developing all-Canada plans on the way to having one global strategy.

Marie LeMans felt the current marketing approach to the Quebec market should be reevaluated because an inappropriate marketing plan may be responsible for the sales slowdown. After all, she said, '80 per cent of the market is French-speaking. It's in the best interest of the company to treat that market as being separate and distinct from the rest of Canada'.

Marie LeMans supported her position by showing that Quebec's per capita consumption of many product categories (in which the firm competes) is above the national average (see Table 1). Research projects conducted by Deluxe Foods also support the 'separate and distinct' argument. Over the years, the firm has found many French–English differences in brand attitudes, lifestyles, usage rates and so on.

LeMans argued that the company should develop a unique Quebec marketing plan for some or all of its brands. She specifically suggested that the French-language advertising plan for a particular brand be developed independently of the plan for English Canada. Currently, the Toronto agency assigned to the brand just translates its English-language ads for the French market. Jessica Walters pointed out that the present advertising approach assured Deluxe Foods of a uniform brand image across Canada. Marie LeMans said she knew what the agency was doing, and that straight translation into Canadian-French may not communicate the same brand image. The discussion that followed suggested that a different brand image might be needed in the French market if the company wanted to stop the brand's decline in sales.

The managers also discussed the food distribution system in Quebec. The major supermarket chains have their lowest market share in that province. Independents are strongest there—the 'mom-and-pop' food stores fast disappearing outside Quebec remain alive and well in the province. Traditionally, these stores have stocked a higher proportion (than supermarkets) of their shelf space with national brands—an advantage for Deluxe Foods.

Finally, various issues related to discount policies, pricing structure, sales promotion and cooperative advertising were discussed. All this suggested that things were different in Quebec—and that future marketing plans should reflect these differences to a greater extent than they do now.

After the meeting, Jessica Walters stayed in her office to think about the situation. Although she agreed with the basic idea that the Quebec market was in many ways different, she wasn't sure how far the company should go in recognizing this fact. She knew that regional differences in food tastes and brand purchases existed not only in Quebec but in other parts of Canada as well. But people are people, after all, with far more similarities than differences, so a Canadian and eventually a global strategy makes some sense too.

Jessica Walters was afraid that giving special status to one region might conflict with top management's objective of achieving standardization whenever possible—one global strategy for Canada, on the way to one worldwide global strategy. She was also worried about the long-term effect of such a policy change on costs, organizational structure and brand image. Still, enough product managers had expressed their concern over the years about the Quebec market to make her wonder if she shouldn't modify the current approach. Perhaps they could experiment with a few brands—and just in Quebec. She could cite the language difference as the reason for trying Quebec rather than any of the other provinces. But Walters realizes that any change of policy could be seen as the beginning of more change, and what would Minneapolis think? Could she explain it successfully there?

Evaluate Deluxe Foods, Ltd.'s present strategy. What should Jessica Walters do now? Explain.

16. Aluminium Basics Co.*

Mark Parcells, newly hired VP of Marketing for Aluminium Basics Co., is reviewing the firm's international distribution arrangements because they don't seem to be very well thought out. He is not sure if anything is wrong, but he feels that the company should follow a global strategy rather than continuing its current policies.

Aluminium Basics, based in Atlanta, Georgia, produces finished aluminium products, such as aluminium ladders, umbrella-type clothes racks, scaffolding and patio tables and chairs that fold flat. Sales in 1998 reached $25 million—primarily to US customers.

Aluminium Basics had decided to try foreign markets. The sales manager, Bonnie Pope, believed the growing affluence of European workers would help the company's products gain market acceptance quickly.

Bonnie's first step in investigating foreign markets was to join a trade mission to Europe—a tour organized by the US Department of Commerce. This trade mission visited Italy, Germany, Denmark, Holland, France and England. During this trip, Bonnie was officially introduced to leading buyers for department store chains, import houses, wholesalers, and buying groups. The two-week trip convinced Bonnie that there was ample buying power to make exporting a profitable opportunity.

On her return to Atlanta, Bonnie's next step was to obtain credit references for the firms she considered potential distributors. To those who were judged creditworthy, she sent letters expressing interest and samples, brochures, prices and other relevant information.

The first orders were from a French wholesaler. Sales in this market totalled 70 000 in the first year. Similar success was achieved in Germany and England. Italy, on the other hand, did not produce any sales. Bonnie felt the semi-luxury nature of the company's products and the lower incomes in Italy encouraged a 'making do' attitude rather than purchase of goods and services that would make life easier.

In the United States, Aluminium Basics distributes through fairly aggressive and well-organized merchant hardware distributors and buying groups, such as cooperative and voluntary hardware chains, who have taken over much of the strategy planning for cooperating producers and retailers. In its foreign markets, however, there is no recognizable pattern. Channel systems vary from country to country. To avoid mixing channels of distribution, Aluminium Basics has only one account in each country. The chosen distributor is the exclusive distributor.

In France, Aluminium Basics distributes through a wholesaler based in Paris. This wholesaler has five salespeople covering the country. The firm specializes in small housewares and has contacts with leading buying groups, wholesalers, and department stores. Bonnie is impressed with the firm's aggressiveness and knowledge of merchandising techniques.

In Germany, Aluminium Basics sells to a Hamburg-based buying group for hardware wholesalers throughout the country. Bonnie felt this group would provide excellent coverage of the market because of its extensive distribution network.

In Denmark, Aluminium Basics' line is sold to a buying group representing a chain of hardware retailers. This group recently expanded to include retailers in Sweden, Finland and Norway. Together this group purchases goods for about 500 hardware retailers. The buying power of Scandinavians is quite high, and it is expected that Aluminium Basics' products will prove very successful there.

In the United Kingdom, Aluminium Basics uses an importer-distributor, who both buys on their own account and acts as a sales agent. This firm sells to department stores and hardware wholesalers. They have not done very well overall, but have done very well with Aluminium Basics' line of patio tables and chairs.

Australia is handled by an importer who operates a chain of discount houses. It heard about Aluminium Basics from a United Kingdom contact. After extensive e-mailing, this firm discovered it could land aluminium patio furniture in Melbourne at prices competitive with Japanese imports. So it started ordering because it wanted to cut prices in a high-priced garden furniture market.

The Argentinian market is handled by an American who came to the United States from Buenos Aires in search of new lines. Aluminium Basics attributes success in Argentina to the efforts of this aggressive and capable agent. He has built a sizeable trade in aluminium ladders.

In Trinidad and Jamaica, Aluminium Basics' products are handled by traders who carry such diversified lines as insurance, apples, plums and fish. They have been successful in selling aluminium ladders. This business grew out of inquiries sent to the US Department of Commerce and in researching its Web site (www.doc.gov), which Bonnie Pope followed up by mail.

Bonnie Pope's export policies for Aluminium Basics are as follows:

---

*Adapted from a case study written by Professor Peter Bantring, McMaster University, Canda.

1. Product: No product modifications will be made in selling to foreign customers. This may be considered later after a substantial sales volume develops.

2. Price: The company does not publish suggested list prices. Distributors add their own markup to their landed costs. Supply prices will be kept as low as possible. This is accomplished by: (a) removing advertising expenses and other strictly domestic overhead charges from price calculations, (b) finding the most economical packages for shipping (smallest volume per unit), and (c) bargaining with carriers to obtain the lowest shipping rates possible.

3. Promotion: The firm does no advertising in foreign markets. Brochures and sales literature already being used in the United States are supplied to foreign distributors, who are encouraged to adapt them or create new materials as required. Aluminium Basics will continue to promote its products by participating in overseas trade shows. These are handled by the sales manager. All enquiries are forwarded to the firm's distributor in that country.

4. Distribution: New distributors will be contacted through foreign trade shows. Bonnie Pope considers large distributors desirable. She feels, however, that they are not as receptive as smaller distributors to a new, unestablished product line. Therefore, she prefers to appoint small distributors. Larger distributors may be appointed after the company has gained a strong consumer franchise in a country.

5. Financing: Aluminium Basics sees no need to provide financial help to distributors. The company views its major contribution as providing good products at the lowest possible prices.

6. Marketing and planning assistance: Bonnie Pope feels that foreign distributors know their own markets best. Therefore, they are best equipped to plan for themselves.

7. Selection of foreign markets: The evaluation of foreign market opportunities for the company's products is based primarily on disposable income and lifestyle patterns. For example, Bonnie fails to see any market in North Africa for Aluminium Basics' products, which she thinks are of a semiluxury nature. She thinks that cheaper products such as wood ladders (often homemade) are preferred to prefabricated aluminium ladders in regions such as North Africa and Southern Europe. Argentina, on the other hand, she thinks is a more highly industrialized market with luxury tastes. Thus, Bonnie sees Aluminium Basics' products as better suited for more highly industrialized and affluent societies.

Evaluate Aluminium Basics' present foreign markets strategies. Should it develop a global strategy? What strategy or strategies should Mark Parcells (the new VP of Marketing) develop? Explain.

17. Romano's Take-Away

Angelina Cello, manager of the Romano's Take-Away, is trying to develop a plan for the 'sick' pizza business she just took over.

Romano's Take-Away (RT) is a pizza take-away and delivery business. RT's business comes from telephone or walk-in orders. In addition to pizzas, RT also sells and delivers a limited selection of soft drinks.

RT has had mixed results during the last three years. It has been obtaining only about half of its orders from residential delivery requests. The shop's new manager, Angelina Cello, believes the problem with residential pizza delivery is due to the location of residential neighbourhoods in the area. Several large industrial plants (mostly car industry related) are located throughout the city. Small, mostly factory-worker neighbourhoods are distributed in between the various plant sites. As a result, RT's location can serve only two or three of these neighbourhoods on one delivery run. Competition is also relevant. RT has several aggressive competitors who advertise heavily, distribute discount coupons, and offer 2-for-1 deals. This aggressive competition is probably why RT's residential sales levelled off in the last year or so. For now, anyway, Angelina feels she knows how to meet this competition and hold onto the present sales level.

Most of the shop's potential seems to be in serving the large industrial plants. Many of these plants work two or three shifts—five days a week. During each work shift, workers are allowed one half-hour lunch break—which usually occurs at 11 a.m., 8 p.m., or 2:30 a.m. (depending on the shift).

Generally, a customer will phone or fax from a plant about 30 minutes before a scheduled lunch break and order several (5 to 10) pizzas for a work group. RT may receive many orders of this size from the same plant (i.e., from different groups of workers). The plant business is very profitable for several reasons. First, a large number of pizzas can be delivered at the same time to the same location, saving transportation costs. Second, plant orders usually involve many different toppings (double cheese, pepperoni, mushrooms) on each pizza. This results in £11 to £14 revenue per pizza.

Despite the profitability of the plant orders, several factors make it difficult to serve the plant market. RT's shop is located 5 to 8 minutes from most of the plant sites, so RT must prepare the orders within 20 to 25 minutes after it receives the telephone order. Often, inadequate staff and/or oven capacity means it is impossible to get all the orders heated at the same time.

Generally, plant workers will wait as long as 10 minutes past the start of their lunch break before ordering from various vending vans that arrive at the plant sites during lunch breaks. (Currently, no other pizza delivery shops are in good positions to serve most plant locations and/or have chosen to compete.) But there have been a few instances when workers refused to pay for pizzas that were only five minutes late! Worse yet, if the same work group gets a couple of late orders, they are lost as future customers. Angelina Cello believes that the inconsistent profitability of the shop is partly the result of such lost customers.

In an effort to rebuild the plant delivery business, Angelina is considering various methods to ensure prompt customer delivery. She thinks that potential demand during lunch breaks is significantly above RT's present capacity. Angelina also knows that if she tries to satisfy all phone or fax orders on some peak days, she won't be able to provide prompt service—and may lose more plant customers.

Angelina has outlined three alternatives that may win back some of the plant business for the shop. She has developed these alternatives to discuss with RT's owner. Each alternative is briefly described below:

Alternative 1: Determine practical capacities during peak volume periods using existing equipment and personnel. Accept orders only up to that capacity and politely decline orders beyond. This approach will ensure prompt customer service and high product quality. It will also minimize losses resulting from customers' rejection of late

deliveries. Financial analysis of this alternative—shown in Table 1—indicates that a potential daily contribution to profit of £1230 could result if this alternative is implemented successfully. This would be profit before promotion costs, overhead and net profit (or loss). Note: Any alternative will require advertising expenditure to reinform potential plant customers that Romano's Take-Away has improved its service and 'wants your business.'

Alternative 2: Add additional equipment (one oven and one delivery car) and hire additional staff to handle peak loads. This approach would ensure timely customer delivery and high product quality—as well as provide additional capacity to handle unmet demand. Table 2 is a conservative estimate of potential daily demand for plant orders compared to current capacity and proposed increased capacity. Table 3 gives the cost of acquiring the additional equipment and relevant information related to depreciation and fixed costs.

Using this alternative, the following additional pizza preparation and delivery personnel costs would be required:

The addition of even more equipment and personnel to handle all unmet demand was not considered in this alternative because the current store is not large enough.

	11 a.m. Break	8 p.m. Break	2:30 a.m. Break	Daily Totals
Current capacity (pizzas)	48	48	48	144
Average selling price per unit	£ 12.50	£ 12.50	£ 12.50	£ 12.50
Sales potential	£ 600	£ 600	£ 600	£ 1800
Variable cost (approximately 40 per cent of selling price)*	240	240	240	720
Contribution margin of pizzas	360	360	360	1080
Beverage sales (2 medium-sized beverages per pizza ordered at 75p a piece)†	72	72	72	216
Cost of beverages (30% per beverage)	22	22	22	66
Contribution margin of beverages	50	50	50	150
Total contribution of pizza and beverages	£ 410	£ 410	£ 410	£ 1230

*The variable cost estimate of 40% of sales includes variable costs of delivery to plant locations.

†Amounts shown are not physical capacities (there is almost unlimited physical capacity), but potential sales volume is constrained by number of pizzas that can be sold.

Table 1 Practical Capacities and Sales Potential of Current Equipment and Personnel

	Estimated Daily Demand	Current Daily Capacity	Proposed Daily Capacity
Pizza units (1 pizza)	320	144	300

Table 2

Capacity and Demand for Plant Customer Market

	Hours Required	Cost per Hour	Total Additional Daily Cost
Delivery personnel	6	6	£36.00
Preparation personnel	8	6	
			48.00
			£84.00

Alternative 3: Add additional equipment and personnel as described in alternative 2, but move to a new location that would reduce delivery lead times to two to five minutes. This move would probably allow RT to handle all unmet demand—because the reduction in delivery time will provide for additional oven time. In fact, RT might have excess capacity using this approach.

Suitable premises are available near about the same number of residential customers (including many of the shop's current residential customers). The available premises are slightly larger than needed. And the rent is higher. Relevant cost information on the proposed store appears below:

Angelina Cello presented the three alternatives to RT's owner—Romano Marino. Romano was pleased that Angelina had done her homework. He decided that Angelina should make the final decision on what to do (in part because she had a profit-sharing agreement with Romano) and offered the following comments and concerns:

1. Romano agreed that the plant market was extremely sensitive to delivery timing. Product quality and pricing, although important, were of less importance.
2. He agreed that plant demand estimates were conservative. 'In fact, they may be 10 to 30 per cent low.'
3. Romano expressed concern that under alternative 2, and especially under alternative 3, much of the store's capacity would go unused over 80 per cent of the time.
4. He was also concerned that RT's shop had a bad reputation with plant customers because the prior shop manager was not sensitive to timely plant delivery. So Romano suggested that Angelina develop a promotion plan to improve RT's reputation in the plants, and be sure that everyone knows that RT has improved its delivery service.

Evaluate Angelina's possible strategies for the shop's plant market. What should Angelina do? Why? Suggest possible promotion plans for your preferred strategy.

Additional rental expense of proposed shop over current store	£ 1 600 per year
Cost of moving to new shop (one-time cost)	£16 000

	Cost	Estimated Useful Life	Salvage Value	Annual Depreciation*	Daily Depreciation†
Delivery car (equipped with pizza warmer)	£11 000	5 years	£1 000	£2 000	£5.71
Pizza oven	£20 000	8 years	£2 000	£2 250	£6.43

*Annual depreciation is calculated on a straight-line basis.

†Daily depreciation assumes a 350-day (plant production) year. All variable expenses related to each piece of equipment (e.g., utilities, gas, oil) are included in the variable cost of a pizza.

Table 3   Cost of Required Additional Assets

GLOSSARY

Single-line (or general-line) wholesalers service wholesalers who carry a narrower line of merchandise than general merchandise wholesalers.

Single-line shops specialize in certain lines of related products rather than a wide assortment—sometimes called limited-line.

Single target market approach segmenting the market and picking one of the homogeneous segments as the firm's target market.

Situation analysis an informal study of what information is already available in the problem area.

Skimming price policy trying to sell the top of the market—the top of the demand curve—at a high price before aiming at more price-sensitive customers.

Social class a group of people who have approximately equal social position as viewed by others in the society.

Social needs needs concerned with love, friendship, status and esteem—things that involve a person's interaction with others.

Social responsibility a firm's obligation to improve its positive effects on society and reduce its negative effects.

Sorting separating products into grades and qualities desired by different target markets.

Source the sender of a message.

Speciality products consumer products that the customer really wants and makes a special effort to find.

Speciality shop a type of conventional limited-line shop—usually small and with a distinct personality.

Speciality wholesalers service wholesalers who carry a very narrow range of products and offer more information and service than other service wholesalers.

Spreadsheet analysis organizing costs, sales and other information into a data table to show how changing the value of one or more numbers affects the other numbers.

Standard Industrial Classification System codes codes used to identify groups of firms in similar lines of business.

Standardization and grading sorting products according to size and quality.

Staples products that are bought often, routinely and without much thought.

Statistical packages easy-to-use computer programs that analyse data.

Status quo objectives 'don't-rock-the-*pricing*-boat' objectives.

Stock a share in the ownership of a company.

Stocking allowances allowances given to middlemen to get shelf space for a product—sometimes called slotting allowances.

Stockturn rate the number of times the average inventory is sold during a year.

Storage the marketing function of holding goods.

Storing function holding goods until customers need them.

Straight rebuy a routine repurchase that may have been made many times before.

Strategic business unit (SBU) an organizational unit (within a larger company) that focuses its efforts on some product-markets and is treated as a separate profit centre.

Strategic (management) planning the managerial process of developing and maintaining a match between an organization's resources and its market opportunities.

Substitutes products that offer the buyer a choice.

Superstores are very large shops that carry not only food, but all goods and services that the consumer purchases routinely.

Supermarkets large stores, which normally cover more than 2500 square metres, that specialize in groceries—with self-service and wide assortments.

Supplies expense items that do not become part of a finished product.

Supply curve the quantity of products that will be supplied at various possible prices.

Supporting salespeople salespeople who help the order-oriented salespeople—but don't try to get orders themselves.

SWOT analysis identifies and lists the firm's strengths and weaknesses and its opportunities and threats.

Target market a fairly homogeneous (similar) group of customers to whom a company wishes to appeal.

Target marketing a marketing mix is tailored to fit some specific target customers.

Target return objective a specific level of profit as an objective.

Target return pricing pricing to cover all costs and achieve a target return.

Tariffs taxes on imported products.

Task method an approach to developing a budget—basing the budget on the job to be done.

Task transfer using telecommunications to move service operations to places where there are pools of skilled workers.

Task utility provided when someone performs a task for someone else—for instance, when a bank handles financial transactions.

Team selling different sales reps working together on a specific account.

Technical specialists supporting salespeople who provide technical assistance to order-oriented salespeople.

Technology the application of science to convert an economy's resources to output.

Telemarketing using the telephone to call on customers or prospects.

Telephone and direct-mail retailing allows consumers to shop at home—usually placing orders by mail or a free long-distance telephone call and charging the purchase to a credit card.

Time series historical records of the fluctuations in economic variables.

Time utility having the product available *when* the customer wants it.

Total cost the sum of total fixed and total variable costs.

Total cost approach evaluating each possible PD system and identifying *all* of the costs of each alternative.

Total fixed cost the sum of those costs that are fixed in total—no matter how much is produced.

Total quality management (TQM) a management approach in which everyone in the organization is concerned about quality, throughout all of the firm's activities, to better serve customer needs.

Total variable cost the sum of those changing expenses that are closely related to output—such as expenses for parts, wages, packaging materials, outgoing freight and sales commissions.

Trade (functional) discount a list price reduction given to channel members for the job they are going to do.

Trade-in allowance a price reduction given for used products when similar new products are bought.

Trademark those words, symbols or marks that are legally registered for use by a single company.

Trade-off analysis is a technique that helps to determine how important certain elements of the company's marketing mix are to customers.

Traditional channel of distribution a channel in which the various channel members make little or no effort to cooperate with each other.

Transport the marketing function of moving goods.

Transporting function the movement of goods from one place to another.

Trend extension extends past experience to predict the future.

Truck wholesalers wholesalers who specialize in delivering products that they stock, in their own trucks.

2/10, net 30 allows a 2 per cent discount off the face value of the invoice if the invoice is paid within 10 days.

Unfair trade practice acts put a lower limit on prices, especially at the wholesale and retail levels.

Uniform delivered pricing making an average freight charge to all buyers.

Unit-pricing placing the price per gramme (or some other standard measure) on or near the product.

Universal functions of marketing buying, selling, transporting, storing, standardizing and grading, financing, risk taking and market information.

Universal product code (UPC) special identifying marks for each product readable by electronic scanners.

Unsought products products that potential customers don't yet want or know they can buy.

Utility the power to satisfy human needs.

Validity the extent to which data measures what it is intended to measure.

Value in use pricing setting prices that will capture some of what customers will save by substituting the firm's product for the one currently being used.

Value pricing setting a fair price level for a marketing mix that really gives the target market superior customer value.

Vendor analysis formal rating of suppliers on all relevant areas of performance.

Vertical integration acquiring firms at different levels of channel activity.

Vertical marketing systems channel systems in which the whole channel focuses on the same target market at the end of the channel.

Virtual corporation the firm is primarily a coordinator—with a good marketing concept—instead of a producer.

Voluntary chains wholesaler-sponsored groups that work with independent retailers.

Wants needs that are learned during a person's life.

Wheel of retailing theory new types of retailers enter the market as low-status, low-margin, low-price operators and then—if successful—evolve into more conventional retailers offering more services with higher operating costs and higher prices.

Wholesalers firms whose main function is providing *wholesaling activities*.

Wholesaling the *activities* of those persons or establishments that sell to retailers and other merchants, and/or to industrial, institutional and commercial users, but who do not sell in large amounts to final consumers.

Wholly owned subsidiary a separate firm owned by a parent company.

World Trade Organization (WTO) the only international body dealing with the rules of trade between nations.

Working capital money to pay for short-term expenses such as employee salaries, advertising, marketing research, inventory storing costs and what the firm owes suppliers.

Zone pricing making an average freight charge to all buyers within specific geographic areas.

ILLUSTRATION CREDITS

Chapter 1

Exhibits 1–3, adapted from R.F. Vizza, T.E. Chambers and E.J. Cook, *Adoption of the Marketing Concept: Fact or Fiction* (New York: Sales Executive Club, Inc., 1967), pp. 13–15.

Ads Dolmio by courtesy of DMB&B London-Europe. Vespa by courtesy of BBDO Europe Ltd. Advertising campaign featuring famous people by courtesy of Young & Rubicam, London.

Chapter 2

Ad Texaco by courtesy of DMB&B, Amsterdam-Benelux.

Chapter 3

Exhibits 3–2, map developed by the authors based on data from US Bureau of Census, Reports WP/94 and WP/94-DD, *World Population Profile: 1994* (Washington, DC: US Government Printing Office, 1994). **3–3**, table based on US Census data including US Bureau of Census, *Statistical Abstract of the United States, 1997* (Washington, DC: US Government Printing Office, 1997). **3–4**, *European Marketing Data and Statistics*, (Euromonitor, London, 1998, pp. 130–131). **3–5**, Y & R; INRA: European Marketing Pocket Book, 1998. **3–6**, Patrick E. Murphy and William A. Staples, 'A modern family life cycle', *Journal of Consumer Research*, June 1979, p. 17. **3–8**, adapted from C. Glenn Walters, Consumer Behavior, (Burr Ridge, IL: Richard D. Irwin, 1979). **3–11**, Joseph T. Plummer, 'The Concept and Application of Life-style Segmentation', *Journal of Marketing*, January 1974, pp. 33-37.

Ads Kookai by courtesy of BBDO Europe Ltd. Uncle Ben's by courtesy of DMB&B London-UK.

Chapter 4

Exhibits 4–1, US Bureau of Census, *Statistical Abstract of the United States 1997*; US Bureau of Census, County Business Patterns 1995, United States (Washington, DC: US Government Printing Office, 1997); *Information Please Almanac, 1998* (Boston, MA: Houghton Mifflin). **4–3**, adapted from Rowland T. Moriarty, Jr and Robert E. Spekman, 'An empirical investigation of the information sources used during the industrial buying process', *Journal of Marketing Research*, May 1984, pp. 134–147.

Ads The Economist by courtesy of BBDO Europe Ltd. Audi A4 by courtesy of BBDO Europe Ltd.

Chapter 5

Exhibits 5–5, adapted from Paul E. Green, Frank J. Carmone and David P. Wachpress, 'On the analysis of qualitative data in marketing research', *Journal of Marketing Research*, February 1977, pp. 52–59.

Ad Ford Couga by courtesy of Young & Rubicam Europe.

Chapter 6

Exhibits 6–2, Igor Ansoff, *Corporate Strategy*, (New York: McGraw-Hill, 1965). **6–13** Russell I. Haley, 'Benefit segmentation: A decision-oriented research tool,' *Journal of Marketing*, July 1968, p. 33.

Ads Ben Sherman by courtesy of Grey International. Fiat Seicento by courtesy of DMB&B London-UK.

Chapter 7

Photo/ads Swatch by courtesy of DMB&B London-UK. *Pagine Gialle* by courtesy of DMB&B Milan-Italy.

Chapter 8

Exhibits 8–1, adapted from Frank R. Bacon, Jr, and Thomas W. Butler, *Planned Innovation* (Ann Arbor, MI: University of Michigan Institute of Science and Technology, 1980). **8–2**, adapted fom Philip Kotler, 'What Consumerism means for marketers', *Harvard Business Review*, May–June 1972, pp. 55-56. **8–3**, A. Shepard, 'Adding brand value', in P. Stobart (ed.), Brand Power (Macmillan, Basingstoke, 1994).

Ad Tiffany by courtesy of McCann-Erickson Worldwide.

Chapter 9

Ad Virgin Vie by courtesy of Grey International.

Chapter 10

Exhibits 10–4, adapted from B.J. La Londe and P.H. Zinzer, *Customer Service: Meaning and Measurement* (Chicago: National Council of Physical Distribution Management, 1976); and D. Phillip Locklin, *Transportation for Management* (Burr Ridge, IL: Richard D. Irwin, 1972). **10–6**, adapted from Louis W. Stern and Adel I. El-Ansary, *Marketing Channels* (Englewood Cliffs, NJ: Prentice Hall, 1977), p. 150.

Chapter 11

Exhibit 11–4, *Retail Marketing Pocket Book* (copyright © NTC Publications, 1998, Henley-on-Thames).

Ad Traditional channels of distribution by courtesy of H & M Presseservice.

Chapter 12

Ad Mars by courtesy of DMB&B London - UK.

Chapter 13

Exhibits 13–2, *Retail Marketing Pocket Book* (copyright © NTC Publications, 1998, Henley-on-Thames). **13–5**, cost data from *Standard Rate and Data*, 1997, and sales estimates from 'Ad revenue growth hits 7% in 1997 to surpass forecasts', *Advertising Age*, 18 May 1998, p. 50; 'The Internet is Mr Case's Neighborhood', *Fortune*, 30 March 1998, pp. 69–80. **13–6**, *Retail Marketing Pocket Book* (copyright © NTC Publications, 1998, Henley-on-Thames). **13–8**, I. Fox and I. Abdullah, 'The advertising agency: functions and directions', in T. Meenaghan and P. O'Sullivan (eds) *Marketing Communications in Ireland* (Oak Tree Press, Dublin, 1995), p. 109.

Ads Kellogg's by courtesy of Leo Burnett . Charitable organizations by courtesy of BBDO Europe Ltd.

Chapter 14

Exhibit 14–2, 'Average promotion mix for consumer and industrial marketing' quoted in P.R. Smith, *Marketing Communications: An Integrated Approach* (Kogan Page, London).

Chapter 15

Exhibits 15–2, L. Cuddihy *et al.*, 'Sales promotion: an Irish perspective' in T. Meenaghan and P. O'Sullivan (eds) *Marketing Communication in Ireland* (Oak Tree Press, Dublin, 1996), p. 443. **15–3**, European Federation for Sales Promotion, *Newsletter*, Issue 1, p. 2. **15–4**, Cuddihy *et al.*, in Meenaghan and O'Sullivan, *op. cit.*, p. 44. 15–5 adapted from M.Baier, *Elements of Direct Marketing* (McGraw-Hill, New York, 1983). **15–6**, P.R. Smyth, *Marketing Communication: An Integrated Approach*

(Kogan Page, London, 1993). **15–7**, M. McGowan, 'Direct marketing: an integrated approach' in Meenaghan and O'Sullivan, *op. cit.*, pp. 532–545 . **15–8**, Association of Postal Administration, 'Usage trends in the European direct mail market', *Postal Direct Marketing Survey* (AEPA, Brussels, 1994). 15–9, AEPA, *op. cit.*

Ad Call centres by courtesy of H & M Presseservice.

Chapter 16

Exhibit 16–6, Exchange Rates, Table 3016, *European Marketing Data and Statistics, 1998* (Euromonitor, London, 1998), pp. 150–151.

Ad Tele2 by courtesy of DMB & B - Germany.

Chapter 17

Ad Opel Corsa by courtesy of McCann-Erickson Worldwide.

Chapter 18

Exhibit 18–5, *Sales and Marketing Management*, 30 August 1993.

Ad Fairy products by courtesy of DMB&B London - UK.

Chapter 20

Exhibits 20–6, Marie Gaudard, Roland Coates and Liz Freeman, 'Accelerating improvement', *Quality Progress*, October 1991, pp. 81–88. Gaudard, Coates and Freeman, *op. cit.*, pp. 81–88.

AUTHOR
INDEX

A

Abrams, B. 399
Abratt, R. 128
Achabal, D.D. 399
Acland, H. 328
Aggarwal, S. 444
Ailawadi, K.L. 261
Akhter, S.H. 399
Akintoye, A. 376
Albers, S. 443
Alberts, W.W. 375
Alden, D.L. 239
Alexander, G. 156
Ali, A. 351
Alsop, R. 399
Ambler, T. 418
Anderrson, P. 64
Anderson, M. 290
Anderson, M.D. 239, 261
Andreasen, A.R. 107
Arens, W.F. 290
Arinze, B. 399
Armstrong, G.M. 313
Arnott, D. 312, 313, 375, 376, 399, 443, 444
Ashford, R. 261, 350, 399, 418, 444
Asif Yaqub, C. 261

B

Babakus, E. 64
Bacon, Jnr., F.R. 181
Baker, M.J. 19, 63
Balasubramanian, S.K. 261
Balls, E. 34
Barber, L. 34
Barnard, N. 64
Barry, T.E. 290
Bartmess, A.D. 443
Batchelor, C. 63
Baxter, A. 34, 128
Beatty, Sharon E. 64
Bello, D. 313
Bello, D.C. 239
Bennett, M. 313
Benson, T. 375
Berbig, P.A. 399
Berry, L.L. 155, 418
Berthon, P. 239
Bessen, J. 107
Besson, M. 312
Bharadwaj, S.G. 350
Bhide, A. 443
Bishop, W.S. 155
Biswas, A. 375
Bitner, M.J. 155
Bivins, T.H. 261
Bixby Cooper, M. 85
Blackledge, C. 34
Blodgett, J.G. 261
Blois, K.J. 351
Boles, J.S. 313
Bonoma, T.V. 418
Boshoff, C. 444
Bourke, K. 261
Bovee, C.L. 290
Boynton, A.C. 443
Brasier, M. 443
Brennan, M. 261
Bristor, J.M. 64
Brock Smith, J. 64
Broderick, A. 350
Brown, A. 128
Brown, H.E. 85

Brown, J. 443
Brown, M. 215
Brown, S. 155
Brown, S.W. 444
Browne, A. 351
Brownlie, D. 418
Brownlie, D.T. 34
Bruce, M. 418
Brucker, R.W. 85
Bruns, Jnr., W.J. 418
Buckley, N. 34
Bunn, M.D. 85
Bunyan, N. 19
Burke, R.R. 181
Butler, B. 197
Butler, Jnr., T.W. 181

C

Calantone, R.J. 156
Cantin, A. 399
Cassell, M. 34
Cecchini 34
Cespedes, F.C. 313
Chan, C. 215, 399
Charan, R. 418
Choobineh, J. 239, 261, 290
Choudhry, Y.A. 399
Churchill, D. 350
Clark, R.W. 313
Coates, R. 444
Coe, B.J. 418
Conant, J.S. 418
Conaty, S. 197
Cooper, R. 181, 418, 443
Corey, B. 181
Corey, R.J. 181
Corfman, K.P. 261
Corzine, R. 34
Coykendall, D.S. 239
Creaton, S. 181
Crittenden, V.L. 443
Cron, W.L. 351
Cuddihy, L. 328
Culp, E. 350

D

Dall'Ollmo Riley, F. 64
Danaher, P.J. 261
Daniel, A.L. 444
Daniel Duck, J. 444
Daniel, S.J. 215
Dant, S.P. 85
Dapiran, P. 34
Darmon, R. 313
Darmon, R.Y. 351
Darnell Lattal, A. 313
Daugherty, P.J. 85, 215
Davidson, I. 34
Davies, B.J. 19
Dawkins, W. 34
Day, G.S. 351, 375
de Burca, S. 313
Dearing, B. 215
Deconinck, J.B. 313
Delener, N. 64
Derrick, S. 328
Derwent, C. 376
DeSarbo, W.S. 128
di Benedetto, C.A. 156
Diamantopoulos, A. 399
Diamond, W.D. 351
Dibb, S. 128

Dickson, P.R. 351
Dion, P. 85
Dion, P.A. 215
Dodwell, D. 34
Donthu, N. 290
Doole, I. 261
Dorin, P.C. 215
Doward, J. 128
Doyle, M. 19
Doyle, S.X. 313
Dreze, X. 350
Dröge, C. 85
Dubinsky, A.J. 313
Dwyer, F. 85

E

Easterling, D. 85
Ehrenberg, A. 64
Emshoff, J.R. 444
Ennew, C. 350
Erhenberg, A.S.C. 328
Eriffmeyer, R.C. 313
Evans, R.H. 399

F

Fahey, A. 290
Fahy, J. 351
Farris, P.W. 261
Feinberg, F. 376
Fenton, Jnr., J.W. 444
Fisher, R.J. 261
Fisk, R.P. 107, 155
Fitzgerald, P. 181
Fitzgerald Bone, P. 261
Fletcher, K. 328
Ford, J.B. 64, 313
Fox, M. 376
Frankenberger, K.D. 375
Frazier, G.L. 351
Freedman, R.J. 313
Freeman, L. 444
French, M.T. 399
Frey, D. 181
Frey, R. 444
Frohlich, H.P. 34
Fuller, D.A. 375
Fuller, J.B. 215
Fullerton, R.A. 181

G

Galvin, P. 398
Gandhi, N. 107
Gardiner, L.R. 443
Gardner, D. 34
Gardner, N. 313
Garrett, A. 34, 156, 351
Gaudard, M. 444
Gendell, P. 376
George, W. 444
Germain, R. 85, 215
Gibson, B.J. 215
Gilbert, F.W. 215
Glassman, M. 444
Glover, D.R. 328
Gnoth, J. 444
Golden, J.E. 399
Goodhardt, G.J. 328
Goodhart, D. 34
Gordon, G.L. 156
Govindarajan, V. 443
Gracie, S. 197
Graham, J.L. 155

Granbois, D.H. 261
Granzin, K.L. 181
Grashof, J.F. 418
Green, D. 34
Gresham, A.B. 215
Griffin, A. 181
Griffith, R.L. 128
Grönroos, C. 19
Grove, S.J. 107
Guido, G. 63
Gummesson, E. 19
Gwyther, M. 239

H
Hair, Jnr., J.F. 313
Halliday, A.L. 156
Hamel, G. 34, 261
Hammond, K. 328
Hardie, B. 375
Hardy, K.G. 85
Harvey, M.G. 291
Hasey, L.M. 215
Hauser, J.R. 181, 418
Hawkins, A. 63
Hayden, F. 328
Hayden, V. 19
Hayes, R.H. 443
Helsen, K. 128
Henke, Jnr., J.W. 853
Hensel, J.S. 444
Henthorne, T.L. 64
Herbig, P. 239, 313
Herbig, P.A. 312
Heskett, J.L. 444
Heslop, L.A. 399
Hill, A. 34
Hill, D. 290
Hill, J.S. 313
Hill, N.C. 215
Hoch, S.J. 63, 350
Hoffman, R.C. 239
Holbert, N.B. 399
Homer, P. 64
Honeycutt, Jnr., E.D. 313
Hooley, G.J. 19
Hoyer, W.D. 64
Huellmantel, A.B. 107
Hunt, K.A. 351
Hutcheson, G. 239

I
Irwin, I.L. 418

J
Jackson, A. 34
Jackson, Barbara P. 375
Jacobs, L.W. 215
Jain, S.C. 350
Jaworski, B.J. 19, 418
Jedidi, K. 128
Jobber, D. 399
Johnston, M.W. 313
Jolson, M.A. 313, 351, 375
Jones, D.T. 443
Jones, M.H. 155
Jung, H.S. 261
Juric, B. 350
Jury, L. 291

K
Kahle, L.R. 64
Kahn, K.B. 443

Kalwani, M.U. 85
Kaminski, P.F. 399
Kanso, A. 291
Kaplan, R.S. 418, 443
Karr, M. 351
Kasper, H. 444
Kasturi Rangan, V. 181
Kaufmann, P.J. 215, 239
Keaveney, S.M. 351
Keiningham, T.L. 444
Kelley, S.W. 444
Kendall, D.L. 399
Kenderdine, J.M. 239
Kenny, D. 181
Kitchen, P. 261
Kohli, K. 19
Kokkinaki, F. 418
Konijnendijk, P.A. 443
Konsynski, B.R. 215
Korgaonkar, P. 313
Kortge, G.D. 181, 375
Kotabe, M. 313
Krachenberg, A.R. 85
Kramer, H.E. 312
Krishna Erramilli, M. 399
Krishnamurthi, L. 375
Krishnan, H.S. 418
Kristiaan, H. 375

L
LaFief, W.C. 444
Lafontaine, F. 239
Lal, R. 181
Lambert, D.M. 418, 444
Lambkin, M. 156, 313
Lane Keller, K. 181
Lapper, R. 34
Laric, M.B. 350
LaTour, M.S. 64
Lawlor, K. 261
Lawrence, P. 399
Lee, A. 291
Lee, D.Y. 261
Lehmann, D.R. 261
Leone, R.P. 239
Leverick, F. 418
Levine, J. 290
Levy, D.T. 376
Littler, D. 418
Locander, W.B. 181
Lohtia, R. 239
Loken, B. 181
Lord, K.R. 290
Lovelock, C.H. 19
Low, G.S. 181
Lundin, J. 215
Lusch, R.F. 239, 418
Lyons, T.F. 85

M
McAfee, B. 444
McCarthy, E.J. 128, 261, 418
McDaniel, S. 215
McFarlan, W.W. 418
McHugh, F. 398
MacInnis, M. 399
McIntyre, S.H. 399
McKechnie, S. 350
McKie, Robin 34
McNaughton, R. 399
McTier Anderson, L. 444
McWilliam, G. 63

McWilliams, R.D. 85
Magrath, A.J. 85, 239
Maier, E.P. 181
Malikn, E. 443
Maltz, A.B. 215
Mandják, T. 376
Marbeau, Y. 63
Marcantonio, A. 291
Marn, M.V. 350
Marsh, D. 34
Maruca, R.F. 156
Maute, M.F. 181
Mead, G. 34
Mears, P. 4443
Meenaghan, T. 261, 291, 313, 328, 399
Meller, P. 350
Mentzer, J.T. 107, 443
Merrell, C. 313
Meyer, C. 444
Milewicz, J. 399
Miller, C.M. 399
Miller, S.J. 85
Millward, D. 19
Milton, C. 34
Monroe, K.B. 376
Montgomery, D.B. 375
Moon, M.A. 313
Morris, M.H. 351, 375
Moutinho, L. 239
Mundy, R.A. 215
Munson, J.M. 85
Myers, J.H. 64

N
Naidu, G.M. 399
Narayandas, N. 85
Nash, P. 291
Naumann, E. 85
Neese, W.T. 290
Nel, D. 444
Nevin, J.R. 351
Nichols, M. 443
Niven, D. 444
Novick, J.A. 215

O
O'Callaghan, R. 215
O'Conor, J. 215
O'Donoghue, R. 398
O'Donohoe, S. 290
Oh, S. 85
O'Hara, B. 313
O'Hara, B.S. 239, 313
Ohbora, T. 399
Ohmae, K. 399
Okonkwo, P.A. 181
Okoroafo, S.C. 399
Olins, R. 181
Oliva, T.A. 181
Ollins, R. 443
Olsen, J.E. 181
Olson, E.M. 444
O'Neal, C.R. 215, 444
Ormsby, J.G. 215
Ostas, D.T. 376
O'Sullivan, P. 261, 291, 313, 328, 399

P
Palumbo, F. 313
Panigyrakis, G. 444
Papasolomou, I. 444
Parasúraman, A. 155, 418

Parks, B. 443
Parry, M.E. 261
Parsons, A. 399
Patterson, L.T. 290
Patterson, P.G. 64
Paun, D. 376
Pennings, J. 443
Perreault, Jnr., W.D. 107
Perreault, W. 128, 261
Pesch, M.J. 443
Peston, R. 34
Petrou, A. 399
Pfeiffer, R. 313
Piercy, N. 444
Piercy, N.F. 418
Pine II, B.J. 443
Pisano, G.P. 443
Pisharodi, R.M. 215
Pitt, L. 239, 290, 444
Plank, R.E. 85
Pol, L.G. 128
Polegato, Rosemary 64
Porter, M.E. 443
Porter Lynch, R. 399
Potter, B. 19
Pozen, R.C. 443
Preble, J.F. 239
Price, L.L. 261
Proctor, T. 444
Puri, S.J. 313
Purk, M.E. 350
Putler, D.S. 375
Putrevu, S. 290

Q
Quelch, J.A. 181, 399

R
Raguraman, K. 215
Ram, S. 261
Rangan, V.K. 215
Rangaswamy, A. 181
Rao, C.P. 399
Rao, K. 215
Rappaport, A. 350
Rawlinson, R. 215
Rawsthorne, P. 34
Reekie, W.D. 351
Reeve, S. 239
Reitsperger, W.D. 215
Reynolds, W.H. 64
Richards, A. 350
Riesenbeck, H. 399
Rink, D.R. 399
Roedder John, D. 181
Rogers, D.S. 215
Rogers, E.M. 64
Rogers, M. 290
Rosiello, R.L. 350
Ross III, J.K. 290
Rossant, J. 443
Rouzies, D. 312
Rubinstein, M. 443
Ruiming Liu 375
Russ, K.R. 313
Rust, R. 444
Rust, R.T. 261
Ryans, A.B. 351

S
Samli, A.C. 215
Sampler, J. 34, 261

Sandretto, M.J. 418
Sandy, W. 399
Sang-Lin Han 85
Schaars, S.P. 156
Schilit, W.K. 443
Schindler, R.M. 376
Schlesinger, L.A. 444
Schmenner, R.W. 443
Schonfeld, Erick 34
Schroeder, R.G. 443
Schultz, D. 261
Schurr, P. 85
Scott, S. 85
Segalla, M. 312
Sengupta, K. 328
Severin, A. 328
Shank, J.K. 443
Shapiro, B.P. 215
Shapiro, P. 375
Shaw, E.H. 19
Shelton, E. 351
Sheth, J. 239
Shim, J.K. 443
Shipley, D. 313
Shoemaker, F. 64
Shwarz, J.S. 34
Shycon, H.N. 444
Siegel, J.G. 443
Simkin, L. 128
Simms, J. 63, 107, 239
Simon, J. 376
Singh, J. 261
Singhapakdi, A. 313
Sink, H.L. 215
Sisodia, R. 239
Skitmore, M. 376
Smith, D.S. 85
Smith, K.H. 290
Soberman, D. 418
Sonnenberg, F.K. 444
Spriggs, M.T. 351
Stam, A. 443
Stank, T.P. 215
Stathakopoulos, V. 418
Stephenson, P.R. 351
Sterling, J.U. 418, 444
Stern, S. 418
Sternthal, B. 291
Stewart, K. 261
Stewart, K.M. 418
Still, R.R. 313
Storbacka, K. 444
Stutts, M.A. 290
Suchard, H.T. 34
Suchard, J.C. 34
Summers, D. 107
Summers, R.O.D. 34
Sumner Smith, D. 34, 239, 443
Surowiecki, J. 181
Sviokla, J.J. 215
Swagler, R. 34
Swartz, T.A. 444
Swenson, M.J. 215
Swift, C.O. 85
Szymanski, D.M. 350

T
Tait, N. 34
Talpade, Salil 64
Tamer Cavusgil, S. 399
Tanner, Jnr., J.F. 313
Tat, P.K. 351

Taylor, R.D. 290
Taylor, W.C. 418
Tellis, G.J. 351
Theus, K.T. 290
Thomas, D. 443
Thomas, M. 418
Townsend, B. 107
Traynor, I. 351
Tredre, R. 443
Tullous, R. 85
Tybout, A.M. 418

U
UiGhallachoir, K. 328
Un Lim, C. 313
Urbany, J.E. 351

V
Vandermerwe, S. 63
Varadarajan, P.R. 350
Veloustou, C. 444
Vesey, J.T. 181
Victor, B. 443
Vignali, C. 19
Viswanathan, M. 444
Vitell, S.J. 313
Vlachoutsicos, C. 399

W
Wagner, William B. 443
Waldrop, J. 64
Wallace, C. 399
Walters, R.G. 261
Washburn, S.A. 418
Watson, R. 239, 290
Webster, F.E. 19
Weinberg, C.B. 19
Wheeler, C. 328
White, D. 398
White, R.D. 215
Whitelock, J. 399
Wilcox, J.B. 351
Wills, J. 215
Wilson, D. 418
Wilson, D.T. 85
Wilton, P. 376
Wiman, A.R. 376
Winklhofer, H. 399
Wolf, M. 34
Womack, J.P. 443
Wong, K. 313
Woolf, M. 313
Wright, J. 328

Y
Yadav, M.S. 376
Yang, Y.S. 239
Yavas, U. 64
Young, J.A. 215
Young, R.R. 215

Z
Zabriskie, N.B. 107
Zahorik, A.J. 444
Zaichkowsky, J.L. 64
Zandpour, F. 291
Zeithaml, V.A. 155
Zoltners, A. 312
Zou, S. 399

SUBJECT INDEX

A

3Com company 145-6
4 'Ps' *see* four 'Ps'

accounting data 457-64
  strategy decisions 431-4
  see also economics fundamentals
accumulating concept (channels of
  distribution) 190
action (AIDA element) 278-9
administered channel systems 192-3
administering prices 336-7
adoption process
  advertising 270
  buying 60-1
  communications 249-51
advertising 264-85
  adoption process 270
  AIDA concept 277-80
  allowances 271-2, 345
  briefs 282
  campaigns, activity flow chart 281
  comparative 271
  cooperative relationships 271-2
  copy platform 277
  corporate 270, 271
  defined 243
  effectiveness measuring 283-4
  ethical issues 272, 285
  expenditure 266-8, 274-5
  global messages 279-80
  government influence 284-5
  importance 266-8
  infomercials 276
  institutional 270, 271
  Internet 277
  Japan 271
  media buying services 280
  media planning 273-7
  message planning 277-80
  objectives 269-71
  promotion objectives 273
  strategy planning 266-70
  targeting 275-7
advertising agencies 280-3
  ethical issues 283
  payment methods 282
advertising managers 244-5
Advertising Standards Authority 287
advertising-led publicity 286, 287
agencies, advertising 280-3
agents (wholesalers) 230, 234-6
AIB Group (of companies) 241-2
AIDA (Attention; Interest; Desire; Action)
  concept
  advertising message planning 277-80
  communication model 249-51
  personal selling 309-10
Allianz company 28
Allied Irish Banks (AIB) company 241-2
AlliedSignal company 78
allowances
  advertising 271-2, 345
  pricing 345-6
Amazon.com (booksellers) 9, 24
arithmetic, marketing 457-64
attention (AIDA element) 277-8
auction companies 236
audit, marketing 414-15
AutoLocate (car) service 225
average variable cost (AVC) 358, 362
average-cost pricing 357-60

B

Baileys (brand) 172-3
BCO Technologies company 424
behaviour *see* buying behaviour
`below-the-line' promotional activity 314-22
Benetton company 23, 24, 272, 421
BEP *see* break-even point
Betz company 78
bid pricing (price setting) 372-3
`bid-rigging' 82
Bordeaux wine 265
brand familiarity 172-3
brand managers 169
brand value, quantifying 174
branding 169-79
  defined 170
  favourable conditions 171-2
  'own label' 79
brands, retailer 176
break-even analysis (price setting) 361-3
break-even point (BEP) 361-3
bribery 26, 83
brokers 236
BskyB company 6-7
budget, promotion 258-9
bulk-breaking (channels of distribution)
  190-1
business customers, promoting to 253-4
business and organizational buying
  behaviour 66-83
business product classes 137, 141-5
  marketing mix planning 186
business product planning 141-5
buying
  adoption process 60-1
  computerised 71
  problem-solving process 58-61, 69-73
  reciprocal 71
  relationships concept 75-9
buying behaviour
  business and organizational 66-83
  consumer 51-62
  model 52, 246
  problem-solving process 58-61, 69-73
buying committees 81
buying contracts 75, 77, 82
buying influences
  cultural/social 56-8
  multiple 73-4

C

CAD *see* computer aided design
capital (finance) 422-6
capital investment items 141-2
car selling, Internet 224-5
cartels 28
cases 467-88
cash discounts (pricing) 344
cash-and-carry wholesalers 232-3
catalogue showroom retailers 222
CCI *see* Cotton Council International
Centraal Beheer company 269
chain of supply, channels of distribution 211
Channel Master company 203
channel systems (channels of distribution)
  192-6
Channel Tunnel 50
channels of distribution
  chain of supply 211
  channel systems 192-6
  conflict 192, 196
  development 182-96

direct 188-9, 191
dual channels 196
electronic data interchange (EDI) 212
horizontal arrangements 195
indirect 189-90
information technology (IT) impact 186-8,
  212
intermediaries' roles 190-6
personal selling 297
product-market commitment concept 191
relationships 210-13
vertical marketing systems 192-3
  see also physical distribution
Charles Schwab (company) 24
Chinese market 394-5
CIS *see* Commonwealth of Independent
  States
Clorox company 210
clustering (segmentation technique) 124
Co-operative Bank 14
Coca-Cola company 199
cola marketing 12-13
combination export managers 236
commercialization (product development)
  167-8
commission merchants 236
committee buying 81
Commonwealth of Independent States
  (CIS) 11
communication process
  customer-initiated 254-6
  electronic media 255-6
  promotion 247-8
communications, marketing 240-59
company forecasts 386
comparative advertising 271
competition
  monopolistic 30, 31
  nature of 452-6
competitive advantage 31-2
competitive advertising 271
competitive environment 12-13, 22, 30-2
competitor analysis 31-2
complementary product pricing (price
  setting) 372
computer aided design (CAD) 166
computerized buying 71
computers *see* electronic data interchange
  (EDI); information technology (IT);
  Internet; Intranets; World Wide Web
  (WWW)
concept testing 165
consultative selling (personal selling) 309
consumer buying behaviour 51-62
consumer environment 36-62
consumer panels 100-1
consumer product classes 136-40
  marketing mix planning 185
consumer product planning 136-40
consumer protection laws 29
consumer spending patterns 46-50
consumerism 26-7
consumers, promoting to 252-3
containerization 206
contract manufacturing (exporting method)
  396
contracts, buying 75, 77, 82
contractual channel systems 192-3
contribution-margin approach, marketing
  cost analysis 411-12, 413
convenience (food) shops 223
cooperative advertising 271-2

cooperative chains (retailers) 227
copy platform, advertising 277
corporate advertising 270, 271
corporate chain shops 227
corporate channel systems 192-3
cost analysis
  accounting 431-4
  marketing plans 407, 410-14
cost of sales (accounting) 458-61
cost structure (price setting) 365-6
cost types (price setting) 358-9
cost-oriented pricing 360-1
Cotton Council International (CCI) 315
counterfeiting 175
credit sales 344-5
crosstabulation technique, marketing
  research 102
cultural buying influences 58
cultural and social environment 29-30
cumulative quantity discounts (pricing) 343
customer-initiated interactive
  communication 254-6

D
data
  accounting 431-4
  consumer expenditure 46, 48-9
  Euromonitor 39
  marketing 403-4, 406-14
  research 90, 95-102
debt financing 425
decision support systems (DSS) 90, 102
decision-making, buying behaviour 56-61
demand curves
  economics 446-53
  price setting 359-60, 368
demand schedules (economics) 446-53
demand and supply concept (economics)
  445-56
demand-backward pricing concept (price
  setting) 371
demand-oriented price setting 369-71
demographic issues 39-50
department stores 221
desire (AIDA element) 278
desk-jobbers (wholesalers) 233
detailers (personal selling) 301
development, market 112
dimensions, market segmentation 115-18
diminishing demand law (economics) 446
direct distribution 188-9, 191
direct marketing 189, 322-7
  characteristics 323-5
  ethical issues 326
  forms 325-6
direct type advertising 271
direct-mail retailing 223, 254
direct-response promotion 254
discount policies (pricing) 343-5
discretionary income 46
Disneyland Paris 379-80
disposable income 45-6
dissonance concept, buying behaviour 61
distribution centre 209
distribution and logistics see channels of
  distribution; physical distribution (PD)
diversification (marketing opportunity) 112
Dixons company 340
drop-shippers (wholesalers) 233
DSS see decision support systems
dual distribution channels 196
Dyson company 168

E
EC see electronic commerce
economic environment 22-3
economic unification 26
economics fundamentals 445-56
  see also accounting data
economy, global 23
EDI see electronic data interchange
elasticity concept (economics) 448, 451, 455
electronic commerce (EC) 187-8
electronic data interchange (EDI) 207, 208
  channels of distribution 212
electronic media, interactive communication
  via 255-6
employees, promoting to 252
'empty nesters' concept 48
EMS see European Media and Marketing
  Survey
environment
  changing market 20-33
  competitive 12-13, 22, 30-2
  consumer 36-62
  cultural and social 29-30
  economic 22-3
  impact 15-16, 20-32
  legal 28-9
  macro 22-30
  political 25-7
  technological 22, 23-5
environmental issues, physical distribution
  (PD) 212-13
ethical issues
  advertising 272, 285
  advertising agencies 283
  consumer beliefs 55
  counterfeiting 175
  direct marketing 326
  government bids 82, 83
  Internet 187
  market segmentation 118
  marketing 14-15, 26, 32
  marketing communications 248-9
  marketing plans 424-5
  marketing research 92-3
  new product planning 160-1
  organizational buying 73
  packaging 177-8
  personal selling 310-11
  physical distribution (PD) 212
  pricing policies 338, 345
  retailing 226
  sales promotion 321
  technology 25
  wholesaling 237
ethnic markets 50
EU see European Union
euro 23, 340-1
Euromonitor data 39
Europe, sales promotion techniques 319
European Commission 28, 82
European Media and Marketing Survey
  (EMS) 274
European retailer groups 228
European Union (EU) 26, 28
exchange rates 340-2
exclusive distribution 193-5
exhibitions 302
expenditure data, consumer 46, 48-9
experience curve pricing 360
export agents 235-6
export commission houses 236
exporting 395-6

exporting facilitators 395-6
external finance sources 423-6

F
factor method (forecasting) 387
family life-cycle 47-9
fashion industry 429
fast moving consumer goods (FMCG) 207
feedback, marketing management process
  403
financial services (personal selling) 310-11
financing marketing plan implementation
  422-6
fishbone diagram (quality issues) 436-7
fitness clubs 235
flexible-price policy (pricing) 337
flowcharts (marketing planning) 393
FMCG see fast moving consumer goods
FOB see free on board pricing
forecasting (marketing planning) 386-9
four 'Ps' 16-17
  marketing implementation problems 405
  marketing planning 380-5, 392-3
  see also marketing mix
Foxfield Mushrooms company 342
fragrance market 37-8
franchising 227-8
free on board (FOB) pricing 346
freight absorption pricing 347
freight forwarders 206
full-cost approach, marketing cost analysis
  411-12
full-line pricing (price setting) 371-2
functional accounts 431-4
functional place, marketing's 420-41
funding see financing marketing plan
  implementation

G
GDP see gross domestic product
general merchandise wholesalers 231
general-line wholesalers 231
generic products 176
genetic modification (GM) 27
Gillette company 167, 274
global economy 23
global marketing perspective 40-1
global messages (advertising) 279-80
glossary 489-501
GM see genetic modification
Goodfellas Pizza company 321-2
goods described 134-5
government influence (advertising) 284-5
government marketing research data 96
government markets 81-3
'green' issues 27
grey markets 347-8
gross domestic product (GDP) 43-7
gross margin
  accounting 458-60
  mark-ups 355
growing markets importance 41-5
guarantees 178-9
Guinness company 40

H
health and fitness industry 235
Hertz company 404-5
heterogeneous shopping products 139
Hewlett Packard company 109-10
Holly Farms company 210
homogeneous shopping products 138

horizontal arrangements (channels of distribution) 195
horizontal cooperation (advertising) 272
House of Hardy company 293-4
human resources 439-41

I

iceberg principle, marketing plans 410
idea generation and evaluation, product development 162-6
ideal market exposure concept 193
image, organization's 287
image importance, retailing 219
import agents 235-6
import commission houses 236
indirect distribution 189-90
indirect type advertising 271
industry sales forecast 386
inflation 22-3
infomercials 276
information see marketing information
information technology (IT)
    channels of distribution 186-8, 212
    marketing plans 402-4, 406
    personal selling 304, 306
    see also electronic commerce (EC); electronic data interchange (EDI); Internet; Intranet; World Wide Web (WWW)
informing (promotion objective) 246-7
institutional advertising 270, 271
intensive distribution 193-4
interactive communication
    customer-initiated 254-6
    Internet 255-6
interest (AIDA element) 278
interest rates (economics) 22-3
intermediaries
    channels of distribution 190-6
    promotion activities 252
    see also agents; middlemen; wholesalers
internal finance sources 425-6
internal marketing concept 252
international market segmentation 123-4
international marketing research 104-5
international opportunities 113
international retailing differences 229
Internet 187-8, 208
    advertising on 277
    impact 24
    interactive communication 255-6
    retailing 224-5
    shopping 71
Intranets 89
introductory price dealing 339
inventory policy 207-9, 356-7
organizational buying 71
Irish Times newspaper 187
ISO 9000 69

J

Japan
    advertising in 271
    retailing 229
JIT see just-in-time concept
joint venturing (exporting method) 396
jury of executive opinion (forecasting) 389
just-in-time (JIT) concept 207, 208, 211-13
    buying 71, 76-7

L

law of diminishing demand (economics) 446
leader pricing (price setting) 370

leasing capital items 142
legal environment 28-9
legal issues 26
    pricing policies 82, 347, 348
Levi-Strauss company 256-7
licensing (exporting method) 396
life-cycles
    family 47-9
    product 145-54
        pricing policies 338-42
        promotions mix 256-8
        retailers 226, 227
life-style analysis 56
limited-function wholesalers 232
limited-line shops 220
list prices 343
lobbying 25-6
location, retailers 228-9
Loctite corporation 383
logistics and distribution 198-213
long-run target return pricing 361
L'Oréal company 401-2

M

macroenvironment 22-30
Magic of Spain company 353-4
mail-order
    companies 223
    wholesalers 233
management contracting (exporting method) 396
managers
    advertising 244-5
    brand 169
    combination export 236
    marketing 245, 403
    product 169
    sales 244
    sales promotion 245
Manchester United Football Club (MUFC) 6-7
manufacturers' agents 235
manufacturers' sales branches 231
marginal analysis (price setting) 363-4, 367-9
marginal cost (price setting) 364-5
marginal revenue (price setting) 364
mark-ups
    accounting 463
    price setting 354-7
market
    development 112
    monitoring importance 146
    opportunities 111-13
    penetration 111-12
    potential (forecasting) 386
    testing 166-7
market environment, changing 20-33
market segmentation, targeting, positioning 38-9, 108-26
marketing
    arithmetic 457-64
    audit 414-15
    communications 240-59
    concept 8-15
    data 403-4, 406-14
    defined 6
    described 4-6
    development stages 7-8
    importance 5
    management job 15-18
    management-oriented 6-7

    orientation 8-18
    role 2-18
marketing cost analysis, marketing plans 407, 410-14
marketing ethics see ethical issues
marketing information 86-105
    personal selling 294, 296
marketing information systems (MIS) 16, 88-91
marketing management process 15-18
marketing managers 245, 403
marketing mix 16-17, 146
    marketing implementation problems 405
    marketing planning 185-6, 380-5, 392-3
    product life-cycles relationship 151
    see also four 'Ps'
marketing planning/plans 15-18, 110-11
    developing 378-97
    financing implementation 422-6
    iceberg principle 410
    implementing and controlling 400-16
    information technology impact 402-4, 406
    international 394-5
    marketing cost analysis 407, 410-14
    marketing mix 185-6, 380-5, 392-3
    performance analysis 407-10
    production issues 426-31
    programme 393-4
    sales analysis 406-10
    strategy planning process (overview) 381
    summary outline 391-2
marketing research 90-105
    international 104-5
    primary data 90, 97-102
    qualitative 97-8
    quantitative 98-102
    secondary data 90, 95-7
    situation analysis 95, 97
    surveys 98-100
    syndicated 102
marketing strategy planning process (overview) 381
marketing's functional place 420-41
markets, customers'/suppliers' views 446-51
Mars company 131-2
mass communication 243
mass customization
    segmentation 428
    targeting technique 114
mass-merchandising retailers 221-3, 229
media buying services 280
media planning (advertising) 273-7
merchandisers (personal selling) 301
merchant wholesalers 230-4, 299
message channel (communication process) 248
message planning, advertising 277-80
Microsoft company 24
middlemen see agents; intermediaries; wholesalers
Mintex Don company 163-4
MIS see marketing information systems
missionary salespeople 301
mix see marketing mix
monitoring markets importance 146
monopolistic competition 30, 31, 454-5
Monsanto company 27
Motion Media Technology company 183
motivation theory 52-6
MUFC see Manchester United Football Club

multinational corporations (exporting method) 396
multiple buying influences concept 73-4

N
national income forecast 386
nationalism 26
natural accounts 431-4
Navico company 427
needs hierarchy 52-3
negotiated contract buying 75, 82
negotiated pricing (price setting) 372-3
net profit (accounting) 458-60
news (press) releases 287-8
Nike company 209
non-cumulative quantity discounts (pricing) 343-4
non-profit organizations 6, 10, 13

O
odd-even pricing (price setting) 370
oligopoly situations 30
  economic issues 454
  price setting 369
  pricing policy 339
Olympic Games 274
one-price policy (pricing) 337
operating statements/ratios (accounting) 458-64
opinion leaders, buying behaviour 57-8
opportunities, market 111-13
order getters/takers, personal selling 297, 298-301
organizational buying 66-83
out-sourcing 429
'own-label' branding 79

P
packaging, strategic importance 176-8
Pareto chart (quality issues) 436
partnerships, buyers and suppliers 78-9
payment methods (advertising agencies) 282
payment terms (pricing) 344
PD see physical distribution
penetration, market 111-12
penetration pricing policy 338, 339
people (resource) 439-41
perception analysis 125-6
perception influence (buying behaviour) 54
performance analysis, marketing plans 407-10
perfume market 37-8
personal selling 243, 292-311
  AIDA concept 309-10
  channels of distribution 297
  financial services 310-11
  information technology 304, 306
  intermediaries 252
  marketing information 294, 296
  professional services 298
  promotions mix 296
  sales situations 297-8
  strategy planning 295-6, 297
  techniques 307-11
persuading (promotion objective) 246-7
pharmaceuticals wholesaling 232
physical distribution (PD) 198-213
  alternatives 202-6
  defined 200
  Eastern Europe 200
  environmental issues 212-13
  ethical issues 212

holistic approach 201-3
service levels 202
trade-off concept 200-1, 209, 212
  see also channels of distribution
pioneering advertising 270
Pizza Hut company 279-80
place (four 'Ps') 182-96
planned obsolescence 160
planned shopping centres 229
planning
  products 130-54, 160-1
  business 141-5
  consumer 136-40
  see also marketing planning/plans;
    strategy planning
political environment 25-7
population issues 41-50
positioning, market 108-26
presenting (personal selling) 308
press (news) releases 287-8
prestige pricing 370-1
price fixing 28
price lining concept (price setting) 371
price setting 352-74
  average cost pricing 357-60
  bid pricing 372-3
  break-even analysis 361-3
  cost types 358-9
  demand-oriented 369-71
  full-line 371-2
  marginal analysis 363-4, 367-9
  mark-ups 354-7
  target return 361
price strategy planning 330-74
price/target market relationship 340
Priceline.com (travel auction) 24
pricing
  objectives 330-7
  retailers' power 331
pricing policies 337-48
  allowances 345-6
  discounts 343-5
  ethical issues 338, 345
  flexibility 337
  legal issues 82, 347, 348
  oligopoly situations 339
    product life-cycle 338-42
primary research data 90, 97-102
PrintKraft company 92
problem-solving process, buying behaviour 58-61, 69-73
Procter and Gamble (P&G) company 331, 394-5
producers' cooperatives 233
producers' order takers (personal selling) 300
product
  advertising 270-1
  defined 132-3
  development 112, 158-79
  generic 176
  liability 165
  planning 130-54, 160-1
  quality 133
product assortment concept 135
product classes
  business 137, 141-5
  consumer 136-40
  marketing mix planning 184-6
  marketing planning 383
product life-cycles 145-54
  marketing planning 384-5
  pricing policies 338-42

promotions mix 256-8
sales promotion 319-20
strategy planning 150-3
product line concept 135
product managers 169
product-bundle pricing (pricing concept) 372
product-market commitment concept 191
production issues, marketing plans 426-31
production orientation 9-13
products, customers' view 446-50
professional services 145
  personal selling 298
profit importance 10
profit and loss statement (accounting) 458-61
profit maximisation
  price setting 366-7
  pricing objective 334-5
profit-oriented objectives (pricing) 334-5
profit/sales relationship 146-7
promotion 240-59
  budget 258-9
  business customers 253-4
  communication process 247-8
  consumers 252-3
  direct-response 254
  employees 252
  objectives 246-7, 249-51, 273
  plans 251-4
promotions mix 244-6
  personal selling, consumer cf. industrial 296
  product life-cycles 256-8
prospecting (personal selling) 307-8
PSSP Needs Hierarchy 53-4
psychographics 56
psychological influences, buying behaviour 52-6
psychological pricing 370
public relations (PR) 245, 285-8
publicity 285-8
  advertising-led 286, 287
  defined 243
'pulling' concept (promotional strategy) 252-3, 272
purchasing see buying
'pushing' concept (promotional strategy) 251-3, 272

Q
qualitative research 97-8
quality issues 435-8
  certification 69
  product 133
quantitative research 98-102
quantity discounts 343
Queue Management Group (company) 67

R
R&D see research and development
rack jobbers (wholesalers) 234
ratios, accounting 462-4
raw materials 143
rebates (pricing) 346
reciprocal buying 71
recycling materials 27
reference group, buying behaviour 57
reference prices (price setting) 369-70
regional shopping centres 229
regrouping (channels of distribution) 190
relationship buying concept 75-9

relative quality concept 133
reminder advertising 271
reminding (promotion objective) 246-7
research see marketing research
research and development (R&D) 24
  customer-focused 163-4
  market guided 168-9
retail order takers (personal selling) 300-1
retailers
  brands 176
  groups, European 228
  life-cycles 226, 227
  location 228-9
  promotion activities 252
  strategy planning 216-30
  types 220-8
retailing 218-30
  future 230
  image importance 219
  international differences 229
  Internet 224-5
  Japan 229
  telephone 223, 302-3
return on assets (ROA) 464
return on investment (ROI) 165, 464

S

Saatchi and Saatchi company 245
sale price (pricing) 345
sales analysis, marketing plans 406-10
sales forecasting 386-7
sales managers 244
Sales and Marketing Management 388
sales promotion 243-4, 314-22
  consumers 320-1
  employees 322
  ethical issues 321
  expenditure 316-17
  intermediaries 321-2
  international context 319
  management 318
  managers 245
  product life-cycle 319-20
  strategic role 316-17
  techniques 319
sales situations, personal selling 297-8
sales territories 303
sales-oriented objectives (pricing) 334, 335-6
sales/profit relationship 146-7
salespeople
  employing 305-6
  quantity 303
  roles 296-7
  supporting 301
schwab.com (investment brokers) 24
scrambled merchandising (retailing) 226
screening (product development) 164
seasonal discounts (pricing) 344
secondary research data 90, 95-7
segmentation
  dimensions 115-18
  market 38-9, 108-26
  mass customization 428
selective distribution 193-4
selling agents 236
selling formula approach (personal selling) 309

senior citizens market 49
service wholesalers 231
services
  companies 80
  described 134-5
  industries 11
  professional 145
share issues (financing) 423-5
shopping centres 229
shopping products concept 138-9
SIC codes see Standard Industrial
  Classification codes
single-line mass-merchandisers 222-3
single-line wholesalers 231
situation analysis (marketing research) 95, 97
skimming policies (pricing) 338-9
Skoda company 87-8
Snickers (brand) 131-2
social buying influences 56-8
social and cultural environment 29-30
social responsibility 14-15
sources of finance 423-6
Soviet Union, former see Commonwealth of
  Independent States
speciality shops 221
speciality wholesalers 231-2
spending patterns, consumer 46-50
spreadsheet analysis (marketing planning)
  390-1
Standard Industrial Classification (SIC)
  codes 79-80
  marketing planning 387
status quo oriented objectives (pricing) 334,
  336, 339
stereotypes, national 50
stocking allowances (pricing) 345
stockouts 428-9
stockturn rate
  accounting 461-2
  price setting 356-7
storage, goods 207-9
strategy planning
  advertising 266-70
  personal selling 295-6, 297
  price 330-74
  product life-cycles 150-3
  retailers/wholesalers 216-37
superstores 222
supply curves/schedules (economics)
  450-2
supply and demand concept (economics)
  445-56
surveys, market research 98-100
SWOT (strengths; weaknesses;
  opportunities; threats) analysis (marketing
  planning) 381
syndicated marketing research 102

T

Tango brand 245-6
target market/price relationship 340
target return objective (pricing) 334, 361
targeting, market 38-9, 108-26
task transfer concept (services firms) 430
team selling, personal selling 301
technical specialists (personal selling) 301

technological base 23-4
technological environment 22, 23-5
technology impact, channels of distribution
  186-8, 212
telemarketing 223, 302-3
telephone surveys, marketing research 99
Tesco company 217-18
test marketing 166-7
total quality management (TQM) 435-8
  see also quality issues
Toys "R" Us company 222-3
TQM see total quality management
trade fairs 302
trade promotion 321-2
trade-in allowance (pricing) 345-6
trade-off analysis (segmentation technique)
  124
trade-off concept, physical distribution (PD)
  200-1, 209, 212
trademark issues 170, 175
traditional channel systems 191-3
transportation 204-7
  see also physical distribution (PD)

U

unification, economic 26
uniform delivered pricing 347
Unilever company 31
unique selling proposition 278
unit-pricing 178
universal product code (UPC) 178
unsought products 140
UPC see universal product code

V

value pricing 342
value in use pricing concept 369
vending machines 223
vendor analysis 72-3
vertical integration 192-3
vertical marketing systems, channels of
  distribution 192-3
virtual corporation concept 429
voluntary chains (retailers) 227
Volvo company 159

W

warehousing 208-9
warranties 178-9
wheel of retailing theory 226
Whirlpool company 101
wholesalers
  defined 230
  promotion activity 252
  strategy planning 230-7
  see also agents; intermediaries; middlemen
wholesalers' order takers (personal selling)
  300
wholly-owned subsidiaries (exporting
  method) 396
World Trade Organization (WTO) 28
World Wide Web (WWW) 24
  interactive communication 255-6

Z

zone pricing 346